Clinical Perspectives on Meaning

Pninit Russo-Netzer
Stefan E. Schulenberg • Alexander Batthyany
Editors

Clinical Perspectives on Meaning

Positive and Existential Psychotherapy

Editors
Pninit Russo-Netzer
Department of Counseling and Human
    Development
University of Haifa
Mount Carmel, Haifa, Israel

Alexander Batthyany
International Academy of Philosophy
University in the Principality of
    Liechtenstein
Vienna, Austria

Stefan E. Schulenberg
Department of Psychology
Clinical-Disaster Research Center
    (UM-CDRC)
University of Mississippi
University, MS, USA

ISBN 978-3-319-41395-2   ISBN 978-3-319-41397-6 (eBook)
DOI 10.1007/978-3-319-41397-6

Library of Congress Control Number: 2016953108

© Springer International Publishing Switzerland 2016
This work is subject to copyright. All rights are reserved by the Publisher, whether the whole or part of the material is concerned, specifically the rights of translation, reprinting, reuse of illustrations, recitation, broadcasting, reproduction on microfilms or in any other physical way, and transmission or information storage and retrieval, electronic adaptation, computer software, or by similar or dissimilar methodology now known or hereafter developed.
The use of general descriptive names, registered names, trademarks, service marks, etc. in this publication does not imply, even in the absence of a specific statement, that such names are exempt from the relevant protective laws and regulations and therefore free for general use.
The publisher, the authors and the editors are safe to assume that the advice and information in this book are believed to be true and accurate at the date of publication. Neither the publisher nor the authors or the editors give a warranty, express or implied, with respect to the material contained herein or for any errors or omissions that may have been made.

Printed on acid-free paper

This Springer imprint is published by Springer Nature
The registered company is Springer International Publishing AG
The registered company address is: Gewerbestrasse 11, 6330 Cham, Switzerland

Preface

We are delighted to offer opening comments on the collection of new contributions in *Clinical Perspectives on Meaning: Positive and Existential Psychotherapy*. As a whole, the book signals important advances in the use of meaning-making activities to improve human lives. We highlight these strides forward via four themes that are evident across the chapters. A first and foremost theme is *building on the legacy of logotherapy*. These chapters include the varieties of present-day therapies that follow in the spirit of Viktor Frankl's remarkable life journey. His insights, embodied in logotherapy, helped people around the world appreciate the life-sustaining strengths that follow from choosing to find, and indeed create, meaning in encounters with very difficult experiences. Contributing authors in this volume extend that early work in multiple ways by linking it to aspects of cognitive-behavior therapy as well as formulations in positive psychology. Across chapters many authors highlight the theoretical and clinical commonalities between existential and positive psychology, suggesting that the former paved the way for the modern approach to positive human functioning. Several bridges connect these two disciplines, from the concepts of resilience and thriving, to goal pursuit and hope, to the model of character strengths and virtues. Other chapters describe the importance of meaning in clinical settings and they offer useful reviews of different types of meaning-centered therapies, along with evidence as to their general effectiveness. Meaning-making in mental health settings is now linked with posttraumatic growth and possible related gains in self-efficacy and positive reappraisal. Other novel interventions include exercises in existential gratitude. Importantly, the absence of meaning—that is, living in an existential vacuum wherein one is prone to boredom—is thoughtfully examined with emphasis on how these conditions can increase risk for substance use disorders. Indeed, the common perspective of all these contributions suggests that meaning in life should be the final and more important aim of any psychotherapeutic approach, from standard cognitive-behavioral therapy, to counseling, to mindfulness techniques to positive psychotherapies. Together, these topics reveal valuable new directions in therapies that take meaning-making seriously and deepen and enrich it via connections to new domains.

A second theme pertains to *meaning-making in the face of physical health challenges*. Contributing authors in this area focus on the challenges of living with chronic illness, where conceptions of healing and suffering require new formulations that seek to address and alleviate the loneliness of illness, while also encouraging the exploration of meaning in a physically compromised life. The field of psycho-oncology is present in other contributing chapters that focus on meaning-centered activities among cancer patients. Therapies in this domain seek to nurture resilience and effective coping and, if need be, help patients face limited time horizons. In this framework, the concept of spirituality and sanctification appears to be particularly linked to meaning-making processes. The pursuit of purpose and peace is framed, as it should be, as fundamental to approaching the end of life. Other traumatic health events, such as spinal cord injury, are included as well. This profoundly life-changing event is presented as offering unique opportunities to bring meaning-making activities into traditional rehabilitation practices, thereby enriching conceptions of adjustment in the aftermath of disability. Importantly, the need to educate doctors and therapists in order to address these existential issues with their patients could provide a new valuable area of development for positive psychology and positive health. Collectively, these diverse chapters signal important new directions in enlightened healthcare.

Outside the therapeutic context, *meaning-making in day-to-day life* is a third prominent theme. Here the reader finds contributions that view meaningful living as a grassroots endeavor embodied by the positive health movement. Such initiatives are intended to bring out the good and noble side of human beings, while also providing skills to transform the dark side of the human experience. Other nonclinical perspectives are elaborated via the character strengths and values emphasized in the positive psychology movement, and its related themes of hope and optimism. Another contribution focuses on a relational understanding of meaning that connects individuals to the life world that they inhabit. This linkage is relevant in educational contexts that involve the teaching of modification techniques intended as tools for volitional self-regulation. Caring is the focus of a further chapter that illuminates paths to meaning and purpose that follow from caring for one's significant others or for one's community. Both types of caring are framed as a kind of self-actualization that occurs via helping others to thrive and in working to make the world a better place. All of these contributions showcase how meaning-making in day-to-day life experience can enrich the human spirit and the human condition.

A final theme reflects questions regarding the *when, where, and how of meaning-making*. Chapters in this part of the book take meaning-making activities outside traditional therapies and practices in health contexts (mental or physical) into new, largely uncharted territories. One chapter focuses on *when* in the life course it may be particularly important to cultivate a sense of purpose in life. The emphasis is on adolescents, where research suggests there is an absence of purpose among many. Strategies are thus suggested for helping to foster purpose in the lives of young people. The question of *where* is evident in a chapter on meaning vis-à-vis multiculturalism—this contribution emphasizes the universal need for meaning, while noting the importance of attending to cultural influences on how individuals think about and find purpose in their lives. The present historical context is rife with ethnopolitical tensions and struggles—contributing authors on this topic examine the possibilities for healthy functioning amidst such strife. Specific attention is given to the possible importance of secondary control, wherein one adjusts aspects of the self and accepts circumstances as they are. The relevance of such a stance for coping with daily stressors related to war exposure is considered. The question of *how* is engaged via a contribution that examines nostalgia—specifically, the use of the past as a resource to help people regulate stress and find meaning and strength from autobiographical experience. The boundaries of meaning-making are pushed in a chapter calling for meaninglessness to be respected for its own integrity. This contribution pushes the question of how into new territory, which recognizes the possibility that not finding meanings or reasons in certain difficult experiences may be its own existential reality that warrants empathic attunement among therapists.

These brief opening observations are meant to convey the depth and breadth of what is included in *Clinical Perspectives on Meaning: Positive and Existential Psychotherapy*. It is an outstanding collection of new contributions that build thoughtfully on the past, while at the same time take the uniquely human capacity for meaning-making to important new places.

Madison, WI, USA　　　　　　　　　　　　　　　　　　　　　　　Carol D. Ryff
Bologna, Italy　　　　　　　　　　　　　　　　　　　　　　　　　Chiara Ruini

Acknowledgment

For Lior, Ariel, Shahaf and Shir, my sources of meaning in life.
– Pninit

For Laura and the cats.
– Stefan

To my co-editors, Pninit and Stefan, for taking the lead on this project, and to Juliane, Leonie and Larissa with love.
– Alex

Contents

Clinical Perspectives on Meaning: Understanding, Coping and Thriving through Science and Practice 1
Pninit Russo-Netzer, Stefan E. Schulenberg, and Alexander Batthyany

Part I Understanding: Contexts, Objectives and Considerations

The Proper Aim of Therapy: Subjective Well-Being, Objective Goodness, or a Meaningful Life? 17
Thaddeus Metz

Seeing Life Through a Sacred Lens: The Spiritual Dimension of Meaning 37
Julie M. Pomerleau, Kenneth I. Pargament, and Annette Mahoney

Working with Meaning in Life in Mental Health Care: A Systematic Literature Review of the Practices and Effectiveness of Meaning-Centred Therapies 59
Joel Vos

Making Meaning in the Context of Ethnopolitical Warfare: Secondary Control as a Resource 89
Emily Stagnaro, Laura E.R. Blackie, Erik G. Helzer, and Eranda Jayawickreme

Multiculturalism and Meaning in Existential and Positive Psychology 111
Louis Hoffman, Nathaniel Granger Jr., and Monica Mansilla

Practices of Meaning-Changing Interventions: A Comprehensive Matrix 131
Dmitry Leontiev

Part II Coping: Integrative Meaning-Oriented Perspectives and Interventions for Human Coping

The Significance of Meaning to Conceptualizations of Resilience and Posttraumatic Growth: Strengthening the Foundation for Research and Practice 149
Lauren N. Weathers, Bethany J. Aiena, Meredith A. Blackwell, and Stefan E. Schulenberg

Working with Meaning in Life in Chronic or Life-Threatening Disease: A Review of Its Relevance and the Effectiveness of Meaning-Centred Therapies 171
Joel Vos

Meaning in Life in the Prevention and Treatment of Substance Use Disorders 201
Efrén Martínez Ortíz and Ivonne Andrea Flórez

Reason, Meaning, and Resilience in the Treatment of Depression: Logotherapy as a Bridge Between Cognitive-Behavior Therapy and Positive Psychology 223
Matti Ameli

Meaning-Centered Psychotherapy in the Oncology and Palliative Care Settings 245
William Breitbart and Melissa Masterson

Meaning Making in the Aftermath of a Spinal Cord Injury 261
Peter Claudio, Simon Kunz, Andreas Hegi, and Daniel Stirnimann

Out, Out, Brief Candle? The Meaning of Meaninglessness 283
Todd DuBose

Part III Thriving: Integrative Meaning-Oriented Perspectives and Interventions for Human Thriving

Meaning, Medicine, and Healing 299
Thomas R. Egnew

Integrative Meaning Therapy: From Logotherapy to Existential Positive Interventions 323
Paul T.P. Wong

Nostalgia as an Existential Intervention: Using the Past to Secure Meaning in the Present and the Future 343
Clay Routledge, Christina Roylance, and Andrew A. Abeyta

Caring and Meaning in Psychotherapy 363
Ofra Mayseless

Character Strengths and Mindfulness as Core Pathways to Meaning in Life.. 383
Hadassah Littman-Ovadia and Ryan M. Niemiec

Strategies for Cultivating Purpose Among Adolescents in Clinical Settings.. 407
Kendall Cotton Bronk and Susan Mangan

Meaning Centered Positive Group Intervention......................... 423
Paul T.P. Wong

Index... 447

Contributors

Andrew A. Abeyta, M.A. Department of Psychology, North Dakota State University, Fargo, ND, USA

Bethany J. Aiena, M.A. Department of Psychology, Clinical-Disaster Research Center (UM-CDRC), University of Mississippi, University, MS, USA

Matti Ameli, M.S. Calle Periodista Azzati, Valencia, Spain

Alexander Batthyany, Ph.D. International Academy of Philosophy, University in the Principality of Liechtenstein, Triesen, Liechtenstein

Laura E.R. Blackie, Ph.D. Department of Psychology, University of Nottingham, University Park, Nottingham, UK

Meredith A. Blackwell, B.A. Department of Psychology, Clinical-Disaster Research Center (UM-CDRC), University of Mississippi, University, MS, USA

William Breitbart, M.D., F.A.P.A., F.A.P.O.S. Department of Psychiatry and Behavioral Sciences, Memorial Sloan Kettering Cancer Center, New York, NY, USA

Peter Claudio, Ph.D. Environment, Participation and Social Integration Unit, Swiss Paraplegic Research (SPF), Nottwil, Switzerland

Department of Health Sciences and Health Policy, University of Lucerne, Lucerne, Switzerland

Kendall Cotton Bronk, Ph.D. Quality of Life Research Center, Claremont Graduate University, Claremont, CA, USA

Todd DuBose, Ph.D. The Chicago School of Professional Psychology, Chicago, IL, USA

Thomas R. Egnew, Ed.D., L.I.C.S.W. Tacoma Family Medicine, Tacoma, WA, USA

Ivonne Andrea Flórez, M.A. Department of Psychology, Clinical-Disaster Research Center (UM-CDRC), University of Mississippi, University, MS, USA

Nathaniel Granger, Jr., Psy.D. Department of Humanistic and Clinical Psychology, Saybrook University, Oakland, CA, USA

Andreas Hegi, lic. Phil. Swiss Paraplegic Center (SPZ), Nottwil, Switzerland

Erik G. Helzer, Ph.D. The Johns Hopkins Carey Business School, Baltimore, MD, USA

Louis Hoffman, Ph.D. Department of Humanistic and Clinical Psychology, Saybrook University, Oakland, CA, USA

Eranda Jayawickreme, Ph.D. Department of Psychology, Wake Forest University, Winston-Salem, NC, USA

Simon Kunz, M.Sc. Environment, Participation and Social Integration Unit, Swiss Paraplegic Research (SPF), Nottwil, Switzerland

Department of Health Sciences and Health Policy, University of Lucerne, Lucerne, Switzerland

Dmitry Leontiev, Ph.D. National Research University Higher School of Economics, Moscow, Russia

Hadassah Littman-Ovadia, Ph.D. Department of Behavioral Sciences and Psychology, Ariel University, Ariel, Israel

Annette Mahoney, Ph.D. Department of Clinical Psychology, Bowling Green State University, Bowling Green, OH, USA

Susan Mangan, M.A. Department of Psychology, Claremont Graduate University, Claremont, CA, USA

Monica Mansilla, Ph.D. Department of Humanistic and Clinical Psychology, Saybrook University, Oakland, CA, USA

Melissa Masterson, M.A. Memorial Sloan Kettering Cancer Center, New York, NY, USA

Ofra Mayseless, Ph.D. Faculty of Education, University of Haifa, Haifa, Israel

Thaddeus Metz, Ph.D. Department of Philosophy, University of Johannesburg, Auckland Park, South Africa

Ryan M. Niemiec, Psy.D. VIA Institute on Character, Cincinnati, OH, USA

Xavier University, Cincinnati, OH, USA

Efrén Martínez Ortíz, Ph.D. Society for the Advancement of Meaning-Centered Psychotherapy, Bogotá, Colombia

Kenneth I. Pargament, Ph.D. Department of Clinical Psychology, Bowling Green State University, Bowling Green, OH, USA

Contributors

Julie M. Pomerleau, B.S. Department of Clinical Psychology, Bowling Green State University, Bowling Green, OH, USA

Clay Routledge, Ph.D. Department of Psychology, North Dakota State University, Fargo, ND, USA

Christina Roylance, M.S. Department of Psychology, North Dakota State University, Fargo, ND, USA

Chiara Ruini, Ph.D. Department of Psychology, University of Bologna, Bologna, Italy

Pninit Russo-Netzer, Ph.D. Department of Counseling and Human Development, University of Haifa, Mount Carmel, Haifa, Israel

Carol D. Ryff, Ph.D. Institute on Aging, 2245 Medical Science Center, University of Wisconsin-Madison, Madison, WI, USA

Stefan E. Schulenberg, Ph.D. Department of Psychology, Clinical-Disaster Research Center (UM-CDRC), University of Mississippi, University, MS, USA

Emily Stagnaro, M.A. Department of Psychology, Wake Forest University, Winston-Salem, NC, USA

Daniel Stirnimann, M.Sc. Spinal Cord Injury Center, Balgrist University Hospital, Zürich, Switzerland

Joel Vos, Ph.D. Department of Psychology, University of Roehampton, London, UK

Lauren N. Weathers, M.A. Department of Psychology, Clinical-Disaster Research Center (UM-CDRC), University of Mississippi, University, MS, USA

Paul T.P. Wong, Ph.D., C.Psych. Meaning-Centered Counselling Institute, Inc., Toronto, ON, Canada

About the Editors

Pninit Russo-Netzer, Ph.D. is a researcher and lecturer at the Department of Counseling and Human Development, University of Haifa. Her main research and practice interests focus on meaning in life, positive psychology, spirituality and spiritual development, positive change, and growth. Dr. Russo-Netzer is a practitioner of positive psychology, a logotherapist (Diplomate Clinician), the head of the academic training program for logotherapy at Tel-Aviv University, and the chairperson of the Logotherapy Association in Israel. She serves as academic advisor and consultant to both academic and nonacademic institutions, conducts workshops, and develops training programs and curricula for various organizations on logotherapy, meaning in life, positive psychology, resilience, and spirituality.

Stefan E. Schulenberg, Ph.D. is a licensed psychologist in the state of Mississippi, a Professor in the University of Mississippi's Psychology Department, and a Diplomate in Logotherapy. Dr. Schulenberg serves as the Director of the University of Mississippi's Clinical-Disaster Research Center (UM-CDRC), an integrated research, teaching, and training center with emphases in disaster mental health and positive psychology. His research interests include clinical-disaster psychology, perceived meaning/purpose in life, positive psychology, and psychological assessment. He conducts workshops and provides training on disaster preparedness, psychological first aid, disaster response, meaning/purpose in life, resilience, and posttraumatic growth.

Alexander Batthyany, Ph.D. holds the Viktor Frankl Chair for Philosophy and Psychology at the International Academy of Philosophy in the Principality of Liechtenstein. He teaches theory of Cognitive Science at Vienna University's Cognitive Science Program and Logotherapy and Existential Analysis at the Department of Psychiatry at Vienna Medical School. Since 2012, Dr. Batthyany is Visiting Professor for Existential Psychotherapy at the Moscow University Institute of Psychoanalysis. He is director of the Viktor Frankl Institute and the Viktor Frankl

Archives in Vienna and first editor of the 14-volume Edition of the Collected Works of Viktor Frankl. Dr. Batthyany has published several books and articles. His works have been translated into more than 10 languages. Dr. Batthyany lectures widely on philosophical and existential psychology, philosophy of mind, and theory of cognitive science.

Clinical Perspectives on Meaning: Understanding, Coping and Thriving through Science and Practice

Pninit Russo-Netzer, Stefan E. Schulenberg, and Alexander Batthyany

Listening to the Unheard Cry for Meaning

> In former days, people frustrated in their will to meaning would probably have turned to a pastor, priest, or rabbi. Today, they crowd clinics and offices. The psychiatrist, then, frequently finds himself in an embarrassing situation, for he now is confronted with human problems rather than with specific clinical symptoms. Man's search for a meaning is not pathological, but rather the surest sign of being truly human. Even if this search is frustrated, it cannot be considered a sign of disease. It is spiritual distress, not mental disease. How should the clinician respond to this challenge? Traditionally, he is not prepared to cope with this situation in any but medical terms. Thus he is forced to conceive of the problem as something pathological. Furthermore, he induces his patient to interpret his plight as a sickness to be cured rather than as a challenge to be met. By so doing, the doctor robs the patient of the potential fruits of his spiritual struggle. (Frankl, 1973, p. 93)

As this quote implies, the will to meaning, a fundamental and basic human need, is relevant to each and every human being. Therapists, clinicians, and scholars are constantly confronted with existential questions, about which existing textbooks and diagnostic manuals carry little, if any, information. This is especially relevant in the fast-paced, digital, and global world of today, where mental health professionals need to address the pressing challenges of cultivating a sense of meaning in everyday life. Despite the mounting research findings underscoring the importance of

---

P. Russo-Netzer, Ph.D. (✉)
Department of Counseling and Human Development, University of Haifa,
199 Aba Khoushy Ave., Mount Carmel 3498838, Israel
e-mail: pninit.russonetzer@gmail.com

S.E. Schulenberg, Ph.D.
Department of Psychology, Clinical-Disaster Research Center (UM-CDRC),
University of Mississippi, University, MS 38677, USA

A. Batthyany, Ph.D.
International Academy of Philosophy, University in the Principality of Liechtenstein,
Triesen, Liechtenstein

© Springer International Publishing Switzerland 2016
P. Russo-Netzer et al. (eds.), *Clinical Perspectives on Meaning*,
DOI 10.1007/978-3-319-41397-6_1

meaning for human coping and thriving (e.g., Damon, 2008; Linley & Joseph, 2011; Melton & Schulenberg, 2008; Ryff & Singer, 1998; Steger, Oishi, & Kashdan, 2009), little research has focused on methods one can follow in order to nurture or reinforce it (Nelson, Fuller, Choi, & Lyubomirsky, 2014).

The current literature discusses the distinction between hedonic and eudaimonic well-being, of which meaning is more closely related to the eudaimonic approach. While hedonic well-being is most commonly understood as the accumulation of positive affective experiences of the individual, eudaimonic well-being is understood as a deeper feeling of striving toward meaning and a virtuous purpose, beyond the experience of positive affect (Friedman, 2012; Ryan & Deci, 2001; Ryff & Singer, 1996; Ryff, Singer, & Dienberg Love, 2004). Eudaimonic well-being can be achieved by pursuing activities that are in congruence with the individual's personal values (Waterman, 1993), or in congruence with the individual's strengths or personality traits (Seligman, 2002). Therefore, an individual will experience meaning and will thrive when he/she pursues activities that are intrinsically meaningful and important, in comparison to pursuing activities motivated by external concerns (i.e., the hedonic approach). Yet, interventions designed to cultivate the meaning component of general well-being have received only scant research attention (Shin & Steger, 2014; Steger, Bundick, & Yeager, 2012).

Interest in meaning-oriented interventions is on the rise, and they are increasingly being used in various settings and contexts by researchers and practitioners alike. However, as of today, no single source provides an integrated, comprehensive overview of the conceptual, theoretical, and practical aspects of this varied work. Moreover, despite extensive research examining the benefits of meaning and purpose for individual growth and development, knowledge regarding its promotion and cultivation is limited (Shin & Steger, 2014). Empirical research is slowly uncovering the many positive psychological, spiritual, and physical effects of meaning and purpose for the individual, contributing to our understanding of areas ranging from academic achievement (DeWitz, Woolsey, & Walsh, 2009) and occupational adjustment (Steger & Dik, 2009; Steger, Pickering, Shin, & Dik, 2010), to happiness (e.g., Ryff & Keyes, 1995; Steger et al., 2009) and life satisfaction (e.g., Drescher et al., 2012; Steger, Frazier, Oishi, & Kaler, 2006; Steger, Kashdan, Sullivan, & Lorentz, 2008). Several criticisms have emerged from Shin and Steger's (2014) review of existing interventions, namely that most do not focus specifically on meaning and purpose but rather on overall happiness or well-being. For example, several happiness-enhancing interventions have been empirically studied including, but not limited to, practicing gratitude (Emmons & McCullough, 2003), forgiveness (McCullough, Pargament, & Thoresen, 2000), and thoughtful self-reflection (King, 2001; Lyubomirsky, Sousa, & Dickerhoof, 2006). Secondly, that they address mainly recuperative and protective aspects of meaning rather than aspects of its wider normative developmental process. And thirdly, that they are built on the basis of conceptual frameworks that are "insufficiently systematic to counter the lack of data about interventions" (p. 91). In addition to Shin and Steger's (2014) attempt to analyze meaning-enhancing interventions, Parks and Biswas-Diener (2013) have attempted to set several of their own criteria in order to integrate and refine current conceptualizations. More specifically, they argue that a successful positive intervention must have the primary goal of building some sort of "positive" target variable (e.g., meaning, among others), empirical evidence must exist proving that the intervention causes some change in the target variable, and in addition, must prove that enhancing this target variable is beneficial to the individual and surrounding society.

Parks and Biswas-Diener (2013) claim that current interventions in the literature do not achieve all of these goals. For example, many interventions focus on creating meaning through writing as a way of helping the individual to form a coherent narrative about his or her life, which is viewed as essential to the experience of meaning (Pennebaker & Seagal, 1999). Conflicting evidence exists as Lyubomirsky et al. (2006) found that in some cases, writing about a positive event actually lowered life satisfaction when compared to controls. More recent approaches focus on personal narratives regarding positive events (e.g., King, 2001; Seligman, Rashid, & Parks, 2006). For example, Sheldon and Lyubomirsky (2006) showed that mere thinking about being one's best possible self (and not actually writing it) was enough to demonstrate benefits. However, this has been shown to backfire for some individuals who are prone to anxiety or depression. These examples demonstrate the lack of empirical evidence demonstrating change in the target variable. In other words, empirical literature is lacking an extension of the application of these interventions and therapeutic mechanisms across a wider variety of contexts and populations (Shin & Steger, 2014).

When considering the psychological operationalization of meaning within different life contexts, it is possible that similar mechanisms are at work. Meaning can take on quite diverse properties and roles, each connected to the different research traditions of meaning-oriented psychologies. According to this narrative, the existential tradition, and especially recent empirical work on experimental existential psychology (e.g., Terror Management Theory, or TMT), views meaning mainly as a buffer against existential anxiety, uncertainty, and the impasses of the conditio humana. In contrast, positive psychology conceptualizes meaning and purpose awareness primarily as an activating mechanism to elicit optimal functioning and satisfaction with life. Another perspective less often addressed in this context is known as the cognitive tradition, which views meaning not so much as a way of coping and striving, but as the matrix by which we decipher and understand the structure of complex things or situations, and in this case, our place in the world.

Prima facie, we encounter what appear to be very different accounts and definitions of what meaning could mean in psychological terms, and yet, on closer inspection it turns out that these three connotations are in no way exclusive, but rather are complementary to each other in that they are different paths that lead to one basic phenomenon. Hence, if we have found that on an applied and clinical level, each of these meaning concepts is related to one another, we have naturally also found a bridge to overcome the apparent, or real, differences between their related psychological theories and disciplines. Indeed, it turns out that each of these potential roles of meaning relates in some way or the other to our general psychological make-up and functioning, and often enough, the quest for one type of distinct meaning clearly relates to another. For example—a number of research studies suggest that lack of meaning awareness is a potent risk factor for substance abuse (e.g., Kinnier, Metha, Keim, & Okey, 1994); other studies suggest that meaning awareness is a potent factor in the treatment of substance abuse disorders (e.g., Klingemann, 1991); and yet another set of studies suggest that people's general life satisfaction is significantly higher if they are existentially fulfilled, and hence are assumed to be less likely to revert to self-destructive behavior (e.g., Newcomb & Harlow, 1986).

Therefore, while conducting theoretical and empirical research it may be possible, and at times even necessary, to address each of these connotations separately, as this type of compartmentalization and specialization no longer works when addressing these same issues in the clinical context, and when dealing with real people. While it may well be that artificial disciplinary or traditional boundaries (such as, for example, positive psychology's notion that meaning is predominantly a positive resource for flourishing and striving, whereas some branches of experimental existential psychology, such as TMT, merely view it as a buffer against mortality anxiety and existential threat) help to further scientific progress in this area through debate and dialogue, they may very well also hinder it. For example, certain preconceived notions inherited from tradition (in one area of psychology), rather than being necessary or inherent parts of the respective theory or discipline itself, blank out certain aspects that may turn out to be crucially important for understanding and addressing some of the unresolved questions regarding the potential role, or roles, of meaning in psychology as understood by another area. Take, for example, the question whether search for meaning is a defense mechanism or a genuine human motivation: traditional existentialist schools of psychotherapy, such as Frankl's logotherapy and existential logotherapy, hold that the search for meaning is an irreducible psychological variable. However, none of these schools so far has come forth with plausible arguments why these two perspectives on meaning describe alternative, rather than complementary models of meaning(s).

Sure enough, some of these questions are likely to remain unanswered insofar as they touch upon philosophical problems which are, in fact, unlikely to be resolved by any amount of rational or empirical inquiry. And yet, from an existential point of view, if we seriously consider the human quest for meaning, the question is no longer merely whether the meaning fulfillment many seem to seek, and some at least sometimes experience, achieves the purpose of equipping us with certain psychological advantages in striving, coping, and defense but also, and with equal relevance, whether human beings genuinely strive for meaning for its own sake, or whether a simpler motive is concealed behind the striving, for which the question of meaning is only a means to an end. Therefore, even if psychology will not be able to, nor is it expected to, resolve questions on the nature of meaning it can, and at least needs to, acknowledge that one of the core issues of research of the construct is whether it is a fundamental variable in our psychological functioning, or whether it is reducible to other, more basic drives and psychological mechanisms, even if only for the sake of intellectual honesty.

Still, it is instructive to understand the reasons and causes for the distinction between positive and existential psychologies of meaning, despite their large thematic and therapeutic overlaps. For example, existential psychologists, especially its European founders and pioneers, such as Ludwig Binswanger (1942), Medard Boss (1957), Viktor E. Frankl (1946), and Viktor Von Gebsattel (1954), made ample use of the phenomenological method, i.e., they were trying to apply Husserl's and Merleau-Ponty's introspectionist psychology to the "metaphysics of everyday life." Against the background of its historical setting, within the context of Europe's tragedies of the past century (i.e., the two World Wars), and the massive collective traumas brought about by the Holocaust, the movement of early European existential psychologists and psychiatrists toward the phenomenological method in psychology with its emphasis on individual experience, narrative, and quest, is understandable. Even more so, this approach seems appropriate when it comes to the attempt to comprehend the individual in his or her search for a place in the world, understanding of one's role in life, and for the relentless question of whether meaning can be found in suffering and tragedy, too.

Simultaneously, and often even within the very same university departments where these early existential psychologists and psychiatrists were trying to grasp the richness and complexity of individual narratives and their deeper meaning, empirical psychologists attempted to establish psychology as a scientific discipline using quantitative rather than qualitative research. This caused a move away from narrative, phenomenological, and other more "subject-based" soft approaches to human psychology (Wertz, 2014). Indeed, once quantitative research methods gained prominence, questions regarding the metaphysics of everyday life may not have seemed worthwhile or even accessible research endeavors, as they did not lend themselves to experimental study and quantitative analysis (at least they did not for a long time—cf. recent developments in experimental existential psychology; Greenberg, Koole, & Pyszczynski, 2004). As a result, for the better part of the second half of the twentieth century, researchers in the field of psychology were prone to ignore the clinical relevance, or even authenticity, of existential questions altogether.

Building on the aforementioned methodological factors, one further reason for this relatively nonchalant handling of existential issues may be that once one is even tentatively willing to get involved in existential questions from a psychological perspective, one is at once confronted with a myriad of philosophical problems about the reality, nature, and type of meaning and purpose in an individual's life—and thus with questions that are, by definition it seems, out of reach for empirical research and quantitative analysis. But ignoring a question of course does not mean that it is not relevant for a deeper understanding of the issues at hand; it only means that within a certain discipline, or within a certain school of thought within this discipline, the question is usually not addressed. And yet it is one thing to claim that certain problems are difficult to grasp, and quite another to claim that it is therefore irrelevant or that it does not exist or that it is reducible to other, better studied, mechanisms.

As a case in point, the past decades have seen an unending stream of popular publications designed to help readers to find meaning and purpose in their lives, and to find their place in the world (e.g., Leider, 2015; Millman, 2011). This outpouring of publications has provided, and continues to provide, constant testimony to the fact that there is a widespread interest in existential questions and, as the renowned existential psychiatrist Viktor Frankl put it, a "will to meaning," or, as described in a critical title of one of his later publications, an "unheard cry for meaning":

> More and more a psychiatrist today is confronted with a new type of patient, a new class of neurosis, a new kind of suffering the most remarkable characteristic of which is the fact that it does not represent a disease in the proper sense of the term. This phenomenon has brought about a change in the function - or should I say mission? - of present day psychiatry. In such cases, the traditional techniques of treatment available to the psychiatrist prove themselves to be less and less applicable. (Frankl, 1973, p. 93)

Hence, after a detour during which the psychological role of the quest for meaning and purpose was first ignored due to the difficulty with which scientific psychologists found it to connect to earlier phenomenological research, subsequently, it was ignored due to the perspective of most of the more orthodox psychological schools of thought, according to which existential questions were under the general suspicion of being either psychologically inconsequential or the expression of sublimation or compensation of more basic drives and needs. Finally, meaning made an unexpected return and once again became a prominent issue within psychology and psychotherapy. As hinted at above, and as demonstrated by the sheer number of recent psychological studies on the question of meaning (Batthyany, 2011; Batthyany & Guttmann, 2005; Schulenberg, Hutzell, Nassif, & Rogina, 2008; Thir, 2012), one likely contributing factor to this renewed interest may be the fact that, since around 1970, psychological thought in general has opened up to new ideas, especially since increasing numbers of academic psychologists began to become concerned with the conceptual and therapeutic limits of orthodox psychoanalysis. At the same time, behaviorism, which for several decades was a particularly strong force within experimental psychology, has lost much of its original dominance. Both developments in the history of ideas of psychology took place largely due to the so-called cognitive turn in the behavioral science, which then soon spread into clinical and experimental psychology (Gardner, 1986).

This turn not only brought about a rediscovery of the central role of internal representations of the world, which logotherapy had identified long before as being crucial for understanding human experience and behavior (Frankl, 1946); the increased openness to less mechanistic or purely psychodynamic models also led researchers to abandon some of their earlier, almost exclusive, focus on deficits, and instead sparked interest in looking again at those inner resources by which real and apparent deficits can be overcome or regulated in a psychologically mature and healthy way. Frankl, too, considered much of the "old psychologies" to be disproportionately concerned with deficits and limits, and held that—put simply—they often tended toward a reductionist pathologism, which attempted to explain even such deeply human and existential concerns, such as the need for meaning and authenticity, not as expressions of human maturity, but as mere compensations for psychological defects and frustrated "lower" needs (Frankl, 1946, 1973). In brief, for a long time, psychology was largely *deficit-based* rather than *resource-oriented*. Frankl, on the other hand, consistently emphasized and appealed to those remaining resources that, even during precarious times in a client's or a patient's life, can exert a protective effect in crisis prevention and a curative influence in crisis intervention. He further held that awareness of individual meaning and purpose is the most potent of such resources, and in turn also the most effective in activating other psychological resources.

For several decades now, positive psychology has tied in with these ideas on a broader level (Seligman & Csikszentmihalyi, 2000). Again, looking at the positive sides of human existence is not an entirely new idea in the history of scientific psychology: in parallel with Frankl and as early as the 1930s, Charlotte Bühler had proposed to study not only the life histories of the mentally ill, but also those of individuals who had remained mentally healthy under the same or similar life conditions, in order to determine which resources they activated. In other words, her proposal was to investigate not just what makes people sick, but also what keeps them healthy (Bühler, 1933). Still, the systematic scientific pursuit of a broad-based, resource-oriented psychology is a relatively new undertaking, and at least to existential psychotherapists, it did not come as a surprise that research in this area would soon find that meaning is a central psychological (and existential) resource (Klingberg, 2009). Thus while the phenomenological method, once so prominent in early European existential psychology, has never quite been rehabilitated in contemporary research, one of its core findings—that human beings are not only concerned with surviving everyday life, but that they are also deeply concerned with the meaning of their lives and their individual future—has been rediscovered. More specifically, one has to take first-person accounts seriously in order to learn something about human nature and motivation which, by other methods, may not be so easily accessible. This, then, is but one example that illustrates that the differences between diverging approaches in psychological modeling of meaning and purpose (as both a resource and a potent coping factor) have been illusory rather than real.

The Clinicians' Perspective

In our earlier volume, we argued that only an increase in research and dialogue between the several branches of meaning-oriented psychology will one day enable us to disentangle this question, and related questions, on the nature and function of meaning and meaning awareness. And while, as a whole, our former volume may have accomplished some advances in this direction, the present volume tackles these questions from yet another set of perspectives, namely the social, applied, and clinical perspectives, without which any debate on the metaphysics of everyday life would be incomplete and easily misleading. It is this application to our everyday lives which brings together all perspectives and forces psychological theorizing out of the ivory tower of armchair philosophy and psychology. Moreover, it assists in bridging the gaps between disciplines and branches of meaning-oriented psychologies, which even the most careful and unbiased reasoning may not be able to achieve. Additionally, the inclusion of these perspectives may ultimately lead to the insight that, given that it is built on the encounter with real humans in real situations, much of the divergence between meaning concepts is based on the fact that life itself is so complex that no one single discipline or research branch will be able to address, let alone understand, human existence and the quest for meaning as a whole.

Yet rather than merely acknowledging that once we put meaning on the landscape of psychological theory, our theorizing will reach a degree of complexity that renders the development of a full-blown explanatory model unlikely. Frankl based his model on the notion of nonreductionism as a heuristic principle. Furthermore, he understood nonreductionism to imply that each aspect or dimension of a human being—the physiological, the psychological, and the noetic (or spiritual)—represents a layer of properties and functions that interact with each other, but nonetheless is ontologically and (at least to a certain extent) causally independent of each other (Frankl, 1946). However, each of these are aspects of what constitutes a human person, and therefore none can be discarded or ignored in our quest to truly align psychology with what it means to be human.

This heuristic also works well as a basis for acknowledging, understanding, and researching the three different functions and concepts of meaning, i.e., striving, coping, and understanding. While each is likely to be, to a certain extent, independent of each other, and none is reducible to the other, they still refer to the one basic existential quest to find a home in this world and to being able to discover one's personal tasks and calling. As the contributions collected in this volume attest to, the nonreductionist approach to meaning in clinical psychology allows for an unbiased and fresh look at the roles meaning, or meanings, have in contemporary and, no doubt, future psychologies.

The work presented in this current volume emphasizes the claim that some of the differences and disagreements between these schools of thought may be illusory rather than real. Moreover, they suggest that once the ideas, methods, and concepts of these schools of thought are translated into and tested in everyday clinical practice, many of these differences lose much of their former grip as it comes to real, and existential, encounters with other human beings and ourselves as part of the therapeutic experience.

About this Book

This book is about personal meaning and purpose in both clinical/therapeutic and empirical contexts. In addition, it presents theory and research concerning the circumstances under which people from all walks of life can find meaning and purpose, and how the presence or absence of awareness of meaning and purpose affects their psychological functioning, mental health, and existential fulfillment. Furthermore, the broader picture regarding meaning interventions painted in this volume serves to enhance both the individual thriving of members within the general public, as well as coping mechanisms within specific populations such as cancer patients, those who have survived ethno-political warfare, and individuals experiencing mental illness. As previously mentioned, while this book is complete in itself, it is the natural development of an earlier volume discussing meaning and purpose and their role in psychological theory and practice (Batthyany & Russo-Netzer, 2014a). In this earlier volume, we gave an overview of the theoretical framing and understanding of meaning and purpose within the two branches of psychology, i.e., positive and existential psychology. In short, we attempted to map out contemporary thinking within meaning-oriented psychologies, while at the same time trying to negotiate the common ground and differences in how both of these research traditions model and conceptualize meaning as a psychological and existential variable:

> An integrative, balanced and holistic view – that takes into account controversies and disagreements, as well as strengths and points of agreement – can provide a more comprehensive understanding of the question of meaning. This "collage" or "montage" of ideas, perspectives and conceptualizations is also manifested in the multicultural landscape and contributions from both well-known and established scholars as well as younger researchers from both fields, in order to present a comprehensive and rich view on the issues discussed. (Batthyany & Russo-Netzer, 2014b, p. 19)

Ultimately, the outcome was much more than merely a collage or a montage. Indeed, we learned much previously undiscovered common territory between the two disciplines than we could have expected to find at the outset. Therefore, one of the outcomes of the debate we had facilitated between researchers and practitioners from both traditions seemed to be that to a large extent, the differences between the two disciplines' theorizing about meaning may, in the end, stem not so much from conceptual points of contention, but rather from their very different backgrounds and respective histories of ideas, different vocabulary for often very similar ideas, and, of course, their different methodologies. An additional reason for the real or apparent disagreements seemed to lie deeper, and more accurately, within the subject itself. If life itself is too complex to be captured by one single discipline, worldview, or outlook, so is the personal meaning that is, in ways yet to be defined, at least a potential part of this life. Hence, given life's immense complexity, it would seem unlikely that different schools of psychology would dedicate equal attention to the same aspects of meaning(s), and it is even less likely that they should reach the same (or even similar) conclusions regarding meaning and purpose and their psychological impact at different stages in life. And yet, while it may be obvious to empirically examine these different meanings within the context of research, how to connect them under the umbrella of the individual's subjective experience of meaning is less clear. The current volume attempts to address this theoretical obstacle.

The building blocks for extending the theoretical bridge between existential and positive psychology can be found in the overarching goals and objective of this book. Insights regarding themes such as resilience, thriving, comprehension, coping, the pursuit of goals, and the practice of logotherapy have been selected in order to emphasize the commonality between the disciplines of existential and positive psychology, as well as ground their contribution to the existing meaning literature in empirical research. Furthermore, additional chapters address the importance of meaning in diverse therapeutic settings and through a range of methods of therapy, as well as offer outlines for facilitating meaning-oriented interventions.

This volume seeks to extend the current literature by addressing novel findings in this rapidly growing and promising area of meaning and purpose by means of providing broad international and interdisciplinary perspectives in order to enhance the empirical findings. Moreover, while the book is practical in nature with respect to therapeutic practices, it is also deeply grounded in the scientific method, and a careful review of theoretical and conceptual literature is provided. As such, each chapter includes a section of "Key Takeaways," points for the reader to reflect on and consider when planning meaning-oriented interventions, as well as offers directions for future research and practice.

Moreover, this volume also explores topics such as spirituality, multiculturalism, posttraumatic growth, and nostalgia as additional areas of interest within the realm of meaning which assist in broadening our understanding and application of the construct in our everyday lives, as well as overall human psychological well-being. Some authors address topics relating to meaning-making while facing physical health challenges, while others focus on integrating meaning into everyday life from the perspective of the positive health movement. In addition, some chapters discuss some of the more technical factors of meaning-making, such as when in life it may be particularly important to cultivate meaning and in which cultures it is valued. Such a diverse and varied examination of the construct encourages the reader to integrate his or her thoughts from both existential and positive psychology perspectives, as well as from clinical and empirical approaches, and guides the theoretical convergence to a unique point of understanding and appreciation for the value of meaning and its pursuit.

Chapter Overview

The title of this introductory chapter captures the book's three main components—Understanding, Coping and Thriving—reflecting a contemporary, threefold perspective regarding meaning in positive and existential psychotherapy. In addition, contributions to this volume represent an international perspective, encompassing a wide range of contexts and countries, from the United States, the United Kingdom, Austria, Israel, Spain, Switzerland, Canada, Russia, South Africa, Colombia, and Italy.

In the first section, the volume addresses "*understanding*," and presents a broad conceptual overview comprised of a host of contexts, objectives, and considerations. Together, these chapters provide an important foundation for applying meaning in therapeutic settings. Chapters include work by Thaddeus Metz, who refers to the aims of therapy as a contribution to a meaningful life, and Julie M. Pomerleau, Kenneth I. Pargament, and Annette Mahoney, who emphasize the importance of the spiritual dimension of meaning. Following these works, Joel Vos presents a framework for working with meaning in life in the field of mental health care through a systematic literature review of current practices. Emily Stagnaro, Laura E.R. Blackie, Erik G. Helzer, and Eranda Jayawickreme examine meaning and control in the context of ethno-political warfare. Louis Hoffman, Nathaniel Granger Jr., and Monica Mansilla highlight multiculturalism and meaning in positive and existential psychology, and finally, Dmitry Leontiev reviews a variety of practices relating to meaning-oriented interventions.

The next two sections present various utilizations of meaning-oriented therapy in the context of human coping and thriving. The second section addresses *"coping"* and suggests meaning-oriented interventions for human coping in a variety of clinical settings, based on positive and existential perspectives. Lauren N. Weathers, Bethany J. Aiena, Meredith A. Blackwell, and Stefan E. Schulenberg begin the section with their discussion on the significance of meaning in conceptualizations of resilience and posttraumatic growth. Joel Vos then reviews the effectiveness of meaning-centered therapies in the context of chronic or life-threatening diseases. Efrén Martínez Ortíz and Ivonne Andrea Flórez present a logotherapeutic approach to the treatment of substance use disorders, and Matti Ameli presents logotherapy as a bridge between cognitive-behavior therapy and positive psychology in the treatment of depression. Next, William Breitbart and Melissa Masterson outline a meaning-centered psychotherapy intervention in the context of oncology and palliative care, Peter Claudio, Simon Kunz, Andreas Hegi, and Daniel Stirnimann discuss the experience of meaning for those with spinal cord injury, and Todd DuBose's chapter concludes this section, addressing the lived meaning of meaninglessness.

The third section addresses *"thriving"* and integrates positive and existential perspectives regarding the application of meaning in order to cultivate human flourishing. This section includes the work of Thomas R. Egnew who addresses meaning in the context of medicine and healing, and Paul T.P. Wong's integrative view of meaning therapy, translating logotherapy into existential positive interventions. Clay Routledge, Christina Roylance, and Andrew A. Abeyta highlight nostalgia as an existential intervention for meaning-making, while Ofra Mayseless considers the importance of caring and meaning in therapy. Following their efforts, Hadassah Littman-Ovadia and Ryan M. Niemiec examine character strengths and mindfulness as core pathways to achieving meaning in life, Kendall Cotton Bronk and Susan Mangan offer strategies for cultivating purpose among adolescents in clinical settings, and finally, Paul T.P. Wong provides an overview of a meaningful living group project as an exemplar of mental health intervention. As editors, it is our hope that these fascinating and thought-provoking chapters will stimulate deeper understanding of that which makes us uniquely human.

References

Batthyany, A. (2011). Over thirty-five years later: Research in logotherapy since 1975. New afterword to: Frankl, V. E. (2011). *Man's search for ultimate meaning*. London: Rider.
Batthyany, A., & Guttmann, D. (2005). *Empirical research in logotherapy and meaning-oriented psychotherapy*. Phoenix, AZ: Zeig, Tucker & Theisen.
Batthyany, A., & Russo-Netzer, P. (2014a). Psychologies of meaning. In A. Batthyany & P. Russo-Netzer (Eds.), *Meaning in existential and positive psychology* (pp. 3–22). New York, NY: Springer.
Batthyany, A., & Russo-Netzer, P. (2014b). *Meaning in existential and positive psychology*. New York, NY: Springer.
Binswanger, L. (1942). *Grundformen und Erkenntnis menschlichen Daseins*. Zürich: Rascher.

Boss, M. (1957). *Daseinsanalyse und Psychoanalyse*. Zürich: Rascher.
Bühler, C. (1933). *Der menschliche Lebenslauf als psychologisches Problem*. Leipzig: Hirzel.
Damon, W. (2008). *The path to purpose*. New York, NY: Free Press.
DeWitz, S. J., Woolsey, M. L., & Walsh, W. B. (2009). College student retention: An exploration of the relationship between self-efficacy beliefs and purpose in life among college students. *Journal of College Student Development, 50*, 19–34.
Drescher, C. F., Baczwaski, B. J., Walters, A. B., Aiena, B. J., Schulenberg, S. E., & Johnson, L. R. (2012). Coping with an ecological disaster: The role of perceived meaning in life and self-efficacy following the Gulf oil spill. *Ecopsychology, 4*, 56–63. doi:10.1089/eco.2012.0009
Emmons, R. A., & McCullough, M. E. (2003). Counting blessings versus burdens: An experimental investigation of gratitude and subjective well-being in daily life. *Journal of Personality and Social Psychology, 84*, 377–389.
Frankl, V. (1946). *Ärztliche Seelsorge. Grundlagen der Logotherapie und Existenzanalyse*. Wien: Deuticke.
Frankl, V. (1973). Psychiatry and man's quest for meaning. *Journal of Religion and Health, 1*, 93–103.
Friedman, E. M. (2012). Well-being, aging, and immunity. In S. Segerstrom (Ed.), *The Oxford handbook of psychoneuroimmunology* (pp. 37–62). New York, NY: Oxford University Press.
Gardner, H. (1986). *The mind's new science: A history of the cognitive revolution*. New York, NY: Basic Books.
Greenberg, J., Koole, S. L., & Pyszczynski, T. (Eds.). (2004). *Handbook of experimental existential psychology*. New York, NY: Guilford Press.
King, L. A. (2001). The health benefits of writing about life goals. *Personality and Social Psychology Bulletin, 27*, 798–807.
Kinnier, R. T., Metha, A. T., Keim, J. S., & Okey, J. L. (1994). Depression, meaninglessness, and substance abuse in "normal" and hospitalized adolescents. *Journal of Alcohol & Drug Education, 39*, 101–111.
Klingberg, H. (2009). Logotherapy, Frankl, and positive psychology. In A. Batthyany & J. Levinson (Eds.), *Empirical research in logotherapy and meaning-oriented psychotherapy*. Phoenix, AZ: Zeig, Tucker & Theisen.
Klingemann, H. K. (1991). The motivation for change from problem alcohol and heroin use. *British Journal of Addiction, 86*, 727–744.
Leider, R. J. (2015). *The power of purpose: Find meaning, live longer, better*. Oakland, CA: Berret-Koehler.
Linley, P. A., & Joseph, S. (2011). Meaning in life and posttraumatic growth. *Journal of Loss and Trauma, 16*, 150–159.
Lyubomirsky, S., Sousa, L., & Dickerhoof, R. (2006). The costs and benefits of writing, talking, and thinking about life's triumphs and defeats. *Journal of Personality and Social Psychology, 90*, 692–708.
McCullough, M. E., Pargament, K. I., & Thoresen, C. E. (2000). The psychology of forgiveness: History, conceptual issues, and overview. In M. E. McCullough, K. I. Pargament, & C. E. Thoresen (Eds.), *Forgiveness: Theory, research, and practice* (pp. 1–14). New York, NY: Guilford.
Melton, A. M. A., & Schulenberg, S. E. (2008). On the measurement of meaning: Logotherapy's empirical contributions to humanistic psychology. *The Humanistic Psychologist, 36*, 31–44. doi:10.1080/08873260701828870
Millman, D. (2011). *The four purposes of life*. New York, NY: H.J. Kramer.
Nelson, S. K., Fuller, J. A., Choi, I., & Lyubomirsky, S. (2014). Beyond self-protection self-affirmation benefits hedonic and eudaimonic well-being. *Personality and Social Psychology Bulletin, 40*, 998–1011.
Newcomb, M. D., & Harlow, L. L. (1986). Life events and substance use among adolescents: Mediating effects of perceived loss of control and meaninglessness in life. *Journal of Personality and Social Psychology, 51*, 564–577.
Parks, A. C., & Biswas-Diener, R. (2013). Positive interventions: Past, present and future. In T. B. Kashdan & J. Ciarrochi (Eds.), *Mindfulness, acceptance, and positive psychology: The seven foundations of well-being* (pp. 140–165). Oakland, CA: Context Press/New Harbinger Publications.

Pennebaker, J. W., & Seagal, J. D. (1999). Forming a story: The health benefits of narrative. *Journal of Clinical Psychology, 55*, 1243–1254.
Ryan, R. M., & Deci, E. L. (2001). On happiness and human potentials: A review of research on hedonic and eudaimonic well-being. *Annual Review of Psychology, 52*, 141–166.
Ryff, C. D., & Keyes, C. L. M. (1995). The structure of well-being revisited. *Journal of Personality and Social Psychology, 69*, 719–727.
Ryff, C. D., & Singer, B. (1996). Psychological well-being: Meaning, measurement, and implications for psychotherapy research. *Psychotherapy and Psychosomatics, 65*, 14–23.
Ryff, C. D., & Singer, B. (1998). The contours of positive human health. *Psychological Inquiry, 9*, 1–28.
Ryff, C. D., Singer, B. H., & Dienberg Love, G. (2004). Positive health: Connecting well-being with biology. *Philosophical Transactions-Royal Society of London Series B Biological Sciences, 359*(1449), 1383–1394.
Schulenberg, S. E., Hutzell, R. R., Nassif, C., & Rogina, J. M. (2008). Logotherapy for clinical practice. *Psychotherapy: Theory, Research, Practice, Training, 45*, 447–463. doi:10.1037/a0014331
Seligman, M. E. P. (2002). Positive psychology, positive prevention, and positive therapy. In C. R. Snyder & S. J. Lopez (Eds.), *Handbook of positive psychology* (pp. 3–9). New York, NY: Oxford University Press.
Seligman, M. E. P., & Csikszentmihalyi, M. (2000). Positive psychology: An introduction. *American Psychologist, 55*, 5–14.
Seligman, M. E. P., Rashid, T., & Parks, A. C. (2006). Positive psychotherapy. *American Psychologist, 61*, 774–788.
Sheldon, K. M., & Lyubomirsky, S. (2006). How to increase and sustain positive emotion: The effects of expressing gratitude and visualizing best possible selves. *Journal of Positive Psychology, 1*, 73–82.
Shin, J. Y., & Steger, M. F. (2014). Promoting meaning and purpose in life. In A. C. Parks & S. M. Schueller (Eds.), *The Wiley-Blackwell handbook of positive psychological interventions* (pp. 90–110). Chichester: Wiley-Blackwell.
Steger, M. F., Bundick, M., & Yeager, D. (2012). Understanding and promoting meaning in life during adolescence. In R. J. R. Levesque (Ed.), *Encyclopedia of adolescence* (pp. 1666–1677). New York, NY: Springer.
Steger, M. F., & Dik, B. J. (2009). If one is searching for meaning in life, does meaning in work help? *Applied Psychology: Health and Well-Being, 1*, 303–320.
Steger, M. F., Frazier, P., Oishi, S., & Kaler, M. (2006). The Meaning in Life Questionnaire: Assessing the presence of and search for meaning in life. *Journal of Counseling Psychology, 53*, 80–93.
Steger, M. F., Kashdan, T. B., Sullivan, B. A., & Lorentz, D. (2008). Understanding the search for meaning in life: Personality, cognitive style, and the dynamic between seeking and experiencing meaning. *Journal of Personality, 76*, 199–228.
Steger, M. F., Oishi, S., & Kashdan, T. B. (2009). Meaning in life across the life span: Levels and correlates of meaning in life from emerging adulthood to older adulthood. *Journal of Positive Psychology, 4*, 43–52.
Steger, M. F., Pickering, N. K., Shin, J. Y., & Dik, B. J. (2010). Calling in work: Secular or sacred? *Journal of Career Assessment, 18*, 82–96.
Thir, M. (2012). *Überblick zum gegenwärtigen Stand der empirischen Evaluierung der psychotherapeutischen Fachrichtung "Logotherapie und Existenzanalyse"*. Wels: Ausbildungsinstitut für Logotherapie und Existenzanalyse, Abile.
Von Gebsattel, V. (1954). *Prolegomena einer medizinischen Anthropologie*. Ausgewählte Aufsätze. Berlin: Springer.
Waterman, A. S. (1993). Two conceptions of happiness: Contrasts of personal expressiveness (eudaimonia) and hedonic enjoyment. *Journal of Personality and Social Psychology, 64*, 678–691.
Wertz, F. J. (2014). Qualitative inquiry in the history of psychology. *Qualitative Psychology, 1*, 4–16.

Part I
Understanding: Contexts, Objectives and Considerations

The Proper Aim of Therapy: Subjective Well-Being, Objective Goodness, or a Meaningful Life?

Thaddeus Metz

Therapy's Final End

What should psychotherapists be aiming to achieve with their clients? In seeking to answer this question, this chapter enquires into whether there is good reason to believe in a certain final end that is appropriate for therapy.

In seeking out the final end of therapy, this chapter is not fundamentally interested in *means* that are particularly useful for attaining it. Making a client feel heard and interpreting a dream s/he has shared are often apt tools for obtaining a certain, ultimate goal, where this chapter is solely concerned to identify what that goal ought to be, not how to achieve it effectively.

Similarly, it is not concerned with moral *constraints* on the way that a therapist ought to pursue the proper aim of therapy. A therapist normally ought to keep facts about a client's past confidential and ought not to engage in a sexual relationship with him/her. These are plausible restrictions on the way a therapist should interact with clients, and clearly do not constitute what the point of the therapy is.

Some might suggest that there are *myriad* points of therapy, varying from client to client. That is of course true at one level, but is quite dubious at another. At a certain level of specificity, each client is of course different and calls for a particular aim on the part of the therapist. Some clients have an interest in overcoming a fear of intimacy, others an addiction, others a tendency to dominate, still others an inclination toward wishful thinking, and so on. However, stepping back, it is plausible to think that there are some commonalities among how clients are badly off and what a therapist ought to be striving to achieve with them. After all, dependence on alcohol is not qualitatively different from addiction to drugs; and then arguably those conditions are not all that distinct from being overly attention seeking or being

---

T. Metz, Ph.D. (✉)
Department of Philosophy, University of Johannesburg,
POB 524, Auckland Park 2006, South Africa
e-mail: tmetz@uj.ac.za

submissive out of an unreasonable fear of abandonment. There are plausibly types of mental illness and hence some general final ends of therapy.

Even if the reader agrees with the point that there are, at a broad or theoretical level, not as many final ends as there are numbers of clients, s/he might still think that there are a *plurality* of general final ends, and not just one that captures the proper aim of therapy for every person who is a suitable client. It is true that there might not be just one. However, it would be intellectually fascinating if there turned out to be only one comprehensive final end of psychotherapy. And if there were just one, knowing what it is would naturally have some practical implications for the way therapy should be conducted.

This chapter therefore seeks to ascertain what *the* final end of therapy might be, on the supposition there may well be one. Specifically, it addresses three prima facie plausible theoretical candidates, and argues that one is preferable to the other two, which are currently more influential among therapists, psychologists, and related enquirers such as philosophers.

According to one of the two dominant approaches, the basic point of therapy should be, roughly, to help clients become clear about what they want deep down and to enable them to achieve it by overcoming mental blockages. The second section spells out this conception of therapy's final end in terms of subjective well-being, explains why it has been so influential, and then presents some counterexamples to it.

The third section takes up the other major theory of what a therapist ought to be aiming to achieve, namely, to psychologically enable clients to live an objectively good life, say, one that involves developing their inherent talents or exhibiting a true/whole/strong self. After presenting counterexamples to this theory, it is noted that combining the two approaches would not avoid the objections, and hence that it would be worth considering a third approach that avoids, and indeed explains, them.

The fourth section advances the novel view that the proper aim of therapy is to mentally facilitate a meaningful life as it is broadly understood by contemporary philosophers. The suggestion is that fostering meaning in life, suitably construed in light of recent work in English-speaking philosophy, is not merely the appropriate final end of existential therapy (e.g., Yalom, 1980) and of logotherapy (Frankl, 1984), but of therapy as such.

The concluding section of the chapter provides an overview of its findings, indicates their limits, and makes some recommendations. It points out that what the two dominant views of therapy's final end have in common is a strict devotion to the client's *welfare*, construed either subjectively or objectively. It notes that seeking to enhance the meaningfulness of a client's life is not identical to—although does largely overlap with—promoting a client's good, and is what enables the favored theory to avoid the problems facing its rivals, while capturing their kernels of truth. However, it also concedes that this chapter has not provided enough evidence to convince a skeptic that there is only one final end of psychotherapy, let alone the one toward which this chapter is sympathetic. At best it shows that the category of meaning in life, as recently construed by philosophers, is under-explored as a ground of therapy's proper aim. Supposing, though, that this chapter has demonstrated that meaning is worth taking seriously as therapy's final end, it closes with some advice addressed to therapists.

Subjective Well-Being

Subjectivism is broadly the view that the proper aim of a therapist depends on the subject, i.e., varies according to the particular client with whom s/he is working. After providing some examples of this approach, and indicating why it is prima facie plausible, this section makes some objections to it, ones that make an objective approach look more attractive by comparison (at least temporarily).

Subjective conceptions of therapy's point differ mainly according to which mental state is taken to ground it. For instance, in one text Sigmund Freud is naturally read as suggesting that the therapist's goal should be to relieve clients of suffering and to help them experience pleasant *feelings* without contortion, disturbance, or other symptoms (1930, pp. 32–33, 48; for similar recent views among contemporary analysts, see Bader, 1994 and Fink, 2010). Consider, too, the suggestion from D. W. Winnicott that one major aim of therapy should be to enable clients to feel alive or to experience vigor (Winnicott, 1955; see also Kohut & Wolf, 1978).[1] Finally, recall the hedonic conception of well-being held by many psychologists, perhaps most famously by Kahneman, Diener, and Schwarz (1999). In short, broadly speaking from all these perspectives, the therapist should be working with a client's mental life with the aim of producing pleasure and reducing pain, or at least alleviating suffering.

Carl Jung has also advanced what appears to be a subjective account of the therapist's proper aim, one focused not so much on the client's feelings or experiences, but rather his/her *goals*. Consider how Jung emphasizes the need for a client to prize his/her "inner voice" (1953, p. 156) or to place "his law above all conventions" (1953, p. 154). Jung also remarks, "The greatness and the liberating effect of all genuine personality consists in this, that it subjects itself of free choice to its vocation …." (1953, p. 155), with the therapist's proper aim being to foster such a way of living. Also worth mentioning, here, are Rollo May's suggestions that it is "the function of the counselor to lead the counselee to an acceptance of responsibility for the conduct and outcome of his or her life" (1989, p. 21) and that "the function of the counselor is to help the counselee be what destiny intended him or her to be" (1989, p. 22), where responsible choices and destinies will vary widely depending on the individuals involved.

For a third kind of subjectivism, consider an approach that focuses on a client's *judgment*. According to one influential version, the therapist's aim should be to enable the client to hold an appraisal of his/her life that is on balance positive. For many, such judgment centrally includes an emotional dimension, so that positive self-appraisal consists of the relative absence of negative emotions and the presence of satisfaction with one's life as a whole. Beyond many psychologists conceiving of happiness in this way (e.g., Diener, Suh, Lucas, & Smith, 1999), those who have

---

[1] The suggestion is not that these perspectives exhaust either Freud's or Winnicott's views (indeed, section three addresses the latter's more objective view that the point of therapy is to live according to a true self); it is rather that their texts occasion awareness of subjective approaches, ones that have been extremely influential. More generally, this chapter is not out to capture the intricacies of any particular *theorist*, but rather to draw on remarks and views so as to illustrate *theories*.

addressed therapy directly have sometimes suggested that its proper aim is to make it psychologically possible for the client to deem his/her life to be at least less bad, and ideally good on the whole. "The job is to make some sense out of the often vague feeling that one's life is not being lived as well as it could be. To what extent can we say that this is the result of an emotional disturbance that can be approached therapeutically?" (Kovel, 1976, p. 34).

For a related view, consider the one that the philosopher Jürgen Habermas seems to propose when he says, "Analytic insights possess validity for the analyst only after they have been accepted as knowledge by the analysand himself" (1971, p. 261). If an interpretation is valid "only to the degree that those who are made the object of individual interpretations *know and recognize themselves* in these interpretations" (Habermas, 1971, pp. 261–262, see also pages 267 and 269), and if an interpretation also includes a view of how a client ought to move forward, then it follows that the proper aim of therapy for a given client is essentially one that s/he has judged to be correct.

This adumbration of types of subjectivism should be enough to illustrate the ways that this general approach has been influential among psychotherapists, psychologists, and philosophers, too. It should also be sufficient to reveal why it has been worth taking seriously as a theory of what therapists ought to be striving for with their clients. First off, a typical client enters therapy because s/he is miserable, cannot achieve what s/he most wants, or is dissatisfied with his/her life, and therapists naturally tend to view themselves as allies in the struggle against conditions experienced as negative by the client.

Second, subjectivism makes good sense of "one of counselling's most sacred rules, which is that the counsellor should respect the client's values" (LeBon, 2001, p. 38; see also p. 107). Instead of imposing his/her own values, the therapist is normally expected to work within the client's set of desires and ideals, the appropriateness of which subjectivism easily explains.

For a third consideration in favor of subjectivism, note that a plausible explanation of what makes something a mental illness or otherwise worth treating is that it interferes with a particular client's subjective orientation in some way. It is plausible to think that: a fear of intimacy is something to overcome because it inhibits a client's ability to feel as much pleasure as s/he could; an addiction is something to beat because it is incompatible with a client's more basic goal in life; an inclination to dominate others is something to rebut because a client is dissatisfied with him/herself for exhibiting it; a fear of being in public is something to deal with because it prevents a client from enjoying what the world has to offer; and a tendency for a client to harm him/herself consequent to feeling abandoned is something to treat because of the suffering involved.

Fourth, and finally, subjective well-being has been, and still remains, the dominant understanding of the nature of happiness by psychologists (so report Adler et al., 2013). Supposing, as is reasonable on the face of it, that the job of a therapist should be to enable his/her client to be happy or to fare well, or at least not to be all that unhappy, a subjective approach is what contemporary psychology on the whole recommends.

However, there are serious objections to any subjective theory, construed as a comprehensive and fundamental account of the final end of psychotherapy. Philosophers and even psychologists sometimes postulate "fantastic" hypothetical counterexamples to it. For instance, if subjective states were all that mattered, then feeding people *soma* in a Brave New World would be appropriate (Adler et al., 2013), as would putting them into an "experience machine," viz., a virtual reality device that would impart only positive feelings and emotions during the course of their lives (Nozick, 1974, pp. 42–45; see also LeBon, 2001, pp. 29–30; cf. Metz, 2013a, pp. 163–179).

Although such thought experiments have their proper place in theoretical reflection, one need not seek out such unrealistic counterexamples in order to question subjectivism. Here are more likely examples, even if they would still be somewhat rare to encounter in an actual therapeutic context.

Consider someone who regularly undergoes manic states, which s/he experiences as pleasant, and who does not "crash hard" after them. Suppose there were a person addicted to heroin who had an unending and regular supply of the drug available. Think about those who exhibit schizoid tendencies, say, who proclaim to "love" a lifelike doll that is ever present and who forgo relationships with "unreliable" persons in favor of it. Reflect for a moment on a psychopath who judges his/her inclination to manipulate others to be just fine. Imagine a narcissist who succeeds in substantially achieving his/her aim of doing whatever it takes to enhance his/her sense of self-worth, including by treating others merely as a means to it. Imagine someone who is histrionic but lucks out in finding someone able and willing to give him/her the attention s/he so desperately craves.

When focusing on subjective factors, the key issue becomes one of *stability*, of encountering a world reliably instrumental for producing pleasure in oneself, achieving one's ends, or fostering satisfaction with one's life. Where the world does not cooperate, as it were, e.g., when an addict cannot obtain the drug or when a narcissist is rejected, then the subject undergoes a negative state. What the cases above show, however, is that mental illness can obtain even when the world *does* cooperate, viz., when the addict has plenty of the drug and the narcissist or psychopath becomes a "successful" CEO. A person can be apt for psychotherapy, e.g., can intuitively be "sick," even in situations where his/her pleasure, goals, or satisfaction are not threatened. If so, then subjectivism cannot be an adequate account of therapy's point.

One might reply on behalf of the subjectivist that it would be wrong for someone to interfere with these individuals. If someone were content being in a "relationship" with a doll, who may rightfully stop him/her?

However, this reply conflates two distinct issues. One issue is whether a person should be forced into therapy or otherwise coerced into changing. The other is whether a person would be a good candidate for therapy in light of a certain conception of therapy's point. Just because someone has strong reason to undergo therapy does not mean that others may legitimately force him/her to do so.

Another reply on behalf of the subjectivist might be to suggest that the above kinds of persons would not be in therapy if they were not undergoing some kind of negative condition such as experiencing pain, or failing to get what they ultimately want, or sensing that their lives are not going well. If someone is seeking out therapy, then *deep down* s/he is undergoing pain, frustration, despair, so the argument goes.

There are two responses to make to this tempting reply. One is that not everyone who is in therapy is there because of "instability," i.e., because his/her positive subjective conditions are being thwarted. A person might seek out a therapist not because s/he finds him/herself disturbed, but rather because others have suggested that s/he see one. That is, s/he might have taken some third-personal advice about him/herself (say, given by the author of this chapter). Or a court might have ordered him/her to undergo some kind of rehabilitation that includes therapy. Or a person might be temporarily confused about what s/he ultimately values, and then finds, upon reflection with a therapist, that s/he really does hate women more than love them and so will continue to act on the former orientation.

Subjectivists might be tending to assume that human nature is essentially good, that what all people *ultimately* prefer is intuitively desirable. But one need not believe in the Freudian id in order to deem that to be a form of wishful thinking. That is true even when focusing on the "preferences which we would keep if we were reflecting under idealized conditions of being well informed, cool, calm, and collected" where "the counselling room provides the perfect arena for such reflection" (LeBon, 2001, pp. 35, 39). Some people are so damaged that their deepest subjective dispositions are fundamentally unhealthy or otherwise merit treatment.[2]

The second response is that the present reply, upon reflection, is not really relevant. The question is not, "Given that people are in therapy, why are they there?"; it is rather, "Given a certain conception of the point of therapy, who should be in it (even if they are not yet)?". The claim in this section is that a subjective conception of therapy's point cannot easily make sense of the intuition that a person could be a good candidate for therapy even if s/he were not disposed toward subjective upset. The lucky addict and narcissist are just two illustrations of individuals who are subjectively well off but who are nonetheless mentally ill or otherwise have reason to seek out therapeutic intervention.

In light of the above counterexamples, there appear to be some conditions in which one ought not take pleasure, some goals that one should give up, and some states with which one has reason to be dissatisfied. Recurrent mania could be pleasant, but it would come at the cost of a loss of groundedness (setting aside the chances of consequent depression). One might be able to achieve consistently the goal of enhancing one's self-interest by means of manipulating others, and feel a great sense of self-satisfaction thereby, but one should not have such a higher-order goal and such a strong emotion. And one might not feel any shame at being subject to a compulsion to receive constant attention from others that one ends up receiving, but it would be reasonable to become the sort of person who does.

---

[2] Note that merely because an attitude is *deep* does not necessarily mean that it is *fixed*. Even if one strongly likes something or takes an interest in it for its own sake, it might still be possible to change one's likes and interests.

These are the kinds of judgments that an adherent to a more objective conception of the point of therapy would make. In particular, they suggest the theory that the point of therapy is to foster a client's welfare, construed in terms that are in an important respect independent of his/her particular feelings, goals, and judgments.

Objective Goodness

The other influential conception of the final end of psychotherapy has been one focused on what would be objectively good for the client. "Objective" here indicates that there are certain ways of being and living that would be desirable for a person, and not merely because s/he would feel pleasure upon exhibiting them, want to do so, or approve of them. Instead, the idea is that there are ways of functioning well that are appropriate "in themselves" and that one perhaps has reason to be pleased by, to want to do, or to approve of, if one does not already.

Such a theoretical approach emerged most clearly in the 1950s, and from those from a variety of clinical and academic backgrounds. On the one hand, there were neo-Freudian analysts, such as Karen Horney, who conceived of the proper aims of therapy as enabling a client to work, to relate to others, and to be responsible (1950), and Erich Fromm, who in one text maintained that the ultimate aim should be to enable clients to love (1956). On the other hand, there were humanist psychologists who advanced objective conceptions of mental health and (at least by implication) of therapy's point. Consider, here, Abraham Maslow having proposed 14 properties of psychological health, such as creativity and moral concern, as elements of self-actualization (1950) and Carl Rogers having advocated a focus on the abilities to cope with stressors and to rely on oneself (1957).

Then there were also the various forms of self-psychology that therapists and psychologists developed in the post-war era. W. R. D. Fairbairn (1958, p. 380) and Anthony Storr (1960, pp. 156–160), for just two examples, focused on the idea that psychopathology consists of a fragmented or conflicted self, with the aim of therapy being to develop synthesis or wholeness in the client's self. D. W. Winnicott distinguished between the true self and the false self, where the therapist should strive to bring out the former (1960; for more recent proponents, see Masterson, 1990; Miller, 1979). And still others emphasized mental health as a strong or firm self as opposed to a weak or feeble one, with Heinz Kohut being one clear example (1977; see also Kohut & Wolf, 1978, pp. 361–363).[3]

Finally, as a contrast to hedonic and more generally subjective approaches to well-being in psychology, *eudaimonism* has become influential of late, particularly among positive psychologists. According to this broad perspective, mental health is a matter of being psychologically able to realize oneself through activities of various

---

[3] Sometimes these thinkers appeal to more than one characterization of a healthy self, the thought being that, say, a disintegrative self is a (kind of a) weak one. It would be interesting to consider elsewhere whether one construal is more apt than the others or is most fundamental.

kinds. For instance, living well might be a matter of exercizing virtue, actualizing one's inherent talents, or living autonomously (e.g., Boniwell & Henry, 2007; Delle Fave, Massimini, & Bassi, 2011; Ryan & Deci, 2001; Ryff, 1989, 2014). Instead of a focus on *states* of feeling pleasure or being satisfied, *eudaimonism* concentrates on *processes* such as certain ways of functioning or interacting that are intrinsically good for a person (Delle Fave et al., 2011).

Another way to understand *eudaimonism* is in terms of higher and lower natures. On the one hand, a person has a lower nature that is either shared with animals or is deemed to be undesirable for being metaphorically animalistic or inhuman. On the other hand, a person also has the capacity to exhibit valuable traits, features that are genuinely human. According to *eudaimonism*, one is living well when one is flourishing as a human in a way that no animal can, say, for playing the piano, exhibiting integrity, or being part of a loving relationship.

Conceiving of the ultimate point of therapy in terms of objective goodness grounds explanations of mental illness that powerfully rival the subjective ones canvassed in the previous section. A fear of intimacy is undesirable not so much because it inhibits a client's pleasure, but rather because it prevents him/her from realizing him/herself as a loving person. An addiction is something to overcome not merely because it conflicts with a deeper goal that a client happens to have, but mainly because it is incompatible with his/her higher (rational) nature. An inclination to dominate others is something to rebut not because a client is dissatisfied with him/herself for exhibiting it, but rather because s/he ought to be dissatisfied with him/herself for being unable to relate to others on egalitarian terms. A fear of being in public is something to deal with not so much because it prevents a client from enjoying what the world has to offer, but rather because it prevents him/her from actualizing him/herself through a variety of potential activities. Finally, a tendency for a client to harm him/herself consequent to feeling abandoned is something to treat not just because of the suffering involved, but because of the weak self or neediness determining his/her interaction with others.

In addition to grounding compelling accounts of conditions that merit psychological intervention, taking an objective approach to therapy's point enables a theorist to avoid the objections facing a focus on subjective well-being. For example, someone addicted to a never-ending supply of heroin might feel pleasure, but would not be *doing* much with his/her life. A narcissist whose desire for self-aggrandizement were routinely satisfied would still be acting consequent to a weak self at the core of his/her character. A person who elects to "love" a doll rather than a person would not be engaging in a relationship, or at least not a genuinely important one.

Despite these substantial advantages accruing to objectivism, it is also vulnerable to counterexamples, if construed as an exhaustive account of what therapists ought ultimately to be striving to achieve with their clients. There are intuitively occasions when it would be right for a therapist to aim to help clients knowingly do what would fail to help them live a life that would be objectively good for them.

What these cases have in common is the idea that sometimes it can be reasonable for clients to want to sacrifice their own objective good. More specifically, there are times when people are sensible to forsake the prospect of an objectively good life for themselves so as to help others.[4] And therapists would not be inappropriate to assist them in doing so.

For a first, "hypothetical" case to make the point clear, consider someone, A, who needs therapy in light of objective considerations, but who knows someone, B, who also needs such therapy. Suppose B cannot afford or otherwise access therapy without A's help, but that for A to help would mean being unable to afford or otherwise access therapy him/herself. And now suppose A is in therapy discussing precisely this situation with his/her therapist, viz., whether A should discontinue therapy so as to enable B to undergo it.

Supposing that A does not need therapy *desperately* more than B, it would be reasonable for a therapist not to discourage A from discontinuing therapy and perhaps for him/her even to help A find ways to make it most efficient for B to obtain it. To do so would appear to be an instance in which the therapist is not acting for the sake of an objectively good life for A.

In reply, the objectivist would surely suggest that in making such a sacrifice for another, A would be *thereby* living objectively well. A would be trading off one sort of objective goodness, which would obtain via therapy, for another, which would obtain by forgoing it.

This is a prima facie compelling reply, but it is not clearly successful. First off, one might question whether making such a sacrifice would really be an instance of objective goodness; if one thinks of the latter in terms of a certain kind of self or character that is extremely hard to develop over time, as in the psychodynamic tradition, then one might well not.

However, let us grant, for the sake of argument, that making such a sacrifice would be to exemplify some objective goodness. The second response, then, is that it would be reasonable for a therapist to help A make such a sacrifice even if A would thereby obtain *less* objective goodness than s/he would if s/he stayed in therapy. Again, granting that making the sacrifice would be good for A, it could well be *better for A* were s/he *not* to make the sacrifice. In such a situation, however, a therapist would not be unreasonable to help A make the sacrifice, or at least not steer him/her away from doing so.

Here is a second counterexample. Imagine a soldier who will soon be going off to war in order to fight for a just cause. S/he is wondering precisely how much sacrifice to make for this cause and for his/her fellow soldiers. In particular, s/he is considering whether to be willing to jump on a grenade, if doing so would save his/her comrades and best enable his/her side to push forward. In this situation, it would be reasonable for a therapist not to try to persuade the client to stay alive. But staying alive would of course be necessary for living objectively well; after all, one cannot play the piano, develop an authentic or integrated self, or be part of a loving relationship if one is dead.

---

[4] Another sort of case, which I lack the space to address in depth here, is one in which a client is inclined to give up objective goodness in favor of a religious, cultural, or other value with which s/he identifies. A medical doctor intuitively can have reason to treat patients in light of their meaningful self-conceptions, and so not to promote their physical health as much as s/he would have otherwise (on which see Orr & Genesen, 1997); similar remarks arguably apply to a therapist.

Again, it is tempting for the objectivist to reply that committing suicide would be an instance of objective goodness. Here, however, it is even less plausible than in the previous case to think that it would be good for him/her *at all*. It is natural to think of *eudaimonia*, self-realization through certain kinds of activities, as something that makes a life worth continuing, but such cannot be something that makes life worth ending (cf. Metz, 2012). And then one is hardly developing a strong self as prescribed by self-psychology if one kills oneself.

These far-fetched cases have been constructed in order to motivate clearly the point that it can sometimes be reasonable for a therapist not to aim for what would be most likely to make a client objectively best off in the long run. More everyday and familiar illustrative cases abound, upon reflection. Consider, for instance, someone trying to make the decision of whether to become chair of an academic department, having to take on administrative burdens and attend dull meetings so that his/her colleagues can avoid doing so. Even if this person would exhibit some moral concern and hence objective goodness by becoming the chair, s/he might be giving up more objective goodness on the whole, as s/he would have made substantial scholarly or creative contributions, or been able to deal with his/her moderate depression, if s/he had had the time and mental freedom.

Less glibly, think about those in the caring professions, such as nurses who elect to face stench, filth, distress, misery, and the like so that such conditions are lessened for others. There can, of course, be some self-realization that comes in the form of emptying bedpans and otherwise caring for others in desperate need. The point is that it could be reasonable for one to empty bedpans even if one would obtain even *more* self-realization if one did not, and furthermore reasonable for a therapist not to counsel a person otherwise and instead to enable him/her to confront the challenges s/he has elected to confront. Similar remarks apply to those who have firmly decided to stay in a marriage that is unfulfilling and even threatens self-esteem a few more years for the sake of their children, and who are seeking help from a therapist in making the best of a situation they have chosen that is, let us suppose, good for the kids but not good for them.

An interesting reply for the objectivist to make at this point would be to contend even if the therapist *as a person* should sometimes help clients forsake their own objective good, s/he ought not do so *as a therapist*. *Qua* therapist, one ought to focus strictly on a client's self-realization or self-development, but sometimes one can have good reason to let go of the role of therapist, so the reply goes.[5]

But is it intuitively the case that one would not be engaging in therapy any longer if one accepted a soldier's firm inclination to commit suicide for a just cause or a parent's unwavering commitment to stay in a crummy relationship? Should one not charge clients for the time spent during which one was enabling them to sacrifice their objective good for the sake of others? Should one be reported to the profession for having engaged in misconduct?

Subjectivists will naturally point out, here, that salient versions of their view can readily accommodate these counterexamples. They appear to be cases in which a

---

[5] I must credit Michael Lacewing for this fascinating suggestion.

therapist should support clients' deepest desires and firmest judgments about their lives, even though their choices might not be objectively good for themselves.

However, despite this advantage, the objections to subjectivism from the previous section remain; it is not just *any* subjective orientation on the part of a client that plausibly orients his/her therapy. That means it would be ideal to develop a theory of therapy's final end that avoids the objections facing both subjectivism and objectivism, while capturing their advantages, something sketched in the following section.

Meaning in Life

The deep lesson to be learned from the previous two sections is that it is implausible to think that the proper aim of a therapist should be reduced to doing *whatever would be good for a client*. Of course, *much* of what a therapist should be doing is equivalent to making a client well off in some sense. However, the objections to subjectivism and objectivism suggest that at least sometimes the point of therapy should not be to maximize a client's happiness, interests, welfare, excellence, or the like, whether subjectively or objectively construed. Against subjectivism, sometimes a client's attitudes are not ones to be promoted, and against objectivism, sometimes a client is sensible to want to sacrifice his/her own self-realization or self-development for the sake of others.

The rest of this chapter articulates a different approach to therapy's final end that promises to capture the kernels of truth in both subjectivism and objectivism while avoiding the counterexamples to them. Whereas subjectivism and objectivism are plausibly understood as theories of well-being, or of what makes a life worth living, the focus here is instead on the category of meaningfulness, as conceived by contemporary Anglo-American philosophers.[6] Often what makes a life meaningful will make it good for the individual whose life it is, but not always.

For many in the field of philosophy these days, talk of "meaning in life" largely connotes ideas about what it would be reasonable for a person to take great pride in, what it would be sensible to admire in others, or what merits reverence, awe, and similar kinds of emotions (Kauppinen, 2012, pp. 353–358; Metz, 2001, 2013a, pp. 24–35; Taylor, 1989). Note how these kinds of ideas differ from what it means to speak of "happiness" or "well-being"; the bare fact of living well does not intuitively merit reactions of esteem, admiration, or respect.

By speaking of a "meaningful life" philosophers do not essentially mean one that is merely *perceived* as meaningful. Some psychologists, for instance, think of a good life as one in which the person *judges* him/herself to be engaging in meaningful activities (e.g., Baumeister & Vohs, 2002; Delle Fave et al., 2011, p. 8). However, instead of focusing on *finding* aspects of a life to be meaningful, consider meaning in a life period, a matter of living in a way that *merits* a certain emotional response

---

[6] And hence not by, say, Viktor Frankl (1984).

such as pride, admiration, or awe. Philosophers tend to find it plausible to suppose that a life could be meaningful but not judged to be by the person living it, with Vincent Van Gogh being a reasonable example, and, conversely, that a life could be found meaningful that was not in fact so, probably Adolf Hitler.

In presenting a substantive conception of what makes an individual's life meaningful, the following draws mainly on work by contemporary English-speaking philosophers. More specifically, it focuses on common ground among many of the most prominent and influential ones to address the topic of meaning in life over the past 25 years or so.[7]

For many philosophers now writing on what constitutes meaning in a person's life, it is thought to largely involve the rigorous exercise of one's intelligence, ideally directed toward the classic triad of "the good, the true, and the beautiful" and in a way that makes for a compelling life story. The following spells out each of the key elements of this terse statement.

Intelligence, or rationality, includes reflecting on one's aims, planning so that many aims are realized in the long run, acting in light of one's deliberation, and exhibiting strength of will. It also includes certain capacities, beyond deliberation and volition, that some readers might suspect are being excluded, such as emotions. Love and artistic expression are sometimes called "irrational" or "nonrational," but these are sensibly deemed to be parts of our rational nature, insofar as they include an element of judgment (e.g., that a beloved is good, that a brushstroke is apt) and can be modified by cognitive reflection (at least indirectly, over time). Many human emotions are, in these ways, forms of rationality that differ substantially from autonomic functions, reflexes, and moods. In short, talk of "emotional intelligence" and "social intelligence" is to be taken literally.

The mere process of rigorously using one's intelligence can probably confer some meaning on one's life; excelling at sports and games can intuitively make one's life meaningful, viz., be something in which to take substantial pride. However, for many in the field, notable meaning normally comes when one's rational nature is positively oriented toward certain *ends* (other than placing a ball into a small space in the face of obstacles), most saliently the following: "goodness," viz., helping others in the form of, say, loving a family, working for a charity, or being employed in a caring profession; "truth," which means informedly reflecting about oneself, society, or nature, perhaps by obtaining a formal education, making a scholarly discovery, or becoming more wise; and "beauty," shorthand for being creative by, for instance, making art objects, decorating a room, or expressing humor.

Finally, another key idea in contemporary philosophical reflection on meaningfulness is that it can inhere in the pattern of one's life or the narrative one's life makes up. For example, there is plausibly meaning in the fact of one's life having progressed over time, from having started out bad in one's adolescence and having ended on a high note in one's old age. For another example, there is intuitively meaning in having redeemed bad parts of a life by making good come of them in later parts. For yet another example, there seems to be meaning in standing up for

---

[7] Which was first spelled out in Metz (2013b), from which the next few paragraphs borrow.

what one believes to be right throughout the course of one's life despite recurrent temptations to do otherwise. These are just three examples of "life stories" that appear meaningful, or at least to merit much greater esteem or admiration than the converse patterns (viz., of starting off well and ending on a low note, seeing good in one's life produce lots of bad, or flip-flopping in an opportunistic way).

Although many professional philosophers currently writing on meaning in life would accept the above ideas, there of course remain substantial differences beyond them. There is disagreement about what, if anything, all three elements of the good, the true, and the beautiful have in common at bottom. There is debate about whether there could be any of these values without God, or whether they can be adequately realized in a physical world, absent a heaven. Some emphasize certain elements of the triad more than others. And theorists naturally tend to conceive of elements of the triad in detailed ways that compete.[8]

Before applying this broad conception of meaning in life to issues of psychotherapy, note some salient ways that it differs from objectivism, its theoretical cousin. The view that one's life is more meaningful, the more one exercises rationality in beneficent, reflective, and creative ways that, as a pattern, make for an interesting life story is not identical to the view that one is mentally healthy or well off insofar as one develops an authentic/integrated/resilient self or realizes oneself through certain activities. To be sure, the latter could instantiate elements of the former. The point is that the latter, at least as characteristically conceived, do not exhaust the former.

For one, a focus on developing a certain kind of self is often considered intrinsic to the client, as a state internal to his/her mind, which is particularly the case for psychodynamic theory and self-psychology. In contrast, much of meaning in a person's life is extrinsic, a matter of a client relating to something beyond, perhaps greater than, him/herself, such as the good, the true, or the beautiful.

For another, neither self-development nor self-realization is usually cashed out in terms of displaying narrative value in one's life. Invariably, a self-focused approach to mental health or well-being concentrates on certain states of mind or activities considered in themselves, and not as a pattern they compose over time. Of course, attention often must be paid to a client's history in order for him/her to develop a particular sort of self; the point is that such attention to a "life story" is merely a means to an end for developmental- or self-psychology, whereas for most theorists of meaning it can be something worth developing for its own sake, with redemption being a key theme.

For a third, meaningfully contributing to the realization of certain ends by the substantial use of one's intelligence need not, and indeed sometimes cannot, be conceived in terms of self-development or self-realization. Returning to the case of Van Gogh, his life was plausibly meaningful (admirable) not merely in virtue of the great paintings he produced during his lifetime, but also the unforeseeable posthumous influence they had on the art world and the more general public. It is quite implausible to think that this *influence*—after Van Gogh's death—was *constituted*

---

[8] These matters are critically explored in Metz (2013a).

by a true/whole/strong self or self-actualization on his part (even if it was *caused by* such a condition).

Consider, now, how the present conception of meaning in life grounds explanations of why certain people intuitively are good candidates for therapy, explanations that contrast with those appealing to what is objectively good for a person. A fear of intimacy is undesirable not merely because it prevents one from realizing oneself as a loving person, but also because it prevents one from participating in a meaningful relationship. An addiction is something to overcome not ultimately because it is incompatible with a person's higher nature, but mainly because it would undermine his/her rationality and particularly his/her ability to exercise it in substantial ways toward the good, the true, or the beautiful. An inclination to dominate others is something to rebut not because one ought to be dissatisfied with oneself for being unable to relate to others on egalitarian terms, but because it is something in which one cannot reasonably take pride and should probably instead feel shame. A fear of being in public is something to deal with not fundamentally because it prevents one from actualizing oneself through a variety of potential activities, but because meaning is largely a matter of relating to something beyond oneself, with isolation (e.g., prison) being a source of meaninglessness. Finally, a tendency for a client to harm him/herself consequent to feeling abandoned is something to treat not just because of the weak self or neediness determining his/her interaction with others, but because these conditions threaten his/her ability to live a life that one could sensibly admire for having made accomplishments.

Supposing these explanations are plausible, the category of meaning cannot, at least as yet, be criticized for failing to capture the major advantages that subjectivism and objectivism claim. It appears at least on a par with them so far. In addition, though, it can easily avoid the counterexamples facing the latter theories.

Recall that subjectivism faces the objection of lucky addicts, narcissists, and the like, those whose attitudes intuitively merit therapy despite not being frustrated by an uncooperative world. The advocate of meaning in life can say that such individuals, even if happy or well off in subjective terms, are not living nearly as meaningfully as they could. The addict with a never-ending supply of heroin would fail to exercise his/her intelligence substantively for, say, creative ends, while the narcissist with a never-ending supply of adoration would fail to do so in positive ways toward others' good.

And then recall that objectivism faces the problem that sometimes it can be apt for a therapist to help clients sacrifice their objective interests for the sake of others, which means that something other than objective goodness can be the point of therapy. The present suggestion is that meaning is a promising category. Why should a therapist enable a client to give up his/her own self-development or self-realization so as to help others? A plausible explanation is that the proper aim of therapy is to foster meaning in life, where such sacrifice can confer substantial meaning.[9] Although it is often said of meaningfulness that it is something worth living for, it can also be something worth dying for (as Joseph Heller has famously suggested in *Catch-22*).

---

[9] The next two sentences are cribbed from Metz (2012, p. 445).

Some meaningful conditions are naturally understood to be able to provide reasons to commit suicide, to let oneself die, or to otherwise make a large sacrifice of one's objective interests, since doing so might impart certain narrative qualities to one's life or produce good consequences for others' lives.

Before concluding, consider a few important objections to this section's hypothesis and replies to them. First off, it appears that a defender of this section's claim is committed to the view that a therapist ought not act for the sake of a client's mental health or psychological well-being, which is of course grossly counterintuitive.

However, the friend of the meaning view is not committed to that way of putting things. Instead, s/he can sensibly maintain that a therapist ought to act for the sake of a client's health or well-being *insofar as it would be expected to contribute to meaning in his/her life*, as it indeed often (but not always) would.

A second concern is whether the present view can make adequate sense of the "sacred rule" mentioned above, viz., that a therapist ought not to impose his/her own values on a client and should instead respect the client's. It might seem that only subjectivism can accommodate that intuition; considerations of meaning in life (as well as objective goodness) instead appear to entail that the therapist is, or should be, an expert on how to live, with few therapists thinking of themselves that way.

In reply, the view that the point of therapy is to foster meaning in a client's life does not require one to hold the view that a therapist invariably knows best. It could be, and probably often is the case, that what would make a particular client's life meaningful is something that can be discovered only in the course of dialogue between the two in a holding environment. Even if a therapist adheres to an abstract view of meaning, what it means for a given individual cannot be known by a therapist independent of drawing a client out, listening carefully to him/her, and considering his/her point of view.

As for the maxim of respecting a client's values, the category of meaning can plausibly account for it. A meaningful relationship between two adults is not one in which one person foists his/her views onto the other or treats the other as incapable. Instead, using one's intelligence in the realm of "the good" normally means doing what is expected to genuinely help another and in ways that the other recognizes and wants.

In addition, it is worth noting that respect for a client's values need not mean unconditional acceptance of them. If a client is keen on cheating on his/her spouse, torturing small animals for fun, acting out of racial hatred, or watching as much TV as s/he can while drinking beer, it would not be unreasonable for a therapist to press him/her on the issue. Inviting a client to consider whether a course of action would be meaningful or merit pursuit can be respectful; a therapist need not, and probably should not, automatically accept whatever his/her client wants deep down (in light of either defenses, on the one hand, or simply a lack of reflectiveness, on the other). Even trying to persuade a client that a certain course of action would be better than another could be respectful of his/her ability to make choices for him/herself, or could otherwise treat him/her as an equal rather than as an inferior.

For a third worry about the category of meaning as a plausible conception of therapy's final end, return to the point that most clients enter therapy because of subjective considerations; they are miserable, cannot obtain what they most want, or are dissatisfied. Sometimes clients do begin therapy because they detect a lack of meaning in their lives, but that appears to be less often the case. Is not the point, or one major point, of therapy simply to relieve suffering?

It would not be unreasonable to posit more than one final end of therapy, as the conclusion notes. However, what those sympathetic to the meaning view can say is that suffering is something to overcome insofar as it is meaningless, reduces meaning, or is an obstacle to meaning. *Pointless* suffering is what should be combated, not suffering as such, or so the reader should consider.

Conclusion

This chapter has supposed that it is reasonable to suspect that there is a single comprehensive final end that is appropriate for psychotherapy, and has considered three accounts of what it might be. It has spelled out and motivated the two dominant theories, namely, of subjective well-being and objective goodness, but then presented counterexamples to them. The counterexamples suggest that a therapist ought not be aiming merely to do what is good for a client, either subjectively or objectively construed. Instead, this chapter has argued that a therapist ought at bottom to be doing what is likely to enhance the meaning in a client's life, understood in light of recent philosophical analysis, where that often, but not always, means doing what would be good for a client in some way.

The reflections in this chapter are probably not sufficient on their own to convince a skeptic that there is a single proper aim of therapy, let alone that the category of meaning in life, as spelled out here, captures it. In particular, one might still be tempted to hold the pluralist view that a therapist ought to promote a balance of subjective well-being, objective goodness, and meaningfulness in a client's life. More work would need to be done in order to see whether meaning can indeed supplant, and not merely supplement, the two dominant theoretical approaches to the proper aim of therapy. The hope is that the reader accepts that such work merits being undertaken.

At the very least, supposing meaning is a plausible contender for a, if not *the*, final end of therapy, there are certain strategies that therapists might usefully keep in mind. For one, they might invoke the terminology developed here in order to help clarify dilemmas for clients. That is, there can be situations in which clients cannot avoid trade-offs between subjective well-being, objective goodness, and meaning in life, and simply being able to name these different, competing values can be a way of obtaining understanding and moving forward.

For another, therapists could invoke "deathbed reflection" on the part of a client, asking him/her to consider what about his/her life s/he would like to be able to take pride in before dying, or what about it s/he would like others to be able to admire in a eulogy. Not only does such a perspective encourage attention to what is intuitively important, but it also fosters reflection on narrative values, including posthumous ones.

For a third, therapists may remember the remark often ascribed to Friedrich Nietzsche, "He who has a why to live can bear almost any how." There will be occasions when clients continue to suffer or do not develop stronger selves, despite substantial therapeutic intervention. Nonetheless, they might still be capable of engaging in meaningful activities, achieving purposes that help others, disclosing truth, or creating beauty, at least from time to time. That would be something for clients, and therapists, to grab on to when times are hard.[10]

Key Takeaways

- There are three theoretical interpretations of the ultimate aim of psychotherapy that are usefully distinguished, which focus on subjective well-being, objective goodness, and a meaningful life, respectively.
- The idea that psychotherapy as such, and not merely a particular instance of it, properly aims to impart meaning to clients' lives is not as popular as the other two approaches and is underdeveloped.
- Meaning in life here is understood in terms of contemporary English-speaking philosophy, where many hold the broad view that one's life is more meaningful, the more one exercises one's rational nature (which includes one's emotional life) in beneficent, reflective, and creative ways that, as a pattern, make for an interesting narrative or "life story."
- The more familiar and influential two theories of therapy's point both focus on what is conceived as good for the client, and it is this welfarist orientation that makes them vulnerable to objection. Sometimes what clients want deep down is not something that a therapist should help them fulfill, and it can also be reasonable for clients to want to sacrifice their own objective interests for the sake of others and for a therapist to assist them in this regard.
- Viewing therapy's point to be to foster meaningfulness avoids the objections facing rival, welfarist theories, while capturing their advantages.
- Supposing that therapy ought largely, if not exclusively, aim to foster meaning in clients' lives, a therapist would usefully invoke talk of "meaning" in order to clarify goals and dilemmas. There can be situations in which clients cannot avoid trade-offs between, e.g., happiness and meaning in life, and naming these competing values can assist self-understanding and decision-making.
- In addition, a therapist could encourage "deathbed reflection" on the part of clients, asking them to consider what about their life they would like to take pride in before dying, or what about it they would like others to admire in a eulogy.

---

[10] For comments on a previous draft of this chapter, the author thanks Dan Stein, Pedro Tabensky, and the editors of this volume. Special thanks to Michael Lacewing.

Such a perspective encourages attention to what is intuitively important, and fosters reflection on narrative values, including posthumous ones.
- Finally, it can be worth reminding clients of the worth of meaningfulness in the face of continued suffering or the inability to develop a suitably strong self. Despite lacking welfare, clients might be able to achieve purposes that help others, disclose truth, or create beauty. That is something for clients, and a therapist, to grab on to when times are hard.

References

Adler, A., Boniwell, I., Gibson, E., Metz, T., Seligman, M., Uchida, Y., et al. (2013). Definitions of terms. In I. Boniwell & S. Alkire (Eds.), *Report on wellbeing and happiness* (pp. 19–34). Thimphu: Centre for Bhutan Studies.
Bader, M. (1994). The tendency to neglect therapeutic aims in psychoanalysis. *Psychoanalytic Quarterly, 63*, 246–270.
Baumeister, R., & Vohs, K. (2002). The pursuit of meaningfulness in life. In C. R. Snyder & S. Lopez (Eds.), *Handbook of positive psychology* (pp. 608–618). Oxford: Oxford University Press.
Boniwell, I., & Henry, J. (2007). Developing conceptions of well-being. *Social Psychology Review, 9*, 3–18.
Delle Fave, A., Massimini, F., & Bassi, M. (2011). *Psychological selection and optimal experience across cultures*. New York, NY: Springer.
Diener, E., Suh, E., Lucas, R., & Smith, H. (1999). Subjective well-being: Three decades of progress. *Psychological Bulletin, 125*, 276–302.
Fairbairn, W. R. D. (1958). On the nature and aims of psychoanalytical treatment. *International Journal of Psychoanalysis, 39*, 374–383.
Fink, B. (2010). Against understanding: Why understanding should not be viewed as an essential aim of psychoanalytic treatment. *Journal of the American Psychoanalytic Association, 58*, 259–285.
Frankl, V. (1984). *Man's search for meaning* (Rev. ed.). New York, NY: Simon & Schuster Inc.
Freud, S. (1930). *Civilization and its discontents*. J. Strachey (Trans.), Repr. New York, NY: W. W. Norton & Company, 1961.
Fromm, E. (1956). *The art of loving*. Repr. New York, NY: Perennial Library, 1989.
Habermas, J. (1971). *Knowledge and human interests*. J. Shapiro (Trans.), Boston, MA: Beacon Press.
Horney, K. (1950). *Neurosis and human growth*. New York, NY: W. W. Norton & Company Inc.
Jung, C. (1953). The development of personality. Repr. In C. Moustakas (Ed.), *The self* (pp. 147–159). New York, NY: Harper Colophon Books, 1956.
Kahneman, D., Diener, E., & Schwarz, N. (1999). *Well-being: Foundations of hedonic psychology*. New York, NY: The Russell Sage Foundation.
Kauppinen, A. (2012). Meaningfulness and time. *Philosophy and Phenomenological Research, 82*, 345–377.
Kohut, H. (1977). *The restoration of the self*. Chicago, IL: The University of Chicago Press.
Kohut, H., & Wolf, E. (1978). The disorders of the self and their treatment. Repr. In P. Ornstein (Ed.), *The search for the self: Selected writings of Heinz Kohut: 1978–1981* (Vol. 3, pp. 359–386). Madison, WI: International Universities Press, 1990.
Kovel, J. (1976). *A complete guide to therapy*. London: Penguin Books Ltd.
LeBon, T. (2001). *Wise therapy*. London: Continuum.
Maslow, A. (1950). Self-actualizing people: A study of psychological health. Repr. In C. Moustakas (Ed.), *The self* (pp. 160–194). New York, NY: Harper Colophon Books, 1956.

Masterson, J. (1990). *The search for the real self*. New York, NY: The Free Press.
May, R. (1989). *The art of counselling*. New York, NY: Gardner Press.
Metz, T. (2001). The concept of a meaningful life. *American Philosophical Quarterly, 38*, 137–153.
Metz, T. (2012). The meaningful and the worthwhile: Clarifying the relationships. *The Philosophical Forum, 43*, 435–448.
Metz, T. (2013a). *Meaning in life: An analytic study*. Oxford: Oxford University Press.
Metz, T. (2013b). Meaning in life as the aim of psychotherapy: A hypothesis. In J. Hicks & C. Routledge (Eds.), *The experience of meaning in life: Classical perspectives, emerging themes, and controversies* (pp. 405–417). Dordrecht: Springer.
Miller, A. (1979). *The drama of the gifted child: The search for the true self*. R. Ward (Trans.), Repr. New York, NY: Basic Books, 1981.
Nozick, R. (1974). *Anarchy, state, and utopia*. New York, NY: Basic Books.
Orr, R., & Genesen, L. (1997). Requests for "inappropriate" treatment based on religious beliefs. *Journal of Medical Ethics, 23*, 143–147.
Rogers, C. (1957). A therapist's view of the good life. Repr. In his *On becoming a person: A therapist's view of psychotherapy* (pp. 183–196). Boston, MA: Houghton Mifflin Company, 1961.
Ryan, R., & Deci, E. (2001). On happiness and human potentials: A review of research on hedonic and eudaimonic well-being. *Annual Review of Psychology, 52*, 141–166.
Ryff, C. (1989). Happiness is everything, or is it? Explorations on the meaning of psychological well-being. *Journal of Personality and Social Psychology, 57*, 1069–1081.
Ryff, C. (2014). Psychological well-being revisited: Advances in the science and practice of eudaimonia. *Psychotherapy and Psychosomatics, 83*, 10–28.
Storr, A. (1960). *The integrity of the personality*. Repr. New York, NY: Ballantine Books, 1992.
Taylor, C. (1989). *Sources of the self: The making of the modern identity*. Cambridge, MA: Harvard University Press.
Winnicott, D. W. (1955). Clinical varieties of transference. Repr. In M. Khan (Ed.), *Through paediatrics to psycho-analysis* (pp. 295–299). London: The Hogarth Press and the Institute of Psychoanalysis, 1978.
Winnicott, D. W. (1960). Ego distortion in terms of true and false self. Repr. In his *The maturational process and the facilitating environment* (pp. 140–152). New York, NY: International Universities Press, 1965.
Yalom, I. (1980). *Existential psychotherapy*. New York, NY: Basic Books.

Seeing Life Through a Sacred Lens: The Spiritual Dimension of Meaning

Julie M. Pomerleau, Kenneth I. Pargament, and Annette Mahoney

Within the fields of social science, theology, and religious studies, definitions of spirituality abound. Advanced scholars within these disciplines have articulated perspectives on the true meaning of spirituality; however, agreement among them is low. We will not resolve these definitional debates about spirituality in this chapter. Instead, we will focus on one aspect of spirituality, sanctification, which can be understood as a way of perceiving a deeper dimension of life. More poetically, sanctification involves the capacity to see life through a sacred lens. This chapter will focus on that capacity, the ways that life as a whole, specific life domains, and particular moments may be colored by a sacred lens, and the implications of this way of seeing for the health of our minds, bodies, and relationships. After reviewing current examples and empirical research findings on sanctification, we conclude that seeing beyond the physical realities of the world to imbue life with a deeper meaning is not only central to our understanding of positive psychology and meaning making, it is also vital to the very essence of what it means to be human.

What Does It Mean to See Life Through a Sacred Lens?

Since our spiritual focus here is on the realm of sanctification, it is critical to know what we mean when we talk about seeing life through this "sacred lens." In a theological context, the term "sanctification" has been used to connote a person being set apart by God to become holy or sacred. In contrast, our focus here is on sanctification as a psychospiritual construct. Sanctification as we use it refers to the ways in which individuals interpret aspects of life as having sacred qualities and/or as

J.M. Pomerleau, B.S. (✉) • K.I. Pargament, Ph.D. • A. Mahoney, Ph.D.
Department of Clinical Psychology, Bowling Green State University, Bowling Green, OH 43403, USA
e-mail: pomerjm@bgsu.edu

being a manifestation of their particular image(s) of God/higher powers. Thus, in moving from a theological to a psychological framework, our focus shifts from a theological understanding of sanctification as a gift handed down from God or higher powers per se to the individual's active role in sanctifying various elements of life by viewing them through a sacred lens.

From this perspective, sanctification refers both to perceiving seemingly ordinary elements of life as being reflective of God or higher powers and/or as possessing extraordinary or divine qualities (Pargament & Mahoney, 2005). One way to visualize the concept of sanctification is through the illustration depicted in Fig. 1. This figure displays a core and ring, with the entire figure representing what we have called "the sacred" in our prior work. Thus, an experience with the sacred may include direct encounters with elements at the core of this figure—that is with theistic deities that many believe is the source of all sacredness or nontheistic transcendent reality. The sacred also includes a multitude of seemingly ordinary experiences that take on extraordinary character due to being viewed as embodying God/a higher power or sacred qualities that reflect the core (Mahoney, Pargament, & Hernandez, 2013; Pargament, 2007). Thinking about it in this way, we see that each person could have a distinctive experience of sanctification due to the different ways in which he or she perceives what lies within this core (e.g., Jesus, Allah, Mother Nature, transcendent reality) and the diverse areas of life that extend this core into his or her ring of sacred entities (e.g., family, art, nature, work, parenting). Though the content of the various objects within the ring may vary between individuals, the general psychological process remains the same. Thus, we define sanctification as the process of "perceiving aspects of life as having divine character and significance" (Pargament & Mahoney, 2005, p. 180).

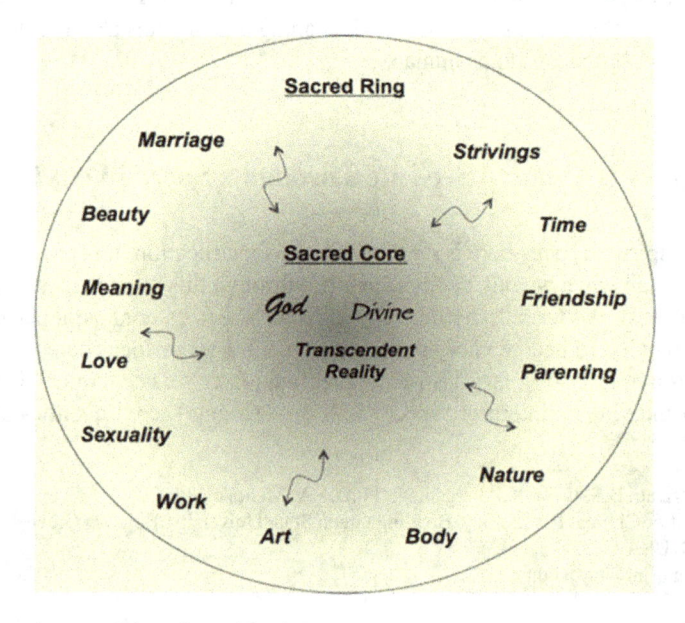

Fig. 1 Sacred core and ring of sanctification

Theistic and Nontheistic Sanctification

Consistent with the prior paragraph, sanctification may occur theistically or nontheistically. Because an individual may view a sanctified object as a manifestation of God/the divine (theistic) or as having sacred qualities (nontheistic), sanctification is possible whether one is a theist or a nontheist (Mahoney et al., 2013). Returning to the image of the sacred core and ring (Fig. 1), one can see that the core contains several different conceptualizations of the source of the sacred (i.e., God, Divine, Transcendent Reality). For theists, this source may be one God or multiple gods/divinities, and sanctification involves perceiving the manifestation or involvement of this divine source in one's life experiences. For example, individuals may think that God was involved in how they met their spouse and/or sense God's presence in their marital relationship. One couple described theistic sanctification in their marital relationship in the following way: "It's a covenant to each other, but more importantly it's a covenant to God. It's a threesome that holds together. You take that third out and it falls apart. So that's I think what for us has really defined our marriage" (Lambert & Dollahite, 2008, p. 601). Notably, theists are not limited to theistic sanctification, but may also perceive objects as possessing nontheistic sacred qualities. For instance, parents may view the birth of their child as a blessing or a miracle and thus regard parenting as a sacred calling.

Though nontheists do not view a particular deity as being at the core, they may sense existence as possessing a transcendent dimension that reflects sacred (divine) qualities such as mystery, ultimacy, and boundlessness. One well-known example of this process comes from Albert Einstein who, though he did not believe in God, recognized and encountered the presence of sacred qualities through his study of physics (1956): "A knowledge of the existence of something we cannot penetrate, of the manifestations of the profoundest reason and the most radiant beauty—it is this knowledge and this emotion that constitute the truly religious attitude; in this sense, and in this alone, I am a deeply religious man" (p. 7). In a similar way, the contemporary philosopher and writer Roger Scruton describes how a religious place can be experienced as sacred by a nonreligious person: "Entering a country church… not necessarily as a believer…and sensing this stored accumulated silence…to think about it as the product of prayer, the distillation of need, anxiety, suffering and perhaps rejoicing too…you seem to be facing into the transcendental" (cited in Regunathan, 2014). Scruton notes the many avenues through which people may encounter a sacred dimension of existence. Thus, because sanctification is so flexible and potentially distinctive to each individual, the experience is open to anyone who can see life through this sacred lens.

It is also important to differentiate sanctification from constructs that address similarly deep and meaningful dimensions of life. Though related in some ways to experiences of importance and value, sanctification should not be confused with other ways of describing feelings of human significance and purpose. Rather, the definition explicitly indicates that the sanctified object is seen as *having divine significance and character*. Thus, the perceived involvement of God or a higher power and/or qualities of divine significance and character distinguishes the concept of sanctification from similar experiences of salient yet nonsacred meaning. One illustration of this point comes from the sanctification of strivings research, in which participants were required to rate the importance of their personal life goals as well as the degree to which they sanctify each striving (Mahoney, Pargament, et al., 2005). Though importance and sanctification were related, they were clearly measuring distinct constructs. In some cases, strivings that were considered to be highly important were not necessarily highly sanctified. Likewise, individuals' ratings of investment in and commitment to their strivings overlapped with but were distinct from their sanctification ratings. Thus, experiencing the sacred in daily life goes beyond being highly committed to an important area of one's life.

How Do Contemporary Scientists Empirically Study Sanctification?

It is necessary at this point to take a step back and briefly explain the methods social scientists use to measure sanctification. Given the diverse and unique aspects of life that people view as being a reflection of God/higher powers or sacred qualities, sanctification may seem an illusive construct to study empirically. However, the measures that researchers have developed to investigate the prevalence and nature of sanctification have been specific and direct, leading to a better scientific understanding of this concept. The first psychospiritual measure of sanctification was created to study the ways in which couples experience their marriages as sacred. Mahoney and colleagues (1999) created a *Sanctification Measure* with two subscales to represent both theistic and nontheistic experiences of the sanctity of marriage. The Manifestation of God (MG) subscale is comprised of items that refer to individuals' perceptions of direct encounters with God in their union (i.e., "I experience God through my marriage"). To measure the prevalence of nontheistic sacred experiences, the Sacred Qualities (SQ) subscale focuses on the ways that one's marriage may take on characteristics of a sacred reality, such as transcendence, ultimacy, and boundlessness (i.e., "My marriage is holy"). Participants rate these items on a scale ranging from *Strongly Agree* to *Strongly Disagree*. Following this initial study on marriage (1999), researchers adapted the Sanctification Measure for use in other domains, including sanctification of work (Walker, Jones, Wuensch, Aziz, & Cope, 2008), social justice (Todd, Houston, & Odahl-Ruan, 2014), and forgiveness (Bell et al., 2014; Davis, Hook, Van Tongeren, & Worthington, 2012). Original and modified versions of the sanctification measures that have been developed by members of our lab to empirically study specific aspects of life including strivings (Mahoney, Pargament, et al., 2005), pregnancy (Mahoney, Pargament, & DeMaris, 2009), marriage (Mahoney et al., 1999, 2009), parenting (Murray-Swank, Mahoney, & Pargament, 2006), sexuality (Murray-Swank, Pargament, & Mahoney, 2005), the body (Mahoney, Carels, et al., 2005), and dreams (Phillips & Pargament, 2002) can be found at our website (Mahoney, 2015). Also, Doehring and colleagues developed the *Perceiving Sacredness in Life Scale* (Doehring et al., 2009) where people reflect on how often they experience God's presence or sacred qualities across life writ large including life in general, nature, all living things, people, ideas or actions, and abstract attributes such as love and hope. Thus, it is clear that this field of research is growing as researchers continue to investigate the process of seeing life through a sacred lens.

Is Seeing Life Through a Sacred Lens Prevalent in Modern Life?

Historical Examples of Sanctification

In the contemporary world it may seem unusual for people to sense the presence of the sacred in seemingly secular areas of life, but we find examples of this process both historically and, as we will show later, in modern times. For example, Alexander Hamilton sanctified human rights as a prelude to and justification for the American Revolution: "The sacred rights of mankind are not to be rummaged for among old parchments or musty records. They are written, as with a sunbeam, in the whole volume of human nature by the hand of the divinity itself and can never be erased or obscured by mortal power" (cited in Chernow, 2005, p. 92). Centuries later, Dr. Martin Luther King, Jr. used this sacred ideal as a foundation for the Civil Rights movement, reminding citizens that the nation's leaders had a "sacred obligation" to uphold the rights established by the Declaration of Independence and the Constitution: "When the architects of our republic wrote the magnificent words of the Constitution and the Declaration of Independence, they were signing a promissory note....that all men, yes, black men as well as white men, would be guaranteed the unalienable rights of life, liberty, and the pursuit of happiness.... Instead of honoring this sacred obligation, America has given the Negro people a bad check, a check which has come back marked 'insufficient funds'" (King, 1963, pp. 1–2). These examples illustrate the way in which regarding something as sacred or as having divine significance can be a normative and powerful theme outside of overtly religious contexts.

Modern Examples of Sanctification

Despite these historical examples, one may doubt that seeing life through a sacred lens is a phenomenon still experienced in the twenty-first century, as we tend to think that American society is becoming increasingly secular. It may seem more likely that sanctification is something accessible only to those who are religiously devout. However, prevalence rates from the current studies of sanctification suggest that sanctification is indeed a common occurrence within the United States, an experience endorsed by the majority of individuals regardless of degree of involvement in religious groups or an affiliation with a religious tradition.

Sanctification of...	Nontheistic	Theistic
Life as a Whole	I feel reverence for all living things.	I see each day, good or bad, as a gift from God.
Life Domains		
Marriage	My marriage reveals the deepest truths of life to me.	I feel God at work in my marriage.
Parenting	Being a mother feels like a deeply spiritual experience.	I sense God's presence in my relationship with my baby.
Body	My body is holy.	My body is created in God's image.
Sexuality	Our sexual relationship connects us to something greater than ourselves.	God's essence is expressed in our sexual relationship.
Moments	-I felt a deep sense of mystery. -This moment felt set apart from everyday life.	N/A

Fig. 2 Example sanctification items

The high prevalence rate of sanctification is unsurprising given that the majority of Americans identify as religious and/or spiritual, suggesting they are involved in the search for the sacred (Pargament & Mahoney, 2005). For example, results from the 2012 National Pew Survey show that 65 % of U.S. adults identify as religious and 18 % as spiritual, with 91 % endorsing belief in God or a Universal Spirit (Pew Research Center, 2012). Though each person's search may involve different pathways, which may or may not include self-identifying as belonging to a religious tradition, most individuals are searching for deeper significance and the manifestation of a divine or higher power or transcendence in their lives. Furthermore, studies of sanctification show that people also commonly report encountering the sacred in daily life both theistically and nontheistically. Various aspects of life can be colored by this sacred lens including life as a whole, specific life domains, and particular moments (Fig. 2).

The Sacred Meaning of Life as a Whole

Though much of the research on sanctification has focused on experiencing the sacred in specific life domains (e.g., marriage, parenting, work, strivings), sanctification is not necessarily limited to these segregated domains, but can reflect a way of viewing life as a whole as sacred. Theologian and minister Frederick Buechner (1992) eloquently summarizes both the specific and holistic experiences of the sacred:

> Taking your children to school and kissing your wife goodbye. Eating lunch with a friend. Trying to do a decent day's work. Hearing the rain patter against the window. There is no event so commonplace but that God is present within it, always hiddenly, always leaving you room to recognize him or not to recognize him, but all the more fascinatingly because of that, all the more compellingly and hauntingly. .... Listen to your life. See it for the fath-

omless mystery that it is. In the boredom and pain of it no less than in the excitement and gladness: touch, taste, smell your way to the holy and hidden heart of it because in the last analysis all moments are key moments, and life itself is grace (p. 2).

Doehring, Pargament, Clarke, and colleagues (2009) examined this notion that "life itself is grace," and studied the ways in which individuals experience the presence of God or the spiritual in their lives as a whole. For example, people often see life as a sacred journey, sense God's presence in their day-to-day existence or natural creation, experience something more sacred in life than simply material existence, find God in life's joys and sorrows, and feel that life has a sacred purpose. Such perceptions are commonplace and are correlated with, but distinctive from, other types of religious practices (e.g., frequency of prayer or service attendance). For instance, in Doehring and Clarke's national survey (2002), most people endorsed sanctifying life as a whole. Seventy-five percent of individuals endorsed theistic sanctification, reporting that they "see God's presence in all of life." Nontheistic sanctification showed similar rates, with 76% of respondents endorsing that they "experience something more sacred than simply material existence" (Doehring & Clarke, 2002). Thus, it seems that people often experience a deeper meaning hidden within the ongoing flow of all of life around them.

The Sacred Meaning of Specific Domains of Modern Life

Sanctification is also rather common when examining people's experiences of the sacred in specific areas of life. Whether regarding their relationships, careers, bodies, personal strivings, or a number of other areas, a substantial number of people report seeing these domains through a sacred lens. Considering sanctified relationships, studies of marital sanctification have found that at least two-thirds of both wives and husbands report viewing their marriage as sacred to some degree, endorsing items such as "I sense God's presence in my relationship with my spouse" and "This marriage is a part of a larger spiritual plan" (Mahoney et al., 1999, 2009). Research has found similarly high prevalence rates in the sanctification of parenting (Brelsford, 2013; Murray-Swank et al., 2006; Weyand, O'Laughlin, & Bennett, 2013) and pregnancy (Mahoney et al., 2009). In these studies, the range of scores tends to be negatively skewed, suggesting that the majority of parents experience family life as sacred, sense a deeper connection to God through their spousal and parental relationships, and believe that God played a role in bringing their children into their lives.

Perceiving nonrelational aspects of life as sacred is also a common occurrence. For example, a study of the sanctification of personal life strivings (Mahoney, Pargament, et al., 2005) had participants identify their top ten personal strivings and rate the degree to which they sanctify them. Findings revealed that the majority of individuals sanctified their top strivings to some degree, viewing those that involved spiritual concerns, family relationships, or helping others as having the most spiritual significance. Similarly, sanctification of work is also prevalent, with studies showing that the majority of people perceive God to be present in their work or see their work as a sacred calling (Carroll, Stewart-Sicking, & Thompson, 2014). Also, most people endorse viewing one's body as sacred or made in a divine image (Benjamins, Ellison, Krause, & Marcum, 2011).

However, we do see variation among levels of sanctification across domains, particularly in the realm of the sanctification of sexuality. Studies examining the degree to which couples sanctify their marital and nonmarital sexual relationships have revealed a broader range of prevalence, from 20 % positively endorsing items such as "I experience God through the sexual bond I have with my spouse," to 75 % agreeing that "The sexual relationship I have with my spouse is sacred to me" (Hernandez, Mahoney, & Pargament, 2011; Murray-Swank et al., 2005). Thus, we see that even though sanctification is indeed a common occurrence, the degree to which people perceive the sacred in their lives also tends to vary depending on individuals' experiences and contexts.

The Sacred Meaning of Moments of Modern Life

Yet another promising area of study focuses on the sanctification of key moments in life. Pargament, Lomax, McGee, and Fang (2014) studied important moments in treatment reported by a sample of mental health providers and a sample of mental health patients. The sample then responded to items that asked about the degree to which participants imbued these moments with sacred qualities, such as transcendence, boundlessness, and ultimacy. Fifty-five percent of the mental health providers, interestingly a largely secular group, perceived their important moment in treatment as sacred. A second study examined clients' experience of sacred moments in treatment using the same methodology. Results showed that 24 % of clients perceived their important moment in treatment as sacred. Thus, it seems that viewing life through a sacred lens is not restricted to general areas of life but may also be experienced in specific moments that convey a deeper meaning.

What Is the Psychosocial Relevance of Sanctification in Modern Life?

With findings showing that sanctification is a fairly common experience, we now want to highlight the implications of seeing life through a sacred lens. Though this construct is applicable to nearly any domain of life, we can identify five common implications of sanctification that cut across domains (Pargament & Mahoney, 2005):

1. People are more likely to invest themselves and their resources (e.g., time, money, energy) in sacred matters. When people sanctify objects, relationships, or actions, they tend to dedicate more of themselves to pursuing them.
2. People tend to work harder to protect and preserve those elements of life they hold sacred, especially in times of threat or conflict. This may mean devoting care to a child or spouse by engaging in less aggression and more problem

solving, or it may take the form of a ritual that protects against the violation of a sacred object.
3. Sacred elements of life tend to elicit spiritual emotions. These emotions may be characterized as feelings of attraction to the sacred object (e.g., love, gratitude, and adoration) or feelings of awe in relation to the sanctified object (e.g., fear, majesty) (Otto, 1928).
4. Sanctified objects and relationships are often resources that people rely on for support and meaning throughout their lives. Across domains, sanctification is linked to greater relationship satisfaction, general well-being, positive affect, and stress-related growth.
5. When people experience a loss or violation of what they hold sacred, they are at risk for powerfully adverse outcomes. Experiences of loss or desecration of a sacred object or betrayal within a sanctified relationship tend to contribute to poorer mental health outcomes than negative life events that are not seen as relevant to the sacred.

In the following sections, we illustrate the ways in which these implications are supported by empirical research on the sanctity of life as a whole, specific life domains, and specific moments. These findings provide evidence in support of our assertion that the capacity to imbue multiple levels of life with a deeper meaning is a core component of the human experience.

Life as a Whole

With the majority of individuals endorsing that they perceive God or the sacred in the daily flow of life, it is important to understand the ways this may shape other aspects of their lives. People who endorsed sanctifying life as a whole tended to have a greater sense of purpose in life and higher self-esteem. They also tended to be more committed to social and community helping and were less likely to have narcissist personality traits (Doehring et al., 2009). These findings suggest that individuals who perceive the sacred in life are able to look beyond themselves and to focus their concern on others. Findings also showed that sanctifying life as a whole was linked with individuals more frequently experiencing pleasant events and more deeply enjoying these events, indicating that perceiving a deeper dimension of life may enhance people's daily lived experiences in a multitude ways.

Specific Domains of Modern Life

Marriage

Given the high prevalence rates of sanctification found in the initial marital sanctification study (Mahoney et al., 1999), researchers have continued to explore the various ways in which sanctification is related to critical relational factors such as commitment and communication. This first study of marital sanctification polled couples living in the Midwest, finding that greater marital sanctification was linked to greater marital adjustment and verbal collaboration, and less marital conflict and verbal aggression by both spouses (Mahoney et al., 1999). Several subsequent quantitative studies have shown similar results, suggesting that sanctification of marriage tends to enhance the relational quality and promote a positive relational process (DeMaris, Mahoney, & Pargament, 2010; Ellison, Henderson, Glenn, & Harkrider, 2011; Lichter & Carmalt, 2009; Stafford, David, & McPherson, 2014). For instance, Ellison and colleagues (2011) examined the role of both general religiousness and sanctification in marital satisfaction in a sample of over one thousand married Texans. Sanctification of marriage strongly predicted higher levels of overall marital quality, relationship commitment, positive emotions, and bonding, as well as lower levels of negative emotion, fully mediating the linkages between general religiousness and these outcomes. Additionally, sanctification neutralized the negative influence of perceived general stress and financial strain on marital quality. Furthermore, a recent study using fixed effects modeling with longitudinal data gathered from 174 couples across the transition to parenthood shows that sanctification of marriage predicted more positive communication skills and warmth by both husbands and wives after taking into account stable characteristics of the partners, such as personality traits or intelligence (Kusner, Mahoney, Pargament, & DeMaris, 2014). Notably, self-reported sanctification was tied to researchers' direct observations of more positive interactions between couples when discussing topics that were likely to trigger conflict. Thus, current scientific evidence indicates that sanctification does not simply act as a proxy measure of general religiousness or other positive attributes of couples but rather is a psychospiritual construct that uniquely predicts better psychosocial and relational health. Together, these findings support the broader implication that regarding a relationship as sacred means one is more likely to invest oneself in it and make attempts to preserve and protect a union.

Several additional studies have found similar results indicating that perceiving one's marital relationship as sacred may serve as a resource for spouses that enhance both their marital bond and their individual well-being. For example, in a study of married couples expecting their first child, greater marital sanctification buffered the effect of perceived inequality between spouses to create marital dissatisfaction, conflict, and anxiety (DeMaris et al., 2010). In a national sample of low-income couples with children, greater marital sanctification was linked to greater commitment, satisfaction, communication, better conflict resolution, and greater commitment to their children, after controlling for other demographic and general religiousness variables (Lichter & Carmalt, 2009). A recent study of highly educated married couples found similar results, with marital sanctification linked to greater marital satisfaction, forgiveness, and more willingness to sacrifice for the relationship (Stafford et al., 2014). Overall, these findings suggest that individuals who perceive their marriage to be sacred often rely on the relationship for support and meaning, invest more of themselves in the relationship, and take steps to preserve their marriage. Thus, those with greater marital sanctification tend to have an enhanced marital experience marked by greater relational happiness and healthier relational processes.

Parenting

Given the noteworthy results emerging from marital sanctification studies, the question arises whether similar findings might emerge in the parent–child relationship. Certainly many parents are highly committed to and invested in their children. Could sanctifying this relationship further strengthen their parent–child bond? To answer this question, researchers modified the original scales to apply to parenting, creating items such as "God is present in my role as a parent" and sampling mothers of 4–6 year-olds in the Midwest (Murray-Swank et al., 2006). Findings showed that viewing one's parental role as sacred was significantly linked to less parental verbal aggression and more consistency in parenting. A similar study showed links between greater parenting sanctification and greater use of positive parenting strategies (Dumas & Nissley-Tsiopinis, 2006). These findings further illustrate that when people hold some aspect of life sacred, they are more diligent in their efforts to do what they believe is necessary to protect it and preserve it from harm. Also, those who view their parental relationship as sacred may be willing to invest more time and energy in their children. Sanctification may be particularly salient in the parent–child relationship, as parents commonly view their children as gifts from God and their parenting as a sacred calling, and thus may simultaneously sanctify their children and their parenting role.

More recently, Weyand et al. (2013) investigated the relationship between sanctification of parenting, child behavior problems, and parental stress. Their findings suggest that viewing one's parental role as sacred moderates the link between behavior problems and parental stress. Thus, for parents with low levels of sanctification, the greater their child's behavior problems, the more stress the parents reported experiencing. However, for parents with high levels of sanctification, greater child behavior problems were not linked with greater stress. These findings suggest that viewing one's parental role through a sacred lens may buffer parents from distress when coping with more challenging behavior problems.

Sexual Behavior

Another domain closely related to the area of marital sanctification is the sanctification of sexual intercourse. A satisfying and healthy sexual relationship plays an important role in overall relationship satisfaction for both married and unmarried romantic partners. Would viewing sexual intercourse as sacred or a connection to the divine make a difference in the quality of sex within a committed relationship? Two initial investigations have examined sexual sanctification in two distinct samples: a community sample of newlywed couples (Hernandez et al., 2011) and sexually active college students in nonmarital romantic relationships (Murray-Swank et al., 2005). The results were quite similar across studies. First, it is notable that viewing sex as sacred was less prevalent than the usual rates of sanctification in other domains such as marriage or parenting. However, despite this lower prevalence, findings showed that those who did more often attribute sacred qualities to their sexual behavior also reported having greater sexual satisfaction and sexual intimacy, more frequent sex, and greater relationship satisfaction (Hernandez et al., 2011; Murray-Swank et al., 2005). These results have also been shown longitudinally in a sample of newlywed couples (Mahoney & Hernandez, 2009). Individuals who endorsed greater sanctification early in the marriage had more frequent sexual intercourse and greater sexual and marital satisfaction 1 year later, and they had smaller declines in sexual functioning over the year.

Given the general tendency for more religious individuals to have less frequent premarital sexual intercourse (Haglund & Fehring, 2010), Murray-Swank et al. (2005) expected to find that unmarried college students who sanctified sexual intercourse would engage less in sexual intercourse as a way of protecting and preserving its special value. However, surprising as they were, these findings underscore the ways sanctification distinguishes itself from more global religious variables. In contrast to the more constraining implications of general religiousness for sexual functioning, sanctification appears to relate to greater investment in and satisfaction with sexuality. To put it more succinctly, sanctification appears to enhance the experience of sexuality within a committed union.

Strivings

One of the most noteworthy domains of study so far is the sanctification of strivings. By strivings, we mean the general goals that people are drawn to in their daily lives; these are the pursuits that tend to receive the most time, commitment, and resources (Emmons, 1986). Just as what one holds sacred is distinctive to each individual, every person has his or her unique configuration of personal strivings. Of course, a few goals tend to be most common—for example, family relationships and career development often rise to the top of the list; nevertheless, people demonstrate considerable variability in their strivings.

In studying this domain, researchers were sensitive to the highly personal and varied nature of personal goals, and had participants generate a list of their own top ten personal strivings (Mahoney, Pargament, et al., 2005). Participants then indicated the degree to which they sanctify each of these strivings as well as the amount of time, commitment, and investment they spent on each striving. Overall, participants reported that they saw their top ten strivings through a sacred lens. Unsurprisingly, the most sanctified strivings were overtly religious or spiritual (e.g., prayer). However, many strivings that are not directly religious/spiritual in nature such as altruistic and family-related strivings (e.g., work on my marriage) were frequently sanctified (Mahoney, Pargament, et al., 2005). Regardless of the type of striving, the two most sanctified strivings were also the ones to which individuals devoted the most time and energy and the ones to which they were most committed and considered to be most important. These findings directly support that people dedicate and invest more of their resources in aspects of life that are held sacred. Also, those strivings that people imbued with more sacred qualities tended to elicit more meaning, joy, and happiness, illustrating how sanctification can elicit spiritual emotions that increase the attraction of the individual to the sanctified object

(Mahoney, Pargament, et al., 2005). However, in this case, sanctifying one's strivings did not relate to greater life satisfaction or better physical or mental health outcomes. Thus, perceiving important personal life goals as manifestations of the divine and imbuing these strivings with sacred qualities related to greater commitment and pursuit of these goals. The lack of positive connection between the sanctification of strivings and health-related outcomes suggests that the pursuit of sacred goals may also be accompanied by sacrifice and some pain.

Work

Given the way in which sanctifying key strivings relates to greater commitment and dedication, it seems plausible that sanctification would function similarly in the workplace. Many people invest a great deal of themselves and their time in cultivating a successful career. An important question follows: does viewing one's work as a sacred calling further enhance this commitment? Anecdotally, we see many instances of this process both among religious and nonreligious figures. For example, many of the saints described a sense that they were called by God to do sacred work or complete a holy mission. Mother Teresa was Albanian by birth but moved to Ireland to answer a divine call to become a missionary sister. Several years later, she reportedly received a strong call from God to start a mission to serve the dying in Calcutta, India, where she worked tirelessly for nearly 50 years despite both practical and spiritual struggles (Teresa, 1995).

Outside of a religious framework, the concept of work as a calling or vocation is also fairly common. The Oxford English dictionary (2015) defines *vocation* (derived from the word *to call*) as "a person's employment or main occupation, especially regarded as particularly worthy and requiring great dedication." Thus, we hear people express a vocation or calling to the field of medicine, education, and other such professions. Leider and Shapiro's (2015) popular new book on career planning speaks to this deeper sense of meaning in work: "Each of us, no matter what we do, has a calling. Of course, some jobs fit more naturally with our calling, but every working situation provides us with some opportunities for fulfilling the urge to give our gifts away. Satisfaction on the job—and ultimately in life—will in part depend on how we take advantage of these meaningful moments" (p. 149). Sanctification in the context of work is closely related to the concept of calling. The theoretical framework of sanctification predicts that those who perceive work as sacred may be more deeply invested in and committed to their work.

Researchers have generated support for this hypothesis. Sanctification of work has been measured with items such as, "God is present in my work," and "My work is sacred." Results of studies show that greater work sanctification relates to greater job satisfaction, higher organizational commitment, and lower intention to leave one's job (Carroll et al., 2014; Walker et al., 2008). Though these findings do not demonstrate a causal relationship between these variables, they are consistent with the theory that perceiving work as having a deeper meaning and purpose than simply generating an income leads employees to invest more in their job duties than would be otherwise expected.

Body

What happens when individuals view their bodies as sacred or perceive God to be involved in their physical health? Though this is a relatively new area of study within psychology, various religious traditions have promoted the idea that the body serves as a dwelling place for the soul and thus should be regarded as a kind of sacred temple. Within the handful of studies that have investigated the role of sanctifying one's body, interesting patterns have emerged. Researchers have tested the theoretical prediction that those individuals who regard their bodies as sacred would be more invested in caring for their physical health. However, studies have found mixed results. On the one hand, some studies have found that greater body sanctification is related to more frequent physical exercise, greater body satisfaction, and greater disapproval of illicit drug use (e.g., Homan & Boyatzis, 2009; Jacobson, Hall, & Anderson, 2013; Mahoney, Carels, et al., 2005). These findings suggest that if individuals perceive their body as sacred, then they are more likely to care for their body in an attempt to preserve and protect it from disease or harm.

However, other large-scale studies in this area have shown different results. For example, Ellison and colleagues (2008) found that as endorsement of body sanctification increased, rates of completing annual medical checkups decreased. Similarly, Benjamins et al. (2011) found that body sanctification was largely unrelated to individuals' use of preventative health services such as cholesterol screenings, flu shots, and colonoscopies. Thus, the perception that the body is a sacred object may encourage people to take better care of themselves physically and respect their bodies mentally. However, the perception that the body is sacred may also encourage the belief that God is able to protect bodies from illness, and thus reduce concerns about utilizing services to detect the warning signs of disease. We are hopeful that future research in this area will clarify this complex and important relationship.

Environment

One study has also examined the sanctification of the environment (Tarakeshwar, Swank, Pargament, & Mahoney, 2001), polling a large national sample of Presbyterian Church members, elders, and clergy. The majority of the sample agreed that "Nature is sacred because it was created by God," and higher endorsement of this item predicted greater participation in nature-preserving activities. Also, individuals who more highly sanctified nature tended to have lower endorsement of the belief that humans take precedence over nature, stronger beliefs that human actions hurt nature, and greater willingness to invest in protecting the environment (Tarakeshwar et al., 2001). These findings further support the broader theme that holding something sacred means one is more likely to take actions to preserve and protect it from harm.

Social Justice

Another promising line of research involves the role of the sanctification in the area of social justice attitudes and activities (Todd, Houston, et al., 2014; Todd, McConnell, & Suffrin, 2014). Researchers have asked whether imbuing social justice efforts with a sense of the sacred relates to more commitment to these endeavors. Results indicate that this may indeed be the case, as sanctification of social justice positively predicted social justice interest and commitment in ways that were not predicted by other religious variables such as being biblically conservative. These are promising findings that illustrate how a theoretical framework of sanctification can contribute greater understanding of a wide range of important life domains.

Sacred Moments in Therapy

Pargament and colleagues' study of sanctification of key moments in life (2014) revealed how important moments in treatment identified by both mental health providers and mental health patients may have pivotal implications. Perceptions of important moments as more sacred by the providers were linked with reports of greater treatment gains, a stronger therapeutic alliance, and higher levels of provider well-being and work motivation. Similar findings were reported by the mental health patients. Sacred moments then may be an important spiritual ingredient of therapeutic change. More generally, sacred moments appear to be a potentially valuable resource, not only for people seeking out help but people providing that help. Findings such as these underscore the importance of extending studies of sanctification to the context of care giving.

Sacred Loss & Desecration

Up to this point we have been focusing on the benefits of viewing life through a sacred lens; however, we must also point out some of the potential risks that accompany sanctification. Though imbuing parts of life with sacred meaning tends to enrich people's life experiences when these objects and relationships remain intact, if sanctified aspects of life are lost (i.e., sacred loss), violated, or harmed (i.e., desecration) the consequences tend to be more severe (Pargament, Magyar, Benore, & Mahoney, 2005). For example, a sacred loss might be the death of a loved one with whom one had a sacred bond, whereas a desecration might be the bombing of a religious space such as a church or temple or discovering a spouse's infidelity in a marriage one held sacred. In each of these cases, the deeper spiritual meaning attached to the object or relationship translates into a greater depth of loss and pain when it is lost or damaged.

Though similar to sanctification, sacred loss and desecration are distinct constructs and have been studied as a separate line of research. One of the first studies in this area (Mahoney et al., 2002) examined the attitudes of college students in Ohio and New York following the 9/11 World Trade Center attack. When asked to rate the degree to which they viewed the attack as a desecration, nearly half of the students endorsed that "this event was both an offence against me and against God," and a third agreed that "something sacred that came from God was dishonored" (Mahoney et al., 2002). In order to better understand the prevalence and implications of these concepts, Pargament and colleagues (2005) asked individuals in a Midwest community sample to identify the most significant personal negative life event they had experienced in the past 2 years. Individuals then rated items that assessed the degree to which they perceived this event to be a sacred loss (e.g., "Something that gave sacred meaning to my life is now missing") or desecration (e.g., "This event ruined a blessing from God") (Pargament et al., 2005). Thirty-eight percent of individuals perceived the negative event as a sacred loss to some degree, whereas 24 % perceived the event as a desecration.

This line of research has also been applied to study the dissolution of romantic and marital relationships. Initial studies have found that over half of college students who experienced a romantic breakup and 74 % of divorced couples perceive the dissolution to be a sacred loss or desecration (Hawley & Mahoney, 2013; Krumrei, Mahoney, & Pargament, 2009). Results across studies have shown a significant link between greater desecration and sacred loss and more emotional distress including greater depression, anger, and intrusive thoughts (Hawley & Mahoney, 2013; Krumrei et al., 2009; Pargament et al., 2005). Also, individuals who experienced a sacred loss tended to report more spiritual growth following the event; however, those who experienced a desecration reported less spiritual growth. Thus, for a significant number of people, perceiving negative events through the lens of sacred meaning has a powerful impact.

It is important especially in clinical settings to recognize that experiencing life as sacred makes facing negative personal events more challenging and painful. However, this does not mean that these negative implications of sacred loss or injury outweigh the benefits of perceiving life through a sacred lens. Faced with a painful event, some individuals are able to rely on spiritual and religious coping to enter into a period of spiritual growth that may lead to deeper insights in the months and years to come. Others may benefit from recognizing that while the object or relationship that manifested the sacred is no longer able to fulfill this role, the entire sphere of the sacred has not been lost, and new and different pathways to experience God/higher powers and/or sacred qualities can be found. Overall, it seems that people who imbue life with sacred meaning experience both the joys and sorrows of life at a deeper level that touches them at the core of their being.

In summary, the research to date suggests that seeing life through a sacred lens is a common experience, one that holds several key implications for human functioning across several domains. People who imbue a dimension of life with sacred status are more likely to show: (1) greater investment of resources in and commitment to the sanctified domain; (2) greater motivation to protect and preserve sacred objects; (3) stronger spiritual emotions; (4) greater support and satisfaction derived from sanctified areas; and (5) heightened risk of adverse outcomes if the sacred is lost or violated.

Broader Implications and Conclusions

How might we understand the great versatility of sanctification and its manifestations in such diverse areas of our lives? Eliade (1961, p. 12) writes, "For those to whom a stone reveals itself as sacred, its immediate reality is transmuted into supernatural reality. In other words, for those who have a religious experience all nature is capable of revealing itself as cosmic sacrality." In this sense, it seems that the power of sanctification lies less in its particular focal point than in the deeper reality revealed through this different way of seeing and experiencing the world. Thus, whether it is a sacred relationship, object, role, or ideal, this way of infusing that which appears to be ordinary with extraordinary meaning and purpose amplifies individuals' experiences of these domains.

Sanctification involves the search for the deeper meaning within everyday experiences and objects. Regardless of the spiritual or religious beliefs underlying this process, the very impulse to look beyond the conventional view to experience a deeper, more nuanced and meaningful dimension is highly valuable in contemporary culture that is rather materialistic and leaves many people persistently dissatisfied and de-moralized. Unfortunately, rather than engage this inner sense of dissatisfaction and uneasiness by facing the challenging existential questions about ultimate meaning and purpose, individuals often distract and numb themselves in order to enjoy the present moment. These distractions can take the form of serious problems, such as addictions. One source of this disillusionment may be the sense of personal disconnection from the deeper dimensions of life, which we propose is an essential part of the human experience. As psychologist Viktor Frankl (1985) asserted: "For too long we have been dreaming a dream from which we are now waking up: the dream that if we just improve the socioeconomic situation of people, everything will be okay, people will become happy. The truth is that as the *struggle for survival* has subsided, the question has emerged: *survival for what*? Ever more people today have the means to live, but no meaning to live for" (p. 121).

How might individuals today reengage with this underlying struggle to find a deeper, more ultimate meaning and purpose in their lives? Though there are many beneficial approaches (e.g., mindfulness or meditation), the process of sanctification may help to frame the seemingly mundane activities of daily living within a deep spiritual dimension. By seeing life through a sacred lens, any moment becomes a potential opportunity to encounter and rediscover something of divine character and significance, fulfilling the human longing for genuine meaning and purpose. Overall, findings in this area of study show that the capacity to sanctify life corresponds with an enriched lived experience of healthier and more satisfying relationships, greater investment and commitment to one's goals, and more satisfaction in pursuing one's most important personal strivings.

These findings also have clinical implications. There is a potential power within sanctification to provide a point of contact between clients' spiritual beliefs and their treatment goals. A critical task for clinicians is to guide clients in identifying their core values and beliefs in order to define their most deeply desired goals and the pathways they take to reach these desired destinations. Helping clients identify those areas in their lives that they hold sacred can facilitate this process (see Pargament, 2007 for illustrations). And as we have stressed, because sanctification can occur theistically or nontheistically, questions about what people perceive as sacred are relevant not only to traditionally religious clients but also to those who define themselves as nontraditional, agnostic, or even atheist. Historically, psychologists have been reluctant to examine spirituality or the sacred dimension of life, perhaps because they themselves are less religious than the general population (Shafranske & Cummings, 2013). Yet, it is becoming clear that many people do see life through a sacred lens and that in many ways imbuing life with sacred meaning is often beneficial. At the same time, the loss or violation of that which is seen as sacred can exacerbate pain, suffering, and violence among individuals and collectives. To appreciate and assist clients in their full humanity as psychological, social, physical, and spiritual beings then, practitioners must also become more facile in seeing life, particularly the lives of their clients, through a sacred lens. Without that spiritual acumen, we overlook a vital dimension of life, one that makes us more deeply human.

Key Takeaways: Potential Implications for Therapy/Helping Professionals

- Assist clients in fostering the capacity to see more deeply, asking clients about what aspects of their life they hold sacred.
- Help clients to prioritize and incorporate what they hold sacred as they formulate therapeutic goals.
- Consider the deeper meaning of problems that involve what clients regard as sacred. For example, in marital therapy with a couple that holds their marriage sacred, encourage spiritual conversation to strengthen intimacy between partners.
- Foster acceptance of diverse spiritual and sacred expressions, recognizing that this construct is relevant not only to traditionally religious clients but also to those who define themselves as nontraditional, agnostic, or even atheist.
- Be open to sacred moments within therapy, recognizing them as an important spiritual ingredient of therapeutic change.

References

Bell, C., Woodruff, E., Davis, D. E., Van Tongeren, D. R., Hook, J. N., & Worthington, E. L., Jr. (2014). Community sanctification of forgiveness. *Journal of Psychology and Theology, 42*(3), 243–251.
Benjamins, M. R., Ellison, C. G., Krause, N. M., & Marcum, J. P. (2011). Religion and preventive service use: Do congregational support and religious beliefs explain the relationship between attendance and utilization? *Journal of Behavioral Medicine, 34*(6), 462–476. doi:10.1007/s10865-011-9318-8
Brelsford, G. M. (2013). Sanctification and spiritual disclosure in parent-child relationships: Implications for family relationship quality. *Journal of Family Psychology, 27*(4), 639–649. doi:10.1037/a0033424
Buechner, F. (1992). *Listening to your life: Daily meditations with Frederick Buechner*. San Francisco, CA: Harper.
Carroll, S. T., Stewart-Sicking, J. A., & Thompson, B. (2014). Sanctification of work: Assessing the role of spirituality in employment attitudes. *Mental Health, Religion & Culture, 17*(6), 545–556. doi:10.1080/13674676.2013.860519
Chernow, R. (2005). *Alexander Hamilton*. New York, NY: Penguin.
Davis, D. E., Hook, J. N., Van Tongeren, D. R., & Worthington, E. L. (2012). Sanctification of forgiveness. *Psychology of Religion and Spirituality, 4*(1), 31–39. doi:10.1037/a0025803
DeMaris, A., Mahoney, A., & Pargament, K. I. (2010). Sanctification of marriage and general religiousness as buffers of the effects of marital inequity. *Journal of Family Issues, 31*(10), 1255–1278. doi:10.1177/0192513X10363888
Doehring, C., & Clarke, A. (2002, August). *Perceiving sacredness in life: Personal, religious, social, and situational predictors*. Paper presented at the annual meeting of the American Psychological Association, Chicago, IL.
Doehring, C., Clarke, A., Pargament, K. I., Hayes, A., Hammer, D., Nickolas, M., & Hughes, P. (2009). Perceiving sacredness in life: Correlates and predictors. *Archive for the Psychology of Religion, 31*(1), 55–73. doi:10.1163/157361209X371492
Dumas, J. E., & Nissley-Tsiopinis, J. (2006). Parental global religiousness, sanctification of parenting, and positive and negative religious coping as predictors of parental and child functioning. *The International Journal for the Psychology of Religion, 16*(4), 289–310. doi:10.1207/s15327582ijpr1604_4
Einstein, A. (1956). *The world as I see it*. New York, NY: Kensington Publishing.
Eliade, M. (1961). *The sacred and the profane* (W. R. Trask, Trans.). New York, NY: Harper & Brothers.
Ellison, C. G., Henderson, A. K., Glenn, N. D., & Harkrider, K. E. (2011). Sanctification, stress, and marital quality. *Family Relations, 60*(4), 404–420. doi:10.1111/j.1741-3729.2011.00658.x
Ellison, C. G., Lee, J., Benjamins, M. R., Krause, N. M., Ryan, D. N., & Marcum, J. P. (2008). Congregational support networks, health beliefs, and annual medical exams: Findings from a nationwide sample of Presbyterians. *Review of Religious Research, 50*(2), 176–193.
Emmons, R. A. (1986). Personal strivings: An approach to personality and subjective well-being. *Journal of Personality and Social Psychology, 51*(5), 1058–1068. doi:10.1037/0022-3514.51.5.1058
Frankl, V. E. (1985). *The unheard cry for meaning: Psychotherapy and humanism*. New York, NY: Washington Square Press.
Haglund, K., & Fehring, R. (2010). The association of religiosity, sexual education and parental factors with risky sexual behavior among adolescents and young adults. *Journal of Religion and Health, 49*(4), 460–472. doi:10.1007/s10943-009-9267-5
Hawley, A. R., & Mahoney, A. (2013). Romantic breakup as a sacred loss and desecration among Christians at a state university. *Journal of Psychology and Christianity, 32*(3), 245–260.

Hernandez, K. M., Mahoney, A., & Pargament, K. I. (2011). Sanctification of sexuality: Implications for newlyweds' marital and sexual quality. *Journal of Family Psychology, 25*(5), 775–780. doi:10.1037/a0025103

Homan, K. J., & Boyatzis, C. J. (2009). Body image in older adults: Links with religion and gender. *Journal of Adult Development, 16*(4), 230–238. doi:10.1007/s10804-009-9069-8

Jacobson, H. L., Hall, M., & Anderson, T. L. (2013). Theology and the body: Sanctification and bodily experiences. *Psychology of Religion and Spirituality, 5*(1), 41–50. doi:10.1037/a0028042

King, M. L., Jr. (1963). *I have a dream.* Retrieved from https://www.archives.gov/press/exhibits/dream-speech

Krumrei, E. J., Mahoney, A., & Pargament, K. I. (2009). Divorce and the divine: The role of spirituality in adjustment to divorce. *Journal of Marriage and Family, 71*(2), 373–383. doi:10.1111/j.1741-3737.2009.00605.x

Kusner, K. G., Mahoney, A., Pargament, K. I., & DeMaris, A. (2014). Sanctification of marriage and spiritual intimacy predicting observed marital interactions across the transition to parenthood. *Journal of Family Psychology, 28*(5), 604–614. doi:10.1037/a0036989

Lambert, N. M., & Dollahite, D. C. (2008). The threefold cord: Marital commitment in religious couples. *Journal of Family Issues, 29*(5), 592–614. doi:10.1177/0192513X07308395

Leider, R. & Shapiro, D. A. (2015). *Work reimagined: Uncover your calling.* Oakland, CA: Berrett-Koehler Publ.

Lichter, D. T., & Carmalt, J. H. (2009). Religion and marital quality among low-income couples. *Social Science Research, 38*(1), 168–187. doi:10.1016/j.ssresearch.2008.07.003

Mahoney, A. (2015). *Constructs and our measures.* Retrieved from https://www.bgsu.edu/arts-and-sciences/psychology/graduate-program/clinical/the-psychology-of-spirituality-and--family/for-researchers/constructs-and-our-measures.html

Mahoney, A., Ano, G., Lynn, Q., Magyar, G. M., McCarthy, S., Pristas, E., & Wachholtz, A. (2002, August). *The devil made them do it? Demonization and desecration in response to the 9/11 Attacks.* Paper presented at the annual meeting of the American Psychological Association, Chicago, IL.

Mahoney, A., Carels, R. A., Pargament, K. I., Wachholtz, A., Leeper, L. E., Kaplar, M., & Frutchey, R. (2005). The sanctification of the body and behavioral health patterns of college students. *The International Journal for the Psychology of Religion, 15*(3), 221–238. doi:10.1207/s15327582ijpr1503_3

Mahoney, A., & Hernandez, K. M. (2009). Sex through a sacred lens: The longitudinal effects of the sanctification of marital sexuality. *National Center for Family & Marriage Research Working Paper Series.* Retrieved from http://www.bgsu.edu/content/dam/BGSU/college-of-arts-and-sciences/NCFMR/documents/WP/WP-09-09.pdf

Mahoney, A., Pargament, K. I., Cole, B., Jewell, T., Magyar, G. M., Tarakeshwar, N., … Phillips, R. (2005). A higher purpose: The sanctification of strivings in a community sample. *The International Journal for the Psychology of Religion, 15*(3), 239–262. doi:10.1207/s15327582ijpr1503_4

Mahoney, A., Pargament, K. I., Jewell, T., Swank, A. B., Scott, E., Emery, E., & Rye, M. (1999). Marriage and the spiritual realm: The role of proximal and distal religious constructs in marital functioning. *Journal of Family Psychology, 13*(3), 321–338. doi:10.1037/0893-3200.13.3.321

Mahoney, A., Pargament, K. I., & DeMaris, A. (2009). Couples viewing marriage and pregnancy through the lens of the sacred: A descriptive study. *Research in the Social Scientific Study of Religion, 20*, 1–46. doi:10.1163/ej.9789004175624.i-334.7

Mahoney, A., Pargament, K. I., & Hernandez, K. M. (2013). Heaven on earth: Beneficial effects of sanctification for individual and interpersonal well-being. In J. Henry (Ed.), *The Oxford handbook of happiness* (pp. 397–410). Oxford: Oxford University Press.

Murray-Swank, N. A., Mahoney, A., & Pargament, K. I. (2006). Sanctification of parenting: Links to corporal punishment and parental warmth among biblically conservative and liberal mothers. *The International Journal for the Psychology of Religion, 16*(4), 271–287. doi:10.1207/s15327582ijpr1604_3

Murray-Swank, N. A., Pargament, K. I., & Mahoney, A. (2005). At the crossroads of sexuality and spirituality: The sanctification of sex by college students. *The International Journal for the Psychology of Religion, 15*(3), 199–219. doi:10.1207/s15327582ijpr1503_2

Otto, R. (1928). *The idea of the holy: An inquiry into the non-rational factor in the idea of the divine and its relation to the rational.* London: Oxford University Press.

Pargament, K. I. (2007). *Spiritually integrated psychotherapy: Understanding and addressing the sacred.* New York, NY: Guilford Press.

Pargament, K. I., Lomax, J. W., McGee, J. S., & Fang, Q. (2014). Sacred moments in psychotherapy from the perspectives of mental health providers and clients: Prevalence, predictors, and consequences. *Spirituality in Clinical Practice, 1*(4), 248–262. doi:10.1037/scp0000043

Pargament, K. I., Magyar, G. M., Benore, E., & Mahoney, A. (2005). Sacrilege: A study of sacred loss and desecration and their implications for health and well-being in a community sample. *Journal for the Scientific Study of Religion, 44*(1), 59–78. doi:10.1111/j.1468-5906.2005.00265.x

Pargament, K. I., & Mahoney, A. (2005). Sacred matters: Sanctification as a vital topic for the psychology of religion. *The International Journal of the Psychology of Religion, 15*(3), 179–198. doi:10.1207/s15327582ijpr1503_1

Pew Research Center. (2012, October 9). *Religion and the unaffiliated.* Retrieved from http://www.pewforum.org/2012/10/09/nones-on-the-rise-religion/#religious-spiritual-or-neither

Phillips, R. E., & Pargament, K. I. (2002). The sanctification of dreams: Prevalence and implications. *Dreaming, 12*(3), 141–153. doi:10.1023/A:1020166208750

Regunathan, S. (2014, December 18). Experiencing the sacred. *The Hindu.* Retrieved from http://www.thehindu.com/features/friday-review/telling-voices-column-roger-scruton/article6704561.ece

Shafranske, E. P., & Cummings, J. P. (2013). Religious and spiritual beliefs, affiliations, and practices of psychologists. In K. I. Pargament & A. Mahoney (Eds.), *APA handbook of psychology, religion, and spirituality (Vol 2): An applied psychology of religion and spirituality* (pp. 23–41). Washington, DC: American Psychological Association. doi:10.1037/14046-002

Stafford, L., David, P., & McPherson, S. (2014). Sanctity of marriage and marital quality. *Journal of Social and Personal Relationships, 31*(1), 54–70. doi:10.1177/0265407513486975

Tarakeshwar, N., Swank, A. B., Pargament, K. I., & Mahoney, A. (2001). The sanctification of nature and theological conservatism: A study of opposing religious correlates of environmentalism. *Review of Religious Research, 42*(4), 387–404. doi:10.2307/3512131

Teresa, M. (1995). *A simple path* (L. Vardey, Compl.). New York, NY: Ballantine Books.

Todd, N. R., Houston, J. D., & Odahl-Ruan, C. A. (2014). Preliminary validation of the sanctification of social justice scale. *Psychology of Religion and Spirituality, 6*(3), 245–256. doi:10.1037/a0036348

Todd, N. R., McConnell, E. A., & Suffrin, R. L. (2014). The role of attitudes toward white privilege and religious beliefs in predicting social justice interest and commitment. *American Journal of Community Psychology, 53*(1-2), 109–121. doi:10.1007/s10464-014-9630-x

Vocation. (2015). In *Oxford English dictionary online.* (2nd ed.), Retrieved from http://www.oed.com

Walker, A. G., Jones, M. N., Wuensch, K. L., Aziz, S., & Cope, J. G. (2008). Sanctifying work: Effects on satisfaction, commitment, and intent to leave. *The International Journal for the Psychology of Religion, 18*(2), 132–145. doi:10.1080/10508610701879480

Weyand, C., O'Laughlin, L., & Bennett, P. (2013). Dimensions of religiousness that influence parenting. *Psychology of Religion and Spirituality, 5*(3), 182–191. doi:10.1037/a0030627

Working with Meaning in Life in Mental Health Care: A Systematic Literature Review of the Practices and Effectiveness of Meaning-Centred Therapies

Joel Vos

Introduction

In all times and cultures, individuals have most likely asked questions about what makes their life meaningful, for example: 'What is important to focus my limited time and energy in life on?' 'How can I live a fulfilling life?' 'What do I really want?' Although sceptical scholars criticise meaning in life as a tenuous construct, research shows that many individuals perceive there to be a larger direction and orientation in their daily lives, and when they lack this experience, they seem more prone to developing depression, anxiety and other psychological problems (cf. Shin & Steger, 2014). Although the answers to these questions differ between individuals, many people construct meaning socially in the context of their wider group, such as the traditional context of a tribe or religion (cf. Chao & Kesebir, 2013; Mikulincer & Shaver, 2013; Neimeyer, 2001; Stillman & Lambert, 2013). However, in our individualistic and secular age, individuals also search for answers inside themselves, focusing on what they see as their authentic true self (cf. Berman, 2009; Schulze, 1992/2005). Consequently, many have turned to therapists for their individual quest for meaning.

Little is known about this new approach, that is, meaning-centred therapy (MCT). It can be asked how psychologically trained meaning-centred therapists support clients to construct a sense of meaning and how effective is their support. This chapter systematically reviews the practices of such therapists and examines their empirical evidence base. As will be described, meaning-centred therapists have traditionally steered away from standardisation and systematic research, as this would not do justice to the totality of the individual's subjective experience; instead, MCT practitioners often base their practices on individual therapy experiences and

J. Vos, Ph.D. (✉)
Department of Psychology, University of Roehampton,
Holybourne Avenue, London SW15 4JD, UK
e-mail: joel.vos@roehampton.ac.uk

philosophy. However, it has recently been argued that systematic empirical research is important for pragmatic reasons such as receiving professional recognition and financial support; with this in mind, empirical MCT studies have been published in recent years (Vos, Cooper, Correia, & Craig, 2015). Therefore, this chapter is based on a systematic literature review of quantitative and qualitative studies on MCT, covering 52,220 citations and 60 trials in 3713 participants, as described elsewhere (Vos & Vitali, 2016).

As this review revealed that some MCT therapists differ in their philosophies and practices, the current chapter starts with an overview of different types of MCT and how these differences have emerged. Subsequently, six fundamental clinical and aetiological assumptions that these schools have in common are described alongside their empirical evidence. This is followed by a review of evidence for the most common therapeutic skills and an overview of the content of the therapy sessions. These MCT types, assumptions, skills and sessions have been identified via thematic analysis (Braun & Clarke, 2006), that is, themes in each individual study are identified, thematic groups across different publications are created, and the most frequently reported themes are presented. Subsequently, this chapter briefly describes the effectiveness of MCT with meta-analyses as detailed elsewhere (Vos & Vitali, 2016). Finally, the findings are critically discussed, followed by recommendations for practitioners.

History and Types of Meaning-Centred Therapies

Founding Fathers of Meaning-Centred Therapies

At the start of psychology as a profession around 1900, meaning-related questions received little attention in psychological treatments, as meaning was considered to be irrelevant, a psychopathological symptom, a defence mechanism or a cognitive bias. This scepticism has been attributed to the mechanistic–deterministic world views of some psychoanalysts and behaviourists of that time, reducing human beings to either steam engines of drives and defences or behavioural–cognitive machines (cf. Lukas, 2014; Marshall & Marshall, 2012). However, psychologists and psychiatrists such as William James, Karl Jaspers and Alfred Adler tried to open this reductionist world view and revealed how existential experiences are essential to the psychological realm. For instance, Adler showed how the experience of meaning is engrained in our personality and fulfils crucial functions in our psychological development. Meaning seems particularly beneficial in situations of suffering, pain or death, which Jaspers (1925/2013) called 'boundary situations in life'. At such inevitable crossroads, we can choose to sink into despair and resignation or take a leap of faith towards 'transcendence', that is, transcending the situation in space and time, accepting our freedom to decide and developing a larger, more authentic and meaningful perspective on life.

Self-transcendence was also at the heart of Frankl's paradigm-shifting book about his experiences as inmate and psychiatrist in Nazi concentration camps, originally entitled 'Saying Yes to Life in Spite of Everything', better known as *Man's Search for Meaning* (1985). Frankl wrote that the inmates' ability to identify meaning and imagine the future affected their longevity. He concluded that meaning in life can be found in every moment of living; life never ceases to have meaning, even in suffering and death. From his experiences, Frankl developed the idea that a prisoner's psychological reactions are not solely the result of his or her life situation but also from the freedom of choice he or she always has, even in severe suffering. That is, every individual has the freedom in every situation to modulate their inner attitude towards it, in a similar way that Jaspers had described the inner leap of faith from despair and resignation towards experiencing a meaning transcending the situation. Life ultimately means taking the responsibility to find the right answer to its problems and to fulfil the tasks which it constantly sets for each individual. Frankl believed that people are primarily driven by a striving to experience meaning in life and that it is this sense of meaning that enables people to overcome painful experiences. Life always has a potential meaning transcending the here and now, even in the most dehumanising and painful moments.

The three conceptual pillars of Frankl's work included the assumption that all individuals have an inner striving towards meaning ('will to meaning'), that everyone is always free to take a stance towards any condition in life ('freedom of will') and that every situation has the potential of being meaningful, even in times of the tragic triad of suffering, guilt and death (Lukas, 2014). Frankl called his new non-deterministic therapeutic approach 'logotherapy' and 'existential analysis'.

Although many techniques and exercises have emerged over the years, three techniques dominated Frankl's work and are still practised by many existential therapists (Correia, Cooper, Berdondini, & Correia, 2014). *First*, paradoxical intentions are based on the assumption that individuals can choose the stance they take towards their psychological difficulties and that their symptoms are exacerbated by avoiding problems or feeling saddened or anxious. Frankl invited clients to deliberate practice or exaggerate a neurotic habit or thought, so that they stopped fighting and instead identified and undermined their problems. This technique has proven to be particularly effective in anxiety disorders (e.g. Hill, 1987). *Second*, de-reflection techniques are based on the assumption that individuals can become obsessed with themselves and their problems, which exacerbates their symptoms. Frankl encouraged clients to distance themselves from themselves and their problems, by stopping reflections and paying attention to the world around them, for instance, via humour and art, and focusing on something meaningful. De-reflection seems similar to defusion in acceptance and commitment therapy, which has been shown to be effective (e.g. Hayes, Luoma, Bond, Masuda, & Lillis, 2006). *Third*, modulation of attitudes ('Einstellungsmodulation') means that clients are stimulated to develop a more positive and meaningful attitude towards the situation; that is, clients change their perspective or coping style to create the opportunity of living a meaningful life *despite* the limitations of daily life which gives them a sense of creative freedom (cf. Lukas, 1986, 2014). One way of transforming attitudes is via Socratic dialogues, which are questions helping clients to become aware of the freedom, creativity and meaning they already have; this technique has been shown to be moderately effective for self-improvement, cultivating virtue in everyday life as well as psychological well-being (Overholser, 2010). These three main meaning-centred techniques have over the years been extended with relational–humanistic skills such as having a respectful approach, empathically exploring clients' life situations and intuitively exploring what is meaningful for them (cf. Lukas, 2014). Furthermore, existential analysts have elaborated a hermeneutic-phenomenological stance, which implies an open description of the client's experiences without imposing on them the therapist's reflections and values (Langle, 2014).

Frankl's Legacy

In contrast with other types of therapies, logotherapy has not developed into one unified therapeutic school (Raskob, 2005). This may be explained by Frankl's belief that logotherapy is a "supplement rather than a substitute for psychotherapy" (1985, p. xii). He also insisted that therapies should not be developed by 'gurus' but by individual therapists (Frankl, 1980/2014). Furthermore, Frankl's anthropology centres around the uniqueness of individual clients, implying that treatments are tailored to individual clients and therefore "a standardised guide would be more hindrance than help" (Lukas, 1986/2014, p. 129). Consequently, there is little standardisation of meaning-centred therapies. For instance, only in recent years have treatment manuals been developed and tested in clinical trials. This lack of research has created the scientifically unsatisfactory situation that there are a large number of meaning-centred practitioners and training institutions worldwide (cf. Correia et al., 2014) which use practices that have not been validated in accordance with current academic standards. Possibly due to this lack of validation, meaning-centred practices only seem to play a marginal role in public mental health care and are excluded from health guidelines such as the British NICE guidelines. Therefore, despite ideological arguments against standardisation and trials, there are pragmatic reasons that justify conducting rigorous outcome studies (Vos, Cooper, et al., 2015). In line with this pragmatic approach, a literature review by the author of this chapter uncovered an exponential growth of the number of MCT trials since the turn of the millennium (Vos & Vitali, 2016). Were there no more than fourteen clinical trials before the year 2000, there are now over 60 studies. Why has meaning in life suddenly become fashionable? Four answers are possible.

First, an impressive body of qualitative and quantitative studies has validated the core assumptions of MCT, namely, that many individuals experience meaning in life, that this experience can be differentiated from other psychological experiences and that it predicts long-term well-being. These studies have been summarised in several handbooks (e.g. Batthyany & Russo-Netzer, 2014; Hicks & Routledge, 2013; Reker & Chamberlain, 2000; Wong, 2012).

Second, meaning is one of the cornerstones of the increasingly popular movement of positive psychology, which transforms mental health care from merely treating mental illness to including positive psychological experiences such as meaning. Many trials have supported positive psychology interventions (Seligman, Steen, Park, & Peterson, 2005). However, some authors argue that positive experiences cannot be artificially disentangled from negative psychological and existential experiences such as awareness of our finitude, and they therefore propose an integrated positive–negative approach (Batthyany & Russo-Netzer, 2014; Ivtzan, Lomas, Hefferon, & Worth, 2015; Kashdan & Biswas-Diener, 2014; Vos, 2013; Wong, 2011).

Third, meaning has been promoted as essential to the personal recovery that all clients undergo in therapy: "recovery is about building a meaningful and satisfying life, as defined by the person themselves, whether or not there are ongoing or recurring symptoms or problems" (Andresen, Oades, & Caputi, 2011, p. 2). This is based on over 70 studies indicating that clients perceive meaning-making as essential to their therapeutic recovery process (Andresen et al., 2011). That is, therapy helped them to live a meaningful life, although their life situation or psychiatric disorder may not be changed. This reminisces of the Jasperian–Franklian transcendence: 'saying yes to life in spite of everything'. This may even suggest that supporting meaning is a common factor of all effective therapies (cf. Goldfried, 1982). Policymakers in several countries including the United Kingdom and United States have promoted the recovery model as more consumer-oriented, pragmatic and cost-effective than the traditional medical-cure model.

Fourth, a large body of studies shows that many clients struggle with meaning-related questions, particularly in response to sudden negative life events. For instance, a majority of individuals report meaning-related questions or request meaning-related support in confrontation with the diagnosis of a chronic or life-threatening disease, the loss of a loved one or a disaster; these individuals seem to benefit from meaning-based coping styles (e.g. Henoch & Danielson, 2009; Lee, Cohen, Edgar, Laizner, & Gagnon, 2004; Neimeyer, 2001; Park, 2010; Park & Folkman, 1997; Schulenberg, Drescher, & Baczwaski, 2014).

Overview of Types of Meaning-Centred Therapy

In the empirical literature, 30 different types of MCT can be identified (Vos & Vitali, 2016).

The first type of therapy explicitly aims to improve meaning in life via systematic and directive techniques such as didactics, guided exercises and relational–humanistic skills. All publications cite Frankl as their basis, although most schools have elaborated their own clinical, aetiological and therapeutic models. Classical logotherapy, general meaning-centred therapies and logo-analysis (e.g. Frankl, Lukas, Fabry, Marshall, Hutzell and Crumbaugh) directly use Frankl's core methods as previously described in standardised, relatively directive manuals for a wide range of clients. Existential analysis has elaborated the logo-therapeutic theory within a phenomenological, client-directed and dialogical approach. It seeks to help clients develop an authentic and responsible attitude towards their lives and contexts, so they can experience themselves freely and thus 'say yes' with an inner consent to the world (feeling we exist), life (feeling life is good and valuable), self (feeling and showing authentic uniqueness) and meaning. Thus existential analysis helps clients to say: 'Yes, I exist, my life is good, I can be myself, and I can achieve my goals' (Langle, 2014, p. 23). Meaning-centred counselling or meaning therapy (Wong, 2013) is a short action-oriented therapeutic approach with specific exercises, based on the theoretical ABCDE model: helping clients to accept events in life, believe in strengths and the possibility of change, commit to actions, discover hidden meanings and evaluate change and progress. Meaning-centred group psychotherapy is a brief manualised group for cancer patients developed by Breitbart and Poppito (2014), which uses specific self-reflection exercises to focus on creating a sense of coherence between the life before and after cancer, grieving over how the disease challenges meaning and explaining and experientially connecting with the three main pathways to meaning proposed by Frankl (see below). Meaning-making interventions involve a narrative approach, helping clients to review their lives and chronologically embed the cancer experience in the historical context of other important life events, which also pays attention to themes such as self-worth, controllability of events, justice, coping and life priorities (Lee et al., 2004). Meaning-based group counselling for bereavement helps individuals to reconstruct meaning during grief over the loss of a loved one (MacKinnon et al., 2013).

Several therapies address meaning as one core aspect of the intervention, sometimes using different terminology such as 'values' or 'life goals', along with other aims and processes in therapy. These studies will not be discussed in the remainder of this chapter to avoid conflation with therapeutic aims and methods not focusing on meaning. Empirical studies suggest modest to large effects for these therapies on improving psychological well-being; the following cited studies are reviews or representative examples: meaning-centred marital and family therapy (Lantz, 2000; Schulenberg, Schnetzer, Winters, & Hutzell, 2010), meaning therapy via the use of photography (Steger, Shim, Barenz, & Shin, 2014), acceptance and commitment therapy (Hayes et al., 2006), structured life review and guided autobiography (Bohlmeijer, Smit, & Cuijpers, 2003), dignity therapy in palliative care (Chochinov et al., 2005), positive psychological interventions (Sin & Lyubomirsky, 2009), goal management intervention (Arends & Bode, 2013), salutogenic therapy (Langeland et al., 2006), spiritual interventions (Anderson et al., 2015), psychosynthesis (no empirical trials found), humanistic and person-centred therapies (Elliott, 2002) and existential therapies (Vos, Craig, & Cooper, 2015). Additionally, several therapies indirectly or peripherally address meaning, with small to moderate psychological effects: hardiness interventions (Maddi, 2014), transactional analysis (Khalil et al., 2007), schema therapy (Masley, Gillanders, Simpson, & Taylor, 2012), hope therapy (Weis & Speridakos, 2011), motivational interviewing (Lundahl, Kunz, Brownell, Tollefson, & Burke, 2010) and Jungian therapies (no systematic trials identified). Meaning is also addressed by nontherapeutic approaches which have not been studied in trials such as life coaching, philosophical counselling, meaning in life education nationwide in Taiwan and occasionally in other countries and art of life education in the Netherlands and Germany (e.g., Kekes, Dohmen, Schmid, Bohlmeijer).

Validation of Clinical–Aetiological Assumptions

The difference between quack therapies and evidence-based therapies is not only that outcome studies prove the effectiveness of the latter but also that there is empirical evidence and conceptual coherence for the underlying clinical and aetiological models and that the therapeutic mechanisms are logically built on these clinical–aetiological models (Kazdin, 2008; Vos, 2014b). A clinical model is the conceptualisation of the main psychological problem that the therapeutic intervention focuses on and an aetiological model describes how this problem has developed. The therapeutic mechanisms should logically follow from these clinical–aetiological models.

It seems difficult to validate the clinical–aetiological assumptions in meaning-centred therapies, as most publications do not explicate these assumptions and do not present one unified model. Most of the evidence is also philosophical-deductive in nature or merely reflects personal therapeutic experiences from key authors. For instance, two of Frankl's three main conceptual pillars are fundamentally unverifiable as these are anthropological and philosophical in nature, i.e. the assumptions that we are free in our decisions and that life is meaningful (Lukas, 1986/2014). The sociological causes of existential frustration and meaning-centred/noogenic neuroses are also difficult to verify empirically (Marshall & Marshall, 2012). Additionally, Frankl has developed a diagnostic system (1999/2005) which has not been systematically validated, although Lukas (2014) has conceptually connected this with psychiatric diagnostic manuals. However, six verifiable aspects can be identified in MCT publications, which will be discussed alongside their empirical evidence.

First, meaning is assumed to be correlated with, but phenomenologically distinct, from other psychological phenomena. This assumption has been confirmed by many questionnaire studies (e.g. Melton & Schulenberg, 2008; Shin & Steger, 2014; Steger, 2012). The MCT publications consistently describe five aspects of meaning, and empirical research confirms that the experience of meaning consists of (1) being motivated by purposes, drives and/or self-transcendence in life; (2) living according to one's own values; (3) understanding and having a sense of coherence of the world, life and self (sometimes associated with 'cosmic meaning'); (4) experiencing one's own life as worthy, significant and relevant ('existential meaning'); (5) committing to goals and actions in daily life ('situational meaning'); and (6) evaluating and adjusting one's way of living ('self-regulation') (e.g., Batthyany & Russo-Netzer, 2014; Reker & Chamberlain, 2000; Wong, 2012). Thus meaning in life seems to be a valid and reliable concept.

Second, all MCT authors hypothesise that humans strive and crave for meaning, and this contains an internal contribution, i.e. the individual who is striving and craving, and an external contribution, i.e. the meaning potential of the situation (Lukas, 1986/2014). Indeed, many individuals search for and/or experience meaning or purpose in life, as confirmed by studies with instruments such as meaning in life questionnaire and purpose in life, although the precise percentages differ per instrument, population and study (e.g. Brandstätter, Baumann, Borasio, & Fegg, 2012; Shin & Steger, 2014; Steger, 2012).

Third, a low sense of meaning is often associated with an overall low psychological well-being and psychopathology, while a strong sense of meaning correlates with better overall well-being in the long term (e.g. Reker & Chamberlain, 2000; Shin & Steger, 2014; Steger, 2012). However, most of this evidence comes from studies with nonexperimental designs, that have not clarified the causal direction (e.g. King, Hicks, Krull, & Del Gaiso, 2006). Nevertheless, indirect evidence for causality may be found through cross-sectional studies which show that, following negative life events, individuals search for meaning. Individual resources of meaning act as resources for coping, since a high level of life meaningfulness seems to act as a buffer against the negative consequences of stress, and meaning-based coping contributes to better psychological adjustment during or after stressful events (e.g. Folkman, 2008; Henoch & Danielson, 2009; Park, 2010). Like Frankl predicted, when individuals are frustrated in roles and activities that they highly value, they seem to experience lower psychological and physical well-being (e.g., Krause, 2004). More specifically, Frankl used the term 'existential vacuum' to describe the result of a long-standing frustration of the will to meaning, characterised by a sense of lack of meaning and purpose, combined with feelings of emptiness and boredom (Lukas, 2014). Frankl cited his own observation that 25 % of European students and 60 % of American students experience this (Marshall & Marshall, 2012). Due to the complexity of this concept, this hypothesis seems difficult to verify (Dyck, 1987), although one study indicated that particularly individuals of young and old age experience existential vacuum (Reker, Peacock, & Wong, 1987).

Fourth, it is assumed that individuals experience meanings as more important when these are concordant with their true or authentic self, instead of when these meanings reflect inauthentic or externally imposed meanings (cf. Schlegel, Smith, & Hirsch, 2013). Although the concept of a true self may be called 'tenuous at best', the perception of a true self is closely related to the experience of 'values consistent with the true self'. Empirical studies show that choices consistent with the true self-concept are more valuable for an individual. Furthermore, perceived true self-knowledge strongly influences what an individual experiences as meaningful and that this is related with satisfaction about decisions and with feeling confident in past and future decisions (Schlegel, Smith, & Hirsch, 2013).

Fifth, Frankl hypothesised that individuals experience an absolute hierarchy in their meanings: certain meanings are more valuable than others. Our 'conscience' can discover this absolute hierarchy of meanings in our life via intuitive sensing ('Spüren'), which is a valuation process in which not only abstract cognitions are involved but our full person with all our senses and experiences (Längle & Bürgi, 2014; Lukas, 1986/2014). This intuitive process would, for instance, imply that we need to peel off the superficial layers of our everyday emotions before we can sense the underlying values in our deeper layers of experiences that resonate with our true selves and the hierarchy of values in the situation (cf. Vos, 2014). Consequently, MCT should not help clients to 'create' meaning in their lives but to help them 'discover' meaning, "like finding the right answer in a multiple choice quiz. Several answers are possible; only one is right. Several interpretations of a situation are possible; only one is true" (Fabry, 1980, p. 53).

Correlational research, indeed, identifies different types of meaning. Illusionary or defensive meanings are, for instance, meanings that correlate with denial and avoidance coping styles, while constructive or authentic meanings correlate with an accepting stance (e.g. Pat-Horenczyk et al., 2015; Schlegel et al., 2013; Zoellner & Maercker, 2006). Additionally, individuals who primarily focus on materialistic–hedonic values experience life as less meaningful and satisfying and experience more long-term psychological problems, while social and transcending values are associated with better well-being (e.g. Baumeister, Vohs, Aaker, & Garbinsky, 2013; Nielsen, 2014; Gantt, & Thayne, 2014). Furthermore, empirical research seems to confirm the existence of an innate functional capacity to intuit what is 'right' and 'wrong' in a situation (Hauser, 2006).

Notwithstanding this correlational and functional evidence, the metaphysical truth underlying the absolute-hierarchy hypothesis cannot be verified. Possibly due to this lack of verifiability, many meaning-centred practitioners have moved away from this Franklian radical absolutism and merely offer a phenomenological exploration of what the client experiences as valuable. These therapists remain metaphysically agnostic about the question how absolute these experiences of the client are. This pragmatic shift seems to answer traditional criticisms that MCT may have authoritarian overtones (May, 1978; Yalom, 1980) and are based on "unvalidated assumptions and unalterable truths" (Cooper, 2003, p. 65). For instance, relativistic MCT therapists mention that on the one hand they recognise their client's wish for clarity about what is truly valuable and what is not, while on the other hand, recognising that in life full metaphysical truth may not be achievable; this dual awareness combines the client's wish for certainty with accepting their existential uncertainty (cf. Vos, 2014).

Sixth, all publications mention that according to Frankl there are three 'main streets' ('Hauptstraße') to a meaningful life, that is, via realising the values of 'experiencing' ('Erlebniswerte'), the values of 'creativity and productivity' ('Schöpferische Werte') and the values of 'inner attitudes' ('Einstellungswerte') (Lukas, 1986/2014). That is, individuals experience many different types of meanings that are unique for them and for their current life situation, but the reason why they experience something as meaningful is because it realises a broader underlying value. For instance, a client may experience her job as meaningful because she highly values being productive and creative, but this value could also be realised in other situations such as being productive in volunteer work or parenting. Thus, meanings are 'values realised in daily life' and 'the most valuable option in the current situation'. In this context, the will to meaning can be defined as 'saying yes to a value', that is, 'a decision to commit to a chosen value' (Längle & Bürgi, 2014, p. 180). Most MCT authors assume that these three most common types of values that individuals experience can be categorised into these three specific groups of universal values. Subsequently, they use this meaning triad as a cornerstone for the treatment manuals: after some introduction sessions, most manuals address one session for each of the three values, which is often followed by sessions in which the three values are translated into concrete goals and actions for daily life.

Although specific definitions differ between authors, the group of values about 'experiencing' describe a wide range of meaningful experiences, such as enjoying nature, music and art, physical well-being, entertainment, relationships and love; on the most fundamental level, value can be found in the human capacity to experience anything at all. 'Creativity and productivity' are not only about our visible contribution to the world via our profession, art or offspring but also about having a creative stance in life such as being able to find creative solutions to difficult life situations. This is also connected with the third group of values relating to 'inner attitudes', and this concerns the inner freedom all of us have to distance ourselves from the situation and decide our response to it. For instance, individuals could act as a victim to a diagnosis of the terminal stage of a disease or instead try to live life meaningfully despite their disease; for example, Frankl (1980/2014) writes that a dying individual has the ability to change his attitude to his situation. This value triad is a cornerstone for many therapy manuals (Vos & Vitali, 2016).

One may argue that these three values can only be philosophically validated, as they reflect three existential modes of being and not three operationalisable aspects. However, it is possible to ask individuals which meanings they experience and subsequently analyse which values their answers reflect. For instance, Lukas conducted such a survey and found that 50 % of the individuals reported experiencing, 25 % creativity–productivity and 25 % inner attitude as main values (Lukas, 1971, in Lukas, 2014). Since Lukas, many researchers have asked individuals in different countries and of different ages what they experience as meaningful. A recent systematic literature review included 79 studies with 2435 participants, which confirmed that individuals indeed experience these three main values (Vos, 2016b). However, other values were more frequently reported as important, which led to a different categorisation (and which appeared to be in line with a smaller review by Wong & Reker in Reker & Chamberlain, 2000). Here, values were categorised in terms of materialistic–hedonic values, self-oriented values, social values, higher/transcendental values and meta-values (see Table 1). This review also revealed the multiple interpretability of values: an individual could, for example, not only pursue sports achievements for the hedonic-pleasurable feelings they evoke but also for the sake of the self and others or to achieve a higher goal. The Franklian value triad does not need to conflict with this quintet. For instance, experiencing, creativity–productivity and certain attitudes could be applied to each of the five categories: creativity–productivity could be realised in the materialistic–hedonic, self-oriented, social and transcending domains of life.

Thus, compared with the Franklian value triad, the value quintet reflects the experience of more clients in multiple studies around the world, while the triad is

Table 1 Overview of life domains and hypothetical underlying values, as identified in a systematic literature review of 79 publications on what individuals' experience as meaningful in life and categorised via thematic analyses (Vos, 2016a)

I. Materialistic–hedonic domain of meaning
Underlying value: the value of having material goods, objective success, nice physical experiences
(a) Material conditions
E.g. finances, housing, possessions, practical daily life activities
(b) Professional and educational success
E.g. general success, professional success, educational success, profession/education-related social status
(c) Hedonic and experiential activities
E.g. hedonism, leisure and joyful activities, peak experiences, sex, nature and animals
(d) Health
E.g. Being healthy, healthy lifestyle, sports
II. Self-oriented sources of meaning
Underlying value: the value of the self
(a) Resilience (coping successfully with difficult life situations)
E.g. flexibility, perseverance and hardiness, accepting challenges, effective coping skills
(b) Self-efficacy
E.g. feeling in control, knowing how to set, experiment and adjust reachable goals in daily life
(c) Self-acceptance
E.g. self-insight, self-acceptance, self-esteem
(d) Creative self-expression
E.g. in work or hobby, such as making music, writing, sports and having a creative dynamic lifestyle
(e) Autonomy
E.g. self-reliance, non-selfish balance with social context
(f) Self-care
III. Social sources of meaning
Underlying value: the value of being connected with others, belonging to a specific community and improving the well-being of others and children in particular
(a) Feeling socially connected
E.g. sociability, friends, family, intimate relationships
(b) Belonging to a specific community
E.g. family, community, history and society
(c) Altruism
E.g. selfless services to others, contribution to society
(d) Taking care of children
E.g. becoming a parent, foster care, working in education
IV. Transcending/higher sources of meaning
Underlying value: values about something larger than their materialistic–hedonic experiences, themselves and other human beings, merely for the sake of that larger value
(a) Purposes
E.g. specific higher purposes, goals or aims in life

(continued)

Table 1 (continued)

(b) Personal growth	
	E.g. self-development (e.g. cognitive, behavioural self-developnment via education, training and therapy), self-transcendence, self-realisation and realising one's highest personal potential consistent
(c) Temporality	
	E.g. future-oriented, sense of coherence and feeling part of the totality of past, present, future, legacy and after-life
(d) Justice & ethics	
	E.g. following ethical standards, being treated in a just way, contributing to a just world
(e) Spirituality & religion	
	E.g. spirituality and religion, beliefs, cosmic meaning, peace harmony and balance
V. The meaning of being here ('meta-meaning')	
Underlying value: the value of being able to have values and the meaning of being able to experience meanings. Thus, this source of meaning does not have a specific content like the other types of meaning but is more abstract, philosophical or spiritual; the mere fact that someone is breathing and is able to make unique decisions within freedom is a gift to which one may feel grateful and may want to respond to with responsible decisions. This type of meaning can be implicitly present and underlying the other types of meaning.	
(a) Being alive: e.g. being born, feeling alive, being until death	
(b) Uniqueness: e.g. the unique individuality of one's own experiences, own life, own world and own self	
(c) Connectedness with the world and others: e.g. being in the world, being in context, being in relationships	
(d) Individual freedom: e.g. freedom of decision, freedom to decide one's attitude towards a limitation situation in life, the possibility to leave a legacy	
(e) Be grateful to life as a gift: e.g. experiencing the mere fact of being born as a gift or miracle that one did not ask for but one regards as highly precious and special and to which one responds with gratitude	
(f) Responsibility: e.g. the individual responsibility for oneself to live a meaningful life according to one's highest values	

based on philosophical assumptions and few empirical studies. However, the majority of MCT manuals are centred around the triad. Consequently, therapists impose their normative selection of values to clients by exploring a non-exhaustive range of possible meanings in life. Subsequently, some clients may feel that MCT is not relevant for them, leading to drop out or smaller effectiveness (cf. Applebaum et al., 2012). For instance, paying only limited attention to hedonic–materialistic values may alienate clients who have never reflected on 'higher values'. Therefore, to be applicable to a wider client population, it could be recommended to structure MCT manuals around this inclusive evidence-based value quintet instead of the traditionally narrow value triad.

In conclusion, meaning-centred practices are based on some unverifiable clinical and aetiological assumptions, but research indicates that individuals experience meaning in life as a multidimensional phenomenon which seems important and predictive of their general well-being. Individuals experience different types of meaning, with hedonistic–materialistic meanings as less beneficial and with social and transcendent meanings as more beneficial for their well-being. This evidence seems to justify offering MCT to clients experiencing meaning-related problems, in particular those in boundary situations in life, who often ask such questions and would benefit from meaning-oriented coping styles.

Therapeutic Skills

What do meaning-centred practitioners actually do when they work with clients, and how is this supported by empirical evidence? Thematic analyses of the literature review divulged 38 skills (see Table 2).

Assessment Skills

These skills are about evaluating the life situation, needs, preferences and capacities of the clients, to develop a specific meaning-related plan together with the clients to help them with the problems they are currently facing in life. More specifically, the practitioner tries to understand how the problems of the client relate to meaning and to ascertain whether the client has the capacity for and could benefit from directly and systematically working with meaning in life. The foundations for a positive therapeutic relationship are laid, and potential iatrogenic damage of the diagnostic process should be avoided, for instance, by not only focusing on the client's weaknesses but also their strengths and positive meanings (e.g. Lukas, 1986/2014). Scientific evidence seems to confirm that—in therapies in general—assessing and tailoring therapy to the needs, skills and wishes of the individual client can to some extent improve the effectiveness of therapies (Eifert, Schulte, Zvolensky, Lejuez, & Lau, 1997; Schulte, 1996), in particular when client and therapist agree on therapeutic goals and processes to achieve these goals (Tryon & Winograd, 2010).

Meaning-Specific Skills

These skills aim at explicating, systematically exploring and improving meaningful aspects of the client's experiences. They include skills that have been shown to be effective in other therapies such as providing psychoeducation, rephrasing/reframing the stories of the clients in terms of meaning, conducting guided exercises and connecting the topic of therapy, namely, meaning, with specific situations in everyday life (cf. Cooper, 2008; Roth & Fonagy, 2013). Frankl and other logotherapists often explicate their belief that the client will be able to find meaning in life again, and studies confirm that an unconditional positive regard and hope are important

Table 2 Overview of therapeutic skills identified via thematic analyses of the studies in a systematic literature review of therapies explicitly and systematically addressing meaning in life (Vos & Vitali, 2016)

PART I. Assessment skills
1. Exploring the client's request for support in a non-reductionist and multidimensional way
2. Assessing the immediate needs and life situation of the client
3. Developing a meaning-oriented case formulation
4. Making shared decisions about goals and method of the meaning-oriented practice
5. Using assessment as the start of the therapeutic process
Part II. Meaning-specific skills
6. Providing didactics about meaning in life
7. Focusing on long-term meaning in life instead of on short-term gratification and pleasures and showing the potential benefits of this focus
8. Identifying and explicating meaning-oriented topics in the experiences of the clients
9. Offering clients a guided discovery of their meaning potential via concrete exercises
10. Showing an unconditional positive regard about the possibility to find meaning in any situation in life
11. Addressing the totality of possible meanings in the client's life, that is:
(a) Exploring multiple potential domains and underlying values how meaning can be experienced in life (e.g. Frankl: experiencing, attitude, productivity and creativity; according to Table 1, materialistic–hedonic, self-oriented, social, transcendent and meta-values)
(b) Experienced in multiple senses (affects, cognitions, behavioural, body)
(c) In different domains in life (work, social, political, etc.)
(d) Internal (e.g. inner attitude) and external (e.g. behaviour)
(e) Hedonic (e.g. pleasure in the here and now) and self-transcending (e.g. social and commitment to a purpose larger than the self, cosmic meaning)
(f) Conscious/explicit and unconscious/implicit meanings
(g) Balancing stress-causing meaning (e.g. positive aspects of stress and striving towards goals) and leisure time (e.g. relaxing after striving and working hard towards goals)
(h) Concrete meanings in daily life (e.g. behaviour and concrete decisions) and abstract meaning (e.g. ideals and values)
(i) Striving towards goals (i.e. linear, goal-directed, future-oriented) and non-goal-directed (i.e. non-linear, e.g. inner attitude and experiencing in the here and now)
(j) Deepening the experiences of these meanings
12. Concretising and specifying meaning in daily life
13. Stimulating effective goal management: (a) help clients to set concrete aims for daily life, (b) make a plan, (c) experiment in daily life, (d) evaluate these experiments, (e) adjust the aims and methods and (f) make long-term commitment to goals
14. Exploring meanings in the client's past, as a potential source for improving self-esteem, hope and inspiration for future meaning
15. Stimulating the client to give his/her own independent-but-connected answer to his/her social context: encouraging the client to develop autonomy and stay connected with his/her social context at the same time (i.e. a 'two-sided approach' or 'multiple partiality').
16. Focusing on meanings that are based on and that stimulate self-esteem, self-love, self-efficacy and worthiness of the self
Part III. Existential skills: explicitly embedding meaning in the broader context of life
17. Recognising and explicitly addressing the existential dimension of the experiences of the client (e.g., the limitations of meaning in life and inevitable mortality)

(continued)

Table 2 (continued)

18.	Stimulating meaning-oriented coping with situations of suffering
19.	Exploring paradoxical feelings about meaning in life and fostering acceptance of paradoxes and tensions
20.	Identifying avoidance and denial of meaning-related topics, exploring the reasons of avoidance and denial and trying to overcome this
21.	Stimulating the client to connect with the bigger temporal picture of past–present–future
22.	Stimulating the client to take up his/her own responsibility for living a meaningful life
23.	Phenomenologically exploring whether there are any hierarchies in the client's experiences of meaning (e.g., in which experiences are more meaningful than others, how authentic are certain meanings)
	Part IV. Relational–humanistic skills: focus on the therapeutic relationship and on a phenomenological exploration of the client's experiences
24.	Using general skills to focus on improving and deepening the therapeutic relationship
25.	Phenomenological exploration of the experiences of the client
26.	Following the tempo of progress of the client
27.	Empathising with the client's struggles in life and stressing that existential struggles are common to all human beings
28.	Tailoring the practice to the needs, skills and wishes of the client
30.	Exploring which meanings the client expresses in the relationship with the practitioner
31.	Helping the client to develop ethical and authentic relationships with others
32.	Having an ethical stance towards the client and his/her situation
	Part V. Spiritual and mindfulness skills: openness to the spiritual–cultural context, focus on acceptance, including experiential exercises (e.g., mindfulness)
33.	Being sensitive to the religious and cultural context of the client
34.	Stimulating de-reflection and self-distancing
35.	Using experiential exercises focusing on inner awareness (e.g., mindfulness)
36.	Stimulating a basic attitude of acceptance on multiple levels:
	(a) Acceptance that specific life events have occurred (emotional acceptance and integrative acceptance which incorporates a negative event with positive aspects of life)
	(b) Acceptance that absolute certainty about what is meaningful for ourselves (absolute existential meaning), about the meaning of the universe (absolute cosmic meaning) and how my life fits into this cosmic 'big plan' (e.g. 'why did this happen to me?') may not be achievable
	(c) Acceptance of the world (e.g. accept physical limitation such as a disease)
	(d) Acceptance of life (e.g. accept own experiences)
	(e) Acceptance of self (e.g. accept and show who they are)
	(f) Acceptance of what they experience as meaningful
37.	Using nonintellectual therapeutic techniques (e.g. art, drama)
38.	Exploring how the client subjectively experiences 'cosmic meaning in life', that is, 'how everything fits into an overall coherent pattern such as the universe or a master plan'

factors in therapy (Farber & Doolin, 2011). Furthermore, it seems beneficial for the client's well-being to focus on long-term meaning in life rather than on short-term gratification and pleasure (cf. Wong, 2013). This often involves focusing on the larger timeline, that is, helping clients to develop a sense of continuity between past, present, future and their possible legacy for future generations. Although the main focus of meaning-centred practices is on the present and the future, the first sessions often review meaningful aspects of the past to enable clients to become aware of their meaning potential again and mourn over lost meanings. Conducting such a life review has shown to be effective (Westerhof, Bohlmeijer, & Webster, 2010).

Many manuals suggest that practitioners should not only help clients find one specific meaning in life but explore meaning potentials in multiple domains in life, experienced in multiple senses, conscious and unconscious. With the exception of the previously mentioned evidence for differentiating levels of meaning, there are no experimental studies on the effectiveness of addressing the totality of meanings. Additionally, several meaning-centred practitioners stimulate effective goal managements, such as helping clients to set concrete aims for their day-to-day lives, to make a plan, to experiment in daily life, to evaluate and adjust the aims and method and to make long-term commitments. The effectiveness of this type of intervention is supported by several trials (e.g., Lapierre, Dubé, Bouffard, & Alain, 2007).

Several manuals address both the importance of the clients' autonomy and their social connections in meaning-making; the effectiveness of this balance between self and context is indicated by multiple studies (e.g., Mikulincer & Shaver, 2013). Furthermore, self-discovery has been described as important by existential analysts, which seems indirectly supported by research indicating that it may be difficult to experience life as meaningful when one is not in touch with oneself and does not experience one's own worthiness (cf. George & Park, 2014; Mikulincer & Shaver, 2013; Schlegel, Smith, & Hirsch, 2013).

Existential Skills

These skills are about MCT therapists embedding the experience of meaning in the broader context of life, although these skills are less often practised by classical logotherapists and meaning-centred psychotherapists. Research confirms that clients experience existential moods and struggle with life's limitations, and it seems beneficial to address these existential moods (e.g., Vos, 2014; Vos, Cooper, et al., 2015). However, studies on the effectiveness of addressing existential themes without simultaneously addressing meaning in life, for example supportive–expressive or experiential–existential therapies, have only small or no significant effects (Vos, Craig, et al., 2015). This suggests that addressing existential limitations—such as freedom of decision and mortality—may help clients to accept life's limitations and create realistic goals and expectations about life as part of, for instance, MCT, but this may not be effective as a stand-alone therapeutic technique.

Meaning-centred therapists often explore the defence mechanisms of clients and help them to find positive meaning in adversity. Several empirical studies confirm that clients cope better with existential frustrations when they focus on larger meanings behind their current life situation or when they change the situational meaning or inner attitude. Research indicates that individuals may indeed respond to existential threats with existential denial and avoidance, for instance, by shifting their attention from the threatening information or experiences (Greenberg & Koole, 2013). Although such defence mechanisms may relieve stress in the short term, they predict a lower sense of meaning and fulfilment about life in the long term (Jim, Richardson, Golden-Kreutz, & Andersen, 2006). Thus, it seems important that individuals can flexibly switch between different styles of coping, so that they could, for instance, temporarily use denial and avoidance to immediately lower their psychological stress levels, but in the long term also use other ways of coping. This coping flexibility predicts better long-term well-being (Cheng, Lau, & Chan, 2014; Vos, 2014). Therefore, it seems beneficial for individuals to learn a dual attitude, which means that they learn to tolerate the possible tensions between their wish for meaning and life's limitations (cf. Vos, 2014; Wong, 2015). For instance, it seems beneficial to have illusions about life—such as feeling invulnerable, immortal and in control—while at the same time being (cognitively) aware of their illusory character (e.g., Janoff-Bulman, 2010). For example, after a negative event it seems beneficial to not maintain the notion of predictability and unchangeability of life but to re-evaluate life, values and goals and find new meaning (e.g., Batthyany & Russo-Netzer, 2014).

Relational–Humanistic Skills

These skills focus on establishing an in-depth, authentic therapeutic relationship, along with reflection on and analysis of the relational encounter, combined with a phenomenological exploration of the client's experiences, which is particularly practised by existential analysts. Empirical research strongly supports the emphasis on the quality of the therapeutic relationship, with the APA Task Force concluding that "the therapy relationship makes substantial and consistent contributions to psychotherapy outcomes independent of the specific type of treatment" (Norcross & Lambert, 2011, p. 423) by means of empathy, congruence and the capacity to repair alliance ruptures (Kolden, Klein, Wang, & Austin, 2011; Safran, Muran, & Eubanks-Carter, 2011).

The phenomenological practices follow from the idea that everyone can intuitively sense meaning through their conscience (see above). The focus on the client's subjective flow of experiencing may help therapist and client to avoid biases and blind spots and do justice to the totality of the client's inner experiences and gain deeper self-awareness ('eidetic reduction'). The phenomenological method traditionally includes temporarily setting aside our assumptions and biases ('rule of epoche'), neutrally describing the phenomena ('rule of description') and avoiding placing any initial hierarchies of significance or importance upon the themes of description ('rule of equalisation') (Spinelli, 2005). Existential analysts use four phenomenological steps in 'personal existential analysis' to help clients with their problems (Langle, 2014): after description of the external facts of the situation, phenomenological analysis explores the client's experiences in more depth, followed by inner positioning in which clients evaluate their inner attitude and values, and finally clients reflect on the responding performance (act) they want to do. Although pure phenomenological therapeutic approaches seem relatively ineffective (Vos, Craig, et al., 2015), specific techniques associated with the phenomenological approach are effective, such as the Socratic dialogue, which helps to elicit what the client already knows instead of pouring information into the client and which is known for its moderate positive psychological effects (e.g., Overholser, 2010).

Spiritual and Mindfulness Skills

These skills regard the therapist's openness to the client's spiritual–cultural context, stimulating de-reflection, self-distancing and a general accepting stance in life, including nonintellectualising exercises such as mindfulness and focusing techniques as developed by Gendlin (1982). Many studies have confirmed the beneficial effects of mindfulness and meditation on the well-being of individuals, in particular for those in stressful life situations such as those caused by a somatic disease (e.g., Hofmann, Sawyer, Witt, & Oh, 2010). There is also some modest evidence for including nonintellectual techniques such as art, drama, poetry and drawing (e.g., Elliott, Greenberg, & Lietaer, 2004). Existential analysts also foster acceptance of world (e.g., accept physical limitations of a disease), life (e.g., accept your own experiences), self (e.g., accept and show who you are) and what clients experience as meaningful; however, these phenomena are unverifiable due to their abstract nature (Langle, 2014).

In conclusion, the publications reviewed revealed 38 different practitioner's skills, ranging from assessment, meaning-specific, existential, relational–humanistic and spiritual–religious skills. Most skills were shown to be supported by empirical research evidence, although some skills were unverifiable or need further validation. In addition, several practitioners integrate evidence-based techniques from other therapeutic approaches such as group psychotherapy (e.g., Leszcz & Yalom, 2005) and pluralistic therapy which focuses on the adequate positive responsiveness of the therapist to the client, such as shared decision-making about the aims, method and structure of sessions (e.g., Cooper, 2015). This review is limited by a risk for self-serving bias, as only evidence confirming the effectiveness of the practitioner's skills was searched for. The results suggest the potential benefits of these meaning-centred practitioner's skills.

Session Structure

How are the therapeutic skills translated into specific therapeutic practices and sessions? Over the years, possibly hundreds of standardised MCT procedures have been published, especially in the *International Forum for Logotherapy*, but most procedures were only described briefly and tested in nonsystematic case studies.

Seventy studies systematically tested clear semi-structured therapy manuals (Vos & Vitali, 2016), which will be the basis of the following overview of therapy sessions. Most manuals described between 5 and 15 sessions and consisted of three phases.

The assessment and introduction phase focuses on understanding the facts of the client's life situation, problems and strengths, exploring hopes and expectations, exploring the relevance and history of meaning for the client and building a constructive therapeutic working alliance. This assumes strong assessment and relational–humanistic skills. Often, acute suffering and recent life events are explored, such as the experience of having a life-threatening physical disease and how life has changed on account of this. This exploration of the recent history frequently focuses on grieving lost meanings or a lost meaning potential, and clients are invited to explore how they could experience meaning despite the loss and thus transcend their suffering in the current life situation. Several manuals position the clients' current experience of suffering and loss in the broader context of their life history, for instance, via an autobiographic life review, and clients may be asked to describe what they experienced as meaningful in the past and how they have overcome previous hardships in life.

The meaning-exploration phase is the backbone of many manuals and consists of systematically exploring clients' values and meaning potential. In this phase, meaning-specific and existential-therapeutic skills are used. Usually, one session is spent on each group of values from the Franklian–Lukassian value triad (one session on the value of experiencing, one on productivity–creativity and one on attitude modulation), although it may be recommended to replace this with the value quintet (see Table 2).

Clients are guided in their explorations of what they experience as valuable and meaningful via practical exercises and direct questions or structured techniques such as the value awareness technique (Hutzell, 1990). The urgency and intuitive hierarchy of values is sometimes strengthened via Yalom's 'write your own epitaph' exercise' or 'death bed experiment', by which clients are asked to imagine that they are dying and to identify how they need to have lived their lives to be able to die with a feeling of meaning and fulfilment (Yalom, 1980). In meaning therapy, fast-forwarding and encouraging clients to imagine the differences that particular choices could make in their life ('what would your life look like?') and 'miracle questions' help overcome limiting thoughts by asking, for instance, what the client would do if money were not an issue or if God granted three wishes in life (Wong, 2013). Clients could be asked to describe their life as a movie, with questions such as 'who would play you?' and 'how would the ending look like?' (Lantz, 2000). Another creative form is to invite clients to bid on a limited number of values (Schulenberg, Hutzell, Nassif, & Rogina, 2008). In existential analysis, techniques are used such as identifying and integrating biographically relevant experiences in the present (biographical existential analysis), exploring and accepting fundamental fears (gates of death method) and imagining living up to values (value-oriented imagery).

The evaluation and application phase aims to evaluate the values and potential meanings that were explored in previous sessions and apply these to everyday life. Clients are, for instance, invited to create an intuitive hierarchy of values and meanings, for example, by drawing a mountain and putting different meanings/ values at different heights reflecting differences in value and authenticity (e.g. Ernzen, 1990). This evaluation is followed by assessing to which extent the clients already live their lives according to this hierarchy and what may need to be changed in their lives to re-create the mountain range exercise in their daily lives. Subsequently, clients are stimulated to translate this into concrete goals and plans and actually experiment with this. The following sessions could help to evaluate these experiments and, if necessary, adjust the aims and methods and make long-term commitments to goals. In this phase, clients are often confronted with limitations in life such as meanings that are difficult or impossible to actualise; in response to this, meaning-centred practitioners use their existential skills to help clients explore and tolerate imperfections, tensions and paradoxes in life, while stimulating pragmatic problem-solving. The last session often explores existential feelings of termination, autonomy and being responsible for their own life (cf. Lukas, 1984/2014).

An average session starts with an emotional check-in and discussion about the previous session and about the homework. The aim of this is to understand any developments in life since the last session and to connect with the emotional process and progress of the client. This is often followed by explicit psychoeducation on the theory and practice of a central topic, for instance, the value of productivity–creativity. Clients are often invited to participate in interactive psychoeducation by giving examples. Often, a guided exercise is performed to help clients apply the theory to their own lives, for instance, by searching for examples of how the theory manifests in their own lives. Some practitioners introduce these exercises with a guided mindfulness exercise to help the clients connect with the topic not only on an intellectual level but also on an experiential-embodied level (e.g. Elliott et al., 2004; Hofmann et al., 2010; Van der Spek et al., 2014). The guided exercise is sometimes followed by exploring hierarchies in the client's experiences and by identifying which examples in their daily life feel most valuable and authentic. This sometimes leads to an evaluation and a decision regarding questions such as 'what do I want to change in my life', 'what can I realistically change', 'what do I need to accept that it cannot be changed', and 'how can I cope with this situation in a positive way?' These questions sometimes lead to the decision to change something in one's life, to set goals and to make a plan for how to achieve them. Most sessions end with homework and an evaluation of the session.

Effectiveness

The systematic literature review on which this chapter is based included 60 trials (total sample $N = 3713$) of which 26 were randomised-controlled trials ($N = 1975$), 15 nonrandomised controlled trials ($N = 709$) and 19 nonrandomised noncontrolled pre-post measurement studies ($N = 1029$). Twenty-five studies with a large risk of bias in selective reporting or presenting unlikely positive study results were not included in these analyses. Samples included physical illness (26 trials), transition moments in life (12 trials), psychiatric diagnosis (8 trials), carers (7 trials), substance misuse (4 trials), and other (3 trials). Studies were conducted in the Middle East (18 trials), North-America (16 trials), South-East Asia (14 trials), Europe (6 trials), South-Africa (3 trials) and South America (2 trials). The average number of sessions was 8.65, with some as short as two sessions and some as long as 52.

The combination of all 60 trials showed large improvements from baseline to immediate post-treatment and follow-up measurement on quality of life (Hedges' g = 1.13, SE = 0.12; g = 0.99, SE = 0.20) and psychological stress (g = 1.21, SE = 0.10; g = 0.67, SE = 0.20), although effects varied between studies (large heterogeneity as indicated by $I^2 > 50$ %). Additional analyses were done in the controlled trials only, which showed large homogeneous effects compared with control groups (mostly active treatment or care as usual, some waiting lists), both immediate and at follow-up on quality of life (g = 1.02, SE = 0.06; g = 1.06, SE = 0.12) and psychological stress (g = 0.94, SE = 0.07, $p < 0.01$; g = 0.84, SE = 0.10). Immediate effects were larger on general quality of life (g = 1.37, SE = 0.12) than on meaning in life (g = 1.18, SE = 0.08), hope and optimism (g = 0.80, SE = 0.13), self-efficacy (g = 0.89, SE = 0.14) and social well-being (g = 0.81, SE = 13).

Additional meta-regression analyses indicated that the improvement in meaning in life strongly predicted a significant decrease in psychological stress ($\beta = -0.56$, $p < 0.001$). This seems to confirm the assumption that meaning-centred therapies reduce psychological stress, *thanks to* explicitly addressing and improving meaning in life in therapy. The more different types of meaning were explicitly explored in MCT, the larger the effects were on both quality-of-life and psychological stress (resp. β =.32, p<.01; β =.21, p<.01). This confirms the recommendation to use the most exhaustive list of meanings -such as the meaning quintet- as the core structure of MCT instead of, for instance, the smaller Franklian triad.

A wide range of moderators were not significant, implying that the effects were similar, for instance, for different types of MCT, control conditions, countries, populations and sample sizes. Larger effects were found in analyses of the 70 trials, when the treatment manuals were more structured, included mindfulness/meditation exercises, explicitly encouraged clients to set and experiment with achievable goals in their daily lives, explicitly discussed one type of meaning per session (e.g., one session on social meanings, one on self-oriented meanings, etc.) instead of using another therapy structure (e.g., existential analysis), explicitly paid attention to self-worth, explicitly addressed existential limitations such as life's finitude and freedom, discussed the totality of time (past, present, future and legacy) and not only the present and/or past and described how a positive therapeutic relationship can be created.

Discussion

What is the evidence base for MCT? First, the meta-analyses indicate that MCT strongly improves the client's existential, psychological, physical and general well-being, not only compared to the baseline measurement but also compared with other active interventions in control groups. These findings are corroborated by the positive effects in studies on therapies that discuss meaning as one of multiple core aspects, which were not included in these analyses, such as acceptance and commitment therapy and dignity therapy (see references above). Second, although several aspects of the clinical and aetiological models are unverifiable, the main assumptions seem valid: individuals experience meaning as important for their well-being, especially in crisis situations in life, and it seems beneficial to support them in exploring higher levels of meaning via social and transcending values. Third, many MCT skills are corroborated by effectiveness studies. Fourth, the meta-regression analyses confirmed the clinical assumption that the well-being of clients improves, thanks to improvements in meaning in life, which is in line with a review of 57 studies that placed meaning at the heart of therapeutic recovery (Andresen et al., 2011). That is, clients seemed to feel much better in many domains of their lives, thanks to their increased sense of meaning in life, which had improved thanks to MCT. In conclusion, these findings seem to indicate that MCT is mostly bona fide (Wampold et al., 1997) and has beneficial effects for many clients.

This review is limited by its focus on effectiveness trials, as case studies, for example, were not described. It is possible that the description of therapeutic skills and their effectiveness are not representative of MCT conducted by therapists rejecting standardisation. However, several manuals were based on the works of key authors such as Frankl, Langle, Lukas and Marshall.

Additionally, conceptual dissimilarities between different MCT schools seemed large, especially regarding the extent to which the practitioner was directive and normative. Despite these differences, the meta-analytic effects seemed statistically homogenous after exclusion of studies with a large risk of bias, and many moderators were tested but shown to be not significant. This seems to suggest a general commonality in the underlying therapeutic practices, as all studies directly and systematically addressed different levels of meaning in life. It is these meaning-centered therapy skills that differentiate meaning-centred practices from other therapeutic approaches such as other existential therapies. The humanistic framework also differentiates meaning-centred practices from behavioural approaches such as acceptance and commitment therapy. However, these are not hard distinctions with other approaches but seem to imply an integrative or pluralistic approach that focuses on being responsive to the individual clients, their needs, preferences and skills (cf. Cooper, 2015). This unity despite diversity seems to indicate that the conceptual differences between meaning-centred schools may be less important than what they have in common. Thus, it may not be necessary to stick to one particular manual, but therapists may develop their own version on the basis of different evidence-based therapy skills (although it remains unclear whether adherence to the manual is important or not, as few studies tested adherence).

Which clients should be offered to work with meaning in life? In most trials, MCT was offered to individuals in boundary situations in life, which is in line with the underlying clinical–aetiological assumptions, stating that particularly individuals in these situations ask meaning-related questions. Some authors, such as Breitbart and Poppito (2014), did not only require their participants to be in a certain boundary situation—such as being patients with advanced cancer—but also to be experiencing clinical levels of depression or anxiety. Although from the perspective of routine outcome monitoring in traditional health services, it is understandable that such clinical diagnoses are used as inclusion criteria, both the clinical–aetiological assumptions and meta-analytic findings would not require clients to have clinical levels of psychopathology. It is recommended to develop meaning-centred screening questionnaires, asking not only whether clients experience meaning in life or search for meaning—which does not directly mean that they need or would like to receive therapy for these issues—but also directly ask them whether they experience meaning-related problems and whether they would like to receive help with these meaning-related topics; we have started to develop such a screening instrument which needs further validation (Vos, 2011, unpublished report). Until such screening instruments are validated, meaning-centred practices could be offered to all individuals who explicitly ask meaning-related questions or who are in boundary situations in life. Subsequently, the therapist could explain the aims and methods of working with meaning in life, and the client and therapist could decide together how much this therapeutic approach fits the needs and preferences of the client. One could argue that clients may not know that they need to work with meaning in life, due to their existential defence mechanisms; therefore, therapists are recommended to be sensitive towards manifest and latent meaning-related themes in the work with their clients and, if needed, to explicate the possible relevance of meaning for the client. The literature review in this chapter does not indicate negative effects of explicitly addressing meaning in life.

A continued concern could be the possibly authoritarian attitude and the unvalidated assumptions of some meaning-centred practitioners, although this review seems to suggest that some practitioners have moved from traditional Franklian radical absolutism to a more relativistic–pragmatic position. It is recommended to base the meaning-centred practices on validated assumptions and continuously check to which extent norms and values of the therapist reflect those of the client, possibly via a meta-therapeutic dialogue (Cooper & McLeod, 2010). Shared decision-making and tailoring the values and aims in therapy seem more consistent than an authoritarian approach with the relational–humanistic skills and values that are at the heart of most meaning-centred manuals. Moreover, the relational–humanistic and phenomenological approach does not exclude the relatively directive use of a structured manual when the client and practitioner have decided together to use this, and the practitioner remains sensitive and phenomenologically open to the micro-experiences of the client (cf. Eifert et al., 1997). This means that on the therapeutic macro level, client and practitioner could decide together on the aims and structure of therapy, which presupposes strong relational–humanistic skills in the therapist. On a meso-level the practitioner could offer—possibly quite directively—structured practices, which require strong meaning-centred skills. On a micro level the practitioner could phenomenologically explore the unique individual experiences of the client and be sensitive to the spiritual–religious experiences of the client, which presupposes strong existential–spiritual skills.

In summary, the evidence in this chapter confirms that a wide range of individuals benefit from a broad range of meaning-centred interventions, supporting the recent surge in MCT. Therefore, the inclusion of meaning-centred practices in mental health-care guidelines is strongly recommended (cf. Vos, 2016a, 2016b).

Key Takeaways

- Develop a therapeutic sensitivity for the important role that meaning often has in the therapeutic recovery of any clients receiving any type of therapy.
- Offer MCT to individuals who explicitly ask meaning-related questions and to individuals who are experiencing negative life events, such as a chronic or life-threatening disease.
- Systematically explore different types of meaning in separate sessions: materialistic–hedonic, self-oriented, social, higher and meta-meanings.
- Develop assessment, meaning-specific, existential, relational–humanistic and spiritual/mindfulness therapeutic skills.
- When offering MCT, include mindfulness/meditation exercises, encourage clients to set and experiment with achievable goals in their daily lives, stimulate self-worth, address existential limitations and the totality of time (past, present, future and legacy) and develop a positive therapeutic relationship.
- Offer MCT to any relevant populations: MCT is, for instance, equally effective in clients with and without psychopathology.
- Be aware of the risk of therapeutic authoritarianism, reflect together with the client whether MCT is the most suited therapy for this client at this moment and explore the client's individual experiences with an open, nonjudgmental attitude.

References

Anderson, N., Heywood-Everett, S., Siddiqi, N., Wright, J., Meredith, J., & McMillan, D. (2015). Faith-adapted psychological therapies for depression and anxiety: Systematic review and meta-analysis. *Journal of Affective Disorders, 176*, 183–196.

Andresen, R., Oades, L. G., & Caputi, P. (2011). *Psychological recovery: Beyond mental illness.* London: John Wiley & Sons.

Applebaum, A. J., Lichtenthal, W. G., Pessin, H. A., Radomski, J. N., Simay Gökbayrak, N., Katz, A. M., & Breitbart, W. (2012). Factors associated with attrition from a randomized controlled trial of meaning-centered group psychotherapy for patients with advanced cancer. *Psychooncology, 21*(11), 1195–1204.

Arends, R. Y., Bode, C., Taal, E., & Van de Laar, M. A. (2013). A goal management intervention for polyarthritis patients: rationale and design of a randomized controlled trial. *BMC musculoskeletal disorders, 14*(1), 1.

Batthyany, A., & Russo-Netzer, P. (Eds.). (2014). *Meaning in positive and existential psychology.* New York, NY: Springer.

Baumeister, R. F., Vohs, K. D., Aaker, J. L., & Garbinsky, E. N. (2013). Some key differences between a happy life and a meaningful life. *The Journal of Positive Psychology, 8*(6), 505–516.

Berman, M. (2009). *The politics of authenticity: Radical individualism and the emergence of modern society.* New York, NY: Verso Books.

Bohlmeijer, E., Smit, F., & Cuijpers, P. (2003). Effects of reminiscence and life review on late-life depression: A meta-analysis. *International Journal of Geriatric Psychiatry, 18*(12), 1088–1094.

Brandstätter, M., Baumann, U., Borasio, G. D., & Fegg, M. J. (2012). Systematic review of meaning in life assessment instruments. *Psycho-Oncology, 21*(10), 1034–1052.

Braun, V., & Clarke, V. (2006). Using thematic analysis in psychology. *Qualitative Research in Psychology, 3*(2), 77–101.

Breitbart, W., & Poppito, S. (2014). *Meaning-centered group psychotherapy for patients with advanced cancer: A treatment manual*. New York, NY: Oxford University Press.

Chao, M. M., & Kesebir, P. (2013). Culture: The grand web of meaning. In J.A. Hicks & C. Routledge (Eds.), *The experience of meaning in life* (pp. 317–331). Dordrecht: Springer.

Cheng, C., Lau, H. P. B., & Chan, M. P. S. (2014). Coping flexibility and psychological adjustment to stressful life changes: A meta-analytic review. *Psychological Bulletin, 140*(6), 1582–1607.

Chochinov, H. M., Hack, T., Hassard, T., Kristjanson, L. J., McClement, S., & Harlos, M. (2005). Dignity therapy: A novel psychotherapeutic intervention for patients near the end of life. *Journal of Clinical Oncology, 23*(24), 5520–5525.

Cooper, M. (2003). *Existential therapies*. London: Sage.

Cooper, M. (2008). *Essential research findings in counselling and psychotherapy: The facts are friendly*. London: Sage.

Cooper, M. (2015). *Existential psychotherapy and counselling: Contributions to a pluralistic practice*. London: Sage.

Cooper, M., & McLeod, J. (2010). *Pluralistic Counselling and psychotherapy*. London: Sage.

Correia, E., Cooper, M., Berdondini, L., & Correia, K. (2014). The worldwide distribution and characteristics of existential counsellors and psychotherapists. *Existential Analysis, 25*(2), 321–337.

Dyck, M. J. (1987). Assessing logotherapeutic constructs: Conceptual and psychometric status of the Purpose in Life and Seeking of Noetic Goals tests. *Clinical Psychology Review, 7*(4), 439–447.

Eifert, G. H., Schulte, D., Zvolensky, M. J., Lejuez, C. W., & Lau, A. W. (1997). Manualized behavior therapy: Merits and challenges. *Behavior Therapy, 28*(4), 499–509.

Elliott, R. (2002). The effectiveness of humanistic therapies: A meta-analysis. In D. J. Cain (Ed.), *Humanistic psychotherapies: Handbook of research and practice*. Washington, DC: American Psychological Association.

Elliott, R., Greenberg, L. S., & Lietaer, G. (2004). Research on experiential psychotherapies. In *Bergin and Garfield's handbook of psychotherapy and behavior change* (Vol. 5, pp. 139–193). New York, NY: John Wiley & Sons.

Ernzen, F. I. (1990). Frankl's mountain range exercise: A logotherapy activity for small groups. *International Forum for Logotherapy, 1*, 20–35.

Fabry, J. B. (1980). *The pursuit of meaning*. New York, NY: Harper & Row Barnes & Noble Import Division.

Farber, B. A., & Doolin, E. M. (2011). Positive regard. *Psychotherapy, 48*(1), 58.

Folkman, S. (2008). The case for positive emotions in the stress process. *Anxiety, Stress, and Coping, 21*(1), 3–14.

Frankl, V. E. (1980/2014). *The will to meaning: Foundations and applications of logotherapy*. New York, NY: Penguin.

Frankl, V. E. (1985). *Man's search for meaning*. New York, NY: Simon and Schuster.

Frankl, V. E. (1986). *The doctor and the soul: From psychotherapy to logotherapy*. London: Vintage.

Gantt, E. E., & Thayne, J. L. (2014). Positive psychology, existential psychology and the presumption of egoism. In A. Batthyany & P. Russo-Netzer (Eds.), *Meaning in positive and existential psychology* (pp. 185–204). New York, NY: Springer.

Gendlin, E. T. (1982). *Focusing*. London: Bantam.

George, L. S., & Park, C. L. (2014). Existential mattering: Bringing attention to a neglected but central aspect of meaning? In A. Batthyany & P. Russo-Netzer (Eds.), *Meaning in positive and existential psychology* (pp. 39–52). New York, NY: Springer.

Goldfried, M. R. (1982). *Converging themes in psychotherapy: Trends in psychodynamic, humanistic, and behavioral practice*. New York, NY: Springer.

Greenberg, J., & Koole, S. L. (Eds.). (2013). *Handbook of experimental existential psychology*. London: Guilford Publications.

Hauser, M. D. (2006). *Moral minds: How nature designed our universal sense of right and wrong*. New York, NY: Ecco.

Hayes, S. C., Luoma, J. B., Bond, F. W., Masuda, A., & Lillis, J. (2006). Acceptance and commitment therapy: Model, processes and outcomes. *Behaviour Research and Therapy, 44*(1), 1–25.

Henoch, I., & Danielson, E. (2009). Existential concerns among patients with cancer and interventions to meet them: An integrative literature review. *Psycho-Oncology, 18*(3), 225–236.

Hicks, J. A., & Routledge, C. (2013). *The experience of meaning in life: Classical perspectives, emerging themes, and controversies*. New York, NY: Springer.

Hill, K. A. (1987). Meta-analysis of paradoxical interventions. *Psychotherapy: Theory, Research, Practice, Training, 24*(2), 266.

Hofmann, S. G., Sawyer, A. T., Witt, A. A., & Oh, D. (2010). The effect of mindfulness-based therapy on anxiety and depression: A meta-analytic review. *Journal of Consulting and Clinical Psychology, 78*(2), 169.

Hutzell, R. R. (1990). The value awareness technique. *A primer of projective techniques of psychological assessment*, 147–156. Chicago

Ivtzan, I., Lomas, T., Hefferon, K., & Worth, P. (2015). *Second wave positive psychology: Embracing the dark side of life*. Routledge.

Janoff-Bulman, R. (2010). *Shattered assumptions*. New York, NY: Simon and Schuster.

Jaspers, K. (1925/2013). *Psychologie der weltanschauungen*. Tubingen: Springer.

Jim, H. S., Richardson, S. A., Golden-Kreutz, D. M., & Andersen, B. L. (2006). Strategies used in coping with a cancer diagnosis predict meaning in life for survivors. *Health Psychology, 25*(6), 753.

Kashdan, T., & Biswas-Diener, R. (2014). *The upside of your dark side: Why being your whole self—Not just your "good" self-drives success and fulfillment*. London: Penguin.

Kazdin, A. E. (2008). Understanding how and why psychotherapy leads to change. *Psychotherapy Research, 19*(4–5), 418–428.

Khalil, E., Callager, P. & James, N. (2007). *Transactional Analysis: a scoping exercise for evidence of outcomes*. Report prepared for the Berne Institute. portal2nottingham.ac.uk/nmp/research/mental…/berne_outcomes.pdf.

King, L. A., Hicks, J. A., Krull, J. L., & Del Gaiso, A. K. (2006). Positive affect and the experience of meaning in life. *Journal of Personality and Social Psychology, 90*(1), 179.

Kolden, G. G., Klein, M. H., Wang, C. C., & Austin, S. (2011). Congruence/genuineness. *Psychotherapy, 48*(1), 65.

Krause, N. (2004). Stressors arising in highly valued roles, meaning in life, and the physical health status of older adults. *The Journals of Gerontology Series B: Psychological Sciences and Social Sciences, 59*(5), S287–S297.

Langeland, E., Riise, T., Hanestad, B. R., Nortvedt, M. W., Kristoffersen, K., & Wahl, A. K. (2006). The effect of salutogenic treatment principles on coping with mental health problems: A randomised controlled trial. *Patient Education and Counseling, 62*(2), 212–219.

Langle, A. (2014). *Lehrbuch zur Existenzanalyse: Grundlagen*. Wien: Facultas.

Längle, A., & Bürgi, D. (2014). *Existentielles coaching – Theoretische Orientierung, Grundlagen und Praxis für Coaching, Organisationsberatung und Supervision*. Wien: Facultas WUV.

Lantz, J. E. (2000). *Meaning-centered marital and family therapy: Learning to bear the beams of love*. New York, NY: Thomas.

Lapierre, S., Dubé, M., Bouffard, L., & Alain, M. (2007). Addressing suicidal ideations through the realization of meaningful personal goals. *Crisis, 28*(1), 16–25.

Lee, V., Cohen, S. R., Edgar, L., Laizner, A. M., & Gagnon, A. J. (2004). Clarifying "meaning" in the context of cancer research: A systematic literature review. *Palliative & Supportive Care, 2*(03), 291–303.

Leszcz, M., & Yalom, I. D. (2005). *The theory and practice of group psychotherapy*. New York, NY: Basic Books.

Lukas, E. (1986/2014). *Meaning in suffering*. Berkeley, CA: Institute of Logotherapy Press.

Lukas, E. (2014). *Lehrbuch der Logotherapie. Menschenbild und Methoden* (3rd ed.). München: Profil.

Lundahl, B. W., Kunz, C., Brownell, C., Tollefson, D., & Burke, B. L. (2010). A meta-analysis of motivational interviewing: Twenty-five years of empirical studies. *Research on Social Work Practice, 1*, 1–20.

MacKinnon, C. J., Milman, E., Smith, N. G., Henry, M., Berish, M., Copeland, L. S., ... Cohen, S. R. (2013). Means to meaning in cancer-related bereavement identifying clinical implications for counseling psychologists. *The Counseling Psychologist, 41*(2), 216–239.

Maddi, S. R. (2014). Hardiness leads to meaningful growth through what is learned when resolving stressful circumstances. In A. Batthyany & P. Russo-Netzer (Eds.), *Meaning in positive and existential psychology* (pp. 291–302). New York, NY: Springer.

Marshall, M., & Marshall, E. (2012). *Logotherapy revisited: Review of the tenets of Viktor E. Frankl's logotherapy*. Ottawa, ON: Create Space Independent Publishing Platform.

Masley, S. A., Gillanders, D. T., Simpson, S. G., & Taylor, M. A. (2012). A systematic review of the evidence base for schema therapy. *Cognitive Behaviour Therapy, 41*(3), 185–202.

May, R. (1978). Response to Bulka's article. *Journal of Humanistic Psychology, 18*(4), 55.

Melton, A. M., & Schulenberg, S. E. (2008). On the measurement of meaning: Logotherapy's empirical contributions to humanistic psychology. *The Humanistic Psychologist, 36*(1), 31–44.

Mikulincer, M., & Shaver, P. R. (2013). Attachment orientations and meaning in life. In J. A. Hicks & C. Routledge (Eds.), *The experience of meaning in life: Classical perspectives, emerging themes, and controversies* (pp. 287–304). New York, NY: Springer.

Neimeyer, R. A. (2001). *Meaning reconstruction & the experience of loss*. New York, NY: American Psychological Association.

Nielsen, T.W. (2014). Finding the keys to meaningful happiness: Beyond being happy or sad is to love. In: A. Batthyany & P. Russo-Netzer (Eds.), *Meaning in positive and existential psychology* (pp. 81–96). NY: Springer.

Norcross, J. C., & Lambert, M. J. (2011). Evidence-based therapy relationships. In J. C. Norcross (Ed.), *Psychotherapy relationships that work: Evidence-based responsiveness* (2nd ed., pp. 3–21). New York, NY: Oxford University.

Overholser, J. C. (2010). Psychotherapy according to the Socratic method: Integrating ancient philosophy with contemporary cognitive therapy. *Journal of Cognitive Psychotherapy, 24*(4), 354–363.

Park, C. L. (2010). Making sense of the meaning literature: An integrative review of meaning making and its effects on adjustment to stressful life events. *Psychological Bulletin, 136*(2), 257.

Park, C. L., & Folkman, S. (1997). Meaning in the context of stress and coping. *Review of General Psychology, 1*(2), 115.

Pat-Horenczyk, R., Perry, S., Hamama-Raz, Y., Ziv, Y., Schramm-Yavin, S., & Stemmer, S. M. (2015). Posttraumatic growth in breast cancer survivors: Constructive and illusory aspects. *Journal of Traumatic Stress, 28*, 214.

Raskob, H. (2005). *Die Logotherapie und Existenzanalyse Vikor Frankls. Systematisch und kritisch*. Wien: Springer.

Reker, G. T. (2000). Theoretical perspective, dimensions, and measurement of existential meaning. In G. T. Reker & K. Chamberlain (Eds.), *Exploring existential meaning: Optimizing human development across the life span* (pp. 39–55). Thousand Oaks, CA: Sage.

Reker, G. T., Peacock, E. J., & Wong, P. T. (1987). Meaning and purpose in life and well-being: A life-span perspective. *Journal of Gerontology, 42*(1), 44–49.

Roth, A., & Fonagy, P. (2013). *What works for whom?: A critical review of psychotherapy research*. London: Guilford Publications.

Safran, J. D., Muran, J. C., & Eubanks-Carter, C. (2011). Repairing alliance ruptures. *Psychotherapy, 48*(1), 80.

Schlegel, R. J., Smith, C. M., & Hirsch, K. A. (2013). Examining the True Self as a Wellspring of Meaning. In The Experience of Meaning in Life (pp. 177–188). Springer Netherlands.

Schulenberg, S. E., Drescher, C. F., & Baczwaski, B. J. (2014). Perceived meaning and disaster mental health: A role for logotherapy in clinical-disaster psychology. In A. Batthyany & P. Russo-Netzer (Eds.), *Meaning in positive and existential psychology* (pp. 251–267). New York, NY: Springer.

Schulenberg, S. E., Hutzell, R. R., Nassif, C., & Rogina, J. M. (2008). Logotherapy for clinical practice. *Psychotherapy: Theory, Research, Practice, Training, 45*(4), 447.

Schulenberg, S. E., Schnetzer, L. W., Winters, M. R., & Hutzell, R. R. (2010). Meaning-centered couples therapy: Logotherapy and intimate relationships. *Journal of Contemporary Psychotherapy, 40*(2), 95–102.

Schulte, D. (1996). Tailor-made and standardized therapy: Complementary tasks in behavior therapy a contrarian view. *Journal of Behavior Therapy and Experimental Psychiatry, 27*(2), 119–126.

Schulze, G. (1992/2005). *Die Erlebnisgesellschaft: Kultursoziologie der Gegenwart*. Berlin: Campus.

Seligman, M. E., Steen, T. A., Park, N., & Peterson, C. (2005). Positive psychology progress: Empirical validation of interventions. *American Psychologist, 60*(5), 410.

Shin, J. Y., & Steger, M. F. (2014). Promoting meaning and purpose in life. In A. C. Parks & S. Schueller (Eds.), *The Wiley Blackwell handbook of positive psychological interventions* (pp. 90–110). Chichester: John Wiley & Sons.

Sin, N. L., & Lyubomirsky, S. (2009). Enhancing well-being and alleviating depressive symptoms with positive psychology interventions: A practice-friendly meta-analysis. *Journal of Clinical Psychology, 65*(5), 467–487.

Spek, N., Uden-Kraan, C. F., Vos, J., Breitbart, W., Tollenaar, R. A., Asperen, C. J., ... & Verdonck-de Leeuw, I. M. (2014). Meaning-centered group psychotherapy in cancer survivors: a feasibility study. *Psycho-Oncology, 23*(7), 827–831.

Spinelli, E. (2005). *The interpreted world: An introduction to phenomenological psychology*. Thousand Oaks, CA: Sage.

Steger, M. F. (2012). Experiencing meaning in life. In P. Wong (Ed.), *The human quest for meaning: Theories, research, and applications*. New York, NY: Springer.

Steger, M. F., Shim, Y., Barenz, J., & Shin, J. Y. (2014). Through the windows of the soul: A pilot study using photography to enhance meaning in life. *Journal of Contextual Behavioral Science, 3*(1), 27–30.

Stillman, T. F., & Lambert, N. M. (2013). The bidirectional relationship of meaning and belonging. In J. A. Hicks & C. Routledge (Eds.), *The experience of meaning in life*. New York, NY: Springer.

Tryon, G. S., & Winograd, G. (2010). Goal consensus and collaboration. Evidence-based therapy relationships. *Psychotherapy, 48*(1), 50–57.

Vos, J. (2011). Opening the psychological black box in genetic counseling. Department of Clinical Genetics, Faculty of Medicine, Leiden University Medical Center (LUMC), Leiden University.

Vos, J., Asperen, C. J., Oosterwijk, J. C., Menko, F. H., Collee, M. J., Garcia, E. G., & Tibben, A. (2013a). The counselees' self-reported request for psychological help in genetic counseling for hereditary breast/ovarian cancer: not only psychopathology matters. *Psycho-Oncology, 22*(4), 902–910.

Vos, J. (2014a). Meaning and existential givens in the lives of cancer patients: A philosophical perspective on psycho-oncology. *Palliative and Supportive Care, 13*(04), 885–900.

Vos, J. (2014b). How to develop and validate conceptual models in psychotherapy research. Presentation at: Research Conference, British Association Counselling & Psychotherapy (BACP), London, UK.

Vos, J. (2016a). Working with meaning in life in individuals with a chronic or life-threatening disease: A review of its relevance and the effectiveness of meaning-centered therapies. In P. Russo-Netzer, S.E. Schulenberg & A. Batthyany (Eds.), *Clinical Perspectives on Meaning*. NY: Springer.

Vos, J. (2016b). Where to find meaning in life: A systematic literature review of survey studies. *Under review*.

Vos, J., Cooper, M., Correia, E., & Craig, M. (2015). Existential therapies: A review of their scientific foundations and efficacy. *Existential Analysis, 26*(1), 49.

Vos, J., Craig, M., & Cooper, M. (2015). Existential therapies: A meta-analysis of their effects on psychological outcomes. *Journal of Consulting and Clinical Psychology, 83*(1), 115.

Vos, J., & Vitali, D. (2016). Psychological treatments supporting clients to live a meaningful life: A meta-analysis of meaning-centered therapies on quality-of-life and psychological-stress. *Under review.*

Wampold, B. E., Mondin, G. W., Moody, M., Stich, F., Benson, K., & Ahn, H. N. (1997). A meta-analysis of outcome studies comparing bona fide psychotherapies. *Psychological Bulletin, 122*(3), 203–213.

Weis, R., & Speridakos, E. C. (2011). A meta-analysis of hope enhancement strategies in clinical and community settings. *Psychology of Well-Being, 1*(1), 1–16.

Westerhof, G. J., Bohlmeijer, E., & Webster, J. D. (2010). Reminiscence and mental health: A review of recent progress in theory, research and interventions. *Ageing and Society, 30*(04), 697–721.

Wong, P. T. (2011). Positive psychology 2.0: Towards a balanced interactive model of the good life. *Canadian Psychology, 52*(2), 69.

Wong, P. T. (Ed.). (2013). *The human quest for meaning: Theories, research, and applications.* New York, NY: Routledge.

Wong, P. T. (2015). The meaning hypothesis of living a good life: Virtue, happiness, and meaning. In: Research working group meeting for Virtue, Happiness, and the Meaning of Life Project, University of South Carolina, Columbia, South Carolina.

Yalom, I. D. (1980). *Existential psychotherapy.* New York, NY: Basic Books.

Zoellner, T., & Maercker, A. (2006). Posttraumatic growth in clinical psychology—A critical review and introduction of a two component model. *Clinical Psychology Review, 26*(5), 626–653.

Making Meaning in the Context of Ethnopolitical Warfare: Secondary Control as a Resource

Emily Stagnaro, Laura E.R. Blackie, Erik G. Helzer, and Eranda Jayawickreme

Meaning in the Context of Ethnopolitical Warfare: Secondary Control as a Resource

> Everything can be taken from a man but one thing: the last of the human freedoms—to choose one's attitude in any given set of circumstances, to choose one's own way. (Viktor Frankl, 1963, p. 65)

Psychologists have a long history of working to understand how people recover and function in the face of significant adversity (Seligman & Csikszentmihalyi, 2000). For example, recent work in personality science has focused on documenting the impact of negative events including unemployment, divorce, and chronic illness on an individual's disposition and well-being (e.g., Diener & Chen, 2011; Lucas, 2007; Luhmann, Hofmann, Eid, & Lucas, 2011; Oishi, Diener, & Lucas, 2007). While clinicians and therapists have tended to have a similar interest, their focus has mostly been on alleviating the distress caused by past adversity. Recent work has proposed applying an integrative approach by using the findings of personality science to identify the dispositional characteristics that could be targeted in interventions to increase well-being after challenging and difficult life experiences (Blackie, Roepke, Forgeard, Jayawickreme, & Fleeson, 2014) and how these

---

E. Stagnaro, M.A. • E. Jayawickreme, Ph.D. (✉)
Department of Psychology, Wake Forest University,
P.O. Box 7778, Winston-Salem, NC 27109, USA
e-mail: jayawide@wfu.edu

L.E.R. Blackie, Ph.D.
Department of Psychology, University of Nottingham,
University Park, Nottingham NG7 2RD, UK

E.G. Helzer, Ph.D.
The Johns Hopkins Carey Business School,
100 International Drive, Baltimore, MD 21202-1099, USA

interventions can be modified for use in refugee populations who face extremely stressful and repeated traumas (Jayawickreme, Jayawickreme, & Seligman, 2012).

The present chapter focuses on the possibilities for adaptive functioning among refugees in the context of ethnopolitical warfare (Jayawickreme, Jayawickreme, et al., 2012), with a particular focus on secondary control as a meaning-making tool for alleviating symptoms of distress and promoting resilience and well-being. We focus on this population due to the unique challenges faced by survivors of ethnopolitical warfare, including displacement, malnutrition, poverty, and the loss of social and material support. These stressors are the result not only of past direct war exposure but also the daily struggles of surviving in refugee camps or warzones (Miller & Rasmussen, 2010). Thus, interventions that can increase adaptive functioning (broadly defined as the alleviation of distress and enhancement of well-being) are desperately needed in a world in which conflict and displacement remain persistent problems. Because displaced individuals have limited direct control over the circumstances that have led to and maintain their displacement, we will consider the value of secondary control—the ability to adjust one's emotional reactions and cognitive appraisals to suit a reality that is presently unchangeable (Morling & Evered, 2006)—as a protective factor while struggling to rebuild life as a refugee. This chapter is based on the premise that refugees are active agents (as opposed to simply victims) in extraordinary circumstances who can learn to harness their own internal resources in an effort to cope and function with the challenges they face (Jayawickreme, Jayawickreme, et al., 2012).

Defining Primary and Secondary Control

Perceived control has long been linked to psychological functioning (Bandura, 1997; Baumeister, 2005; Deci & Ryan, 1995). Previous research has found that a sense of control contributes significantly to successful adjustment (Thompson, Collins, Newcomb, & Hunt, 1996), coping (Compas et al., 2015), resilience (Diehl & Hay, 2010), and overall well-being (Helzer & Jayawickreme, 2015). Due to the complexity of the construct, control has been defined and operationalized in multiple ways in the literature (see Skinner, 1996 for a review), resulting in confusion about which aspect(s) of perceived control is responsible for its positive effects.

Rothbaum, Weisz, and Snyder's (1982) model of control divides the construct to include two types of perceived control, primary and secondary. Primary control is engaged when an individual acts to alter their environment to better suit their needs. Secondary control is engaged when an individual chooses to make internal adjustments by altering expectations, goals, and motivations, in order to better suit their circumstances. Applied in a clinically oriented context, a person who exercises primary control to combat life dissatisfaction would take active, intentional steps to change the objective circumstances of daily life—evaluating and changing aspects of their social relationships, workplace situation, or family life. In contrast, secondary control strategies involve the person reconciling himself or herself to the present reality while exploring alternative ways of operating within that reality. Typically these efforts involve intentional cognitive changes, such as reframing or searching for benefits and opportunities in the present circumstances. Secondary control strategies may foster a sense of agency, enhancing the perception of control by releasing the person from the direct grip of the situation: though immediate circumstances are not within the person's direct control, secondary control efforts allow the person to control how he or she is affected by circumstances. This final point is key to the ideas advanced in this chapter. In the refugee context, secondary control may function not as a strategy of resignation, but in fact a tool for promoting a sense of control when faced with objectively traumatic situations.

We note here that the precise definition of secondary control has been long debated. For the purposes of this chapter, we adopt Morling and Evered's (2006) definition, highlighting the adaptive dual process of secondary control, which includes both acceptance of and adjustment to a given situation. We note that acceptance here does not mean a passive fatalism but instead constitutes acknowledging the situation for the reality that it is. That said, acceptance alone may not always be adaptive (Thompson et al., 1996), highlighting the important role that both components play in facilitating adjustment.

The work of Connor-Smith and colleagues (Connor-Smith & Compas, 2004; Connor-Smith, Compas, Wadsworth, Thomsen, & Saltzman, 2000) considers the role of secondary control in coping. While they do consider passive voluntary acceptance responses to stress to be secondary control, the measure they utilize, the Response to Stress Questionnaire (RSQ), includes items measuring both acceptance and adaptation, each of which has been linked to improved coping (Connor-Smith et al., 2000; Connor-Smith & Compas, 2004). It is also important to distinguish secondary control from what we can term "tertiary control," or trying to align with and gain a sense of control through a benevolent god or higher power. While trusting that a higher power is in control and has a plan can be a part of acceptance, it is important for individuals to feel they are capable of working within that plan. For example, one study of cancer patients found that religiousness was associated with improved coping but was mediated through coping self-efficacy. Without a concurrent increase in self-efficacy, asking a higher power to intercede was maladaptive (Pérez & Smith, 2015).

There are several other notable conceptions of secondary control found in the literature. Skinner (2007) objects to the concept being included under the umbrella of control, finding the construct more akin to accommodation. However, we maintain that secondary control increases perceptions of control, precisely because it involves the *alteration* of one's psychology. Heckhausen and Schulz have focused on secondary control being utilized as tool to compensate for loss of or as strategy to maintain a sense of control after attempts at gaining primary control have failed (Heckhausen, 1997; Heckhausen & Schulz, 1995). Additionally, secondary control seems to be most adaptive under circumstances where an ability to take primary control is unavailable. While primary and secondary control can work together to bring about optimal outcomes, recent research suggests that secondary control offers unique benefits (Farber, Mirsalimi, Williams, & McDaniel, 2003; Guo, Gan, & Tong, 2013; Helzer & Jayawickreme, 2015).

Morling and Evered (2006) discuss the subtypes of secondary control considered by Rothbaum and colleagues (1982), *interpretive secondary control* being the most relevant to the current topic. Interpretive secondary control is used to understand, accept, and find meaning in a situation. However, a distinction must be made between meaning-making as discussed by Park and Folkman (1997) and meaning-making through secondary control from the perspective of Morling and Evered (2006):

> Thus, both our view of secondary control and Park and Folkman's view of meaning making suggest that some aspect of the self is adjusting, that an event is accepted, and that people desire consistency. One difference is that Park and Folkman are mainly interested in how individuals strive for coherence and fit between global and situational meaning, both of which are cognitive constructs within the self. Secondary control researchers are mainly interested in how people strive for coherence and fit between the self and an external environment. (Morling & Evered, 2006, p. 282)

This distinction, focusing on alterations to the self through engagement with the environment rather than making adjustments to a broader worldview (Morling & Evered, 2006), is one reason to expect that meaning-making through secondary control has benefits to offer over and above resolving internal inconsistencies. Specifically, we believe that utilizing secondary control as a tool for meaning-making vis-à-vis adjustment of the self to present circumstances can also contribute to a sense of control and to the related constructs of agency and self-efficacy. Consistent with this, Steger, Owens, and Park (2015) found that, among Vietnam veterans, goal violations, which constitute threats to agency and control, are more damaging in terms of mental health than belief violations, which involve no threat to agency. These findings also suggest that interventions targeting acceptance of what cannot be changed, restoration of self-efficacy in achieving goals, and considering alternate routes to achieve those goals (Steger et al., 2015)—all of which can be accomplished through secondary control—may confer additional benefits over those which only focus on repairing internal meaning systems. Given the unique nature of the refugee experience, secondary control may be especially important for promoting adaptive functioning in the context of ethnopolitical warfare, where direct control over one's environment is minimal, and individuals must cope with stressors related to both direct war exposure and to the chronic stressors of daily life (Miller & Rasmussen, 2014; Rawlence, 2016).

The Diversity of Refugee Experiences

When discussing the nature of the refugee experience, it is important to note that not all refugee experiences are equivalent. Specifically, the causes of displacement, the objective outcomes of displacement, and what it means for a given refugee population to successfully function will vary from context to context. Thus, while there will be some shared experiences that will likely be relevant to most refugee populations (such as loss of resources, displacement, and trauma exposure), there are other differences that need to be considered when determining proper assessment and intervention design.

What Are the Causes of Displacement?

Chirot and Seligman (2000) established a scale of intensity for ethnopolitical conflicts with six specific levels, four of which are associated with some form of conflict. Individual cases of conflict can move up and down the scale depending on the severity of the conflict. The six levels they identified were as follows:

1. Genocide
2. Major ethnopolitical warfare that stopped short of genocide (i.e., that did not lead to the mass killing of specific populations)
3. Low-level ethnopolitical war
4. Ethnopolitical conflict without war but with occasional violence
5. No serious conflict despite high level of awareness about and important political role of ethnic, religious, and regional differences
6. Past conflict followed by reconciliation

Each of the top three levels have been associated with significant refugee movement, whether in Rwanda in 1994 (genocide), Sri Lanka until 2009 (major ethnopolitical warfare), or the West Bank and Gaza Strip (low-level ethnopolitical war). One important point to highlight here is that the type of ethnopolitical conflict that prompted migration will vary from context to context, and researchers should be mindful of this context, as this will have implications for the mental health implications of having been exposed to that conflict (e.g., Jayawickreme, Jayawickreme, Atanasov, Goonasekera, & Foa, 2012).

What Are the Outcomes of Displacement?

The distinction between levels of conflict points to a second equivalent question for refugee movements over the course of modern history: What are the major long-term outcomes of refugee movement? At first glance, it may seem that there would be only three outcomes for migrants forced from their homeland: they would either successfully form communities in the host territory, they may struggle to adapt to life in a new host country, or they would suffer further persecution despite the fact that they had left their home country. However, a preliminary evaluation of different refugee outcomes in recent human history suggests a more extensive set of outcomes. Such long-term outcomes of forced migration could include return to one's homeland (as happened with the relocation of German refugees after the end of World War II), endurance in a pervasive state of displacement (e.g., the situation of Guatemalan refugees in Mexico (Cheng & Chudoba, 2003) or the Somalian refugees in Kenya (Rawlence, 2016)), permanent settlement without assimilation (the situation of various communities in the Middle East), the founding of a new country of settlement (the founding of Israel by Jewish communities in 1947), the successful assimilation of new communities (arguably the Vietnamese and Irish communities in the USA), and extra-genocide outcomes (such as the pogroms faced by the Jewish communities in the early part of the twentieth century).

This represents a very preliminary set of outcomes, and further work needs to be done in order to ascertain to validity and sufficiency of the set described. For one, given the Jewish community's history of being survivors of constant migration and persecution, it could be that they may represent one of a small number of examples for some of these outcomes. Moreover, given that much refugee research has focused on populations displaced following World War II, previous examples of forced migration before 1939 as well as examples of forced migration outside Europe should ideally be evaluated with a view toward reducing or potentially even increasing the number of possible outcomes for refugee populations. With a more complete list of outcomes, it would then be possible to identify factors that lead to positive outcomes in different scenarios. For example, in the context of the modern political landscape, what factors would differentially predict positive outcomes for international refugees, internally displaced persons, and the growing group of transnational migrants (Levitt & Jaworsky, 2007)? Other factors that would be important in this context would be the reasons for migration, the skills they brought with them, and the attitude of the host country.

What Does It Mean for Refugees to Do "Well"?

A third point that bears highlighting here is the fact that how well refugees function following the experience of ethnopolitical warfare will depend not only on the nature of the conflict and the type of settlement following the conflict but also on what it means for a refugee to do "well" in any given context. For example, what it means for a refugee to be resilient in the face of adversity depends on the domain of functioning one is assessing (e.g., life satisfaction, symptoms of depression, functional impairment). Much resilience research has operationalized resilience in terms of stable levels of depressive symptoms (Bonanno, Kennedy, Galatzer-Levy, Lude, & Elfström, 2012), for example, but these may not be the most relevant measures of functioning critical to refugee well-being. Researchers doing work on refugee populations should ensure that an appropriate breadth of important domains of functioning is assessed (Luthar & Brown, 2007). Additionally, it is possible that doing well in one relevant domain of functioning can coexist with significant struggles in others (Infurna & Luthar, 2015). Being careful to select the most appropriate and context-specific measures of functioning is therefore especially important when working with refugee populations (Jayawickreme, Jayawickreme, et al., 2012).

It is important to note that the experience of the refugee is part of a wider history of human migration that has played an important and positive role in the growth and evolution of human civilization. The phenomenon of forced migration is as old as human history:

> Throughout human history, individual and group migration has played an important role in the social evolution of human society by contributing to cultural and biological diversity. This diversity has permitted human beings to thrive in the face of adversity by providing an ever-changing set of perspectives and solutions to pressing environmental demands.

Within this context, opinions and judgments about the merits of human migration are historically irrelevant. Migration has been and will continue to be an integral part of the human response to threat and opportunity, even in the face of obvious hardships and hazards that are part of the departure, transit, arrival, and resettlement phases of migration. The "promise" has always superseded the "peril," regardless of the migratory patterns and legal status of the migrant. Thus, whether settlers, contract workers, professional transients, illegal immigrants, asylum seekers, or refugees—or any of their ancient analogs—migrants have been a major source of social evolution. (Jablensky et al., 1994, p. 327)

Forced population movements have been a commonplace practice since the beginning of human history, as in the expulsion of Moses and his followers from Egypt and the "social death" of banishment in classical Greece. Interestingly, the phenomenon of being "cast out" of one's community is seen across primates, including communities of rhesus macaque (Maestripieri, 2007). However, Malkki (1995) argues that the concept of the "refugee" as a social category and global legal issue has only existed in the wake of World War II, when more than seven million Europeans were unable to return to their homelands (Marrus, 2002). It is interesting to note that, when the United Nations first defined the "refugee" in 1951 in terms of an individual fleeing his or her nation due to a well-founded fear of persecution, the resulting convention did not cover refugees outside of Europe (Hein, 1993). Before refugees became seen as an international humanitarian concern, they were considered as a military problem during the last years of World War II and the immediate postwar years, with refugees coming under the jurisdiction of the Displaced Persons Branch of the Supreme Headquarters Allied Expeditionary Force (Malkki, 1995; Proudfoot, 1956).

The Psychological Experience of Refugees

However, the recognition of the refugee plight as a humanitarian issue led to a focus on their assessment through the lens of the medical model. Much of the research with refugee populations has thus focused on documenting the traumas these populations have faced and how these traumas have impacted mental health. The main objectives have been detailing symptoms and correlates of psychological stress caused by trauma and developing diagnostic tools of psychopathology (Miller & Rasco, 2004). The introduction of a clinical characterization of symptoms seen post-trauma, with the addition of post-traumatic stress disorder (PTSD) to the third edition of the *Diagnostic Statistical Manual* (American Psychiatric Association, 1980), has led to a focus on the "medical model" in refugee research (Jayawickreme, Jayawickreme, et al., 2012). From the perspective of many Western clinicians, the goal of refugee interventions is to treat symptoms of mental illness and to alleviate distress through therapy. However, Summerfield (1999) has argued that refugee populations rarely pursue such treatment for their symptoms, if symptoms are present at all. While many may suffer from symptoms of PTSD, it is unlikely that they consider these symptoms to be their most pressing challenge in daily functioning (Summerfield, 1999). While refugees may have left the trauma of direct war exposure, focusing on only past trauma may cause clinicians to overlook an overwhelming number of ongoing current stressors that may also be traumatizing, such as loss of friends or family, loss of economic resources, and limited control over their circumstances (Miller & Rasmussen, 2014). While interventions to alleviate distress are important where appropriate, many displaced individuals manage to function in spite of their distress. Understanding which skills and strategies may promote resilience in those select individuals is important to improving interventions for those experiencing distress or living in adverse situations .

From Victims to Survivors: Redefining Refugees

During the past decade, the emerging field of positive psychology (Jayawickreme, Forgeard, & Seligman, 2012; Seligman & Csikszentmihalyi, 2000) has supported and stimulated research aimed at redressing the imbalance between psychopathology and disease relative to human strengths and well-being (Jayawickreme, Forgeard, et al., 2012). This research has furthered the goal of creating "a psychology of positive human functioning... that achieves a scientific understanding and effective interventions to build thriving individuals, families and communities" (Seligman, 2002, p. 5). Positive psychology's focus on promoting wellness and strengths has also stimulated research exploring how trauma may promote positive personal growth (e.g., Blackie, Jayawickreme, Forgeard, & Jayawickreme, 2015; Tedeschi & Calhoun, 2004).

The domination of the aforementioned "medical model" in mental health research among refugee populations and victims of ethnopolitical conflict—a model that has emphasized the diagnosis of psychiatric disorders—has led to at least two serious limitations in our understanding of the well-being of refugees (Jayawickreme, Jayawickreme, et al., 2012). First, some researchers have argued that this research paradigm obscures the fact that most refugees do not show evidence of a diagnosable psychiatric disorder and even those that do continue to function effectively (e.g., Miller, Kulkarni, & Kushner, 2006; Summerfield, 2005). Limited work has focused on how some individuals caught up in ethnopolitical conflict are able to continue functioning adaptively in the wake of extreme situations or on which resources and skills may facilitate such functioning. Yet, factors that make such resilience possible have been largely ignored due to a focus on concepts of loss, separation, stress, and trauma, all of which emphasize what is lacking for refugees to maintain adequate levels of well-being. This issue contributes in no small way to the second limitation: most disorder-focused interventions are designed to alleviate psychological distress while ignoring the promotion of "positive" skills and strategies that may enable refugees to maintain an adequate level of psychological functioning and promote improvements in subjective well-being.

Positive psychology thus has the potential to make a serious and important contribution to research on displaced populations; but so, too, does the experience of political refugees have the potential to make an important contribution to positive psychology. As Ryff and Singer (2002) have pointed out, positive human functioning is most remarkable when seen in contexts of significant life challenge and adversity. Understanding which resources are important for resilience in the context of ethnopolitical conflict has important consequences for understanding the coping mechanisms individuals use in times of war and conflict (Jayawickreme, Jayawickreme, et al., 2012), as well as other extreme hardships people face throughout life. In general resources such as self-esteem, optimism, personal control, and a sense of meaning have been shown to act as a buffer against stressful life events (Taylor, Kemeny, Reed, Bower, & Gruenewald, 2000). Such resources may also serve a protective role in preserving well-being when confronted with adversity. For example, Blackie et al. (2015) found that personal growth initiative—the intentional desire to develop as a person and the confidence to set goals that enable personal growth—was negatively associated with functional impairment when controlling for depression, post-traumatic stress disorder, and other demographic factors among survivors of the 1994 Rwandan genocide. However, while people can adapt relatively well to isolated incidents of trauma, adapting to a long-term situation involving significant resource loss may be much harder (Hobfoll, Johnson, Ennis, & Jackson, 2003)—a reality that is faced by displaced refugee populations.

Security, Meaning, and Coping

With regard to refugee populations, one could argue that security is among the most important and salient psychological needs, insofar as their status as individuals-in-flight would seem to preclude any possibility of fulfilling this need to any significant degree. Indeed, the UNHCR State of the World's Refugees report cites psychological security as an important resource and one that refugees the world over lack (UNHCR, 2006). Moreover, the UNDP Human Development Report for 1994 focused on the question of human security and argued that it was a vital need at an individual level:

> The concept of security has for too long been interpreted narrowly: as security of territory from external aggression, or as protection of national interests in foreign policy or as global security from the threat of a nuclear holocaust. It has been related more to nation-states than to people … who sought security in their daily lives. For many of them, security symbolizes protection from the threat of disease, hunger, unemployment, crime, social conflict, political repression and environmental hazards. (UNDP, 1994, p. 22)

The relative importance of psychological security among refugee populations remains an open question. While Leaning and Arie (2000) have attempted to subsume psychological security within other needs such as autonomy and self-sufficiency, it remains unclear whether psychological security in and of itself predicts psychological distress or well-being. Evaluating the role of psychological security in refugee well-being remains an important (and thus far) unanswered empirical question.

In terms of related evidence, Maslow (1954) identified five fundamental needs: physical health, security, self-esteem, love-belongingness, and self-actualization. Maslow held that security—the search for structure and order—was an important factor as humans needed to feel a sense of predictability and order in their lives. Wahba and Bridwell (1973) have argued that human psychological needs can be divided into positive "enhancement" or "growth" needs on the one hand and "deficiency" or "security" needs on the other. Supporting this view, an assessment of important psychological needs (Sheldon, Elliot, Kim, & Kasser, 2001) found that not having one's security needs met (along with competence and self-esteem needs) was related to unsatisfying events, although it was not related to satisfying events. One interpretation, following Maslow (1954) and Sheldon and colleagues (2001), is that the need for security may have to be fulfilled before growth and positive experiences become possible. Moreover, when individuals struggle with significant adversity, they may crave the security, safety, and predictability of their lives, which they previously took for granted (APA, 2001). As Sheldon et al. (2001) themselves note, "when things go wrong, people may strongly wish for the safety and predictability that they often take for granted" (p. 336).

While the importance of security for positive psychology is not immediately apparent—given its lack of relation to satisfying events in Sheldon et al.'s (2001) study—fulfilling this need for refugee populations may be an important prerequisite for their ability to adapt to adversity and experience well-being. Moreover, the concept of security, as discussed by Maslow (1954), may overlap with the concept of meaning. It is broadly accepted that having a sense of meaning—that life has purpose, functions in an understandable way, and is significant (Baumeister, 1991; Heintzelman & King, 2014)—is a positive and valuable experience (McAdams, 2013). Aside from the intuitive belief that meaning in life is worth seeking, a variety of positive outcomes have been empirically linked to the sense that life has meaning. Positive physical outcomes are associated with meaning and purpose in life (see Roepke, Jayawickreme, & Riffle, 2014 for a review). The presence of meaning in life also positively correlates with positive psychological outcomes, such as positive affect, satisfaction with life (Steger, Oishi, & Kashdan, 2009), and subjective well-being (Zika & Chamberlain, 1987).

Park and Folkman (1997) have divided meaning into two categories: global and situational. Global meaning is the more general understanding of the world, assumptions, and expectations, such as "Good things happen to good people" or "I am in control of my destiny." Situational meaning is the appraisal of a particular event, such as it being good or bad, significant or not. Distress is experienced when an event's situational meaning does not fit into an individual's global meaning, and this distress can be relieved through reappraisal of the event or alterations to global meaning (Park & Folkman, 1997). Meaning-focused coping does not directly address external circumstances or negative emotions but is focused on bringing global and situational meaning into alignment (Park & Folkman, 1997). Park's (2010) review of meaning-making highlights the importance of the meaning that is made, showing that findings suggest that adaptive meaning-making is needed to aid in recovery and psychological adjustment.

This view of meaning is supported by research and suggests that meaning-making, by either altering an existing global framework to accommodate an event or adjusting the appraised meaning of the event in order for it to fit into a global framework, is an adaptive form of coping (Guo et al., 2013; Park & Folkman, 1997; Park, Riley, & Snyder, 2012). Guo et al. (2013) found that, for earthquake victims, whose foundational beliefs about life may have been called into question by the destruction of their home or the loss of a loved one, focusing on determining the meaning of the event was more beneficial than focusing on the problem or addressing the negative emotions it caused. Steger et al. (2015) found support for the meaning-making model (Park, 2010; Park & Folkman, 1997) in their study of Vietnam veterans, showing that meaning-making was important for post-trauma adjustment. We speculate here that meaning-making through secondary control can offer unique benefits that may aid foster refugee resilience. In particular, secondary control-focused techniques targeting acceptance of what cannot be changed, leading to consideration of alternate routes to achieve important life goals, may facilitate post-trauma adjustment.

The Importance of Perceiving Control

Not surprisingly, little is known about the risk factors and protective factors associated with successful coping among refugee populations. Mollica, Cui, McInnes, and Massagli (2002) found that, among Cambodian refugees, positive work status was a protective factor against major depression, and religious practices were a strong protective factor against PTSD. One possible explanation for this finding was that work enabled the refugees to perceive some control over their lives. Moreover, caregiving for other camp members emerged as a risk factor for PTSD. The link between religious practices and reduced emotional distress has also been noted among Bhutanese refugees in Nepal (Shrestha et al., 1998). The strong relationship between religious practices and better mental health is not surprising, given that religious and spiritual practices can help bolster global meaning through its contribution to an individual's worldview. Religious beliefs assist the individual in finding meaning and understanding in their loss (Davis, Nolen-Hoeksema, & Larson, 1998; McIntosh, Silver, & Wortman, 1993), usually through the ascription of the stressful event to a greater plan of a higher power. However, while religion can spur on making sense of the evening, it had limited value in promoting benefit-finding (Davis et al., 1998).

The association between positive work status and better mental health outcomes may be explained as an example of reactive problem-focused coping. Engaging in economic activity may serve to increase a refugee's perceived control and self-efficacy and further improve his or her sense of control over the environment. The benefits of similar forms of self-directed behavior have also been examining with regard to the question of self-settlement. Self-settlement allows refugees to integrate into the host community, as opposed to remaining within a refugee camp. Most refugees in the world today are accommodated within refugee camps, where they do not (or, in most instances, are not allowed to) engage in economic activity and remain dependent on aid, the provision of which is undependable, erratic, and inadequate (Harrell-Bond, 2000; Verdirame & Harrell-Bond, 2005).

The importance of facilitating human control—even at the expense of other psychological services—is highlighted by a study of two cohorts of families from the same town of origin and the same socioeconomic background who had survived internment at a Bosnian concentration camp (Eastmond, 1998). Half of these families were sent to an area with temporary employment opportunities and no psychological services, while the other half were sent to an area that had a number of psychological services but no job opportunities. After 1 year, the families who had found work were doing significantly better than the second group, the majority of whom remained on sick leave.

The benefits of control become evident when one considers the lives of most refugees today. Many of them are compelled to remain within the confines of refugee camps, since receiving assistance is conditional on remaining within the settlement (Hovil, 2002). This approach has been condemned as the "warehousing" of refugees and denying their rights (Black, 1998; Dunn, 2015; Van Damme, 1995; Verdirame, 1999), and there is some evidence that self-settled refugees are able to facilitate their own enablement—that is, achieve the goals that they have set for themselves (Maddux, 2002)—without burdening the community in which they settle. For example, despite the nominal security that camps are supposed to provide, self-settled refugees in Uganda are able to make decisions about their own security, use their skills and knowledge to enrich themselves and the communities that they live in, work, pay taxes, and contribute to the economy (Hovil, 2007). This successful pattern of self-settlement has also been noted in Zambia (Hansen, 1979), Eastern Sudan (Kok, 1989), and Guinea (Black, 1998). While the success of such programs is dependent to a great degree on how receptive the host population is to refugee settlement, as well on the security situation, it would seem that in many instances refugee camps take for granted the notion that refugees are victims of external circumstances and can potentially end up inadvertently promoting a sense of helplessness among its members. This helplessness can arguably be seen in the Dadaab refugee camp in eastern Kenya, where some of the camp's inhabitants speak of experiencing a depressive feeling they term *buufis*—a sense of longing to be resettled so powerful it makes them unable in invest in their present life (Horst, 2006; Rawlence, 2016). In light of positive psychology's emphasis on the notion that individuals are self-initiating and transactional agents for change in themselves and others, the benefits of self-settlement over camp settlement whenever possible would greatly assist refugee populations with coping successfully with their current situation. Moreover, such self-settlement programs afford the opportunity for refugees to generate meaning in their everyday lives.

Secondary Control as a Resource in Adversity

In this context, it is worth speculating how secondary control can be a unique resource for maintaining well-being among individuals undergoing significant adversity, such as victims of ethnopolitical warfare. We note that secondary control can be beneficial in at least the following ways:

1. Secondary control can reduce immediate distress associated with uncontrollable, negative circumstances by helping refugees accept and adjust their selves to the new environment.
2. Secondary control can create growth and meaning in the face of adversity, vis-à-vis changing the self (e.g., personality change, Jayawickreme & Blackie, 2014).
3. Secondary control can assist in the adjustment to a new and possibly long-term environment.
4. Secondary control can reveal other opportunities that do not fit with one's current expectations ("opening doors" that were not previously perceived).
5. Secondary control can facilitate opportunities for deploying primary control in the service of pursuing new opportunities.

Perhaps the best example of secondary control providing meaning along with other empowering benefits in the context of ethnopolitical warfare is found in the writings of psychiatrist and concentration camp survivor, Viktor Frankl. Frankl, speaking of his time in concentration camps, says, "…there were always choices to make. Every day, every hour, offered the opportunity to make a decision, a decision which determined whether you would or would not submit to those powers which threatened to rob you of your very self, your inner freedom…" (Frankl, 1963, p. 64). Frankl felt that he maintained a sense of control over his view of and response to his circumstances by choosing to shift his outlook. He found that fellow prisoners who had what he called a "will to meaning," a desire to seek out a reason to survive, were more likely to do so. Finding a purpose was something that every individual must do for themselves, and Frankl believed that finding such meaning was possible under any circumstances.

Although firsthand exposure to war itself is directly associated with negative outcomes, a great deal of research has focused on the way that daily stressors caused by major traumas such as ethnopolitical warfare (such as the stress caused by lack of housing, access to food, or access to employment) impact individuals (Miller & Rasmussen, 2010). In this day-to-day stress, which often lasts long after the conflict has ended, resilience may confer many benefits (Bonanno, 2004), and it is here that we feel secondary control can play a unique role. In fact the original article by Rothbaum and colleagues (1982) and the review from Morling and Evered (2006) note the complex relationship between primary and secondary control. Exertions of primary control are necessary for gaining access to necessities, but secondary control may be useful in maintaining a resilient attitude when attempting these tasks, either by enriching those attempts with broader meaning or by increasing a sense of agency within the person.

While we believe that secondary control can be beneficial on its own, it also provides the ability to see new opportunities for taking primary control. Displaced refugees must make many internal adjustments to successfully adapt to daily struggles. Through acceptance of the constraints placed upon them by their current plight, refugees may find power in their ability to adjust to these circumstances, pursuing new goals suited to their circumstances. A good example of this comes from a Somali refugee in Nairobi. She and her three children were forced to flee their home to avoid fighting. Sharing a single room with her children and another family, acceptance and adaptation to her circumstances—*secondary control*—is crucial to her family's survival. While she had been a nurse at home, she now sets up a small grill where she cooks food to sell in the streets—*primary control*—allowing her to provide a modest income for her family (Offer, 2010). Both primary and secondary controls appear to be working together. However, in light of the previous discussion on coping, a more general question may be asked: which refugees are more likely to utilize and benefit from primary control, and which refugees are more likely to utilize and benefit from secondary control? Both the cause for refugee status and the long-term contexts or outcomes vary widely among refugees.

The structural and material challenges faced by refugees are undeniably the most pressing. As refugees wait for their country to rebuild or as programs are being put in place to assist refugees while the fighting they have fled continues, one thing that can be offered is skills that help to maintain or enhance resilience. There are a number of existing interventions that we believe operate by encouraging meaning-making through the use of secondary control. While the aforementioned examples of the Somali nurse and Viktor Frankl could represent outliers, and their work may have helped hone skills that enabled an uncommon ability to adapt, we do believe that secondary control is a resource that can be cultivated through interventions.

Future Directions

In this chapter, we have discussed the possible benefits of promoting secondary control as a resource for promoting well-being among refugees fleeing ethnopolitical warfare. A danger that is not lost on us, however, is that the recommendation of a strategy premised upon acceptance and adjustment may come across as trite and even privileged in light of the objectively terrible situations faced by refugees fleeing ethnopolitical warfare. This is obviously not our intention. Ultimately, the successful resolution of the refugees' displacement and the guaranteeing of their material security will go a long way toward providing for their well-being. Yet, this process can woefully take decades to accomplish, which points to the need for psychological interventions that may help refugees cope with their circumstances, while restoring in them a sense of agency. Moreover, the wisdom of secondary control, such as it is, is that it should be applicable to even the worst situations. We would argue that utilizing the tool of secondary control in the context of ethnopolitical conflict confers unique benefits to the person in the horrible situation, while remaining cognizant of the objective horror of their situation.

So, what *is* secondary control good for in situations of ethnopolitical warfare? We believe that secondary control can restore a sense of power amid chaos. The quote that begins this chapter emphasizes the potential power and liberation that comes from recognizing that even in the most horrible situations a person can take steps to restore his or her a sense of agency, a capability that is increasingly implicated as a key ingredient to psychological well-being. Moreover, as our illustrative examples above have highlighted, this realization that one can maintain some sense of control in even the most dire situations may in fact lead to a cascade effect, whereby reclaiming a greater level of control over specific life domains can be a catalyst for greater self-empowerment.

While little research has directly manipulated secondary control, some relevant intervention programs point to promising future directions. While grounded in a different conceptual tradition, Acceptance and Commitment Therapy (ACT; Hayes, Strosahl, & Wilson, 1999) has, as one component, an active focus on acceptance of one's current condition. Additionally, Frankl's own logotherapy focuses on the importance of meaning (Frankl, 1963). Frankl wrote that maintaining a future goal was instrumental in motivating prisoners to stay alive in concentration camps and argued that people need an internal tension, a reason to strive and struggle toward a goal. Both primary and secondary control may be important tools in fostering this consistent striving in the face of significant adversity. While Frankl did not propose a specific meaning for life, he believed that there was strength to feeling a sense of purpose in every moment. Logotherapy encourages shifting perspective and advises that even suffering, when viewed from a particular point of view, can be infused with meaning (Frankl, 1963). The techniques utilized in logotherapy include paradoxical intention, which involved self-distancing through humor and absurdity; dereflection, which involves shifting the individual's attention away from symptom causing distress and redirecting it toward a motivating/meaningful area; and attitude modification. It is possible that this therapy may function as a positive addition to cognitive-behavioral therapy, although more research is needed (Ameli & Dattilio, 2013).

Changing the self by choosing to focus on the resources one has may enhance well-being. One specific adjustment that can be made in order to alter an event's meaning and maintain the motivation to move forward is trying to see the benefits of the situation, however limited (Anderson, Kay, & Fitzsimons, 2013). One example of this comes from a refugee who fled the Congo and had to make a life in a Nairobi apartment with seven other family members. While she said life is a struggle, she noted that it was better to be in a peaceful country (Offer, 2010). Even though her life was harder in many ways and she would likely prefer to be home, she saw certain benefits conferred by even these challenging circumstances. Recent research suggests that finding and appreciating advantages may also be beneficial to those who have experienced trauma. In one study, individuals with neuromuscular disease were encouraged to list life events they were grateful for over the past week for 9 weeks. Gratitude was linked to increased positive affect, and listing "blessings" led to increased offering and seeking of personal and emotional support, suggesting there may be important interpersonal benefits from choosing to focus on what is not lacking (Emmons & McCullough, 2003).

Discussed throughout this chapter, and of relevant to refugee populations, is the importance of *perceptions* of agency and self-efficacy, which are central to maintaining a sense of control. As we noted earlier in this chapter, threats to agency and control are more damaging in terms of mental health than belief violations, which involve no threat to agency (Steger et al., 2015). Such research suggests that developing secondary control-focused interventions targeting acceptance of what cannot be changed, leading to restoration of self-efficacy in achieving goals by considering alternate routes to achieve those goals, may be an exciting avenue for future research. Perceptions of increased agency and self-efficacy, therefore, are key outcomes to be targeted in meaning-making interventions to enhance secondary control in the midst of adversity.

We note however that, while these interventions may be uniquely beneficial to displaced populations, clinicians need to be cautious before implementing interventions of secondary control following severe trauma. For individuals suffering from symptoms of post-traumatic stress disorder, for example, evidence-based interventions intended to treat these symptoms should first be utilized. Interventions to increase well-being and adaptability would only be appropriate to use with those who had already been properly treated for mental disorders such as PTSD or for those who have managed to maintain a relatively functional level of mental health.

Conclusion

This chapter has discussed the shortcomings of the medical model approach to survivors of ethnopolitical warfare and the benefits of identifying tools that can promote well-being among refugee populations. Much of the research in refugee mental health has been imbalanced, caused in part by the overdominance of the psychiatric traumatological approach and the PTSD concept. While this program of research has resulted in a wealth of knowledge, it has also led to a lopsided perspective on refugee mental health. We have also outlined how primary and secondary control is conceptualized in the literature and why secondary control may be a tool that is particularly well suited to refugee populations. Though further research is necessary, we believe that findings support the position that utilizing secondary control to accept and adapt to challenging circumstances through meaning-making may help to bolster resources that may be particularly beneficial to resilience in refugee populations, including meaning in life, a sense of control, self-efficacy, and agency.

Key Takeaways

- The medical model approach to refugees has led to a lack of understanding about the skills and strategies that allow some people to function in spite of their distress. Rather than focusing only on diagnosing and treating illness, refugees would be better served by the addition of interventions designed to promote well-being and maintain functioning.
- How well refugees function following the experience of ethnopolitical warfare will depend not only on the nature of the conflict and the type of settlement following the conflict but also on what it means for a refugee to do "well" in any given context. Being careful to select the most appropriate and context-specific measures of functioning is therefore especially important when working with refugee populations.
- A sense of control contributes to successful adjustment, coping, resilience, and overall well-being. Research suggests that factors contributing to refugees' sense of control may serve a protective function and lead to improved outcomes. However, the context of ethnopolitical conflict is particularly lacking in opportunities for individuals to control their circumstances.
- Secondary control is engaged when an individual accepts and actively adapts to the reality of a situation by altering expectations, goals, and motivations, in order to better suit circumstances. Secondary control is not a passive response and has proved to have benefits above and beyond those of primary control (i.e., acting on the environment to make it better suited to the individual).
- Interventions that target meaning-making through the use of secondary control may be particularly well suited to the refugee experience, serving to bolster resilience, a sense of control, agency, and self-efficacy.

Acknowledgment This publication was made possible through the support of grant #24322 from the John Templeton Foundation awarded to Eranda Jayawickreme. The opinions expressed in this publication are those of the authors and do not necessarily reflect the views of the John Templeton Foundation.

References

Ameli, M., & Dattilio, F. M. (2013). Enhancing cognitive behavior therapy with logotherapy: Techniques for clinical practice. *Psychotherapy, 50*(3), 387–391.

American Psychiatric Association. (1980). *Diagnostic and statistical manual of mental disorders* (3rd ed.). Arlington, VA: American Psychiatric Publishing.

American Psychological Association. (2001). *What makes people the happiest? Researchers say it's not money or popularity*. Press release (2/11/2001).

Anderson, J. E., Kay, A. C., & Fitzsimons, G. M. (2013). Finding silver linings: Meaning making as a compensatory response to negative experiences. In K. D. Markman, T. Proulx, & M. J. Lindberg (Eds.), *The psychology of meaning* (pp. 279–295). Washington, DC: American Psychological Association.

Bandura, A. (1997). *Self-efficacy: The exercise of control.* New York, NY: W.H. Freeman & Company.

Baumeister, R. F. (1991). *Meanings of life.* New York, NY: Guilford Press.

Baumeister, R. F. (2005). *The cultural animal: Human nature, meaning, and social life.* Oxford: Oxford University Press.

Black, R. (1998). Refugee camps not really reconsidered: A reply to Crisp and Jacobsen. *Forced Migration Review, 3,* 31.

Blackie, L. E. R., Jayawickreme, E., Forgeard, M. J., & Jayawickreme, N. (2015). The protective function of personal growth initiative among a genocide-affected population in Rwanda. *Psychological Trauma: Theory, Research, Practice, and Policy, 7*(4), 333–339.

Blackie, L. E. R., Roepke, A. M., Forgeard, M. J., Jayawickreme, E., & Fleeson, W. (2014). Act well to be well: The promise of changing personality states to promote well-being. In A. C. Parks & S. M. Schueller (Eds.), *The Wiley Blackwell handbook of positive psychological interventions* (pp. 462–474). Oxford: Wiley-Blackwell.

Bonanno, G. A. (2004). Loss, trauma, and human resilience: Have we underestimated the human capacity to thrive after extremely aversive events? *American Psychologist, 59*(1), 20–27.

Bonanno, G. A., Kennedy, P., Galatzer-Levy, I. R., Lude, P., & Elfström, M. L. (2012). Trajectories of resilience, depression, and anxiety following spinal cord injury. *Rehabilitation Psychology, 57*(3), 236–247.

Cheng, C., & Chudoba, J. (2003). *New issues in refugee research* (No. 86). Working Paper.

Chirot, D., & Seligman, M. E. P. (2000). *Ethnopolitical warfare: Causes, consequences, and possible solutions.* Washington, DC: American Psychological Association.

Compas, B. E., Bemis, H., Gerhardt, C. A., Dunn, M. J., Rodriguez, E. M., Desjardins, L., ... Vannatta, K. (2015). Mothers and fathers coping with their children's cancer: Individual and interpersonal processes. *Health Psychology, 34*(8), 783–793.

Connor-Smith, J. K., & Compas, B. E. (2004). Coping as a moderator of relations between reactivity to interpersonal stress, health status, and internalizing problems. *Cognitive Therapy and Research, 28*(3), 347–368.

Connor-Smith, J. K., Compas, B. E., Wadsworth, M. E., Thomsen, A. H., & Saltzman, H. (2000). Responses to stress in adolescence: Measurement of coping and involuntary stress responses. *Journal of Consulting and Clinical Psychology, 68*(6), 976–992.

Davis, C. G., Nolen-Hoeksema, S., & Larson, J. (1998). Making sense of loss and benefiting from the experience: Two construals of meaning. *Journal of Personality and Social Psychology, 75*(2), 561–574.

Deci, E. L., & Ryan, R. M. (1995). Human autonomy: The basis for true self-esteem. In M. Kernis (Ed.), *Efficacy, agency, and self-esteem* (pp. 31–49). New York, NY: Plenum.

Diener, E., & Chan, M. Y. (2011). Happy people live longer: Subjective well-being contributes to health and longevity. *Applied Psychology: Health and Well-Being, 3*(1), 1–43.

Diehl, M., & Hay, E. L. (2010). Risk and resilience factors in coping with daily stress in adulthood: The role of age, self-concept incoherence, and personal control. *Developmental Psychology, 46*(5), 1132–1146.

Dunn, E. (2015, September 28). The Failure of Refugee Camps. *Boston Review.*

Eastmond, M. (1998). Nationalist discourses and the construction of difference: Bosnian Muslim refugees in Sweden. *Journal of Refugee Studies, 11*(2), 161–181.

Emmons, R. A., & McCullough, M. E. (2003). Counting blessings versus burdens: An experimental investigation of gratitude and subjective well-being in daily life. *Journal of Personality and Social Psychology, 84*(2), 377–389.

Farber, E. W., Mirsalimi, H., Williams, K. A., & McDaniel, J. S. (2003). Meaning of illness and psychological adjustment to HIV/AIDS. *Psychosomatics, 44*(6), 485–491.

Frankl, V. (1963). *Man's search for meaning: An introduction to Logotherapy* (I. Lasch, Trans.). New York, NY: Pocket.

Guo, M., Gan, Y., & Tong, J. (2013). The role of meaning-focused coping in significant loss. *Anxiety, Stress & Coping, 26*(1), 87–102.

Hansen, A. (1979). Managing refugees: Zambia's response to Angolan refugees 1966–1977*. *Disasters, 3*(4), 375–380.
Harrell-Bond, B. (2000). Are refugee camps good for children?. In *New Issues in Refugee Research: Working Paper* (Vol. 29). UN. High Commissioner for Refugees (UNHCR).
Hayes, S. C., Strosahl, K. D., & Wilson, K. G. (1999). Acceptance and commitment therapy: An experiential approach to behavior change. Guilford Press.
Heckhausen, J. (1997). Developmental regulation across adulthood: Primary and secondary control of age-related challenges. *Developmental Psychology, 33*(1), 176–187.
Heckhausen, J., & Schulz, R. (1995). A life-span theory of control. *Psychological Review, 102*(2), 284–304.
Hein, J. (1993). Refugees, immigrants, and the state. *Annual Review of Sociology, 19*, 43–59.
Heintzelman, S. J., & King, L. A. (2014). Life is pretty meaningful. *American Psychologist, 69*(6), 561–574.
Helzer, E. G., & Jayawickreme, E. (2015). Control and the 'good life': Primary and secondary control as distinct indicators of well-being. *Social Psychological and Personality Science, 6*(6), 653–660.
Hobfoll, S. E., Johnson, R. J., Ennis, N., & Jackson, A. P. (2003). Resource loss, resource gain, and emotional outcomes among inner city women. *Journal of Personality and Social Psychology, 84*(3), 632–643.
Horst, C. (2006). Buufis amongst Somalis in Dadaab: The transnational and historical logics behind resettlement dreams. *Journal of Refugee Studies, 19*(2), 143–157.
Hovil, L. (2002). Free to stay, free to go?: Movement, seclusion and integration of refugees in Moyo district. *Refugee Law Project*.
Hovil, L. (2007). Self-settled refugees in Uganda: An alternative approach to displacement? *Journal of Refugee Studies, 20*, 599–620.
Infurna, F. J., & Luthar, S. S. (2015). Resilience to major life stressors is not as common as thought. *Perspectives on Psychological Science, 11*(2), 175–194.
Jablensky, A., Marsella, A. J., Ekbald, S., Jansson, B., Levi, L., & Bornemann, T. (1994). Refugee mental health and well-being: Conclusions and recommendations. In A. J. Marsella et al. (Eds.), *Amidst peril and pain: The mental health and well-being of the world's refugees* (pp. 327–340). Washington, DC: American Psychological Association.
Jayawickreme, E., & Blackie, L. E. (2014). Post-traumatic growth as positive personality change: Evidence, controversies and future directions. *European Journal of Personality, 28*(4), 312–331.
Jayawickreme, E., Forgeard, M. J. C., & Seligman, M. E. P. (2012). The engine of well-being. *Review of General Psychology, 16*, 327–342.
Jayawickreme, N., Jayawickreme, E., Atanasov, P., Goonasekera, M. A., & Foa, E. B. (2012). Are culturally specific measures of trauma-related anxiety and depression needed? The case of Sri Lanka. *Psychological Assessment, 24*(4), 791–800.
Jayawickreme, E., Jayawickreme, N., & Seligman, M. E. P. (2012). From victims to survivors: The positive psychology of refugee mental health. In K. M. Gow & M. J. Celinski (Eds.), *Mass trauma: Impact and recovery issues* (pp. 313–330). New York: Nova Science Publishers.
Kok, W. (1989). Self-settled refugees and the socio-economic impact of their presence on Kassala, Eastern Sudan. *Journal of Refugee Studies, 2*(4), 419–440.
Leaning, J., & Arie, S. (2000). *Human security in crisis and transition: A background document of definition and application*. Arlington, VA: CERTI.
Levitt, P., & Jaworsky, B. N. (2007). Transnational migration studies: Past developments and future trends. *Annual Review of Sociology, 33*, 129–156.
Lucas, R. E. (2007). Long-term disability is associated with lasting changes in subjective well-being: Evidence from two nationally representative longitudinal studies. *Journal of Personality and Social Psychology, 92*, 717–730.
Luhmann, M., Hofmann, W., Eid, M., & Lucas, R. E. (2012). Subjective well-being and adaptation to life events: a meta-analysis. *Journal of personality and social psychology, 102*(3), 592–615.

Luthar, S. S., & Brown, P. J. (2007). Maximizing resilience through diverse levels of inquiry: Prevailing paradigms, possibilities, and priorities for the future. *Development and Psychopathology, 19*(03), 931–955.

Maddux, J. E. (2002). Stopping the "madness": Positive psychology and the deconstruction of the illness ideology and the DSM. In C. R. Snyder & S. J. Lopez (Eds.), *Handbook of positive psychology* (pp. 13–25). New York, NY: Oxford University Press.

Maestripieri, D. (2007). *Macachiavellian intelligence: How Rhesus Macaques and humans have conquered the world*. Chicago, IL: University of Chicago Press.

Malkki, L. H. (1995). Refugees and exile: From "refugee studies" to the natural order of things. *Annual Review of Anthropology, 24*, 495–523.

Marrus, M. R. (2002). *The unwanted: European refugees in the twentieth century*. Philadelphia, PA: Temple University Press.

Maslow, A. H. (1954). *Motivation and personality*. New York, NY: Harper & Collins.

McAdams, D. P. (2013). How actors, agents, and authors find meaning in life. In K. Markman, T. Proulx, & M. J. Lindberg (Eds.), *The psychology of meaning* (pp. 171–190). Washington, DC: American Psychological Association.

McIntosh, D. N., Silver, R. C., & Wortman, C. B. (1993). Religion's role in adjustment to a negative life event: Coping with the loss of a child. *Journal of Personality and Social Psychology, 65*(4), 812–821.

Miller, K. E., Kulkarni, M., & Kushner, H. (2006). Beyond trauma-focused psychiatric epidemiology: Bridging research and practice with war-affected populations. *American Journal of Orthopsychiatry, 76*(4), 409–422.

Miller, K. E., & Rasco, L. M. (Eds.). (2004). *The mental health of refugees: Ecological approaches to healing and adaptation*. Mahwah, NJ: Erlbaum.

Miller, K. E., & Rasmussen, A. (2010). War exposure, daily stressors, and mental health in conflict and post-conflict settings: Bridging the divide between trauma-focused and psychosocial frameworks. *Social Science & Medicine, 70*(1), 7–16.

Miller, K. E., & Rasmussen, A. (2014). War experiences, daily stressors and mental health five years on: Elaborations and future directions. *Intervention, 12*, 33–42.

Mollica, R. F., Cui, X., McInnes, K., & Massagli, M. P. (2002). Science-based policy for psychosocial interventions in refugee camps. *Journal of Nervous and Mental Disease, 190*(3), 158–166.

Morling, B., & Evered, S. (2006). Secondary control reviewed and defined. *Psychological Bulletin, 132*(2), 269–296.

Offer, J. (2010, February 22). *The daily struggles of refugee life in Nairobi*. Retrieved from http://www.rescue.org/blog/daily-struggles-refugee-life-nairobi-photos.

Office of the United Nations High Commissioner for Refugees. (2006). *The state of the world's refugees 2006: Human displacement in the new millennium*. New York, NY: Oxford University Press.

Oishi, S., Diener, E., & Lucas, R. E. (2007). The optimum level of well-being: Can people be too happy?. *Perspectives on psychological science, 2*(4), 346–360.

Park, C. L. (2010). Making sense of the meaning literature: An integrative review of meaning making and its effects on adjustment to stressful life events. *Psychological Bulletin, 136*(2), 257–301.

Park, C. L., & Folkman, S. (1997). Meaning in the context of stress and coping. *Review of General Psychology, 1*(2), 115–144.

Park, C. L., Riley, K. E., & Snyder, L. B. (2012). Meaning making coping, making sense, and post-traumatic growth following the 9/11 terrorist attacks. *The Journal of Positive Psychology, 7*(3), 198–207.

Pérez, J. E., & Smith, A. R. (2015). Intrinsic religiousness and well-being among cancer patients: The mediating role of control-related religious coping and self-efficacy for coping with cancer. *Journal of Behavioral Medicine, 38*(2), 183–193.

Proudfoot, M. (1956). *European refugees: 1939-52: A study in forced population movement*. London: Faber & Faber.

Rawlence, B. (2016). *City of thorns: Nine lives in the World's largest refugee camp*. New York, NY: Macmillan.

Roepke, A. M., Jayawickreme, E., & Riffle, O. M. (2014). Meaning and health: A systematic review. *Applied Research in Quality of Life, 9*(4), 1055–1079.

Rothbaum, F., Weisz, J. R., & Snyder, S. S. (1982). Changing the world and changing the self: A two-process model of perceived control. *Journal of Personality and Social Psychology, 42*(1), 5–37.

Ryff, C. D., & Singer, B. (2002). From social structure to biology: Integrative science in pursuit of human health and well-being. In C. R. Snyder & S. J. Lopez (Eds.), *Handbook of positive psychology* (pp. 541–555). New York, NY: Oxford University Press.

Seligman, M. E. P. (2002). Positive psychology, positive prevention, and positive therapy. In C. R. Snyder & S. J. Lopez (Eds.), *Handbook of positive psychology* (pp. 3–9). New York, NY: Oxford University Press.

Seligman, M. E. P., & Csikszentmihalyi, M. (2000). Positive psychology: An introduction. *American Psychologist, 55,* 5–14.

Sheldon, K. M., Elliot, A. J., Kim, Y., & Kasser, T. (2001). What is satisfying about satisfying events? Testing 10 candidate psychological needs. *Journal of Personality and Social Psychology, 80,* 325–339.

Shrestha, N. M., Sharma, B., Van Ommeren, M. H., Regmi, S., Makaji, R., Komproe, I. H., ... deNew Jong, J. T. V. M. (1998). Impact of torture on refugees displaced within the developing world: Symptomatology among Bhutanese refugees in Nepal. *Journal of the American Medical Association, 280,* 443–448.

Skinner, E. A. (1996). A guide to constructs of control. *Journal of Personality and Social Psychology, 71*(3), 549.

Skinner, E. A. (2007). Secondary control critiqued: Is it secondary? Is it control? Comment on Morling and Evered (2006). *Psychological Bulletin, 133*(6), 911–916.

Steger, M. F., Oishi, S., & Kashdan, T. B. (2009). Meaning in life across the life span: Levels and correlates of meaning in life from emerging adulthood to older adulthood. *The Journal of Positive Psychology, 4*(1), 43–52.

Steger, M. F., Owens, G. P., & Park, C. L. (2015). Violations of war: Testing the meaning-making model among Vietnam veterans. *Journal of Clinical Psychology, 71*(1), 105–116.

Summerfield, D. (1999). A critique of seven assumptions behind psychological trauma programmes in war-affected areas. *Social Science & Medicine, 48*(10), 1449–1462.

Summerfield, D. (2005). What exactly is emergency or disaster "mental health"? *Bulletin of the World Health Organization, 83*(1), 76–77.

Taylor, S. E., Kemeny, M. E., Reed, G. M., Bower, J. E., & Gruenewald, T. L. (2000). Psychological resources, positive illusions, and health. *American Psychologist, 55*(1), 99–109.

Tedeschi, R. G., & Calhoun, L. G. (2004). Posttraumatic growth: Conceptual foundations and empirical evidence. *Psychological Inquiry, 15*(1), 1–18.

Thompson, S. C., Collins, M. A., Newcomb, M. D., & Hunt, W. (1996). On fighting versus accepting stressful circumstances: Primary and secondary control among HIV-positive men in prison. *Journal of Personality and Social Psychology, 70*(6), 1307–1317.

United Nations Development Programme. (1994). *Human development report 1994*. New York, NY; Oxford: Oxford University Press.

Van Damme, W. (1995). Do refugees belong in camps? Experiences from Goma and Ghana. *The Lancet, 346,* 306–346.

Verdirame, G. (1999). Human rights and refugees: The case of Kenya. *Journal of Refugee Studies, 12,* 54–74.

Verdirame, G., & Harrell-Bond, B. E. (2005). *Rights in exile: Janus-faced humanitarianism* (No. 17). Berghahn Books.

Wahba, M. A., & Bridwell, L. (1973). Maslow's need hierarchy theory: A review of research. *Proceedings of the Annual Convention of the American Psychological Association,* 571–572.

Zika, S., & Chamberlain, K. (1987). Relation of hassles and personality to subjective well-being. *Journal of Personality and Social Psychology, 53*(1), 155–162.

Multiculturalism and Meaning in Existential and Positive Psychology

Louis Hoffman, Nathaniel Granger Jr, and Monica Mansilla

Existential psychology and positive psychology share much in their history and value system. Since their inception, both have been critical of the excessive focus on pathologizing and dysfunction in mainstream psychology. Although they focus their critique and emergent alternatives differently, meaning is a central concept in both positive psychology and existential psychology. Within positive psychology, a primary focus has been on the role of meaning in promoting happiness, well-being, and health. Within existential psychology, meaning is understood as playing an important role in dealing with suffering and coping as well as being essential for well-being.

Meaning itself is not a simple construct (MacKenzie & Baumeister, 2014). While meaning is a universal human concern, answers to the question of meaning require a personal and cultural response (Hoffman, 2009a). There is no universal meaning to which everyone ascribes. In this chapter, we begin with an exploration of the relationship between existential psychology, positive psychology, and multicultural psychology. Building from this foundation, we draw upon these approaches to examine cultural variations in meaning and clinical applications.

Meaning as a Bridge Between Existential Psychology and Positive Psychology

As is evident, there is a significant difference between the *meaning of life* and the *meaning of a sentence or a piece of art*, even if the topic is the meaning of life. In this chapter, we are concerned with the former type of meaning, which can be

---

L. Hoffman, Ph.D. (✉) • N. Granger Jr., Psy.D. • M. Mansilla, Ph.D.
Department of Humanistic and Clinical Psychology, Saybrook University,
475 14th Street, 9th Floor, Oakland, CA 94612, USA
e-mail: lhoffman@saybrook.edu

understood as a foundational concern of human existence, or an existential given (Heery, 2009; Hoffman, 2009b; Yalom, 1980). MacKenzie and Baumeister (2014), in a basic definition of meaning, state "Meaning is that which connects ideas and objects to each other in a predictable and relatively stable way… meaning of life is a special usage of meaning that superimposes meaning onto one's life" (p. 26). While this description may be adequate on a purely descriptive or technical level, it does inspire the depth of significance that meaning of life serves in one's life. Frankl (1984) as well as other existential thinkers (Hoffman, 2009b; Hoffman, Vallejos, Cleare-Hoffman, & Rubin, 2015; Wong, 2014) maintain that meaning is a fundamental question, if not *the* fundamental question, of human existence. As such, it has greater importance than happiness, success, or financial security.

Paul Tillich (1957) places meaning in the context of an *ultimate concern*, which deepens the definition provided by MacKenzie and Baumeister. As an ultimate concern, meaning is a driving force in one's psychological functioning and behavior. Emmons (1999), building upon Tillich's work, discussed ultimate concerns to refer to the "multiple personal goals that a person might possess in striving toward the sacred" (p. 6). Although Tillich and Emmons place the idea of ultimate concern(s) in the context of spirituality, they allow for spirituality to be broadly defined inclusive of what many would consider to be secular, such as nationalism and economic well-being. The essence of an ultimate concern is that it is something which grasps the individual and guides their life and choices, even when not recognized by the individual. Similarly, Frankl (2000) speaks of the *will to meaning* as occupying a "central place in the motivational theory of logotherapy" (p. 85). From this perspective, meaning is a central concept for understanding human existence. Similarly, positive psychology has increasingly recognized meaning as central to understanding human flourishing and well-being (Mascaro, 2014; Nielsen, 2014; Steger, 2013; Steger, Shin, Shim, & Fitch-Martin, 2013). Given the central place of meaning in existential psychology and positive psychology, it can serve as a natural bridge between these two approaches.

Differences and Clarifications

Existential psychology is considered part of the third force of psychology, labeled humanistic psychology. Even more than existential psychology, it would seem that humanistic psychology and positive psychology would be natural allies; however, this has not always been the case (Bohart & Greening, 2001; Churchill, 2014; Friedman, 2008; Robbins, 2008, 2015; Waterman, 2013a). The history of the differences has been thoroughly dealt with elsewhere (see Batthyany & Russo-Netzer, 2014; Robbins, 2008, 2015); therefore, we will focus on clarifying two issues relevant to this chapter.

Kim, Seto, Davis, and Hicks (2014) state, "From our perspective, experimental existential psychologists have primarily examined variables that contribute to a sense of *meaninglessness* (e.g., Yalom, 1980)" (p. 221). In citing Yalom as the example, it is important to recognize that while Yalom is a widely recognized existential psychologist, he is not representative of the broader field of existential psychology that includes various approaches (see Cooper, 2003). Yalom focuses more on negative aspects of meaning (i.e., meaninglessness), which is not representative of many existential perspectives (Greening, 1992; Heery, 2009; Helminiak, Hoffman, & Dodson, 2012). Other existential approaches are more inclusive and comprehensive in their applications of the value of meaning in psychological health. However, Yalom (1980), too, recognized that meaning promotes well-being and was more than just a buffer against suffering.

Robbins (2008, 2015) identified divergent views of well-being and the good life as differences between positive psychology and humanistic psychology, which includes existential psychology. In the early development of positive psychology, much focus was placed on hedonic well-being, which can be "defined in terms of the ratio of pleasure to pain" (Robbins, 2008, p. 100). This view of well-being has important limitations. Humanistic and existential approaches embody a eudaimonic view of well-being rooted in character, ethics, and virtues. Frankl (1984), for instance, maintained that happiness becomes more difficult to attain when one's goal is to be happy. Instead, he believed that happiness was best achieved through living well, which includes living consistent with one's character and values, maintaining healthy relationships, accepting oneself, and seeking personal and collective growth. Positive psychology has become more inclusive of a eudaimonic view of well-being over time (Ryff & Singer, 2008; Waterman, 2013b), which, as Robbins (2008) points out, is more consistent with humanistic and existential psychology. Our interest in this chapter is the eudaimonic view of well-being, which is particularly relevant when considering multicultural issues.

While the differences between positive psychology and humanistic/existential psychology have been consistently identified over time, further examination of these differences suggests that they represent degrees of difference and preferences more than absolute distinctions. Furthermore, positive psychology appears to have gravitated in a direction that, while retaining important differences, is increasingly similar to humanistic and existential psychology.

Points of Convergence

Waterman (2013a), in a review of the differences between humanistic psychology and positive psychology, concludes that, "Because of this philosophical divide, adherents to the two perspectives [of humanistic psychology and positive psychology] may best be advised to pursue separately their shared desire to understand and promote human potentials and well-being" (p. 124). While Waterman was intentional in stating he was not discouraging collaboration, he based much of his appraisal on the lack of success in reaching collaboration as well as what he believed were unbridgeable differences. Despite this, the convergences between positive psychology and humanistic/existential psychology far outweigh the discordances

(Linley & Joseph, 2004). Furthermore, distinctions are narrowing. We hold a more optimistic perspective of the potential for collaboration and convergence.

The most evident similarity between humanistic/existential psychology and positive psychology is the emphasis on well-being and human flourishing. An emergent similarity is the concern for virtue or character. Existential thought has long been concerned with character (Frankl, 1984; Hoffman, 2009b; Jaspers, 1947/2001; Mendelowitz, 2008; Nietzsche, 1885/1966). Similarly, character strengths and virtues have increasingly become a focus within positive psychology (Peterson & Seligman, 2004).

A third point of convergence between positive psychology and existential psychology is the focus on meaning. While some have maintained that existential psychology focused on meaning solely in reference to meaning as a way of coping with suffering and meaninglessness (Kim et al., 2014), this is accurate with a limited number of existential scholars. The inclusion of meaning in conceptions of well-being is most notable in the work of Viktor Frankl and the legacy of logotherapy; however, existential psychology is replete with examples of meaning being valuable in well-being as well as coping (Hoffman, 2009b; Maddi, 2014; Wong, 2012, 2014).

Existential Psychology, Positive Psychology, and Multiculturalism

Existential psychology and positive psychology have struggled with embracing multiculturalism. Recent movements are beginning to address this critical oversight. In an increasingly pluralistic society, it is imperative that all approaches to psychology integrate multicultural viewpoints. This integration ought not be a superficial engagement, but one that helps inform and transform the psychological theory and its applications. If existential psychology and positive psychology are to remain influential and relevant, they must embrace multiculturalism. At the same time, these approaches to psychology have something to offer multicultural psychology.

Positive Psychology and Multiculturalism

Positive psychology has received criticism for its failure to address multicultural issues as well as the discounting of the need to consider culture by a few positive psychologists (Christopher & Howe, 2014; Downey & Chang, 2014; Ho et al., 2014; Pedrotti, Edwards, & Lopez, 2009). Pedrotti et al. (2009) noted that positive psychology has taken two approaches to culture. The first, represented by Peterson and Seligman (2004), advocated for a culture-free perspective that asserted objectivity and universality in the identification of various personality strengths. However, even if there is agreement about the value of a construct across cultures, the meaning and experience of that construct still can vary widely (Tanner, 1997). Any claims of universality of specific meanings are dependent upon thin and fragile meanings that quickly lose their value. Recently, a culturally embedded perspective has emerged in positive psychology (Pedrotti et al., 2009). Pedrotti and colleagues advocate that although, "strengths can be found in all cultures and societies,... strengths may manifest differently depending upon the cultural context" (p. 51). Although it has been less influential historically, this perspective represents an important development in positive psychology that is gaining influence.

Positive psychology and multicultural psychology focus on the meaning of being human. Positive psychology focuses on human significance explored from the perspective of one's highest human potential, while multicultural psychology views meaning as largely embedded within particular cultures, including when different cultures live in the same geographical region, as is the case in the study of multiculturalism (Sandage, Hill, & Vang, 2003). Various attempts have been made to advance the understanding of human potential from both perspectives.

Positive psychology focused on the study of strengths and virtues. This is different from other mainstream psychology approaches that discuss strengths and virtues from a descriptive and/or developmental perspective, such as the descriptive explanation of moral development presented by Lawrence Kohlberg (1981) and modified with feminist considerations by Carol Gilligan (1977). Multicultural psychology, when focusing on human potential, approaches strength and virtue as understood from a cultural perspective, while giving significant consideration to implicit and explicit cultural meanings that vary or converge between cultures living in the same country or region. Multicultural psychology differs from cultural psychology's focus on the in-depth study of one specific culture. It also differs from cross-cultural psychology's focus on comparisons of differences and similarities across cultures.

Multicultural psychology can be understood as an ecological system integrated through an array of cultures whose interactions are impacted and molded by the meanings of each group and by the historical meanings internalized by the group's interaction with other cultures. Such is the case of African, Latino, and Chinese Americans' understanding of their sense of virtue and strength based on the meanings and values of their cultural ancestry, which are also influenced by the US culture, including the experience of prejudice and discrimination (Neville & Mobley, 2001). Further alluding to globalization, multicultural psychology focuses on the world as a macro-system of cultural diversity that explains how the majority of Western-focused research continues to promote individualistic values over collectivistic ones while undermining the comparable legitimacy of non-Western perceptions of virtue and strength (Neville & Mobley, 2001; Sandage et al., 2003; Vontress & Epp, 2014). For instance, the focus on individual meaning often implicitly, if not explicitly, devalues collective approaches to meaning and meaning systems. Seligman and Csikszentmihalyi (2000) proposed positive psychology as the primary science behind the discovery and study of strengths and virtues that transcend culture, enhance individual and social significance, and "promote positive experiences and emotions" (p. 556). However, Pedrotti et al. (2009) have offered more culturally sensitive alternatives.

In the culture-free approach to positive psychology, culture and diversity have been significantly disregarded. In addition, multiculturalism as an ecological system has been further neglected and misunderstood given that cultural studies in positive psychology have primarily focused on cross-cultural understandings of strengths and virtues, which often entails generalizing to the culture of those whose cultural home is no longer the culture's country of origin. Most significantly, positive psychology has largely ignored the impact that interculture and intra-cultural exchange has on the personal attribution and meaning of virtue and strength that might differ from culture to culture (Pedrotti & Edwards, 2014). Recent attempts have been made to explore the intersection of multiculturalism with positive psychology, including various studies in the United States where virtues and strengths, such as forgiveness, fulfillment, and well-being, have been considered among Chinese, Latino, indigenous Hmong, and African American populations (Sandage et al., 2003; Sheu, 2014; Sundararajan, 2008; see also Pedrotti & Edwards, 2014). Yet, positive psychology is still in need of further development of a deeper embracement with multicultural psychology.

Existential Psychology and Multiculturalism

Existential psychology and multicultural psychology share much of a common history (Hoffman, Cleare-Hoffman, & Jackson, 2014; Jackson, 2012). Similar to positive psychology, existential psychology and multicultural psychology began partially as critiques of mainstream psychology. Both felt marginalized from the American Psychological Association and much of conventional psychology. Furthermore, existential psychology showed interest in issues of culture well before this was popular in the field of psychology. Despite these convergences, existential psychology struggled to integrate multicultural perspectives and attract individuals from diverse cultural groups (Hoffman, 2016; Hoffman, Cleare-Hoffman, et al., 2014).

Hoffman, Cleare-Hoffman, et al. (2014) identified several problems within humanistic and existential psychology that have created barriers to becoming more multicultural. Referring to these as "humanistic microaggressions," they discussed (1) an individualistic bias, (2) viewing multiculturalism as an unnecessary conversation due to the focus on subjective experience (compare with positive psychology's culture-free approach), and (3) a lack of genuineness and mutuality in attempts to become more diverse.

Existential psychology has, however, made significant strides toward increasing the depth of engagement with multicultural issues and perspectives. International dialogues, in particular, have played an important role in advancing recognition of the value of multicultural awareness (Hoffman, Yang, Kaklauskas, & Chan, 2009; Yang & Hoffman, 2011). In particular, international dialogues have emphasized the importance of (1) cultural critique, (2) identification of necessary adaptations to particular cultural contexts in which existential therapy is applied, (3) identification of indigenous thought and systems sharing values with existential psychology, and (4) dialogue and integration with indigenous approaches (Yang & Hoffman, 2014). Hoffman, Cleare-Hoffman, et al. (2014) note the importance of increased focus on multiculturalism in existential training and conference programming, which have helped make important advancements. However, existential psychology, too, is still in need of further development with multicultural engagement.

Multicultural Variations in Meaning

Tanner (1997) identifies "Culture as the meaning dimension of social life" (p. 31). Culture and meaning are irrevocably intertwined in an intricate and complex relationship. It is impossible to understand culture apart from meaning or meaning apart from culture. In this section, we draw upon existential psychology and positive psychology to examine meaning from a multicultural perspective.

Myth and Meaning

In *The Cry for Myth*, Rollo May (1991) initiated an existential perspective on meaning and culture. Myths can be understood as important sources of meaning and could even be construed as meaning systems. Although myths may not be literally true and cannot be proven to be true, they point toward important personal and cultural truths or meanings. *The Cry for Myth* represents May's attempt to elucidate important shared cultural meanings through an analysis of Western cultural myths. Literature, movies, music, and many other expressive forms are representative of myths. Not all works of art rise to a level where they could be considered cultural myths. However, some works of art resonate with the broader culture to the degree that they could be considered cultural myths.

In *Existential Psychology East-West*, Hoffman et al. (2009) extended May's work through analyses of several specific cultural myths extending beyond the Western paradigm (Chan, 2009; Cleare-Hoffman, 2009; Kaklauskas & Olson, 2009). In an attempt to apply May's theory with deeper cultural engagement, Hoffman (2009a) advocated that there are a number of universal challenges that all people face, commonly referred to as the existential givens (see also Greening, 1992; Heery, 2009; Yalom, 1980). While these challenges or questions may be universal, the answer to them requires both a personal and cultural response (Hoffman, 2009a). Cultural myths identify or express shared cultural meanings, particularly in response to common struggles, such as the existential givens. An examination of particular cultural symbols and myths is one way to deepen the examination pertaining to how meaning is embedded in and interpreted through culture.

Freedom, Courage, and Meaning. Cleare-Hoffman (2009) provided an existential analysis of the Bahamian festival of Junkanoo, which could be identified as a cultural mythology connected to the existential given of freedom. Freedom can be conceived at the social and political levels, such as pertaining to political rights or being free from external constraints. However, freedom can also be considered at the existential level, such as the freedom to choose how one will respond to the lack of other types of freedom (Frankl, 1984). These different types of freedom inevitably intersect. Junkanoo is a Bahamian festival originated by African slaves in the Bahamas. The festival was, in part, a way to retain their West African culture; however, it also represented a celebration of freedom. For the African slaves in the Bahamas, they were given 3 days off a year from their forced work. On two of these 3 days, Boxing Day and New Year's Day, they celebrated Junkanoo, which was a celebration of their freedom. Given the context, this is a powerful expression of freedom.

While freedom can be valued by many different cultures, the meaning and experience of freedom widely varies. For individuals and cultures who have never had their social and political freedom significantly challenged, freedom will be experienced differently than by those who have endured slavery, imprisonment, or other losses of freedom. Freedom is experienced vastly different by those who experience financial and other forms of privilege than by those who are in a lower socioeconomic status and lacking in other forms of privilege (i.e., racial, gender, religious, etc.).

In light of this, the meaning of Junkanoo becomes much more complex, particularly in light of the existential given of freedom. According to May (1981), "Freedom is thus more than a value itself: *it underlies the possibility of valuing*; *it is basic to our capacity to value*" (p. 6). Freedom, in other words, is essential to the concept of meaning. To assert one's freedom is an act of courage. May is talking about freedom at the existential level; however, existential freedom is impacted by social and political freedom. While no limitations on social and political freedom can completely destroy one's existential freedom, one's experience of existential freedom is necessarily impacted by one's social and political freedom.

The distinction in freedom is more evident when contextualized in a comparison between Bahamian slaves and individuals with privilege. Privilege is commonly associated with *White privilege*, understood as resulting from "an identifiable racial hierarchy that creates a system of social advantages or 'special rights' for Whites based primarily on race rather than merit" (Neville, Worthington, & Spanierman, 2001, p. 261). We can speak of many other forms of privilege, including gender, religious, social economic status, and sexual orientation. A wealthy White heterosexual Christian male benefits from various types of privilege in the United States and most of Western culture. While privilege is most recognizable in extreme examples, its impact remains relevant at more nuanced levels.

In the United States, all cultural groups do not experience the same political and social freedoms. Only recently have lesbian, gay, bisexual, transgender, and queer (LGBTQ) individuals been granted the freedom to marry. Many people of color do not experience the same freedom to live wherever they would choose without being subjected to significant prejudice and discrimination. Similarly, many Black and Latino males as well as many Muslims do not experience the same *freedom from* various experiences, such as being pulled over by the police for looking suspicious due to the color of their skin or receiving extra scrutiny when passing through security. For individuals with privileged backgrounds, it makes sense to utilize the political and legal systems to advocate for their rights and freedoms. However, for many marginalized groups, the political and legal systems have not been sources of protection and, oftentimes, have been experienced as sources of oppression (Hoffman, Granger, Vallejos, & Moats, 2016). In order to advocate for their freedom, it has been necessary to speak out in ways that draw attention to the injustices and impingements upon their freedom.

At the time of this writing, there has been an increased period of protests about police violence, particularly as it has disproportionally impacted people of color.[1] The protests are understood and experienced differently by many people of privilege and people from marginalized groups (Hoffman, et al., 2016). It is common for people coming from privileged backgrounds to criticize protestors for any behaviors that break the law or create inconvenience for others. They would, it seems, prefer for protesters to advocate through the political and legal system instead of protests. However, this fails to take into account that the political and legal systems have not protected marginalized groups the way it has privileged groups. If the protests were quiet and civil, or comprised of merely writing letters to legislatures, it is unlikely that it would draw enough attention to bring about any significant change. As stated by Martin Luther King, Jr. (1967), "riot is the language of the unheard" (p. 7). For individuals with privilege, freedom comes with fewer constraints, anxieties, and fears; freedom requires less courage.

Ethnicity and privilege significantly influence the meaning associated with the recent protests. Frequently, when such issues are discussed rationally or debated, individuals become more rooted in their positions instead of moving toward empathy, understanding, and change (Hoffman & Granger, 2015). This has a greater impact upon the individuals lacking privilege who are advocating for change as compared with the individuals who are impacted less and not motivated to seek change. In this context, to seek freedom is to assert meaning. The protests, much like the Bahamian festival of Junkanoo, can be powerful expressions and sources of collective meaning. They represent a way of transforming one's suffering into positive change while bringing meaning and honor to those who have lost their lives. Furthermore, they can be symbolic of self-esteem, pride in one's culture, and the courage to stand up for oneself.

---

[1] The increased frequency of protests began after George Zimmerman, acting as part of a neighborhood watch group, shot and killed Trayvon Martin, an unarmed Black teenager. Subsequently, several other unarmed Black males were killed by police officers, including Michael Brown, Tamir Rice (age 12), Eric Garner, and numerous others. Many of the individuals who killed the unarmed Black males were not indicted or not convicted, increasing the outrage. Compared to previous similar incidents, these more recent events have been widely publicized through the national media as well as social media.

Identity, Character, and the Construction of Meaning

Existential psychology and positive psychology are both concerned with character and integrity (Mendelowitz, 2008; Peterson & Seligman, 2004), which has important implications for meaning. For Frankl (1984), the good life is the meaningful life, and meaning is an important basis for attaining happiness. Character in this context can be a basis for meaning and the good life. The ongoing struggle for civil rights in the United States has a parallel psychological struggle for marginalized groups. It is common for people from marginalized groups to experience being viewed as having a deficit in character based upon prejudices or falling outside the normal behavior as defined by the majority group. LGBTQ individuals may be perceived as lacking character relevant to sexual morality. Many people of color are viewed as being lazy and dependent upon the government as well as frequently labeled as suspicious and more likely engaged in criminal activity. This struggle continues to be immortalized in the words of Martin Luther King, Jr., who dreamed that people would "Not be judged by the color of their skin but by the content of their character" (King, 2001). Judgments based on skin color make genuine character invisible. Dealing with the myriad of prejudgmental views of character determined by prejudice and, in turn, acts of racism create psychological tension in individuals who feel invisible.

A common struggle for people of color and other individuals in marginalized groups is feeling the pressure to conform, which often results in a loss of identity through attempts to adapt to pressures from the mainstream. DuBois (1903/1994), in his classic *The Souls of Black Folk*, stated, "[the African American] simply wishes to make it possible for a man to be both a Negro and an American, without being cursed and spit upon by his fellows, without having the doors of opportunity closed roughly in his face" (p. 3). Sadly, this statement continues to ring true today. The conflict, however, has shifted from an explicit to a more implicit level of communication.

Meaning variations relative to culture are governed by context to the extent that even subtle fluctuations in language usage, such as pitch, can be defense mechanisms so inherent among individuals of one group that they often go unnoticed by members of another group. Because of their experiences with racism, sexism, and heterosexism, many marginalized groups have developed heightened perceptual wisdom that allows them to more accurately discern the hidden rules of language (Sue & Sue, 2003) and, along with it, important hidden or subtle levels of meaning. At times, this discernment has been misconstrued as paranoia; however, this power of perception has been an important skill developed that allows people from marginalized groups to protect themselves.

Heightened perceptual wisdom has been associated with the ability to accurately read nonverbal communications (Hanna, Talley, & Guindon, 2000). Interestingly, people of color and women have been found to be better "readers" of nonverbal cues than White men (Jenkins, 1982; Pearson, 1985; Weber, 1985). Given this, they are more likely to create meaning in part through a different process. According to Sue

(2010), the greater attunement to nonverbal communication connects with the need of those with less power in interpersonal relationships to understand those who have the power in order to influence or determine their lives. According to Payne (2012), most rules are hidden and represent the unspoken cues and habits of a group. Knowing and following the rules, even if primarily at an implicit level, is part of belonging to the group. These rules, too, can be a way of exerting power. According to Sue (2010), many people of color, women, and those who are LGBTQ lose their identity through pressure to act White, male, or straight or to leave aspects of their cultural identity behind. These pressures are often communicated through implicit, nonverbal communication.

Nonverbal and implicit communications have significant implications for the construction of meaning. Granger's (2011) research on the impact of racial microaggressions among African American males in higher education speaks to the power of the implicit in multicultural communication. His research provided evidence that microaggressions, which often occur at the implicit and nonverbal levels of communication, can have significant impact upon African American males including impacting the meaning they associate with education and their valuing of themselves. Similarly, Hoffman and Cleare-Hoffman (2011) discuss cultural differences in the way emotions are experienced and expressed (see also Campos & Shenhav, 2014). Individuals who come from cultural backgrounds that are more emotionally expressive are frequently viewed as having emotional problems based upon their different style of embodying and communicating emotions. Instead of being recognized as a cultural difference, these cultural differences are pathologized. When one's cultural approach to emotional expression is pathologized, this can have implications for cultural identity development and the meaning one places on their cultural group. Additionally, it can have implications for one's self-esteem and self-concept. The de-emphasis on pathologizing in existential psychology and positive psychology, along with existential psychology's avoidance of pathologizing emotions in general (Hoffman, 2009b), can be beneficial in working with clients who have had negative experiences around cultural variations pertaining to the expression of emotion.

While pathologizing can have negative consequences for self-identity and meaning, Horne, Puckett, Apter, and Levitt (2014) note that many LGBTQ individuals have strengths rooted in the complex meanings they derive in part from their minority sexual orientation. Similarly, Boscoe-Huffman (2010) found that a perceived negative impact from religious individuals and organizations relevant to one's sexual orientation was associated with stronger relationships for same-sex couples. While this meaning often emerges through suffering, it is often rooted in relationships and engagement with the LGBTQ community. Furthermore, as this meaning develops, it serves to promote well-being as well as aiding resiliency.

For clinicians, it is not sufficient to recognize that meaning can play a role in facilitating well-being as well as serving as a protective factor when experiencing prejudice and discrimination. If solely rooted in this recognition, it becomes easy to encourage superficial approaches to meaning that are not as likely to be well received by clients and are less likely to be sustaining. The development of meaning in the face of prejudice and discrimination is a complex and nuanced process. For many individuals, it may involve one's cultural identity development as well as other aspects of one's identity, relationships within one's own cultural group as well as relationships with those in other cultural groups, and working through challenges to one's worldview and views of human nature. Additionally, there may be complexities pertaining to cultural variations in the experience and expression of emotions, differences in family dynamics, and other cultural differences.

It is not sufficient for clinicians to be aware of the universality of the existential givens or character strengths and virtues. Rather, clinicians must be aware of the cultural variations in how these are understood, experienced, and applied. Concepts familiar to clinicians may be experienced quite differently by individuals from other cultures.

Clinical Applications

The preceding history and foundation provides a basis to consider approaches for addressing meaning with multicultural considerations. Frankl (1984) did not believe that all forms of meaning were equal. He prioritized meaning derived from work, love/relationship, or attained through suffering. Similarly, Hoffman has differentiated between sustaining meaning and non-sustaining meaning (Hoffman, 2009b; Hoffman, Stewart, Warren, & Meek, 2014). Accordingly, sustaining meaning is better able to help one cope with trauma and suffering. Additionally, sustaining meaning is more likely to result in well-being and flourishing. Given that not all types of meaning are equal, it is important that clinicians are able to recognize and work with the complexity of meaning and meaning systems with particular consideration to culture.

Analyzing Meaning

> What is the ideal for mental health, then? A lived, compelling illusion that does not lie about life, death, and reality, one honest enough to follow its own commandments: I mean, not to kill, not to take the lives of others to justify itself. (Becker, 1972, p. 204)

Hoffman (2009b) advocates that the Becker quote above provides important insight relevant to analyzing meaning in the context of well-being. Well-being, or the ideal for mental health, is an illusion according to Becker, or what May (1991) called myth. In other words, it is not something that is necessarily provable, but is something that guides one's life and is embodied (see also Emmons, 1999; Tillich, 1957). Meaning has the potential to be constructive or destructive. This, in part, is why character, integrity, and virtues need to be considered along with meaning. Finally, Becker's quote suggests that some types of meaning may not be sustainable, or may not be as effective in terms of coping and promoting well-being. The role of the therapist is not merely to help clients discover or create meaning, but also to analyze their meaning.

As clients consider their current meaning systems, and consider changes to their meaning systems, it is important to recognize that adding meaning is not as simple as merely ascribing to a particular meaning. Tillich (1957) refers to being grasped by or surrendering to the ultimate concern. This indicates a meaning that is holistically embodied, not just cognitively ascribed to. At times, there may be a discrepancy between what clients state as their meaning or ultimate concern, and what is evident as their ultimate concern through analysis of their values, emotions, and behaviors. For example, people may state that family and relationships are their primary meaning, yet financial security or respect from others serves as a more primary influence upon their emotions and behaviors. A skilled therapist can work with a client to help them examine whether they are not living in accordance with their values, which often creates anxiety and guilt, or whether they are not fully aware of their deeper implicit meanings. Additionally, therapists can help clients recognize conflicting meanings and values. Building from this recognition, clients can work to reconsider their meaning systems and their choices.

Individual and Collective Meaning

In the United States and much of the West, there generally is a bias toward individual meanings and freedoms over collective meanings and freedoms. These biases can even emerge within the therapy process. Clients adhering to cultural meaning systems may even be pathologized in accordance with this bias. For example, clients who follow their cultural values may be labeled as "enmeshed" or viewed as not having successfully individuated from their family of origin. When working with clients to analyze and evaluate their meaning systems, therapists intentionally, or even unintentionally, push them toward individual meaning systems. Consider the following vignette:

> Feng is a Chinese college student attending a university in the United States. While going to college, he is also working many hours in order to send money back to his parents in China. He was an only child and his parents often worked long hours to make enough money for him to go to college in the United States. His friends encourage him to spend more of the money he is making on himself. Although he begins taking his friends' advice, he becomes preoccupied with feelings of guilt for doing this. When his parents find out they become upset and say he is being selfish. Feng's anxiety further increases and he seeks therapy at the university's counseling center.

In this vignette, Feng is struggling between different cultures and meaning systems. From a Western psychology perspective, many therapists might view Feng as being overly dependent and encourage him to make his own decisions based upon what he wants; however, this may be in conflict with his values and meaning system. In many cultures that are often identified as collectivist, the values of harmony and the family's happiness are prioritized over the happiness of the individual. This is preference, not pathology. As Chan (2009) notes, values such as harmony are quite beautiful when they are openly ascribed to; however, they can also become problematic, especially when they are forced as a defense against anxiety and fear. It is not the value itself, but rather the particular expression of the value that is the problem. For Feng, valuing his family's happiness over his own is not necessarily the problem. Therapists working with diverse clients must be able to recognize and appreciate diverse forms of meaning. Often, without some cultural knowledge of the differences, these therapists may not recognize these different values when they are presented.

Meaning, Prejudice, Discrimination, and Microaggressions

Therapists, particularly therapists with limited training and development on multicultural issues, often struggle dealing with clients who are experiencing prejudice and discrimination. Meaning can be an important variable in helping clients face prejudice and discrimination; however, misapplications can be problematic. Prilleltensky and Fox (1997), as well as Hillman and Venture (1992), warn that therapists often end up promoting and reinforcing the status quo (i.e., prejudice and discrimination) when working with clients who are facing injustices, such as prejudice and discrimination. Consider the following brief vignette:

> Khalil is a 28-year old Muslim man originally from Pakistan. He relocated with his family as a child and is now a United States citizen. He was referred to therapy by his employer. In recent months, Khalil began experiencing frequent microaggressions from his colleagues and supervisor, including people being critical of his religion, his daily prayers, and asking if he knew any terrorists. His supervisor became concerned when Khalil started to become irritable in response to these microaggressions. Even though he appeared less angry and more controlled than many of the perpetrators of these statements, his supervisor called Khalil in to discuss his anger issues. Khalil was warned that his irritability, as well as his daily prayers, were making his co-workers uncomfortable and he was told that he could lose his job if he did not find ways to get along better with his peers without making them uncomfortable. He was referred to therapy for anger management.

In this vignette, the implicit message in the referral suggests the therapist should help the client to improve his ability to cope with the prejudice he is experiencing and better control his irritability in the face of this. To accomplish this implicit goal from the referral source, the therapist could assist Khalil in developing coping strategies as well as meaning in the face of suffering caused by the inappropriate actions. From a hedonic well-being perspective (i.e., decreasing negative emotions, increasing positive emotions), this approach could be considered successful if the client became less negatively impacted by his co-workers' and supervisor's actions. Various meaning strategies, including helping Khalil see himself as a survivor or taking the high road, may help provide meaning that would help him cope with his current situation. However, from the perspective of critical psychology, this could be seen as empowering the status quo and an oppressive system. Similarly, from a eudaimonic perspective, this could be understood as sacrificing character, integrity, and deeper sources of meaning in order to achieve a more superficial happiness.

A therapy strategy emphasizing eudaimonic meaning and well-being would prioritize different strategies. As noted previously, eudaimonic perspectives value character, integrity, and values, suggesting a different starting point although not necessarily a different end. The therapist embracing this approach would begin by collaborating with the client to clarify Khalil's values and the implications of various responses to his situation, which is, in essence, an analysis of meaning. It may be, in considering the breadth of options, that Khalil's preference is the hedonic approach to using meaning to cope with suffering. However, it is also possible that Khalil may find deeper meaning through alternative ways to respond, including considering ways to confront the prejudice and discrimination in a manner consistent with his integrity and character.

In the Bahamian festival of Junkanoo and the protest movements, such as Black Lives Matter, deep and sustaining meaning can be found in standing up to and embracing suffering. This is distinct from utilizing meaning as a coping mechanism, but rather represents finding meaning through suffering. These meanings transform the experience of suffering (Hoffman, 2009b) while also promoting well-being and even a sense of joy. From an existential perspective it is too simplistic to categorize emotions as "good or bad," "pleasant or unpleasant." Emotions are complex experiences, and suffering and joy are often intimately connected. It is possible that Khalil may find greater joy through finding ways to confront and challenge the oppressive system in which he is experiencing prejudice and discrimination.

As is hopefully evident, the contrast presented between the hedonic and eudaimonic strategies is somewhat oversimplified in order to illustrate the difference. Engaging in a meaning and values analysis may lead Khalil to find meaning that would help him cope with his situation and keep his job. Particularly if he needs the job to support his family and does not have other employment options, this may be the way he chooses to face his situation. As therapists concerned with meaning, it is important to avoid imposing the therapist's meanings upon clients and, instead, work with them to find the meanings they choose to embrace. These choices are often influenced by one's culture. When this is the case, it is important that therapists do not pathologize client decisions to align with and embrace their cultural values.

Conclusion and Key Takeaways

Meaning is an important, although somewhat neglected, concept in examining multicultural issues in psychology. Being culturally competent as a therapist is about more than just respecting differences. Therapists must possess the knowledge and skills to implement a culturally sensitive attitude. This is true for positive psychologists and existential psychologists as well. In this chapter, building upon some theoretical foundations, we discussed several practical implications for working with diverse clients pertaining to meaning:

- When analyzing meaning, therapists must be able to recognize cultural variations in meaning, including varied sources of meaning and different ways that particular meanings can be understood and experienced in diverse cultural contexts.

- Much of Western psychology, including existential and positive psychology, has privileged individualist perspectives on meaning. Especially when working with diverse clientele, therapists need to be careful to not devalue collective sources of meaning.
- Hedonic and eudaimonic views of well-being may, at times, connect with cultural differences. It is important for therapists to recognize the difference between hedonic and eudaimonic approaches to dealing with complex meanings.
- Many psychological constructs with meanings that are often taken for granted as being universal, such as freedom and responsibility, have significant cultural variations. Without some cultural knowledge base, it can be difficult to recognize these differences when they present themselves. It is important that therapists develop an adequate foundation of cultural knowledge and remain open to continued learning in order to practice in a culturally sensitive manner.

Acknowledgment The authors would like to thank Heatherlyn Cleare-Hoffman and Brent Dean Robbins for the feedback on various drafts of the manuscript.

References

Batthyany, A., & Russo-Netzer, P. (Eds.). (2014). *Meaning in positive and existential psychology*. New York, NY: Springer.

Becker, E. (1972). *The denial of death*. New York, NY: The Free Press.

Bohart, A., & Greening, T. (2001). Comment: Humanistic psychology and positive psychology. *American Psychologist, 34*, 357–367.

Boscoe-Huffman, S. (2010). *An examination of religious impact on the support and maintenance of same-sex relationships* (doctoral dissertation). ProQuest Dissertations and Thesis database (UMI No. 756746035).

Campos, B., & Shenhav, S. (2014). Relationships in multicultural contexts. In J. T. Pedrotti & L. M. Edwards (Eds.), *Perspectives on the intersection of multicultural and positive psychology* (pp. 93–105). New York, NY: Springer.

Chan, A. (2009). In harmony with the sky: Implications for existential psychology. In L. Hoffman, M. Yang, F. J. Kaklauskas, & A. Chan (Eds.), *Existential psychology East-West* (pp. 307–325). Colorado Springs, CO: University of the Rockies Press.

Christopher, J. C., & Howe, K. L. (2014). Future directions for a more multiculturally competent (and humble) positive psychology. In J. T. Pedrotti & L. M. Edwards (Eds.), *Perspectives on the intersection of multicultural and positive psychology* (pp. 253–266). New York, NY: Springer.

Churchill, S. D. (2014). At the crossroads of humanistic psychology and positive psychology. *The Humanistic Psychologist, 42*, 1–5. doi:10.1080/08873267.2014.891902

Cleare-Hoffman, H. (2009). Junkanoo: A Bahamian cultural myth. In L. Hoffman, M. Yang, F. J. Kaklauskas, & A. Chan (Eds.), *Existential psychology East-West* (pp. 363–372). Colorado Springs, CO: University of the Rockies Press.

Cooper, M. (2003). *Existential therapies*. Thousand Oaks, CA: Sage.

Downey, C. A., & Chang, E. C. (2014). History of cultural context in positive psychology: We finally come to the start of the journey. In J. T. Pedrotti & L. M. Edwards (Eds.), *Perspectives on the intersection of multiculturalism and positive psychology* (pp. 3–16). New York, NY: Springer.

DuBois, W. E. B. (1994). *The souls of black folk*. New York, NY: Dover (Original work published in 1903).

Emmons, R. A. (1999). *The psychology of ultimate concerns: Motivation and spirituality in personality*. New York, NY: Guilford Press.

Frankl, V. E. (1984). *Man's search for meaning* (3rd ed.). New York, NY: Touchstone.

Frankl, V. E. (2000). *Man's search for ultimate meaning*. Cambridge, MA: Perseus.

Friedman, H. (2008). Humanistic and positive psychology: The methodological and epistemological divide. *The Humanistic Psychologist, 36*, 113–126.

Gilligan, C. (1977). In a different voice: Women's conceptions of self and of morality. *Harvard Educational Review, 47*(4), 481–517.

Granger, N. (2011). *Perceptions of racial microaggressions among African American males in higher education: A heuristic inquiry*. Ann Arbor, MI: ProQuest LLC.

Greening, T. (1992). Existential challenges and responses. *The Humanistic Psychologist, 20*(1), 111–115.

Hanna, F. J., Talley, W. B., & Guindon, M. H. (2000). The power of perception: Toward a model of cultural oppression and liberation. *Journal of Counseling and Development, 78*, 430–446.

Heery, M. (2009). Global authenticity. In L. Hoffman, M. Yang, F. J. Kaklauskas, & A. Chan (Eds.), *Existential psychology East-West* (pp. 205–219). Colorado Springs, CO: University of the Rockies Press.

Helminiak, D., Hoffman, L., & Dodson, E. (2012). A critique of the "theistic psychology" movement as exemplified in Bartz (2009) "Theistic Existential Psychology.". *The Humanistic Psychologist, 40*, 179–196. doi:10.1080/08873267.2012.672351

Hillman, J., & Venture, M. (1992). *We've had a hundred years of psychotherapy – And the world's getting worse*. San Francisco, CA: Harper.

Ho, S. M. Y., Rochelle, T. L., Law, L. S. C., Duan, W., Bai, Y., & Shih, S.-M. (2014). Methodological issues in positive psychology research with diverse populations: Exploring strengths among Chinese adults. In A. Batthyany & P. Russo-Netzer (Eds.), *Meaning in positive and existential psychology* (pp. 45–57). New York, NY: Springer.

Hoffman, L. (2009a). Gordo's ghost: An introduction to existential perspectives on myths. In L. Hoffman, M. Yang, F. J. Kaklauskas, & A. Chan (Eds.), *Existential psychology East-West* (pp. 259–274). Colorado Springs, CO: University of the Rockies Press.

Hoffman, L. (2009b). Introduction to existential psychotherapy in a cross-cultural context: An East-West dialogue. In L. Hoffman, M. Yang, F. J. Kaklauskas, & A. Chan (Eds.), *Existential psychology East-West* (pp. 1–67). Colorado Springs, CO: University of the Rockies Press.

Hoffman, L. (2016). Multiculturalism and humanistic psychology: From neglected to epistemological and ontological diversity. *The Humanistic Psychologist, 44*, 56–71.

Hoffman, L., & Cleare-Hoffman, H. P. (2011). Existential therapy and emotions: Lessons from cross-cultural exchange. *The Humanistic Psychologist, 39*, 261–267.

Hoffman, L., Cleare-Hoffman, H. P., & Jackson, T. (2014). Humanistic psychology and multiculturalism: History, current status, and advancements. In K. J. Schneider, J. F. Pierson, & J. F. T. Bugental (Eds.), *The handbook of humanistic psychology: Theory, research, and practice* (2nd ed., pp. 41–55). Thousand Oaks, CA: Sage.

Hoffman, L., & Granger, N., Jr. (2015). Introduction. In L. Hoffman & N. Granger Jr. (Eds.), *Stay awhile: Poetic narratives on multiculturalism and diversity* (pp. 9–17). Colorado Springs, CO: University Professors Press.

Hoffman, L., Granger, N., Jr., Vallejos, L., & Moats, M. (2016). An existential-humanistic perspective on Black Lives Matter and contemporary protest movements. *Journal of Humanistic Psychology*. doi:10.1177/0022167816652273

Hoffman, L., & Mansilla, M. (2015). Rebooting positive psychology [Review of perspectives on the intersection of multiculturalism and positive psychology]. *PsycCRITIQUES-Contemporary Psychology: APA Review of Books, 60*(25). doi:10.1037/a0039265

Hoffman, L., Stewart, S., Warren, D. M., & Meek, L. (2014). Toward a sustainable myth of self: An existential response to the postmodern condition. In K. J. Schneider, J. F. Pierson, & J. F. T. Bugental (Eds.), *The handbook of humanistic psychology: Theory, research, and practice* (2nd ed., pp. 105–133). Thousand Oaks, CA: Sage.

Hoffman, L., Vallejos, L., Cleare-Hoffman, H. P., & Rubin, S. (2015). Emotion, relationship, and meaning as core existential practice: Evidence-based foundations. *Journal of Contemporary Psychotherapy, 45*, 11–20. doi:10.1007/s10879-014-9277-9

Hoffman, L., Yang, M., Kaklauskas, F. J., & Chan, A. (Eds.). (2009). *Existential psychology East-West*. Colorado Springs, CO: University of the Rockies Press.

Horne, S. G., Puckett, J. A., Apter, R., & Levitt, H. (2014). Positive psychology and LGBTQ populations. In J. T. Pedrotti & L. Edwards (Eds.), *Perspectives on the intersection of positive psychology and multiculturalism* (pp. 189–204). New York: Springer.

Jackson, T. (2012, March). The tale of two cities: Humanistic psychology within a cultural context. In L. Hoffman (Chair), *The collective and individual in humanistic psychology: Implications of moving beyond the individualistic bias*. Symposium presented at the 5th Annual Society for Humanistic Psychology Conference, Pittsburgh, PA.

Jaspers, K. (2001). *The question of German guilt* (E. B. Ashton, Trans.). New York, NY: Fordham University Press. (Original work published in 1947).

Jenkins, A. H. (1982). *The psychology of the Afro-American*. New York, NY: Pergamon.

Kaklauskas, F. J., & Olson, E. (2009). Kisagotami, Buddha, and mustard seeds: An existential psychological perspective. In L. Hoffman, M. Yang, F. J. Kaklauskas, & A. Chan (Eds.), *Existential psychology East-West* (pp. 351–362). Colorado Springs, CO: University of the Rockies Press.

Kim, J., Seto, E., Davis, W. E., & Hicks, J. A. (2014). Positive and existential psychological approaches to the experience of meaning in life. In A. Batthyany & P. Russo-Netzer (Eds.), *Meaning in positive and existential psychology* (pp. 221–233). New York, NY: Springer.

King, M. L., Jr. (1967). *The other America* (speech transcript). Retrieved from http://auroraforum.stanford.edu/files/transcripts/Aurora_Forum_Transcript_Martin_Luther_King_The_Other_America_Speech_at_Stanford_04.15.07.pdf

King, M. L., Jr. (2001). I have a dream. In C. Carson & K. Shepard (Eds.), *A call to conscience: The landmark speeches of Dr. Martin Luther King, Jr*. New York, NY: Hachette Book Group.

Kohlberg, L. (1981). *Essays on moral development. Vol. I: The philosophy of moral development*. San Francisco, CA: Harper & Row.

Linley, P., & Joseph, S. (2004). Preface. In P. Linley & S. Joseph (Eds.), *Positive psychology in practice* (pp. xv–xvi). Hoboken, NJ: Wiley.

MacKenzie, M. J., & Baumeister, R. F. (2014). Meaning in life: Nature, needs, and myths. In A. Batthyany & P. Russo-Netzer (Eds.), *Meaning in positive and existential psychology* (pp. 25–37). New York, NY: Springer.

Maddi, S. R. (2014). Hardiness leads to meaningful growth through what is learned when resolving stressful circumstances. In A. Batthyany & P. Russo-Netzer (Eds.), *Meaning in positive and existential psychology* (pp. 291–302). New York, NY: Springer.

Mascaro, N. (2014). Meaning sensitive psychotherapy: Binding clinical, existential, and positive psychological perspectives. In A. Batthyany & P. Russo-Netzer (Eds.), *Meaning in positive and existential psychology* (pp. 269–289). New York, NY: Springer.

May, R. (1981). *Freedom and destiny*. New York, NY: Norton & Company.

May, R. (1991). *The cry for myth*. New York, NY: Delta.

Mendelowitz, E. (2008). *Ethics and Lao-Tzu: Intimations of character*. Colorado Springs, CO: University of the Rockies Press.

Neville, H. A., & Mobley, M. (2001). Social identities in contexts: An ecological model of multicultural counseling psychology processes. *The Counseling Psychologist, 29*, 471–486.

Neville, H. A., Worthington, R. L., & Spanierman, L. B. (2001). Race, power, and multicultural counseling psychology: Understanding White privilege and color-blind racial attitudes. In J. G. Ponterotto, J. M. Casas, L. A. Suzuki, & C. M. Alexander (Eds.), *Handbook of multicultural counseling* (2nd ed., pp. 257–288). Thousand Oaks, CA: Sage.

Nielsen, T. W. (2014). Finding the keys to meaningful happiness: Beyond being happy or sad is to love. In A. Batthyany & P. Russo-Netzer (Eds.), *Meaning in positive and existential psychology* (pp. 81–93). New York, NY: Springer.

Nietzsche, F. (1966). *Thus spoke Zarathustra: A book for none and all* (W. Kaufmann, Trans.). New York, NY: Penguin Books. (Original work published in 1885).
Payne, R. K. (2012). *A framework for understanding poverty: 10 actions to educate students.* Highlands, TX: aha! Process.
Pearson, J. C. (1985). *Gender and communication.* Dubuque, IA: W. C. Brown.
Pedrotti, J. T., & Edwards, L. M. (Eds.). (2014). *Perspectives on the intersection of multiculturalism and positive psychology.* New York, NY: Springer.
Pedrotti, J. T., Edwards, L. M., & Lopez, S. J. (2009). Positive psychology within a cultural context. In P. E. Nathan (Ed.), *Oxford handbook of positive psychology* (pp. 49–57). New York, NY: Oxford University Press.
Peterson, C., & Seligman, M. E. P. (2004). *Character strengths and virtues: A handbook and classification.* Washington, DC: American Psychological Association.
Prilleltensky, I., & Fox, D. (1997). Introducing critical psychology: Values, assumptions, and the status quo. In D. Fox & I. Prilleltensky (Eds.), *Critical psychology: An introduction* (pp. 3–20). Thousand Oaks, CA: Sage.
Robbins, B. D. (2008). What is the good life? Positive psychology and the renaissance of humanistic psychology. *The Humanistic Psychologist, 36,* 96–112. doi:10.1080/08873260802110988
Robbins, B. D. (2015). Building bridges between humanistic and positive psychology. In S. Joseph (Ed.), *Positive psychology in practice: Promoting human flourishing in work, health, education, and everyday life* (2nd ed., pp. 31–45). Hoboken, NJ: Wiley.
Ryff, C. D., & Singer, B. H. (2008). Know thyself and become what you are: A eudaimonic approach to psychological well-being. *Journal of Happiness Studies, 9,* 13–39.
Sandage, S. J., Hill, P. C., & Vang, H. C. (2003). Toward a multicultural positive psychology: Indigenous forgiveness and Hmong culture. *The Counseling Psychologist, 31*(5), 564–592. doi:10.1177/0011000003256350
Seligman, M. E. P., & Csikszentmihalyi, M. (2000). Positive psychology: An introduction. *American Psychologist, 55,* 5–14.
Sheu, H. B. (2014). Affective well-being viewed through a lens of race and ethnicity. In J.T. Pedrotti & L. M. Edwards (Eds.), *Perspectives on the intersection of multiculturalism and positive psychology* (pp. xv–xviii). London: Springer.
Steger, M. F. (2013). Assessing meaning and quality of life. In K. F. Geisinger (Ed.), *APA handbook of testing and assessment in psychology* (Vol. 2, pp. 489–499). Washington, DC: American Psychological Association.
Steger, M. F., Shin, J. Y., Shim, Y., & Fitch-Martin, A. (2013). Is meaning in life a flagship indicator of well-being? In A. S. Waterman (Ed.), *The best within us: Positive psychology perspectives on eudaimonia* (pp. 159–182). Washington, DC: American Psychological Association.
Sue, D. W. (2010). *Microaggressions in everyday life: Race, gender, and sexual orientation.* Hoboken, NJ: Wiley.
Sue, D. W., & Sue, D. (2003). *Counseling the culturally diverse: Theory and practice* (4th ed.). New York, NY: John Wiley & Sons.
Sundararajan, L. (2008). Toward a reflexive positive psychology: Insights from the Chinese Buddhist notion of emptiness. *Theory & Psychology, 18*(5), 655–674. doi:10.1177/0959354308093400
Tanner, K. (1997). *Theories of culture: A new agenda for theology.* Minneapolis, MN: Fortress Press.
Tillich, P. (1957). *Dynamics of faith.* New York, NY: Harper Touchstone.
Vontress, C. E., & Epp, L. R. (2014). Existential cross-cultural counseling: The courage to be an existential counselor. In K. J. Schneider, J. F. T. Pierson, & J. Bugental (Eds.), *Handbook of humanistic psychology: Theory, research, and practice* (2nd ed., pp. 473–489). Thousand Oaks, CA: Sage.
Waterman, A. S. (2013a). The humanistic psychology-positive psychology divide: Contrasts in philosophical foundations. *American Psychologist, 68,* 124–133. doi:10.1037/a0032168
Waterman, A. S. (Ed.). (2013b). *The best within us: Positive psychology perspectives on eudaimonia.* Washington, DC: American Psychological Association.

Weber, S. N. (1985). The need to be: The socio-cultural significance of Black language. In L. A. Samovar & R. E. Porter (Eds.), *Intercultural communication: A reader* (pp. 232–242). Belmont, CA: Wadsworth.

Wong, P. T. P. (2012). Toward a dual-systems model of what makes life worth living. In P. T. P. Wong (Ed.), *The human quest for meaning: Theories, research, and applications* (2nd ed., pp. 3–22). New York, NY: Routledge.

Wong, P. T. P. (2014). Viktor Frankl's meaning-seeking model and positive psychology. In A. Batthyany & P. Russo-Netzer (Eds.), *Meaning in positive and existential psychology* (pp. 149–184). New York, NY: Springer.

Yalom, I. D. (1980). *Existential psychotherapy*. New York, NY: Basic Books.

Yang, M., & Hoffman, L. (2011). Introduction to the special section on the First International Conference on Existential Psychology. *The Humanistic Psychologist, 39*, 236–239.

Yang, M., & Hoffman, L. (2014, August). *Training and practice in an international context*. In C. N. Shealy (Chair), International humanistic psychology: Implications and applications for research and practice. Symposium presented at the 122nd Annual Convention of the American Psychological Association, Washington, DC.

Practices of Meaning-Changing Interventions: A Comprehensive Matrix

Dmitry Leontiev

The problem of personal meaning seems to be now at the peak of its popularity (see, e.g., Schnell, 2014). In the past century, a number of mostly marginal approaches tried to make sense of this multifaceted concept, without much reference to each other (Leontiev, 1996); Viktor Frankl's (1969) logotherapy was the most convincing among them, and it has added the issue of meaning to the agenda of human sciences and public discourse. Nevertheless, by the end of the last century meaning was not a welcome topic in academic publications. It was positive psychology that made this issue academically legitimate after Martin Seligman (2002) announced meaningful life as one of the three aspects of the life worth living, probably the most important one. A period of latency resulted in seven books on meaning being released by major publishers between 2012 and 2015 as compared to only four having been published during the previous 30 years! (see Leontiev, 2016b).

Much has been said about the complexity of the issue; psychologists are still far from a uniform definition, though we are progressing in this direction (ibid.). In my attempts to make ends meet by finding the common denominator between different views, I advocate the relational, or referential, view of meaning (Baumeister, 1991; Leontiev, 2013; Leontiev, 2016a; Nuttin, 1984). According to this view, the meaning of something is its relation to a broader superordinate context; all individual meanings are parts of an integrated network depicted through the metaphor of a web (Baumeister, 1991) or mycelium (Leontiev, 2013).

Here I would like to focus on the issue of whether meaning can be deliberately changed, directly or indirectly. This is the problem of meaning-focused intervention we often face not only in professional psychotherapy and counseling settings, but also in our everyday lives. By intervention I mean a deliberate action to modify a

---

D. Leontiev, Ph.D. (✉)
National Research University Higher School of Economics,
20 Myasnitskaya str., Moscow 101000, Russia
e-mail: dleontiev@hse.ru

process that might occur naturally, without any intervention, in order to direct it in a desirable direction or to make it fit some desirable parameters.

In the first part of this chapter, I discuss the general models of naturally occurring and deliberate meaning dynamics. This allows distinguishing the bases for classifying the forms of meaning-focused interventions. In the second part, I explicate an attempt at such a classification that may serve as a helpful heuristic tool for both researchers and practitioners.

Meaning and Meaning-Making

First, we need to define the original process to be modified, meaning-making, departing from the referential or relational viewpoint mentioned above.

The basic structure of meaning includes three components: the carrier of meaning (meaning of what?), the source of meaning (superordinate meaning-making context), and the relationship between them due to which the carrier gets its meaning from the source. The contexts may be impersonal and purely semantic, and we define the semantic meaning of something by verbalization, calling it by name. There may also be personal, existential contexts that give the carrier its personal meaning due to its place and role in the person's life. For instance, if I speak of my life as the carrier in question, the semantic meaning refers to the answer to the question, what is life, and the personal meaning refers to the answer to the question, what makes my life meaningful rather than meaningless.

It follows that different contexts suggest different meanings of the same carrier. To get an insight into something's meaning we have to reconstruct its source and relationship to the latter. To change the meaning of something we need to connect it to a different context.

The referential approach allows us to transcend the old dichotomy of seeking vs. construing meaning. We cannot speak of the meaning of something without placing it into some context. We may (1) find this context (and the meaning made by it) without seeking, as something self-evident; (2) seek and discover it, if it is not self-evident; (3) let it be imposed by other people or cultural frameworks (religions, ideologies, scientific or lay theories, myths, etc.); (4) deliberately construe it through our mental work. In all four cases some new meaning-making relationship is established between the carrier and the source; what differs is the way it is established: passively or actively, naturally or deliberately, having other people involved or not. Neither the carrier nor the source changes in the process, in any of the four variants. It is only the relationship between them that emerges as the outcome of this process.

Other-Intervention and Self-Intervention

Meaning-focused intervention is not only a way to help another person, but also a powerful self-help tool, the mental work of self-development. Indeed, we often face not only the task of discovering meaning but also that of changing the meaning of something for ourselves, e.g., trying to find any meaning in something we must do against our wishes, or trying to devaluate the broken relationship to make the divorce less painful. In processes such as positive reappraisal (Lazarus, 1966), construct revision (Kelly, 1970), situational reconstruction (Maddi & Kobasa, 1984), Socratic dialogue (Frankl, 1969), attitude modulation (Lukas, 2002), etc., we find a way, sometimes with the help of a counselor or therapist, sometimes on our own, to reconnect the current action to different meaning-making contexts, thus changing its meaning.

An important point is that the ways and devices we apply to our own mind and behavior for the reconstruction of meaning mirror the ones we apply to others to modify their meanings. This follows from Lev Vygotsky's (1983) cultural-historical theory that says, in particular, that a growing child learns to apply to others the techniques of controlling behavior they have previously applied to him/her; still later, he/she learns to apply these techniques to him/herself. In this way, the techniques of interpersonal control (manipulation, education) are transformed into the techniques of self-control, and the learning of imposed meanings is transformed into the self-construction of personal meaning. It will be demonstrated below that interpersonal meaning relations modification techniques (MRMT) used in education and manipulation do mirror intrapersonal MRMT as tools of volitional self-regulation (see also Leontiev, 1999).

Volition as Meaning-Focused Self-Regulation

The theory of volition as meaning-focused self-regulation has been developed by Russian scholar Vyacheslav Ivannikov (1991). Ivannikov combined two theoretical ideas of his predecessors. The first was Lev Vygotsky's distinction between lower and higher human mental functions: the former are involuntary and function on an impulsive basis; the latter are deliberate, voluntary, and mediated by their structure (Vygotsky, 1983; see also Aidman & Leontiev, 1991). This distinction is close to a more recent distinction of reflexive and reflective regulations (Carver & Scheier, 2002) or hot and cool regulatory systems (Metcalfe & Mischel, 1999). The second idea was Alexei N. Leontiev's theory (1978) of the meaning-making function of human motives, recently transformed by the present author into a theory of meaning and meaning relationships as the basis of all human motivation: incentives can direct and drive actions only because and inasmuch as they make sense, carrying some personal meaning in the context of the person's life-world (see Leontiev, 2012). If the meaning connection between them and our needs is broken, they lose their motivational power, like a stash of gold found by Robinson Crusoe on a ruined ship that cannot carry him away to where he can spend it.

Based on these ideas, Ivannikov's (1991) main argument was the following: the mechanism of voluntary regulation is a deliberate alteration of the personal meaning of a motive by linking it to additional meaning-making contexts. In other words, if we are aware that the motivation for doing something required from us is insufficient, we find or construe additional meaning-making contexts to connect our action to them, and this gives additional meaning and hence additional motivating power to the object of our activity. A prototype example can be found in Kurt Lewin's analysis of motivation for a child's behavior. Lewin (1935) stated that the inclusion of a task into another context, connecting it to something important for a child, may radically change "*the meaning, and together with it the valence, of the task*" (p. 168; italics added). This, Lewin says, is the only type of motivational intervention that implies no negative side consequences.

Ivannikov (1991) listed eight types of such meaning-based motivational interventions: (1) reappraisal of the significance of a motive; (2) changing the role or social position; (3) anticipation of the consequences of an action or nonaction; (4) appealing to symbols, rituals, other people, or a deity for support; (5) connecting the action to new motives and goals; (6) inclusion of the action in a more comprehensive and significant activity; (7) conditioning the action by the opportunity to subsequently fulfill something desired; (8) promises and oaths, self-approval or disapproval, comparison to other people, or fictional characters.

This list was composed on an inductive rather than on a deductive basis. Some of the devices listed are just other names for the general idea of connecting to a larger meaning-making context (1, 5, 6); others refer to specific types of meaning sources to connect the current action: social values and expectations (2, 4), anticipated future time perspective (3, 7), and self-conception (8). Very often the person does not see the connection of the current action to a distant perspective, to social norms and values, or to one's self-esteem, and its meaning is limited to immediate benefits and threats. However, when the work of volitional regulation allows these connections to be established, the stakes go up and the urge to fulfill the task becomes stronger. When John Locke (Locke, 1690/1999) three centuries ago discussed the question of why we often make bad choices we later regret, he found the following cause: we fail to anticipate the distant consequences of our actions and consider only immediate, usually beneficial, or pleasurable outcomes. Reconstructing and anticipating more distant consequences thus provide a cognitive tactic of connecting to broader contexts that may not only increase but also decrease the meaning and hence the motivating power of some goals.

In volitional self-regulation we apply meaning-focused interventions to ourselves in the same way we apply them to others. Such interventions may be restrictive, aimed at disconnecting the situation from broader meaning-making contexts; say, for example, when a salesperson urges us to hurry a decision because discounts are only active that day, or when a leader of a destructive sect urges his or her followers not to read anything except for special sectarian literature. The similarity of self-directed and other-directed interventions will be visible when I proceed with the classification of specific meaning-making practices.

Dimensions of Classification for Meaning-Focused Interventions

The distinction between *self-directed* vs. *other-directed* intervention is just one of several possible categorical dimensions for classifying meaning-focused interventions. Some other dimensions are to be specified before composing the list of intervention techniques.

The second important distinction is *formative* vs. *facilitative* intervention. The former refers to the type of interventions aimed at a special foreseeable outcome to be attained by a known algorithm. This type of intervention is best exemplified by skills training, programmed learning, cognitive-behavioral therapy, and neurolinguistic programming, among others. Facilitative interventions stimulate the processes of change but cannot determine their direction and outcomes. All kinds of group processes, from focus groups to group therapy, are based on facilitators turning all inputs from group members into mutual interventions of this kind. The latter, facilitation processes, can be formalized and put into algorithms only to a limited degree. Socrates' metaphor for this kind of psychological help was maieutics; that is, obstetrics. A facilitator is not the one who gives birth to a new insight, but rather a midwife assisting in this process. Facilitative interventions cannot bring a useful result per se; they may only push the client's psychological processes in the direction of growing complexity and self-organization, making him or her capable of solving problems of greater complexity than before. Existential problems can never be solved, to be sure, but the desired outcome would be elaborating a way of integrating these insoluble problems into one's world view and life strategy. Formative meaning-focused interventions are, accordingly, aimed at creating some definite, prescribed meaning, as in case of advertising or propaganda. Facilitative interventions do not claim to control the outcomes. It is the meaning-making process, rather than the meanings made, that is the target of these influences, supposing that more developed and elaborated meaning-making processes will help the person to make more flexible, diverse, and relevant meanings.

One more dimension refers to the intervention effect, namely, whether it is provided ad hoc, here and now, to modify the ongoing meaning-making processes and to provide an immediate result, or whether it is supposed to modify some latent psychological structures and process to bear fruits in the future. For example, if a friend or relative is planning to go into business or begin a personal relationship with a person who does not deserve to be trusted, I can share some discreditable information to make this person immediately change his/her mind. Perhaps, though, the issue is not urgent; I might just suspect that they may get involved in some relationship more than would be safe for them, and so I share the same discreditable information to encourage them to modify their attitude and prevent eventual erroneous decisions in the future. Accordingly, the intervention may be *immediate or prolonged by its effect*.

The fourth distinction of meaning-focused interventions refers to the mechanisms of interventions: *meaning insight* vs. *meaning making*. Meaning insight refers to the awareness of a meaning-making framework and the meaning connections of a given object, like discovering the hidden meaning of suppressed experiences in psychoanalysis or other interpretive work. Meaning making refers to the inclusion of new elements in an existing framework, like making sense of a goal through establishing its connection with some actual motive.

Some of these distinctions seem to overlap. However, to show their heuristic value, I combine all of them in Table 1; each cell of the table refers to some form of meaning-focused intervention. The next section will be devoted to providing phenomenological examples for each cell.

Table 1 Classification of meaning-focused interventions

		Meaning making		Meaning insight	
		Self-directed	Other-directed	Self-directed	Other-directed
Immediate effect	formative	1. Psychological defense (Freud), volitional regulation (Ivannikov)	2. Conditioning, priming.	9. Prejudiced interpretation	10. Prejudiced interpretation
Immediate effect	facilitative	3. Self-discipline training	4. Will education	11. Self-insight	12. Psychoanalysis
Prolonged effect	formative	5. Self-persuasion, search of merits or demerits in the object of an attitude	6. Stressing the merits (advertising) or demerits (defamation) of the object of an attitude	13. Positive reinterpretation (Peseschkian), positive reappraisal (Lazarus), Pollyanna effect	14. Socratic dialogue (Frankl)
Prolonged effect	facilitative	7. Meaning-based choice	8. Training of meaning-based choice	15. Focusing	16. In-depth psychotherapy

Meaning Relations Modification Techniques 1: Meaning-Making Devices

Probably the most typical everyday tactics of meaning-focused intervention are located in the upper left quadrant (1–4). They refer to the mechanisms of volitional regulation as presented above. Formative effects (1–2) result in changing the actual meaning of the current action, situation, or some object. The classic example of cell (1) is the famous Aesop's fable # 15 often used to illustrate rationalization as a defense mechanism: a fox who failed to reach grapes that were hanging too high devaluated the target, persuading himself that the grapes were unripe. Indeed, this alters its meaning and justifies cancelling the attempt without a feeling of failure. An opposite situation of (1) is exemplified by the volitional intervention techniques listed by Ivannikov (1991; see above); all of them connect the current action with an additional motive, thus providing its meaning with extra investments.

Cell (2) refers to the use of similar devices in the context of interpersonal manipulation, including parents' control over the actions of their children. The simplest ways are those of conditioning: a promise of a reward to make the meaning of the desirable action more attractive and a threat of punishment to make the meaning of undesirable action aversive. However, there may be more complicated effects when the imposed meaning interacts with other meanings of the same action. In the case of reward, if an action that has been rewarded already had an intrinsic positive meaning for a child (or an adult), the extrinsically imposed meaning of a reward undermines, rather than adds to, the positive meaning (Ryan & Deci, 2000). In the case of punishment, a paradoxical reversal effect may take the form of a "forbidden fruit" effect: what is forbidden is perceived as the most valuable, and the growth of negative meaning due to the threat of punishment is counterbalanced by the growth of positive meaning due to the increase in the perceived value of the forbidden option.

Another example of this type of intervention can be exemplified by the well-known experimental technique of priming: "researchers increasingly recognize active meaning-making as an integral component in priming phenomena" (Fujita & Trope, 2014, p. 75). The essence of priming is implicitly imposing a definite meaning-making context for the subsequent task that changes the meaning of this task beyond the participant's awareness. For example, the reminder of money makes the subsequent behavior more egocentric and alienated (Vohs, Mead, & Goode, 2006). Sometimes, however, priming may bring about the effects of a facilitative type (Cell 4), e.g., the reminder of death has been shown to stimulate the sense of meaning and value of life (King, Hicks, & Abdelkhalik, 2009).

Cells (3) and (4) refer to the capacity for altering the meaning of something beyond the actual context by changing a stable attitude to it, be it self-directed (3) or other-directed (4). Cell (3) corresponds to the training of the self-controlled capacity of mobilization/demobilization through adding meaning-making connections or disconnecting the action from meaning-making sources that have been described above as the capacity of volitional regulation. Cell (4) refers to other-directed training of this capacity in education or coaching.

Formative self-correcting intervention aimed at emphasizing the merits or demerits of some intentional object in order to change one's behavior regarding this object (cell 5) can be found in many contexts, e.g., in attempts to give up smoking or drinking, though such interventions are not often effective. In the practice of athletic games or competitions, sometimes the devaluation of a rival, demonstrating their worthlessness, may be helpful for strengthening self-confidence. On other occasions, just the opposite might be the case; emphasizing their strengths can be the most effective strategy for relevant self-mobilization and preparation for the contest. Both these opposing strategies exemplify changing the personal meaning of the rival and thus the attitude to this rival, regulating one's efforts. Both of these meaning-correction devices, of discrediting or idealizing one's rival, have been described in chess (Krogius, 1981).

Similar idealization may have the nature of unconscious defenses aimed at preventing the attitude to the object of romantic or passionate love from eventual devaluation; in this case not only the incoming information but often even the evidence of our senses is discredited if they threaten to shake the pedestal of the object of our love. This process was described by Stendhal (1822) as the crystallization of a loving attitude. There are multiple descriptions of similar effects in fiction such as in the famous discussion of Panurg's marriage (Rabelais, 1894): the character reinterprets in a favorable way all advice and omens suggesting misfortune in the intended marriage, even though the bride is not yet defined.

A special form of this type of intervention is the correction of the meaning of oneself, or self-regard. Most typically, this dynamic is aimed at maintaining high self-esteem, neglecting all doubts, but sometimes low self-esteem and belief in one's inferiority is defended with equal passion and sophistication.

What is placed into cell 6 is an analogous other-directed strategy aimed at convincing another person of the merits or demerits of the object of his or her attitude. It is self-evident that this strategy mirrors the previous one. However, its most typical domain of application refers to mass influences such as commercial advertising and political propaganda. Meaning-focused manipulation underlies the success of commercial sales or political recruitment, because it construes or lays bare meaning connections between the goods, service, or image to be sold and the target audience's needs, values, and life-world at large. This is in line with the popular aphorism among marketers: what we sell is not drills but rather holes of a specific diameter.

In commercial advertising mostly positive rhetoric is in use whereas in political marketing, besides positive rhetoric in favor of the desirable candidate, negative rhetoric addressed to competitors is also broadly used. There may also be sophisticated devices of false devaluation in the market, to make others believe that a highly desirable asset is worth nothing. The latter case is illustrated by an historical anecdote about a highly successful manipulation implemented by Nathan Rothschild, one of the founders of the Rothschild business empire. Having received, in 1815, news of the British victory over Napoleon at Waterloo earlier than anyone else in London, he immediately started selling off British Treasure stocks. Other stock players, knowing that Rothschild was perfectly informed, decided that Napoleon had triumphed and started selling their stock too; their price fell to near zero, panic broke out, and Rothschild bought huge amounts of Treasury funds very cheaply before London discovered the truth.

In Cell 7 we find facilitative intervention focused on the attitude toward some objects is characteristic of some situations of choice. Choice is reducing uncertainty in one's conduct that results in some action or forbearance of action (unlike decision making, which refers to reducing uncertainty in one's mind and results in judgment). Every instance of choice contains more than one option and the choice results in the implementation of one of them and the rejection of the others.

Leontiev and Pilipko (1995) have classified instances of choice according to the structure of options. In the case of *a simple choice* all available options and the criteria for their comparison are given to the person; the point is only in providing the necessary calculations to define the optimal choice (this is possible, in principle). *Meaning-related choice* refers to situations in which options are mostly present, but the criteria for their comparison are ambiguous or not evident. The point is first elaborating the criteria to evaluate and compare options. However, there are no ways to do it fully rationally; it sets the task of discovering personal meaning not only for every option but also for each criterion for their comparison. To do this, one has to reconstruct a common space for all the criteria in order to compare and prioritize them. For instance, in situations of consumer choice it is not always evident which criterion will be the most important: price, quality, style, simplicity of the purchase process, fashion, and public opinion, etc. Shall we choose the most fashionable suit, the lowest-priced one, the most luxurious, the most fade-resistant, or the most stylish or individually tailored? Shall I vote for the most popular candidate, the youngest, the most experienced, the best looking, the wealthiest, the best speaker, the best thinker? Shall I choose a spouse for emotional comfort, for childbirth, for household maintenance, or just for sex? When this task of decoding the meaning of the criteria is solved (this is not easy and can never be completed with certainty — there is no "correct" solution), comparing options is not a big deal. More complicated still is *existential choice*: in this case not only are criteria not evident, but the options themselves are not offered as a finite list; many of them are to be construed, departing from one's wishes, values, and expectations. Vocational choice is a typical example.

Meaning-related choice is essentially the inner mental work (choice work) aimed at discovering the meanings of every option in a way that would make them comparable. This form of choice has been investigated in a study with university students choosing the topic of their yearly research work (Leontiev & Pilipko, 1995). To assess the meaning-relatedness of their choice, the students were asked to write down the arguments for and against the actual options they were considering, and then rank them. The arguments were classified by their content, some of them being meaning-related (what would be the meaningful effect of this choice) and some not (lucky opportunity, actual skills, others' advice or example, or no clear reason). It was found, in particular, that the proportion of meaning-related arguments is much greater in more mature students who attended the university not immediately after high school but after a period of postsecondary employment and/or military service.

Cell 8 refers to the same procedure of meaning-related be used for other-directed intervention. A part of the aforementioned study (Leontiev & Pilipko, 1995) was elaborating and applying a procedure of meaningful choice training designed for the development of the capacity for meaning-related choice, in which we unfolded and explicated the mental work on the comparison of arguments and finding their meaning. For this purpose we composed a set of ten topics for yearly research projects picked from actual offerings of different professors, trying to provide maximal variety among them, and asked the participants of the experimental group to write down and rank the arguments *pro* and *contra* each option. Then they repeated this procedure with the topic they were actually considering at the time. The control group did not explicate the arguments for various topics; instead, they completed some personality inventories and then repeated the explication of arguments for and against the topic they were actually considering. As we assumed, in the experimental group both the total number of arguments referring to one's actual topic and the proportion of meaning-related arguments among them significantly increased after the training, unlike in the control group. A similar procedure has been successfully applied by the authors in individual counseling (ibid.).

Meaning Relations Modification Techniques 2: Meaning Insight Devices

The right part of Table 1 presents the types of interventions aimed at achieving awareness of already existing meaning relations.

Prejudiced interpretation as the example of a biased insight into one's own meaning is placed into Cell 9. Leontiev (1978) defined "the sense-making task" as the challenge of becoming aware of the motives that give personal meaning to objects, events, or actions. Motives, indeed, make the immediate meaning-making context; there may, however, be broader meaning-making contexts beyond and above the actual motives. The solution of this task becomes an instance of formative self-interventions when the solution of this task is prejudiced, or channeled in a different stereotyped direction. For example, a racially prejudiced person would be more likely to interpret as threatening the unclear and ambiguous behavior of a person of different race than the same behavior exhibited by someone of their own race.

Cell (10) refers to prejudiced interpretation of another person's experiences or behavior, which is a widespread target of criticism against psychoanalysis. Having elaborated a sophisticated technique for interpretation of hidden meanings, orthodox psychoanalysis subdued this interpretation into a rather rigid theoretical explanatory model that has been partly overcome in some subsequent theoretical developments. The apocryphal citation falsely ascribed to Freud (see http://quoteinvestigator.com/2011/08/12/just-a-cigar/) says that sometimes a cigar is just a cigar, rather than a phallic symbol, thus responding to the widespread practice of "wild" psychoanalytic interpretations of everything solely in the context of sexual drives. It is not an intervention in the strict meaning of the word; rather, it is a sincere attempt to channel the awareness of meaning relations into a definite meaning-making context, in this case a sexual one. Salvatore Maddi (1974) has wittingly demonstrated the way such a prejudiced interpretation can be reverted against psychoanalysis itself. Maddi has discovered professional faults in Freud's treating the famous case of Dora, and then offered his interpretation of these faults as motivated by Freud's latent sexual problems.

In some cases, placed into Cell 11, these efforts at finding meaning are not restricted by an a priori theoretical or worldview frame. Reflexive self-analysis, aimed at discovering nonevident meanings of one's experiences or behavior, is the case. When Freud was analyzing his own dreams or memory lapses before he came to his rigid metapsychological theory he was doing this kind of work, as do many self-reflecting persons, whether they accept psychoanalytic theory and methodology or not. What we are doing in this case is figuring out the broader meaning-making contexts to which our actual emotionally loaded experiences or actions are connected, to figure out what is the actual reason for their emergence.

The same kind of reflexive discovery of meaning-making contexts may be directed to the experiences or actions of another person; this case is placed into Cell 12. This is the case with unbiased psychoanalytic or similar types of interpretation, provided they are not channeled by rigid theoretical premises; otherwise, they would fit into cell 10. In both this and the previous example, the discovery of unpredetermined and sometimes unexpected meaning-making connections and contexts contributes to the broadening and enhancement of the analysand's life-world. Ancient Greeks used to say that after knowing oneself no one would stay the same. The point is that the core of our self-knowledge, as well as of another person's knowledge, is an understanding (always a limited one, to be sure) of the framework of meaning connections.

Formative self-directed meaning insight with prolonged effects, placed into Cell 13, is most typically exemplified by reinterpreting of negative events into positive ones. This type of self-directed intervention is well-known as "Pollyanna effect"—finding a positive side in everything that seems negative. In psychology and psychotherapy, such devices have been described many times in different theoretical contexts. For example, positive reappraisal has been described as one of the most effective constructive coping strategies (Lazarus, 1966). Still more developed is the type of reinterpretation promoted in Nossrat Peseschkian's positive psychotherapy, in which acceptance of, and coming to peace with, one's problems are attained through finding positive sides of every clinical symptom. So depression is positively reinterpreted as the capacity for deep emotional reactions to conflicts; laziness as the capacity to escape the pressure of achievement; aggression as the capacity to respond in an emotionally uninhibited way; frigidity as the capacity to say "no" with one's body, etc. (Peseschkian, 1987).

To be sure, positive reinterpretation is not a panacea and is not always helpful. This is, however, true for any type of intervention, especially formative ones.

Formative other-directed meaning insights that refer to Cell 14 can be best illustrated by the Socratic dialogue technique, one of the most complicated tools of logotherapy, for it requires an extraordinarily high level of comprehension on the side of the therapist. Characteristic of Socratic dialogue is that Socrates (or, in the example below, Frankl) knows the answer but behaves as if they do not know it, encouraging the partner to complete some complicated mental work of sense-making in a controlled direction. Here is a famous case to illustrate this: "An example of meaningful suffering drawn from my own practice is the story of the old general practitioner who consulted me because of his depression after his wife died. Using the form of Socratic dialogue, I asked him what would have happened if he rather than his wife had died first. 'How she would have suffered', he said. I replied, 'Don't you see, Doctor, that great suffering has been spared her, and it is you who have spared her this suffering; but now, you have to pay for it by surviving and mourning her'. Our dialogue induced him to discover a meaning in his suffering, the meaning of a sacrifice for the sake of his wife" (Frankl, 1969, pp. 118–119).

Self-facilitation of meaning connection insight beyond lay self-analysis, placed into Cell 15, is the target of focusing psychotherapy (Gendlin, 1981). Gendlin has elaborated this profound technique for self-analysis based on his theory of experiencing and meaning-making (Gendlin, 1962) as a complicated procedure leading to awareness of the meaning of the experiences initially represented as a vague, bodily felt sense. This felt sense contains meaning in itself, but it requires special focusing work following specific guidelines for some time to uncover the hidden meaning. A nontherapeutic example can be religious conversion, especially in crises, which helps to believe that there must be some meaning rather than specifying this meaning (see, e.g., Miller & C'de Baca, 2001; Park & Edmondson, 2012). Finding a new meaning whatever it could be when the existing meaning is destroyed in traumatic dissociation is treated recently as the universal mechanism of adversarial growth and the predictor of thriving in stressful or adverse situations (e.g., Emmons, 1999; Janoff-Bulman & Frantz, 1997; Joseph & Linley, 2008).

Cell 16 of Table 1 refers to other-directed meaning insight interventions of a similar type. In a sense, it is the most challenging type of meaning-focused intervention—helping another person to extend their awareness of meaning-making contexts to come to a sustainable new vision that cannot be foreseen and designed by the helper; the point is just to facilitate one's capacity for meaning insights without limitations. This kind of work forms a part of most approaches to in-depth dynamic psychotherapy, including psychodynamic, Gestalt, existential, etc. In its purest form, this type of intervention has been described as life enhancement (LE) methodology (Leontiev, 2015). An LE approach reminds us of Socratic dialogue; however, in this case there is no "right" answer or underlying value or worldview presumptions. The focus of LE work is increasing the flexibility of rigid channels of experience processing, including meaning connections, questioning the stereotyped meaning structures from word meanings to worldview generalizations. This encourages the restructuring of meaning frameworks that can never be planned and predicted at the beginning of the work.

Conclusion

The list of meaning-focused intervention techniques explicated above suggests that there are more similarities than differences in meaning-making and meaning-insight devices. Indeed, deliberate, controlled, selective awareness of definite meaning connections and contexts that suggests attributing a definite meaning to the object or action in question (9–10, 13–14) is similar to the artificial creation of such contexts associated with the corresponding meaning (1–2, 5–6). The difference between these two cases is that in the former the awareness of meaning connections is necessarily present, while in the latter it is rather an exception and even undesirable, as in cases of priming that are nothing but the hidden connecting of a definite content with a definite meaning-making context. Besides, the direction of the meaning-making process is the reverse in both cases. In the former case, the meaning to be analyzed is given, and based on this, meaning-making contexts are constructed or reconstructed; in the latter, it is the context that is given, and based on that, meaning connections with the content in question are construed that define its meaning.

A special case of meaning-making is rectifying meaning connections, often used in advertising. In this case the promoted goods are placed in a significant and attractive meaning-making context such as success, beauty, sexuality, youth, etc., while weak and multiply mediated connections of these goods (such as a shampoo) with desirable effects are presented as strong, close, immediate, and decisive. It is a combination of meaning-making and meaning insight, because it does not create qualitatively new meaning connections but reconstructs them in a dynamic way, inflating an actually existing weak connection.

I hope that this attempt of classifying meaning-changing interventions may contribute to the construction of a common language for scholars and professionals from different fields. This is fairly consistent with the nature of meaning as a "*divine knot holding the things together*" (de Saint-Exupery, 1948, pp. 257, 277, 286).

Key Takeaways

- The concept of meaning does not specifically refer to an existential problem field; rather, it may serve as an umbrella concept for explaining varied forms of psychological interventions that have been studied in diverse theoretical and applied contexts, making a common denominator between them.
- Meaning-changing interventions are aimed at changing the connection of a target oblect to a meaning-making context, through its awareness or otherwise.
- Meaning-changing interventions can be classified on the following dimensions: self-directed vs. other-directed; making an immediate short-term effect or a prolonged effect; formative vs. facilitative; meaning-making vs. meaning insight.
- Self-directed interventions (like voluntary self-discipline) do mirror other-directed interventions (like education or marketing), which allows treating them in a single explanatory scheme.
- A relational view of meaning may serve as the basis for treating all kinds of meaning-making processes, including both finding and creating meaning, within a unified framework.

Acknowledgment The chapter was prepared within the framework of a subsidy granted to the HSE by the Government of the Russian Federation for the implementation of the Global Competitiveness Program.

References

Aidman, E. V., & Leontiev, D. A. (1991). From being motivated to motivating oneself: A Vygotskian perspective. *Studies in Soviet Thought, 42*, 137–151.

Baumeister, R. F. (1991). *The meanings of life*. New York, NY: Guilford.

Carver, C. S., & Scheier, M. F. (2002). Control processes and self-organization as complementary principles underlying behavior. *Personality and Social Psychology Review, 6*, 304–315.

de Saint-Exupery, A. (1948). *Citadelle*. Paris: Gallimard.

Emmons, R. A. (1999). *The psychology of ultimate concerns*. New York, NY: Guilford.

Frankl, V. (1969). *The will to meaning: Foundations and applications of logotherapy*. New York, NY: Plume press.

Fujita, K., & Trope, Y. (2014). Structured versus unstructured regulation: On procedural mindsets and the mechanisms of priming effects. In D. C. Molden (Ed.), *Understanding priming effects in social psychology* (pp. 70–89). New York, NY: Guilford.

Gendlin, E. T. (1962). *Experiencing and the creation of meaning: A philosophical and psychological approach to the subjective*. New York, NY: The Free press of Glencoe.

Gendlin, E. T. (1981). *Focusing* (2nd ed.). Toronto, ON: Bantam Books.

Ivannikov, V. A. (1991). *Psikhologicheskie mekhanizmy volevoi regulatsii (Psychological mechanisms of voluntary regulation)*. Moscow: Moscow University Press.

Janoff-Bulman, R., & Frantz, C. M. (1997). The impact of trauma on meaning: From meaningless world to meaningful life. In M. Power & C. Brewin (Eds.), *The transformation of meaning in psychological therapies: Integrating theory and practice* (pp. 91–106). Chichester: Wiley.

Joseph, S., & Linley, P. A. (2008). Reflections on theory and practice in trauma, recovery, and growth: A paradigm shift for the field of traumatic stress. In S. Joseph & P. A. Linley (Eds.), *Trauma, recovery, and growth: Positive psychological perspectives on posttraumatic stress* (pp. 339–356). Hoboken, NJ: John Wiley & Sons.

Kelly, G. A. (1970). A brief introduction to personal construct theory. In D. Bannister (Ed.), *Perspectives in personal construct theory* (pp. 1–29). London; New York, NY: Academic.

King, L. A., Hicks, J. A., & Abdelkhalik, J. (2009). Death, life, scarcity, and value: An alternative perspective on the meaning of death. *Psychological Science, 20*, 1459–1462.

Krogius, N. V. (1981). Vzaimoobuslovlennost poznaniya ludmi drug druga I samopoznaniya v konfliktnoi deyatelnosti (Interrelatedness of mutual cognition and self-cognition in conflict-related activity). In A. Bodalev (Ed.), *Psikhologiya mezhlichnostnogo poznaniya (Psychology of interpersonal cognition)* (pp. 66–80). Moscow: Pedagogika.

Lazarus, R. (1966). *Psychological stress and the coping process*. New York, NY: McGraw-Hill.

Leontiev, A. N. (1978). *Activity, consciousness, and personality*. Englewood Cliffs, NJ: Prentice-Hall.

Leontiev, D. A. (1996). Dimensions of the meaning/sense concept in the psychological context. In C. Tolman, F. Cherry, R. van Hezewijk, & I. Lubek (Eds.), *Problems of theoretical psychology* (pp. 130–142). New York, NY: Captus University Publications.

Leontiev, D. A. (1999). *Psikhologiya smysla (The psychology of personal meaning)*. Moscow: Smysl.

Leontiev, D. A. (2012). Personal meaning as the basis of motivational processes. In D. Leontiev (Ed.), *Motivation, consciousness, and self-regulation* (pp. 65–78). New York, NY: Nova.

Leontiev, D. A. (2013). Personal meaning: A challenge for psychology. *The Journal of Positive Psychology, 8*, 459–470.

Leontiev, D. A. (2015). Experience processing as an aspect of existential psychotherapy: Life enhancement methodology. *Journal of Contemporary Psychotherapy, 45*, 49–58.

Leontiev, D. A. (2016a). The Divine Knot: A relational view on meaning. *Journal of Constructivist Psychology*.

Leontiev, D. A. (2016b). Converging paths toward meaning. *Journal of Constructivist Psychology*.

Leontiev, D. A., & Pilipko, N. V. (1995). Vybor kak deyatelnost: Lichnostnye determinanty i vozmozhnosti formirovaniya (Choice as activity: Its personality determinants and possibilities of training). *Voprosy Psikhologii, 1*, 97–110.

Lewin, K. (1935). *A dynamic theory of personality: Selected papers*. New York, NY: McGraw-Hill.

Locke, J. (1999). *An essay concerning human understanding* (First published 1690). Philadelphia, PA: The Pennsylvania State University.

Lukas, E. (2002). *Lehrbuch der Logotherapie (Logotherapy textbook)* (2nd ed.). Muenchen: Profil.

Maddi, S. (1974). The victimization of Dora. *Psychology Today, 8*(4), 90–100.

Maddi, S. R., & Kobasa, S. C. (1984). *The hardy executive: Health under stress*. Homewood, IL: Dow Jones-Irwin.

Metcalfe, J., & Mischel, W. (1999). A hot/cool system analysis of delay of gratification: Dynamics of willpower. *Psychological Review, 106*, 3–19.

Miller, W. R., & C'de Baca, J. (2001). *Quantum change: When epiphanies and sudden insights transform ordinary lives*. New York, NY: Guilford Press.

Nuttin, J. (1984). *Motivation, planning, and action: A relational theory of behavior dynamics*. Leuven; Hillsdale, NJ: Leuven University Press; Lawrence Erlbaum Associates.

Park, C. R., & Edmondson, D. (2012). Religion as a source of meaning. In P. R. Shaver & M. Mikulincer (Eds.), *Meaning, mortality, and choice: Social psychology of existential concerns* (pp. 145–162). Washington, DC: APA Press.

Peseschkian, N. (1987). *Positive psychotherapy: Theory and practice of a new method*. Berlin: Springer.

Rabelais, F. (1894). *Gargantua and Pantagruel* (T. Urquhart, & P. A. Motteux, Trans.). Retrieved from https://www.gutenberg.org/files/1200/1200-h/1200-h.htm.

Ryan, R., & Deci, E. (2000). When rewards compete with nature: The undermining of intrinsic motivation and self-regulation. In C. Sansone & J. M. Harackiewicz (Eds.), *Intrinsic and extrinsic motivation: The search for optimal motivation and performance* (pp. 13–54). San Diego, CA: Academic Press.

Schnell, T. (2014). An empirical approach to existential psychology: Meaning in life operationalized. In S. Kreitler & T. Urbanek (Eds.), *Conceptions of meaning* (pp. 173–194). New York, NY: Nova Science.
Seligman, M. E. P. (2002). *Authentic happiness*. New York, NY: The Free Press.
Stendhal. (1822). *On love*. New York, NY: Penguin.
Vohs, K. D., Mead, N. L., & Goode, M. R. (2006). The psychological consequences of money. *Science, 314*, 1154–1156.
Vygotsky, L. S. (1983). Istoriya razvitiya vysshikh psikhicheskikh funktsii (History of development of higher mental functions). In *Vygotsky L. S. Sobranie sochineniy (Collected works)* (Vol. 3, pp. 5–328). Moscow: Pedagogika.

Part II
Coping: Integrative Meaning-Oriented Perspectives and Interventions for Human Coping

The Significance of Meaning to Conceptualizations of Resilience and Posttraumatic Growth: Strengthening the Foundation for Research and Practice

Lauren N. Weathers, Bethany J. Aiena, Meredith A. Blackwell, and Stefan E. Schulenberg

The primary aim of this chapter is to discuss meaning's relationship with resilience and posttraumatic growth; ultimately asserting that meaning may serve as a catalyst for both outcomes. Cultivating a sense of meaning is integral to perceiving life as being fulfilling and is a means of adaptively coping with a range of potentially traumatic events that may occur throughout the course of one's life.

This current effort is an extension of a series of workshops and written works in the areas of meaning, resilience, and posttraumatic growth (Schulenberg, 2014a, 2014b, 2014c; Schulenberg, Drescher, & Baczwaski, 2014; Schulenberg, Hutzell, Nassif, & Rogina, 2008). From our efforts in studying outcomes post Hurricane Katrina (Hirschel & Schulenberg, 2009, 2010; Schulenberg, Dellinger, et al. 2008; Schulenberg, Drescher, et al., 2014), we discovered that self-efficacy significantly and negatively correlates with posttraumatic stress symptoms in Hurricane Katrina survivors (Hirschel & Schulenberg, 2009). In addition, through our collaboration with the Mississippi Department of Mental Health in response to the Deepwater Horizon oil spill, we learned that concepts such as perceived meaning in life, self-efficacy, and resilience all appear to be significant protective factors (Aiena, Baczwaski, Schulenberg, & Buchanan, 2015; Aiena, Buchanan, Smith, & Schulenberg, 2015; Drescher et al., 2012). This research further inspired us, here at the University of Mississippi's Clinical-Disaster Research Center (UM-CDRC), to study the effect protective factors have on survivors of disasters, specifically concepts that stimulate resilience and recovery during and after the occurrence of a disaster. We have also become interested in whether these factors similarly promote

---

L.N. Weathers, M.A. (✉) • B.J. Aiena, M.A. • M.A. Blackwell, B.A.
S.E. Schulenberg, Ph.D.
Department of Psychology, Clinical-Disaster Research Center (UM-CDRC),
University of Mississippi, University, MS 38677, USA
e-mail: lnweathe@go.olemiss.edu

disaster preparedness. Through our work, we have taken a particular interest in the concept of meaning in relation to resilience and posttraumatic growth. While the context we consider is one of disaster mental health, culled from experiences with natural and technological disasters such as Hurricane Katrina and the Deepwater Horizon oil spill (e.g., Aiena et al., 2015; Drescher et al., 2012; Schulenberg, Drescher, et al., 2014; Schulenberg, Smith, Drescher, & Buchanan, 2015), the discussion has implications for other kinds of events as well.

Traumatic Events

A traumatic event is a circumstance that challenges a person's adaptive resources, as well as his or her understanding of the world and how he or she fits into it (Janoff-Bulman, 1992). The *DSM-5* further defined a traumatic event as exposure to actual or threatened death, serious injury, or sexual violence through direct experience, witnessing the event in person, learning that the event happened to a close friend or family member, or experiencing repeated or extreme exposure to the aftermath of an event, such as in the case of a first responder (American Psychiatric Association, 2013). Some researchers have reported that 40–70 % of individuals will experience a potentially traumatic event in their lifetime (Breslau, 2009; Resnick, Falsetti, Kilpatrick, & Freedy, 1996), whereas other sources estimate the prevalence of traumatic event exposure to be nearly 90 % (American Psychiatric Association, 2013; Kilpatrick et al., 2013).

While some people use the term "disaster" synonymously with "trauma," as a means of referencing a traumatic experience, a disaster is one example of a potential trauma (McFarlane & Norris, 2006). McFarlane and Norris defined a disaster as a "potentially traumatic event that is collectively experienced, has an acute onset, and is time-delimited; disasters may be attributed to natural, technological, or human causes" (p. 4). Thus, events that constitute a disaster include natural occurrences such as tornadoes, hurricanes, and earthquakes, or they may be occurrences that are technological or man-made in origin, such as in the case of oil spills, fires, explosions, etc. McFarlane and Norris acknowledged that while not all disasters result in death or injury, they have the potential to do so. The extreme stress and disruption of a disaster to an individual's psychological and physical health, coupled with effects to the surrounding physical, economic, and social environment, can lead to suffering long after the event has passed. While anyone may experience a severe stress reaction following such an occurrence, women, non-White, and impoverished individuals are at increased risk (Halpern & Tramontin, 2007; Hawkins, Zinzow, Amstadter, Danielson, & Ruggiero, 2009; Kimerling, Mack, & Alvarez, 2009).

However, not everyone who experiences a potentially traumatic event such as a natural or technological disaster will develop long-term negative effects, a few examples being depression, anxiety, general stress, or posttraumatic stress (Aiena et al., 2015; Drescher, Schulenberg, & Smith, 2014). Levels of recovery and resilience are high following a disaster (Bonanno, Brewin, Kaniasty, & La Greca, 2010), so much so that recovery is the generally expected response. In short, people are remarkably resilient. Moreover, the use of protective resources can alleviate the negative effects of adverse circumstances (Aiena et al., 2015; Dursun, Steger, Bentele, & Schulenberg, 2016; Zakour, 2012). One potential protective resource receiving increased attention in the literature is the concept of meaning in life.

Meaning in Life

Meaning is the "degree to which people have achieved comprehension (through making sense of their lives and experience, developing a coherent mental model of their selves, the world around them, and their fit and interactions with the world) and have achieved purpose (through discerning, committing to, and pursuing overarching lifelong goals, aims, and aspirations)" (Steger, Shin, Shim, & Fitch-Martin, 2013, p. 166). Meaning involves a sense of coherence, or understanding, a sense of significance, or value, as well as a sense of direction, or purpose (e.g., Lomas, Hefferon, & Ivtzan, 2014). Many researchers have studied meaning's essential ties to human health and well-being (Melton & Schulenberg, 2008; Ryff & Singer, 1998a, 1998b; Savolaine & Granello, 2002; Spiegel & Fawzy, 2002; Zika & Chamberlain, 1992). Overall, meaning in life predicts elevated levels of hope and subjective well-being (Yalçın & Malkoç, 2015). Moreover, meaning in life is linked to physical health and positively related to self-reported general health (Brassai, Piko, & Steger, 2012; Krause, 2007; Steger, Mann, Michels, & Cooper, 2009). Meaning also contributes to overall wellness by making individuals aware of social support, providing a sense of identity and values, facilitating health-promoting behaviors, and inoculating against stress (Ryff & Singer, 1998b; Savolaine & Granello, 2002; Schulenberg, Hutzell, et al., 2008).

Meaning-making is a resource to help reconcile a person's experience with his or her previous worldview following a potentially traumatic experience; that is, meaning in life can be used across experiences, including negative ones, serving as a driving force or reason to continue moving forward when confronted with a traumatic stressor. An individual's sense of meaning depends on his or her specific context and values (Frankl, 1965), and as a result, people can uniquely construct their own meaning (Frankl, 1966). A growing number of researchers cite meaning as an essential facet of what makes an individual resilient when dealing with adversity (Aiena et al., 2015; Wagnild, 2009; Wong & Wong, 2012).

Resilience

Resilience is the capacity to adapt to stressors and restore balance to one's life when confronted with a stressor (Bonanno, 2004; Wagnild & Young, 1993). Resilient individuals are able to harness internal and environmental resources that allow them to maintain a sense of well-being, even under conditions of severe stress (Southwick, Bonanno, Masten, Panter-Brick, & Yehuda, 2014; Southwick & Charney, 2012a, 2012b; Wong & Wong, 2012).

While work in resilience continues to proliferate, and while it is a concept that many researchers and practitioners consider to be essential to understanding trauma-related responses, it is still in the early stages as a science (Shahar, 2012). Research on resilience began as examinations of adjustment to chronic adversity in children (Garmezy, 1993; Masten, 2001; Rutter, 1987; Werner, 1984), but efforts have been expanded considerably to study resilience in relation to a wider range of potentially traumatic events, such as natural and technological disasters, and examining resilience across the lifespan (Aiena et al., 2015; Bonanno & Diminich, 2013). Recently, studies have found resilience to be positively correlated with well-being, optimism, self-esteem, gratitude, and positive affect, and negatively correlated with posttraumatic stress, general psychological distress, and generalized anxiety (Arnetz, Rofa, Arnetz, Ventimiglia, & Jamil, 2013; Baldwin, Jackson, Okoh, & Cannon, 2011; Christopher, 2000; Fredrickson, Tugade, Waugh, & Larkin, 2003; Nishi, Uehara, Kondo, & Matsuoka, 2010; Scali et al., 2012; Tugade & Fredrickson, 2004).

Resilience is often conceptualized as multiple protective factors that work together (Herbert, Manjula, & Philip, 2013; Lyons, 1991; Wagnild & Young, 1990). For example, Wagnild (2009) designated five characteristics that comprise the "Resilience Core": perseverance, equanimity, meaningfulness, self-reliance, and existential aloneness. Perseverance is the ability to continue on even in the face of setbacks. People who possess equanimity are characterized as having a stable view of life and their experiences and often have a sense of humor. Meaningfulness is when people recognize that their lives have purpose and significance. People who are self-reliant recognize their personal strengths and can rely on those strengths to guide their actions. Finally, existential aloneness is the recognition that while some experiences can be shared with other people, one must be able to confront and manage other experiences alone. Wagnild (2009) theorized that meaning provides a foundation for the other four resilience characteristics, making it perhaps the most essential resource.

With perseverance, the steadfastness to continue moving forward despite experiencing adversities, to have a sense of meaning or purpose in life drives individuals to press on when confronted with hardship, even when undergoing setbacks (Frankl, 1959/2006). Equanimity, or having a stable view of one's life, is evident when a person recognizes that life is not all good or all bad. A sense of meaning allows an individual to make sense of a potentially traumatic event, and to recognize that while an event was distressing, there are lessons that can be learned. One event does not define a person or determine the outcome of all future events in a person's life. As for self-reliance and existential aloneness, these aspects of resilience focus on each individual's unique journey through life and the ability to rely on one's self to overcome obstacles. With self-reliance, people recognize their own strengths and weaknesses. They are also confident in their abilities, using them to guide their actions. With existential aloneness, people who recognize their worth and strengths can use this knowledge to bounce back and carry on from an event that has caused hardship. With respect to freedom of the will, every individual has the capacity to choose how he or she will respond to external circumstances (Lukas & Hirsch, 2002; Melton & Schulenberg, 2008). Individuals with a defined sense of purpose will be better able to recognize, foster, and utilize their own strengths when working toward goals and will be better able to respond to negative circumstances.

According to Wong and Wong (2012), effective resilience-building efforts should be meaning-centered for two primary reasons. The first reason is that resilience, by nature, is a multifaceted construct that is comprised of multiple positive psychological concepts, meaning being one example. The second reason has to do with the aims of a meaning-centered approach (e.g., development of character strengths, moral strength, compassion for others, and supportive social ecologies), which would lead to greater individual resilience. Damon (2008) demonstrated that a key component that enables young people to respond resiliently to adversity is when they develop a sense of purpose and meaning that helps them transcend self-interest. Living a meaningful life gives people reasons to bounce back during difficult times (Frankl, 1959/2006; Wong, 2010). Clearly, meaning plays an important role in a person's capacity to be resilient. However, as will be demonstrated, meaning is also an important aspect of the related concept of posttraumatic growth. While resilience is the ability to bounce back or recover from stressors, some people demonstrate the capacity to thrive following the experience of a potentially traumatic event, a trajectory referred to in the literature as posttraumatic growth.

Posttraumatic Growth

Traumatic events present challenges to peoples' views of themselves and their views of the world. People may learn that the world is not always a safe place. Bad things can happen to good people, and so on. Such challenges to views of self and the world and how these views are threatened and are reformed are essential to conceptualizations of posttraumatic growth (Janoff-Bulman, 1992; Park, 2016; Steger & Park, 2012; Tedeschi, Calhoun, & Groleau, 2015). Posttraumatic growth is the positive psychological change that some people perceive or experience as a result of a negative life event (Calhoun & Tedeschi, 1999, 2001, 2013). Furthermore, posttraumatic growth is positively correlated with character strengths whereby an increase in the number of traumatic events leads to higher endorsements of character strengths and posttraumatic growth (Peterson, Park, Pole, D'Andrea, & Seligman, 2008). The term is often synonymous with stress-related growth (Park, Cohen, & Murch, 1996), adversarial growth (Linley & Joseph, 2004), perceived benefits (McMillen & Fisher, 1998), thriving (Abraído-Lanza, Guier, & Colón, 1998), and enrichment (Bannink, 2014). For the sake of parsimony we employ the term posttraumatic growth as it is the most well-known.

With respect to posttraumatic growth and meaning, research is being conducted to examine these concepts in relation to one another (Dursun et al., 2016; Triplett, Tedeschi, Cann, Calhoun, & Reeve, 2012). Researchers have found that there may be an indirect path from growth to life satisfaction via meaning in life (Triplett et al., 2012). One reason for the relationship between these two concepts becomes increasingly clear when the foundations of posttraumatic growth are examined in greater detail. Simply stated, posttraumatic growth has theoretical roots in meaning and purpose in life. This idea becomes all the more evident when one examines the facets of posttraumatic growth as measured by the Posttraumatic Growth Inventory (PTGI; Tedeschi & Calhoun, 1996). Posttraumatic growth is associated with people who perceive or experience positive reappraisal (reflective rumination), self-efficacy (a greater sense of personal strength), enhanced relationships, a greater appreciation of life or a sense of life's possibilities, and spiritual development following a potentially traumatic experience (Tedeschi & Calhoun, 1996, 2004). Each of these aspects of posttraumatic growth is closely associated with the concept of meaning. The following section briefly describes each aspect of posttraumatic growth and points to some of the avenues where meaning and posttraumatic growth intersect with one another.

Positive Reappraisal (Reflective Rumination). Positive reappraisal, also known as reflective rumination or positive reframing, refers to how one takes a negative event and strives to find a positive aspect from the experience (e.g., Helgeson, Reynolds, & Tomich, 2006). Cognitive efforts to find positive and constructive (rather than destructive) aspects of a traumatic experience may make one more likely to perceive or experience growth (rather than distress) following a potentially traumatic event (Triplett et al., 2012). Positive reappraisal is an important part of meaning-making in such circumstances, and is directly in line with Frankl's (1959/2006, 1990; Lukas & Hirsch, 2002) stance that life has meaning under all circumstances, even those involving unavoidable suffering. Frankl commonly noted in his works that suffering ceases to be suffering the moment a person discovers meaning in the experience. Through one's attitudinal stance, over time an individual may come to view the event as something that has meaning (i.e., an opportunity for growth, an opportunity to learn one's strengths, self-transcendence—an opportunity to help others, perspective—an opportunity to recognize what is truly important in life).

Rumination occurs when one thinks over and over about one aspect of an event—thus rumination is a conscious process that can occur given environmental cues related to a particular occurrence (Martin & Tesser, 1996). Rumination is a complicated process that can be defined or experienced as intrusive, nonconstructive, or psychologically harmful on the one hand, or deliberate, reflective, and constructive on the other hand (e.g., Horowitz, 1986; Lyubomirsky, Caldwell, & Nolen-Hoeksema, 1998; Taku, Cann, Tedeschi, & Calhoun, 2009). For instance, in the former case, people whose ruminations and self-reflections are negative/self-derogatory are less likely to experience posttraumatic growth. Brooding in this way is associated with maladaptive cognitive processing that can lead to negative affect (Moberly & Watkins, 2008), depression (Burwell & Shirk, 2007), and suicidal ideation (Chan, Miranda, & Surrence, 2009). Essentially, some forms of rumination may exacerbate posttraumatic stress symptoms. Alternatively, in the latter case, for some people persistent processing, or attempting to build new schemas, goals, and meanings, is associated with growth (Tedeschi & Calhoun, 2004). After a potentially traumatic event, some people report distressing intrusive thoughts, striving to comprehend what happened, hoping to discover meaning in the situation (Tedeschi & Calhoun, 2005). Thinking about the traumatic event and potential positive consequences (reflective rumination) may facilitate clarity, adaptively reorganizing views of the self and the world. When done with intention, reflective rumination is considered to be an aspect of posttraumatic growth (Tedeschi & Calhoun, 1996).

Self-Efficacy (Personal Strength). Self-efficacy is a person's perception of his or her ability to organize and execute actions necessary to manage a particular situation (Bandura, 1994). As such, self-efficacy has been well documented as a significant facilitator of posttraumatic growth considering many different contexts, including terrorism and war survivors (Hall et al., 2010), natural disaster survivors (Cieslak et al., 2009; Compton, 2013), and survivors of life-threatening illness (Mystakidou et al., 2015; Zhai, Huang, Gao, Jiang, & Xu, 2014).

There are two primary reasons why there is an emphasis on self-efficacy in a time of adversity. First, self-efficacy is important in recovery as it helps deter people from feeling hopeless and lacking in control. Secondly, research has shown that self-efficacy is an important trait to promote self-protective measures, and ultimately prevent revictimization in interpersonal trauma (Ball & Martin, 2012; Orchowski, Gidycz, & Raffle, 2008), as well as promoting emergency preparedness for larger-scale natural disasters (Burns, 2015; Paton, Smith, & Johnston, 2005). In addition to the link with posttraumatic growth, self-efficacy is positively related to meaning (Blackburn & Owens, 2015; Jafary, Farahbakhsh, Shafiabadi, & Delavar, 2011) and appears to mediate the relationship between conscientiousness and meaning in life. Along these lines, Lightsey and colleagues (2014) theorized that conscientiousness and self-efficacy build meaning by increasing the frequency of positive thoughts and decreasing the frequency of negative thoughts when it comes to one's purpose and value, ultimately finding that self-efficacy does, indeed, mediate the relationship between conscientiousness and meaning.

Self-efficacy is a means of empowerment, with a focus on what people can do in specific circumstances to assist themselves or others. Self-efficacy involves purposeful, goal-oriented behavior, as does meaning. When a potentially traumatic experience does occur, people often wonder about the steps they may take to help themselves, or those steps that may be taken to help others. Helping in times of severe stress provides a sense of purpose, a sense of value, a sense of significance. We learn how we can make a difference, not only to ourselves but also to others. We learn that we can be effective agents of change. We can be proactive. We can learn to overcome adversity and help others to do so. We can be "Somebody," to ourselves and/or to someone else, that is, discovering "a personal identity, a meaning for existence, a place in life, a worthwhile cause" (Crumbaugh, 1973/1988, p. ix). Thus, one would expect meaning to be significantly and positively related to self-efficacy. People who perceive meaning from their experiences are likely to be more goal-directed, with a defined sense of values and a congruence of fit between their values and goals (Schulenberg, Hutzell, et al., 2008). Alternatively, people who value safety, security, and helping others in times of hardship are likely to discover a sense of meaning via the taking of positive steps in response to a potentially traumatic event. One would expect each of these concepts to inform, or stimulate, the other.

Indeed, studies have demonstrated meaning and self-efficacy's close relationship to one another along these lines, as well as their relationship to reported life satisfaction following adverse circumstances such as the Deepwater Horizon oil spill (Aiena et al., 2015; Drescher et al., 2012; Schulenberg et al., 2015). Thus, meaning and self-efficacy appear to be critically important to one another, and both concepts are likely essential to fostering personal growth in response to adversity.

Enhanced Relationships. Another area of growth following a potentially traumatic event includes relationships with others (Calhoun & Tedeschi, 1999). In terms of relationships with others, people typically feel an enhanced closeness due to a need to talk about and process the event. As a result, there is a greater level of self-disclosure, which makes socialization more gratifying and, due to the inherent vulnerability of self-disclosure, enhances the perception of emotional intimacy and closeness. Telling one's story following a potentially traumatic event enhances one's coping by gradual exposure to the associated fear and loss; disclosure may be helpful as it provides time and a means for processing one's experiences (Niederhoffer & Pennebaker, 2009; Zakour, 2012). When people who have experienced a potentially traumatic event have empathetic listeners who facilitate positive responses and interactions, they are better able to reconstruct their self-concept (Lepore, 2001). Likewise, Lakey and Cohen (2000) theorized that when people who have experienced a potentially traumatic event actively seek and receive social support, they are more likely to evaluate the event as less distressful because the support received tends to be associated with adaptive problem-solving and positive coping. As a result, enhanced relationships promote growth following experiences of extreme adversity.

Consequently, posttraumatic growth is perceived to be greater when people are able to access their social support, including their social network, community resources, and family environment (e.g., Hobfoll et al., 2007; Vranceanu, Hobfoll, & Johnson, 2007). The perceived and received social support mobilization model holds that community cohesion following a potentially traumatic event has therapeutic and positive effects on individuals within the community (Kaniasty, 2012). Moreover, concern may lessen the chance of people experiencing adverse psychological outcomes associated with disasters, leading to "… levels of integration, productivity, and capacity for growth" (p. 692; see also Quarantelli, 1985). Essentially, in order for post-event well-being to occur from a social perspective, people need to perceive that they have social support, that the community is cohesive, that people are benevolent, and that there is efficacy of mutual helping (Kaniasty, 2012). In this fashion, social support is a protective factor against the experience of negative psychological effects following a potentially traumatic event. Alternatively, withdrawing from social support is often associated with negative psychological effects.

Related to enhanced relationships, meaning in life has been linked to more proactive, social behavior and a sense of belonging (Florez, Schulenberg, & Stewart, 2016; Lambert et al., 2013; Melton & Schulenberg, 2008; Steger et al., 2009). Positive social interaction is a component that can add to one's sense of meaning (Krause, 2007). Stillman and colleagues (2009) experimentally determined that when people are excluded from social activities, whether the interaction is via computer or face-to-face, their perception of meaning diminishes. Sherman and Simonton (2012) also reported that higher personal meaning has been associated with an increase in close intimate relations. Moreover, in older individuals, anticipated support (i.e., people will be there to help them in the future if they need them) predicts meaning over time (Krause, 2007). Thus, meaning appears to play a key role in how enhanced relationships lead to growth following the experience of a potentially traumatic event.

Greater Appreciation of Life (Sense of Life's Possibilities). Posttraumatic growth is frequently associated with greater appreciation of life, or a sense of new directions or opportunities (i.e., seeing possibilities inherent in new and/or different paths; Tedeschi & Calhoun, 1996, 2004). People who experience potentially traumatic events and who subsequently perceive or experience posttraumatic growth often believe that the lives they were living before the event were insubstantial in comparison to their lives post-event (Tedeschi & Calhoun, 2012). Potentially traumatic events often serve as a "wake-up call" to what is truly important in life, thus offering a sense of perspective. People may realize that they are not using their time as they would like, perhaps not spending as much time with family and friends as they would like, or not working in jobs that they enjoy and that provide a sense of meaning or purpose. A potentially traumatic event may galvanize people, inspiring them, motivating them, and encouraging them to spend their time and energy differently post-disaster (and perhaps more consistently with their values).

A greater appreciation of life, and the recognition that life presents new possibilities, new opportunities perhaps previously unrecognized, in turn leads to growth toward more meaningful (and wiser) living (Tedeschi & Calhoun, 2012). Links between life appreciation and the recognition of new possibilities theoretically and anecdotally are related to a greater sense of meaning. There is research support as well, which has been noted in a number of studies or reviews. For instance, meaning is associated with greater life satisfaction, happiness, empowerment, and gratitude (Bronk, 2014; Drescher et al., 2012; Melton & Schulenberg, 2008; Schulenberg, Hutzell, et al., 2008; Volkert, Schulz, Brütt, & Andreas, 2014), each of which allow for a greater appreciation of life and the recognition and consideration of new possibilities, thus increasing the chance that a person will experience posttraumatic growth after a potentially traumatic event.

Spiritual Development. Amidst the process of discovering meaning in a potentially traumatic event, many people identify spiritual or religious development as an essential aspect of recovery (De Castella & Simmonds, 2013; Taku, Tedeschi, & Cann, 2015). Spirituality, "the yearning within the human being for meaning, for that which is greater than the encapsulated individual" and religion, the "complex pattern of writings, rituals and ethical codes that are deemed necessary for spiritual fulfillment" (Thorne, 2001, p. 438), are often what people seek to make sense of their experiences. In times of adversity, people ask questions such as "Why did this happen to me?", "Was this a random occurrence?", "Who is to blame?", "Is it a part of God's plan?", "What purpose does the event serve?", and "What can I learn from it?" In such cases it is not unusual for people to rely on their spirituality for comfort. Some people may find solace in their views, perhaps growing closer to their pre-event beliefs (e.g., turning to their faith for support), while in other instances people may question the accuracy of their pre-event beliefs (e.g., "Why would God let this happen to me?"; Exline, Park, Smyth, & Carey, 2011).

In terms of posttraumatic growth, the process of trying to comprehend a potentially traumatic event may lead to a strengthening of one's spiritual beliefs (Andrykowski, 1992; Garlick, Wall, Corwin, & Koopman, 2011). Spirituality affords some people a greater sense of comprehension as to why an event may have occurred, or a sense of peace in terms of being unable to discover a reason (Tsai, El-Gabalawy, Sledge, Southwick, & Pietrzak, 2015). Spirituality thus allows some people to reconcile their pre-event and post-event views of the self and the world. People often report a stronger sense of spirituality following a potentially traumatic event, noting that their spirituality helped them to discover meaning in the experience (Ai, Cascio, Santangelo, & Evans-Campbell, 2005).

Here, too, meaning is strongly linked with this domain of growth. Researchers have consistently demonstrated a link between presence of meaning and a sense of spirituality and well-being (Ivtzan, Chan, Gardner, & Prashar, 2013; Khumalo, Wissing, & Schutte, 2014; Park, 2012; Tsai et al., 2015). Spirituality creates a framework for how people view the self, the world, and the self's relation to the world. Thus, it is logical that those with high levels of spirituality, and therefore, a sense of certainty about themselves and their place in the world, would also experience high levels of meaning and purpose in life. Such attitudinal and behavioral stances following an event help people to seek and value greater levels of growth personally, interpersonally, and spiritually, lessening the likelihood that people may dwell on material losses (De Castella & Simmonds, 2013).

Strengthening the Foundation for Research and Practice

Our perspective is that positive coping mechanisms that have been consistently linked to resilience and posttraumatic growth can conceivably be seen as components of an overarching sense of meaning. In this chapter, meaning has been shown to be an important aspect of resilience, and it has been woven throughout the facets that comprise posttraumatic growth. Resilience and posttraumatic growth may not just be cooccurring protective processes, but rather factors that are encompassed by meaning, or are by-products of meaning. With the likelihood for people to experience a potentially traumatic event in their lifetime, as well as the importance for people to experience a positive recovery trajectory post-event (or at the very least a return to pre-disaster levels of functioning), it is imperative that researchers give these constructs more attention, investigating the significance of meaning to resilience and posttraumatic growth across a range of trauma-related contexts.

In the field of disaster mental health, resilience and posttraumatic growth have had a much larger presence than meaning to this point. Thus, a potentially important protective factor against the negative sequelae of a traumatic event is being largely overshadowed in the literature. Additionally, clinicians may overlook an important aspect of intervention that could enhance treatment efficacy following a disaster, which could improve the likelihood that positive outcomes will be obtained in both the short and long term. Meaning may even help to psychologically "inoculate" people prior to the occurrence of such an event, as well as facilitate preparedness for future disasters. While we have primarily studied meaning in life, resilience, and posttraumatic growth related to natural and technological disasters, we believe these concepts are likely to be key with respect to a range of potentially traumatic events.

Consequently, new research needs to be conducted to better illuminate our understanding of how a sense of meaning or purpose in life contributes to resilience and posttraumatic growth. While some researchers have asserted the importance of meaning or purpose in life in relation to resilience (Aiena et al., 2015; Park, 2013; Steger & Park, 2012; Wagnild, 2009) and posttraumatic growth (Cann, Calhoun, Tedeschi, & Solomon, 2010; Park, 2010; Tedeschi & Calhoun, 1995; Triplett et al., 2012), more studies are needed to rigorously examine the contributions that meaning may offer with respect to promoting these two concepts.

Clinically, it is also evident that there is a growing need to examine meaning as a potential facilitator of resilience and posttraumatic growth. In our view, meaning should be considered on "equal footing" with resilience and posttraumatic growth. It is promising that there is movement in the literature in this direction (Aiena et al., 2015; Dursun et al., 2016). Meaning in life has become a concept that has been linked to the facilitation and augmentation of happiness, and is one way for clinicians to increase overall levels of client happiness (Lent, 2004; Ryff & Singer, 1998a; Steger, Frazier, Oishi, & Kaler, 2006). Indeed, meaning is "crucial for a flourishing life" (Lomas et al., 2014, p. 42) and something that "everyone can find and experience" (Smith, Vicuna, & Emmanuel, 2015, p. 263). With the incorporation of meaning in resilience-based and posttraumatic growth-based interventions, the systematic benefits of this combination can be better studied and understood.

Meaning-making interventions could involve clinicians encouraging clients to learn adaptive emotion-regulation skills, consider the event in a reflective and positive manner, and seek to understand how the event has affected their core beliefs, as well as illuminating how a return to pre-event functioning (and potential growth) can occur, thus bolstering well-being and life satisfaction (Triplett et al., 2012). It is essential that any treatment approach be tailor-made to meet the needs of individual clients, taking into account their unique contexts, resources, and capacities. By way of an example of a potentially helpful means of facilitating adaptive reflection, clinicians may ask clients to recall previous successes in difficult situations, inquiring as to the nature of talents, strengths, and resources that were employed, and whether a given client learned something from the experience that could be useful in the current situation (Bannink, 2014). From such exercises, clients may come to realize that they have resources, strengths, and experiences that they may have forgotten about, and which may be accessed as a means of coping with their current situation. They may discover meaning in past suffering experiences and learn how these difficulties may be of use in overcoming other stressors. Potentially traumatic events create opportunities for people to see a different perspective, note what is truly important, and may serve as a catalyst to change one's values, goals, and priorities (Schulenberg, 2014a, 2014b, 2014c).

Considering meaning's relevance in such circumstances is consistent with clinicians who work with clients via a broad range of strengths-based approaches (i.e., positive clinical psychology). When clinicians employ strengths-based approaches they may in turn help clients find meaning in multiple areas of their lives, as well as teach them how to identify, prioritize, and adaptively apply their strengths in given situations. Therefore, strengths-based approaches, with an emphasis on meaning and purpose in life, are an essential means to guide case formulations and treatment efforts, complementing more traditional clinical approaches that tend to focus on symptom reduction.

As an example of the synergy between strengths-based approaches and more traditional, clinical approaches, cognitive restructuring (e.g., Taylor, 1983) is a tool clinicians can use to facilitate clients overcoming a potentially traumatic event and which meaning in life can be incorporated. People who experience such events are active agents in cognitively adapting to the event and thus reaching a psychological equilibrium. In this way, the event is challenging one's perception of meaning, one's sense of mastery, and also one's sense of self-esteem. Thus, people are motivated to make sense of the event, develop a sense of mastery over the event, and restore a sense of self-esteem after the event (Taylor & Brown, 1988). By conducting cognitive restructuring work, clinicians can bolster resources and effect positive therapeutic outcomes. For example, how individuals make sense of what happened to them following a traumatic event appears to be a strong predictor of how well they cope with and recover from the event. Moreover, deliberate thinking that focuses on what meaning or purpose can be taken from the event can influence revised life narratives, which may then lead to growth (Calhoun, Cann, & Tedeschi, 2010). People who are unable to reappraise their situation in a positive light or who have difficulty discovering a meaning in the situation may become "cognitively stuck." That is, it would be much more difficult for them to discover meaning or positively reframe a negative situation, thus hampering their ability to recover and perceive growth in response. An example of a reappraisal exercise clinicians may find to be appropriate for use with some clients is having them visualize themselves as older and wiser and looking back on the event and brainstorming what advice they would give themselves as a means of facilitating recovery (Bannink, 2014).

People who are able to positively reappraise their situation, who are able to discover meaning in their experience, would be expected to perceive some aspect of growth from the event. After all, while people cannot control their biology (in the sense of what they were born with), and while they may not be able to change their circumstances, they retain the ability to choose how they will respond to their circumstances (Frankl, 1959/2006; Schulenberg, 2014a, 2014b, 2014c). Clearly, meaning, resilience, and posttraumatic growth are critically important concepts for researchers and practitioners to consider throughout the course of trauma-related work. For clinicians and researchers who are interested in learning more about the applications of meaning, resilience, and posttraumatic growth in the context of trauma, Southwick, Litz, Charney, and Friedman (2011); Southwick and Charney (2012a); Kent, Davis, and Reich (2014); Calhoun and Tedeschi (2013); Bannink (2014); Werdel and Wicks (2012); and Joseph and Linley (2008) are suggested as useful places to begin.

Summary and Conclusions

Despite the fact that meaning is essential to human health and well-being, there are no one-size-fits-all interventions within this line of clinical work. Each person is unique, with a unique series of life experiences, requiring a tailor-made, research-supported treatment approach. It is important to understand individual differences in how people react to potentially traumatic events and how unique strengths, capacities, resources, and values may be brought to bear on a given situation. There is undoubtedly merit in the integration of meaning into resilience-based and post-traumatic growth-based interventions. As scientific and clinical interest in meaning, resilience, and posttraumatic growth continues to evolve, we must strive to better understand these concepts, how best to define and assess them, and how to effectively incorporate them into clinical interventions and empirical studies. We must work toward greater enlightenment of their interrelationships with one another. Researchers who examine resilience or posttraumatic growth should take special care to consider meaning and what it may contribute to the study of interest. Similarly, clinicians could readily include modules on meaning-making and purposeful living with many different kinds of presenting issues, and incorporate meaning in cognitive processing work with clients. Meaning-making (Park, 2016; Park & Folkman, 1997), which involves reframing an event so that it is less discordant from one's perception of meaning prior to the event, allows for the discovery and conceptualization of new, adaptive meaning systems post-event (Park, 2016). Meaning-based interventions could thus conceivably enhance resilience-based and posttraumatic growth-based interventions, helping clients to cultivate and maintain positive short- and long-term benefits.

Finally, much of this discussion is written with a focus as to what should be done *after* an event has occurred. In disaster mental health the question is not *if* a disaster will occur, but *when* it will occur (Schulenberg, Dellinger, et al., 2008). Thus, we argue for an assertive, proactive stance with respect to the significance of meaning and meaning-making. Meaning and meaning-making are not just important at the individual, group, and family level, but also in clinical contexts, societal and educational levels, and from a skill-building approach that may be employed in schools and other community contexts. Within these contexts, there should be an emphasis *before* the occurrence of an event. Taking the initiative in such a manner, we may better serve society, providing essential tools for living meaningful, flourishing lives, and galvanizing resilience and posttraumatic growth in times of adversity.

Key Takeaways

- Meaning contributes to overall wellness by facilitating awareness of social support, providing a sense of identity and values, facilitating health-promoting behaviors, and inoculating against stress.
- Many researchers cite meaning as an essential facet of what makes an individual resilient, resiliency being the capacity to adapt to stressors and restore balance to one's life when confronted with adversity.
- Posttraumatic growth, the positive perceived or actual change that people may experience as a result of a negative life event, has theoretical roots in meaning and purpose in life.
- Research needs to be conducted to better clarify our understanding of how a sense of meaning and purpose in life contributes to resilience and posttraumatic growth.
- With the incorporation of meaning into resilience-based and posttraumatic growth-based interventions, the systematic benefits of this combination can be better studied and understood.
- Meaning-making interventions could involve clinicians encouraging clients to learn adaptive emotion-regulation skills, consider the disaster in a reflective and positive manner, and seek to understand how the event has affected their core beliefs, illuminating how a return to pre-event functioning (and potential growth) can occur.

References

Abraído-Lanza, A. F., Guier, C., & Colón, R. M. (1998). Psychological thriving among Latinas with chronic illness. *The Journal of Social Issues, 54*, 405–424. doi:10.1111/j.1540-4560.1998.tb01227.x

Ai, A. L., Cascio, T., Santangelo, L. K., & Evans-Campbell, T. (2005). Hope, meaning, and growth following the September 11, 2001, terrorist attacks. *Journal of Interpersonal Violence, 20*, 523–548.

Aiena, B. J., Baczwaski, B. J., Schulenberg, S. E., & Buchanan, E. M. (2015). Psychometric properties of the 14-Item Resilience Scale: A tale of two samples. *Journal of Personality Assessment, 97*, 297–300. doi:10.1080/00223891.2014.951445

Aiena, B. J., Buchanan, E. M., Smith, C. V., & Schulenberg, S. E. (2015). Meaning, resilience, and traumatic stress after the Deepwater Horizon oil spill: A study of Mississippi coastal residents seeking mental health services. *Journal of Clinical Psychology*. doi:10.1002/jclp.22232

American Psychiatric Association. (2013). *Diagnostic and statistical manual of mental disorders* (5th ed.). Washington, DC: Author.

Andrykowski, M. A. (1992, August). *Positive psychosocial adjustment among cancer survivors*. Paper presented at the Annual Convention of the American Psychological Association, Washington, DC.

Arnetz, J., Rofa, Y., Arnetz, B., Ventimiglia, M., & Jamil, H. (2013). Resilience as a protective factor against the development of psychopathology among refugees. *Journal of Nervous and Mental Disease, 201*, 167–172. doi:10.1097/NMD.0b013e3182848afe

Baldwin, D. R., Jackson, D., Okoh, I., & Cannon, R. L. (2011). Resiliency and optimism: An African American senior citizen's perspective. *Journal of Black Psychology, 37,* 24–41. doi:10.1177/0095798410364394

Ball, K., & Martin, J. (2012). Self-defense training and traditional martial arts: Influences on self-efficacy and fear related to sexual victimization. *Sport, Exercise, and Performance Psychology, 1,* 135–144. doi:10.1037/a0025745

Bandura, A. (1994). Social cognitive theory of mass communication. In J. Bryant & D. Zillman (Eds.), *Media effects: Advances in theory and research* (pp. 61–90). Hillsdale, NJ: Lawrence Erlbaum Associates.

Bannink, F. (2014). *Post traumatic success: Positive psychology and solution-focused strategies to help clients survive and thrive.* New York, NY: W.W. Norton & Co.

Blackburn, L., & Owens, G. P. (2015). The effect of self efficacy and meaning in life on Posttraumatic Stress Disorder and depression severity among veterans. *Journal of Clinical Psychology, 71,* 219–228. doi:10.1002/jclp.22133

Bonanno, G. A. (2004). Loss, trauma, and human resilience. *American Psychologist, 59,* 20–28. doi:10.1037/0003-066X.591.20

Bonanno, G. A., Brewin, C. R., Kaniasty, K., & La Greca, A. M. (2010). Weighing the costs of disaster consequences, risks, and resilience in individuals, families, and communities. *Psychological Science in the Public Interest, 11,* 1–49. doi:10.1177/1529100610387086

Bonanno, G. A., & Diminich, E. D. (2013). Annual research review: Positive adjustment to adversity—Trajectories of minimal–impact resilience and emergent resilience. *Journal of Child Psychology and Psychiatry, 54,* 378–401. doi:10.1111/jcpp.12021

Brassai, L., Piko, B. F., & Steger, M. F. (2012). Existential attitudes and Eastern European adolescents' problem and health behaviors: Highlighting the role of the search for meaning in life. *The Psychological Record, 62,* 719–734.

Breslau, N. (2009). The epidemiology of trauma, PTSD, and other posttrauma disorders. *Trauma, Violence & Abuse, 10,* 198–210. doi:10.1177/1524838009334448

Bronk, K. C. (2014). *Purpose in life: A critical component of optimal youth development.* New York, NY: Springer Science + Business Media. doi:10.1007/978-94-007-7491-9

Burns, K. M. (2015). Emergency preparedness self-efficacy and the ongoing threat of disasters. (Doctoral dissertation). *Dissertation Abstracts International, 76.*

Burwell, R. A., & Shirk, S. R. (2007). Subtypes of rumination in adolescence: Associations between brooding, reflection, depressive symptoms and coping. *Journal of Clinical Child and Adolescent Psychology, 36,* 56–65. doi:10.1080/15374410709336568

Calhoun, L. G., Cann, A., & Tedeschi, R. G. (2010). The posttraumatic growth model: Sociocultural considerations. In T. Weiss & R. Berger (Eds.), *Posttraumatic growth and culturally competent practice: Lessons learned from around the globe* (pp. 1–14). Hoboken, NJ: John Wiley & Sons.

Calhoun, L. G., & Tedeschi, R. G. (1999). *Facilitating posttraumatic growth.* Mahwah, NJ: Lawrence Erlbaum Associates.

Calhoun, L. G., & Tedeschi, R. G. (2001). Posttraumatic growth: The positive lessons of loss. In R. A. Neimeyer (Ed.), *Meaning reconstruction and the experience of loss* (pp. 157–172). Washington, DC: American Psychological Association.

Calhoun, L. G., & Tedeschi, R. G. (2013). *Posttraumatic growth in clinical practice.* New York, NY: Routledge.

Cann, A., Calhoun, L. G., Tedeschi, R. G., & Solomon, D. T. (2010). Posttraumatic growth and depreciation as independent experiences and predictors of well-being. *Journal of Loss and Trauma, 15,* 151–166. doi:10.1080/15325020903375826

Chan, S., Miranda, R., & Surrence, K. (2009). Subtypes of rumination in the relationship between negative life events and suicidal ideation. *Archives of Suicide Research, 13,* 123–135. doi:10.1080/13811110902835015

Christopher, K. A. (2000). Determinants of psychological well-being in Irish immigrants. *Western Journal of Nursing Research, 22,* 123–143. doi:10.1177/01939450022044322

Cieslak, R., Benight, C., Schmidt, N., Luszczynska, A., Curtin, E., Clark, R. A., & Kissinger, P. (2009). Predicting posttraumatic growth among Hurricane Katrina survivors living with HIV: The role of self-efficacy, social support, and PTSD symptoms. *Anxiety, Stress & Coping, 22*, 449–463. doi:10.1080/10615800802403815

Compton, D. (2013). Traumatic adjustment and meaning-making processes. *Dissertation Abstracts International, 73*.

Crumbaugh, J. C. (1973/1988). *Everything to gain: A guide to self-fulfillment through logoanalysis*. Berkeley, CA: Institute of Logotherapy Press.

Damon, W. (2008). *The path to purpose: Helping our children find their calling in life*. New York, NY: Free Press.

De Castella, R. G., & Simmonds, J. G. (2013). There's a deeper level of meaning as to what suffering's all about: Experiences of religious and spiritual growth following trauma. *Mental Health, Religion & Culture, 16*, 536–556.

Drescher, C. F., Baczwaski, B. J., Walters, A., Aiena, B. J., Schulenberg, S. E., & Johnson, L. R. (2012). Coping with an ecological disaster: The role of perceived meaning in life and self-efficacy following the Gulf oil spill. *Ecopsychology, 4*, 56–63. doi:10.1089/eco.2012.0009

Drescher, C. F., Schulenberg, S. E., & Smith, C. V. (2014). The Deepwater Horizon oil spill and the Mississippi Gulf Coast: Mental health in the context of a technological disaster. *American Journal of Orthopsychiatry, 84*, 142–151. doi:10.1037/h0099382

Dursun, P., Steger, M. F., Bentele, C., & Schulenberg, S. E. (2016). Meaning and posttraumatic growth among survivors of the September 2013 Colorado floods. *Journal of Clinical Psychology*. doi:10.1002/jclp.22344

Exline, J. J., Park, C. L., Smyth, J. M., & Carey, M. P. (2011). Anger toward god: Social-cognitive predictors, prevalence, and links with adjustment to bereavement and cancer. *Journal of Personality and Social Psychology, 100*, 129–148. doi:10.1037/a0021716

Florez, I. A., Schulenberg, S. E., & Stewart, T. L. (2016). Meaning and automatic stereotyping: Advancing an agenda for research. In A. Batthyany (Ed.), *Logotherapy and Existential Analysis: Proceedings of the Viktor Frankl Institute, Vienna* (Vol. 1, pp. 107–124). Switzerland: Springer International Publishing. doi:10.1007/978-3-319-29424-7_11

Frankl, V. E. (1959/2006). *Man's search for meaning* (Rev. ed.). Boston, MA: Beacon Press.

Frankl, V. E. (1965). *The doctor and the soul: From psychotherapy to logotherapy*. New York, NY: Vintage Books.

Frankl, V. E. (1966). What is meant by meaning? *Journal of Existentialism, 7*, 21–28.

Frankl, V. E. (1990). Logotherapy and the challenge of suffering. In K. Hoeller (Ed.), *Readings in existential psychology and psychiatry* (pp. 63–67). Seattle, WA: Kluwer Academic Publishers.

Fredrickson, B. L., Tugade, M. M., Waugh, C. E., & Larkin, G. R. (2003). What good are positive emotions in crisis? A prospective study of resilience and emotions following the terrorist attacks on the United States on September 11th, 2001. *Journal of Personality and Social Psychology, 84*, 365–376. doi:10.1037/0022-3514.84.2.365

Garlick, M., Wall, K., Corwin, D., & Koopman, C. (2011). Psycho-spiritual integrative therapy for women with primary breast cancer. *Journal of Clinical Psychology in Medical Settings, 18*, 78–90. doi:10.1007/s10880-011-9224-9

Garmezy, N. (1993). Children in poverty: Resilience despite risk. *Psychiatry, 56*, 127–136.

Hall, B. J., Hobfoll, S. E., Canetti, D., Johnson, R. J., Palmieri, P. A., & Galea, S. (2010). Exploring the association between posttraumatic growth and PTSD: National Study of Jews and Arabs following the 2006 Israeli-Hezbollah War. *Journal of Nervous and Mental Disease, 198*, 180–186. doi:10.1097/NMD.0b013e3181d1411b

Halpern, J., & Tramontin, M. (2007). *Disaster mental health: Theory and practice*. Belmont, CA: Thomson Brooks/Cole.

Hawkins, A. O., Zinzow, H. M., Amstadter, A. B., Danielson, C. K., & Ruggiero, K. J. (2009). Factors associated with exposure and response to disasters among marginalized populations. In Y. Neria, S. Galea, & F. H. Norris (Eds.), *Mental health and disasters* (pp. 277–290). New York, NY: Cambridge University Press.

Helgeson, V. S., Reynolds, K. A., & Tomich, P. L. (2006). A meta-analytic review of benefit finding and growth. *Journal of Consulting and Clinical Psychology, 74*, 797–816. doi:10.1037/0022-006x.74.5.797

Herbert, H. S., Manjula, M., & Philip, M. (2013). Resilience and factors contributing to resilience among the offsprings of parents with schizophrenia. *Psychological Studies, 58*, 1–9. doi:10.1007/s12646-012-0168-4

Hirschel, M. J., & Schulenberg, S. E. (2009). Hurricane Katrina's impact on the Mississippi Gulf Coast: General self-efficacy's relationship to PTSD prevalence and severity. *Psychological Services, 6*, 293–303. doi:10.1037/a0017467

Hirschel, M. J., & Schulenberg, S. E. (2010). On the viability of PTSD Checklist (PCL) short form use: Analyses from Mississippi Gulf Coast Hurricane Katrina survivors. *Psychological Assessment, 22*, 460–464. doi:10.1037/a0018336

Hobfoll, S. E., Hall, B. J., Canetti-Nisim, D., Galea, S., Johnson, R. J., & Palmieri, P. A. (2007). Refining our understanding of traumatic growth in the face of terrorism: Moving from meaning cognitions to doing what is meaningful. *Applied Psychology: An International Review, 56*, 345–366.

Horowitz, M. J. (1986). *Stress response syndromes* (2nd ed.). New York, NY: Jason Aronson.

Ivtzan, I., Chan, C. P., Gardner, H. E., & Prashar, K. (2013). Linking religion and spirituality with psychological well-being: Examining self-actualisation, meaning in life, and personal growth initiative. *Journal of Religion and Health, 52*, 915–929. doi:10.1007/s10943-011-9540-2

Jafary, F., Farahbakhsh, K., Shafiabadi, A., & Delavar, A. (2011). Quality of life and menopause: Developing a theoretical model based on meaning in life, self-efficacy beliefs, and body image. *Aging & Mental Health, 15*, 630–637. doi:10.1080/13607863.2010.548056

Janoff-Bulman, R. (1992). *Shattered assumptions: Towards a new psychology of trauma*. New York, NY: Free Press.

Joseph, S., & Linley, P. A. (Eds.). (2008). *Trauma, recovery, and growth: Positive psychological perspectives on posttraumatic stress*. Hoboken, NJ: John Wiley & Sons.

Kaniasty, K. (2012). Predicting social psychological well-being following trauma: The role of postdisaster social support. *Psychological Trauma: Theory, Research, Practice, and Policy, 4*, 22–33. doi:10.1037/a0021412

Kent, M., Davis, M. C., & Reich, J. W. (Eds.). (2014). *The resilience handbook: Approaches to stress and trauma*. New York, NY: Routledge.

Khumalo, I. P., Wissing, M. P., & Schutte, L. (2014). Presence of meaning and search for meaning as mediators between spirituality and psychological well-being in a South African sample. *Journal of Psychology in Africa, 24*, 61–72.

Kilpatrick, D. G., Resnick, H. S., Milanak, M. E., Miller, M. W., Keyes, K. M., & Friedman, M. J. (2013). National estimates of exposure to traumatic events and PTSD prevalence using DSM-IV and DSM-5 criteria. *Journal of Traumatic Stress, 26*, 537–547.

Kimerling, R., Mack, K. P., & Alvarez, J. (2009). Women and disasters. In Y. Neria, S. Galea, & F. H. Norris (Eds.), *Mental health and disasters* (pp. 203–217). New York, NY: Cambridge University Press.

Krause, N. (2007). Longitudinal study of social support and meaning in life. *Psychology and Aging, 22*, 456–469. doi:10.1037/0882-7974.22.3.456

Lakey, B., & Cohen, S. (2000). Social support theory and measurement. In S. Cohen, L. G. Underwood, & B. Gottlieb (Eds.), *Social support measurement and intervention* (pp. 29–52). New York, NY: Oxford University Press.

Lambert, N. M., Stillman, T. F., Hicks, J. A., Kamble, S., Baumeister, R. F., & Fincham, F. D. (2013). To belong is to matter: Sense of belonging enhances meaning in life. *Personality and Social Psychology Bulletin, 39*, 1418–1427. doi:10.1177/0146167213499186

Lent, R. W. (2004). Toward a unifying theoretical and practical perspective on well-being and psychosocial adjustment. *Journal of Counseling Psychology, 51*, 482–509. doi:10.1037/0022-0167.51.4.482

Lepore, S. J. (2001). A social–cognitive processing model of emotional adjustment to cancer. In A. Baum & B. L. Andersen (Eds.), *Psychosocial interventions for cancer* (pp. 99–116). Washington, DC: American Psychological Association. doi:10.1037/10402-006

Lightsey, O. R., Boyraz, G., Ervin, A., Rarey, E., Gharghani, G. G., & Maxwell, D. (2014). Generalized self-efficacy, positive cognitions, and negative cognitions as mediators of the relationship between conscientiousness and meaning in life. *Canadian Journal of Behavioural Science, 46*, 436–445. doi:10.1037/a0034022

Linley, P. A., & Joseph, S. (2004). Positive change following trauma and adversity: A review. *Journal of Traumatic Stress, 17*, 11–21. doi:10.1023/B:JOTS.0000014671.27856.7e

Lomas, T., Hefferon, K., & Ivtzan, I. (2014). *Applied positive psychology: Integrated positive practice*. Los Angeles, CA: Sage.

Lukas, E., & Hirsch, B. Z. (2002). Logotherapy. In F. W. Kaslow (Ed.-In-Chief), & R. F. Massey & S. D. Massey (Vol. Eds.), *Comprehensive handbook of psychotherapy: Vol. 3. Interpersonal/humanistic/existential* (pp. 333–356). New York, NY: John Wiley & Sons.

Lyons, J. (1991). Strategies for assessing the potential for positive adjustment following trauma. *Journal of Traumatic Stress, 4*, 93–111.

Lyubomirsky, S., Caldwell, N. D., & Nolen-Hoeksema, S. (1998). Effects of ruminative and distracting responses to depressed mood on retrieval of autobiographical memories. *Journal of Personality and Social Psychology, 75*, 166–177. doi:10.1037/0022-3514.75.1.166

Martin, L. L., & Tesser, A. (1996). Some ruminative thoughts. In R. S. Wyer (Ed.), *Advances in social cognition* (Vol. IX, pp. 1–47). Mahwah, NJ: Lawrence Erlbaum Associates.

Masten, A. S. (2001). Ordinary magic: Resilience processes in development. *American Psychologist, 56*, 227–238. doi:10.1037/0003-066x.56.3.227

McFarlane, A. C., & Norris, F. H. (2006). Definitions and concepts in disaster research. In F. H. Norris, S. Galea, M. J. Friedman, & P. J. Watson (Eds.), *Methods for disaster mental health research* (pp. 3–19). New York, NY: Guilford Press.

McMillen, J. C., & Fisher, R. H. (1998). The Perceived Benefits Scales: Measuring perceived positive life changes after negative events. *Social Work Research, 22*, 173–187.

Melton, A. M. A., & Schulenberg, S. E. (2008). On the measurement of meaning: Logotherapy's empirical contributions to humanistic psychology. *The Humanistic Psychologist, 36*, 31–44. doi:10.1080/08873260701828870

Moberly, N. J., & Watkins, E. R. (2008). Ruminative self-focus and negative affect: An experience sampling study. *Journal of Abnormal Psychology, 117*, 314–323. doi:10.1037/0021-843X.117.2.314

Mystakidou, K., Parpa, E., Tsilika, E., Panagiotou, I., Theodorakis, P. N., Galanos, A., & Gouliamos, A. (2015). Self-efficacy and its relationship to posttraumatic stress symptoms and posttraumatic growth in cancer patients. *Journal of Loss and Trauma, 20*, 160–170. doi:10.1080/15325024.2013.838892

Niederhoffer, K. G., & Pennebaker, J. W. (2009). Sharing one's story: On the benefits of writing or talking about emotional experience. In S. J. Lopez & C. R. Snyder (Eds.), *Oxford handbook of positive psychology* (2nd ed., pp. 621–632). New York, NY: Oxford University Press.

Nishi, D., Uehara, R., Kondo, M., & Matsuoka, Y. (2010). Reliability and validity of the Japanese version of the Resilience Scale and its short version. *BMC Research Notes, 3*, 310–315. doi:10.1186/1756-0500-3-310

Orchowski, L. M., Gidycz, C. A., & Raffle, H. (2008). Evaluation of a sexual assault risk reduction and self-defense program: A prospective analysis of a revised protocol. *Psychology of Women Quarterly, 32*, 204–218. doi:10.1111/j.1471-6402.2008.00425.x

Park, C. L. (2010). Making sense of the meaning literature: An integrative review of meaning making and its effects on adjustment to stressful life events. *Psychological Bulletin, 136*, 257–301. doi:10.1037/a0018301

Park, C. L. (2012). Meaning, spirituality, and growth: Protective and resilience factors in health and illness. In A. Baum, T. A. Revenson, & J. Singer (Eds.), *Handbook of health psychology* (2nd ed., pp. 405–429). New York, NY: Psychology Press.

Park, C. L. (2013). Trauma and meaning making: Converging conceptualizations and emerging evidence. In J. A. Hicks & C. Routledge (Eds.), *The experience of meaning in life: Classical perspectives, emerging theories, and controversies* (pp. 61–76). New York, NY: Springer. doi:10.1007/978-94-007-6527-6_5

Park, C. L. (2016). Meaning making in the context of disasters. *Journal of Clinical Psychology*. doi:10.1002/jclp.22270

Park, C. L., Cohen, L. H., & Murch, R. L. (1996). Assessment and prediction of stress–related growth. *Journal of Personality, 64*, 71–105.

Park, C. L., & Folkman, S. (1997). Meaning in the context of stress and coping. *Review of General Psychology, 1*, 115–144.

Paton, D., Smith, L., & Johnston, D. (2005). When good intentions turn bad: Promoting natural hazard preparedness. *Australian Journal of Emergency Management, 20*, 25–30.

Peterson, C., Park, N., Pole, N., D'Andrea, W., & Seligman, M. (2008). Strengths of character and posttraumatic growth. *Journal of Traumatic Stress, 21*, 214–217.

Quarantelli, E. L. (1985). An assessment of conflicting views on mental health: The consequences of traumatic events. In C. Figley (Ed.), *Trauma and its wake* (pp. 173–217). New York, NY: Brunner/Mazel.

Resnick, H. S., Falsetti, S. A., Kilpatrick, D. G., & Freedy, J. R. (1996). Assessment of rape and other civilian trauma-related PTSD: Emphasis on assessment of potentially traumatic events. In T. W. Miller (Ed.), *Theory and assessment of stressful life events* (pp. 235–271). Madison, CT: International Universities Press.

Rutter, M. (1987). Psychosocial resilience and protective mechanisms. *American Journal of Orthopsychiatry, 57*, 316–331. doi:10.1111/j.1939-0025.1987.tb03541.x

Ryff, C. D., & Singer, B. (1998a). The contours of positive human health. *Psychological Inquiry, 9*, 1–28.

Ryff, C. D., & Singer, B. (1998b). The role of purpose in life and personal growth in positive human health. In P. T. P. Wong & P. S. Fry (Eds.), *The human quest for meaning: A handbook of psychological research and clinical applications* (pp. 213–235). Mahwah, NJ: Lawrence Erlbaum Associates.

Savolaine, J., & Granello, P. F. (2002). The function of meaning and purpose for individual wellness. *Journal of Humanistic Counseling Education and Development, 41*, 178–189.

Scali, J., Gandubert, C., Ritchie, K., Soulier, M., Anceline, M. L., & Chadieu, I. (2012). Measuring resilience in adult women using the 10-Items Connor-Davidson Resilience Scale (CD-RISC). Role of trauma exposure and anxiety disorders. *Plos One, 7*, 1–7. doi:10.1371/journal.pone.0039879

Schulenberg, S. E. (2014a, May). *Meaning and disaster mental health*. Paper presented at the 2nd International Conference on Logotherapy & Existential Analysis, Vienna, Austria.

Schulenberg, S. E. (2014b, July). *Disaster mental health and positive psychology: Meaning-making and resilience following traumatic events*. Workshop presented at the 8th Biennial Conference of the International Network on Personal Meaning, Vancouver, BC, Canada.

Schulenberg, S. E. (2014c, August). *Recovering from natural and technological disasters: Meaning as catalyst for resilience and posttraumatic growth*. Paper presented at the 4th Colombian Congress on Logotherapy and Existential Analysis, Bogota, Colombia.

Schulenberg, S. E., Dellinger, K. A., Koestler, A. J., Kinnell, A. M. K., Swanson, D. A., Van Boening, M. V., & Forgette, R. G. (2008). Psychologists and Hurricane Katrina: Natural disaster response through training, public education, and research. *Training and Education in Professional Psychology, 2*, 83–88. doi:10.1037/1931-3918.2.2.83

Schulenberg, S. E., Drescher, C. F., & Baczwaski, B. J. (2014). Perceived meaning and disaster mental health: A role for logotherapy in clinical-disaster psychology. In A. Batthyany & P. Russo-Netzer (Eds.), *Meaning in positive and existential psychology* (pp. 251–267). New York, NY: Springer. doi:10.1007/978-1-4939-0308-5_15

Schulenberg, S. E., Hutzell, R. R., Nassif, C., & Rogina, J. M. (2008). Logotherapy for clinical practice. *Psychotherapy: Theory, Research, Practice, Training, 45*, 447–463. doi:10.1037/a0014331

Schulenberg, S. E., Smith, C. V., Drescher, C. F., & Buchanan, E. M. (2015). Assessment of meaning in adolescents receiving clinical services in Mississippi following the Deepwater Horizon oil spill: An application of the Purpose in Life test—Short Form (PIL-SF). *Journal of Clinical Psychology*. doi:10.1002/jclp.22240

Shahar, G. (2012). A social-clinical psychological statement on resilience: Introduction to the special issue. *Journal of Social and Clinical Psychology, 31*, 535–541. doi:10.1521/jscp.2012.31.6.535

Sherman, A. C., & Simonton, S. (2012). Effects of personal meaning among patients in primary and specialized care: Associations with psychosocial and physical outcomes. *Psychology & Health, 27*, 475–490. doi:10.1080/08870446.2011.592983

Smith, B. W., Vicuna, B., & Emmanuel, G. (2015). The role of positive psychology in fostering spiritual development and a sense of calling in college. In J. C. Wade, L. I. Marks, & R. D. Hetzel (Eds.), *Positive psychology on the college campus* (pp. 261–278). Oxford: Oxford University Press.

Southwick, S. M., Bonanno, G. A., Masten, A. S., Panter-Brick, C., & Yehuda, R. (2014). Resilience definitions, theory, and challenges: Interdisciplinary perspectives. *European Journal of Psychotraumatology, 5*, 1–14. doi:10.3402/ejpt.v5.25338

Southwick, S. M., & Charney, D. S. (2012a). *Resilience: The science of mastering life's greatest challenges*. Cambridge: Cambridge University Press.

Southwick, S. M., & Charney, D. S. (2012b). The science of resilience: Implications for the prevention and treatment of depression. *Science, 338*, 79–82. doi:10.1126/science.1222942

Southwick, S. M., Litz, B. T., Charney, D., & Friedman, M. J. (Eds.). (2011). *Resilience and mental health: Challenges across the lifespan*. New York, NY: Cambridge University Press.

Spiegel, D., & Fawzy, F. I. (2002). Psychosocial interventions and prognosis in cancer. In H. G. Koenig & H. J. Cohen (Eds.), *The link between religion and health: Psychoneuroimmunology and the faith factor* (pp. 84–100). New York, NY: Oxford University Press.

Steger, M. F., Frazier, P., Oishi, S., & Kaler, M. (2006). The Meaning in Life Questionnaire: Assessing the presence of and search for meaning in life. *Journal of Counseling Psychology, 53*, 80–93.

Steger, M. F., Mann, J. R., Michels, P., & Cooper, T. C. (2009). Meaning in life, anxiety, depression, and general health among smoking cessation patients. *Journal of Psychosomatic Research, 67*, 353–358. doi:10.1016/j.jpsychores.2009.02.006

Steger, M. F., & Park, C. L. (2012). The creation of meaning following trauma: Meaning making and trajectories of distress and recovery. In R. A. McMackin, E. Newman, J. M. Fogler, & T. M. Keane (Eds.), *Trauma therapy in context: The science and craft of evidence-based practice* (pp. 171–191). Washington, DC: American Psychological Association. doi:10.1037/13746-008

Steger, M. F., Shin, J. Y., Shim, Y., & Fitch-Martin, A. (2013). Is meaning in life a flagship indicator of well-being? In A. Waterman (Ed.), *The best within us: Positive psychology perspectives on eudaimonia* (pp. 159–182). Washington, DC: American Psychological Association. doi:10.1037/14092-009

Stillman, T. F., Baumeister, R. F., Lambert, N. M., Crescioni, A. W., DeWall, C. N., & Fincham, F. D. (2009). Alone and without purpose: Life loses meaning following social exclusion. *Journal of Experimental Social Psychology, 45*, 686–694. doi:10.1016/j.jesp.2009.03.007

Taku, K., Cann, A., Tedeschi, R. G., & Calhoun, L. G. (2009). Intrusive versus deliberate rumination in posttraumatic growth across US and Japanese samples. *Anxiety, Stress, & Coping, 22*, 129–136. doi:10.1080/10615800802317841

Taku, K., Tedeschi, R. G., & Cann, A. (2015). Relationships of posttraumatic growth and stress responses in bereaved young adults. *Journal of Loss & Trauma, 20*, 56–71. doi:10.1080/15325024.2013.824306

Taylor, S. E. (1983). Adjustment to threatening events: A theory of cognitive adaptation. *American Psychologist, 38*, 1161–1173.

Taylor, S. E., & Brown, J. (1988). Illusion and well-being: A social psychological perspective on mental health. *Psychological Bulletin, 103*, 193–210. doi:10.1037/0033-2909.103.2.193

Tedeschi, R. G., & Calhoun, L. G. (1995). *Trauma and transformation: Growing in the aftermath of suffering*. Thousand Oaks, CA: Sage.

Tedeschi, R. G., & Calhoun, L. G. (1996). The Posttraumatic Growth Inventory: Measuring the positive legacy of trauma. *Journal of Traumatic Stress, 9*, 455–472. doi:10.1002/jts.2490090305

Tedeschi, R. G., & Calhoun, L. G. (2004). Posttraumatic growth: Conceptual foundations and empirical evidence. *Psychological Inquiry, 15*, 1–18. doi:10.1207/s15327965pli1501_01

Tedeschi, R. G., & Calhoun, L. G. (2005). Special issue: Editorial note. *Traumatology, 11*, 207–208. doi:10.1177/153476560501100401

Tedeschi, R. G., & Calhoun, L. G. (2012). Pathways to personal transformation: Theoretical and empirical developments. In P. T. P. Wong (Ed.), *The human quest for meaning: Theories, research, and applications* (2nd ed., pp. 559–572). New York, NY: Routledge.

Tedeschi, R., Calhoun, L., & Groleau, J. (2015). Clinical applications of posttraumatic growth. In S. Joseph (Ed.), *Positive psychology in practice: Promoting human flourishing in work, health, education, and everyday life* (2nd ed., pp. 503–518). Hoboken, NJ: John Wiley & Sons.

Thorne, B. (2001). A personal view: The prophetic nature of pastoral counselling. *British Journal of Guidance and Counselling, 29*, 43–45. doi:10.1080/03069880127015

Triplett, K. N., Tedeschi, R. G., Cann, A., Calhoun, L. G., & Reeve, C. L. (2012). Posttraumatic growth, meaning in life, and life satisfaction in response to trauma. *Psychological Trauma: Theory, Research, Practice, and Policy, 4*, 400–410. doi:10.1037/a0024204

Tsai, J., El-Gabalawy, R., Sledge, W. H., Southwick, S., & Pietrzak, R. H. (2015). Post-traumatic growth among veterans in the USA: Results from the National Health and Resilience in Veterans Study. *Psychological Medicine, 45*, 165–179. doi:10.1017/S0033291714001202

Tugade, M. M., & Fredrickson, B. L. (2004). Resilient individuals use positive emotions to bounce back from negative emotional experiences. *Journal of Personality and Social Psychology, 86*, 320–333. doi:10.1037/0022-3514.86.2.320

Volkert, J., Schulz, H., Brütt, A. L., & Andreas, S. (2014). Meaning in life: Relationship to clinical diagnosis and psychotherapy outcome. *Journal of Clinical Psychology, 70*, 528–535. doi:10.1002/jclp.22053

Vranceanu, A.-M., Hobfoll, S. E., & Johnson, R. J. (2007). Child multi-type maltreatment and associated depression and PTSD symptoms: The role of social support and stress. *Child Abuse & Neglect, 31*, 71–84. doi:10.1016/j.chiabu.2006.04.010

Wagnild, G. (2009). *The Resilience Scale user's guide for the US English version of the Resilience Scale and the 14-Item Resilience Scale (RS-14)*. Worden, MT: Resilience Center.

Wagnild, G., & Young, H. M. (1990). Resilience among older women. *Journal of Nursing Scholarship, 22*, 252–255. doi:10.1111/j.1547-5069.1990.tb00224.x

Wagnild, G., & Young, H. (1993). Development and psychometric evaluation of the Resilience Scale. *Journal of Nursing Measurement, 1*, 165–178.

Werdel, M. B., & Wicks, R. J. (2012). *Primer on posttraumatic growth: An introduction and guide*. Hoboken, NJ: John Wiley & Sons.

Werner, E. E. (1984). Resilient children. *Young Child, 40*, 68–72.

Wong, P. T. P. (2010). Meaning therapy: An integrative and positive existential psychotherapy. *Journal of Contemporary Psychotherapy, 40*, 85–93. doi:10.1007/s10879-009-9132-6

Wong, P. T. P., & Wong, L. C. J. (2012). A meaning-centered approach to building youth resilience. In P. T. P. Wong (Ed.), *The human quest for meaning: Theories, research, and applications* (2nd ed., pp. 585–617). New York, NY: Routledge.

Yalçın, İ., & Malkoç, A. (2015). The relationship between meaning in life and subjective well-being: Forgiveness and hope as mediators. *Journal of Happiness Studies, 16*, 915–929. doi:10.1007/s10902-014-9540-5

Zakour, M. J. (2012). Coping with loss and overcoming trauma. In J. L. Framingham & M. L. Teasley (Eds.), *Behavioral health response to disasters* (pp. 91–113). Boca Raton, FL: CRC Press.

Zhai, J., Huang, Y., Gao, X., Jiang, H., & Xu, J. (2014). Post-trauma growth in a mainland Chinese population with chronic skin disease. *International Journal of Dermatology, 53*, 450–457. doi:10.1111/j.1365-4632.2012.05734.x

Zika, S., & Chamberlain, K. (1992). On the relation between meaning in life and psychological well-being. *British Journal of Psychology, 83*, 133–145. doi:10.1111/j.2044-8295.1992.tb02429.x

Working with Meaning in Life in Chronic or Life-Threatening Disease: A Review of Its Relevance and the Effectiveness of Meaning-Centred Therapies

Joel Vos

Introduction

Two years ago, 36-year-old Emma received a diagnosis of breast cancer. Initially, the prognosis seemed positive after breast-conserving surgery, but recently doctors have brought her bad news. They have identified metastases and it is uncertain whether cure is possible this time. After the first operation, Emma had shown a brave face and seemed to deny the impact of cancer: "I needed to fight; I could not let my emotions overwhelm me." For instance, as soon as her physical health allowed, she continued to work as a nurse and even started working longer night shifts. But after the diagnosis of the metastases "Something broke inside me: everything started to feel meaningless. Why would I work so many hours? Why work at all? Why fight? (…) I am too tired to see my daughter play football; I cannot be a good mother anymore. (…) It's all relative isn't it? One day you are a good employee and mother and the next day you are nothing anymore. One day going to your work seems important to you, but the next day it does not. Thus possibly, nothing in life is certain. (…) What do I do? In which direction should I go in life now?" (Anonymised case from private counselling practice)

Meaning seems to be at the heart of the experience of many those with a chronic or life-threatening disease. Emma's story shows how a diagnosis can cast a totally different perspective on life and makes everything that was once meaningful suddenly feel relative. The illness may also hinder engaging in meaningful activities such as cheering at your daughter's sports field, because you lack the energy or your mobility is restricted. It seems unavoidable that physically ill patients may start experiencing symptoms of depression and anxiety, as staring at the sun blinds everyone (Yalom, 2008).

This attention to the patient's sense of meaning seems at odds with stereotypical medical care, putting a label of psychopathology on such existential questions and

J. Vos, Ph.D. (✉)
Department of Psychology, University of Roehampton,
Holybourne Avenue, London SW15 4JD, UK
e-mail: joel.vos@roehampton.ac.uk

referring patients to psychopharmacological treatment or a psychological therapy to change cognitive biases, behavioural avoidance or poor stress management. Consequently, too often patients feel that their voice is not heard in such a medical system as their experience that "the meaning of everything" has changed is not taken seriously (cf. Henoch & Danielson, 2009). For example, Emma told me about her previous cognitive therapist: "My fear of death is not the result of a bad cognition: It is the reality of my finitude that I am facing, and my struggles are about the almost impossible task of building a meaningful life while I am facing my death—a literally life-saving task!" After several sessions Emma realised that "Society tells you are crazy, doctors tell you are crazy, friends tell you are crazy. Even your therapist tells you are crazy! But what you are experiencing is actually a normal response to an abnormal situation."

This chapter gives voice to the role of meaning in the experiences of patients with a chronic or life-threatening disease. Not only will the relevance of meaning be discussed but also the effectiveness of directly addressing meaning in psychological treatments. This aim is achieved by reviewing the empirical literature, in particular the literature about the effectiveness of traditional psychological therapies, dominant meaning-centred models in health and medical psychology and effectiveness studies on meaning-centred practices. Most figures will focus on the UK as a case study, which may, however, be generalised to other countries, although more research is warranted.

Time for Change: The Failure of Traditional Treatments

More than 30 % of all individuals in the UK live with a chronic or life-threatening disease such as cancer, cardiovascular disease or chronic pain, and this percentage is rapidly increasing due to modern lifestyles and the ageing population; of these physically ill individuals, almost 40 % also experience mental health problems during their disease history such as psychological stress, depression, anxiety or adjustment difficulties (Cimpean & Drake, 2011; Mitchell et al., 2011). Mental health problems are associated with poorer health outcomes, lower quality of life and increased health-care costs by interacting with and exacerbating physical illness and even shortening survival time. Co-morbid mental health problems raise the total health-care costs by at least 45 % for each person with a long-term physical condition (Naylor et al., 2012). Consequently, between 12 and 18 % of all expenditure of the national health services on long-term physical conditions is linked to poor mental health and well-being, i.e., between £8 billion and £13 billion in England each year (Naylor et al., 2012). For these reasons, the British government prioritises psychological care for people with long-term health conditions, and a national health-care review recommends that integrated forms of care for people with co-morbid mental and physical health problems should be "one of the top ten priorities for clinical commissioning groups" (Imison et al., 2011).

Although guidelines of, for instance, the British National Health Service (NHS) are clear about the fact that effective psychological support should be available to physically ill patients, most guidelines do not specify which specific type of psychological treatment should be offered. A first reason for this imprecision may be that different patients have different needs. Second, relatively few empirical studies have examined the effectiveness of psychotherapeutic care with the rigour of randomised controlled trials in, for instance, cancer, cardiovascular disease and chronic pain patients. Third, meta-analyses suggest inconsistent findings between studies and confounding, biased study designs (e.g., Cuijpers, Van Straten, Bohlmeijer, Hollon, & Andersson, 2010; Lepore & Coyne, 2006). Recent meta-analyses conclude that the effects of traditional psychological treatments—such as cognitive-behavioural therapy—for physically ill patients on their psychological well-being are at their best small to moderate (e.g., Beltman, Voshaar, & Speckens, 2010; Eccleston, Williams, & Morley, 2009; Faller et al., 2013; Hart et al., 2012; McCracken & Vowles, 2014; Van Straten, Geraedts, Verdonck-de Leeuw, Andersson, & Cuijpers, 2010; Whalley et al., 2011). To put this in a broader context: some exceptional individual studies have large effect sizes, and most psychological treatments are more effective than pharmacotherapy or no treatment.

Why do most psychological treatments only have modest effects on the well-being of patients with a chronic or life-threatening disease? One answer may be found by examining the underlying clinical and aetiological assumptions of these traditional psychological treatments. That is, it has been argued that one of the differences between quack therapies and evidence-based therapies is not only that outcome studies prove their effectiveness but also that there is empirical evidence and conceptual coherence for the underlying clinical and aetiological models and that the therapeutic mechanisms are logically built on these clinical–aetiological models (Kazdin, 2008; Vos, 2015). A clinical model conceptualises the main psychological problem that the therapy focuses on, and an aetiological model describes how this problem developed; the therapeutic mechanisms should logically follow from these clinical–aetiological models.

It may be argued that there is inconsistency in these populations between the evidence-based clinical–aetiological models, on the one hand, and the therapeutic mechanisms in the psychological treatments, on the other. The psychological treatments that are applied were not initially developed and tailored to physically ill patients but were generalisations of treatments for physically healthy individuals with mental health problems. However, several studies indicate that the experience and aetiology of the psychological problems in physically ill patients cannot be generalised from those in physically healthy individuals with primarily psychological concerns (e.g., Alderson, Foy, Glidewell, McLintock, & House, 2012). The differences between these populations would imply a different type of mental health care tailored to the unique experiences and aetiology of physically ill patients.

For example, the psychological therapy most frequently offered in the NHS for patients with cancer, cardiovascular disease (CVD) and chronic pain is cognitive-behavioural therapy, which teaches cognitive and behavioural skills. More recently, this approach has also started to include practices such as mindfulness/meditation to improve the patient's stress management skills; while the effects of these interventions are promising, they are still relatively small (e.g., Powers, Vörding, & Emmelkamp, 2009; Veehof, Oskam, Schreurs, & Bohlmeijer, 2011). Of course, some individuals will benefit from these interventions, as their psychological problems originate in negative thought patterns, unconstructive behaviour and a lack of stress reduction skills, which were possibly already present before they became physically ill (preexisting neuroticism; Schneider et al., 2010). However, the majority of physically ill individuals were not mentally ill before they became physically ill, and therefore the aetiology and treatment of their mental health problems may be different from those with pre-existing neuroticism (cf. Lepore & Coyne, 2006).

Thus, the main hypothesis in this chapter is that the usual psychological treatments for individuals with a chronic or life-threatening disease are at their best moderately effective because they do not directly and systematically address the unique concerns of this population, which centre on the question "How can I live a meaningful and satisfying life despite my disease?" It has been hypothesised that meaning, however, is at the core of the clinical and aetiological models of these patients' psychological concerns. Therefore, meaning-centred treatment may be more effective than the usual care provided for this population.

The Integrated Meaning-Centred Clinical–Aetiological Model

To support the hypothesis that meaning is relevant for this population, this section reviews and subsequently integrates six frequently cited perspectives in health and medical psychology, along with their empirical support.

The Assumptive Worlds Perspective

We usually live our daily lives with many illusions about ourselves and our world, but it becomes difficult to maintain our belief in these assumptions when we develop a physical disease. That is, most individuals seem to have the three main assumptions that "the world is benevolent, the world is meaningful, and the self is worthy," and consequently they expect themselves and the world around them to remain decent and meaningful under all circumstances (Brewin & Holmes, 2003; Janoff-Bulman, 1992). The benevolence of the world entails that they believe that the world around them is good, and more particularly it gives "good fortune and positive outcomes" with the idea that "all people have an inner goodness" (Janoff-Bulman, 1992, p. 35). The meaningfulness of the world means that events in life are intelligible, and, more precisely, that the purpose of events can be explained and that there is a fair distribution of negative events happening in response to bad behaviour and positive events in response to good behaviour. Thus, it is perceived as unfair or wrong when an unjust event happens to an undeserving person. The self is regarded as positive, moral and successful and is able to control for positive or negative outcomes. Although we may cognitively know that these are mere illusions—for instance, we know the fact that all of us will die one day—we often feel and act as if these illusions are true. The reason why we believe in these illusions in our everyday lives may be a pragmatic and socially reinforced way of coping with our existential reality; it seems, for instance, not pragmatic to be continuously aware of our vulnerability and finitude, as this may evoke so much existential anxiety that we might possibly not dare to cross the street because of the risk of dying (cf. Greenberg & Koole, 2013).

However, a chronic or life-threatening disease can shatter these assumptions, especially if this disease is diagnosed unexpectedly or has developed quickly, as a result of an accident, for example. This shattering of fundamental assumptions can be emotionally stressful, especially for those who previously had strong positive beliefs (Brewin & Holmes, 2003). Several empirical studies confirm that the psychological stress and symptoms of psychopathology that patients may experience in the aftermath of a traumatic event, such as the diagnosis of a chronic or life-threatening disease, are related to the shattering of their fundamental assumptions about life (DePrince & Freyd, 2002; Park, 2010; Park, Edmondson, Fenster, & Blank, 2008). Other studies on the self-regulation theory confirm that the ways in which individuals monitor, evaluate and change their behaviour are often driven by assumptions; for instance, when individuals fail to have genuine control in life, they seem to fall back on defensive attributions of control and illusions of control (Fenton-O'Creevy, Nicholson, Soane, & Willman, 2003). More in particular, the way in which, for instance, coronary heart disease patients perceive the extent of control over their disease, their sense of coherence and life's timeline predicts their quality of life and level of psychological stress (Foxwell, Morley, & Frizelle, 2013).

From the perspective of assumptive worlds, the psychological treatment of this population should focus on creating new assumptions or modifying old assumptions (e.g., Brewin & Holmes, 2003; Janoff-Bulman, 1992). After a negative event, it seems beneficial to not maintain the notion of predictability and unchangeability of life but to re-evaluate one's life, values and goals and to find new meaning in life (e.g., Batthyany & Russo-Netzer, 2014; Park et al., 2008). In other words, positive growth after adversity seems to focus on coping with duality in life (e.g., Zoellner & Maercker, 2006). Individuals may be supported to develop a dual attitude, which on the one hand acknowledges the undeniable reality of their disease and on the other recognises the necessity of having illusions as beneficial for their everyday life and well-being (Vos, 2014). The patient could be taught to go back and forth between different perspectives on life, which has been called "existential plasticity" and which has been metaphorically compared with the movie *The Matrix*, in which the main character flexibly moves between reality and an illusionary world; the possibility that patients could develop such a dual awareness is confirmed by research on dual emotional–cognitive processes and on tolerating ambiguities (Vos, 2014). Additionally, patients could be supported in tolerating the tensions between illusions and reality, mourn over the "lost paradise" of the old assumptive world and develop a sense of trust and hope that it will be possible to live a meaningful life again, despite life's limitations (Vos, 2014). This assumptive world framework seems to fit with the aims and methods of different treatment modalities, although meaning-centred treatments seem to focus most directly on coping with the Janus face of being ill and systematically re-creating meaningful assumptions.

The Change Perspective

The change perspective is a specification of the assumptive worlds perspective and suggests that becoming ill makes individuals aware of what is meaningful to them and changes where and how they experience meaning in life. This is in contrast to people's ordinary existence in which they are usually not explicitly aware of what gives their lives meaning; most individuals usually act intuitively on the basis of a pre-reflective understanding of what is meaningful to them (Vos, 2014). Thus, in ordinary life situations, people do not need a self-reflective homunculus making decisions and giving orders about which meaningful activities to engage in. To the contrary, reflecting too much on what is meaningful to us in everyday life (hyper-reflection) can create a cognitive distance from our activities and the implicit meanings of our daily life, which could subsequently create a sense of meaninglessness (Lukas, 2006); Heidegger calls this "not being at home"; instead of "being *in* the situation," hyper-reflective patients feel they are "*with* the situation" in their thoughts (Vos, 2014).

Thus, speaking about meaning seems to some extent artificial, with some phenomenologically-oriented authors arguing that "meaning in life" is a tenuous and artificial construct. Although individuals may not need to have reflected on meaning before they are able to live a meaningful daily life, when they are asked, they are able to identify a general direction or orientation in life (e.g., Brandstätter, Baumann, Borasio, & Fegg, 2012; Park & George, 2013). Furthermore, research indicates that the experience of meaning entails motivation, values, understanding, self-worth, action-directed goals and self-regulation (e.g., Batthyany & Russo-Netzer, 2014; Wong, 2012).

When individuals are confronted with boundary situations in life such as a chronic or life-threatening disease, they often start to reflect on what is meaningful to them. That is, they are not embedded anymore in an unreflected manner in the context that had made sense to them in their daily lives before, but now they start to reflect and ask questions about meaning (Vos, 2014). For instance, surveys in many countries have shown that a majority of patients with a chronic or life-threatening disease start to ask questions about meaning, regardless of the type and stage of their disease (e.g., Harrison, Young, Price, Butow, & Solomon, 2009; Henoch & Danielson, 2009; LeMay & Wilson, 2008; Vehling et al., 2012; Wexler & Corn, 2012). Figure 1 shows a simplified overview of meaning-related changes that patients reported in these studies.

First, changes may occur in specific meanings in life. That is, some specific aspects of their lives that had felt meaningful to them in the past may still feel equally valuable, whereas other aspects may feel less valuable. Moreover, new meanings

```
Possible consequences:

Chronic or                                    Specific previous meanings stay the same
life-threatening ──▶ Confronted with          A specific previous meaning becomes         ⎤ Changes in the
disease              life's boundaries        more valuable                                 experience of
                                              A specific previous meaning feels less valuable  specific
                                              One or more previous meanings become unattainable meanings in life
                                              Something new starts to feel more valuable   ⎦
                     * Physical
                     * Emotional              General priorities in life change
                     * Personality
                     * Meaning                Experiencing life more intensively
                     * Spirituality
                                              Becoming aware of what authenticity and true self are
                                                                                          ⎤ Changes in the
                                              Such a narrow focus on the disease and the treatment general
                                              that other meaningful aspects of life are forgotten or denied perception of
                                              Reflecting so much about life that it becomes difficult life in general
                                              to submerge oneself in ordinary meaningful life
                                              (hyper-reflection)
                                              Becoming aware of how meanings are created in general
                                              and relativizing all possible meanings in life ⎦
```

Fig. 1 Possible changes in the sense of meaning in life in individuals with a chronic or life-threatening disease

may arise, or previous meanings may have become unattainable. For instance, the symptoms and treatment of a physical disease may limit the patients' possibilities to realise their goals and may, for instance, complicate being a good partner or parent (Lee, Cohen, Edgar, Laizner, & Gagnon, 2004). An individual may, for instance, focus on being a cancer patient and forget that he or she is also a parent, an employee, a friend, etc. Therefore, a disease is often experienced as a threat to one's self-value and self-integrity as a person (Henoch & Danielson, 2009). Emma's example shows how her work suddenly felt less important, while going to her daughter's football match became more important, although she did not have enough energy to actually go to the football field (cf. Van der Spek et al., 2013). Another possible change is that an individual focuses so much on the disease and the medical treatment that other meaningful aspects of life are forgotten or denied. "I had primarily become a patient and had forgotten that I am also a daughter, mother, friend, employee and music-lover." Emma told about the immediate response to her second diagnosis. This forgetting or temporary bracketing of meaning in life may be understandable from an evolutionary perspective as a fight-or-flight response, as all attention, energy and other physical resources are needed for fighting.

Second, some patients ask such meaning-related questions for the first time in life, especially when they are young, which can be unsettling. Being diagnosed with a chronic or life-threatening disease can cast a totally different perspective on life (Helgeson, Reynolds, & Tomich, 2006; Henoch & Danielson, 2009). For instance, a large body of literature on post-traumatic growth shows that after the diagnosis of a chronic or life-threatening disease, the general priorities in life may change, life may be experienced more intensively and patients may become more aware of what they experience as authentic and as their true self (e.g., Calhoun & Tedeschi, 2014). This changed perspective on life seems to determine how and where an individual experiences meaning in life; for instance, empirical studies indicate that choices that feel consistent with what individuals consider as "authentic" or "consistent with their true self-concept" are more valuable for an individual and that perceived true self-knowledge strongly influences what an individual experiences as meaningful (Schlegel, Smith, & Hirsch, 2013).

The assumptive worlds theory asserts that the patients' perspective on life may change when they start to realise that the assumptions of their previous ordinary daily life were mere "illusions." Consequently, individuals may start relativising all possible meanings in life and experience life as meaningless (Vos, 2014). That is, Jaspers (1925/2013) wrote that the confrontation with life's physical, emotional and existential boundaries can teach patients general lessons about life, such as "not only this specific situation can change, but all possible situations in life are fundamentally changeable" and "not only this specific meaning can change, but everything that feels meaningful is changeable." Like Emma said: "One day going to your work seems important to you, but the next day it doesn't. Thus possibly, nothing in life is certain." This awareness may be metaphorically compared with looking at a Persian carpet not from above, where the meaningful patterns can be seen, but from below, where the stitches and loose threads ordinary meaningful life again, and they may are visible (cf. Vos, 2014). This existential awareness makes it difficult for patients to submerge into ordinary meaningful life again, and they may become stuck in continuous reflections about life (hyper-reflection).

Thus, many patients seem to experience changes in specific meanings, but also their general perspective on life may change. But, do patients also experience these changes as problematic? Research indicates that meaning-related changes indeed lead to psychological stress, depression and anxiety, and these changes in meaning are some of the main reasons why some patients ask for therapeutic support (e.g., Vos et al. 2014; Wexler & Corn, 2012). Additionally, a review of 47 studies of physically ill patients showed moderately strong correlations between meaning in life and the level of psychological stress and psychopathology (Steger, 2012; Winger, Adams, & Mosher, 2016).

In summary, a majority of individuals with a chronic or life-threatening disease report changes in specific meanings or in their general perspective on life, and these meaning-related concerns seem to lead to psychological stress. One of the main reasons why patients want to receive therapeutic help relates to the following question: "How can I live a meaningful and satisfying life despite the practical, physical and emotional limitations of my disease?" Although many patients ask for meaning-related support, their needs are often unmet by the usual treatments. These unfulfilled requests for help can lead to higher levels of depression, lower quality of life and shorter survival time (Park & Hwang, 2012). Unattended existential suffering may be regarded as "one of the most debilitating conditions" that occur in patients with a life-threatening disease (Boston, Bruce, & Schreiber, 2011) and may lead to demoralisation, suicidal ideation or a wish for a hastened death (Kissane, 2001). Therefore, it may be recommended that therapists directly address the possible changes that patients may experience in specific meanings and in their global perspective on life.

The Existential Coping Perspective

The existential coping perspective describes how individuals may focus on larger meanings in life as a defence mechanism and coping style.

First, many studies, including cognitive laboratory experiments, have shown that individuals use meaning in life to cope with existential threats such as being confronted with physical disease or death (Greenberg & Koole, 2013; Vos, 2014). For instance, pain can trigger existential anxiety, i.e., fears related to dying and not knowing how to live a meaningful life due to physical limitations, and focusing on meaningful behaviour and thoughts can help patients cope with such existential fears (cf. Strang, 1998).

Second, many studies put meaning-centred skills at the core of adequate coping with physical diseases (e.g., Lee et al., 2004; Park & Folkman, 1997). For instance, when confronted with a chronic or life-threatening disease, people may first appraise the situation as relevant or irrelevant for them (primary appraisal) and evaluate their personal sources to deal with it (secondary appraisal). These appraisal processes subsequently interact strongly with their meaning in life (tertiary appraisal). When individuals experience a situation as discongruent with their global meaning, distress will arise. For instance, if someone highly values having a job but experiences cancer as a threat to working, he or she will experience distress. Therefore, the level of distress often shows to be unrelated to the objective prognosis of a disease but is strongly related to the meaningful re-appraisal of the disease (Laubmeier & Zakowski, 2004). A large review of empirical studies confirms the restorative function of meaning and other positive emotions with respect to physiological, psychological and social coping resources; that is, individuals seem to benefit from coping processes that generate positive emotions such as benefit finding and reminding, adaptive goal processes, reordering priorities and infusing ordinary events with positive meaning (Folkman, 2008). Thus, well-being seems to depend on the extent to which a patient is able to integrate cancer into his or her global meaning via tertiary appraisal (Wong, 2010). Discongruence between disease and global meaning in life can be solved by re-appraisal of the global meaning. For instance, Emma reordered her fundamental values in life: her job was not as important as her health and her family; despite not being physically able to work, she still experienced meaning in her motherhood. Thus, after a period of perceived meaninglessness, a physically ill patient may undergo a personal transition by developing new specific meanings and, by doing so, learning to live with the disease.

Thus, patients seem to negotiate between the situational meaning and the global meaning in life, trying to accommodate or assimilate the physical changes in the wider framework about what they experience as meaningful in general. This model has been verified by studies showing how physically ill patients benefit from meaning-based coping; additionally, re-creating a sense of meaning in life has been shown to be crucial in maintaining and enhancing someone's level of well-being and is strongly negatively correlated with stress, depression and demoralisation (e.g., Visser, Garssen, & Vingerhoets, 2010; Winger et al., 2016). Additionally, several studies indicate that it is not one particular coping style, for example, being dominantly using active or denial strategies, but it is the flexibility of coping that predicts whether physically ill individuals will experience positive change, such as having a broad coping repertoire, a well-balanced coping profile, cross-situational variability in strategy deployment or a good strategy–situation fit (Cheng, Lau, & Chan, 2014). Therefore, it could be recommended that therapists assess and address existential defence mechanisms, e.g., pretending that nothing has happened, and stimulate flexible meaning-based coping; for instance, therapists could explore how the disease experience relates to the patient's sense of meaning and could encourage new flexible ways of living a meaningful life despite being ill.

The Transcending Perspective

The transcending perspective explains why meaning-focused coping can be beneficial for physically ill patients as they develop a sense of meaning to overcome the limitations and changes of their life situation. For instance, King, Hicks, Krull, and Del Gaiso (2006) concluded that when physically ill patients improve their skills in living a meaningful daily life, they are able to transcend their situation and cease to be narrowly focused on their pain and other physical limitations, which may subsequently lead to better physical well-being. Engaging in meaningful activities does not only offer distraction from the painful life situation but also helps the patient to see the disease within a broader context and become aware of the meanings that are still possible. Moreover, meaning seems to be an important aspect of what clients experience as a positive recovery process in therapeutic treatments, in particular in unchangeable life situations such as physical illness (e.g., Bennett, Breeze, & Neilson, 2014). Creating a sense of coherence in time and space has shown to be important for the well-being of individuals (Antonovsky, 1998).

This is reminiscent of Frankl's belief that we always have freedom of choice, even in times of the "tragic triad" of suffering, guilt and death, as "every individual has the freedom in every situation to modulate his inner attitude towards it" (Lukas, 2006, p. 54). This is similar to Jaspers' (1925/2013) idea that individuals can take an inner leap of faith from despair and resignation towards experiencing a meaning that transcends the situation. When the external situation is unchangeable, the internal situation may still be changeable. For example, during the course of the sessions, Emma started to realise that the meaning of her motherhood does not require external actions but mainly an inner transformation, as she did not need to be at her daughter's football match but could, for instance, reflect on the achievements of raising her daughter and sharing pleasant memories. Therefore, Frankl recommended that therapists help clients to develop a larger perspective and connect with something more important and meaningful than the current situation.

The Motivation Perspective

This perspective focuses on the motivation of patients to make specific lifestyle changes, such as engaging in physical exercise, changing their diet or giving up smoking, especially when they are able to connect the lifestyle change to a larger meaning in their lives. Physically ill patients seem to benefit psychologically and physically from connecting specific health-related goals with general goals in life. Research has, for instance, shown that the most beneficial strategy is to adjust health-related goals to one's personal ability and circumstances (e.g., Arends, Bode, Taal, & Van de Laar, 2013).

To elucidate this idea further, although being physically active and doing specific exercises are well-known beneficial factors for physical recovery (Warburton, Nicol, & Bredin, 2006), many individuals do not adhere to the recommendations, for instance, because they are afraid of movement, have particular beliefs about exercise, experience practical problems or lack motivation. For this reason, the most successful physical activity and exercise programmes include motivation techniques (Teixeira, Carraça, Markland, Silva, & Ryan, 2012). There are many examples in the literature of how patients could be motivated to change their health behaviour. For example, the trans-theoretical model describes how individuals go through different stages in the change process, starting with pre-contemplation (not ready for change), contemplation (getting ready for change), preparation (ready for change), action, maintenance and termination (Armitage, 2009; Prochaska & Velicer, 1997). Via a range of activities, the patients' relative weighing of the pros and cons of changing moves in favour of change, while simultaneously they start to feel confident that they can actually make the change (increased self-efficacy). The trans-theoretical model hypothesises that health interventions are more effective when they are tailored to the specific stage of the individual patient. This has, for example, been validated with regard to physical activity and exercise programmes (Marshall & Biddle, 2001).

In addition to this trans-theoretical model, the tertiary appraisal model adds the hypothesis that patients will change their behaviour when they see how a specific change can help them realise a larger meaning in life, via iterative steps in the appraisal process. That is, individuals may not be motivated to change their behaviour only for the sake of their physical well-being, but they may become motivated when they see how this change can help them live a more meaningful and satisfying life in general. For instance, in a study of adolescents, meaning in life seemed to play a protective motivational role with regard to health-risk behaviours such as illicit drug and sedatives use, binge-drinking, unsafe sex and lack of exercise and diet control (Brassai, Piko, & Steger, 2011). Another example is Emma who became only motivated to stop spending all day in bed when she realised that getting out of her bedroom could give her the opportunity of going for walks with her daughter and visiting her friends, which she experienced as very meaningful. Thus, the experience of meaning in life seems to be the condition and framework within which individuals are motivated for actual behaviour change. In Frankl's words, citing the philosopher Nietzsche, "He who has a *why* to live for can bear almost any *how*" (1946/1985).

To some extent, connecting behaviour change with a larger meaning in life is also the aim of motivational interviewing, where via a wide range of cognitive and relationship-focused therapeutic techniques, patients are encouraged to consider what they might gain through behaviour change and to explore inconsistencies with their personal values or goals. The vision of a better future might subsequently increase their motivation for change. Motivational interviewing has been shown to have modest effects in terms of helping physically ill patients improve their health behaviour (Lundahl et al., 2013). However, this assumes that patients are to some extent already aware of what is meaningful to them, and in motivational interviews, the discussion of global meaning in life often seems to be reduced to specific goals. Therefore, if motivated lifestyle changes are important, therapists may consider more systematically exploring what is fundamentally meaningful for their clients.

The Biological Perspective

Research shows that higher levels of meaning in life are associated with better physical health (Roepke, Jayawickreme, & Riffle, 2014) and that individuals feeling frustrated in roles and activities that they highly value, for instance, due to physical limitations, may experience a deterioration of their physical health (e.g., Krause, 2004b). Research consistently shows moderately strong correlations between meaning in life and a range of biomarkers, such as stress hormones, immune system functioning, physical energy, slower growth of tumour cells and longer survival time (Bower, Kemeny, Taylor, & Fahey, 2003; Chida & Steptoe, 2008; Ryff et al., 2006; Ryff, Singer, & Love, 2004).

However, the number of relevant publications remains relatively small; researchers test relatively simplistic pathways between mental health and physical outcomes and only test a small range of biomarkers without the inclusion of potentially confounding variables such as the side effects of medication. The precise causal relationships between meaning in life and biomedical well-being also need to be studied further; most models hypothesise, for instance, that meaning leads to better stress management, which subsequently lowers cortisol levels, which finally may interact with other biological processes.

Meaning has been described as an important factor of biopsychosocial resilience which can be of crucial importance for gene–environment interactions with various epigenetic plasticity genes and meaning change mechanisms relating to resilience (Davydov, Stewart, Ritchie, & Chaudieu, 2010). Several studies confirm that a sense of meaning contributes to biological resilience; for instance, one longitudinal study of 773 HIV+ patients showed that the level of meaning predicted CD4+ cell count decline, HIV-related mortality and time to death at 5-year follow-up (Ickovics et al., 2006). Furthermore, meta-analyses of controlled trials (Vos & Vitali, 2016) showed that meaning-centred treatments have large short-term effects and moderate long-term effects on self-reported physical well-being (resp. Hedges' $g=0.81$, $SE=0.29$; $k=8$ trials; $g=0.53$, $SE=0.11$, $k=4$). Immediate effects on blood pressure, stress hormones and survival time were large both immediately and at follow-up in three trials ($g=0.86$, $SE=0.31$, $k=3$; $g=1.20$, $SE=0.26$, $k=1$).

These studies show that meaning in life and physical well-being are related, although the precise relationships between them need further examination. Meaning seems to be a significant factor in the biomedical recovery of physically ill patients, and supporting them to experience meaning improves their physical well-being.

Integrated Summary

Over the last few decades, researchers and practitioners have started to move away from a mere biological and biopsychosocial clinical–aetiological model of physically ill patients to a biopsycho-existential model, which places the goal of helping patients to live a meaningful life despite their disease at its centre (e.g., Breitbart & Alici, 2009). This clinical–aetiological model is an integration of the previously outlined six dominant perspectives in health and medical psychology. Figure 2 visualises this "integrated meaning-centred clinical–aetiological model of mental health care for individuals with a chronic or life-threatening physical disease."

The life situation of all human beings may be characterised by the duality of our fundamental assumptions in ordinary daily life on the one hand and the reality of our life on the other. These fundamental assumptions are usually unreflected and automatic, and we do not need to make conscious decisions to live a meaningful and satisfying life; that is, we are submerged in our daily life activities based on a pre-reflective understanding of what is meaningful and valuable for us. More specifically, living a meaningful and satisfying life means that individuals are motivated towards the activities they do and which they experience as valuable, and they have the ability to adequately regulate their behaviour and emotions, which will lead them to specific action-directed goals in life. We are able to act intuitively without reflection, because the context of our lives feels stable and we have no need to step outside of our routine and reflect. We stay in this ordinary daily life mode as long as we are able to experience positive assumptions about life (wish for illusions), meaning (will to meaning) and certainty (need for certainty). For instance, we commit ourselves to meaningful activities such as our job or having and raising children because we assume that our life will not suddenly radically change, as, for instance, due to becoming ill or dying, and we assume that we can control our life and that we are worthy to listen to what feels meaningful to ourselves. Thus, the fundamental assumptions of the benevolence and meaningfulness of the world and the worthiness of our self create the stable context in which we can submerge ourselves without reflection in the meaningful activities of our daily life. Hence, the experience of meaning is intertwined with individuals' understanding of the world and having a sense of worthiness of the self.

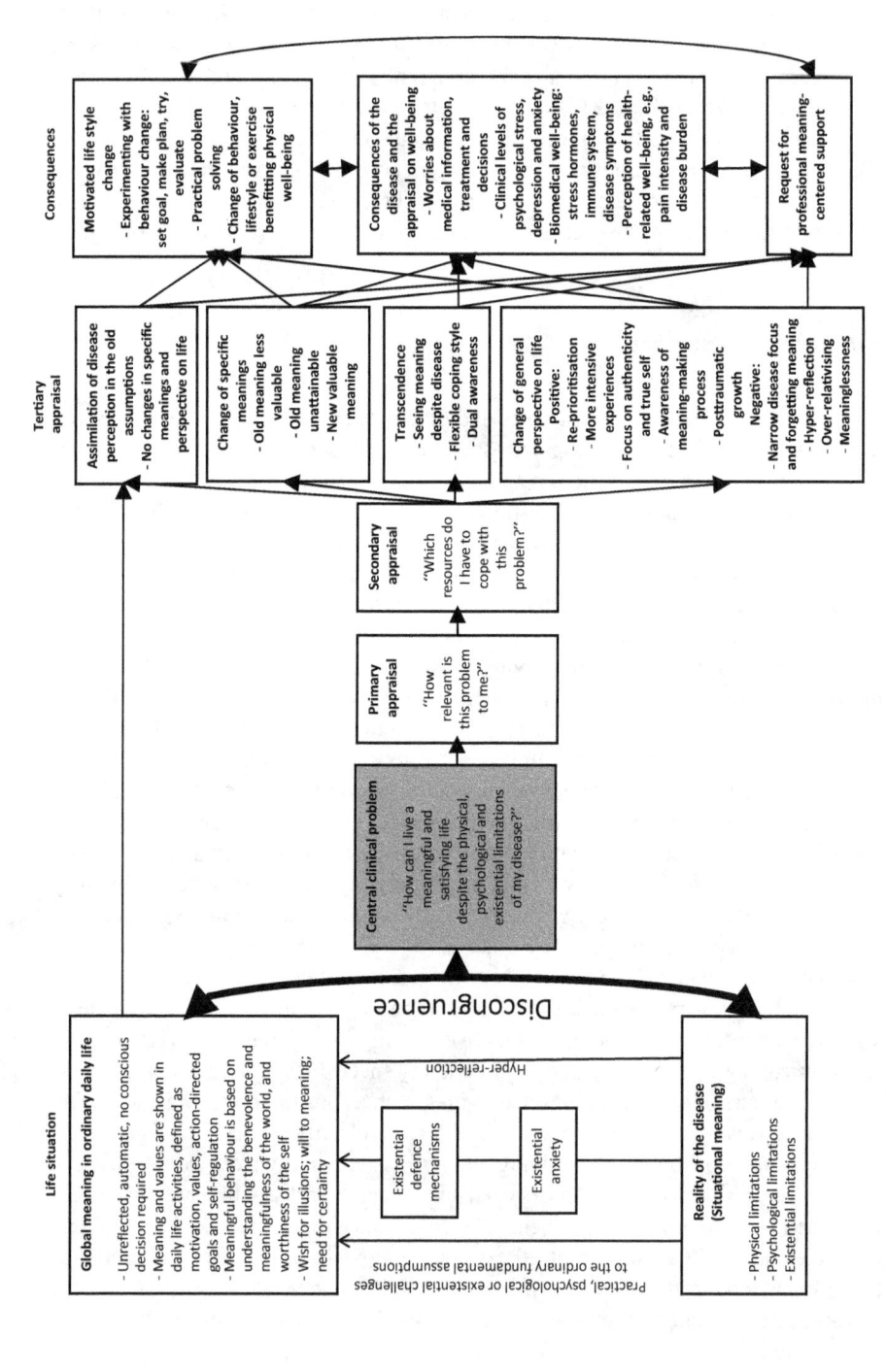

Fig. 2 The integrated meaning-centred clinical–aetiological model of mental health care for individuals with a chronic or life-threatening physical disease

Like all individuals, those with a chronic or life-threatening disease experience that their fundamental assumptions are challenged by reality, and in particular by the physical, emotional and existential limitations of their disease. For instance, Emma was physically unable to work any longer (physical limitations), had difficulties in coping with her emotions (emotional limitations) and social relationships (social limitations) and felt overwhelmed by the idea that she could die (existential limitations). These limitations cannot only challenge everyday-life assumptions, they can also evoke existential anxiety, which individuals can try to deny or avoid (defence mechanisms), for instance, by clasping onto what feels meaningful to them, as meaning may be used as a defence against the anxiety evoked by the limitations of the disease. Finally, the disease seems to eject the patients from the unreflected illusionary situation of their daily life, as the disease directly or indirectly urges individuals to reflect on their fundamental assumptions (hyper-reflection).

The life situation of these patients could lead to the experience of discongruence between the assumptions in ordinary daily life and the reality of their disease. This experience of discongruence is the central clinical problem, which may be formulated as the question, "How can I live a meaningful and satisfying life despite the physical, psychological and existential limitations of my disease?" Individuals can answer this question in different ways, depending on their appraisal of the relevance of this question for them (primary appraisal) and depending on the available internal and external resources to cope with the question (secondary appraisal).

Tertiary appraisal entails four partially overlapping ways to solve the discongruence. First, patients can assimilate their experience of the limitations within their existing assumptions and make no change in any specific meanings and perspectives on life; this is what Emma did when she continued "with business as usual" after the first diagnosis of cancer. Second, individuals can change specific meanings: specific previous meanings become less valuable or unattainable, or something else starts to feel more meaningful and valuable. Third, individuals can transcend the situation by focusing on what is meaningful in their lives despite their disease, use a flexible coping style and develop an awareness and acceptance of the duality between their ordinary life assumptions and the reality of their disease. Fourth, individuals may change their general perspective on life. For instance, priorities could change, they can experience life more intensively, focus more on what they experience as authentic and their true self and become aware of how the meaning-making process works (seeing the carpet from below). Such changes may be called "posttraumatic growth." However, negative changes may also occur. Patients may reflect so much on life that it becomes difficult to submerge themselves again in a naïve way in their ordinary meaningful life. Finally, patients could start to see all meanings and values in life as relative and feel overwhelmed by life's meaninglessness.

These appraisal processes can have several consequences in the lives of physically ill patients. First, they can start to feel motivated to change their lives, for instance, by experimenting with behaviour change (setting goals, making a plan, acting, evaluating) and practical problem solving. Second, the changes in meanings and perspectives on life can influence their psychological and biomedical well-being;

they could, for instance, start worrying about their medical situation, experience clinical depression or anxiety, have high levels of stress hormones and suboptimal immune system functioning and perceive their pain and disease burden as worse. Third, patients may request professional support to cope with these life changes, consequences for well-being, appraisal processes and the underlying question of "How can I live a meaningful and satisfying life despite my disease?"

Meaning in Common Physical Diseases

The previous section showed how meaning seems relevant for physically ill patients in general. The relevance of meaning for specific diseases and how meaning-centred treatments could add to existing health-care services are further questions to be addressed. This section focuses on these questions with regard to individuals with cancer, cardiovascular disease, chronic pain and heritable diseases.

However, the relatively clear picture that we will sketch on the basis of the scientific literature may not be reflected in the daily clinical practice of health-care services for long-term health conditions. In reality, there are often relatively unclear pathways of referral and treatment, and the waiting lists are sometimes so long that not all patients will receive the requested service. Therefore, health services often focus on patients with the most complex debilitating problems and co-morbid psychological, physical, social and occupational problems. Given their focus on complex cases, the programmes of these services are often multidisciplinary in nature and are provided by a broad team of psychologists, physiotherapists, medical specialists and spiritual care personnel. These multidisciplinary programmes are often based on holistic models of care, integrating expertise from these different disciplines and offering multiple modules such as psycho-educational groups and intensive individual counselling. Overall, a large number of studies show that multidisciplinary health services for individuals with chronic pain and cardiovascular disease have some moderate effects (Wood et al., 2008). However, the findings from these trials are difficult to generalise because they often have unclear referral pathways and strongly depend on local variables, such as unique members of staff with specific expertise, and there are concerns about the quality of the coordination and evaluation of some multidisciplinary teams (e.g., Fleissig, Jenkins, Catt, & Fallowfield, 2006). Furthermore, as only overall effects have been tested, it is unclear which specific aspects of the interventions are helpful and which are less helpful. Therefore, the following literature review will only describe uni-disciplinary psychological treatments, and its conclusions may indicate which specific psychological interventions are evidence-based and could be integrated into larger multidisciplinary programmes.

Cancer

Worldwide, cancer is one of the diseases with the largest incidence and prevalence. In 2012, an estimated 14.1 million new cases of cancer occurred worldwide, 8.2 million people died from cancer, and 32.5 million people diagnosed with cancer within the previous 5 years were still alive by the end of 2012 (cancerresearch.uk.org). Although the precise figures about the psychological concerns of these patients differ per instrument and population as targeted by different studies, it is estimated that between one fifth and one third of all cancer patients experience clinical levels of depression and anxiety (Krebber, 2014; Walker et al., 2013). Thus, worldwide millions of new cancer patients experience significant psychological problems. The subsequent care of cancer patients has radically changed in the last century, from mere medical treatment, to psychological support for psychiatric problems such as anxiety and depression as well as care for existential-spiritual concerns (Breitbart & Alici, 2009). Numerous psychological treatments with different therapeutic approaches have been developed, but recent meta-analyses conclude that with regard to most psychological treatments for physically ill patients, their effects on people's psychological well-being are at best small to moderate (Faller et al., 2013; Hart et al., 2012; Van Straten et al., 2010). The combination of a large population of cancer patients with psychological problems and lagging effects seems to justify the continued development of new, possibly more effective, types of support.

Many studies describe oncology patients with regard to changes in specific meanings and their general perspective on life. For instance, a review of 109 studies showed that a majority of cancer patients struggle to maintain self-identity and values in life and as well as with creating a sense of purpose (Henoch & Danielson, 2009). Consequently, cancer patients report that meaning is one of the most central clinical concerns. Between 50 and 70 % of patients in one study reported that they would like to receive help with remaining hopeful, staying independent in the face of illness, dealing with the unpredictability of the future, maintaining a sense of control, finding a sense of purpose and meaning and dealing with changes to their bodies (Soothill et al., 2001). When asked what they want to receive psychological treatment for, 51 % said help to overcome fears, 42 % said help to find hope, 40 % said help to find meaning in life, 40 % said help to find peace of mind and 39 % said help to find spiritual resources (Moadel et al., 1999). When cancer patients are able to experience meaning—with or without the support of a psychologist—they are better adjusted to cancer, experience a better quality of life and lower depression and anxiety of up to 50 % (Winger et al., 2016). Moreover, in the terminal stages of cancer, they experience a decreased desire for a hastened death, less depression and less suicidal ideation (Breitbart et al., 2000). Given this importance of meaning for cancer patients, many meaning-centred therapies have been developed and validated for cancer patients, as will be discussed in the next section of this chapter (Vos & Vitali, 2016).

Cardiovascular Disease (CVD)

The incidence and prevalence of CVD has increased rapidly in recent decades, and statistics have begun to include higher mortality rates for CVD than for cancer. In Europe, between 30 and 50% of all individuals die from CVD (bhf.org.uk). Being diagnosed with CVD after a heart attack or stroke is associated with heightened levels of psychological stress, depression and anxiety (Konstam, Moser, & De Jong, 2005), although it is unclear whether this psychological stress is the cause or consequence of CVD, or both. It is widely recognised that reducing stress and mental health problems is crucial to the recovery and prevention of further cardiac illness (Whalley et al., 2011). Although few studies are available, the psychological problems of CVD patients are clearly associated with underlying meaning-related questions, for instance, regarding lifestyle changes and the inability to participate in activities that were meaningful in the past (e.g., Beery et al., 2002; Dornelas, 2008). Moreover, the relevance of meaning for CVD patients is demonstrated by the fact that those individuals who are able to live a meaningful and satisfying life are better at controlling their heart failure, report fewer psychological problems (Park et al., 2008; Vollman, LaMontagne, & Wallston, 2009) and have fewer CVD-associated risk factors such as high HDL/cholesterol levels (Doster, Harvey, Riley, Goven, & Moorefield, 2002).

However, only 24 psychological treatments for CVD patients have been found in systematic literature reviews and none of these included meaning-centred interventions; these studies did not show consistent positive effects on psychological and physical outcomes (Whalley et al., 2011). Thus, there are no consistent effective treatments for CVD patients, although psychological stress reduction seems crucial to improve mortality rates. Given the important role of meaning for CVD patients, it seems relevant to develop and validate meaning-centred treatment for these individuals. There are no known trials on meaning-centred treatments for CVD patients, except for a positive feasibility study by the University of Roehampton in London and the Liverpool Heart and Chest Hospital (Vos & Hutchinson, 2015).

Chronic Pain

Up to 19% of all Europeans suffer from chronic pain, lasting for at least a period between 3 and 6 months (Debono et al., 2013). Half of them do not receive adequate treatment (Breivik, Collett, Ventafridda, Cohen, & Gallacher, 2006), as effective medical treatment is often unavailable or inadequate in terms of pain reduction. Consequently, many patients are often forced to live with pain instead of trying to get rid of pain (Severeijns, Vlaeyen, van den Hout, & Weber, 2001). Research suggests that a majority of chronic pain patients have difficulties effectively managing their pain in their daily lives (Breivik et al., 2006). Coping inadequately with pain not only leads to the continuation of the pain experience but also to higher health-care costs, lower job productivity and higher societal costs (Breivik et al., 2006; Severeijns et al., 2001). For instance, chronic pain often disrupts patients' roles within their families, their relationships and careers and sometimes even causes them to withdraw from society (Turk & Flor, 1999). Thus, many patients experience difficulties living a meaningful and satisfying life, due to their chronic pain, which seems to be at the core of their clinical concerns.

As a logical implication, several psychological treatments have been developed for chronic pain patients. The most frequently offered therapies are cognitive-behavioural therapy and Acceptance and Commitment Therapy, although the evidence supporting their effectiveness on pain intensity and emotional and physical well-being in chronic pain patients is weak (Eccleston et al., 2009; McCracken & Vowles, 2014; Powers et al., 2009; Veehof et al., 2011). A review of the literature indicates that there are no strongly effective therapies for chronic pain patients, although specific aspects of interventions may work with certain individuals. One possible reason for this limited lack of effectiveness is that these treatments do not systematically help chronic pain patients to live a meaningful and satisfying life, but instead focus, for instance, on improving thought processes or aiming for stress reduction. However, "creating meaning out of chaos" has been identified by patients and practitioners to be at the clinical core of adequately coping and appraising chronic pain (Bullington, Nordemar, Nordemar, & Sjöström-Flanagan, 2003). As noted before, King et al. (2006) reported that when individuals improve their skills to live a meaningful daily life, they cease to be narrowly focused on their pain. Moreover, up to 50% of all chronic pain patients report problems with experiencing their lives as meaningful due to their physical suffering (e.g., Glover-Graf, Marini, Baker, & Buck, 2007; Gudmannsdottir & Halldorsdottir, 2009). Therefore, Dezutter, Luyckx and Wachholtz (2015) suggested that meaning-centred group treatments would be "the ideal starting point and the encouraged direction" (p. 253) for novel psychotherapeutic interventions for chronic pain patients.

Heritable Diseases

Recent advances in medical technology have increased our knowledge of risk factors contributing to the development of a chronic or life-threatening disease. For instance, genetic testing may reveal pathogenic mutations in the DNA-structure that are inherited from parents and that could be passed on to the next generation (Vos, 2011). Genetic tests are available to test for high penetrant genes for diseases such as heritable breast and ovarian cancer, which could imply a risk between 40 and 80% to develop cancer during a person's lifetime. However, the pathogenic genetic profile of many other diseases is unknown or consists of a combination of multiple small genetic mutations in interaction with environmental and lifestyle factors.

Given the complexity of the genetic information, it is understandable that many patients misinterpret it (Vos, 2011). However, the accuracy of their understanding only seems to depend to a small extent on the way the DNA test result was communicated or on the patients' educational level and cognitive skills (Vos, 2011). By contrast, patients have a much more accurate perception of the medical information when they have a stronger sense of purpose in life, wonder less frequently what the meaning in their life is and feel that they currently live a meaningful life. Their accuracy is furthermore predicted by their assumptions about the meaningfulness of the world and the worthiness of the self, in particular by having an optimistic, autonomous, accepting sense of self, not having an excessive need for certainty and structure in life and reacting positively to a lack of structure. Thus, having a sense of meaning of the self and the world seems to help patients to interpret health risk information realistically, possibly because they do not perceive the risks as a threat to their general sense of meaning in life and do not need to distort the medical information to fit with their meaning framework.

Several studies have shown that cancer patients feel somewhat distressed after DNA test result disclosure, but this distress seldom reaches psychopathological levels, and it usually significantly decreases after several months; despite this relatively low level of clinical levels of stress, approximately one fifth of all patients would like to receive psychological help (Vos, 2011). Their level of psychological stress is not the only reason why they request this support, but they also have questions about understanding and coping with the medical information, and they have existential concerns which include experiencing a lack of purpose in life, low self-acceptance and an unfulfilled wish for certainty (Vos, 2011). Thus, meaning seems clinically relevant and predicts long-term adjustment and well-being. This suggests that the psychological care may not only be limited for patients with psychopathology but also for those with meaning-related questions (Vos, 2011). It seems particularly important to develop meaning-centred treatments in genetic counselling. In general, there are few systematic therapy trials in genetic counselling, and the findings only suggest modest effect sizes.

Meaning-Centred Therapies

Previous sections of this chapter suggest that meaning is at the heart of the clinical–aetiological models of the psychological concerns of individuals with a chronic or life-threatening disease. However, the usual course of psychological care for this population, such as cognitive-behavioural therapy, addresses some meaning-related aspects, but the therapeutic model is not specifically tailored to these clinical–aetiological models. By contrast, meaning-centred therapy (MCT) directly and systematically focuses on helping physically ill patients to live a meaningful and satisfying life despite their disease. Therefore, several meaning-centred treatments have been developed and validated for physically ill patients.

Many MCT therapists base their work on Austrian psychiatrist Viktor Frankl, who introduced a meaning-centred non-reductionist psychological treatment known as logotherapy and existential analysis (Vos, 2016). As described above, self-transcendence is a core aspect of this intervention, which means that individuals do not stare endlessly at the—often unchangeable—limitations of their life situation but focus on a greater meaning behind the situation. Frankl assumed that all individuals have an inner striving towards meaning (will to meaning), that everyone is free to take a stance towards any conditions in life (freedom of will) and that every situation has the potential of being meaningful, even in times of suffering, guilt and death (Lukas, 2006).

Over the years, many different types of meaning-centred practices have evolved, as the review in another chapter describes (Vos, 2016). The most common therapies are general Franklian therapies and meaning-centred psychotherapies which directly translate aspects of Frankl's work into standardised brief manuals, most frequently for physically ill patients. They aim at improving meaning in life via systematic and direct techniques such as psycho-education, guided exercises and relational–humanistic skills. Many other therapeutic approaches have included meaning as one of their core concepts and have shown moderate to large existential and psychological effects in physically ill patients; these include dignity therapy, life review interventions and Acceptance and Commitment Therapy (Vos, 2016). To prevent conflation with other therapeutic aims and methods, this chapter focuses on general Franklian therapy and meaning-centred psychotherapy (e.g., Breitbart & Poppito, 2014).

Meaning-centred therapists following this approach use a combination of therapeutic skills, of which many are supported by empirical evidence (Vos, 2016). These skills seem directly connected to the integrated meaning-centred clinical–aetiological model of physical diseases (cf. Fig. 2). *Assessment skills* are about evaluating the life situation, the needs, preferences and capacities of clients such as identifying the central clinical questions that clients want to work on in therapy. *Meaning-specific skills* aim at systematically exploring meaningful aspects in the stories of clients such as rephrasing/reframing their stories in terms of meaning, exploring their appraisal processes, providing psycho-education about changes in specific meanings and general perspective on life and normalising by explaining how the reality of their disease has challenged their ordinary life experiences. Clients are encouraged to transcend their situation with the help of guided exercises, unconditional positive regard and through creating hope for the possibility of experiencing meaning. Additionally, MCT therapists often connect meaning with specific situations in everyday life and stimulate effective goal management to foster, for instance, motivated lifestyle changes. That is to say, they help clients set specific aims, make plans, experiment in their everyday life, evaluate and adjust their aims and methods and make long-term commitments. This entails a shift in focus from short-term gratification and pleasure-seeking to long-term meaning in life, which seems beneficial for patient well-being (cf. Batthyany & Russo-Netzer, 2014). *Existential skills* are about supporting clients in developing a beneficial general perspective on life, for instance, by embedding the disease experience in their broader context of life, for example, skills for coping with existential anxiety and mortality and exploring existential defence mechanisms such as denial of death. *Relational–humanistic skills* focus on the creation of a positive therapeutic relationship and on the phenomenological exploration of patient experiences, which helps in analysing the disease-related changes in life and identifying meaning-related topics in their stories. *Spiritual and mindfulness skills* concern the therapist's openness to the patient's spiritual–cultural context. They involve de-reflection, self-distancing and a generally accepting stance in life and non-intellectualising exercises such as mindfulness. These skills may stop hyper-reflection and foster the development of an authentic sense of meaning. In summary, MCT helps clients to systematically explore possible answers to their central clinical concern, namely, the question "How can I live a meaningful and satisfying life despite the limitations of my life situation?"

Most trials on MCT include 5–15 sessions with three phases. The assessment and introduction phase focuses on understanding the facts of a given patient's life situation; on problems and strengths; on the creation of hope, the exploration of the relevance and history of meaning for the patient; and on building a constructive therapeutic working alliance. The meaning-exploration phase is the backbone of many manuals and consists of systematically exploring the patients' values and meaning potential via psycho-education, group discussions, questions, guided experiential exercises and homework. Usually, one session addresses the value of experiencing, others the value of productivity/creativity and the value of attitude modulation; however, a review of empirical studies of what patients experience as valuable meanings only partially confirmed this triad and suggested to extend it to five separate sessions focusing on hedonic–materialistic values, self-oriented values, social values, transcending values and meta-values (Vos, 2016). The evaluation and application phase aims to evaluate the values and potential meanings that were explored in the previous sessions and apply these to the patients' daily life.

A systematic literature review on MCT yielded 19 pre-post trials without control groups and 41 controlled trials (Vos, 2016). Of these controlled trials, 15 studies were conducted with cancer patients and nine with patients with other physical diseases such as spinal injuries. We did not find any statistically significant differences between meaning-centred therapies for patients with and without a chronic or life-threatening disease, and therefore the following findings are for both populations together. The effects were large compared with the control groups (mostly active treatment or care as usual, some waiting lists), both immediate and at follow-up on quality of life ($g=1.02$, SE$=0.06$; $g=1.06$, SE$=0.12$) and psychological stress ($g=0.94$, SE$=0.07$, $g=0.84$, SE$=0.10$). Immediate effects were larger for general quality of life ($g=1.37$, SE$=0.12$) than for meaning in life ($g=1.18$, SE$=0.08$), hope and optimism ($g=0.80$, SE$=0.13$), self-efficacy ($g=0.89$, SE$=0.14$) and social well-being ($g=0.81$, SE$=13$). This indicates that MCT not only reduces the psychological consequences of the disease but also improves the tertiary appraisal processes of clients, by supporting the transformation of specific meanings, transcending the situation and improving their general perspective on life (cf. Fig. 1). These therapeutic changes may be attributed to helping clients find a satisfactory answer to their central clinical question, "How can I live a meaningful and satisfying life despite my disease?" Moderation analyses indicated that MCT was significantly more effective when therapists used the above-mentioned skills such as discussing one meaning per session, discussing existential themes and experimenting with achievable daily life goals. Furthermore, the decrease in psychological stress was explained by improvements in meaning in life ($\beta=-0.56$, $p<0.001$). Thus, these trials confirm the therapeutic effectiveness of MCT based on the integrated meaning-centred clinical–aetiological model of physical diseases.

Discussion

This chapter reviewed the relevance and effectiveness of working with meaning in the psychological treatment of individuals with a chronic or life-threatening disease. It was hypothesised that traditional psychological treatments for these individuals are at best moderately effective, because they do not directly and systematically address meaning in life. The empirical studies reviewed in this chapter demonstrate that meaning is a core aspect of the clinical and aetiological model of this population. For instance, a disease can undermine fundamental assumptions that patients have about meaning in life and change where and how they experience meaning in life. Patients can use meaning as a beneficial way of coping with and transcending the limitations of their disease. Moreover, meaning is also often associated with better hormonal and immunological functioning. The relevance of this integrated meaning-centred clinical–aetiological model was specified for cancer, cardiovascular disease disease, chronic pain and heritable diseases. This overview showed that for each of these diseases, patients ask meaning-related questions, and their level of meaning is related to their general well-being. However standard psychological treatments do not directly and systematically address the topic of meaning, which may explain the relatively small effect sizes of these treatments. These findings justify the development of meaning-centred treatments for physically ill patients. Meta-analyses evidence that MCT has large effects on existential, psychological and physical outcomes compared with control groups. In conclusion, working with meaning is not only relevant but also effective for many individuals with a chronic or life-threatening disease.

This review is limited by a self-serving bias, as only evidence was sought in support of the hypothesis that working with meaning is relevant and effective in this population. Further research is warranted to validate the relevance and effectiveness of working therapeutically with meaning.

Another limitation of this chapter is that MCT may not apply to every individual. Some clients may, for example, struggle with negative cognitions or require stress reduction techniques, which implies different clinical–aetiological and therapeutic models. A therapist needs to systematically assess and discuss the applicability of MCT with the client. Additionally, Längle (2014) suggests that it is important to first solve basic problems such as health, safety and security before the theme of meaning in life can be addressed. For this reason, many practitioners do not offer MCT in the first year after a diagnosis of a chronic or life-threatening disease, when clients often seem mentally absorbed with practical and medical questions. However, this decision is not supported by evidence, as there are not enough studies to confirm that MCT is more effective in the medium or long term than in the short term. This is understandable, as patients seem to ask questions about meaning at any stage of their disease (e.g., Vehling et al., 2012). Several studies also suggest that many patients experience an existential crisis during the first year after their diagnosis, for instance, during treatment in a hospital. Although individual therapists offer MCT at the bedside and the models presented in this chapter seem to justify their practices, the effectiveness of this meaning-centred bedside approach still needs to be empirically validated (Vos & Breitbart, 2011). It may also be necessary to work first on psychological or personality problems that existed before the onset of the physical disease, as some studies indicate that such pre-existing problems predict the size of the psychological impact of the physical disease and the effectiveness of psychological treatment in this population in general (Schneider et al., 2010).

Some patients may also experience difficulties with the usual talking approach of either meaning-centred practices or any other psychological treatments. For instance, many patients experience cognitive problems such as the loss of short-term memory or linguistic limitations after a stroke or after receiving chemotherapy. In such situations, the precise formulations and the total format of the treatment need to be creatively adjusted to the skills of the client, and non-verbal and behavioural formats such as drawing exercises may be considered (cf. Breitbart & Alici, 2009). More research is needed focusing on working with meaning in cognitively and linguistically impaired individuals.

In sum, it may be recommended to do a holistic assessment of the clinical problems and their underlying causes in individual patients, assess their needs and skills and subsequently refer them to specific treatment modules or offer tailored treatment. Such a multidisciplinary approach is in line with the multidisciplinary approach of many health services in the UK.

This review has also shown how MCT shares many clinical, aetiological and therapeutic assumptions with other therapeutic approaches, such as motivational interviewing interventions and Acceptance and Commitment Therapy (Sharp, Schulenberg, Wilson, & Murrell, 2004). However, what makes MCT unique? MCT gives more explicit and longer attention to values and meaning-related issues and offers a more systematic and direct evaluation of possible sources of meaning in life. This seems particularly helpful for individuals who experience substantial changes in their meanings or general perspective on life and who are in an existential crisis, feel demoralised or are overwhelmed by a sense of meaninglessness (cf. Fig. 1). The broader exploration of meaning and the transcending perspective of MCT may also prevent hyper-reflection, which seems more likely to occur in problem-centred approaches where the sessions may overly focus on problems (cf. Sharp et al., 2004). MCT also seems more strongly embedded in a non-deterministic humanistic approach which focuses on the therapeutic relationship and an open phenomenological exploration of the patient's experiences. Although a structured manual can be used, the intervention is tailored to the client and an open space is offered for clients to explore their unique experiences. Although MCT also offers some practical problem-solving skills, it tends more towards an insight-focused approach with attention to existential processes and defence mechanisms. MCT's perspective on suffering also seems to differ from other approaches (Sharp et al., 2004) as it is regarded as an existential problem, i.e., a normal but inevitable part of life rather than an experience that can be changed by more constructive ways of thinking and behaving. This perspective implies, for instance, that the practitioner tries to normalise the experiences of patients and helps them to accept the fact that the reality of suffering cannot be changed, not even by psychological techniques. Meaning is also assumed to be a uniquely irreplaceable experience for individuals, that is, patients intuitively perceive differences in value and authenticity, and the treatments help them to discover what feels "right to them". Thus, the aim of MCT is not to replace any lost meanings with a random new meaning but with a meaning that feels connected to the client's true self (Vos, 2014). This meaning of meaning seems in contrast with approaches, such as Acceptance and Commitment Therapy and motivational interviewing, those that regard meanings and values from a social-constructivist perspective as verbal contingencies (Sharp et al., 2004).

Despite the limitations of this chapter and recommendations for further research, the findings indicate that MCT is an effective alternative to traditional psychological treatments and a beneficial addition to multidisciplinary programmes. Therapists are recommended to offer MCT in the standard care of individuals with a chronic or life-threatening disease. The beneficial effects on both psychological stress and physical well-being indicates that MCT is able to cut—at least partially—the vicious cycle of health-related stress interacting with and exacerbating physical illness and shorter survival time. This makes MCT a clinically relevant and potentially cost-effective intervention which may be considered for inclusion in guidelines by national health services and health insurances.

Key Takeaways

- Therapists should ask themselves whether traditional psychological treatments are adequately tailored to the unique clinical–aetiological needs of physically ill patients.
- Meaning-related questions should be regarded as a normal response to a chronic or life-threatening disease.
- The standard assessment of physically ill patients should include specific questions about meaning and general perspectives on life.
- Physically ill patients should be offered systematic support with their quest for meaning.
- To treat physically ill patients, therapists need to develop specific assessment, meaning-specific, existential, relational–humanistic and spiritual–mindfulness skills.
- Meaning-centred therapy should be considered for inclusion in health guidelines.

References

Alderson, S. L., Foy, R., Glidewell, L., McLintock, K., & House, A. (2012). How patients understand depression associated with chronic physical disease. *BMC Family Practice, 13*(1), 41–51.

Antonovsky, A. (1998). The sense of coherence: An historical and future perspective. In H. I. McCubbin, E. A. Thompson, A. I. Thompson, & J. E. Fromer (Eds.), *Stress, coping, and health in families: Sense of coherence and resiliency* (pp. 3–20). Thousand Oaks, CA: Sage.

Arends, R. Y., Bode, C., Taal, E., & Van de Laar, M. A. (2013). The role of goal management for successful adaptation to arthritis. *Patient Education and Counseling, 93*(1), 130–138.

Armitage, C. J. (2009). Is there utility in the transtheoretical model? *British Journal of Health Psychology, 14*(2), 195–210.

Batthyany, A., & Russo-Netzer, P. (Eds.). (2014). *Meaning in positive and existential psychology.* New York, NY: Springer.

Beery, T. A., Baas, L. S., Fowler, C., & Allen, G. (2002). Spirituality in persons with heart failure. *Journal of Holistic Nursing, 20*(1), 5–25.

Beltman, M. W., Voshaar, R. C. O., & Speckens, A. E. (2010). Cognitive–behavioural therapy for depression in people with a somatic disease: Meta-analysis of randomised controlled trials. *British Journal of Psychiatry, 197*(1), 11–19.

Bennett, B., Breeze, J., & Neilson, T. (2014). Applying the recovery model to physical rehabilitation. *Nursing Standard, 28*(23), 37–43.

Boston, P., Bruce, A., & Schreiber, R. (2011). Existential suffering in the palliative care setting: An integrated literature review. *Journal of Pain and Symptom Management, 41*(3), 604–618.

Bower, J. E., Kemeny, M. E., Taylor, S. E., & Fahey, J. L. (2003). Finding positive meaning and its association with natural killer cell cytotoxicity among participants in a bereavement-related disclosure intervention. *Annals of Behavioral Medicine, 25*(2), 146–155.

Brandstätter, M., Baumann, U., Borasio, G. D., & Fegg, M. J. (2012). Systematic review of meaning in life assessment instruments. *Psycho-Oncology, 21*(10), 1034–1052.

Brassai, L., Piko, B. F., & Steger, M. F. (2011). Meaning in life: Is it a protective factor for adolescents' psychological health? *International Journal of Behavioral Medicine, 18*(1), 44–51.

Breitbart, W., Rosenfeld, B., Pessin, H., Kaim, M., Funesti-Esch, J., Galietta, M., et al. (2000). Depression, hopelessness, and desire for hastened death in terminally ill patients with cancer. *JAMA: Journal of the American Medical Association, 284*(22), 2907–2911.

Breitbart, W. S., & Alici, Y. (2009). Psycho-oncology. *Harvard Review of Psychiatry, 17*(6), 361–376.

Breitbart, W., & Poppito, S. (2014). *Meaning-centered group psychotherapy for patients with advanced cancer: A treatment manual.* New York, NY: Oxford University Press.

Breivik, H., Collett, B., Ventafridda, V., Cohen, R., & Gallacher, D. (2006). Survey of chronic pain in Europe: Prevalence, impact on daily life, and treatment. *European Journal of Pain, 10*(4), 287–333.

Brewin, C., & Holmes, E. (2003). Psychological theories of posttraumatic stress disorder. *Clinical Psychology Review, 23*, 339–376.

Bullington, J., Nordemar, R., Nordemar, K., & Sjöström-Flanagan, C. (2003). Meaning out of chaos: A way to understand chronic pain. *Scandinavian Journal of Caring Sciences, 17*(4), 325–331.

Calhoun, L. G., & Tedeschi, R. G. (Eds.). (2014). *Handbook of posttraumatic growth: Research and practice.* New York, NY: Routledge.

Cheng, C., Lau, H. P. B., & Chan, M. P. S. (2014). Coping flexibility and psychological adjustment to stressful life changes: A meta-analytic review. *Psychological Bulletin, 140*(6), 1582–1607.

Chida, Y., & Steptoe, A. (2008). Positive psychological well-being and mortality: A quantitative review of prospective observational studies. *Psychosomatic Medicine, 70*(7), 741–756.

Cimpean, D., & Drake, R. E. (2011). Treating co-morbid medical conditions and anxiety/depression. *Epidemiology and Psychiatric Sciences, 20*(2), 141–150.

Cuijpers, P., Van Straten, A., Bohlmeijer, E., Hollon, S. D., & Andersson, G. (2010). The effects of psychotherapy for adult depression are overestimated: A meta-analysis of study quality and effect size. *Psychological Medicine, 40*(2), 211–223.

Davydov, D. M., Stewart, R., Ritchie, K., & Chaudieu, I. (2010). Resilience and mental health. *Clinical Psychology Review, 30*(5), 479–495.

Debono, D. J., Hoeksema, L. J., & Hobbs, R. D. (2013). Caring for patients with chronic pain: Pearls and pitfalls. *Journal of the American Osteopathic Association, 113*(8), 620–627.

DePrince, A., & Freyd, J. (2002). The harm of trauma. In J. Kauffman (Ed.), *Loss of the Assumptive World: A theory of traumatic loss* (pp. 71–82). New York, NY: Brunner-Routledge.

Dezutter, J., Luyckx, K., & Wachholtz, A. (2015). Meaning in life in chronic pain patients over time: Associations with pain experience and well-being. *Journal of Behavioral Medicine, 38*(2), 384–396.

Dornelas, E. A. (2008). *Psychotherapy with cardiac patients: Behavioral cardiology in practice.* New York, NY: American Psychological Association.

Doster, J. A., Harvey, M. B., Riley, C. A., Goven, A. J., & Moorefield, R. (2002). Spirituality and cardiovascular risk. *Journal of Religion and Health, 41*(1), 69–79.

Eccleston, C., Williams, A. C., & Morley, S. (2009). Psychological therapies for the management of chronic pain (excluding headache) in adults. *Cochrane Database of Systematic Reviews, 2*, 1–105.

Faller, H., Schuler, M., Richard, M., Heckl, U., Weis, J., & Küffner, R. (2013). Effects of psycho-oncologic interventions on emotional distress and quality of life in adult patients with cancer: Systematic review and meta-analysis. *Journal of Clinical Oncology, 2*, 20–40.

Fenton-O'Creevy, M., Nicholson, N., Soane, E., & Willman, P. (2003). Trading on illusions: Unrealistic perceptions of control and trading performance. *Journal of Occupational and Organizational Psychology, 76*(1), 53–68.

Fleissig, A., Jenkins, V., Catt, S., & Fallowfield, L. (2006). Multidisciplinary teams in cancer care: Are they effective in the UK? *The Lancet Oncology, 7*(11), 935–943.

Folkman, S. (2008). The case for positive emotions in the stress process. *Anxiety, Stress, and Coping, 21*(1), 3–14.

Foxwell, R., Morley, C., & Frizelle, D. (2013). Illness perceptions, mood and quality of life: A systematic review of coronary heart disease patients. *Journal of Psychosomatic Research, 75*(3), 211–222.

Frankl, V. E. (1946/1985). *Man's search for meaning.* New York, NY: Simon and Schuster.

Glover-Graf, N. M., Marini, I., Baker, J., & Buck, T. (2007). Religious and spiritual beliefs and practices of persons with chronic pain. *Rehabilitation Counseling Bulletin, 51*(1), 21–33.

Greenberg, J., & Koole, S. L. (Eds.). (2013). *Handbook of experimental existential psychology.* New York, NY: Guilford Publications.

Gudmannsdottir, G. D., & Halldorsdottir, S. (2009). Primacy of existential pain and suffering in residents in chronic pain in nursing homes: A phenomenological study. *Scandinavian Journal of Caring Sciences, 23*(2), 317–327.

Harrison, J. D., Young, J. M., Price, M. A., Butow, P. N., & Solomon, M. J. (2009). What are the unmet supportive care needs of people with cancer? A systematic review. *Supportive Care in Cancer, 17*(8), 1117–1128.

Hart, S. L., Hoyt, M. A., Diefenbach, M., Anderson, D. R., Kilbourn, K. M., Craft, L. L., ... Stanton, A. L. (2012). Meta-analysis of efficacy of interventions for elevated depressive symptoms in adults diagnosed with cancer. *Journal of the National Cancer Institute, 2*, 205–220.

Helgeson, V. S., Reynolds, K. A., & Tomich, P. L. (2006). A meta-analytic review of benefit finding and growth. *Journal of Consulting and Clinical Psychology, 74*(5), 797–816.

Henoch, I., & Danielson, E. (2009). Existential concerns among patients with cancer and interventions to meet them: An integrative literature review. *Psycho-Oncology, 18*(3), 225–236.

Ickovics, J. R., Milan, S., Boland, R., Schoenbaum, E., Schuman, P., Vlahov, D., & HIV Epidemiology Research Study (HERS) Group. (2006). Psychological resources protect health: 5-year survival and immune function among HIV-infected women from four US cities. *Aids, 20*(14), 1851–1860.

Imison, C., Naylor, C., Goodwin, N., Buck, D., Curry, N., Addicott, R., & Zollinger-Read, P. (2011). *Transforming our health care system.* London: The King's Fund.

Janoff-Bulman, R. (1992). *Shattered assumptions.* New York, NY: Free Press.

Jaspers, K. (1925/2013). *Psychologie der weltanschauungen.* New York, NY: Springer.

Kazdin, A. E. (2008). Understanding how and why psychotherapy leads to change. *Psychotherapy Research, 19*, 418–428.

King, L. A., Hicks, J. A., Krull, J. L., & Del Gaiso, A. K. (2006). Positive affect and the experience of meaning in life. *Journal of Personality and Social Psychology, 90*(1), 179–196.

Kissane, D. (2001). Demoralisation—A useful conceptualisation of existential distress in the elderly. *Australasian Journal on Ageing, 20*(3), 110–111.

Konstam, V., Moser, D. K., & De Jong, M. J. (2005). Depression and anxiety in heart failure. *Journal of Cardiac Failure, 11*(6), 455–463.

Krause, N. (2004b). Stressors arising in highly valued roles, meaning in life, and the physical health status of older adults. *The Journals of Gerontology Series B: Psychological Sciences and Social Sciences, 59*(5), S287–S297.

Krebber, A. M. H., Buffart, L. M., Kleijn, G., Riepma, I. C., Bree, R., Leemans, C. R., et al. (2014). Prevalence of depression in cancer patients: A meta-analysis of diagnostic interviews and self-report instruments. *Psycho-Oncology, 23*(2), 121–130.

Längle, A. (2014). *Lehrbuch zur Existenzanalyse: Grundlagen*. Wien: Facultas.

Laubmeier, K. K., & Zakowski, S. G. (2004). The role of objective versus perceived life threat in the psychological adjustment to cancer. *Psychology & Health, 19*(4), 425–437.

Lee, V., Cohen, S. R., Edgar, L., Laizner, A. M., & Gagnon, A. J. (2004). Clarifying "meaning" in the context of cancer research: A systematic literature review. *Palliative & Supportive Care, 2*(3), 291–303.

LeMay, K., & Wilson, K. G. (2008). Treatment of existential distress in life threatening illness: A review of manualized interventions. *Clinical Psychology Review, 28*, 472–493.

Lepore, S. J., & Coyne, J. C. (2006). Psychological interventions for distress in cancer patients: A review of reviews. *Annals of Behavioral Medicine, 32*(2), 85–92.

Lukas, E. (2006). *Lehrbuch der Logotherapie. Menschenbild und Methoden*. Munchen: Profil.

Lundahl, B., Moleni, T., Burke, B. L., Butters, R., Tollefson, D., Butler, C., & Rollnick, S. (2013). Motivational interviewing in medical care settings: A systematic review and meta-analysis of randomized controlled trials. *Patient Education and Counseling, 93*(2), 157–168.

Marshall, S. J., & Biddle, S. J. (2001). The transtheoretical model of behavior change: A meta-analysis of applications to physical activity and exercise. *Annals of Behavioral Medicine, 23*(4), 229–246.

McCracken, L. M., & Vowles, K. E. (2014). Acceptance and Commitment Therapy and mindfulness for chronic pain: Model, process, and progress. *American Psychologist, 69*(2), 178–187.

Mitchell, A. J., Chan, M., Bhatti, H., Halton, M., Grassi, L., Johansen, C., et al. (2011). Prevalence of depression, anxiety, and adjustment disorder in oncological, haematological, and palliative-care settings: A meta-analysis of 94 interview-based studies. *The Lancet Oncology, 12*(2), 160–174.

Moadel, A., Morgan, C., Fatone, A., Grennan, J., Carter, J., Laruffa, G., et al. (1999). Seeking meaning and hope: Self-reported spiritual and existential needs among an ethnically-diverse cancer patient population. *Psycho-Oncology, 8*(5), 378–385.

Naylor, C., Parsonage, M., McDaid, D., Knapp, M., Fossey, M., & Galea, A. (2012). *Long-term conditions and mental health: The cost of co-morbidities*. London: The King's Fund.

Park, C. L. (2010). Making sense of the meaning literature: An integrative review of meaning making and its effects on adjustment to stressful life events. *Psychological Bulletin, 136*(2), 257–301.

Park, C. L., Edmondson, D., Fenster, J. R., & Blank, T. O. (2008). Meaning making and psychological adjustment following cancer: The mediating roles of growth, life meaning, and restored just-world beliefs. *Journal of Consulting and Clinical Psychology, 76*(5), 863–875.

Park, C. L., & Folkman, S. (1997). Meaning in the context of stress and coping. *Review of General Psychology, 1*(2), 115–144.

Park, C. L., & George, L. S. (2013). Assessing meaning and meaning making in the context of stressful life events: Measurement tools and approaches. *The Journal of Positive Psychology, 8*(6), 483–504.

Park, B. W., & Hwang, S. Y. (2012). Unmet needs of breast cancer patients relative to survival duration. *Yonsei Medical Journal, 53*(1), 118–125.

Powers, M. B., Vörding, M. B., & Emmelkamp, P. M. (2009). Acceptance and Commitment Therapy: A meta-analytic review. *Psychotherapy and Psychosomatics, 78*(2), 73–80.

Prochaska, J. O., & Velicer, W. F. (1997). The transtheoretical model of health behavior change. *American Journal Health Promotion, 12*(1), 38–48.

Roepke, A. M., Jayawickreme, E., & Riffle, O. M. (2014). Meaning and health: A systematic review. *Applied Research in Quality of Life, 9*(4), 1055–1079.

Ryff, C. D., Dienberg Love, G., Urry, H. L., Muller, D., Rosenkranz, M. A., Friedman, E. M., ... Singer, B. (2006). Psychological well-being and ill-being: Do they have distinct or mirrored biological correlates? *Psychotherapy and Psychosomatics, 75*(2), 85–95.

Ryff, C. D., Singer, B. H., & Love, G. D. (2004). Positive health: Connecting well-being with biology. *Philosophical Transactions-Royal Society of London Series B Biological Sciences, 359*(1449), 1383–1394.

Schlegel, R. J., Smith, C. M., & Hirsch, K. A. (2013). Examining the true self as a wellspring of meaning. In J. A. Hicks & C. Routledge (Eds.), *The experience of meaning in life* (pp. 177–188). Dordrecht: Springer.

Schneider, S., Moyer, A., Knapp-Oliver, S., Sohl, S., Cannella, D., & Targhetta, V. (2010). Pre-intervention distress moderates the efficacy of psychosocial treatment for cancer patients: A meta-analysis. *Journal of Behavioral Medicine, 33*(1), 1–14.

Severeijns, R., Vlaeyen, J. W., van den Hout, M. A., & Weber, W. E. (2001). Pain catastrophizing predicts pain intensity, disability, and psychological distress independent of the level of physical impairment. *Clinical Journal of Pain, 17*(2), 165–172.

Sharp, W., Schulenberg, S. E., Wilson, K. G., & Murrell, A. R. (2004). Logotherapy and Acceptance and Commitment Therapy (ACT): An initial comparison of values-centered approaches. *The International Forum for Logotherapy, 27*(2), 98–105.

Soothill, K., Morris, S., Harman, J., Francis, B., Thomas, C., & McIllmurray, M. (2001). The significant unmet needs of cancer patients: Probing psychosocial concerns. *Supportive Care in Cancer, 9*(8), 597–605.

Steger, M. F. (2012). Experiencing meaning in life. In P. T. P. Wong (Ed.), *The human quest for meaning: Theories, research, and applications* (2nd ed., pp. 165–184). New York, NY: Routledge.

Strang, P. (1998). Cancer pain—A provoker of emotional, social and existential distress. *Acta Oncologica, 37*(7-8), 641–644.

Teixeira, P. J., Carraça, E. V., Markland, D., Silva, M. N., & Ryan, R. M. (2012). Exercise, physical activity, and self-determination theory: A systematic review. *International Journal of Behavioural Nutrition and Physical Activity, 9*(1), 78–88.

Turk, D. C., & Flor, H. (1999). Chronic pain: A biobehavioral perspective. In R. J. Gatchel & D. C. Turk (Eds.), *Psychosocial factors in pain: Critical perspectives* (pp. 18–34). New York, NY: Guilford.

Van der Spek, N., Vos, J., van Uden-Kraan, C. F., Breitbart, W., Tollenaar, R. A. E. M., Cuijpers, P., & Verdonck-de Leeuw, I. M. (2013). Meaning making in cancer survivors: A focus group study. *PLoS One, 8*(9), 1–7.

Van Straten, A., Geraedts, A., Verdonck-de Leeuw, I., Andersson, G., & Cuijpers, P. (2010). Psychological treatment of depressive symptoms in patients with medical disorders: A meta-analysis. *Journal of Psychosomatic Research, 69*(1), 23–32.

Veehof, M. M., Oskam, M.-J., Schreurs, K. M., & Bohlmeijer, E. T. (2011). Acceptance-based interventions for the treatment of chronic pain: A systematic review and meta-analysis. *Pain, 152*(3), 533–542.

Vehling, S., Lehmann, C., Oechsle, K., Bokemeyer, C., Krull, A., Koch, U., & Mehnert, A. (2012). Is advanced cancer associated with demoralization and lower global meaning? The role of tumor stage and physical problems in explaining existential distress in cancer patients. *Psycho-Oncology, 21*(1), 54–63.

Visser, A., Garssen, B., & Vingerhoets, A. (2010). Spirituality and well-being in cancer patients: A review. *Psycho-Oncology, 19*(6), 565–572.

Vollman, M. W., LaMontagne, L. L., & Wallston, K. A. (2009). Existential well-being predicts perceived control in adults with heart failure. *Applied Nursing Research, 22*(3), 198–203.

Vos, J., & Breitbart, W. (2011). *Meaning-centered psychotherapy at the bedside.* Paper Presented at the World Conference of the International Psycho Oncology Society (IPOS), Antalya, Turkey.

Vos, J. (2011). *Opening the psychological black box in genetic counseling*. Leiden: Department of Clinical Genetics, Faculty of Medicine, Leiden University Medical Center (LUMC), Leiden University.

Vos, J., Asperen, C. J., Oosterwijk, J. C., Menko, F. H., Collee, M. J., Garcia, E. G., et al. (2013b). The counselees' self-reported request for psychological help in genetic counseling for hereditary breast/ovarian cancer: Not only psychopathology matters. *Psycho-Oncology, 22*(4), 902–910.

Vos, J. (2014). Meaning and existential givens in the lives of cancer patients: A philosophical perspective on psycho-oncology. *Palliative & Supportive Care, 12*(9), 1–16.

Vos, J. (2015). *How to develop and evaluate the conceptual structure of articles: A systematic literature review of the top 100 articles in clinical psychology, psychotherapy and counselling. Internal Report*. London: University of Roehampton.

Vos, J. (2016). Working with meaning in life in mental health care: A systematic literature review of the practices and effectiveness of meaning-centered therapies. In P. Russo-Netzer, S. E. Schulenberg, & A. Batthyany (Eds.), *To thrive, to cope, to understand – Meaning in positive and existential psychotherapy*. Switzerland: Springer International Publishing.

Vos, J., & Hutchinson, Z. (2015). *Meaning oriented psychotherapy for physically ill patients: Overview, exercises and a case study*. Workshop at the Annual Conference of the Division of Counselling Psychology of the British Psychology Society.

Vos, J., & Vitali, D. (2016). Psychological treatments supporting clients to live a meaningful life: A meta-analysis of meaning-centered therapies on quality-of-life and psychologicalstress. Manuscript submitted for publication.

Walker, J., Hansen, C. H., Martin, P., Sawhney, A., Thekkumpurath, P., Beale, C., et al. (2013). Prevalence of depression in adults with cancer: A systematic review. *Annals of Oncology, 24*(4), 895–900.

Warburton, D. E., Nicol, C. W., & Bredin, S. S. (2006). Health benefits of physical activity: The evidence. *Canadian Medical Association Journal, 174*(6), 801–809.

Wexler, I. D., & Corn, B. W. (2012). An existential approach to oncology: Meeting the needs of our patients. *Current Opinion in Supportive and Palliative Care, 6*(2), 275–279.

Whalley, B., Rees, K., Davies, P., Bennett, P., Ebrahim, S., Liu, Z., ... Taylor, R. S. (2011). Psychological interventions for coronary heart disease. *Cochrane Database of Systematic Reviews, (8)*, CD002902.

Winger, J. G., Adams, R. N., & Mosher, C. E. (2016). Relations of meaning in life and sense of coherence to distress in cancer patients: A meta-analysis. *Psycho-Oncology, 25*, 2–10.

Wong, P. T. P. (2010). Meaning therapy: An integrative and positive existential psychotherapy. *Journal of Contemporary Psychotherapy, 40*(2), 85–93.

Wong, P. T. P. (Ed.). (2012). *The human quest for meaning: Theories, research, and applications* (2nd ed.). New York, NY: Routledge.

Wood, D. A., Kotseva, K., Connolly, S., Jennings, C., Mead, A., Jones, J., ... EUROACTION Study Group. (2008). Nurse-coordinated multidisciplinary, family-based cardiovascular disease prevention programme for patients with coronary heart disease and asymptomatic individuals at high risk of cardiovascular disease: A paired, cluster-randomised controlled trial. *The Lancet, 371*(9629), 1999–2012.

Yalom, I. D. (2008). *Staring at the sun: Overcoming the terror of death*. London: Jossey-Bass.

Zoellner, T., & Maercker, A. (2006). Posttraumatic growth in clinical psychology—A critical review and introduction of a two component model. *Clinical Psychology Review, 26*(5), 626–653.

Meaning in Life in the Prevention and Treatment of Substance Use Disorders

Efrén Martínez Ortíz and Ivonne Andrea Flórez

Substance use disorders (SUD), or substance-related disorders, are one of the biggest problems in public health around the world (UNODC, 2014). In 2014, the United Nations Office on Drugs and Crime (UNODC) estimated that between 10 and 13 % of the world's entire population, approximately 16 to 39 million individuals, suffers from SUD (UNODC, 2014). The UNODC also established that the cost of addictions ranges from $200 to $250 million dollars annually and only one out of five people suffering from SUD receives adequate treatment for recovery (UNODC, 2014).

Several authors have proposed that SUD, or addictions, not only affects individuals' physical and psychological functioning, but also a spiritual dimension related to meaning in life (Becoña, 2002; Calafat, Gómez, Juan, & Becoña, 2007; Lyons, Deane, Caputi, & Kelly, 2011; Lyons, Frank, & Kelly, 2010; Marsh, Smith, Piek, & Saunders, 2003; Piedmont, 2004; Thompson, 2012; Wiklund, 2008a, 2008b). Viktor Frankl (1994), the founder of logotherapy, posited that individuals abuse substances to deal with existential vacuum, or feelings of meaninglessness. He defined meaning as the degree to which individuals perceive life as coherent and significant, and whether they behave consistently with established valuable life goals (Frankl, 1959/1984). According to Frankl, the main causative factors associated with the development of an addiction are proneness to boredom, a meaningless life, and the use of maladaptive coping strategies associated with distress (Frankl, 1959/1984; Thompson, 2012).

E.M. Ortíz, Ph.D. (✉)
Society for the Advancement of Meaning-Centered Psychotherapy,
Cra. 14a #101 – 11 Oficina 403, Bogotá, Colombia
e-mail: yortizo@hotmail.com

I.A. Flórez, M.A.
Department of Psychology, Clinical-Disaster Research Center (UM-CDRC),
University of Mississippi, University, MS 38677, USA

Even though it is well known that addictions are caused by an interaction of biological, environmental, and psychological variables (Sloboda, Glantz, & Tarter, 2012), several research findings have validated the assumption that substance abuse is associated with perceived lack of meaning (Hart & Carey, 2014; Marsh et al., 2003; Noblejas de la Flor, 1997; Roos, Kirouac, Pearson, Fink, & Witkiewitz, 2015). There is a strong relationship between meaninglessness and drug use and abuse, and severity of SUD symptoms across the lifespan (Addad & Himi, 2008; Newcomb & Harlow, 1986; Noblejas de la Flor, 1997; Rahman, 2001; Schnetzer, Schulenberg, & Buchanan, 2013).

Specifically, perceived lack of meaning in life has been suggested to be a risk factor in youth substance use (Hart & Carey, 2014; Konkoly, Bachner, Martos, & Kushnir, 2009; Palfai, Ralston, & Wright, 2011; Schnetzer et al., 2013). In adolescents, the establishment of meaningful goals is associated with decreased frequency of alcohol use (Lecci, MacLean, & Croteau, 2002), fewer reports of alcohol abuse symptoms, and fewer negative consequences due to alcohol use (Palfai et al., 2011; Palfai & Weafer, 2006). Moreover, in teenagers that use alcohol as a coping strategy, drinking is a predictor of alcohol-related problems (Lecci et al., 2002).

In college samples, correlational studies have indicated that higher scores on measures of perceived meaning are associated with decreases in the use of alcohol, tobacco, marijuana, and cocaine (Hart & Carey, 2014; Konkoly et al., 2009; Martin, MacKinnon, Johnson, & Rohsenow, 2011; Minehan, Newcomb, & Galaif, 2000; Schnetzer et al., 2013). Meaning in life also mediates the relationship between drug use and depression, stress, boredom, and perceived control and power (Harlow, Newcomb, & Bentler, 1986; Minehan et al., 2000; Newcomb & Harlow, 1986). These findings suggest that in the presence of other risk variables, such as depression and stress, the absence of meaning in life increases the likelihood of experiencing drug abuse. Interestingly, Newcomb and Harlow (1986) also found that the presence or absence of meaning has a stronger impact on the relationship between stress and alcohol use in early adolescence when compared to late adolescence. Therefore, it appears that in early adolescence there is a greater vulnerability associated with the use of alcohol to cope with feelings of meaninglessness, and thus, meaning-centered interventions to prevent substance use should be implemented before this stage.

Similarly, in a study comparing a sample of adolescents in high schools with a group of adolescents that were hospitalized for mental health issues, the authors found that adolescents receiving inpatient treatment reported significantly lower levels of self-esteem and meaning in life (Kinnier et al., 1994). Moreover, in the two groups of adolescents, meaning in life was again a significant mediator variable between depression and substance use (Kinnier et al., 1994). The results suggested that higher levels of depression predicted lower levels of meaning in life, which in turn had a direct effect on higher levels of substance use. In this study, the presence or absence of meaning accounted for 33 % in the variance of drug use for the group of hospitalized adolescents (Kinnier et al., 1994).

Overall, these findings suggest that meaning in life is a protective factor for substance abuse among adolescents and college students. On the contrary, the absence of meaning is associated with an increased likelihood of developing a substance use disorder (Frankl, 1959/1984; Thompson, 2012). Despite the supporting evidence, a review of the literature did not uncover any published experimental studies exploring the effectiveness of meaning-centered interventions in reducing substance use problems in adolescent or college student samples. This research gap hinders any causal assumption about the role of meaning in the prevention of youth substance use and SUD. Moreover, it highlights the importance of setting a research agenda to examine logotherapeutic preventive interventions in children and young adolescents.

In terms of gender differences, some studies have evidenced particularities in the association between meaning in life and drug use in males and females. For instance, Schnetzer et al. (2013) found that in males, meaning was a significant mediator between depression and alcohol use. However, this finding was not replicated in females. Additionally, Harlow et al. (1986) found that in the absence of meaning women seem to use drugs more often as a coping mechanism, whereas men appear to engage in suicidal ideation more frequently. Similarly, Schlesinger, Susman, and Koenigsberg (1990) determined that when comparing males and females suffering from alcoholism, women reported significantly lower meaning in life scores than men did. These studies suggest potential gender differences in the relationship between meaning and substance abuse that are important to consider when planning interventions.

Findings are less clear when it comes to the role of meaning over the development of an addiction (Hart & Carey, 2014; Roos et al., 2015). Even though there is strong evidence showing lower levels of perceived meaning in individuals diagnosed with SUD, some empirical findings have failed to validate this association under certain conditions (Hart & Carey, 2014; Kinnier et al., 1994; Nicholson et al., 1994; Noblejas de la Flor, 1997; Rahman, 2001; Schnetzer et al., 2013). Specifically, in individuals initiating treatment, some studies have not found a significant correlation between levels of meaning and current alcohol consumption, daily alcohol consumption, total alcohol use over the last 3 months, alcohol blood levels, and the total number of abstinence days since the initiation of treatment (Brown, Ashcroft, & Miller 1998; Osaka, Morita, Nakatani, & Fujisawa, 2008; Waisberg & Porter, 1994). Along the same lines, Martin et al. (2011) did not find any significant correlation between perceived meaning in life and reported cocaine and alcohol use before entering treatment.

Considering that most of the studies showing mixed findings were conducted with clients initiating treatment, it can be argued that these individuals could boost their levels of meaning to reduce cognitive dissonance produced by drug use. In fact, the absence of meaning becomes more salient as individuals with an SUD problem stop using drugs and begin treatment (Hart & Carey, 2014; Martínez, 2002). To validate this hypothesis, in future studies it will be important to measure changes in the perception of meaning throughout the course of addiction. It is also important to assess how individuals define and conceptualize sources of meaning before and after treatment (Hart & Carey, 2014).

Regarding the potential benefit of meaning in the treatment of addiction, perceived meaning in life is a significant predictor of treatment outcome and motivation to change in recovery (Carroll, 1993; Krentzman, Farkas, & Townsend, 2010; Noblejas de la Flor, 1997). Empirical findings have evidenced that levels of perceived meaning in life increase significantly over the course of treatment (Roos et al., 2015). This is true even in treatment programs that do not directly address meaning in their interventions (Flora & Stalikas, 2012; Noblejas de la Flor, 1997; Waisberg & Porter, 1994).

In a longitudinal study, Robinson, Cranford, Webb, and Brower (2007) found that levels of meaning in life increased significantly after 6 months of treatment. The study was conducted with 123 individuals with alcoholism receiving outpatient treatment based on Alcoholics Anonymous (A.A.) principles. Results also indicated that when there was a one-unit increment in scores of presence of meaning, there was a 3% decrease in the likelihood of re-engaging in a substance abuse pattern. In this sample, enhanced meaning was associated with an average of a 12% decreased likelihood of re-engaging in compulsive alcohol use. After 6 months of treatment, meaninglessness was a significant predictor of alcohol abuse.

Additionally, in members of A.A. and individuals receiving inpatient treatment, longer abstinence periods have been related to greater meaning in life (Carroll, 1993; Krentzman et al., 2010). Krentzman et al. (2010) found that for every one-point increment in meaning scores, there was a 2% higher likelihood that individuals would remain sober after 12 months of treatment. When increments of meaning scores were above the group mean, the likelihood of individuals remaining abstinent increased to 3.9%. The authors also found that higher levels of meaning had a stronger effect in Black individuals when compared to White individuals. In Black individuals there was a 4.4% increment for every unit change in meaning scores. These findings are suggestive of potential differences in the way meaning interacts with distinct cultural and vulnerability factors (Brown et al., 1998).

Similarly, Miller (1998) found that meaning in life, or the lack thereof, significantly predicted cocaine and alcohol relapse after treatment. Meaning also significantly predicted the number of days in which cocaine and alcohol were used following 6 months of treatment. Moreover, in individuals with cocaine addiction, higher perceived meaning in life reported at the beginning of treatment was associated with better treatment outcomes, lower relapse rates, and decreased frequency of alcohol and cocaine use. Meaning significantly predicted these variables even after controlling for depression, substance use severity, and age (Krentzman et al., 2010).

More importantly, in a recent publication of a longitudinal analysis of secondary data using latent growth curve models, Roos et al. (2015) found that meaning in life and temptation to drink were significantly and negatively related across time. Participants were recruited from the Matching Alcohol Treatments to Client Heterogeneity Project (Project MATCH Research Group, 1997). Analyses were conducted with 1729 individuals receiving treatment for alcohol use disorder (AUD). Participants were allocated to one of three different treatment approaches: motivational enhancement therapy, cognitive-behavioral therapy, or 12-step facilitation therapy. Data on meaning and temptation to drink were collected at the beginning of treatment, at the end of treatment (3 months after baseline), and at 9 and 15 months following the beginning of treatment.

Results indicated that regardless of the treatment condition, over the course of treatment higher levels of meaning in life were significantly related to decreased reported temptation to drink. At the 15-month follow-up, decreases in meaning in life and increases in temptation to drink were significantly related to greater intensity and frequency of drinking (Roos et al., 2015). Moreover, individuals reporting lower levels of meaning and greater temptation to drink were more likely to report increased negative consequences due to alcohol use. This study suggested that meaning in life is a relevant target for treatment and recovery. The findings of this study further form a strong argument for increased research efforts to validate meaning-based interventions in the treatment of SUD (Roos et al., 2015).

Along the same lines, subsequent to treatment addiction, meaning has also been found to be related to better functioning and quality of life (Hart, 2009; Robinson, Krentzman, Webb, & Brower, 2011). In Hart's (2009) study, after 2 years of treatment participants were asked about their perceived improvement in functioning (interpersonal, personal, and community functioning) since completion of treatment. They were also asked to report as to their current perception of meaning, quality of life, and spirituality. Hart found that individuals' quality of life was positively and significantly related to perceived meaning. Moreover, perceived improvement in functioning was associated with higher levels of meaning in life 2 years after treatment. In addition, Robinson et al. (2011) found that over the course of 6 months positive changes in meaning in life in individuals diagnosed with SUD predicted improvement of drinking outcomes and a greater percentage of days abstinent at 9 months after baseline.

Overall, these findings support the potential role of meaning in life in decreasing abstinence rates, promoting better recovery, and decreasing vulnerability to relapse when coping with stress and cravings (Laudet, Morgen, & White, 2006; Piderman, Schneekloth, & Pankratz, 2008; Robinson et al., 2011). Thus, increased meaning in life during the course of treatment may account for successful outcomes and improvement of symptoms (Amodeo, Kurtz, & Cutter, 1992; Carroll, 1993; Chen, 2006; Krentzman et al., 2010; Noblejas de la Flor, 1997; Waisberg & Porter, 1994).

In fact, most treatment approaches to SUD, implicitly or explicitly, intervene with an individual's perceived levels of meaning in life at different stages of therapy. For instance, programs such as motivational interviewing (McCambridge & Strang, 2005), self-support groups of A.A. and N.A. (Narcotics Anonymous; Laudet et al., 2006; Majer, 1992), and some forms of cognitive-behavioral therapy address aspects related to finding meaning and purpose in life (Grosse & Castonguay, 2005). These models of treatment focus on meaning-related aspects by establishing or enhancing an individual's sense of personal coherence, meaningful goals in therapy, values clarification to facilitate motivation to change, and self-transcendent behaviors that go beyond the desire to use substances (Hayes et al., 2004; Hettema, Steele, & Miller, 2005; Laudet et al., 2006).

Of specific relevance for this chapter are the treatment models that incorporate meaning in life as a fundamental component of intervention (Martínez, 1999, 2002, 2004, 2009a, 2009b; Somov, 2007; Thompson, 2012). In the next section, we highlight the contribution of meaning-centered psychotherapy, or logotherapeutic approaches, in the treatment of SUD.

Logotherapy in the Treatment of SUD

Since Frankl first suggested the importance of addressing meaning in the treatment of addictions (Frankl, 1994), a number of logotherapeutic interventions for the treatment of addictions have been developed (Hart, 2009; Martínez, 2013; Somov, 2007; Thompson, 2012; Wiklund, 2008a). In the context of SUD, some logotherapeutic developments include individual and group protocols to enhance meaning in life, as well as meaning-based groups to promote skill building and relapse prevention (Martínez, 2004, 2005, 2009b; Somov, 2007; Thompson, 2012).

According to Wiklund (2008b), an individual suffering from an addiction experiences difficulties discovering meaning in life. These problems are associated with feelings of guilt and shame that hinder the perception that life can be meaningful and that the individual is worthy of good things (Addad & Himi, 2008). Thus, Wiklund (2008b) asserted that attempts to discover meaning in the beginning stages of treatment are often limited by feelings of worthlessness and negative perceptions of the self. He further proposed that the first step in treating clients is to facilitate a positive and hopeful self-reference framework to interpret the world, which is later used as a building block to discover meaning (Thompson, 2012). In logotherapy, meaning is presented as a question that clients need to answer (Wiklund, 2008a). Clients are constantly challenged to discover meaning in their lives and actualize values (Thompson, 2012). Furthermore, purposeful goals and consistency with values become the fundamental factors to promote treatment adherence and maintenance of positive outcomes (Flora & Stalikas, 2012; Lyons et al., 2011; Martínez, 2013; Noblejas de la Flor, 1997; Wiklund, 2008a).

In addition, during treatment the therapist addresses the client's existential vacuum, which becomes more salient when he or she stops consuming substances, using the drive for meaning to motivate change and the establishment of new goals (Martínez, 2002; Thompson, 2012). Then, the therapist helps the client to also find the meaning of suffering caused by addiction, discover new sources of meaning and values, and develop new projects based on what is personally meaningful (Ford, 1996; Thompson, 2012). In regards to relapse prevention, an individual's perception of the presence of meaning, and the possibility of actualizing meaning and values in daily activities, have the potential of reducing vulnerability to relapse (Martínez, 2009b; Roos et al., 2015). From a theory of meaning, when individuals are aware of their need for meaning, drug use is no longer a priority as it becomes a threat to engaging in a life worth living (Ford, 1996; Thompson, 2012).

In spite of compelling evidence suggesting the important role of meaning in the prevention and treatment of SUD, there do not appear to be any validated meaning-based treatment programs established. Without empirically valid protocols and manuals, the diffusion of such important interventions is limited as researchers and practitioners often overlook advances in logotherapy (Martínez & Flórez, 2015). Thus, there is a growing need for empirically-based logotherapeutic clinical protocols focusing on substance-related disorders (Martínez & Flórez, 2015). The next step is for meaning-centered clinicians to evaluate their interventions, engage in on-going research efforts to evaluate treatment, and diffuse findings through publications and presentations (Schulenberg & Flórez, 2013).

With this in mind, a logotherapeutic model for the treatment of SUD is introduced. This model of treatment was developed by the El Colectivo Aquí y Ahora Foundation (CAYA), located in Bogotá, Colombia. Following this introduction, preliminary findings are reported as to levels of perceived meaning in life in individuals that completed CAYA's logotherapeutic treatment model for addiction versus individuals that received another form of treatment.

CAYA's Logotherapeutic Treatment Model

CAYA is a foundation that specializes in the treatment of substance abuse disorders in adolescents and adults. The organization has been providing inpatient and outpatient therapeutic services for addictions for more than two decades (Martínez, 2005; Martínez et al., 2015). The therapeutic model was designed based on literature reviews about addiction as well as empirical findings that indicate best practices for the treatment of SUD (Martínez, 2005; Martínez et al., 2015). To implement the program, mental health providers receive clinical training in logotherapy. The treatment program is a multi-component model that focuses on four major axes of intervention: meaning in life, motivation to change, personality traits, and relapse prevention. These four axes of intervention constantly interact to strengthen treatment goals and skill building in clients.

The first axis of intervention constitutes the philosophical core of the program. It highlights the importance of meaning in life and existential analyses in the treatment of SUD (Galanter, 2006; Roos et al., 2015). The existence of this focus of intervention is based on research findings that confirm a significant association between absence of meaning and substance use (Galanter, 2006; Roos et al., 2015). Moreover, the theoretical framework of the program is based on Frankl's logotherapy theory, which sustains that the development of SUD is related to existential vacuum (Frankl, 1959/1984). Within this axis, the logotherapeutic theoretical and practical advancements developed by Martínez (2002, 2009c) are integrated. Specifically, during treatment the therapist conducts an existential analysis of the client's addictions (Martínez, 2002), assesses his or her current use of personal resources (namely self-distancing self-projection, and self-transcendence; see Martínez & Flórez, 2015), and forms a strong therapeutic relationship from a logotherapeutic perspective (Martínez & Flórez, 2015).

The second axis of intervention of the CAYA model focuses on the motivation to change (Martínez, 2013). The client's motivation to stop using substances and receive treatment is a vital component for treatment adherence and maintenance of change (McCambridge & Strang, 2005). CAYA integrates Miller and Rollnick's (2004) principles of motivational interviewing (see also Hettema et al., 2005) with Frankl's theory of logotherapy, in which a *will to meaning* becomes a motivational force in the process of recovery (1994). Depending on the developmental stage of the client (e.g., teenagers vs. adults), CAYA's treatment model focuses on specific motivational sources associated with each client (Martínez et al., 2015). In therapy, the emotional and social expectations of drug use and abstinence are explored to attribute new significance to reasons that underlie substance use (Martínez, 2002). For instance, the belief that using drugs helps people be more social is replaced with more realistic information on how people behave inadequately in social situations while under the influence of alcohol and drugs.

The third axis of intervention addresses comorbid mental health problems that augment vulnerability for relapse, particularly those related to personality. In the CAYA model, personality problems that manifest in rigidity of behavior are considered to contribute to the progression of addictions, and thus they are important to include in the treatment of SUD (Martínez, 2002). CAYA's theoretical model further suggests that in a number of individuals diagnosed with SUD, the presence of a Personality Disorder (PD) precedes and underlies substance abuse problems (Martínez, 2011). This assumption has been supported by a growing body of research confirming a significant relationship between PD and SUD (Pettinati, Pierce, Belden, & Meyers, 1999; Trull, Jahng, Tomko, Wood, & Sher, 2010; Van Den Bosch & Verheul, 2007). There is a greater prevalence of PD in individuals suffering from substance abuse disorders (Bosch, Verheul, & Brink, 2001; Trull et al., 2010; Van Den Bosch & Verheul, 2007). Approximately 44 % of individuals diagnosed with alcohol dependency also have a PD. Moreover, 79 % of individuals diagnosed with opioid addiction also meet criteria for a PD diagnosis (Van Den Bosch & Verheul, 2007). In addition, in a study conducted by Pettinati et al. (1999) it was found that individuals diagnosed with PD had a higher likelihood of relapse regardless of positive outcomes obtained in treatment. From a logotherapy perspective, it is also assumed that an inauthentic personality leads to the use of maladaptive coping strategies such as drug use (Martínez, 2011; Martínez & Flórez, 2015). Based on this view, CAYA's logotherapeutic model aims to promote an authentic personality by replacing rigid patterns of behaviors with flexible and adaptive responses (Martínez, 2005; Martínez et al., 2015). This process of change is conducted through the mobilization of self-distancing and self-regulation as well as individualized exposure exercises in which clients are asked to implement a new coping strategy to replace a rigid behavior of escape and avoidance of distress.

The fourth and final axis of intervention focuses entirely on relapse prevention (Martínez, 2009a). In the treatment of SUD, relapse is often common following treatment (Marlatt, Parks, & Witkiewitz, 2002; McKay, 2001; Miller, Walters, & Bennett, 2001). For instance, 50–58 % of young adults relapse during the first 6 months following treatment (Chassin, Flora, & King, 2004; Cornelius et al., 2003; Maisto, Pollock, Cornelius, & Martin, 2003). Moreover, treatment models of SUD that do not incorporate relapse prevention programs report lower long-term abstinence rates and more intense relapse episodes (Rawson et al., 2002; Witkiewitz & Marlatt, 2004). Thus, treatment targets individual risk factors in order to decrease the likelihood of relapse, identifies protective factors in order to facilitate relapse prevention, and teaches specific strategies to cope with high-risk situations (Godley, Dennis, Godley, & Funk, 2004; Martínez, 2004). Relapse prevention is anchored to meaning, values, and the promotion of self-transcendent behavior to decrease the saliency of cravings and motivation to drink (Martínez, 2004).

Implementation of the CAYA Model of Treatment

CAYA's logotherapeutic model for the treatment of addictions is implemented over the course of 3 months of inpatient treatment. The program includes individual, family, and group therapy, in which each treatment modality interacts to target each of the four axes noted previously. The program delivers 10 family psychotherapy sessions and 36 multifamily sessions (with several families of individuals suffering from SUD). In the multifamily sessions, the mental health providers offer psychoeducation and address specific common treatment needs (Martínez, 2005; Martínez et al., 2015). The client also receives approximately 16 individual sessions of meaning-centered psychotherapy (at least one individual session weekly) and 320 group therapy sessions over a 3-month period of inpatient treatment (Martínez et al., 2015). After treatment is completed, there is a 1-year period of individual, group, and family follow-up for relapse prevention (Martínez, 2005; Martínez et al., 2015).

The program is implemented in three consecutive phases. The initial phase starts during the first week of treatment and lasts from 4 to 6 weeks. The main objectives of this phase are to develop a clear case formulation of the phenomenology of the client, consolidate the therapeutic relationship, and augment motivation to change. Through assessment and continuous observation the mental health provider focuses on a case formulation that identifies (1) the client's perceived meaning in life, (2) the level of spiritual resources being displayed, (3) the client's maladaptive coping strategies that lead to an inauthentic personality, and (4) the client's history of substance abuse as well as other symptoms of psychopathology. Additionally, in individual and group therapy, the processes of self-distancing and motivation to change are mobilized through activities in which clients establish reasons for sobriety, understand the freedom and responsibility of finding meaning, identify inadequate coping strategies, and take perspective of their symptoms. The CAYA model uses two manuals that are given to clients for them to reflect on their substance abuse history as it relates to meaning and to train them to identify values and meaningful activities.

In these manuals, clients are asked to respond to a series of questions about their substance use that prompt them to think about the reasons to change and the consequences of their use (e.g., "What concerns you about your substance use?, What situations in your life indicate that changing might be a good idea?, How would you like your life to be if you change?, What is likely to happen if you do not change?, What is the best thing that can happen to you if you change?," etc.). The manuals also contain exercises in which clients are asked to reflect on the steps that are necessary for change. For instance, clients are asked to write and address three letters to themselves with respect to how they are doing 1, 5, and 10 years (a different time corresponding to each of the three letters) after having recovered from addiction. In these letters, clients detail how their current self is doing with respect to maintaining sobriety. Letters also prompt clients to write about their feelings, their fears, their relationships with loved ones, and what they have accomplished since they recovered.

Once the therapist has a clear case formulation, the second phase of treatment begins, lasting from week 4 to week 10. In the second phase, the therapist continues to address the client's motivation to change and strengthens the therapeutic relationship. However, in this phase there is a greater emphasis on helping the client change inadequate maladaptive coping strategies for more adequate coping strategies through processes of self-distancing (self-comprehension, self-regulation, and self-projection; see Martínez & Flórez, 2015). To this end, the therapist develops a treatment plan that includes in vivo exposure to activities that evoke old maladaptive coping strategies (i.e., activities that create feelings of distress in clients). Through these activities, the client attributes new meanings to situations associated with subjective threats, and practices the implementation of new, increasingly effective strategies in the presence of undesired feelings (e.g., a client with fear of evaluation is asked to give several speeches in public). In this phase, the client learns to use self-comprehension (the ability to objectively see oneself and assume a healthy stance upon such observation), self-regulation (the ability to monitor and regulate cognitive and emotional processes), and self-projection (the ability to perceive oneself differently in the future) to cope with difficult situations and move forward toward a more authentic personality (see Martínez & Flórez, 2015).

In the third and final stage, which lasts approximately from the 11th to the 16th week of treatment, the therapist focuses specifically on strengthening commitment to change, preventing relapse, and augmenting processes of self-transcendence for a meaningful life. The therapist praises and validates the client's progress, and encourages the client to establish a plan to maintain change after completion of treatment. For relapse prevention, the therapist implements a six-session manual (Martínez, 2005) in which the client anticipates obstacles to maintaining sobriety; signs of relapse; and high-risk situations, places, and behaviors for relapse, as well as develops plans to adequately cope with these situations in order to prevent possible setbacks that could trigger previous maladaptive patterns of living. An example of an activity useful for relapse prevention is known as humoristic cognitive reframing. In humoristic cognitive reframing, the client generates an alternative funny thought to a thought associated with using drugs (humoristic cognitive reframing: "I want to get high, maybe I should go and climb."). This is similar to Frankl's paradoxical intention technique, in which a client's sense of humor is used to facilitate self-distancing and as a means to alleviate the emotional burden of thoughts associated with substances. Lastly, during this phase there is a great emphasis on mobilizing self-transcendence resources (affectation and commitment) oriented to meaning. Through affectation the client gets in touch with his or her ability to be moved by the presence of values and meaning. Through commitment, the client is directed toward giving himself or herself to a cause or a higher power that brings a sense of meaning. Using the meaning in life manual given to them during treatment, clients learn to identify creative, experiential and attitudinal values and establish actions consistent with these values. Moreover, to facilitate values clarification, they are asked to monitor and register the meaning of the moment of different past, present, and future instances of their lives.

Over the course of treatment, group therapy is the main intervention modality in the CAYA model of rehabilitation. Every day (except for weekends) there are seven group interventions in which the following groups rotate each week:

- The existential group: This group consists of a 16-session protocol that focuses on the meaning of life and the meaning of suffering.
- The meaning in life group: This group consists of an 8-session protocol that focuses on the topics of freedom, responsibility, will to meaning (inner drive to discover meaning), values, optimism, and ultimate meaning.
- The dereflection group: This group consists of an 8-session protocol directed to augment the perception of meaning and redirect attention away from symptoms and toward valuable and positive activities.
- The existential growth group: This group consists of a 90-session protocol that teaches clients a logotherapy perspective of relapse prevention, motivation to change, meaning in life, and an authentic personality.
- The relapse prevention group: This group consists of a 16-session protocol that focuses on relapse prevention.
- The experiential group: This group is a daily group in which clients are exposed to personalized therapeutic activities that are shared with the group and target each client's specific maladaptive strategies (e.g., a client that fears evaluation gives a presentation to the group, a client that engages in aggression discusses assertiveness and strategies to be appropriately assertive).
- The gathering group: A daily morning group that promotes self-distancing and responsibility.

The objective of these groups is to build within the client a model of logotherapy that constitutes the overall framework of recovery and facilitates the objectives of the three phases of treatment.

The CAYA foundation understands the importance of directing research efforts to validate treatment and identify mechanisms of change. As a result, CAYA is invested in conducting research to evaluate treatment objectives and outcomes. Currently, CAYA is conducting an ongoing investigation to evaluate treatment effectiveness over 2 years of follow-up. Moreover, CAYA is initiating a study about the influence that each of the four axes of treatment has on treatment outcome. In the next section of the chapter, preliminary findings are presented of an investigation that evaluated the effects that the CAYA logotherapeutic model had in augmenting perceived meaning in life in a group of individuals with SUD.

Meaning in Life Following Treatment for SUD

This study had a quasi-experimental nonequivalent group design (Shadish, Cook, & Campbell, 2002). In the study, changes of meaning in life pre- and post-treatment were compared in individuals that participated in the CAYA treatment program

(Group 1, or G1) versus individuals that received a 12-step inpatient treatment program with medication management (Group 2, or G2). It was expected that following both treatments individuals were going to experience significant changes in meaning. Furthermore, it was hypothesized that participants receiving logotherapeutic treatment were going to show greater changes in meaning scores after treatment.

Participants

The study sample consisted of 81 participants seeking treatment for SUD. The inclusion criteria consisted of individuals who voluntarily participated in either of the two treatment programs during the first 6 months of 2014. In the two treatment programs, the CAYA program and the 12-step inpatient program, all of the individuals that were receiving treatment consented to participate. There were no incentives for participation. Moreover, the study followed the ethical guidelines stipulated by the Colombian psychological legislation.

Participants' ages ranged from 14 to 57 years old, with a mean age of 25.68 years ($SD = 10.74$) and a median age of 22. With respect to gender, 70.4% of participants identified as males and 29.6% identified as females. Group 1 was composed of 31 participants (38% of the total sample, 64.5% males and 35.5% females). Group 2 was composed of 50 participants (61% of the total sample, 74% males and 26% females).

Measures

The Meaning in Life Dimensional Scale (MLDS; Martínez, Trujillo, Díaz del Castillo, & Osma, 2011) was used to measure meaning in life. The MLDS is an 18-item self-report scale presented in Spanish. In this scale, meaning is defined as a subjective sense of coherence and vital purpose. The aim of the questionnaire is to identify an individual's current perception and experience of meaning. It employs a 4-point Likert-type response format ranging from 0 (completely disagree) to 3 (completely agree). Total MLDS scores range from 0 to 54. Higher total scores are indicative of greater perceived meaning in life. As an example, one of the items is: *"I have discovered clear goals in my life."*

For interpretation of the measure, total MLDS scores are classified via four levels of perceived meaning in life: search for meaning, medium level of meaning, high level of meaning, and plenitude. The search for meaning level refers to those individuals that are having difficulties discovering meaning and setting valuable life goals. The medium level corresponds to people that report perceiving meaning in life, but that also indicate moments of confusion with life goals and lack of perceived coherence. The high level of meaning is associated with individuals that experience a purposeful life most of the time and perceive their lives as coherent and significant. Finally, the plenitude level of meaning includes individuals that perceive they are pursuing meaningful and clear goals and their lives are full of purpose, personal coherence, and significance.

To calculate the classification score, each participant's mean score is computed. A mean total score ranging from 0 to 2 is classified as being within the search for meaning level, a mean total score from 2 to 2.34 falls within the medium level, a score from 2.35 to 2.64 is classified at the high level of meaning, and a score from 2.65 to 3 corresponds to the plenitude level of meaning. The measure was designed to be used for both research and clinical proposes. The validation of the scale was conducted with 820 individuals from Colombia, with an age range of 20 to 70 years old (Martínez et al., 2011). Exploratory factor analysis suggested a two-dimensional structure: existential coherence and purpose in life. Moreover, the internal consistency coefficient reported for the MLDS was 0.94 (Martínez et al., 2011).

Procedures

Participants were contacted through each treatment program. Both treatment models have a duration of 90 days and include individual, group, and family therapy. After obtaining informed consent, participants received the standard treatment program for each of the group conditions. Participants receiving the CAYA model of treatment participated in all therapeutic modalities and activities described previously. Participants receiving the 12-step model of treatment were educated according to standard A.A./N.A. philosophy (Galanter, 2007). The mental health providers that implemented the treatments also administered the self-report measures. Data were collected at the beginning and at the end of treatment.

Results

After data collection, statistical analyses were performed using SPSS statistical software (Meyers, Gamst, & Guarino, 2013). All of the responses were included. Pre- and post-descriptive statistics for the MLDS were obtained for the overall sample and each treatment group. Results are presented in terms of participants' changes in levels of meaning. To compare significance of changes in levels of meaning for individual cases the McNemar test was used. Then, to compare mean group differences, t-test statistics were calculated.

At the beginning of treatment, in the overall sample, 58% of the participants' scores fell in the search for meaning level, whereas only 4.9% of the participants' scores fell in the plenitude level of meaning. As for changes in levels of meaning for each group, Fig. 1 shows the classification of individual levels of meaning for G1 and G2 at pre-test and post-test in terms of percentages. As indicated in the graph, for G1 there was an increase of 19.4% of participants in the plenitude level of meaning after

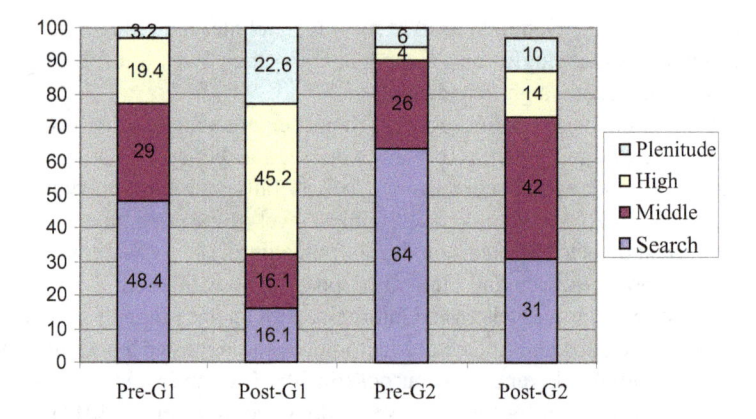

Fig. 1 Classification of individuals' levels of meaning by percentage. G1 = logotherapeutic intervention, G2 = 12-step treatment program

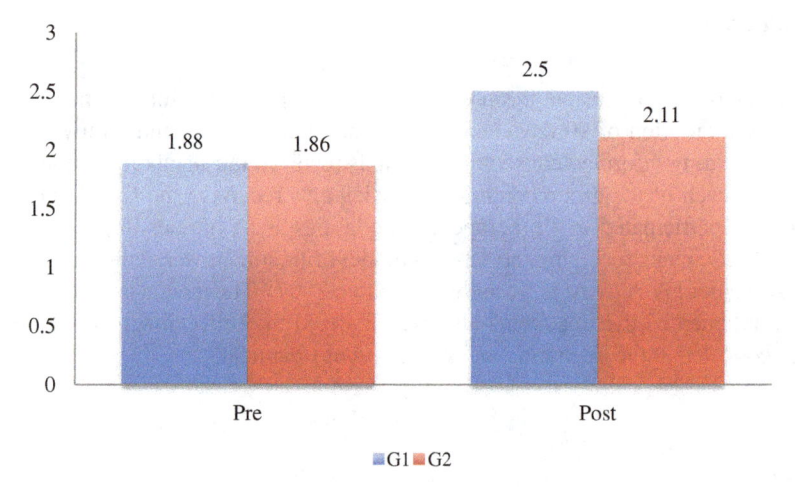

Fig. 2 MLDS pre- and post-test median scores for G1 and G2. G1 = logotherapeutic intervention, G2 = 12-step treatment program

treatment. Moreover, following treatment there was a decrease of 32.3 % of participants in the search for meaning level. In the G2 treatment condition there was an increase of 4 % of participants in the plenitude level of meaning and a decrease of 33 % of participants in the search for meaning level after treatment.

The McNemar test for matched-paired samples was used to test for statistically significant differences in individual changes in levels of meaning. A significant difference was found for changes in levels of meaning following treatment in individuals in the G1 treatment condition ($p < 0.001$). However, for individuals in the G2 treatment condition, changes in levels of meaning after treatment were not statistically significant ($p = 0.092$). In terms of the overall MLDS scores for each treatment group, the G1 condition started with a median score of 1.88 and the G2 condition started with a median score of 1.86 (Fig. 2). There were no statistically significant group differences between G1 and G2's pre-test scores. At post-test, G1's median score was 2.5, whereas G2's median score was 2.1.

A paired-samples *t*-test was conducted to compare mean differences on MLDS pre-test and post-test scores for each group. The mean comparison is different than the changes in levels of meaning comparison presented above in which the McNemar test was used. Using a paired-samples *t*-test, the overall mean differences were analyzed without consideration for individuals' classification of meaning levels. Changes in median scores from pre-test to post-test using the overall mean and not individual changes in levels of meaning were statistically significant for both groups (G1 pre $M=1.88$, $SD=0.55$, post $M=2.5$, $SD=0.33$, $t(30)=5.8$, $p<0.001$; G2 pre $M=1.86$, $SD=0.53$, post $M=2.1$, $SD=0.52$, $t(49)=4.1$, $p<0.001$). Thus, in both treatment groups, there was significant improvement in meaning scores after treatment. Finally, an independent samples *t*-test was conducted to compare MLDS post-test scores between groups. There was a statistically significant difference between G1 and G2 scores; $t(79)=2.58$, $p<0.01$. These results suggest that the G1 treatment condition was superior to the G2 treatment condition with respect to improving participants' perceived meaning in life.

Discussion

This study compared changes in levels of meaning in individuals receiving two different treatment modalities for SUD, the CAYA model and a 12-step therapeutic model that follows A.A./N.A. guidelines and which incorporates medication management. The hypothesis of the study was that for both groups statistically significant changes in meaning were going to be observed following treatment. Additionally, it was anticipated that individuals receiving the CAYA treatment model were going to report significantly greater changes in meaning when compared to individuals receiving a standard 12-step model of treatment.

Results indicated that in both treatment conditions participants reported greater levels of meaning when compared to their baseline scores. Findings indicate that regardless of differences in these models of intervention, efforts to treat SUD are associated with improvements in perceived meaning in life. This hypothesis has also been supported in previous studies, in which changes in meaning were associated with improvements in SUD symptoms across distinct treatment approaches (Roos et al., 2015). Findings provide validation for Frankl's initial suggestion that meaning in life plays an important role in the recovery of substance use disorders. These results also suggest that interventions targeting symptoms of SUD are tapping, directly or indirectly, meaning-related issues (Roos et al., 2015).

As anticipated, results also confirmed that the logotherapeutic model was superior to the 12-step inpatient treatment program with medication management in enhancing perception of meaning. These findings suggest that a treatment model for SUD that incorporates a theory of meaning and meaning-centered interventions is more effective in increasing perception of meaning than a standard 12-step model of treatment. In the CAYA model, over the course of treatment, meaning-related issues and existential concerns are explicitly addressed. In addition, inpatient clients learn about Frankl's theory of meaning and participate in weekly meaning in life groups throughout treatment. Findings also support the effectiveness of CAYA's model with respect to enhancing participants' levels of meaning in life.

Overall, these preliminary findings strengthen the argument for implementing meaning-based interventions in the treatment of addictions. Potentially, the benefits of incorporating meaning-centered interventions go beyond increasing meaning perception and reducing SUD symptoms as meaning is associated with protective factors for mental health problems such as depression, anxiety, and posttraumatic stress disorder, as well as with positive functioning across several life domains (Ortíz, Schulenberg, & Pacciola, 2013). With this in mind, meaning-based interventions may boost other significant mediators of change to protect against relapse and promote better functioning and adjustment following treatment (DeWitz, Woolsey, & Walsh, 2009; Drescher et al., 2012; Halama, 2003; Schulenberg, Hutzell, Nassif, & Rogina, 2008; Steger, Kashdan, & Oishi, 2008).

In terms of the limitations of the study, causality cannot be inferred because there was not a random allocation of participants for each treatment condition. Moreover, individual differences between groups were not accounted for, and thus, results can be confounded by pre-existing variables interacting with treatment effects. In addition, due to the multi-component nature of the CAYA treatment model, it cannot be concluded that the active component associated with changes in meaning is the meaning-based intervention. Rather, treatment effectiveness in enhancing perceived meaning could be attributed to the interactive effect of the four axes of intervention.

Therefore, for future studies it is important to conduct increasingly rigorous research designed to disentangle the effects of treatment components. In addition, to decrease confounds, it is important to control for variables such as therapeutic relationship and therapist training, as well as other important variables such as an individual's social support. Finally, in this study there were no data examined as to SUD severity or with regard to changes in symptom presentation over the course of treatment. In the future, the relationship between meaning in life and changes in SUD symptoms during the course of the CAYA inpatient treatment program needs to be systematically explored.

Final Comments

There seems to be compelling evidence advocating for the incorporation of meaning-centered interventions in the treatment and prevention of SUD. However, more rigorous research is needed as empirical findings are still not definitive (Hart & Carey, 2014; Roos et al., 2015). Amongst the biggest limitations of the current body of knowledge about the role of meaning in SUD is that the majority of studies are correlational. Thus, they do not validate that the absence of meaning is a casual factor in the onset of SUD (Hart & Carey, 2014). Furthermore, the lack of randomized controlled trials validating meaning-centered interventions limits empirical support for the applicability and efficacy of these interventions in the treatment of addiction (Hart & Carey, 2014).

Other limitations found in the literature are the ambiguity and lack of consensus as to the definition of meaning. In some studies, meaning is interpreted as spirituality or a search for a higher power. Although some research has supported a strong relationship between meaning and spiritual values, meaning is not synonymous with spirituality, and meaning-based interventions are independent from spiritual or religious models. This confusion of terms has misguided research and practice. Moreover, it has hindered clarification of the specific role of meaning in SUD recovery.

Additionally, longitudinal studies that use advanced statistical analyses are needed to explore changes in meaning over the course of the addiction process (Hart & Carey, 2014). All of the reported studies have been conducted either in a "normal" population of adolescents and college students, people who are less likely to present with SUD, or in populations that are already seeking treatment. Therefore, there is a gap in the dynamics of meaning and substance use disorder at different stages of its progression.

There is also scarce research that explores how distinct components of meaning in life relate to SUD treatment and prevention. For instance, conceptually meaning has cognitive, affective, and behavioral components that encompass different aspects of a meaningful life. The study of how such components relate to substance use would yield important findings to inform meaning-centered interventions. For instance, future studies should focus on the mediational role of values, goal setting, sense of purpose, sense of coherence, positive affect, positive thinking, and other adaptive meaning-based coping strategies.

To conclude, although there are still several limitations in the research on meaning in life in addictions, the current body of knowledge evidences the importance of meaning-centered interventions in the treatment and prevention of addictions. The preliminary empirical results of recent investigations constitute a solid foundation to direct efforts to experimental designs and the validation of interventions.

Key Takeaways

- Based on the literature review demonstrating that meaning is a protector factor for substance use disorders across the lifespan, it is important to recognize the role of meaning in life in both preventive and treatment interventions for adolescents and adults. For instance, in regards to the prevention of SUD, given that the absence of meaning is a risk factor for the development of substance use, assessment of levels of meaning in adolescents can help identify vulnerable individuals who would benefit from more specific interventions to prevent future alcohol and drug use. Thus, it is important to incorporate formal evaluation of perceived meaning, values, and sense of purpose in preventive and health promotion programs.

- Similarly, during preventive efforts related to substance abuse it is important to incorporate psychoeducation on values, meaning, and goal-congruent behavior adapted to different developmental stages. For instance, programs can include activities oriented toward identifying individuals' sources of meaning, their valued goals and ideals, and further emphasize the dissonance between such values and substance use.
- In the treatment of SUD, ongoing formal monitoring of levels of meaning in life and symptoms is recommended. This can be done through valid self-report measures and the documentation of qualitative reports obtained from observations and perceived changes in clients. Assessment is vital to tracking progress, identifying specific needs for intervention, and evaluating the interaction of meaning in life and symptoms.
- For mental health providers implementing logotherapeutic interventions, it is recommended that they incorporate a program evaluation of treatment outcomes, have clear documentation of treatment procedures, and establish a routine follow-up with clients after treatment for validation and further diffusion of meaning-centered approaches. Initially, findings from program evaluation can be compared to research data on treatment outcomes and abstinence rates following other SUD treatments. Ideally, these models of treatment should be tested against other treatments and evidence-based practices.
- In treatment, meaning-based interventions can be included at every stage, through individual, as well as group therapy. Brief psychoeducation on meaning, using Frankl's theory of logotherapy, can be beneficial. Moreover, group therapy can be oriented to enhance the perception of meaning in recovery and to help clients make sense of their addictions by putting their suffering in the service of something or someone meaningful to them.
- At the beginning of treatment, clients may be reluctant to think about meaning and values because doing so might confront them with past failures at actualizing their values and goals due to drug use. Moreover, at the beginning of treatment the clients' symptoms and resistance to change may keep them from discovering what is meaningful. Thus, it is important for the mental health provider to recognize the best way in which to introduce the topic of meaning to clients, and be aware of any resistance. At the beginning, therapists may find it useful to focus on restoring a sense of dignity and worth in clients before establishing goals oriented to meaning.
- In treatment, clients should be provided with opportunities to actualize their values (e.g., with their families/loved ones, by serving others, through accomplishing tasks, etc.) and to develop clear, concrete, and realistic meaningful goals during and following treatment. In therapy, clients should identify and delineate the specific steps needed to attain such goals.
- Lastly, mental health providers should be careful not to impose their own meaning and values onto clients. Thus, past, present, and future sources of meaning should be explored using Socratic questioning and clients' narratives on what is important to them (see Martínez & Flórez, 2015).

References

Addad, M., & Himi, H. (2008). Meaning of life and drug use among Israeli teenagers. *The International Forum for Logotherapy, 31*, 43–47.

Amodeo, M., Kurtz, N., & Cutter, H. S. (1992). Abstinence, reasons for not drinking, and life satisfaction. *Substance Use & Misuse, 27*, 707–716.

Becoña, E. (2002). *Bases científicas de la prevención de las drogodependencias*. Madrid: Ministerio del Interior.

Brown, J. M., Ashcroft, F. G., & Miller, W. R. (1998). Purpose in life among alcoholics: A comparison of three ethnic groups. *Alcoholism Treatment Quarterly, 16*, 1–11.

Calafat, A., Gómez, C., Juan, M., & Becoña, E. (2007). Weekend nightlife recreational habits: Prominent intrapersonal "risk factors" for drug use? *Substance Use & Misuse, 42*, 1443–1454.

Carroll, S. (1993). Spirituality and purpose in life in alcoholism recovery. *Journal of Studies on Alcohol, 54*, 297–301.

Chassin, L., Flora, D. B., & King, K. M. (2004). Trajectories of alcohol and drug use and dependence from adolescence to adulthood: The effects of familial alcoholism and personality. *Journal of Abnormal Psychology, 113*, 483–498.

Chen, G. (2006). Social support, spiritual program, and addiction recovery. *International Journal of Offender Therapy and Comparative Criminology, 50*, 306–323.

Cornelius, J., Maisto, S., Pollock, N., Martin, C., Salloum, K., & Clark, D. (2003). Rapid relapse generally follows treatment for substance use disorders among adolescents. *Addictive Behaviors, 28*, 381–386.

DeWitz, J. S., Woolsey, L. M., & Walsh, B. W. (2009). College student retention: An exploration of the relationship between self-efficacy beliefs and purpose in life among college students. *Journal of College Student Development, 50*, 19–34.

Drescher, C. F., Baczwaski, B. J., Walters, A. B., Aiena, B. J., Schulenberg, S. E., & Johnson, L. R. (2012). Coping with an ecological disaster: The role of perceived meaning in life and self-efficacy following the Gulf oil spill. *Ecopsychology, 4*, 56–63.

Flora, K., & Stalikas, A. (2012). Factors affecting substance abuse treatment in Greece and their course during therapy. *Addictive Behaviors, 37*, 1358–1364.

Ford, G. (1996). An existential model for promoting life change. *Journal of Substance Abuse Treatment, 13*, 151–158.

Frankl, V. E. (1959/1984). *Man's search for meaning*. New York, NY: Washington Square Press.

Frankl, V. (1994). *El hombre doliente. Fundamentos antropológicos de la psicoterapia*. Barcelona: Herder.

Galanter, M. (2006). Spirituality and addiction: A research and clinical perspective. *The American Journal on Addictions, 15*, 286–292.

Galanter, M. (2007). Spirituality and recovery in 12-step programs: An empirical model. *Journal of Substance Abuse Treatment, 33*, 265–272.

Godley, S., Dennis, M., Godley, M., & Funk, R. (2004). Thirty-month relapse trajectory cluster groups among adolescents discharged from out-patient treatment. *Addiction, 99*, 129–139.

Grosse, M., & Castonguay, L. (2005). Relationship and techniques in cognitive-behavioral therapy—A motivational approach. *Psychotherapy: Theory, Research, Practice, Training, 42*, 443–455.

Halama, P. (2003). Meaning and hope: Two factors of positive psychological functioning in late adulthood. *Studia Psychologica, 45*, 103–110.

Harlow, L. L., Newcomb, M. D., & Bentler, P. M. (1986). Depression, self-derogation, substance use, and suicide ideation: Lack of purpose in life as a mediational factor. *Journal of Clinical Psychology, 42*, 5–21.

Hart, K. E., Singh, T. (2009). An existential model of flourishing subsequent to treatment for addiction: The importance of living a meaningful and spiritual life. *Illness, Crisis, and Loss, 17*, 125–147.

Hart, K., & Carey, T. (2014). Ebb and flow in the sense of meaningful purpose: A lifespan perspective on alcohol and other drug involvement. In A. Batthyany & P. Russo-Netzer (Eds.), *Meaning in positive and existential psychology* (pp. 347–413). New York, NY: Springer.

Hayes, S. C., Wilson, K. G., Gifford, E. V., Bissett, R., Piasecki, M., Batten, S. V., ... Gregg, J. (2004). A preliminary trial of twelve-step facilitation and Acceptance and Commitment Therapy with polysubstance-abusing methadone-maintained opiate addicts. *Behavior Therapy, 35*, 667–688.

Hettema, J., Steele, J., & Miller, W. (2005). Motivational interviewing. *Annual Review of Clinical Psychology, 1*, 91–111.

Kinnier, R., Metha, A., Keim, J., Okey, J., Adler-Tabia, R., Berry, M., & Mulvenon, S. (1994). Depression, meaninglessness, and substance abuse in "normal" and hospitalized adolescents. *Journal of Alcohol and Drug Education, 39*, 101–111.

Konkoly, T., Bachner, Y., Martos, T., & Kushnir, T. (2009). Meaning in life: Does it play a role in smoking? *Substance Use and Misuse, 44*, 1566–1577.

Krentzman, A. R., Farkas, K. J., & Townsend, A. L. (2010). Spirituality, religiousness, and alcoholism treatment outcomes: A comparison between Black and White participants. *Alcoholism Treatment Quarterly, 28*, 128–150.

Laudet, A., Morgen, K., & White, W. (2006). The role of social supports, spirituality, religiousness, life meaning and affiliation with 12-step fellowships in quality of life satisfaction among individuals in recovery from alcohol and drug problems. *Alcoholism Treatment Quarterly, 24*, 33–73.

Lecci, L., MacLean, M. G., & Croteau, N. (2002). Personal goals as predictors of college student drinking motives, alcohol use and related problems. *Journal of Studies on Alcohol, 63*, 620–630.

Lyons, G., Deane, F., Caputi, P., & Kelly, P. (2011). Spirituality and the treatment of substance use disorders: An exploration of forgiveness, resentment and purpose in life. *Addiction Research & Theory, 19*, 459–469.

Lyons, G., Frank, D., & Kelly, P. (2010). Forgiveness and purpose in life as spiritual mechanisms of recovery from substance use disorders. *Addiction Research and Theory, 18*, 528–543.

Maisto, S., Pollock, N., Cornelius, K., & Martin, C. (2003). Alcohol relapse as a function of relapse definition in a clinical sample of adolescents. *Addictive Behaviors, 28*, 449–459.

Majer, J. M. (1992). Assessing the logotherapeutic value of 12-step therapy. *The International Forum for Logotherapy, 15*, 86–89.

Marlatt, A., Parks, G., & Witkiewitz, K. (2002). *Clinical guidelines for implementing relapse prevention therapy*. The Behavioral Health Recovery Project. Illinois Department of Human Services, Office of Alcoholism and Substance Abuse.

Marsh, A., Smith, L., Piek, J., & Saunders, B. (2003). The Purpose in Life scale: Psychometric properties for social drinkers and drinkers in alcohol treatment. *Educational and Psychological Measurement, 63*, 859–871.

Martin, R., MacKinnon, S., Johnson, J., & Rohsenow, D. (2011). Purpose in life predicts treatment outcome among adult cocaine abusers in treatment. *Journal of Substance Abuse Treatment, 40*, 183–188.

Martínez, E. (1999). *Logoterapia: Una alternativa ante la frustración existencial y las adicciones*. Bogotá: Editorial CAA.

Martínez, E. (2002). *Acción y elección: Logoterapia, logoterapia de grupo y una visión de las drogodependencias*. Bogotá: Editorial CAA.

Martínez, E. (2004). *Prevención de recaídas desde una perspectiva logoterapeutica. En: Desafíos y retos contra las adicciones*. España: Plan Nacional de Drogas de España.

Martínez, E. (2005). *Manual de prevención de recaídas*. Bogotá: Editorial CAA.

Martínez, E. (2009a). Modelo Logoterapeutico-ambulatorio en adicciones. In S. Sáenz (Ed.), *Logoterapia en acción. Aplicaciones prácticas* (435–450). Buenos Aires: San Pablo.

Martínez, E. (2009b). *Prevención de recaídas: Un libro de herramientas para personas en recuperación*. Buenos Aires: Editorial CAA.

Martínez, E. (2009c). *En busca del sentido: Manual del facilitador*. Bogotá: Editorial SAPS.

Martínez, E. (2011). *Los modos de ser inauténticos. Psicoterapia Centrada en el Sentido de los Trastornos de la personalidad.* Bogotá: Manual Moderno.
Martínez, E. (2013). *Preparándome para superar la adicción: Manual para aumentar la motivación para el cambio en adolescentes con problemas de adicción.* Bogotá: Editorial CAA.
Martínez, E., Camacho, S., Flórez, I., Riveros, M., Rodríguez, J., & Castellanos, C. (2015). *Adicciones y sentido de vida.* Modelo CAYA de recuperación. Bogotá: Editorial CAA.
Martínez, E. Y., & Flórez, I. A. (2015). Meaning-centered psychotherapy: A Socratic clinical practice. *Journal of Contemporary Psychotherapy, 45,* 37–48.
Martínez, E., Trujillo, A., Díaz del Castillo, J., & Osma, J. (2011). Desarrollo y estructura de la escala dimensional del sentido de vida. *Acta Colombiana de Psicología, 14,* 113–119.
McCambridge, J., & Strang, J. (2005). The efficacy of single-session motivational interviewing in reducing drug consumption and perceptions of drug-related risk and harm among young people: Results from a multi-site cluster randomized trial. *Addiction, 99,* 39–52.
McKay, J. R. (2001). Effectiveness of continuing care interventions for substance abusers: Implications for the study of long-term effects. *Evaluation Review, 25,* 211–232.
Meyers, L. S., Gamst, G., & Guarino, A. J. (2013). *Applied multivariate research: Design and interpretation* (2nd ed.). Washington, DC: Sage.
Miller, W. (1998). Researching the spiritual dimensions of alcohol and other drug problems. *Addiction, 93,* 979–990.
Miller, W. R., & Rollnick, S. (2004). Talking oneself into change: Motivational interviewing, stages of change, and the therapeutic process. *Journal of Cognitive Psychotherapy, 18,* 299–308.
Miller, W. R., Walters, S. T., & Bennett, M. E. (2001). How effective is alcoholism treatment in the United States. *Journal of Studies on Alcohol, 62,* 211–220.
Minehan, J., Newcomb, M., & Galaif, E. (2000). Predictors of adolescent drug use: Cognitive abilities, coping strategies, and purpose in life. *Journal of Child & Adolescent Substance Abuse, 10,* 33–52.
Newcomb, M. D., & Harlow, L. L. (1986). Life events and substance use among adolescents: Mediating effects of perceived loss of control and meaninglessness in life. *Journal of Personality and Social Psychology, 51,* 564–577.
Nicholson, T., Higgins, W., Turner, P., James, S., Stickle, F., & Pruitt, T. (1994). The relation between meaning in life and the occurrence of drug abuse: A retrospective study. *Psychology of Addictive Behaviors, 8,* 24–28.
Noblejas de la Flor, M. (1997). Meaning levels and drug abuse-therapy: An empirical study. *The International Forum for Logotherapy, 20,* 46–52.
Ortíz, E. M., Schulenberg, S. E., & Pacciola, A. (2013). Introducción a la psicoterapia centrada en el sentido o psicoterapia de orientación logoterapéutica. In E. M. Ortiz (Ed.), *Manual de psicoterapia con enfoque logoterapéutico* (pp. 23–40). Bogotá: Editorial El Manual Moderno.
Osaka, Y., Morita, N., Nakatani, Y., & Fujisawa, K. (2008). Correlation between addictive behaviors and mental health in university students. *Psychiatry and Clinical Neurosciences, 62,* 84–92.
Palfai, T. P., Ralston, T. E., & Wright, L. L. (2011). Understanding university student drinking in the context of life goal pursuits: The mediational role of enhancement motives. *Personality and Individual Differences, 50,* 169–174.
Palfai, T. P., & Weafer, J. (2006). College student drinking and meaning in the pursuit of life goals. *Psychology of Addictive Behaviors, 20,* 131–134.
Pettinati, H. M., Pierce, J. D., Belden, P. P., & Meyers, K. (1999). The relationship of Axis II personality disorders to other known predictors of addiction treatment outcome. *The American Journal on Addictions, 8,* 136–147.
Piderman, K., Schneekloth, T., & Pankratz, V. (2008). Spirituality during alcoholism treatment and continuous abstinence for one year. *International Journal of Psychiatry in Medicine, 38,* 391–406.
Piedmont, R. L. (2004). Spiritual transcendence as a predictor of psychosocial outcome from an outpatient substance abuse program. *Psychological Addictive Behavior, 18,* 213–222.
Project MATCH Research Group. (1997). Matching alcoholism treatments to client heterogeneity: Project MATCH posttreatment drinking outcomes. *Journal of Studies on Alcohol, 58,* 7–29.

Rahman, T. (2001). Mental health and purpose in life of drug addicts in Bangladesh. *The International Forum for Logotherapy, 24*, 83–97.

Rawson, R. A., Huber, A., McCann, M., Shoptaw, S., Farabee, D., Reiber, C., & Ling, W. (2002). A comparison of contingency management and cognitive-behavioral approaches during methadone maintenance treatment for cocaine dependence. *Archives of General Psychiatry, 59*, 817–824.

Robinson, E., Cranford, J., Webb, J., & Brower, K. (2007). Six-month changes in spirituality, religiousness, and heavy drinking in a treatment-seeking sample. *Journal of Studies on Alcohol and Drugs, 68*, 282–290.

Robinson, E. A. R., Krentzman, A. R., Webb, J. R., & Brower, K. J. (2011). Six-month changes in spirituality and religiousness in alcoholics predict drinking outcomes at nine months. *Journal of Studies on Alcohol and Drugs, 72*, 660–668.

Roos, C. R., Kirouac, M., Pearson, M. R., Fink, B. C., & Witkiewitz, K. (2015). Examining temptation to drink from an existential perspective: Associations among temptation, purpose in life, and drinking outcomes. *Psychology of Addictive Behaviors, 29*, 716–724.

Schlesinger, S., Susman, M., & Koenigsberg, J. (1990). Self-esteem and purpose in life: A comparative study of women alcoholics. *Journal of Alcohol and Drug Education, 36*, 127–141.

Schnetzer, L. W., Schulenberg, S. E., & Buchanan, E. M. (2013). Differential associations among alcohol use, depression and perceived life meaning in male and female college students. *Journal of Substance Use, 18*, 311–319.

Schulenberg, S. E., & Flórez, I. A. (2013). Advancing logotherapy as a science: A research imperative—Part two. *The International Forum for Logotherapy, 36*, 41–50.

Schulenberg, S. E., Hutzell, R. R., Nassif, C., & Rogina, J. M. (2008). Logotherapy for clinical practice. *Psychotherapy: Theory, Research, Practice, Training, 45*, 447–463.

Shadish, W., Cook, T., & Campbell, D. (2002). *Experimental and quasi-experimental designs for generalized causal inference*. Belmont, CA: Wadsworth Cengage Learning.

Sloboda, Z., Glantz, M. D., & Tarter, R. E. (2012). Revisiting the concepts of risk and protective factors for understanding the etiology and development of substance use and substance use disorders: Implications for prevention. *Substance Use & Misuse, 47*, 944–962.

Somov, P. G. (2007). Meaning of life group: Group application of logotherapy for substance use treatment. *Journal for Specialists in Group Work, 32*, 316–345.

Steger, M. F., Kashdan, T. B., & Oishi, S. (2008). Being good by doing good: Daily eudaimonic activity and well-being correlates, mediators, and temporal relations. *Journal of Research in Personality, 42*, 22–42.

Thompson, G. (2012). A meaning-centered therapy for addictions. *International Journal of Mental Health Addiction, 10*, 428–440.

Trull, T. J., Jahng, S., Tomko, R. L., Wood, P. K., & Sher, K. J. (2010). Revised NESARC personality disorder diagnoses: Gender, prevalence, and comorbidity with substance dependence disorders. *Journal of Personality Disorders, 24*, 412–426.

UNODC. (2014). *World drug report*. United Nations Office on Drugs and Crime. Retrieved from http://www.unodc.org/documents/wdr2014/World_Drug_Report_2014_web.pdf

van Den Bosch, L. M., & Verheul, R. (2007). Patients with addiction and personality disorder: Treatment outcomes and clinical implications. *Current Opinion in Psychiatry, 20*, 67–71.

van Den Bosch, L. M. C., Verheul, R., & van den Brink, W. (2001). Substance abuse in borderline personality disorder: Clinical and etiological correlates. *Journal of Personality Disorders, 15*, 416–424.

Waisberg, J. L., & Porter, J. E. (1994). Purpose in life and outcome of treatment for alcohol dependence. *British Journal of Clinical Psychology, 33*, 49–63.

Wiklund, L. (2008a). Existential aspects of living with addiction—Part I: Meeting challenges. *Journal of Clinical Nursing, 17*, 2426–2434.

Wiklund, L. (2008b). Existential aspects of living with addiction—Part II: Caring needs, a hermeneutic expansion of qualitative findings. *Journal of Clinical Nursing, 17*, 2435–2443.

Witkiewitz, K., & Marlatt, G. A. (2004). Relapse prevention for alcohol and drug problems: That was Zen, this is Tao. *American Psychologist, 59*, 224–235.

Reason, Meaning, and Resilience in the Treatment of Depression: Logotherapy as a Bridge Between Cognitive-Behavior Therapy and Positive Psychology

Matti Ameli

Introduction

The concept of meaning has generated interest in past years. Its understanding, definition, and functionality differ between different schools of psychotherapy. Meaning as defined within logotherapy's framework could be a potential link between cognitive-behavior therapy and positive psychology.

After offering an overview of Beck's model of cognitive-behavior therapy, positive psychology and logotherapy, including their respective views of the concept of meaning, the similarities and differences between logotherapy and both Beck's model of cognitive-behavior therapy and positive psychology will be highlighted. The role of meaning as a bridge between cognitive-behavior therapy and positive psychology, along with ideas for integrating the three approaches, will be discussed and an integrative model for depression will be presented. The chapter concludes with reflections regarding the benefits of a broad and holistic integrative approach to psychotherapy.

Overview of Cognitive-Behavior Therapy

Various forms of cognitive-behavioral therapy have been proposed. The rational emotive behavior therapy (REBT) pioneered by Albert Ellis in 1955 and the cognitive-behavior model developed by Aaron T. Beck in the early 1960s are two well-known approaches (Beck, 1995; Martínez, Rodríguez, Díaz del castillo, & Pacciolla, 2015). This chapter will focus on Beck's model due to its flexibility, wide range of applications, and substantial empirical support (Beck, 1995; Beck & Haigh, 2014).

M. Ameli, M.S. (✉)
Calle Periodista Azzati 5, 4A, 46002, Valencia, Spain
e-mail: matti_ameli@yahoo.com

The Cognitive-Behavior Model

According to the model, people's perceptions or thoughts about situations largely determine their emotional and behavioral reactions. Through cognitive-behavior therapy (Beck, Rush, Shaw, & Emery, 1979; Beck & Weishaar, 1989), clients learn to identify, evaluate (against objective data and facts), and modify their automatic thoughts, assumptions, and core beliefs so their thinking becomes more realistic and adaptive. This process is called cognitive restructuring. The therapeutic change occurs at three interactive levels: cognitive, behavioral, and affective. The cognitive change facilitates behavioral change by allowing the client to adopt a risk-taking perspective and in turn putting into practice the new behaviors helps to validate that perspective. Emotions can be moderated by considering alternative interpretations of the situation (based on objective evidence and facts) and in turn emotions influence cognitive change given that learning is more prominent when emotions are triggered (Beck & Weishaar, 1989).

Cognitive-behavior therapy is empirically based and has been proven effective by a large number of clinical trials for a wide variety of psychiatric disorders (Beck, 1995; Beck & Haigh, 2014).

Therapeutic Process

A strong and sound therapeutic alliance is a key element of cognitive-behavior therapy (Beck, 1995). The therapist and the client collaborate as a team and set the goals for therapy as well as the agenda for each session together. Beck (1995) highlights the importance of a warm, caring, empathetic, and genuine therapeutic relationship.

The two main strategies used are collaborative empiricism and guided discovery (Beck & Weishaar, 1989). Through collaborative empiricism, the client takes up the role of a "scientist" and tests the validity of his/her thoughts and beliefs against objective data and evidence. Through the process of guided discovery, the therapist serves as a guide to help the client clarify his/her problematic thoughts and behaviors and set up behavioral experiments to test hypotheses based on those thoughts and behaviors. A gentle Socratic questioning style is usually used to help clients identify, evaluate, and respond to their automatic thoughts and beliefs. The Socratic questioning consists of a series of open-ended questions to help clients take distance toward their dysfunctional thoughts and explore objective evidence to evaluate them. A variety of other techniques are also used based on the client's individual case conceptualization and goals.

Cognitive-behavior therapy is an active, structured, action-oriented, and time-limited approach. Homework assignments play a key role. Clients are taught to become their "own therapist" through the acquisition and practice of cognitive, behavioral, and emotional regulation skills (Beck, 1995). Beck's model is flexible and open to techniques from other orientations.

The Generic Cognitive Model (GCM)

Recently, an updated and broader model called the generic cognitive model (GCM) has been proposed by Beck and Haigh (2014). At the theoretical level, the new model includes additions such as the continuity between adaptation and maladaptation, a theory of modes (self-expansive and self-protective), dual information processing (automatic and reflective), schema activation, and attentional focus. At the applied clinical level, the generic cognitive model is based on four interacting components: situation, biased belief, focus, and maladaptive behavior. The applied model could serve as a template for clinicians to develop a rapid case conceptualizations for a variety of clinical settings. Beck and Haigh (2014) suggest that the optimum therapeutic intervention is one that focuses on each of the four clinical components.

For belief interventions, cognitive restructuring and behavioral experiments are mainly used. Focus interventions include a variety of cognitive, behavioral, and attentional strategies. Mindfulness-based interventions are also included as part of those interventions. Behavioral interventions generally use behavioral methods along with cognitive restructuring. Beck and Haigh (2014) believe the generic cognitive model has the potential to be the only empirically supported theory of psychopathology, since its components could be easily subjected to empirical investigation.

Meaning in Cognitive-Behavior Therapy

In the frame of the cognitive-behavior approach, meaning is primarily viewed as a cognitive process to develop a rational view of the self, others, and the world. Through the therapeutic process, clients are taught to identify the meaning they attach to their erroneous thoughts and beliefs (e.g., Client: "I can't do this". Therapist: "what does that mean for you?" Client: "I am inadequate"), evaluate that meaning against objective data and come up with a rational alternative. Meaning is used to make sense of and understand at the intellectual level, with the aim of developing realistic and adaptive thinking.

In recent years, importance has been given to the concept of values, especially within the schizophrenia treatment protocol. The latest *recovery-oriented cognitive therapy* (Perivoliotis, Grant, & Beck, in press) highlights the importance of combining cognitive-behavior therapy with a humanistic approach in order to help clients discover their key core values and improve their daily lives by engaging with the world. The updated cognitive-behavior therapy for psychosis referred to as *recovery and strengths-oriented cognitive behavior therapy for psychosis* (Wright et al., 2014) integrates concepts from third wave approaches. The goal is to enhance strengths and work toward values and a more meaningful life. This model goes beyond the rational and coping model.

Overview of Positive Psychology

Positive psychology is a new empirically based scientific movement introduced by the psychologist Martin Seligman in 1998. It is defined as "the scientific study of positive experiences and positive individual traits, and the institutions that facilitate their development" (Duckworth, Steen, & Seligman, 2005, p. 630).

Positive psychology categorizes happiness into three domains that are neither exclusive nor exhaustive: the pleasant life, the engaged life, and the meaningful life (Seligman, Rashid, & Parks, 2006). The pleasant life consists of having positive emotions such as satisfaction, joy, fulfillment, hope, faith and optimism, about the present, past, and future. It represents the hedonic theories of happiness. The engaged life is using one's positive traits such as strengths and talents, engaging and getting absorbed in work, leisure, or intimate relations. The meaningful life consists of using one's strengths for a higher purpose, to serve something considered bigger than oneself. Positive psychology techniques are used to enrich each of these three domains. A "full life", or well-lived life, is one that includes these three domains (Seligman et al., 2006). Recently, Seligman (2011) proposed the PERMA model which includes the following measurable elements: positive emotion, engagement, relationships, meaning and purpose, and accomplishment. According to Seligman et al. (2006), increasing positive emotion, engagement, and meaning could create a buffer against depression and possibly other disorders.

Positive Interventions and Tools

Positive interventions refer to systematic approaches that use clients' strengths and assets to overcome challenges (Rashid, 2009). They are based on three assumptions (Rashid & Seligman, 2013): first, clients desire growth and happiness, not only the avoiding of anxiety and misery; second, positive resources are genuine assets, not merely psychological defense mechanisms; and third, an effective therapeutic relationship includes discussion and focus on positive resources, not only an analysis of deficits and weaknesses. Rashid (2009) points out that positive interventions complement the clinical work.

A series of tools including interviews, inventories, scales, and narrative strategies are used to assess strengths-based constructs. Rashid and Ostermann (2009) outline the steps for conducting strengths-based assessment. The Values In Action Inventory of Strengths (VIA-IS; Peterson & Seligman, 2004) is a widely used, psychometrically sound 240-item self-report questionnaire for adults. It assesses 24 character strengths in about 25 min. For the assessment of strengths use, the 14-item Strengths Use Scale (Govindji & Linley, 2007) has been found to be a reliable and valid instrument (Wood, Linely, Maltby, Kashdan, & Hurling, 2011). Strengths use increases positive affect and is a good longitudinal predictor of well-being (Wood et al., 2011).

Positive interventions have been tested on individuals with depression. Positive psychotherapy (Seligman et al., 2006) and well-being therapy (Fava & Ruini, 2003) have shown good results (Sin & Lyubomirsky, 2009). Positive psychotherapy broadens the scope of traditional psychotherapy by integrating positive resources in treating psychopathology (Rashid & Seligman, 2013). It suggests that building positive emotions, engagement, and meaning could alleviate depression, and help buffer against the reoccurrence of negative symptoms (Seligman et al., 2006). Positive psychotherapy was used both in group and individual formats, with small samples of students (Seligman et al., 2006). In the group format, exercises such as *using strengths*, *writing three good things*, and *gratitude visits* were tested with cases of mild to moderate depression. Results showed a significant decrease in symptoms through 1 year follow-up (Seligman et al., 2006). In the individual format, focus was put on both positive and negative symptoms (positive psychotherapy was a supplement to other treatment approaches). A 14-session outline including exercises related to *signature strengths*, *gratitude*, *forgiveness*, *optimism*, *hope*, and *meaning* was tested with a small sample of severely depressed students. Results showed higher remission rates compared to traditional treatments (Seligman et al., 2006). Although more research is necessary with larger samples, these results suggest that positive psychotherapy may be a useful supplement to depression treatment protocols (Seligman et al., 2006).

Another useful approach for the treatment of depression is well-being therapy, developed by Fava and Ruini (2003). It is a short-term strategy rooted in positive psychology constructs that extends over eight sessions, and is based on Ryff's (1989) model of psychological well-being (Ruini & Fava, 2004). Well-being therapy aims at reinforcing beliefs that promote well-being by emphasizing self-monitoring of well-being episodes, and improving six dimensions of psychological well being: autonomy, personal growth, environmental mastery, purpose in life, positive relations, and self-acceptance (Fava & Ruini, 2003). Ruini and Fava (2004) reported a study with a small sample of 20 patients with affective disorders (including major depression) where well-being therapy led to both a greater reduction of residual symptoms and a greater increase in psychological well-being, in comparison with cognitive-behavior therapy. Another study with a sample of 40 patients with recurrent major depression showed that when well-being therapy was an adjunct to cognitive-behavior therapy, the relapse rate was significantly lower (Ruini & Fava, 2004). Although more research is necessary with larger samples, these results suggest that well-being therapy has the potential to be a good complement to cognitive-behavior therapy for the treatment of depression.

In terms of research, a meta-analysis of 51 positive psychology interventions showed that they significantly enhance well-being and decrease depressive symptoms (Sin & Lyubomirsky, 2009). Results revealed that individual therapy offered over a relatively long period of time, using a variety of positive exercises with emphasis on regular practice, is the most effective format. Sin, Della Porta, and Lyubomirsky (2011) pointed out that most positive interventions have been tested with non-clinical samples and do not necessarily benefit individuals in clinical contexts. Their study shows that, for example, writing letters of gratitude (a well documented positive exercise) was counterproductive for dysphoric individuals and diminished their well-being. They recommended tailoring positive interventions to the resources, needs, and preferences of individuals presenting with depressive symptoms (Sin et al., 2011).

Therapeutic Process

In the framework of positive psychotherapy, a positive relationship is built with clients by encouraging them to describe themselves through a real life situation that shows them at their best. The VIA-IS is used to help clients identify their signature strengths. Then, through collaboration, the therapist and client design new ways of using client strengths in relevant areas such as work, friendship, love, etc. (Seligman et al., 2006). The goal of several positive psychotherapy exercises is to reorient capacities such as attention, memory, or expectations away from the negative and toward the positive (Seligman et al., 2006). The following factors could moderate the efficacy of positive interventions (Sin et al., 2011): therapeutic guidance, length of intervention and continued practice, outcome expectations, person-activity fit, social support, and depression status. Sin and Lyubomirsky (2009) recommended that practitioners assign multiple positive activities, take into account clients' cultural background and unique inclinations, and encourage continuous practice to turn learned strategies into healthy habits.

Positive psychotherapy is presented as a descriptive approach based on scientific evidence. It is not a one-size-fits-all approach and is not appropriate for all clients in all situations, like any other approach. Outcome studies are necessary for generalizability.

Meaning in Positive Psychology

The meaningful life consists of using one's signature strengths and talents in service of something bigger than the self, such as family, community, religion, politics, etc. (Seligman et al., 2006). Seligman et al. (2006) described studies with depressed patients that show that the pursuit of meaning and engagement is strongly correlated with less depression and greater life satisfaction, whereas the pursuit of happiness is marginally correlated with less depression and greater life satisfaction. They suggested that lack of meaning could be a cause of depression, and interventions that build meaning would relieve depression (Seligman et al., 2006).

A primary instrument used to measure meaning is the Meaning in Life Questionnaire (MLQ; Steger, Frazier, Oishi, & Kaler, 2006). The MLQ is a valid and reliable 10-item, two-subscale instrument that measures presence of meaning and search for meaning in life. *Presence of meaning* evaluates the degree of perceived meaning and *search for meaning* assesses the extent to which a person engages in search for meaning (Steger et al., 2006). Meaning is defined as "the sense made of, and significance felt regarding, the nature of one's being and existence" (Steger et al., 2006, p. 81). The MLQ has been used in many different cultural contexts (O'Donnell, Shim, Barenz, & Steger, 2014).

In a review of the MLQ, O'Donnell et al. (2014) reported that presence of meaning is positively correlated with psychological well-being, hope, optimism and life satisfaction, and negatively correlated with anxiety, depression, and posttraumatic stress. The MLQ also has utility with individuals presenting with serious mental illnesses such as major depressive disorder, bipolar disorder, and schizophrenia (Schulenberg, Strack, & Buchanan, 2011). O'Donnell, Shim, Barenz, and Steger (2015) also highlighted the utility of the MLQ for individual therapy and recommended it for interventions in logotherapy, a meaning-centered approach to psychotherapy.

Happiness and Meaningfulness

A recent empirical investigation with a sample of 397 adults identified some differences between a happy life and a meaningful life (Baumeister, Vohs, Aaker, & Garbinsky, 2013). Results showed that although happiness and meaningfulness are positively correlated, and that many factors such as feeling productive or connection to others contribute similarly to both, they are distinct and sometimes even at odds with each other. Their findings suggested that happiness is mostly about feeling good in the present and about satisfying one's wants and needs, whereas meaningfulness involves integrating past, present, and future, focusing on expressing and reflecting on the self, and, in particular, reaching beyond oneself to do positive things for others. Baumeister et al. (2013) pointed out that these results are consistent with the hypothesis that happiness tends to be natural and self-focused, whereas meaning is mostly cultural and outwardly focused. They highlighted meaning as a key element that makes us uniquely human, and argued that not all people seek happiness. They referred to the downsides of the pursuit of happiness and the benefits that may arise from negative feelings. They recommended that positive psychology focus on researching and understanding meaningfulness and its differences with happiness (Baumeister et al., 2013).

Wong (2014) also shared interesting reflections regarding the concept of meaning in positive psychology. He noted that although meaning is an important component of positive psychology, its use in the framework of happiness orientation prevents the understanding that the pursuit of meaning could actually be at odds with the pursuit of happiness, because there is a contradiction: in order to serve a higher cause, one needs to transcend self-interest (Wong, 2014). Wong asserted that the view of meaning within the model of positive psychology is limited and prevents the full understanding of the value of meaning in human issues. He criticized the almost exclusive cognitive focus of most current meaning-making models in making sense of the world in negative situations, and emphasized the need for a comprehensive and coherent theoretical framework to apprehend meaning in positive psychology. He proposed to advance both research and applications by better understanding meaning seeking based on Viktor Frankl's theory of search for meaning, that is, logotherapy (Wong, 2014).

Overview of Logotherapy

Logotherapy was pioneered by the Austrian neurologist and psychiatrist Viktor Frankl (1905–1997) during the 1930s. The Viktor Frankl Institute of Vienna defines logotherapy as "an internationally acknowledged and empirically based meaning-centered approach to psychotherapy" (Batthyany, n.d., Viktorfrankl.org). Frankl (1969) viewed logotherapy as an open, collaborative approach that could be combined with other psychotherapeutic orientations.

Fundamental Tenets

Logotherapy envisions the human person in three overlapping dimensions: somatic, psychological, and spiritual. Frankl (1969) referred to the spiritual dimension as "noetic" to avoid religious connotations. The noetic dimension is the site of authentically human phenomena such as self-distancing, self-transcendence, humor, love, and gratitude. In contrast with the first two dimensions where our reactions are often automatic, in the third dimension, we can choose how to behave (Lukas, 1998). Intentionality is the key factor that makes human beings unpredictable. Frankl's theory is based on the premise that human beings are motivated by a "will to meaning", an inner pull to discover meaning in life. The fundamental tenets of logotherapy are freedom of will, will to meaning, and meaning in life (Frankl, 1969). *Freedom of will* asserts that human beings have the freedom to choose their response within the limits of given possibilities, under all life circumstances. *Will to meaning* points out that the main motivation of human beings is to search for the meaning and purpose in their lives. *Meaning in life* highlights that life has meaning under all circumstances, even in unavoidable suffering and misery. Other important concepts in logotherapy are responsibility, healthy core, and tragic optimism (Frankl, 1959/1984). *Responsibility* is considered as the essence of human existence, reflecting our actions and behaviors to life challenges. *Healthy core* refers to the part that remains intact in spite of illness. *Tragic optimism* implies remaining optimistic through hope, faith, and love in spite of the inevitable tragic triad of pain, guilt, and death, in order to raise above suffering and turn the negative into positive or tragedy into personal triumph.

Therapeutic Process

The goal of the logotherapist is to tap into unique human capacities such as intentionality, responsibility, and freedom of choice, and to broaden clients' visual scope to help them discover and actualize the meaning potentials in their lives. The two primary, healthy resources accessed by the main logotherapeutic techniques are self-distancing (the ability to detach from one's self and differentiate between one's self and one's symptoms) and self-transcendence (the ability to live for something greater than the self). Martínez and Flórez (2014) described the phases of the meaning-centered therapeutic process and highlighted the clients' capacity to accept discomfort and to use healthy, existential resources as a key factor in producing change.

The three main techniques used in logotherapy are paradoxical intention (using self-distancing through humor to counteract anticipatory anxiety), dereflection (shifting the focus of attention toward meaning through self-transcendence), and attitude modification (challenging a negative attitude by activating the will to meaning through Socratic dialogue). Paradoxical intention, validated empirically for sleep disorders, agoraphobia, and public speaking anxiety (Schulenberg, 2003), has similarities with exposure techniques and anticipates some of the behavioral techniques such as implosion and satiation (Frankl, 2004). Dereflection is an important part of Frankl's sexual model proposed in 1947 that predates Masters and Johnson's sexual therapy model, developed in 1970 (Ameli & Dattilio, 2013; Schulenberg, Nassif, Hutzell, & Rogina, 2008).

Lukas (1998) pointed out that modifying an internal attitude leads to behavioral change and outlined the steps for "meaning sensitization" for cases of existential vacuum and a guideline for cases involving unavoidable suffering. Martínez and Flórez (2014) provided specific examples of how Socratic dialogue could be implemented to mobilize clients' spiritual resources. Another interesting tool is the *Values Awareness Technique* (VAT) developed by Hutzell and Eggert (1989/2009), where the goal is to help people discover their personally meaningful values hierarchy (based on Frankl's categorical values), as well as to define meaningful goals for the short, intermediate, and long term, aligning them with their values. Recently, Rogina (2015) proposed a seven-step *noogenic activation* clinical process to mobilize the noetic dimension and tap into clients' healthy core in order to facilitate meaningful change.

Meaning in Logotherapy

Meaning is based on self-transcendence, on transcending self-interest and reaching beyond one's self to serve a cause or others. According to Frankl (1959/1984), in contrast with Maslow's concept of self-actualization, happiness cannot be pursued nor is it the end goal; it is a by-product of self-transcendence. Lukas (2015) pointed out that the discovery of a meaning to be fulfilled is key to an individual's psychological health.

Meaning in logotherapy is inherent to the noetic dimension, to what makes us human. It cannot be invented; it needs to be discovered in the world (Frankl, 1959/1984). There are various levels of meaning (Fabry, 1994; Lukas, 2015). *Ultimate meaning* presupposes the existence of a universal order that cannot be comprehended from a rational perspective. *Meaning contents of one's life* (Lukas, 2015) refers to *being for something* (a task, a mission, a work, etc.) or *being for someone* (caring for family, children, etc.). The *meaning of the moment* may be recognized and responded to by each unique individual in a unique situation. We can discover meaning in life in three different ways known as the categorical values. These categorical values are comprised of the *creative values*, the *experiential values*, and the *attitudinal values* (Frankl, 1959/1984). The creative values consist of what we give to the world, like accomplishing a task, creating a work, or doing a good deed. The experiential values are what we take from the world, like the experience of truth, beauty, and love toward another human being. It could be actualized through nature, culture, art, music and literature, and through loving relationships. The attitudinal values reflect the stand we take toward an unchangeable situation or unavoidable suffering. When the will to meaning is frustrated or blocked and a person is incapable of finding a meaning or purpose in his/her life, there is a perception of emptiness, hopelessness, or despair that Frankl (1969) called *existential vacuum*. Some of the symptoms of this condition include apathy and boredom, and it may lead to aggression, addiction, and depression. Frankl (2004) defined *noogenic neurosis* as a clinical condition where the psychological symptoms are a result of existential conflicts. He proposed logotherapy as the specific therapy for the treatment of existential problems. Logotherapy is offered as a nonspecific or collaborative therapy for other types of issues.

"Search for meaning" has been included in the newest *Diagnostic and Statistical Manual of Mental Disorders, Fifth Edition* (*DSM-5*; American Psychiatric Association, 2013) among the features of a "normal" personality (Marshall, 2014). In clinical practice, logotherapy has been found to be useful with problems such as depression, anxiety, alcohol/drug addiction, and despair associated with incurable disease (Schulenberg et al., 2008). Schulenberg, Drescher, and Baczwaski (2014) also highlighted the potential value of logotherapy in coping with adversity and promoting posttraumatic growth in the framework of disaster mental health.

In terms of research, a large number of studies have been conducted to validate the main logotherapeutic concepts and tools (Batthyany & Guttmann, 2006). The most investigated psychometric tool to assess meaning is the Purpose in Life test (PIL), developed by Crumbaugh and Maholick in 1964. It measures the degree to which a person experiences a sense of personal meaning. PIL scores correlate positively with measures of self-control, life satisfaction, self-acceptance, emotional stability, and resilience, and they are correlated negatively with anxiety and depression (Melton & Schulenberg, 2008). The Purpose in Life test-Short Form (PIL-SF; Schulenberg & Melton, 2010; Schulenberg, Strack, et al., 2011) is a brief four-item version of the PIL. The PIL-SF is a valid and reliable instrument that offers unique psychometric contributions beyond other meaning assessment tools (Schulenberg, Strack, et al., 2011). It has been used as a measure of perceived meaning with both clinical and non-clinical samples in various research areas, such as alcohol use, resilience, and disaster mental health. Results show a strong relationship between perceived meaning and alcohol use among college students, and an interaction between meaning and depression in predicting alcohol use in males (Schnetzer, Schulenberg, & Buchanan, 2013). In the framework of a technological/ecological disaster, perceived meaning in life was shown to be predictive of life satisfaction after the spill, and may actually be a stronger predictor than self-efficacy in some cases (Drescher et al., 2012).

The 14-item Resilience Scale (RS-14; Wagnild, 2009) is another interesting instrument that correlates with perceived meaning in life and shows substantial overlap with PIL-SF, correlating at 0.67–0.69 and sharing 45–48 % of the variance (Aiena, Baczwaski, Schulenberg, & Buchanan, 2015).

Research supports logotherapy's assertion that meaning is crucial to the human experience (O'Donnell et al., 2015). The need for increasingly rigorous research is emphasized to validate the logotherapeutic model across diverse populations and disorders (Martínez & Flórez, 2014; Melton & Schulenberg, 2008) and test it against empirically robust therapeutic models (Martínez & Flórez, 2014).

Areas of Similarities and Differences Between the Three Approaches

Cognitive-Behavior Therapy and Positive Psychology: Similarities and Differences

Cognitive-behavior therapy and positive psychology are empirically based and rely on rigorous scientific research. They both favor a "natural" self, motivated toward satisfying wants and needs (Baumeister et al., 2013; Wong, 2014). They share areas of similarities such as an emphasis on therapeutic alliance, a focus on discrete goals and present issues, and a collaborative approach (Karwoski, Garrat, & Llardi, 2006). Several cognitive-behavioral techniques such as pleasant activities scheduling, relaxation techniques, and problem solving may also be used in positive psychology interventions (Karwoski et al., 2006). The main difference between both approaches is their focus. Cognitive-behavior therapy aims primarily to overcome disorders and reduce distress and positive psychology focuses on increasing well-being using a strengths-based approach.

The two approaches seem compatible and complementary and their integration has been proposed in several models such as well-being therapy (Fava & Ruini, 2003), the integrative model for depression (Karwoski et al., 2006), and positive CBT (Bannink, 2012). Cognitive-behavior therapy and positive psychology have also developed resilience models, drawing on research in both fields. Ann Masten, one of the pioneers in the study of resilience, defined it as "a class of phenomena characterized by good outcomes in spite of serious threats to adaptation of development" (Masten, 2001, p. 228). Resilience is a process, and Yates and Masten (2004) highlighted the importance of applying positive psychology in resilience interventions in order to promote prevention and competence in addition to symptom alleviation. Tugade and Fredrickson (2004) reported various studies that confirm the broaden-and-build theory (Fredrickson, 2001) that takes into account the adaptive function of both positive and negative emotions, and according to which resilient individuals use positive emotions to cope and bounce back from negative experiences. Reivich and Shatté (2002) offered a seven-step program, based mostly on cognitive-behavior strategies, to build resilience. Padesky and Mooney (2012) proposed a four-step cognitive-behavior therapy model to build and strengthen resilience.

Positive interventions and tools seem to be a good adjunct to broaden the scope of cognitive-behavior therapy beyond treatment, toward well-being and resilience.

Logotherapy and Cognitive-Behavior Therapy: Similarities and Differences

Logotherapy has anticipated some of the concepts of cognitive-behavior therapy. The two approaches present many similarities and a high degree of compatibility (Ameli, 2016; Ameli & Dattilio, 2013). They both emphasize that modifying internal maladaptive attitudes leads to behavioral change, their main goal is to resolve present issues, and a caring and warm therapeutic alliance is emphasized. Both approaches are active, participative, and collaborative, using a process of guided discovery without the therapist imposing his/her personal concepts of reason or meaning. In terms of techniques, both approaches are sound, brief, solution-focused and take into account empirical research.

There are also major differences between cognitive-behavior therapy and logotherapy (Ameli, 2016). Logotherapy goes beyond learning principles, reinforcement, rationality and cognition, taking into account the uniquely human noetic dimension. The primary focus of logotherapy is to discover life meaning and purpose versus modifying erroneous thinking patterns and reducing distress in cognitive-behavior therapy. Logotherapy is values-based, mobilizing clients' healthy resources, strengths, and aims to facilitate well-being. Martínez et al. (2015) pointed out that the vision of the human person according to cognitive-behavior therapy tends to be deterministic and reactive whereas logotherapy emphasizes a proactive and intentional view.

The integration of logotherapy with cognitive-behavior therapy has been proposed by several authors such as Lukas (1986), Hutchinson and Chapman (2005), Hutzell (2009), and Ameli and Dattilio (2013). For a summary of these proposals see Ameli (2016). Recently, Marshall (2014) proposed to incorporate *freedom of will* for the diagnosis and treatment of personality disorders and recommended combining cognitive-behavior therapy with logotherapy to help clients in the process of search for meaning. Lukas (1986) envisioned a "fruitful symbiosis" between cognitive-behavior therapy and logotherapy, and considered that their future depends on the motivation of their respective representatives to combine them.

Logotherapy and Positive Psychology: Similarities and Differences

Logotherapy and positive psychology have much in common. They are both future-oriented and strengths-focused, they both consider meaning as an important element of well-being, and they have both garnered psychometric support through meaning-based assessment (Lewis, 2012; Schulenberg et al., 2008; Wong, 2014). Both approaches consider the lack of perceived meaning as a potential cause of depression and propose meaning-based interventions as a means of alleviating symptoms of depression. In terms of their foundation, Lewis (2012) pointed out that the concept of experiential values is similar to the pleasant life and the concept of creative values is similar to the engaged life. In positive psychology, a full life is the one that enriches and integrates these three types of life (pleasant, engaged, and meaningful), and in logotherapy a meaningful life is one where the three types of values (experiential, creative, and attitudinal) are actualized to the highest degree. What Seligman calls "strengths", Frankl calls "values" and both orientations use instruments to identify strengths or values: the Values Awareness Technique (VAT; Hutzell & Eggert, 1989/2009) is used in logotherapy, and the Values In Action Scale (VIA-IS; Peterson & Seligman, 2004) in positive psychology.

There are also major differences between logotherapy and positive psychology. According to Lewis (2012), logotherapy is a form of therapy developed through clinical practice that insists on a genuine human dimension, in contrast with positive psychology which was developed through empirical studies. Wong (2011, 2014) pointed out that logotherapy promotes a spiritual-existential perspective ("spiritual self") while positive psychology prioritizes a cognitive-behavioral perspective ("natural self"). Self-transcendence is the essence of being fully human in logotherapy, the main motivation and an end in itself, whereas happiness and well-being tend to be the end goal in positive psychology and self-transcendence an instrument to reach well-being. In logotherapy, meaning seeking is spiritual and aimed toward self-transcendence, whereas meaning seeking in positive psychology involves a cognitive process to facilitate understanding and life purpose (Wong, 2014).

The integration of positive psychology with logotherapy and the existential approach in general has also been considered (Batthyany & Russo-Netzer, 2014). Schulenberg et al. (2008) suggested incorporating the clinical work done in logotherapy into positive psychology, since what each brings to the table can inform one another. Bretherton and Ørner (2004) focused on the positive aspects of the existential approach, referring to concepts such as meaning, posttraumatic growth, and concern for society. They recommended the inclusion of existential concepts in further development of positive psychology. Wong (2014) suggested further exploring and understanding the concept of meaning and search for meaning within the framework of logotherapy, in order to arrive at a coherent and comprehensive theoretical framework for meaning in positive psychology. He asserted that positive psychology could benefit from Frankl's deep insights and theory of meaning, and that logotherapy could benefit from positive psychology's rigorous meaning-related research. According to Wong, the integration of the spiritual dimension toward self-transcendence and a "spiritually oriented positive psychology" could be beneficial to the positive movement (Wong, 2014).

Wong (2009, 2011) made a compelling case for an existential positive psychology that broadens the scope of positive psychology and integrates the whole spectrum of human experiences, both positives and negatives, both challenges and potentials. He proposed *positive psychology 2.0* as a more complete model of the good life, where a *meaning mindset* (that embraces also negativity) is promoted versus the *happiness mindset* (Wong, 2011). Following Wong's ideas and other critics regarding the excessive positive polarization and focus on the bright side, a *second wave positive psychology* has emerged (Ivtzan, Lomas, Hefferon, & Worth, 2015; Lomas & Ivtzan, 2015). This second wave proposes a more nuanced approach to the concepts of positive and negative, focusing on the dialectical nature of well-being. Lomas and Ivtzan (2015) identified the three key components of the dialectical nature as the principal of appraisal (challenge with categorizing phenomena as positive or negative), the principal of co-valence (experiences are a mix of positive and negative factors), and the principal of complementarity (well-being is a function of a complex interaction between bright and dark aspects). They provide several case studies to illustrate these principles (Lomas & Ivtzan, 2015). Along the same lines, Kashdan and Biswas-Diener (2014) proposed the concept of *wholeness*, instead of happiness, as a healthy living state. Wholeness is an emotional state that includes both positive and negative emotions. According to these authors, unpleasant emotions should be acknowledged and experienced because tolerating psychological discomfort could help people become stronger, happier, and more resilient in the long term (Kashdan & Biswas-Diener, 2014).

The influence of existential concepts in second wave positive psychology makes it closer and more compatible with logotherapy. Wong (2014) recommended future research to integrate logotherapy and positive psychology for the benefit of both psychology and society.

Logotherapy as a Bridge Between Cognitive-Behavior Therapy and Positive Psychology

Logotherapy is compatible and complementary to both cognitive-behavior therapy and positive psychology. Its tri-dimensional view of human beings and will to meaning framework broadens the scope of both approaches, making cognitive-behavior therapy sensitive to freedom of choice and existential meaning, and positive psychology sensitive to self-transcendence and the dark side of life, emphasized also in second wave positive psychology. It appears to be a potent and enriching bridge between these two orientations at the clinical level.

Toward an Integrative Model of Clinical Intervention: Cognitive-Behavior Therapy, Logotherapy and Positive Psychology

The generic cognitive model (Beck & Haigh, 2014) is empirically based and could serve as an expandable template for integration. At the theoretical level, logotherapy could be included at two levels: (1) intentionality based on freedom of choice could be a feature within the reflective system; and (2) meaning could be added on a second continuum, similar to the adaptive function. The meaning continuum would move from meaningful to meaningless. The interesting feature about the continuum is that it takes into account the degree of adaptability and meaningfulness instead of categorizing in terms of positive and negative. Resilience, based on concepts and research drawn from the three approaches, could be considered a feature within the self-expansive mode.

At the clinical level, two more components could be included (in addition to situation, biased belief, focus, and maladaptive behavior), *meaningfulness* based on logotherapy's theoretical framework and *resilience*. Interventions for meaning assessment and discovery would include logotherapy techniques and tools as well as positive psychology's strategies. Instruments such as the PIL-SF (Schulenberg, Schnetzer, & Buchanan, 2011), the MLQ (Steger et al., 2006), and the VAT (Hutzell & Eggert, 1989/2009) have demonstrated utility. The concept of meaning could also be integrated within each separate intervention area (situation, belief, focus, and behavior). Meaning related to a specific situation could be considered. The degree of meaningfulness of beliefs could be assessed, in order to promote both realistic and meaningful beliefs. In the focus category, the dereflection technique could be added as an attentional strategy to refocus on meaningful areas. In the behavior category, intentional meaningful behaviors and actions could be promoted. As for resilience, it could be considered at two levels. It could be assessed at the beginning of therapy, using for example the 14-item Resilience Scale (RS-14; Wagnild, 2009), along with the possession and use of strengths by measures such as the VIA-IS (Peterson & Seligman, 2004) and the Strength Use Scale (Govindji & Linley, 2007). Such data could be helpful in better tailoring therapy to the client because individual strengths and potentials would be taken into account as part of the case conceptualization. Resilience could also be included as part of a relapse prevention strategy. Moreover, logotherapeutic and positive interventions could be implemented to create a meaningful life and build resilience.

As part of the therapeutic process, although many clients seeking help might use the word happiness as their goal, it would be unwise for the therapist to assume that they all have the same definition or the same objective. An astute therapist would first seek to understand the client's definition and then as part of psychoeducation, provide definitions and information based on research regarding both the concepts of happiness and meaningfulness, including their upsides and downsides. As the person responsible for his/her life, the client could choose his/her preference, assuming both positive and negative consequences in the short and long term. Happiness should not be the exclusive pursuit of the client, nor imposed on clients through the therapist's assumption that everybody wants to be happy. As therapists, we also have the responsibility to support those clients who consider themselves not very happy, to move forward in spite of difficulties and challenges. Examples include clients experiencing chronic or serious illness or those who have meaningful tasks that require self-sacrifice, such as single parents working and raising children without a support system. Logotherapy and its concept of meaning based on self-transcendence would potentially be a useful adjunct in such cases. For clients with severe disorders such as schizophrenia, logotherapy could help tap into healthy areas, assisting clients in discovering meaning in spite of suffering.

For a more balanced therapeutic approach, it would be interesting to use concepts from second wave positive psychology such as *wholeness* (Kashdan & Biswas-Diener, 2014), and considering well-being as the interaction between negative and positive emotions (Ivtzan et al., 2015; Lomas & Ivtzan, 2015; Wong, 2011).

Example of an Integrative Clinical Model for Depression

The three approaches offer treatment guidelines and tools for the treatment of depression. Cognitive-behavior therapy has an empirically supported and well-established protocol to reduce distress. Positive psychology has developed a strengths-based outline to directly increase positive emotions, character strengths, and meaning. Logotherapy is a specific meaning-centered therapy for cases of depression related to a sense of meaninglessness, and is also a good adjunct for treating depression associated with other factors. Steps for *meaning sensitization* have been outlined by Lukas (1998), with cases illustrated in her writings (Lukas, 1986, 2014, 2015). Moreover, Martínez (2013) developed *training in meaning perception*, Ungar (2002) illustrated a logotherapeutic treatment protocol in a case of somatogenic, endogenous depression, and Ameli and Dattilio (2013) offered ideas of how to integrate logotherapy with Beck's depression protocol.

The following steps are proposed as a general guideline for an integrative model of depression, considering input from the three approaches:

1. Broad case conceptualization: relevant instruments from cognitive-behavior therapy, logotherapy and positive psychology are used to assess the type and severity of depression, and highlight both client areas of weakness and strengths in the intervention areas of the generic cognitive model, including meaningfulness and resilience. The goal would be to develop a map of strengths and weaknesses, problems, and potentials.

2. Creation of an optimal, individualized treatment plan: clarify the areas of strengths and limitations and, based on the client's characteristics, identify the relevant techniques and strategies from the three approaches in order to motivate the client, draw on his/her strengths throughout the treatment process, help him/her to overcome weaknesses, and build meaning and resilience. Emphasis is placed on establishing a warm and genuine therapeutic relationship and prioritizing the client's unique attributes within the tri-dimensional view (biological, psychological, and noetic).
3. Explanation of hypotheses, the treatment plan, and goal setting: provide a coherent and clear explanation of the problematic symptoms based on the client's individual map and set therapeutic goals collaboratively. One idea would be to explain that therapy has three objectives:

    (a) Help the client detect maladaptive beliefs and behaviors that are working to maintain depression. Assist the client in learning how to turn them into more reasonable and adaptive ones. The main objective would be to address what is not working in order to minimize distress, through primarily cognitive-behavioral techniques.
    (b) Help the client identify and refocus attention on unique strengths, values and positive opportunities and use them to convert reasonable thoughts into meaningful, motivating, and proactive decisions, actions, and attitudes. The goal would be to use the concept of meaning in order to tap into potentials as a means of enhancing well-being, using strategies from logotherapy and positive psychology.
    (c) Help the client build resilience and create a meaningful life plan, inviting him/her to reflect and learn from the experience of depression, which is possible in spite of any suffering experienced. Clients are encouraged to practice their strengths, and increase positive emotions, engagement, and meaning. Research and tools from the three approaches would be beneficial in this stage.

4. Psychoeducation: provide a brief and clear explanation of the three approaches as well as their relevant techniques and goals. Explain the differences between happiness and meaningfulness based on research findings, and introduce concepts such as wholeness (Kashdan & Biswas-Diener, 2014) and the dialectical nature of well-being (Lomas & Ivtzan, 2015; Wong, 2011) from second wave positive psychology.
5. Integrative treatment plan (see Ameli & Dattilio, 2013): combine pleasurable and meaningful activities based on client values (creative, experiential, and attitudinal). Moreover, combine cognitive restructuring with attitude modification to generate both adaptive and meaningful thoughts and beliefs, and use dereflection as a refocusing strategy to counteract rumination. For severe depression associated with suicide, finding meaning could be a key first step (prior to cognitive behavioral interventions), to help clients shift their attitude and hold on to life (Ameli & Dattilio, 2013). Also, as proposed by Karwoski et al. (2006), cultivating hope is helpful to motivate clients and reduce depressive symptoms.

6. Relapse prevention: reflection through Socratic dialogue regarding the possible meaning of the depression within the client's life, what he/she has learned from depression in spite of any suffering experienced, and the attitude he/she can choose to prevent the onset of another depression. In addition, emphasis is placed on the design of a meaningful and purposeful life plan (the VAT could be valuable), as well as a training program geared toward building well-being and resilience using a variety of relevant positive psychology tools and exercises. Examples include practicing strengths in different situations, or gratitude exercises, taking into account the cultural background, needs and preferences of the client. Emphasis should be placed on regular and continuous practice of the skills learned in therapy, especially the positive exercises, in order to turn them into adaptive habits.

Conclusion

Logotherapy is a collaborative, meaning-centered, and empirically supported approach to psychotherapy with broad clinical applications. It emphasizes the unique human dimension. It shares multiple similarities with both cognitive-behavior therapy and positive psychology, fitting well with both orientations. These approaches complement and would also benefit from one another.

Logotherapy offers a coherent and sound theoretical framework for understanding meaning that goes beyond rationality and positive emotions. Meaning is essentially a bridge between cognitive-behavior therapy and positive psychology. It broadens the scope of cognitive-behavior therapy beyond rationality, enriching positive psychology's framework through self-transcendence and an emphasis on meaning associated with negative experiences, challenges, and struggles as potential sources of growth and resilience. Bridging reason and resilience through meaning facilitates the shift from a natural and rational self to a self-transcending and meaning-oriented self. The recent second wave positive psychology movement (Ivtzan et al., 2015; Lomas & Ivtzan, 2015; Wong, 2011) offers a more balanced view that includes both bright and dark aspects of emotion, considering negative experiences and emotions as opportunities for positive transformation. Positive and negative features are context sensitive and could be viewed on a continuum. They are both valuable in clinical practice. For instance, in many cases negative emotions are a good source of learning.

In this chapter, ideas are offered for integrating cognitive-behavior therapy, logotherapy, and positive psychology using Beck's new generic cognitive model as a template. It would be interesting to establish collaboration between experts in the three fields, in order to review, refine, and test the ideas proposed, and validate a model that would include the best of reason, meaning, and resilience (a reasonable, meaningful, and potent guide for treating depression). Integrating cognitive-behavior therapy, logotherapy, and positive psychology would lead to a more balanced, holistic, and unified psychotherapy, with a broad view of human beings, where both opportunities and challenges are taken into account and meaning potentials are emphasized across situations.

Over the past few years, spiritually-based practices such as mindfulness, rooted in Buddhism, and other concepts such as compassion, acceptance, and loving-kindness have been included in scientific protocols as part of third-wave behavior therapies. It seems that science is looking for wisdom to enhance psychological treatments. That wisdom is an inherent part of logotherapy, a psychotherapy that includes the noetic spiritual dimension, promoting meaning as a unique human feature. Therefore, it would be useful to take into account the wealth of knowledge that logotherapy offers in order to expand our understanding of the clinical applications of meaning.

Key Takeaways

- Adopt a tri-dimensional view of clients (bio-psycho-noetic) and identify what makes them unique, their specific strengths and potential.
- Take time to build a genuine, caring, and warm therapeutic relationship.
- Be open to an integrative approach, consider both negative and positive emotions, and include interventions focused on both reducing distress and increasing well-being.
- Become familiar with assessment tools and techniques used in cognitive-behavior therapy, logotherapy and positive psychology, and implement them in the different stages of depression treatment, considering clients' unique characteristics and needs.
- Cultivate a curiosity about the concept of meaning, include it in the cognitive-behavior therapy depression protocol and explain its benefits to clients.
- Draw on clients' strengths and values throughout therapy and tailor positive psychology interventions emphasizing regular practice. Consider also implementing concepts from second wave positive psychology.

References

Aiena, B. J., Baczwaski, B. J., Schulenberg, S. E., & Buchanan, E. M. (2015). Measuring resilience with the RS-14: A tale of two samples. *Journal of Personality Assessment, 97*, 291–300.

Ameli, M. (2016). Integrating logotherapy with cognitive behavior therapy: A worthy challenge. In A. Batthyany (Ed.), *Logotherapy and existential analysis: Proceedings of the Viktor Frankl Institute Vienna* (Vol. 1, pp. 197–217). Cham: Springer International Publishing.

Ameli, M., & Dattilio, F. M. (2013). Enhancing cognitive behavior therapy with logotherapy: Techniques for clinical practice. *Psychotherapy, 50*, 387–391.

American Psychiatric Association. (2013). *Diagnostic and statistical manual of mental disorders* (5th ed.). Washington, DC: Author.

Bannink, F. P. (2012). *Practicing positive CBT: From reducing distress to building success*. Oxford: Wiley.

Batthyany, A. (n.d.) *What is logotherapy and existential analysis?* Retrieved March 25, 2016, from The official website of the Viktor Frankl institute Vienna, www.viktorfrankl.org.

Batthyany, A., & Guttmann, D. (2006). *Empirical research on logotherapy and meaning-oriented psychotherapy. An annotated bibliography*. Phoenix: Zeig Tucker.

Batthyany, A., & Russo-Netzer, P. (2014). *Meaning in positive and existential psychology*. New York, NY: Springer.

Baumeister, R. F., Vohs, K. D., Aaker, J. L., & Garbinsky, E. N. (2013). Some key differences between a happy life and a meaningful life. *Journal of Positive Psychology, 8*, 505–516.

Beck, J. S. (1995). *Cognitive therapy: Basics and beyond*. New York, NY: Guilford Press.

Beck, A. T., & Haigh, E. A. P. (2014). Advances in cognitive theory and therapy: The Generic Cognitive Model. *The Annual Review of Clinical Psychology, 10*, 1–24.

Beck, A. T., Rush, A. J., Shaw, B. F., & Emery, G. (1979). *Cognitive therapy of depression*. New York, NY: Guilford Press.

Beck, A. T., & Weishaar, M. (1989). Cognitive therapy. In A. Freeman, K. M. Simon, L. E. Beutler, & H. Arkowitz (Eds.), *Comprehensive handbook of cognitive therapy* (pp. 21–36). New York, NY: Plenum Press.

Bretherton, R., & Ørner, R. J. (2004). Positive psychology and psychotherapy: An existential approach. In P. A. Linley & S. Joseph (Eds.), *Positive psychology in practice* (pp. 420–430). Hoboken, NJ: Wiley.

Drescher, C. F., Baczwaski, B. J., Walters, A. B., Aiena, B. J., Schulenberg, S. E., & Johnson, L. R. (2012). Coping with an ecological disaster: The role of perceived meaning in life and self-efficacy following the Gulf oil spill. *Ecopsychology, 4*, 56–63.

Duckworth, A. L., Steen, T. A., & Seligman, A. E. P. (2005). Positive psychology in clinical practice. *Annual Review of Clinical Psychology, 1*, 629–651.

Fabry, J. B. (1994). *The pursuit of meaning*. Abilene, TX: Institute of Logotherapy Press.

Fava, G. A., & Ruini, C. (2003). Development and characteristics of a well-being enhancing psychotherapeutic strategy: Well-being therapy. *Journal of Behavior Therapy and Experimental Psychiatry, 34*, 45–63.

Frankl, V. E. (1959/1984). *Man's search for meaning*. Boston, MA: Beacon Press.

Frankl, V. E. (1969). *The will to meaning: Foundations and applications of Logotherapy*. New York, NY: World Publishing.

Frankl, V. E. (2004). *On the theory and therapy of mental disorders*. New York, NY: Brunner-Routledge.

Fredrickson, B. L. (2001). The role of positive emotions in positive psychology: The Broaden-and-Build theory of positive emotions. *American Psychologist, 56*, 218–226.

Govindji, R., & Linley, P. A. (2007). Strengths use, self-concordance and well-being: Implications for strengths coaching and coaching psychologists. *International Coaching Psychology Review, 2*, 143–153.

Hutchinson, G. T., & Chapman, B. P. (2005). Logotherapy-enhanced REBT: An integration of discovery and reason. *Journal of Contemporary Psychotherapy, 35*, 145–159.

Hutzell, R. R. (2009). Why cognitive psychotherapists in the USA benefit from learning logotherapy. In A. Batthyany & J. Levinson (Eds.), *Existential psychotherapy of meaning: Handbook of logotherapy and existential analysis* (pp. 225–231). Phoenix: Zeig Tucker & Theisen.

Hutzell, R. R., & Eggert, M. D. (1989/2009). *A workbook to increase your meaningful and purposeful goals (2009 PDF Edition)*. Retrieved January 1, 2012, from http://www.viktorfrankl.org/source/hutzell_workbook_2009.pdf.

Ivtzan, I., Lomas, T., Hefferon, K., & Worth, P. (2015). *Second wave positive psychology: Embracing the dark side of life*. London: Routledge.

Karwoski, L., Garrat, G. M., & Llardi, S. S. (2006). On the integration of cognitive-behavioral therapy for depression and positive psychology. *Journal of Cognitive Psychotherapy, 20*, 159–170.

Kashdan, T., & Biswas-Diener, R. (2014). *The upside of your dark side: Why being your whole self—Not just your "good" self—drives success and fulfillment*. New York, NY: Penguin.

Lewis, M. H. (2012). Logo talk Episode 36, *Logotherapy and positive psychology*. An online podcast at http://www.logotalk.net.
Lomas, T., & Ivtzan, I. (2015). Second wave positive psychology: Exploring the positive–negative dialectics of wellbeing. *Journal of Happiness Studies, 16*, 1–16.
Lukas, E. (1986). *Meaningful living: A logotherapeutic guide to health*. New York, NY: Grove.
Lukas, E. (1998). *Logotherapy textbook: Meaning-centered psychotherapy*. Toronto, ON: Liberty Press.
Lukas, E. (2014). *Meaning in suffering*. Charlottesville, VA: Purpose Research.
Lukas, E. (2015). *The therapist and the soul: From fate to freedom*. Charlottesville, VA: Purpose Research.
Marshall, E. (2014). Freedom of will and personality: A logotherapeutic approach to the diagnosis and treatment of personality disorders. *The International Forum for Logotherapy, 37*, 71–75.
Martínez, E. (2013). El diálogo socrático en la psicoterapia centrada en el sentido. In E. Martínez (Ed.), *Manual de psicoterapia con enfoque logoterapeutico* (pp. 235–256). Bogotá: Manual Moderno.
Martínez, E., & Flórez, I. (2014). Meaning-centered psychotherapy: A Socratic clinical practice. *Journal of Contemporary Psychotherapy, 45*, 37–48.
Martínez, E., Rodríguez, J., Díaz del castillo, J. P., & Pacciolla, A. (2015). *Vivir a la manera existencial*. Bogotá: SAPS.
Masten, A. S. (2001). Ordinary magic: Resilience processes in development. *American Psychologist, 56*, 227–238.
Melton, A. M. A., & Schulenberg, S. E. (2008). On the measurement of meaning: Logotherapy's empirical contributions to Humanistic Psychology. *The Humanistic Psychologist, 36*, 21–44.
O'Donnell, M. B., Shim, Y., Barenz, J. D., & Steger, M. F. (2014). Revisiting the Meaning in Life Questionnaire, Part 1: Psychometrics, health, and special populations. *The International Forum for Logotherapy, 37*, 96–105.
O'Donnell, M. B., Shim, Y., Barenz, J. D., & Steger, M. F. (2015). Revisiting the Meaning in Life Questionnaire, Part 2: Intervention research and clinical relevance. *The International Forum for Logotherapy, 38*, 41–48.
Padesky, C. A., & Mooney, K. A. (2012). Strengths-based cognitive-behavior therapy: A four-step model to build resilience. *Clinical Psychology and Psychotherapy, 19*, 283–290.
Perivoliotis, D., Grant, P. M., & Beck, A. T. (in press). *Recovery-oriented cognitive therapy for schizophrenia: A comprehensive treatment manual*. New York, NY: Guilford Press.
Peterson, C., & Seligman, M. E. P. (2004). *Character strengths and virtues: A classification and handbook*. Washington, DC: American Psychological Association.
Rashid, T. (2009). Positive interventions in clinical practice. *Journal of Clinical Psychology, 65*, 461–466.
Rashid, T., & Ostermann, R. F. (2009). Strength-based assessment in clinical practice. *Journal of Clinical Psychology, 65*, 488–498.
Rashid, T., & Seligman, M. E. P. (2013). Positive psychotherapy. In R. J. Corsini & D. Wedding (Eds.), *Current psychotherapies* (pp. 461–498). Belmont, CA: Cengage.
Reivich, K., & Shatté, A. (2002). *The Resilience Factor: 7 Essential skills for overcoming life's inevitable obstacles*. New York, NY: Broadway Books.
Rogina, J. M. (2015). Noogenic activation in the clinical practice of logotherapy and existential analysis (LTEA) to facilitate meaningful change. *The International Forum for Logotherapy, 38*, 1–7.
Ruini, C., & Fava, G. A. (2004). Clinical applications of well-being therapy. In P. A. Linley & S. Joseph (Eds.), *Positive psychology in practice* (pp. 371–387). Hoboken, NJ: Wiley.
Ryff, C. D. (1989). Happiness is everything, or is it? Explorations on the meaning of psychological well-being. *Journal of Personality and Social Psychology, 57*, 1069–1081.
Schnetzer, L. W., Schulenberg, S. E., & Buchanan, E. M. (2013). Differential associations among alcohol use, depression and perceived life meaning in male and female college students. *Journal of Substance Use, 18*, 311–319.

Schulenberg, S. E. (2003). Empirical research and Logotherapy. *Psychological Reports, 93*, 307–319.

Schulenberg, S. E., Drescher, C. F., & Baczwaski, B. J. (2014). Perceived meaning and disaster mental health: A role for logotherapy in clinical-disaster psychology. In A. Batthyany & P. Russo-Netzer (Eds.), *Meaning in positive and existential psychology* (pp. 251–267). New York, NY: Springer.

Schulenberg, S. E., & Melton, A. M. A. (2010). A confirmatory factor-analytic evaluation of the Purpose in Life test: Preliminary psychometric support for a replicable two-factor model. *Journal of Happiness Studies, 11*, 95–111.

Schulenberg, S. E., Nassif, C., Hutzell, R. R., & Rogina, J. M. (2008). Logotherapy for clinical practice. *Psychotherapy: Theory, Research, Practice, Training, 45*, 447–463.

Schulenberg, S. E., Schnetzer, L. W., & Buchanan, E. M. (2011). The Purpose in Life test Short-Form: Development and psychometric support. *Journal of Happiness Studies, 12*, 861–876.

Schulenberg, S. E., Strack, K. M., & Buchanan, E. M. (2011). The Meaning in Life Questionnaire: Psychometric properties with individuals with serious mental illness in an inpatient setting. *Journal of Clinical Psychology, 67*, 1210–1219.

Seligman, M. E. P. (2011). *Flourish: A new visionary understanding of happiness and well being*. New York, NY: Free Press.

Seligman, M. E. P., Rashid, T., & Parks, A. C. (2006). Positive psychotherapy. *American Psychologist, 61*, 774–788.

Sin, N. L., Della Porta, M. D., & Lyubomirsky, S. (2011). Tailoring positive psychology interventions to treat depressed individuals. In S. I. Donaldson, M. Csikszentmihalyi, & J. Nakamura (Eds.), *Review of applied positive psychology: Improving everyday life, health, schools, work, and society* (pp. 79–96). New York, NY: Routledge.

Sin, N. L., & Lyubomirsky, S. (2009). Enhancing well-being and alleviating depressive symptoms with positive psychology interventions: A practice-friendly meta-analysis. *Journal of Clinical Psychology, 65*, 467–487.

Steger, M. F., Frazier, P., Oishi, S., & Kaler, M. (2006). The Meaning in Life Questionnaire: Assessing the presence of and search for meaning in life. *Journal of Counseling Psychology, 53*, 80–93.

Tugade, M. M., & Fredrickson, B. L. (2004). Resilient individuals use positive emotions to bounce back from negative emotional experiences. *Journal of Personality and Social Psychology, 86*, 320–333.

Ungar, M. (2002). A logotherapy treatment protocol for major depressive disorder. *The International Forum for Logotherapy, 25*, 3–10.

Wagnild, G. (2009). *The resilience scale user's guide for the US English version of the resilience scale and the 14-item resilience scale (RS–14)*. Worden, MT: Resilience Center.

Wong, P. T. P. (2009). Existential positive psychology. In S. J. Lopez (Ed.), *Encyclopedia of positive psychology* (Vol. 1, pp. 361–368). Oxford, UK: Wiley Blackwell.

Wong, P. T. P. (2011). Positive psychology 2.0: Towards a balanced interactive model of the good life. *Canadian Psychology, 52*, 69–81.

Wong, P. T. P. (2014). Viktor Frankl's meaning seeking model and positive psychology. In A. Batthyany & P. Russo-Netzer (Eds.), *Meaning in existential and positive psychology* (pp. 149–184). New York, NY: Springer.

Wood, A. M., Linely, P. A., Maltby, J., Kashdan, T. B., & Hurling, R. (2011). Using personal and psychological strengths leads to increases in well-being over time: A longitudinal study and the development of the Strengths Use Questionnaire. *Personality and Individual Differences, 50*, 15–19.

Wright, N. P., Turkington, D., Kelly, O. P., Davies, D., Jacobs, A. M., & Hopton, J. (2014). *Treating psychosis: A clinician's guide to integrating Acceptance and Commitment Therapy, compassion-focused therapy, and mindfulness approaches within the cognitive behavioral therapy tradition*. Oakland, CA: New Harbinger Publications.

Yates, T. M., & Masten, A. S. (2004). Fostering the future: Resilience theory and the practice of positive psychology. In P. A. Linley & S. Joseph (Eds.), *Positive psychology in practice* (pp. 521–578). Hoboken, NJ: Wiley.

Meaning-Centered Psychotherapy in the Oncology and Palliative Care Settings

William Breitbart and Melissa Masterson

Introduction

Physical, psychological, and spiritual domains of end-of-life care have been identified as priorities by both medical professional organizations and cancer patients themselves. Two milestone Institute of Medicine (IOM) reports, "Approaching death: Improving care at the end of life" (1997) and "Improving palliative care for cancer" (2001), as well as the National Consensus Project for Quality of Palliative Care Clinical Practice Guidelines (2004) and the National Quality Forum (2006) recommendations for preferred practices for palliative and hospice care identified spiritual well-being (psychological, psychiatric, spiritual, and existential domains of care) as core domains of quality end-of-life care.

Facing a diagnosis of advanced cancer is challenging for even the most resilient individuals. Distress associated with this diagnosis can manifest in many ways including physical symptoms, psychological symptoms, and spiritual/existential symptoms.

Existential concerns are a major issue among the advanced cancer population as feelings regarding one's mortality are brought to the forefront. A consensus conference on improving the quality of spiritual care as a dimension of palliative care was recently held (Puchalski et al., 2009). This conference was formed under the central

---

W. Breitbart, M.D., F.A.P.A., F.A.P.O.S. (✉)
Department of Psychiatry and Behavioral Sciences, Memorial Sloan Kettering Cancer Center, 641 Lexington Avenue, New York, NY 10021, USA
e-mail: breitbaw@mskcc.org

M. Masterson, M.A.
Memorial Sloan Kettering Cancer Center,
641 Lexington Avenue, New York, NY 10022, USA

premise that spiritual care is a fundamental component of end-of-life support. Importantly, the consensus panel explicitly recommended psychotherapy approaches that focus on meaning to address spiritual/existential issues for end-of-life care.

Theoretical Background of Meaning-Centered Psychotherapy

Nearly 15 years ago, our research group at Memorial Sloan Kettering Cancer Center began to understand that a meaning-centered approach to psychosocial care was imperative to alleviate distress among advanced cancer patients. For those patients who are in fact facing death, meaning and the preservation of meaning are not only clinically and spiritually/existentially important but are central concepts to therapeutic intervention. Meaning-centered psychotherapy (MCP) was conceived at the intersection of a baffling clinical problem and inspiration. Clinically, we witnessed despair and hopelessness take hold of our advanced cancer patients and, consequently, the emergence of the desire for hastened death. What we found most surprising was that although 45 % expressing a desire for hastened death were struggling with a clinical depression (Breitbart et al., 2000), a significant percentage were not clinically depressed, but rather facing an existential crisis encompassing a loss of meaning, value, purpose, and hope.

When our research group as well as others demonstrated the central role that meaning plays in diminishing psychosocial distress and despair at the end of life, we were inspired to develop a meaning-centered intervention. This effort led us to the work of Viktor Frankl, his concepts of logotherapy (Frankl, 1955, 1959, 1969, 1975), and pioneers in existential philosophy and psychiatry. We found Frankl's concepts of meaning and spirituality to be powerful tools that could be utilized in our psychotherapeutic work with advanced cancer patients facing existential issues at the end of life. Frankl's main contributions have been increased awareness of the spiritual component of human experience and the central importance of meaning (or the will to meaning) as a motivating force in human psychology. Frankl's basic concepts include:

1. Meaning of life—life has meaning and never ceases to have meaning even up to the last moment of life, and while meaning may change in this context, it never ceases to exist.
2. Will to meaning—the desire to find meaning in human existence is a primary instinct and basic motivation for human behavior.
3. Freedom of will—we have the freedom to find meaning in existence and to choose our attitude toward suffering.
4. The three main sources of meaning in life are derived from creativity (work and deeds), experience (art, nature, humor, love, relationships, roles), and attitude (the attitude one takes toward suffering and existential problems).
5. Meaning exists in a historical context; thus legacy (past, present, and future) is a critical element in sustaining or enhancing meaning.

Meaning-Centered Psychotherapy (MCP)

Model of MCP

Based on Viktor Frankl's logotherapy and the principles above, we developed the "meaning-centered psychotherapy" to help patients with advanced cancer sustain or enhance a sense of meaning, peace, and purpose in their lives even as they approach the end of life (Breitbart, 2002; Breitbart, Gibson, Poppito, & Berg, 2004; Greenstein & Breitbart, 2000). This intervention is based on a theoretical model in which the enhancement of meaning results in improved quality of life and reduced distress, despair, and suffering. The figure below depicts the model underlying our MCP intervention, in which enhanced meaning is conceptualized as the catalyst for improved psychosocial outcomes.

Figure 1 depicts the model underlying the MCP intervention, much of which has been supported by published research. Specifically, meaning is viewed as both an intermediary outcome and a mediator of changes in these important psychosocial outcomes. Religious faith is not expected to directly impact psychosocial outcomes, but may moderate the intermediary outcome of meaning (see, e.g., Nelson, Rosenfeld, Breitbart, & Galietta, 2002, indicating that religious faith does not provide unique contribution to enhanced psychosocial outcomes after controlling for spirituality). This model also presumes that other factors will impact response to a meaning-based intervention, including prognostic awareness, psychosocial treatment preference, and therapeutic alliance. We recognize that the directionality of many of the variables included in this model could potentially be bidirectional; however, we present the model we believe underlies the intervention.

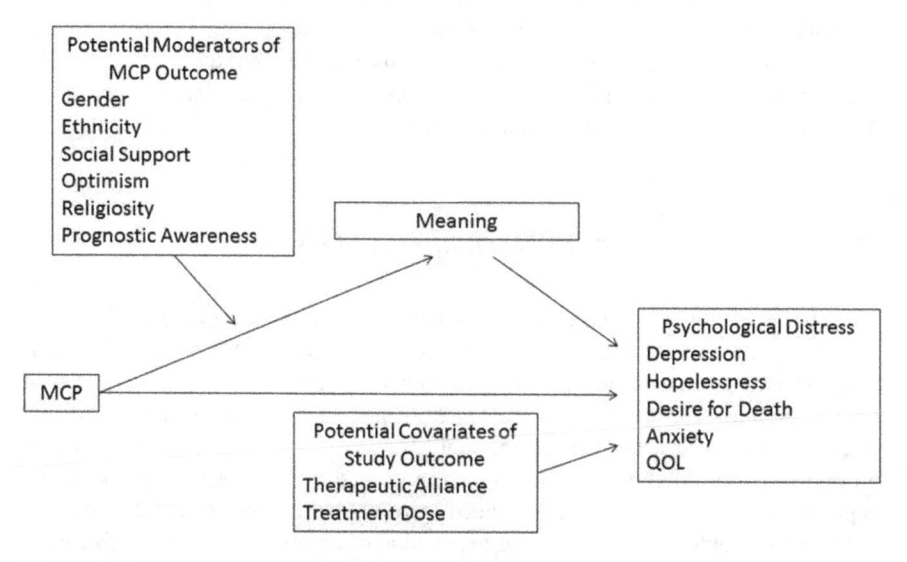

Fig. 1 Study model—mediators and moderators of treatment outcome

In order to target the despair and hopelessness driving the desire for hastened death, a number of existential concepts were called upon that do not directly involve meaning, but serve as a critical framework for conducting the therapeutic work of MCP. Although the MCP intervention is literally centered on meaning and sources of meaning, the richness of the therapeutic content is due to the integration of meaning and the theories of existential philosophy and psychotherapy. The therapeutic value of MCP would be limited without the contribution of existential concepts such as death anxiety, freedom, responsibility, choice, creativity, identity, authenticity, existential guilt, transcendence, transformation, mortality, and existential isolation. These concepts inform the intervention and are utilized to reinforce the goals of MCP related to the search, connection, and creation of meaning.

Appropriate Participants for MCP

While the majority of advanced cancer patients could benefit from participation in MCP, the intervention is best suited for individuals with moderate to extreme distress, as indicated by a score of 4 or higher on the distress thermometer (NCCN Clinical Practice Guidelines in Oncology). The distress thermometer is a brief screening tool that assesses the patient's level of current distress by asking, "Please note your current distress on a scale from 0 to 10," where 0 is "no distress" and 10 is "extreme distress." When the source of the patient's distress is emotional or spiritual/religious in nature, MCP may be a particularly efficacious intervention. Furthermore, MCP is currently delivered in the outpatient setting, and therefore, patients with physical limitations sufficient to preclude participation in the outpatient setting are not suited for this intervention. The patient's physical limitations are assessed using the Karnofsky Performance Rating Scale (KPRS). KPRS scores range from 0, "dead," to 100, "normal, no complaints: no evidence of disease." Scores below 60—"requires considerable assistance and frequent medical care"—deem a participant inappropriate for study participation in the outpatient setting.

Meaning-Centered Group Psychotherapy (MCGP)

Since its inception, MCP has been tested and demonstrated to be an effective intervention in a group format. Meaning-centered group psychotherapy (MCGP) was tested in a randomized clinical trial with advanced cancer patients. The format of MCGP includes eight 1 ½ hour weekly sessions; each session includes didactic teaching, discussions, and an experiential exercise component. Didactic teaching introduces group members to the themes presented in each session, while group experiential exercises allow for enhanced learning and homework practice outside of sessions. Elements of support and expression of emotion that characterize most psychotherapeutic groups are inevitably present in each session but are limited by

Table 1 Individual meaning-centered psychotherapy session topics and themes

Session #1: Concepts and Sources of Meaning	
Introductions and Overview	
Session #2: Cancer and Meaning	
Identity Before and After Cancer Diagnosis	
Session #3: Historical Sources of Meaning	
"Life as a Legacy" that has been given	
"Life as a Legacy" that one lives and will give	
Session #4: Attitudinal Sources of Meaning	
Encountering Life's Limitations	
Session #5: Creative Sources of Meaning	
Creativity, Courage, and Responsibility	
Session #6: Experiential Sources of Meaning	
Connecting with Life through Love, Beauty, and Humor	
Session #7: Transitions	
Final Group Reflections and Hopes for the Future	

the psycho-educational focus of MCGP. Each session is focused on a specific theme related to meaning and advanced cancer (Table 1). Our research team received several National Cancer Institute grants to rigorously test the efficacy of MCGP in advanced cancer patients (refer to Breitbart et al., 2010, 2015, for comprehensive results). In summary, stronger treatment effects were observed for MCGP compared with supportive group psychotherapy for quality of life, spiritual well-being, depression, hopelessness, desire for hastened death, and physical symptom distress (Breitbart et al., 2010, 2015). MCGP proved to be a highly effective intervention, increasing a sense of meaning, spiritual well-being, and hope, while decreasing end-of-life despair (Breitbart et al., 2010, 2015). For information regarding session content, refer to the *Meaning-Centered Group Psychotherapy Treatment Manual* (Breitbart & Poppito, 2014a).

Challenges of MCGP

While the group format of MCGP has been effective for advanced patients with a wide range of cancers, it is not without its challenges. Due to the structure of the MCGP sessions, in which each subsequent session builds upon the last, attendance at each session is crucial in order to fully benefit from the intervention. The rigid schedule necessary to conduct outpatient group sessions of MCGP, coupled with the physical limitation inherent in this population, resulted in high rates of missed sessions and high levels of attrition. In order to solve the problems presented by offering MCP in a group format, Individual Meaning-Centered Psychotherapy (IMCP) was developed. IMCP has the potential to address the unmet need for one-on-one flexible interventions critical to advanced cancer populations. It represents an opportunity to provide an effective intervention for existential and spiritual suffering that can be practically delivered.

Individual Meaning-Centered Psychotherapy (IMCP)

IMCP is a seven-session individual intervention, which utilizes didactics, discussions, and experiential exercises that focus on specific themes related to both meaning and advanced cancer. IMCP serves three major purposes: (1) to promote a supportive environment for cancer patients to explore personal issues and feelings surrounding their illness on a one-to-one therapeutic basis, (2) to facilitate a greater understanding of possible sources of meaning both before and after a diagnosis of cancer, and (3) to aid patients in their discovery and maintenance of a sense of meaning in life during illness. The ultimate goal of this intervention is to optimize coping through the pursuit of an enhanced sense of meaning and purpose. As Frankl points out, the possibility of creating or experiencing meaning exists until the last moment of life.

In the pilot study of IMCP for patients with advanced cancer, 120 patients with stage III or IV cancer were randomly assigned to seven sessions of either IMCP or therapeutic massage (Breitbart et al., 2012). Participants were assessed for spiritual well-being and quality of life, as well as anxiety, depression, hopelessness, and symptom burden. Posttreatment, cancer patients in the IMCP group reported significantly greater improvement in the primary study outcomes, spiritual well-being, and quality of life (Breitbart et al., 2012). Furthermore, IMCP patients demonstrated greater improvements in symptom burden and symptom-related distress than patients in the therapeutic massage group.

The intervention is intended to help broaden the scope of possible sources of meaning through the combination of (1) didactic teaching of the philosophy of meaning on which the intervention is based, (2) session exercises and homework for each participant to complete, and (3) open-ended discussion, which may include the therapist's interpretive insights and comments. However, it is important for clinicians to understand that meaning making is an individualized process, and therefore, it is the individual member's responsibility to use these sessions to actively explore and discover the sources of meaning in their own right. In this format, patients are not passive recipients of the intervention, but are active participants in the process itself, bringing to the table their own experiences, beliefs, and hopes that shape their journey to enhanced meaning and purpose. Although session topics remain the same within both individual and group formats, IMCP includes seven sessions, while MCGP is an eight-session intervention. The third topic, Historical Sources of Meaning and Legacy, is covered over two sessions in the group format to ensure ample time for each group member to participate in the often lengthy discussion of one's legacy. A list of session topics for the individual format of MCP (seven-session format) can be found in Table 1.

In the following section, an overview of each session is provided. For a comprehensive guide to session content, refer to the *Individual Meaning-Centered Psychotherapy Treatment Manual* (Breitbart & Poppito, 2014b).

Session 1: Concepts and Sources of Meaning

The initial session of IMCP includes a series of introductions. During this session, introductions between the patient and therapist occur in addition to introductions between the patient and the intervention. IMCP is a therapeutic program drastically different from traditional forms of psychotherapy; therefore, it is imperative that the therapist spend time in the first session orienting the patient to the structure, logistics, and goals of the intervention. Following introductions, the therapist welcomes the patient to share his/her cancer story, beginning at the time of diagnosis and continuing to the present day. The therapist should encourage the patient to describe how he/she has been affected physically, emotionally, and socially. The remainder of the session focuses on the concept of meaning. Patients are asked to provide their own definition of meaning to help the therapist better understand how the patient connects to and defines meaning in his/her own life. Following this exercise, the therapist offers a definition developed by our research team to offer the patient additional ways to think about the concept of meaning. Furthermore, the patient's meaningful moments in his/her life are explored, and rapport begins to build between the therapist and patient in this first session.

Session 2: Cancer and Meaning

In session 2, the main goal is to explore the topic of *"Cancer* and *Meaning"* in light of the guiding theme: *Identity—before* and *after diagnosis*. In order to reflect upon the origins of meaning in each person's life, it is important to start with their own understanding of who they are. This session will help to reveal the patient's authentic sense of identity, and what made his/her personal experiences meaningful. The experiential exercise for session 2 explores what makes this individual who they are and how cancer has impacted their identity (Breitbart & Poppito, 2014b). What the patient is most likely to discover through this exercise is that the core aspects of his/her identity after cancer are strikingly similar to their identity prior to cancer. Furthermore, it is the role of the clinician to attend to these themes and highlight them as characteristics that have persevered despite a life-altering diagnosis of advanced illness (Breitbart & Poppito, 2014b). The following IMCP excerpt from session 2 exemplifies the type of interaction that can occur:

Patient: *I am someone who loves her family and friends. I am an optimistic person. I am someone who was comfortable in their own skin. I am someone who loves to explore New York City.*
Interventionist: *Tell me a little more about being optimistic and how that characterizes who you are.*
Patient: *I think I'm always a hopeful person in general, like glass half full, and I guess when I was reading this, I noticed personality characteristics, so I knew also that I had to compare it, and so that's where I wrote that down because I feel*

> like the cancer is kind of eating away at that optimistic thing because of the worry and the fear. I try to stay strong to my true self, but this other angle creeps in. But on the positive side, cancer has really intensified my relationships with people and has also made me aware and reminded me to be a more generous person. It is just mind blowing the amount of people who want to bring us meals and ask me how I'm doing and ask my husband how he is doing, and people have given us monetary donations. And I keep telling people don't worry I'm fine; I don't need a meal; I'm functioning; feed your own family, but they all insist and want to do something. So it's always in my head that I need to pay it forward, and it really is a wonderful thing.
>
> Interventionist: *Absolutely.*
> Patient: *It's something wonderful to come out of a really shitty thing.*
> Interventionist: *Yes it is, and recognizing that and taking that approach is attitude.*
> Patient: *Yes, yes, it is.*
> Interventionist: *Out of something so negative, but out of it, something so beautiful that the things that are most important to you have become more intense and more meaningful, and it has given you the opportunity, the illness has, to see the world as a more wonderful place than you thought it was before your illness.*
> Patient: *I think I took it for granted, and I don't take it for granted anymore.*
> Interventionist: *And that is a great thing that has come out of this, this after cancer identity. What strikes me is that you said you were kind of surprised when you look at this after cancer part and thought, wow, three out of these four things aren't affected by cancer or at least aren't affected by cancer in a bad way. It goes to show that from such a profound challenge that can challenge you physically and psychologically, the core of who you are and the things that make you, you, haven't changed. And in fact you are now someone who argues less and loves more, who sees the world and people as being caring and generous, and wants to give back to the world. I think that is incredible.*
> Patient: *Yes, I agree. It is nice to be reminded of that, these, almost the positives that have come out of cancer.*

Session 3: Historical Sources of Meaning—"Life as a Living Legacy"

The main goal for session 3 is to introduce and explore the topic of *Historical Sources of Meaning* and the guiding theme: *Life as a living legacy*. Following the discussion of identity in the previous session, session 3 serves as an opportunity to explore the context in which identity developed through the exploration of legacy. In IMCP, we present the idea of legacy through three temporal parts: (1) the legacy that has been given from the past, (2) the legacy that one lives in the present, and finally (3) the legacy that one will give in the future (Breitbart & Poppito, 2014b). The experiential exercise for session 3 allows the patient to have the opportunity to explore and express meaningful past experiences in order to uncover the historical context of his/her living legacy.

For some patients, discussion of the "legacy given" will be a nice trip down memory lane, while for others it may include difficult experiences related to unmet needs, losses, or disappointments. Whether memories are awesome or dreadful, it is undeniable that this legacy is a part of who our patients are. Our role as therapists is to bear witness to the patient's story; the experience of telling the story may be comforting and transformative for a patient who is struggling physically and emotionally (Breitbart & Poppito, 2014b).

Furthermore, this session explores the present and future components of legacy. Through this process, the patient can begin to witness his/her living legacy as a cohesive whole by integrating past memories with present accomplishments toward future contributions (Breitbart & Poppito, 2014b). The therapist should help the patient find the thread that weaves through his/her past, present, and future legacy while listening for themes of hardship, loss, and adversity that can be reflected upon in the next session discussing life's limitations.

Session 4: Attitudinal Sources of Meaning—"Encountering Life's Limitations"

The main goal for session 4 is to explore the topic of *Attitudinal Sources of Meaning* and the guiding theme: *Encountering Life's Limitations*. Session 4 is centered on Viktor Frankl's core theoretical belief that our last vestige of human freedom is our capacity to choose our attitude toward suffering and life's limitations in any given situation. Furthermore, the session focuses on Frankl's belief that meaning and suffering are not mutually exclusive, but that one has the potential to find meaning in life through suffering. The attitudinal source of meaning is offered to patients as a way in which they can take control of their life in a meaningful way during a time in which the illness has likely stripped from them their sense of peace and control. The experiential exercise for this session allows the patient to reflect on times when he/she has faced obstacles and limitations in the past. It is the role of the therapist to point out how the patient has chosen his/her attitude in the past and how he/she can continue to use this source of meaning to face the challenges presented by illness (Breitbart & Poppito, 2014b). The review of how the patient has turned tragedies into triumphs in the past bolsters strength and self-efficacy regarding the patient's ability to combat the obstacles and limitations that lie ahead.

The following IMCP excerpt exemplifies the type of interaction that occurs during the session 4 experiential exercise:

Patient: *I think the tragic loss of both my parents shortly after I graduated from college. My father passed away when I was 19 ½ and my mom 1 year later. I had two brothers who were a great support to me, and 1 year before my mom passed, I met my dear husband, who I married 1 month after her death. I gathered the strength to bear the loss of my parents drawing on the values and love passed onto me by my dear mom and dad. They left a whole lifetime of values with me, and that is what helped me get through this. That and my husband coming into my life just a year previous, so I was very lucky in that respect. I don't know what would have happened if I hadn't met him at that point; life would have went a very different way maybe, but I was able to gather a lot of strength then and I got through it. It was really balanced by a wonderful time in my life, during a tragic situation.*

Interventionist: *It sounds like you fell in love in the wake of grief.*

Patient: *Exactly, when I think back, I think it is an amazing thing that happened. He never met my father, but met my mother when she was not herself. I fell in love with my husband the second he opened the door for a blind date; that was a gift from God. I have had a lot of gifts from God.*

Interventionist: *So meeting him and the love that you experienced with him certainly gave you strength, and it sounds like your brothers were also pillars of strength for you during that time. It really seems that the way you have always been able to cope with losses and limitations in the past is through the support of your family. When I came in today, I saw your children all around your chemo suite, and I think it is such a touching and beautiful example of how you continue to utilize the strength found in your family to face the current limitations presented by your illness.*

Patient: *I couldn't get through this without them; they are so amazing.*

The homework assigned in session 4 is a long-term homework assignment intended to build upon the work done thus far and further explore the concept of "Life as a Legacy." Additional information on this long-term homework assignment can be found in the *Individual Meaning-Centered Psychotherapy Treatment Manual* (Breitbart & Poppito, 2014b).

Session 5: Creative Sources of Meaning—"Actively Engaging in Life via Creativity and Responsibility"

The main goal for session 5 is to introduce and explore the topic of *Creative Sources of Meaning* and the guiding theme: "*Actively engaging in life* via *creativity* and *responsibility.*"

It is the role of the clinician in this session to provide psycho-education regarding the relationship between creativity, courage, and responsibility. As humans, our existence calls us to create, and our ability to respond to this creative calling forms the basis for taking responsibility for our lives. Creativity and responsibility, therefore, are inextricably linked. While creativity requires action, the beauty of this source of meaning is that it continually gives us second chances to start over, make amends, forge new paths, traverse uncharted territories, and transcend our given bounds.

The challenge of creativity is that it takes a good deal of courage, tenacity, and inner fortitude to continually risk putting oneself out there in the face of uncertainty and doubt. It takes a great deal of courage to confront an advanced stage cancer diagnosis and find the energy and inner resolve to move ahead in spite of an uncertain future. Patients may feel existential guilt when they ignore this creative calling and fail to respond to life. It is imperative to normalize the guilt that patients may experience as well as to foster strength by helping patients to acknowledge their day-to-day ability to create as courageous. By the end of session 5, the patient should have a solid understanding of the significance of "creativity and responsibility" as important sources of meaning in life (Breitbart & Poppito, 2014b).

Session 6: Experiential Sources of Meaning—"Connecting with Life"

The main goal for session 6 is to introduce and explore the topic of *Experiential Sources of Meaning* by way of the guiding theme: *Connecting with Life*. Thus far, the sources of meaning introduced have required active involvement in life; experiential sources embody more passive engagement with life. Creative and attitudinal sources ask us to *give to life*, while experiential sources call us to *give ourselves over* to the lightness of being alive (Breitbart & Poppito, 2014b). There are three major ways in which we connect to life—through love, beauty, and humor. During the experiential exercise for session 6, patients are invited to provide examples of ways they connect to these sources of meaning. Following engagement in this exercise, it is the role of the therapist to reflect on the fact that experiential sources of meaning remain accessible despite limited physical capabilities or emotional hardship (Breitbart & Poppito, 2014b). As the illness progresses, patients may find comfort in these sources of meaning that require little activity to access. By the end of session 6, the patient should have a solid understanding of the significance of connecting with life through experiential sources of meaning.

Session 7: Transitions and Hopes for the Future

The final seventh session allows for time to reflect upon the experience of engaging in this intervention over the previous six sessions. The patient's thoughts and feelings surrounding the finality of this therapeutic experience in light of facing important transitions and endings in their own life should be explored (Breitbart & Poppito, 2014b). Furthermore, these themes can be explored through the sharing of the meaningful experiences within the treatment process. The exercise for session 7 facilitates discussion of transitions and the future.

The following IMCP excerpt exemplifies the type of interaction that occurs during the final session:

Patient: *I never thought that I was a strong person, but I think you made me realize that I am.*

Interventionist: *You have overcome so much. Not only have you overcome obstacles but you have gone the extra mile to create the life that you want despite the limitations you have faced. You have showed me that when life wasn't really giving you what you wanted and what you needed, you went out and found it; you went out and created it. That is attitude.*

Patient: *Did I tell you that my boss and dear friend had adopted a baby from China?*
Interventionist: *Yes, and you were asked to be her godmother?*
Patient: *Yes. I was there yesterday, and this baby that we brought over together is now 17 years old. I forgot the joy the child brought me, and she came trotting down the lobby and started hugging and kissing me, and I thought I am so lucky. Even if I don't see her that often, I am so lucky. She brought great joy to my life.*
Interventionist: *That is wonderful, and I am so struck by that because in our last session, we talked about these experiential sources of meaning and of love.*
Patient: *And I didn't put that down! I needed to realize how much I love that child.*
Interventionist: *So in thinking about some of the themes we have discussed such as love, in general, what was this experience going through meaning-centered psychotherapy like for you?*
Patient: *You know what is interesting, I never really talked about my husband until these sessions, but at my last memoir class, the prompt was about looking at a painting and looking through the painting. The bottom line is that I have a picture of the shore near where we met, and for the first time in my life, I wrote about him. My class and instructor were so struck that I had never mentioned him, and I think that I did that because I was able to open up with you.*
Interventionist: *So what did it feel like to write about him and to have the story of you and him witnessed by others?*
Patient: *It felt so good that they loved it. Professionally, I love having the ability to write and be appreciated for it, but emotionally, I loved writing that story.*
Interventionist: *It is so wonderful that you were able to open up to others and connect that way.*
Patient: *It was so rewarding. I think overall, over these seven sessions, I have opened up.*
Interventionist: *I have certainly noticed. Which is why I think we have made some progress, and I encourage you to explore how opening up and connecting to others can provide you with freedom and take you on a unique journey through the rest of your life.*

Future Directions of MCP

MCP for Caregivers (MCP-C)

In recent years, there has been growing recognition of the unmet needs of the informal caregivers of our patients. The literature shows that structured, goal-oriented, integrative, and time-limited interventions are best suited for informal caregivers of cancer patients (Applebaum & Breitbart, 2013). Currently, we are developing Meaning-Centered Psychotherapy for Cancer Caregivers (MCP-C). The goal of MCP-C is to explore critical sources of meaning in the caregiver's life in an attempt to alleviate existential distress experienced by caregivers who are providing practical and emotional support to patients while coping with their own feelings related to the illness (Applebaum, Kulikowski, & Breitbart, 2015). Previous studies have called for the development of interventions delivered in alternative modalities to increase the number of informal caregivers that can access services (Applebaum & Breitbart, 2013). Therefore, clinical trials are currently underway to evaluate the efficacy of MCP-C delivered over the Internet.

MCGP for Breast Cancer Survivors (MCGP-BCS)

In partnership with the American Cancer Society, members of our team are testing an innovative application of the meaning-centered group (MCG) approach in a new but critically important and large population: breast cancer survivors. This adaptation of MCP consists of eight sessions, which address existential issues that cancer survivors commonly face. It focuses on the future, and life survivors would like to create, using some behavioral strategies to assist survivors with getting "unstuck." We are currently evaluating the delivery of MCG for breast cancer survivors (MCG-BCS) through a virtual group format that involves the use of telephones and computers to connect potentially geographically diverse posttreatment group members who are, thus, not able to return to their cancer treatment center frequently. MCG-BCS has the potential to address the challenges in finding meaning that many breast cancer survivors face.

MCP for Bereaved Parents

The loss of a child is arguably the most devastating type of bereavement, leaving parents of the child in turmoil and suffering intense grief. Due to the existential distress commonly experienced by bereaved parents, a meaning-centered approach is fitting (Lichtenthal & Breitbart, 2015). We are currently evaluating the efficacy of meaning-centered grief therapy for parents bereaved by cancer to address the challenges in finding meaning in their lives and loss that parents frequently face. This intervention involves 16 one-on-one sessions, building upon the principles of MCP and adding content specific to coping with grief. It is designed to assist parents with recognizing their ability to choose their attitude in the face of their grief and suffering, to connect with important sources of meaning in their lives from which they may have become disconnected, and to help them continue their connection to their deceased child (Lichtenthal & Breitbart, 2015).

MCP for Adolescents and Young Adults with Cancer

Adolescents and young adults facing cancer make up a unique and specialized population of cancer patients. Adolescence and young adulthood are critical periods of development in the search for meaning, purpose, and identity. As adolescents and young adults battle cancer, they may face developmental challenges and barriers to finding meaning and a coherent sense of identity due to life disruption from their diagnosis and course of treatment. The adaptation of MCP for the adolescent and young adult population accounts for these unique developmental tasks and may provide relief to the existential distress experienced by these patients. Content derived from qualitative semi-structured interviews with adolescents and young adults focusing on identity, meaning, and purpose is being used to adapt MCP for the adolescent and young adult population.

MCGP in Cancer Survivors (MCGP-CS)

Research has shown that meaning-focused coping may be a helpful tool in effectively adjusting to cancer; patients who experience their lives as meaningful report better adjustment to the cancer experience, better quality of life, and better overall psychological functioning (Park, Edomondson, Fenster, & Blank, 2008; Tomich & Helgeson, 2002). Based on our research in advanced cancer, a research group in the Netherlands worked to adapt meaning-centered group psychotherapy to address the needs of individuals struggling to adjust to life after cancer (Van der Spek et al., 2014). Results from the most recent feasibility study indicate that MCGP-CS is feasible, patients were highly compliant, and patients reported satisfaction following the intervention (Van der Spek et al., 2014). Further evaluation is underway to establish the effectiveness of MCGP-CS in a larger randomized controlled clinical trial.

Key Takeaways

- Meaning-centered psychotherapy was developed when meaning was first identified by our research group and others as a central tool in diminishing psychosocial distress and despair at the end of life.
- MCP is based on Viktor Frankl's logotherapy and was developed to help patients with advanced cancer to sustain or enhance a sense of meaning, peace, and purpose in their lives even as they approach the end of life (Breitbart, 2002; Breitbart et al., 2004; Greenstein & Breitbart, 2000).
- MCP is based on a theoretical model in which the enhancement of meaning results in improved quality of life and reduced distress, despair, and suffering.
- MCP has shown to be a highly effective intervention for existential distress among cancer patients, specifically improving quality of life and spiritual well-being, while diminishing depression, hopelessness, and the desire for hastened death (Breitbart et al., 2010, 2015).
- The core principles that have contributed to its success in treating advanced cancer patients have been utilized and built upon to generate solutions for a wider population, including cancer survivors, young adults, caregivers, and bereaved parents.

References

Applebaum, A. J., & Breitbart, W. (2013). Care for the cancer caregiver: A systematic review. *Palliative and Supportive Care, 11*(3), 231–252.

Applebaum, A. J., Kulikowski, J., & Breitbart, W. (2015). Meaning-centered psychotherapy for cancer caregivers (MCP-C): Rationale and overview. *Palliative and Supportive Care, 13*(6), 1631–1641.

Breitbart, W. (2002). Spirituality and meaning in supportive care: Spirituality and meaning-centered group psychotherapy interventions in advanced cancer. *Supportive Care in Cancer, 10*(4), 272–280.

Breitbart, W., Gibson, C., Poppito, S. R., & Berg, A. (2004). Psychotherapeutic interventions at the end of life: a focus on meaning and spirituality. *Canadian Journal of Psychiatry, 49*(6), 366–372.

Breitbart, W., & Poppito, S. (2014a). *Meaning centered group psychotherapy treatment manual.* New York, NY: Oxford University Press.

Breitbart, W., & Poppito, S. (2014b). *Individual meaning centered psychotherapy treatment manual.* New York, NY: Oxford University Press.

Breitbart, W., Poppito, S., Rosenfeld, B., Vickers, A. J., Li, Y., Abbey, J., ... Cassileth, B. R. (2012). Pilot randomized controlled trial of individual meaning-centered psychotherapy for patients with advanced cancer. *Journal of Clinical Oncology, 30*(12), 1304–1309.

Breitbart, W., Rosenfeld, B., Gibson, C., Pessin, H., Poppito, S., Nelson, C., ... Olden, M. (2010). Meaning-centered group psychotherapy for patients with advanced cancer: A pilot randomized controlled trial. *Psycho-Oncology, 19*(1), 21–28.

Breitbart, W., Rosenfeld, B., Pessin, H., Applebaum, A., Kulikowski, J., & Lichtenthal, W. G. (2015). Meaning-centered group psychotherapy: An effective intervention for improving psychological well-being in patients with advanced cancer. *Journal of Clinical Oncology, 33*(7), 749–754.

Breitbart, W., Rosenfeld, B., Pessin, H., Kaim, M., Funesti-Esch, J., Galietta, M., ... Brescia, R. (2000). Depression, hopelessness, and desire for hastened death in terminally ill patients with cancer. *JAMA, 284*(22), 2907–2911.

Frankl, V. E. (1955/1986). *The doctor and the soul.* New York, NY: Random House.

Frankl, V. E. (1959/1992). *Man's search for meaning* (4th ed.). Boston, MA: Beacon Press.

Frankl, V. E. (1969/1988). *The will to meaning: Foundations and applications of logotherapy, expanded edition.* New York, NY: Penguin Books.

Frankl, V. E. (1975/1997). *Man's search for ultimate meaning.* New York, NY: Plenum Press.

Field, M.J. & Cassel, C.K. (1997). (Eds.). Approaching Death: Improving Care at the End of Life. Washington, DC: National Academy Press.

Foley, K.F. & Gelband, H. (Eds.). (2001). Improving palliative Care in Cancer. Washington DC National Accademy Press: Institute of Medicine National Cancer Policy Board.

Greenstein, M., & Breitbart, W. (2000). Cancer and the experience of meaning: A group psychotherapy program for people with cancer. *American Journal of Psychotherapy, 54*(4), 486–500.

Lichtenthal, W., & Breitbart, W. (2015). The central role of meaning in adjustment to the loss of a child to cancer: Implications for the development of meaning-centered grief therapy. *Supportive and Palliative Care, 9*(1), 46–51.

National Consensus project for Quality Palliative care (2004). Clinical Practice Guidelines for Quality Palliative Care. www.nationalconsensusproject.org.

National Quality Forum (2006). A National Framework and Preferred Practice for palliative Care and Hospice Care Quality. Washington DC National Quality Forum.

Nelson, C. J., Rosenfeld, B., Breitbart, W., & Galietta, M. (2002). Spirituality, religion, and depression in the terminally ill. *Psychosomatics, 43*(3), 213–220.

Park, C. L., Edomondson, D., Fenster, J. R., & Blank, T. O. (2008). Meaning making and psychological adjustment following cancer: The mediating roles of growth, life meaning, and restored just-world beliefs. *Counseling and Clinical Psychology, 76*(5), 863–875.

Puchalski, C., Ferrell, B., Virani, R., Otis-Green, S., Baird, P., Bull, J., … Sulmasy, D. (2009). Improving the quality of spiritual care as a dimension of palliative care: The report of the consensus conference. *Journal of Palliative Medicine, 12*(10), 885–904.

Tomich, P. L., & Helgeson, V. S. (2002). Five years later: A cross-sectional comparison of breast cancer survivors with healthy women. *Psychooncology, 11*(2), 154–169.

Van der Spek, N., van Uden-Kraan, C. F., Vos, J., Breitbart, W., Tollenaar, R. A., van Asperen, C. J., … Verdonck-de Leeuw, I. M. (2014). Meaning-centered group psychotherapy in cancer survivors: A feasibility study. *Psychooncology, 23*(7), 827–831.

Meaning Making in the Aftermath of a Spinal Cord Injury

Peter Claudio, Simon Kunz, Andreas Hegi, and Daniel Stirnimann

Introduction

Adverse life events happen every day. The impact of such events can be detrimental and can have a severe effect on an individual's life. Within this context, the meaning-making process and its components have drawn considerable attention. The interest in the understanding of this process is grounded in the aim to support affected individuals, to strengthen and to facilitate what is necessary, and to provide help, if needed. Using the onset of a spinal cord injury (SCI) as a case in point, this chapter will use Park's meaning-making model (2010) to structure current knowledge on the relevance of meaning and meaning making in the adjustment process after SCI onset.

What Is a Spinal Cord Injury?

Spinal cord injury (SCI) is an example of an acute, profoundly life-changing event with a traumatic or nontraumatic etiology (Lin et al., 2010). The term "traumatic" injury is used to denote the sudden onset of SCI, such as by car crash, sport

---

P. Claudio, Ph.D. (✉) • S. Kunz, M.Sc.
Environment, Participation and Social Integration Unit, Swiss Paraplegic Research (SPF), Guido A. Zäch-Strasse 4, 6207 Nottwil, Switzerland

Department of Health Sciences and Health Policy, University of Lucerne, Frohburgstrasse 3, 6002 Lucerne, Switzerland
e-mail: claudio.peter@paraplegie.ch

A. Hegi, lic. phil.
Swiss Paraplegic Center (SPZ), Guido A. Zäch-Strasse 1, 6207 Nottwil, Switzerland

D. Stirnimann, M.Sc.
Spinal Cord Injury Center, Balgrist University Hospital, Forchstrasse 340, 8008 Zürich, Switzerland

accidents, or falls. Nontraumatic etiologies of SCI may comprise surgical interventions or other health conditions, such as cancer, which may lead to SCI. An SCI can be complete or incomplete: A complete injury means a complete loss of sensory or movement-related functions below the lesion. In contrast, individuals with an incomplete SCI own residual sensory or movement-related functioning nerves (Kirshblum, Campagnolo, & DeLisa, 2002). SCI is a rare health condition. Recent estimated global incidence lies between 40 and 80 new cases per million per year (World Health Organization, 2013). A traumatic SCI is likely to occur among men, especially young adults and the elderly. However, a comprehensive summary of the best available data by the World Health Organization (WHO) shows that basic epidemiological data is sparse, especially in low- and middle-income countries (World Health Organization, 2013).

The impact of SCI on the lived experience of the person is severe, affecting all dimensions of an individual's life. Generally, the higher a lesion, the more extensive the range of physical impairments. Physical impairments not only comprise movement of legs, arms, or hands, but also bladder, bowel, and sexual functions may be negatively affected. The consequences of these impairments for activities and social participation are serious. Walking, moving around, and traveling may be completely restricted or only pursued with considerable efforts (Lin et al., 2010). Modifications of the dwelling or vehicles adapted for the needs of the individuals may help to regain former habitation quality, social participation, and connectedness with friends and family. Reeducation and vocational trainings may be necessary. Many possibilities to keep a sense of autonomy and social integration, however, are also dependent upon the social environment, the cultural background of a society, accessibility of public transport, as well as generally held beliefs and attitudes toward disability within the society (World Health Organization, 2013).

It is not surprising that several individuals with SCI may report elevated levels of depression, anxiety, or symptoms of post-traumatic stress disorder, levels that lie above the general population (Craig, Tran, & Middleton, 2009). However, the low proportion may stimulate contemplation: Recent studies showed that different trajectories are observed following SCI onset. While a majority of individuals seem to maintain or regain comparatively high levels of well-being or good mental health following the injury, a minority, but still considerable proportion (~25 %), reports chronic or increasing levels of distress and low quality of life (Bonanno, Kennedy, Galatzer-Levy, Lude, & Elfström, 2012). On the one hand, these numbers are an impressive testimonial for the resilience that human beings show following traumatic events. On the other hand, these numbers should not be taken as underestimation of the considerable life changes and turmoil that persons with SCI may experience.

Meaning and the process of meaning-making have received substantial attention in trauma-related research and may explain the different trajectories following trauma onset. But what exactly is the role of the meaning-making process in the adjustment to SCI? In the next sections, we will provide an overview of the role of several meaning-related domains, using the meaning-making model as a frame of reference (Park, 2010).

The Meaning-Making Model

Inspired by and consolidating common tenets of former theoretical perspectives, including the seminal work of Janoff-Bulman (1992), Taylor (1983), Lazarus and Folkman (1984), Joseph and Linley (2005), and several others, Park proposed the meaning-making model (Fig. 1) to illustrate and describe the adjustment process following trauma (Park, 2010). Within this context, Park defines meaning making as "the restoration of meaning in the context of highly stressful situations" (Park, 2010, p. 257). Within the meaning-making model, several meaning-related domains are differentiated. In the following sections we will briefly introduce these domains using the terms "traumatic," "critical," or "stressful life event" as synonyms. Following the structure and the domains of the meaning-making model, we will then provide an overview on the findings of psychosocial research conducted in the SCI context.

Global Meaning: Beliefs, Goals, and Subjective Feelings

Global meaning captures the general schemata of a given person, representing comparatively stable beliefs and attitudes on how the self and the world work and are. Park suggests three major areas that represent global meaning: (1) beliefs, (2) goals, and (3) subjective feelings. The three areas of global meaning can be seen as

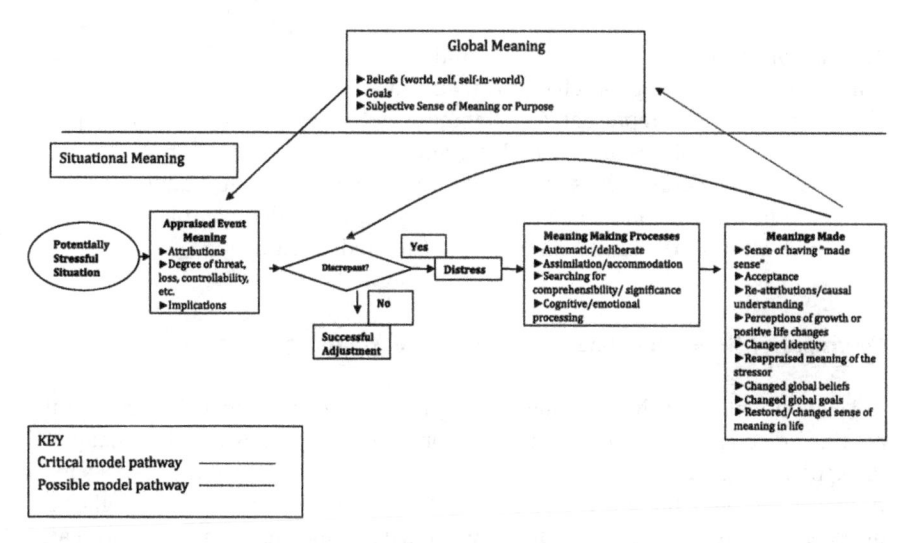

Fig. 1 The meaning-making model (Park, 2010). Copyright © 2010 by the American Psychological Association. Reproduced with permission. The official citation that should be used in referencing this material is Park C. L. (2010) Making sense of the meaning literature: An integrative review of meaning making and its effects on adjustment to stressful life events. *Psychological Bulletin, 136*(2), 257–301. The use of APA information does not imply endorsement by APA

the hardware of a person or the background of an individual's life story, influenced by childhood experiences but also potentially challenged by critical life events, including SCI.

Global beliefs may encompass a person's sense of control, the perceived predictability of events, or views on the self and the world. Hence, similar to filters, general beliefs influence how an individual interprets what happens to and around him or herself. Global goals are hierarchically organized and comprise a person's wishes and aims in life. They may refer to life domains such as relationships, work, power, or knowledge (Park, 2010). The term "subjective feelings" might be misleading, because this category doesn't capture current experienced emotions, but an individual's general sense of meaning or purpose in life. We will henceforth use "sense of purpose" to allude to this area of global meaning.

Situational Meaning: The Context of a Particular Event

The component situational meaning comprises several domains and processes that are triggered by the occurrence of a critical life event. Hence, while global meaning represents "what is already there," situational meaning embodies "what happens" within an individual in the aftermath of trauma.

Appraised Event Meaning

This domain encompasses the appraisal of the stressful situation. Primary appraisals reflect how threatening or challenging a situation is seen by the individual. Secondary appraisals represent the extent to which a person believes to be capable or in possession of resources to deal with the stressful situation (Lazarus & Folkman, 1984). Further types of appraisals are, for example, attributions of blame, the extent to which an individual perceives a situation under control, and the possible implications the situation may have for the individual.

Discrepancy Between Global and Situational Meaning

A key assumption of the meaning-making model is that individuals ascertain the potential discrepancy or fit between the global, previously possessed meaning and the appraised, situational meaning of trauma. The more the implications of a stressful situation contradict previously held global beliefs or goals, i.e., the higher the discrepancy between situational and global meaning, the higher the distress created by the situation. The experienced distress induces efforts to reduce the gap between global and situational meaning and starts the meaning-making process.

Meaning-Making Processes

Park defines meaning-making processes as "the processes in which people engage to reduce the discrepancy" between global and situational meaning (Park, 2010, p. 259). Discrepancy is resolved either by changes in global or situational meaning. Various categorizations have been adopted to describe and differentiate the meaning-making process, including automatic vs. deliberate processes, assimilation vs. accommodation processes, or search for comprehensibility vs. search for significance. The categorizations highlight different specific aspects, but they may overlap in content. But what do they capture?

An example for automatic processes is intrusive thoughts or the avoidance of reminders of the event. Deliberate processes may include coping, such as problem-oriented coping toward the stress-inducing situation. They may further comprise downward and upward comparisons (i.e., comparing the current situation with someone who is worse or better off). In addition, the revision of previously held aspirations has also been suggested as a deliberate process to reduce the discrepancy between situational and global meaning.

Assimilation processes involve changing the meaning of the stressful situation, which facilitates the retention of previously held beliefs, goals, and sense of purpose. Accommodative processes, in contrast, comprise revisions in global meaning following the experience of a traumatic event. Here, an event has consequences on previously held global beliefs, goals, or sense of purpose.

Meaning-making processes may also involve the search for comprehensibility and the search for significance (Janoff-Bulman & McPherson, 1997; Taylor, 1983). Comprehensibility may be captured by the question "Why did it happen?", while significance may be best described with the question "What does it mean for me now?" (Park, 2010).

Meanings Made

Within the meaning-making model, "meanings made" are conceptualized as outcomes or products of the meaning-making process, i.e., "end results or changes derived from attempts to reduce discrepancies or violations between appraised and global meaning" (Park, 2010, p. 260). Again, several forms of meanings made can be identified. A sense of having "made sense" is frequently observed among survivors of a traumatic event. However, the variability in what is understood with "made sense" is considerable, and meanings made may be more accurately conceptualized with other variables. Acceptance of what has happened is an example of a more specific meaning made, although, again, differences may be seen in how and when an individual accepts the stressful situation and its consequences. Meanings made may also comprise a reappraised meaning or causal understanding of the traumatic event or a changed identity, i.e., the integration of the event into the identity and belief system. Perceptions of positive changes following a traumatic event, termed posttraumatic growth (PTG), represent one of the most popular conceptualizations of meanings made. Accounts of PTG allude to different sub-domains, such as an increased appreciation of life with changing values and life perspectives, enhanced relationships, or a feeling of greater personal strength (Joseph, 2013; Tedeschi & Calhoun, 2004). Commonly used synonyms for PTG are, for example, benefit finding (Affleck & Tennen, 1996) or stress-related growth (Park, Cohen, & Murch, 1996).

Indicators of Adjustment

The meaning-making model posits that the resolution of the discrepancy between the global and situational meaning leads to "successful adjustment." The term adjustment will not be further elaborated, but in alignment with common rehabilitation goals, we will mainly focus on indicators of well-being and mental health as indicators of adjustment.

The Meaning-Making Model Applied in SCI: What Do We Know?

How are domains of the meaning-making model associated with adjustment, and what do we know about the meaning-making process following SCI? Hereafter, we will align the overview with the global and situational model components. We will, hence, first focus on aspects related to global meaning; second, describe how affected individuals appraise SCI (appraised event meaning); third, illustrate the findings on the meaning-making process; and finally, discuss meanings made in the aftermath of SCI. Of note, with only few exceptions, research studies did not explicitly refer to the domains included or terms used in the meaning-making model. Rather, we assigned the studies to the domains on the basis of the definitions used in the model.

Global Meaning in SCI: How Is Global Meaning Associated with Adjustment?

Research on global beliefs and attitudes toward the self or the world have received considerable attention, mainly with the focus on how they relate to adjustment. Evidence stems from quantitative research investigating, e.g., locus of control, self-esteem, sense of coherence, or general self-efficacy among individuals with SCI. Systematic literature reviews suggest that higher levels of self-esteem, sense of coherence, or general self-efficacy are consistently associated with better mental health and well-being (Peter, Muller, Cieza, & Geyh, 2012; Post & van Leeuwen, 2012). While examined less extensively, similar positive associations with mental health and well-being were found for higher purpose in life and spirituality (Peter et al., 2012; van Leeuwen, Post, et al., 2012). Purpose in life was even a significant predictor of reduced mortality in a longitudinal study (Krause, Carter, Zhai, & Reed, 2009).

Does the level of self-efficacy, purpose in life, or sense of coherence influence how an individual appraises his or her own injury as posited by the meaning-making model? Only a few studies investigated this aspect, but yield support for this assumption. For example, individuals with high levels of self-efficacy and purpose in life appraised their injury rather as challenge and to lesser extents as loss, leading to better well-being and mental health (e.g. Peter, Muller, Cieza, et al., 2014).

Situational Meaning

Appraised Event Meaning: How Do Affected Individuals Appraise SCI?

A wide range of appraisals have been investigated, showing that individuals appraise their own injury and its consequences differently. But how are these appraisals associated with adjustment? The findings of quantitative studies yield inconsistent results. For example, self-blame and a perceived avoidability of the injury are inconsistently associated with well-being and mental health (van Leeuwen, Kraaijeveld, et al., 2012). Studies have identified significant associations between overwhelming disbelief, fearful despondency, negative perceptions of one's disability, or threat and loss appraisals with lower life satisfaction and mental health (Kennedy, Smithson, et al., 2010; Peter, Muller, Post, et al., 2014). However, these are bivariate associations, and only a few appraisals remain significant predictors of well-being in multivariate analyses (van Leeuwen, Kraaijeveld, Lindeman, & Post, 2012).

Discrepancy Between Global and Situational Meaning

Impressive accounts of how SCI may call into question previously held beliefs and trigger a meaning-making process come from a qualitative study. Carpenter (1994) used the term "transformative learning" to describe a process of critical self-reflection, allowing a "more inclusive, discriminating, and integrative understanding of one's experience" following SCI. The situation "calls a halt to life as previously known and demands attention and a change in the individual's perspective of reality" (Carpenter, 1994, p. 625). This cognitive process is described by a participant of the study as follows:

> I was like a computer with a blank disk and was programmed with a whole set of rules and beliefs, positive and negative stuff, by my parents. Then, when I grew up, I had to take that

and blunder my way through life. It goes right back to our roots, and we sort of unthinkingly accept it and keep perpetuating the same old stuff. Well, the accident happened, and I had to do some major rethinking, because none of that stuff was any help in this situation. (Carpenter, 1994, p. 626)

These statements reflect a discrepancy between global and situational meaning, as globally held beliefs were not considered helpful to master the new life situation. The study participant mentioned how decisive the early years of child- and adulthood are in shaping a person's beliefs. Similarly, Carpenter underlined the role of the sociocultural context, under which the global beliefs had been shaped. She argued that "their meaning perspectives were derived from a society that, it is generally agreed, places great value on youth, vigor, physical attractiveness, employment, and independence […] In such a society, there are powerful stigmas and little esteem associated with persons who lack these characteristics and the capacity for cure" (Carpenter, 1994, p. 625). Not only did the study participant see some global beliefs as irrelevant for his or her own current situation but also as inadequate reproductions of the reality or the world. This started the meaning-making process where previously held global beliefs were questioned.

Meaning-Making Process: How Do Persons Deal with SCI?

Automatic vs. Deliberate Processes. Among the automatic processes, intrusive thoughts have received considerable attention. They have mostly been conceptualized as symptoms of post-traumatic stress disorder, i.e., as sequelae of SCI, but also as long-term indicators of complications in the adjustment process (Kennedy & Duff, 2001; Krause, Saunders, & Newman, 2010). For example, intrusive thoughts were used as a proxy for the severity/impact of disability and related to negative affectivity and worse psychosocial adjustment (Martz, Livneh, Priebe, Wuermser, & Ottomanelli, 2005).

Research on deliberate processes revealed that individuals with SCI rely on both downward and upward comparisons. Downward comparisons use persons as a point of reference who are in the same or worse situation. These comparisons can motivate: "They were very important actually and I did feel incredibly lucky. Seeing other people, that's, it's probably a millimeter against me being in the same position. Um and the more I realized that I could improve and others couldn't, it made me push myself more" (Perrier, Smith, & Latimer-Cheung, 2013, p. 2089). It is true that a number of persons with SCI also express gaining motivation by upward comparison. A woman living with SCI for several years "expressed that she was thankful for seeing the possibility of functioning well, by meeting a volunteer who was experiencing SCI who demonstrated her independence by driving her car and working effectively for people with similar illnesses" (Chun & Lee, 2008, p. 885). Nonetheless, not everyone believes it is helpful to compare oneself with others: "I mean, there are people out there who have more than you and yet are worse off than you, I mean, they just give up. I think it's best to go your own way and try not to compare yourself with others" (Carpenter, 1994, p. 622).

Social comparisons have received little attention in quantitative research (van Leeuwen, Kraaijeveld, et al., 2012). A study found strong associations between both upward contrasts (reacting negatively when seeing others who are better off) and downward identification (identifying with persons who are worse off) with higher levels of depression. In contrast, the complementary views, i.e., downward contrasts and upward identification, were not associated with mental health of the study participants (Buunk, Zurriaga, & Gonzalez, 2006).

Considerable efforts have been directed toward the understanding of coping and its effect on adjustment, however, yielding inconsistent findings. A recent systematic literature review revealed inconsistent associations between passive and emotion-focused coping on one side and mental health and well-being on the other side (van Leeuwen, Kraaijeveld, et al., 2012). Similarly, contrary to expectations, an active, problem-focused coping style is not associated with well-being (van Leeuwen, Kraaijeveld, et al., 2012). Different higher-order coping categorizations have been used. For example, Park suggested positive reappraisal and spiritual coping as meaning-making coping strategies (Folkman, 1997; Park, 2010). Yet, positive reappraisals are typically allocated to the problem-focused coping categorization. Overall, current findings put a question mark on the role and impact of coping. However, the allocation of specific coping strategies to higher-order coping categories may attenuate the positive effect of the specific coping strategies, such as acceptance (van Leeuwen, Kraaijeveld, et al., 2012).

In contrast to the associations with commonly assessed adjustment indicators, meaning-making-related coping strategies, active coping as well as religious or spiritual coping, have been consistently positively associated with greater PTG. The overall findings suggest that after an initial phase in which avoidant coping may be helpful to absorb the initial shock, problem-oriented coping strategies play an important role in the meaning-making process leading to PTG (Elfström, Kreuter, Rydén, Persson, & Sullivan, 2002; McMillen & Cook, 2003; Pollard & Kennedy, 2007).

Assimilation vs. Accommodation Processes. Very few studies explicitly allude to assimilation or accommodation processes after SCI. The authors of a Dutch study operationalized assimilative coping with tenacious goal pursuit, while flexible goal adjustment represented the revision of personal preferences and goals and hence accommodative coping (van Lankveld, van Diemen, & van Nes, 2011). The study showed that persons with flexible goals, i.e., adjusting their preferences and goals after SCI, reported better mental health. No association with mental health was found for assimilative coping.

Searching for Comprehensibility vs. Significance. The search for comprehensibility and for significance of an injury involves questions such as "why did it happen" or "what does this mean for my life now" (Taylor, 1983). Illustrations for the individual's search can be found in qualitative studies (Hammell, 2007). For example, a theme circles around the question of survival and whether the injury represents a miracle, luck, or just coincidence: "Is this a coincidence or is this a signal or should I ... eh stop to live my good life ... because maybe I haven't gone deep enough into it (life) [...] or is it only a coincidence ... [...] Well, actually I really believe that there are some signals here ... I must say so, because I find it conspicuous that this should happen, and … in a way one could say that I think I had reached a point of too much fun and games and the good life" (Lohne, 2009, p. 72).

Meanings Made: What Changes Do Individuals Perceive After SCI?

Immediately following spinal cord injury, a whole series of "I am's," such as "I am tall," "I am an athlete," or "I am a fisherman," are no longer relevant, and a loss or threat of identity is experienced (Carpenter, 1994, p. 622). Individuals may struggle with their new identity after disability onset: "You lose that sense of 'Who am I? Is this the way I have to lead my life now?'" (Levins, Redenbach, & Dyck, 2004, p. 501). Hence, restoring the self and identity can be an important but difficult journey. By engaging in everyday activities, individuals may have opportunities to reconstruct their identity, regain self-esteem, and develop new habits by themselves but also with support from others (Isaksson & Prellwitz, 2010).

However, not all persons get their sense of identity back or find a revised, satisfying self-perception. In a case study, the life story of a young man was explored. His body and its performance had always been at the center of his life, enabling him to outperform others in sports or do tough, demanding jobs. SCI completely left him alone, in despair, years after the injury. He perceived his body as "lost," not belonging to him, and said that life "stopped the day" the rugby accident happened (Smith & Sparkes, 2008, p. 222).

SCI does not necessarily impact an individual's life goals. A qualitative study showed that having a productive and full life remained the main goal of the affected persons (DeSanto-Madeya, 2006). A way back to normality has frequently been identified as a main goal, with vocational reintegration as a symbol for what normality is about. Hence, being a member of a workforce is not a main goal due to financial aspects, but serves the purpose of leading a normal life. Many individuals talk about "resuming employment as inner (visible to self) and outer (visible to others) sign of returning to 'normal' life after SCI" (Hay-Smith, Dickson, Nunnerley, & Anne Sinnott, 2013, p. 1440). Employment may not be the highest or most urgent priority after SCI but rather "the final piece of the puzzle to fit in" or "the icing on the cake" (Hay-Smith et al., 2013, p. 1440).

Changes in how individuals appraise SCI, i.e., reappraisals of cause or consequences of SCI, have been observed. Some persons state that the injury happened for a reason and put their faith to God. They believed that their purpose on earth was not over yet, that they have a task to fulfill, and that there is a reason why the injury happened (DeSanto-Madeya, 2006). A research team led by Paul Kennedy prospectively investigated whether appraisals change in the course of first rehabilitation and then later in the community setting. Across the sample, there was a significant change in "threat" and "loss" appraisals from 6 to 12 weeks after injury, but no further change 1 year and 2 years post-injury, indicating that changes arise early after injury (Kennedy, Lude, Elfstrom, & Smithson, 2010, 2012). However, these findings are based on sample-based mean values and hence do not necessarily reflect changes within an individual.

The development of new values, beliefs, and perspectives was a topic frequently identified in qualitative studies (Hammell, 2007). The injury led to the re-estimation of life itself and the person's values and priorities in life. For example, individuals with SCI reported that they were now aware that they were not invincible. They perceived themselves as more vulnerable and indicated taking more precautionary steps in day-to-day life (McColl et al., 2000a, 2000b).

PTG, i.e., positive psychological changes, are frequently perceived in the aftermath of traumatic events, with an estimated range between 30 and 70 percent of the affected individuals (Linley & Joseph, 2004). Within SCI, McMillen and Cook (2003) declared that 79% of individuals experienced that some things changed for the better after their injury. In what life domains do individuals with SCI perceive PTG? Chun and Lee (2008) identified three salient themes: the experience of meaningful family relationships, the experience of meaningful engagement, and a greater appreciation of life. A more nuanced analysis of positive changes identified 13 PTG themes, with greater appreciation of life and of personal relationships, as well as changes in their personality as the most prevalent positive changes following SCI (Kennedy, Lude, Elfström, & Cox, 2013). Importantly, several respondents stated that they gained nothing from the experience of an SCI. This demonstrates that experiences of positive changes are not undergone by every individual after SCI.

PTG has typically been measured with retrospective accounts, using instruments such as the Posttraumatic Growth Inventory (Tedeschi & Calhoun, 1996). The retrospective approach has been criticized due to its potential biased coverage and difficulty to appreciate past states of being. Longitudinal cohort studies involving repeating assessments of current states are one solution to such criticism. An Australian cohort study showed that individuals with SCI reported lower levels of self-esteem than a control group and revealed that these lower levels remained stable over 2 years post-injury. The same study showed that locus of control changed significantly during clinical rehabilitation, but not in the 2 years following rehabilitation discharge (Craig, Hancock, & Chang, 1994). A recent Dutch study examined the longitudinal development of psychological factors, including self-efficacy, mastery, optimism, and purpose in life. Individuals reported these aspects 4 weeks after admission to clinical rehabilitation, prior to rehabilitation discharge, and at least half a year after discharge. Changes within persons in self-efficacy, mastery, optimism, and purpose in life were observed over time and partly associated with better mental health (van Leeuwen, Edelaar-Peeters, Peter, Stiggelbout, & Post, 2015). Overall, the longitudinal studies indicate that beliefs and goals can change following SCI. However, there are no pre-SCI assessments, and hence it cannot be estimated whether a positive change reflects a trend to the previous level (i.e., resilience) or an even higher state (i.e., PTG).

Open Issues in the Study of Meaning Making in the Aftermath of SCI

Assessment of the Hypothesized Discrepancy Between Global and Situational Meaning

The perceived discrepancy is expressed in personal accounts of individuals affected by SCI, for example, with questions such as "Who am I? Is this the way I have to lead my life now?" (Levins et al., 2004, p. 501). However, the discrepancy has not been investigated with standardized questionnaires. This is surprising, because the amount of shattered schemata and beliefs are viewed as prerequisites for the development of PTG (Janoff-Bulman, 2006), a topic that has received considerable attention in SCI research. Yet, in some studies discrepancy was assessed indirectly. For example, in an intriguing study using mixed methods, individuals with SCI expressed a considerable degree of life change caused by SCI. This degree of life change was used as operationalization of the discrepancy that interferes with subsequent adjustment. An increase in psychological well-being was related to less life change, implying that those who reported greater psychological adjustment viewed their life as more continuous following the SCI, regardless of injury severity (deRoon-Cassini, de St Aubin, Valvano, Hastings, & Brasel, 2013). Longitudinal, quantitative studies may complement and enable more population-based estimations regarding the perceived discrepancy and its progress over time. Measures such as the Core Beliefs Inventory could be used to assess the disruption of global meaning after trauma onset (Cann et al., 2010).

Do "Meanings Made" Lead to Good Adjustment?

The question of the adaptive significance of meanings made has received considerable attention, especially in relation to PTG. Even though the term "growth" has a positive connotation, there are good reasons to question it and two perspectives have emerged. Some theorists see PTG as adaptive per definition, independently whether they are thought to represent "positive illusions" (e.g., Taylor, 1988; Taylor & Brown, 1994) or real changes which leave individuals with positive meaning in life (e.g., Joseph & Linley, 2005; Tedeschi & Calhoun, 2004). Others doubt that PTG is generally adaptive and differentiate the effect of real and illusory PTG, as described in the "Janus face model of self-perceived growth" (Zoellner & Maercker, 2006, p. 639). In this model, real changes are expected to be related to better mental health. In contrast, illusory perceptions may help to bear the immediate emotional response to trauma in the short-term but may have negative impacts on adjustment in the long run.

Do research findings reveal evidence for the adaptive significance of PTG? Literature reviews disclose mixed findings in different trauma populations regarding the relationship of PTG with adjustment (e.g., Barskova & Oesterreich, 2009;

Zoellner & Maercker, 2006). SCI research mirrors these inconsistent findings. For example, three cross-sectional studies examined the relation of perceived PTG with levels of depression. Whereas two of them found no significant association (Kalpakjian et al., 2014; McMillen & Cook, 2003), the third study reported a significant negative correlation (Min et al., 2014). Taken together, these findings show weak support for the assumption of a beneficial impact of perceived PTG on adjustment after SCI.

Do All Individuals Search for a Meaning, and Is the Search for a Meaning a Prerequisite for Finding Meaning and Good Adjustment?

The effects of searching for meaning on finding meaning and their relationships with mental health and well-being in individuals with SCI were examined in an intriguing longitudinal study (Davis & Novoa, 2013). The study showed that people who searched more frequently for meaning were more likely to report finding meaning. However, finding meaning did not decrease or terminate the search for meaning. This may suggest that people constantly scrutinize their life situation and the meaning that they have given to SCI onset. Interestingly, individuals who found some meaning tended to show improvements in adjustment over time, and those who reported more frequent searching tended to report declining adjustment over the course of time. When searching was most frequent, people tended to experience more depressive symptoms; when people reported greater meaning, they tended to report fewer depressive symptoms (Davis & Novoa, 2013). Thus, searching for meaning may also be viewed as missing meaning or the inability to accept the disability.

Strikingly, in the same study, a considerable proportion of the study participants did not make efforts to search for meaning, but were adjusting well to SCI, indicating that searching for meaning seemed frequently occurring, but not "necessary" for the adjustment process. It could be hypothesized that these people already possess a worldview or beliefs that allow for unpredictable events to happen, leading only to a limited perceived discrepancy between global and situational meaning. Alternatively, the assumption of the meaning-making model may not be correct insofar as all persons respond to SCI onset with a meaning-making process. Indeed, not all theorists consider meaning making as a necessary or sufficient precondition for successful adjustment to trauma (e.g., Bonanno, Papa, Lalande, Zhang, & Noll, 2005).

In Davis and Novoa's (2013) study, searching for meaning was not significantly associated with greater perceived growth, suggesting that actively searching for meaning is not a prerequisite for growth. It is worth noting that perceptions of growth were stable, both in terms of relative rank and in terms of mean levels (Davis & Novoa, 2013). Similarly, PTG sample means did not change significantly from 12 weeks to 1 or 2 years post-injury (Kennedy et al., 2012). These findings may be the consequence of PTG measures being insensitive to change. However, they may also indicate that PTG is established early after injury and remains considerably stable over time, which questions whether meanings made result from a long meaning-making process.

Where Is the Social Environment?

Considerable evidence has been gathered for the role and impact of global and situational meaning in the aftermath of SCI in relation to well-being or mental health. However, the meaning-making model falls short in depicting how meaning making and related processes are supported, inhibited, or facilitated by the social environment. For example, social support has positive effects on physical and mental health in individuals with SCI (Muller, Peter, Cieza, & Geyh, 2012). The support of family or friends can help an affected individual to regain a positive outlook, redefine goals, or give room for distractions in the initial period after disability onset. The availability and quality of social support can also build the basis for the adequate use of coping strategies. In one study, coping effectiveness training was compared with a supportive group therapy in a randomized controlled trial. Both intervention arms improved mental health, but no difference between the two interventions was found (Duchnick, Letsch, & Curtiss, 2009). Overall, representing the background of every individual and shaping his or her global beliefs, the role of the social environment needs clarification.

The Intervention Perspective: What Works and What Could Work?

An SCI is characterized by the occurrence of a wide range of consequences, and affected individuals may experience different issues or stressors as most urgent or upsetting. Hence, different techniques reflecting the wide range of possible issues and emerging topics are adopted by the health professionals to support these individuals. Substantial differences exist between the organizational structure and the therapeutic offers of the rehabilitation clinics, even within one country. The work of mental health professionals is not necessarily an integral part of the rehabilitation process of all affected individuals, i.e., not all individuals welcome (or have) the possibility to speak to a mental health professional.

A primary objective of psychosocial interventions, such as cognitive-behavioral therapy (CBT) or coping effectiveness training, is the enhancement of mental health and quality of life (Post & van Leeuwen, 2012). The main target of CBT is cognitions that result from long-standing beliefs and assumptions about the self and the world and that are preventing improvements in terms of mental health (Hunot et al., 2013). Following the assumptions of CBT, changing the negative cognitions that are aroused by an event (situational meaning) leads to better emotional responses. CBT can also comprise relaxation techniques or pleasurable activities.

Recent systematic literature reviews and meta-analyses suggest a positive impact of CBT on mental health and quality of life of individuals with SCI (Dorstyn, Mathias, & Denson, 2011; Mehta et al., 2011; Perkes, Bowman, & Penkala, 2014). These reviews, however, have also identified several knowledge gaps. For example, evidence shows a positive effect of CBT on mental health in the short term, but long-term effects have hardly been examined (Dorstyn et al., 2011). Also, in order to identify which specific CBT components may be particularly beneficial, further testing is needed (Mehta et al., 2011; Perkes et al., 2014). CBT was only effective in individuals with severe levels of distress in one study, suggesting that a targeted approach may be appropriate (Craig, Hancock, Chang, & Dickson, 1998). Overall, these findings indicate that other interventions may be used, alone or in addition to CBT or coping interventions, to improve the lived experience of the individuals with SCI. Nonetheless, because of the methodological limitations, efficacy studies with larger sample sizes should be conducted to improve the state of evidence (Perkes et al., 2014).

Other interventions aimed to restore beliefs directly related to consequences of SCI (situational meaning), such as self-efficacy for active living, or global beliefs (global meaning), such as general self-efficacy or self-esteem (Arbour-Nicitopoulos, Ginis, & Latimer, 2009; Kennedy, Taylor, & Hindson, 2006; Latimer, Ginis, & Arbour, 2006; Rose, Piatt, Zahl, & Kim, 2008; Zahl, Compton, Kim, & Rosenbluth, 2008). Interventions successfully strengthening self-efficacy of individuals with SCI comprised physical activity, sports, or active living programs or consisted of a multimodal wellness workshop intervention (Kennedy et al., 2006; Latimer et al., 2006). CBT or an active living workshop did not successfully restore self-esteem. However, these studies used small sample sizes, consisting of only a few persons with low self-esteem levels (Craig, Hancock, Dickson, & Chang, 1997; Zahl et al., 2008). Overall, multimodal interventions targeting self-efficacy yielded promising findings, but the overall evidence on the efficacy of such treatments is still weak.

What could we learn from other approaches adopted in other populations? Several psychotherapeutic approaches, such as so-called "third wave" behavior therapies (Hayes, 2004), have not been tested in the SCI population, but show promising results for the treatment of depression in comparison to other psychological therapies (Hunot et al., 2013; Ruiz, 2012). One of these therapies is acceptance and commitment therapy (ACT). Rather than changing cognitions, the primary aim of ACT is to foster the acceptance of unwanted thoughts and feelings and to target commitment and action toward predefined goals which correspond to an individual's personal values (Sharp, 2012). The specific focus on personal values, the commitment to related goals, and the acceptance of one's experiences may also prove useful in the context of SCI. From the perspective of the meaning-making model, ACT concentrates on global meaning by targeting goals and values. The acceptance of thoughts and feelings, however, is more difficult to allocate. Within the meaning-making model, acceptance is defined as an outcome, i.e., a meaning made. However, in the context of ACT, it may rather represent a strategy to cope with unpleasant thoughts and feelings and hence the meaning-making process.

Similar to ACT, findings also support the effectiveness of mindfulness (Bohlmeijer, Roemer, Cuijpers, & Smit, 2007; Grossman, Niemann, Schmidt, & Walach, 2004) and positive psychology exercises, such as the gratitude letter, for the general population and for persons with psychosocial problems (Bolier et al., 2013). However, the adoption of these interventions for the SCI context is only starting, e.g., in individuals with SCI or other physical disabilities and chronic pain (e.g., Muller et al., 2016). Additional important input with a specific focus on searching and finding meaning comes from research with other populations. For instance, a meaning-centered group psychotherapy approach aiming to increase a sense of meaning in life in people with advanced or terminal cancer showed improvements in quality of life, depression, and hopelessness (Breitbart et al., 2015). The translation of such interventions to the SCI context seems indicated. However, searching for meaning may not be adequate intervention targets for all individuals with SCI, and hence a tailored approach may be advisable (Davis & Novoa, 2013).

Given the outlined state of evidence both for the SCI context and beyond, what should we take into consideration when planning interventions for individuals with SCI? Current evidence suggests that a sole focus on components of situational meaning, such as appraisals, or meaning-making processes, such as coping, may not sufficiently support individuals with SCI. The time point of the intervention may be decisive. The successful coping effectiveness training was conducted with inpatients, and the multimodal interventions strengthening self-efficacy were conducted with individuals living in the community. Interventions should be targeted to subgroups, e.g., individuals with low self-esteem, to optimize benefits and to avoid undermining inherent resilience. Correspondingly, facilitating the search for meaning may prove useful for some individuals, but not others. A more extensive approach toward the enhancement of mental health and well-being could include a stronger focus on fostering a sense of purpose and defining and committing to goals which accord to one's own values. A mindful attitude toward the self, the appraised meaning of SCI, and the meaning-making process may enable an individual to regain pre-event levels of well-being.

Future Research on Meaning After SCI: What Do We (Not) Know?

The literature on meaning and the meaning-making process following SCI is broad but fragmented. Specific aspects of the lived experience of SCI have been examined, but frequently without incorporating the investigated research question into the larger meaning-making framework or other adjustment models (see Livneh & Martz, 2012). The main strength of the meaning-making model lies in its emphasis on meaning making as a key aspect of the adjustment process following trauma, the comprehensive enumeration of cognitive and emotional processes, and its testable assumptions. Yet, the conceptualization of the model domains is challenging and needs clarification. For example, reappraisal coping was conceptualized as part of the meaning-making process, but the reappraisal of one's life situation after SCI was seen as a meaning made. Explicit references to specific models or model domains are indicated and could help to put single-study findings into a larger perspective (Davis & Novoa, 2013; deRoon-Cassini et al., 2013).

Global meaning: Considerable support has been found for the role of global beliefs, goals, and a sense of purpose in terms of adjustment. Less is known regarding the proposed impact of global meaning on different domains of situational meaning, such as the appraisal of trauma. Further, changes in global beliefs, goals, or sense of purpose have been retrospectively perceived, but longitudinal prospective data are needed to strengthen the overall evidence.

Discrepancy between situational and global meaning as a cause of distress: This key assumption of the meaning-making model has received little attention. Anecdotal evidence exists in the form of personal statements of affected individuals, but a quantitative approach to investigate this issue has hardly been adopted.

Meaning-making process: Both qualitative and quantitative studies have revealed evidence of the role of appraisals, including intrusive thoughts or down- and upward comparisons, and coping. However, findings are inconsistent and multivariate analyses frequently do not confirm the bivariate associations between appraisals and coping with various indicators of adjustment. Hence, the role of process variables within the SCI adjustment process has yet to be elucidated. In addition, challenges remain in the conceptualization of specific variables, especially coping.

Relevance of searching and finding meaning for the SCI adjustment process: Although both searching and finding meaning following SCI onset are key factors of the meaning-making model, evidence suggests that (1) some people do not search for meaning but adjust well to SCI and (2) finding meaning, or meanings made such as PTG, is not consistently associated with better well-being or mental health. Hence, searching and finding meaning may not be adequate intervention targets for all individuals with SCI (Davis & Novoa, 2013).

Key Takeaways

- Evidence of the associations between the various domains of the meaning-making model and adjustment after SCI is broad and reasonably strong. The key assumption of the model- the greater the discrepancy between situational and global meaning, the greater the distress- has received little attention in scientific research.
- Not everyone searches for meaning, and some individuals with SCI are doing well without searching for meaning. Hence, the search for meaning should not necessarily be stimulated in all individuals. A targeted approach is needed.
- In general, evidence of the effectiveness of psychosocial interventions aiming to foster mental health in individuals with SCI is weak and fragmented. Promising results have been shown for multimodal interventions strengthening self-efficacy.

CBT has positive effects on mental health in the short-term, but little attention has been paid to the examination of long-term effects.
- Considering the promising findings observed in other populations, third wave CBT, ACT, mindfulness, and positive psychology interventions may also prove useful in improving adjustment to SCI.

References

Affleck, G., & Tennen, H. (1996). Construing benefits from adversity: Adaptational significance and dispositional underpinnings. *Journal of Personality, 64*(4), 899–922.

Arbour-Nicitopoulos, K. P., Ginis, K. A., & Latimer, A. E. (2009). Planning, leisure-time physical activity, and coping self-efficacy in persons with spinal cord injury: A randomized controlled trial. *Archives of Physical Medicine and Rehabilitation, 90*(12), 2003–2011.

Barskova, T., & Oesterreich, R. (2009). Post-traumatic growth in people living with a serious medical condition and its relations to physical and mental health: A systematic review. *Disability and Rehabilitation, 31*(21), 1709–1733.

Bohlmeijer, E., Roemer, M., Cuijpers, P., & Smit, F. (2007). The effects of reminiscence on psychological well-being in older adults: A meta-analysis. *Aging & Mental Health, 11*, 291–300.

Bolier, L., Haverman, M., Westerhof, G. J., Riper, H., Smit, F., & Bohlmeijer, E. (2013). Positive psychology interventions: A meta-analysis of randomized controlled studies. *BMC Public Health, 13*, 119–139.

Bonanno, G. A., Kennedy, P., Galatzer-Levy, I. R., Lude, P., & Elfström, M. L. (2012). Trajectories of resilience, depression, and anxiety following spinal cord injury. *Rehabilitation Psychology, 57*(3), 236–247.

Bonanno, G. A., Papa, A., Lalande, K., Zhang, N., & Noll, J. G. (2005). Grief processing and deliberate grief avoidance: A prospective comparison of bereaved spouses and parents in the United States and the People's Republic of China. *Journal of Consulting and Clinical Psychology, 73*(1), 86–98.

Breitbart, W., Rosenfeld, B., Pessin, H., Applebaum, A., Kulikowski, J., & Lichtenthal, W. G. (2015). Meaning-centered group psychotherapy: An effective intervention for improving psychological well-being in patients with advanced cancer. *Journal of Clinical Oncology, 33*(7), 749–754.

Buunk, A., Zurriaga, R., & Gonzalez, P. (2006). Social comparison, coping and depression in people with spinal cord injury. *Psychology & Health, 21*, 791–807.

Cann, A., Calhoun, L. G., Tedeschi, R. G., Kilmer, R. P., Gil-Rivas, V., Vishnevsky, T., & Danhauer, S. C. (2010). The Core Beliefs Inventory: A brief measure of disruption in the assumptive world. *Anxiety, Stress, and Coping, 23*(1), 19–34.

Carpenter, C. (1994). The experience of spinal cord injury: The individual's perspective--Implications for rehabilitation practice. *Physical Therapy, 74*(7), 614–628.

Chun, S., & Lee, Y. (2008). The experience of posttraumatic growth for people with spinal cord injury. *Qualitative Health Research, 18*(7), 877–890.

Craig, A. R., Hancock, K., Chang, E., & Dickson, H. (1998). Immunizing against depression and anxiety after spinal cord injury. *Archives of Physical Medicine and Rehabilitation, 79*(4), 375–377.

Craig, A. R., Hancock, K., Dickson, H., & Chang, E. (1997). Long-term psychological outcomes in spinal cord injured persons: Results of a controlled trial using cognitive behavior therapy. *Archives of Physical Medicine and Rehabilitation, 78*, 33–38.

Craig, A. R., Hancock, K., & Chang, E. (1994). The influence of spinal cord injury on coping styles and self-perceptions two years after the injury. *The Australian and New Zealand Journal of Psychiatry, 28*(2), 307–312.

Craig, A., Tran, Y., & Middleton, J. (2009). Psychological morbidity and spinal cord injury: A systematic review. *Spinal Cord, 47*(2), 108–114.

Davis, C. G., & Novoa, D. C. (2013). Meaning-making following spinal cord injury: Individual differences and within-person change. *Rehabilitation Psychology, 58*(2), 166–177.

deRoon-Cassini, T. A., de St Aubin, E., Valvano, A. K., Hastings, J., & Brasel, K. J. (2013). Meaning-making appraisals relevant to adjustment for veterans with spinal cord injury. *Psychological Services, 10*(2), 186–193.

DeSanto-Madeya, S. (2006). The meaning of living with spinal cord injury 5 to 10 years after the injury. *Western Journal of Nursing Research, 28*(3), 265–289.

Dorstyn, D., Mathias, J., & Denson, L. (2011). Efficacy of cognitive behavior therapy for the management of psychological outcomes following spinal cord injury: A meta-analysis. *Journal of Health Psychology, 16*(2), 374–391.

Duchnick, J., Letsch, E. A., & Curtiss, G. (2009). Coping effectiveness training during acute rehabilitation of spinal cord injury/dysfunction: A randomized clinical trial. *Rehabilitation Psychology, 54*, 123–132.

Elfström, M. L., Kreuter, M., Rydén, A., Persson, L.-O., & Sullivan, M. (2002). Effects of coping on psychological outcome when controlling for background variables: A study of traumatically spinal cord lesioned persons. *Spinal Cord, 40*(8), 408–415.

Folkman, S. (1997). Positive psychological states and coping with severe stress. *Social Science & Medicine, 45*, 1207–1221.

Grossman, P., Niemann, L., Schmidt, S., & Walach, H. (2004). Mindfulness-based stress reduction and health benefits: A meta-analysis. *Journal of Psychosomatic Research, 57*, 35–43.

Hammell, K. W. (2007). Quality of life after spinal cord injury: A meta-synthesis of qualitative findings. *Spinal Cord, 45*(2), 124–139.

Hayes, S. C. (2004). Acceptance and commitment therapy, relational frame theory, and the third wave of behavior therapy. *Behavior Therapy, 35*, 639–665.

Hay-Smith, E. J., Dickson, B., Nunnerley, J., & Anne Sinnott, K. (2013). "The final piece of the puzzle to fit in": An interpretative phenomenological analysis of the return to employment in New Zealand after spinal cord injury. *Disability and Rehabilitation, 35*(17), 1436–1446.

Hunot, V., Moore, T. H., Caldwell, D. M., Furukawa, T. A., Davies, P., Jones, H., ... Churchill, R. (2013). 'Third wave' cognitive and behavioural therapies versus other psychological therapies for depression. *The Cochrane Database of Systematic Reviews, (10)*, CD008704.

Isaksson, G., & Prellwitz, M. (2010). One woman's story about her everyday life after a spinal cord injury. *Disability and Rehabilitation, 32*(16), 1376–1386.

Janoff-Bulman, R. (1992). *Shattered assumptions: Towards a new psychology of trauma*. New York, NY: Free Press.

Janoff-Bulman, R. (2006). Schema-change perspectives on posttraumatic growth. In L. G. Calhoun & R. G. Tedeschi (Eds.), *Handbook of posttraumatic growth - Research and practice* (pp. 81–99). Mahwah, NJ: Lawrence Erlbaum Associates.

Janoff-Bulman, R., & McPherson, F. C. (1997). The impact of trauma on meaning: From meaningless world to meaningful life. In M. J. Power & C. R. Brewin (Eds.), *Transformation of meaning in psychological therapies: Integrating theory and practice* (pp. 91–106). New York, NY: John Wiley & Sons.

Joseph, S. (2013). *What doesn't kill us - The new psychology of posttraumatic growth*. New York, NY: Basic Books.

Joseph, S., & Linley, P. A. (2005). Positive adjustment to threatening events: An organismic valuing theory of growth through adversity. *Review of General Psychology, 9*(3), 262–280.

Kalpakjian, C. Z., McCullumsmith, C. B., Fann, J. R., Richards, J. S., Stoelb, B. L., Heinemann, A. W., & Bombardier, C. H. (2014). Post-traumatic growth following spinal cord injury. *The Journal of Spinal Cord Medicine, 37*(2), 218–225.

Kennedy, P., & Duff, J. (2001). Post traumatic stress disorder and spinal cord injuries. *Spinal Cord, 39*(1), 1–10.

Kennedy, P., Lude, P., Elfström, M. L., & Cox, A. (2013). Perceptions of gain following spinal cord injury: A qualitative analysis. *Topics in Spinal Cord Injury Rehabilitation, 19*(3), 202–210.

Kennedy, P., Lude, P., Elfstrom, M. L., & Smithson, E. (2010). Cognitive appraisals, coping and quality of life outcomes: A multi-centre study of spinal cord injury rehabilitation. *Spinal Cord, 48*(10), 762–769.

Kennedy, P., Lude, P., Elfstrom, M. L., & Smithson, E. (2012). Appraisals, coping and adjustment pre and post SCI rehabilitation: A 2-year follow-up study. *Spinal Cord, 50*(2), 112–118.

Kennedy, P., Smithson, E., McClelland, M., Short, D., Royle, J., & Wilson, C. (2010). Life satisfaction, appraisals and functional outcomes in spinal cord-injured people living in the community. *Spinal Cord, 48*(2), 144–148.

Kennedy, P., Taylor, N., & Hindson, L. (2006). A pilot investigation of a psychosocial activity course for people with spinal cord injuries. *Psychology, Health & Medicine, 11*(1), 91–99.

Kirshblum, S., Campagnolo, D. I., & DeLisa, J. A. (2002). *Spinal cord medicine*. Philadelphia, PA: Lippincott Williams & Wilkins.

Krause, J. S., Carter, R., Zhai, Y., & Reed, K. (2009). Psychologic factors and risk of mortality after spinal cord injury. *Archives of Physical Medicine and Rehabilitation, 90*(4), 628–633.

Krause, J. S., Saunders, L. L., & Newman, S. (2010). Posttraumatic stress disorder and spinal cord injury. *Archives of Physical Medicine and Rehabilitation, 91*(8), 1182–1187.

Latimer, A. E., Ginis, K. A. M., & Arbour, K. P. (2006). The efficacy of an implementation intention intervention for promoting physical activity among individuals with spinal cord injury: A randomized controlled trial. *Rehabilitation Psychology, 51*, 273–280.

Lazarus, R. S., & Folkman, S. (1984). *Stress, appraisal, and coping*. New York, NY: Springer Publishing.

Levins, S. M., Redenbach, D. M., & Dyck, I. (2004). Individual and societal influences on participation in physical activity following spinal cord injury: A qualitative study. *Physical Therapy, 84*(6), 496–509.

Lin, V. W., Cardenas, D., Bono, C. M., Frost, F. S., Hammond, M. C., Lindblom, L. B., ... Woolsey, R. M. (2010). *Spinal cord medicine: Principles and practice* (2nd ed.). New York, NY: Demos Medical Publishing.

Linley, P. A., & Joseph, S. (2004). Positive change following trauma and adversity: A review. *Journal of Traumatic Stress, 17*(1), 11–21.

Livneh, H., & Martz, E. (2012). Adjustment to chronic illness and disability: Theoretical perspectives, empirical findings, and unresolved issues. In P. Kennedy (Ed.), *The Oxford handbook of rehabilitation psychology* (pp. 47–87). New York, NY: Oxford University Press.

Lohne, V. (2009). The incomprehensible injury--Interpretations of patients' narratives concerning experiences with an acute and dramatic spinal cord injury. *Scandinavian Journal of Caring Sciences, 23*(1), 67–75.

Martz, E., Livneh, H., Priebe, M., Wuermser, L. A., & Ottomanelli, L. (2005). Predictors of psychosocial adaptation among people with spinal cord injury or disorder. *Archives of Physical Medicine and Rehabilitation, 86*(6), 1182–1192.

McColl, M. A., Bickenbach, J., Johnston, J., Nishihama, S., Schumaker, M., Smith, K., ... Yealland, B. (2000a). Changes in spiritual beliefs after traumatic disability. *Archives of Physical Medicine and Rehabilitation, 81*(6), 817–823.

McColl, M. A., Bickenbach, J., Johnston, J., Nishihama, S., Schumaker, M., Smith, K., ... Yealland, B. (2000b). Spiritual issues associated with traumatic-onset disability. *Disability and Rehabilitation, 22*(12), 555–564.

McMillen, J. C., & Cook, C. L. (2003). The positive by-products of spinal cord injury and their correlates. *Rehabilitation Psychology, 48*(2), 77–85.

Mehta, S., Orenczuk, S., Hansen, K. T., Aubut, J. A., Hitzig, S. L., Legassic, M., & Teasell, R. W. (2011). An evidence-based review of the effectiveness of cognitive behavioral therapy for psychosocial issues post-spinal cord injury. *Rehabilitation Psychology, 56*(1), 15–25.

Min, J. -A., Lee, C. -U., Hwang, S. -I., Shin, J. -I., Lee, B. -S., Han, S. -H., ... Chae, J. -H. (2014). The moderation of resilience on the negative effect of pain on depression and post-traumatic growth in individuals with spinal cord injury. *Disability and Rehabilitation, 36*(14), 1196–1202.

Muller, R., Gertz, K. J., Molton, I. R., Terrill, A. L., Bombardier, C. H., Ehde, D. M., & Jensen, M. P. (2016). Effects of a tailored positive psychology intervention on well-being and pain in individuals with chronic pain and a physical disability: A feasibility trial. *The Clinical Journal of Pain, 32*(1), 32–44.

Muller, R., Peter, C., Cieza, A., & Geyh, S. (2012). The role of social support and social skills in people with spinal cord injury--A systematic review of the literature. *Spinal Cord, 50*(2), 94–106.

Park, C. L. (2010). Making sense of the meaning literature: An integrative review of meaning making and its effects on adjustment to stressful life events. *Psychological Bulletin, 136*(2), 257–301.

Park, C. L., Cohen, L. H., & Murch, R. L. (1996). Assessment and prediction of stress-related growth. *Journal of Personality, 64*(1), 71–105.

Perkes, S. J., Bowman, J., & Penkala, S. (2014). Psychological therapies for the management of co-morbid depression following a spinal cord injury: A systematic review. *Journal of Health Psychology, 19*(12), 1597–1612.

Perrier, M. J., Smith, B. M., & Latimer-Cheung, A. E. (2013). Narrative environments and the capacity of disability narratives to motivate leisure-time physical activity among individuals with spinal cord injury. *Disability and Rehabilitation, 35*(24), 2089–2096.

Peter, C., Muller, R., Cieza, A., Post, M. W., van Leeuwen, C. M., Werner, C. S., & Geyh, S. (2014). Modeling life satisfaction in spinal cord injury: The role of psychological resources. *Quality of Life Research, 23*(10), 2693–2705.

Peter, C., Muller, R., Cieza, A., & Geyh, S. (2012). Psychological resources in spinal cord injury: A systematic literature review. *Spinal Cord, 50*(3), 188–201.

Peter, C., Muller, R., Post, M. W., van Leeuwen, C. M., Werner, C. S., & Geyh, S. (2014). Psychological resources, appraisals, and coping and their relationship to participation in spinal cord injury: A path analysis. *Archives of Physical Medicine and Rehabilitation, 95*(9), 1662–1671.

Pollard, C., & Kennedy, P. (2007). A longitudinal analysis of emotional impact, coping strategies and post-traumatic psychological growth following spinal cord injury: A 10-year review. *British Journal of Health Psychology, 12*(3), 347–362.

Post, M. W. M., & van Leeuwen, C. M. C. (2012). Psychosocial issues in spinal cord injury: A review. *Spinal Cord, 50*(5), 382–389.

Rose, A., Piatt, J. A., Zahl, M., & Kim, K. (2008). The effect of a self-efficacy based forum on life satisfaction for individuals with spinal cord injury or disease. *Annual in Therapeutic Recreation, 16*, 49–56.

Ruiz, F. J. (2012). Acceptance and Commitment Therapy versus traditional cognitive behavioral therapy: A systematic review and meta-analysis of current empirical evidence. *International Journal of Psychology & Psychological Therapy, 12*(2), 333–357.

Sharp, K. (2012). A review of acceptance and commitment therapy with anxiety disorders. *International Journal of Psychology & Psychological Therapy, 12*(3), 359–372.

Smith, B., & Sparkes, A. C. (2008). Changing bodies, changing narratives and the consequences of tellability: A case study of becoming disabled through sport. *Sociology of Health & Illness, 30*(2), 217–236.

Taylor, S. E. (1983). Adjustment to threatening events: A theory of cognitive adaptation. *American Psychologist, 38*(11), 1161–1171.

Taylor, S. E. (1988). Illusion and well-being: A social psychological perspective on mental health. *Psychological Bulletin, 103*(2), 193–210.

Taylor, S. E., & Brown, J. D. (1994). Positive illusions and well-being revisited: Separating fact from fiction. *Psychological Bulletin, 116*(1), 21–27.

Tedeschi, R. G., & Calhoun, L. G. (1996). The Posttraumatic Growth Inventory: Measuring the positive legacy of trauma. *Journal of Traumatic Stress, 9*(3), 455–472.

Tedeschi, R. G., & Calhoun, L. G. (2004). Posttraumatic growth: Conceptual foundations and empirical evidence. *Psychological Inquiry, 15*(1), 1–18.

van Lankveld, W., van Diemen, T., & van Nes, I. (2011). Coping with spinal cord injury: Tenacious goal pursuit and flexible goal adjustment. *Journal of Rehabilitation Medicine, 43*(10), 923–929.

van Leeuwen, C. M. C., Edelaar-Peeters, Y., Peter, C., Stiggelbout, A. M., & Post, M. W. M. (2015). Psychosocial factors and mental health in persons with SCI: An exploration of change or stability. *Journal of Rehabilitation Medicine, 47*(6), 531–537.

van Leeuwen, C. M. C., Kraaijeveld, S., Lindeman, E., & Post, M. W. (2012). Associations between psychological factors and quality of life ratings in persons with spinal cord injury: A systematic review. *Spinal Cord, 50*(3), 174–187.

van Leeuwen, C. M. C., Post, M. W. M., Westers, P., van der Woude, L. H., de Groot, S., Sluis, T., ... Lindeman, E. (2012). Relationships between activities, participation, personal factors, mental health, and life satisfaction in persons with spinal cord injury. *Archives of Physical Medicine and Rehabilitation, 93*(1), 82–89.

World Health Organization. (2013). *International perspectives on spinal cord injury*. Geneva: WHO.

Zahl, M. L., Compton, D. M., Kim, K., & Rosenbluth, J. P. (2008). SCI/D forum to increase active living: The effect of a self-efficacy and self-affirmation based SCI/D forum on active living in adults with spinal cord injury/disease. *SCI Psychosocial Process, 21*, 5–13.

Zoellner, T., & Maercker, A. (2006). Posttraumatic growth in clinical psychology - A critical review and introduction of a two component model. *Clinical Psychology Review, 26*(5), 626–653.

Out, Out, Brief Candle? The Meaning of Meaninglessness

Todd DuBose

Perhaps the most challenging situation in a person's life is to live through, or care for, the experience of meaninglessness, or lived, existential nihilism. Nihilism, as I am using the word in these reflections, is the lived experience of a flat absence of any felt significance or motivation by which to engage life in other than basic functions of endurance—at most. Nihilism is too often reduced to mere depression and "treated," thus often missing the broader and unresolvable existential challenges this state provides for those going through this experience. What does one do (how can one "be," how can one care) when nothing matters?

There are potentially lethal consequences of handling these moments, made all the more sharply edged when one's approach to care is meaning-centric. Nevertheless, I invite us on a perilous but necessary journey to let "meaninglessness" show itself, in its own way, as it is, and explore along the way our potential fears, anxieties, resignations, and hopelessness in doing so. It is often the case that the existential literature views existence as meaninglessness until we make meaning of it, with therapeutic care being a process of helping someone retrieve, find, or create meaning. Even in a meta-analysis (Bergner, 1998) on addressing the therapeutic care of meaninglessness and in the more familiar synopsis of therapeutic interventions with meaninglessness by Irvin Yalom (1980) in his book, *Existential Psychotherapy*, the focus is on correction, curing, healing, altering, and moving beyond meaninglessness. Yalom (1980) is accurate in noting that "meaninglessness is rarely mentioned as a clinical entity because it is generally considered to be a manifestation of some other … clinical syndrome" (p. 449). Not much else has advanced our approach to the topic in substantial ways. The literature suggests we need meaning to thrive, if not merely live, with Viktor Frankl (1985) being the most

---

T. DuBose, Ph.D. (✉)
The Chicago School of Professional Psychology,
325 North Wells, Suite 316, Chicago, IL 60654, USA
e-mail: tdubose@thechicagoschool.edu

well-known proponent of this view. This perspective continues as a status quo in "treating" meaninglessness. In spite of a long-standing thread in existential literature highlighting the inescapable quality of meaninglessness at times in our lives, Michael Allen Fox (2009), in his excellent book, *The Remarkable Existentialists*, synopsizes the task at hand: "existentialism is a concerted attempt to *combat* nihilism and *move beyond* it" (p. 292, italics are mine).

This conviction is all the more shared by the growing literature on positive psychology, where both existential therapy and positive psychology team up to explore the possibility of securing meaning, albeit with existential psychologists looking at causes of meaninglessness and positive psychologists looking at bolstering meaning (Kim, Seto, Davis, & Hicks, 2014). But with any positing of a prescribed way of caring, though, some voice is most often overlooked. I believe this is the case with the experience of meaninglessness and hence this chapter. Meaninglessness, if it *is* noticed, is viewed as the culprit or nemesis that thwarts meaning, a pathogen to correct, extract, cure, avoid, or jettison from our lives *so as to have* a meaningful life. My reflections in this chapter, though, ask us to consider different understandings of meaning and meaninglessness as well as a different kind of therapeutic approach to meaninglessness.

In order to better understand meaninglessness, we need to hold at bay our typical framings and responses to meaninglessness, including our need to fix it, rescue it, and see it as pathological or as an unfortunate and temporary road block on the way to hope and meaning. Containing our presumptions, though, allows us to possibly see that meaninglessness has its own significance. Therapeutic care, from this perspective, then, calls us to let go of, or expand, our understanding of meaningful ways of living to include those ways of living that do *not* have an *arche* (principle, purpose, "oughtness") or *telos* (design, order, direction) (Schurmann, 1987). Said differently, the experience of having not felt purpose or direction or concern or plan for how and if to live is itself a meaningful experience. If we can respect the paradoxical integrity of the meaning of meaninglessness, then perhaps we can dispense with what may be a false dichotomy: meaning versus meaninglessness.

If this false dichotomy is deconstructed, then therapeutic care would avoid slippage into a process of deficit correction yet remain committed to the task of collaboratively understanding and clarifying how one lives out even the meaning of meaninglessness. Put another way, therapeutic care would entail sitting vigil with someone in touch with the experience of meaninglessness—as someone in touch with meaninglessness—which is experienced in various manifestations as *being nothing special*, without intent to pathologize or correct this experience. So, before unpacking this point further and getting to therapeutic care per se, an exploration of many assumptions about meaning may be helpful in understanding how meaninglessness as being nothing special is itself meaningful.

There are many common assumptions about the concept of meaning in philosophical and psychological literature and among the general public's opinions that I believe are misunderstandings of this phenomenon as lived, with the consequence of misunderstanding meaninglessness. I will list these assumptions and then address each one. The first assumption is that meaning is only a positive experience, that is to say, an experience that is inspirational, fulfilling, enhancing, worthy, and enlivening. The second assumption is that meaning is something created, lost, or found. The third assumption is that meaninglessness is a privation or an absence of meaning, a type of aberrant pathology or pathogen to repair, fix, transform, or cure, which leads to a fourth and final assumption of concern, which is that the therapeutic task operates from a deficit-correction model that aims to cure meaninglessness with meaning.

When we say that an experience is meaningful, we usually mean that it is enhancing, inspirational, emotionally moving in a positive way, and, basically, pleasant or fulfilling. We even scale meaning and purpose in life through assessments with ranked privileging of such experiences (e.g., Meaning in Life Questionnaire [MLQ] and Purpose in Life [PIL] assessment instruments) (Crumbaugh & Maholick, 1964; Steger, Frazier, Oishi, & Kaler, 2006). Contemporary studies on the science of meaning still focus on thriving and altruism (Flanagan, 2009). What if the word, *meaningful*, could be defined as that which is impactful or memorable or any kind of mattering and include disturbing if not devastating experiences as well?

If we relegate meaning to only positive experiences, we slip into defining meaninglessness as a privation, an absence, a malfunction, an abnormality, or a disfigurement of meaning, a stance that carries forward remnants of an ancient Manichean Gnostic worldview that bifurcates good (spiritual and immaterial) and evil (physical and material). In this case, though, the contradistinction between meaning and meaninglessness is bifurcated by privileging the good-as-meaningful, or that which is inspirational, enhancing, certain, complete, special, worthy, conclusive, and sensible, against evil-as-meaninglessness, or that which is flat, apathetic, worthless, generic, leveled, banal, mundane, insubstantial, mutable, groundless, uncertain, and unknowing. Manichean Gnostic deliverance, then, means ridding or freeing oneself from the contaminating materialism of meaninglessness in order to reside in the purity of ethereal meaning. This stance joins other hierarchical bifurcations, such as sacred over secular, good over evil, and healthy over ill, all addressed with soteriologies (plans of redemption) predicated on a deficit-correction, or purification, model of care.

An alternative to thinking of meaning and meaninglessness as binary opposites, with the former being hierarchically privileged over the latter, would be to dispense with the bifurcation all together in favor of describing *significance as inherently ontological*. By ontological, I agree with Eric Craig's (2012) definition as "those characteristics or conditions of human being that obtain for every moment of every human being's existence" (p. 13). Each moment is inherently significant in some way or another, including moments, as paradoxically as it sounds, of *in*significance.

If ontological, and thus in every situation, at all times, for everyone, then meaning is neither created, lost, nor found—it is there. If we view meaning as something that can be created, lost, or found, and if equated solely with enhancing, inspiring, and other positive experiences, then meaning is reduced to a kind of existential cocaine. This reading of meaning is a humanistic reading back into the existential understanding of meaning and "forgets" meaning's ontological nature as intentional, interpreting-interpreted, perceiving-receiving existence, which can be special or not. By viewing meaninglessness as an abnormative part of existence, rather than another experience to be engaged like any other experience, we iatrogenically could increase someone's suffering going through it. The irony of this situation is that our "care" is intended as good, when it is often experienced as harmful.

Meaninglessness, therefore, is not the absence or privation of meaning but a *different kind* of meaning. Although evaluative and devaluative assessments are applied to each moment of significance, long before positive or negative valuations occur, significance is already and always being lived out prereflectively in light of the limitations and possibilities of any given situation. This process in itself is neither good nor bad, but simply "is," albeit an "isness" that is significant in one way or another for me, or you, or someone else, or something else. Even if "matter of fact," it is nonetheless meaningful-as-matter of fact. Hence, in order to destigmatize meaninglessness, we will have to shift our discourse and nomenclature from meaninglessness as "the absence of" what is normed, as represented in "less," "a," "ab," or "an," to a different discourse that is hospitable toward this lived experience as having an integrity of its own, as put this way by the wisdom of a taxi driver in conversation with me on the way to work:

> How's it going today? Ah, ok I guess. It's hard to get up on Monday morning as gray and rainy as it is and go to work after such a beautiful weekend. Yeah, well, we have to do what we have to do, don't we? If it rains, just open your umbrella.

This and other brief encounters that I will offer as poetic interludes throughout the chapter come from my own clinical work and are used in these reflections in illustrative ways; they are, of course, cloaked and disidentified for respectful concerns for confidentiality. As phenomenologically-oriented therapists in such situations, that is, as therapists who remain open to the significance of an event showing itself in its own way, we wouldn't look at inspiration and joy as experiences to fix or correct, so why should we do so with flatness, disinterest, or a "whatever" comportment? We would simply stay with the experience in a process of engaged understanding so as to create a clearing for any experience to unfold through descriptive clarification, lighting up its significance, even if its significance is an experience of insignificance. Our engaged care trusts what shows itself in this unfolding, what *aletheia* would ensue, which can only happen if we treat such experiences with respect and bracket any hermeneutic of suspicion that harbors a plan of executing the negative and installing the positive.

The very relativity of what is considered meaningful and meaningless is evidence of the ontic nature of these valuations in themselves and the call to remember being as interpreted-interpreting in each and every moment. To be clear, neither special nor not so special experiences are ontological but only the process that we live out significance. In his reflections on meaning and meaninglessness, Ernesto Spinelli (2015) rightly notes that "one of the great strengths of existential phenomenology is that it can avoid imposing a divide between meaning and meaninglessness … wherein each extreme is of equal standing and import" (p. 37).

The other difficulty with viewing meaning as created, lost, or found is that the self-made human being, so central to most understandings of existential thought read through a humanistic lens that is predicated on enhancement and actualization, or an existential stance particularly based on Jean-Paul Sartre's position that any meaning in life is up to us to create (Sartre, 1956), forgets that the self is decentered. Who we are is how we are in situations. We do constitute but are also simultaneously co-constituted by our situatedness, our world which is our web of meaning. Thinking we create meaning ex nihilo (from nothing) is blatant, unowned existential plagiarism, an oxymoron if there ever was one.

The convergence of multiple events, happenstances, and decisions that provide the opportunity for any situation to occur in which we find ourselves are mostly beyond our control, though nevertheless provide a clearing for us to experience meaning, including the meaning of meaninglessness. Our task, then, is not to go in search of meaning, like riding an ox while looking for an ox (to borrow an image from Eastern thought), or to provide a therapeutic bump of existential cocaine, but *to notice and clarify what kind of meaning is being lived in each moment*, whether inspirational or flattening, enhancing or stifling, vibrant or still, and special or not, all the while remaining horizontal and inclusive of whatever shows itself. Approaching therapeutic care as an attunement to lived meaning of our ontological givenness privileges no one experience over another, knowing that any lived experience has a say to heed, including the meaning of being nothing special.

Before proceeding in detail about therapeutic care, I want to describe the meaning of meaninglessness as the experience of *being nothing special*. My interests lie in discerning its phenomenological expression in therapeutic encounters and in how to care for meaninglessness as a lived expression of being nothing special in a way that does not drift back into a deficit-correction model of cure or a transformation of nothingness into somethingness.

The lived experience of being nothing special is both a confession and an embedded wish. It is a confession of worthlessness, a failed attempt at worth as defined by particular rank-ordered scales of measurement. Meaninglessness as being nothing special is the experience of being reduced to a kind of *mere* functionality, or detached "thingness," dispensable, replaceable, and disposable. It is being *just* a commodity, *just* a cog, or *just* a census datum.

Being special, on the other hand, would also mean to live an existence that is not a mere exchangeable, generic expendable "thing" but a lived experience of indispensable uniqueness, whose worth stands "as is," beyond rank-ordered scales of valuation. What is hoped for is to feel unique, special, and prized, either about oneself or about the idols on which we rest our hope. What is often inspirational is when we experience intimacy or connection (particularly being known and valued) with what seems eternal, ultimate, immutable, sustainable, invincible, or noncontingent.

This yearn for transcendence as connection with these experiences is as much a part of our thrown existential condition as the experience of ourselves as nothing special. Neither the yearn to be special nor the experience of being nothing special is a pathological experience. The former is not narcissism nor the latter depression. This is the human condition, a synthetic outcome, as Kierkegaard noted, of being finite, yet whose finitude includes transcendence (Kierkegaard, 1941). In our choosing, we experience both infinitude in the possibility of choosing multiple choices at hand and our finitude in the nonnegotiability of a choice's singularity.

These experiences are not polarities but dialectical (their identities are interdependent) and ontological (again, inherent to the human condition). There is no need to fix either experience but only to understand their lived significance in particular situations. So, as ontological beings, we are *both* nothing special *and* special. There is no need to see the latter as an achievement or the former as an illness. An attuned therapist clears space for both experiences to have their say. Nevertheless, when something special, either ourselves or someone else, or some event or situation or time in history or role in society, falls as an idol, we are left with the experience of being nothing special.

Being nothing special includes being nothing unique, nothing that lasts, nothing of significant value, nothing indispensable, or nothing sustainable. This is the experience of flattened mundaneness and banality. This is Kierkegaard's leveled crowd, Nietzsche's herd, Heidegger's *Das Mann*, and Sartre's nausea. It's an existence that *merely* does things, *just* to function, with *nothing but* what is instrumentally necessary. It is a lived experience of *oh well* and *whatever*. Life is decontextualized and generic. There is no niche, no "thisness" for me, for you, for it, for us. It is what is left when idols fall and the rank-ordered scales of measurement are not met and when the rank-ordered scales of measurement themselves no longer matter. As one person seeking care remarked:

> I don't even care that I don't care. What was inspiring is now as transient as anything else, so I will save my foolish hope. What was noble and worth living for has been exposed as a sedimented storefront for usury. 'So what?' dominates. When the smoke and mirrors are gone, life shows itself as biodegradable. Why not sleep while the parade passes by? Parades end as well. Tubas rest silently in the corner. Costumes are shelved. Formations disperse. So why march at all? Low Serotonin or high attunement to 'whatever?' Life is without salt and pepper, like eating a disposable paper plate. Nothing calls to me anymore, it should, but doesn't even when others remind me how grateful I should be.

The lived experience of meaninglessness-as-nothing-special is a post-idolatrous experience that exposes the potential idolatrous nature of meaning-centric living. Meaning as idolatry forgets contingency and the relativity of circumstances, contexts, events, and situations. It takes life for granted and looks surprised when life's mutability shows itself. The finitude that paradoxically provides the possibility of specialness is overridden by the search for peak experiences. Therapeutic encouragement of such experiences merely sets up others for the fall of idols.

Qoheleth, the teacher or preacher, and author of the biblical text, *Ecclesiastes*, understands the experience of being nothing special and how we set up the fall of idols. The word associated with meaninglessness in his work is vanity or vapor, according to which translation used, with the Hebrew word being *hevel*, meaning insubstantiability: nothing lasts, we can't predict or control, assume, guarantee, or take for granted how things will be. We find at the heart of Qoheleth's reflections that everything has its time and purpose but only for a while. We are called by Qoheleth to engage life in spite of its transitoriness and in spite of not being able to predict and control it. Having had the privilege of translating and studying

Ecclesiastes with Dr. Phyllis Trible (1988) at Union Theological Seminary, I remember asking her out of my own existential angst, "Why hope, if all is vanity? Should we expect anything?" And she wisely said, "Expect, but don't hold expectations as certainties" (personal communication).

Meaninglessness is a lived confession that there are no idols and that nothing is special, at least not forever. But rather than pathologize this experience, its meaning can be respected and discerned. The pull is strong to correct the situation by treating someone as special but doing so paradoxically nullifies his or her special way of taking up a nonnegotiable, existential experience that at times does not feel special. Why can't this experience be respected? I say, "at times," as ontological, temporal beings living an existence that is *hevel*, or transient, *both* feelings of being special and not being special occur and are transitory. Both experiences, nonetheless, are significant. Hence, *in a meaning-centered way of caring, making the goal to "find meaning" will, paradoxically, encourage a lack of empathic attunement for being nothing special in the world* and, hence, leaving someone existentially abandoned at (perhaps) the most difficult time of his or her life—a presumption that itself should be bracketed.

Inattending to our specialness is as much an ontological oversight as inattending to *not* being special. Therapeutic care, therefore, clarifies the lived meaning of both being special and not being special, of wanting to live and not wanting to live, without privileging one state of existence over another. We know that the meta-analysis of evidence-based best practice points to the quality of the therapeutic relationship as the most important factor in therapeutic factors contributing to successful outcomes (American Psychological Association, 2006). But let us press this further regarding what is meant by "quality" and how it relates to what I am suggesting.

The quality of the therapeutic relationship rests on the care, honesty, empathy, and attunement of the therapist to another's struggles. One suffers in an interrelational way, either with other people or in relation to life circumstances, such as in this person's situation:

> You could still smell the embedded odor of burnt wood in her clothes during my visit. Her entire family was killed in a recent fire. She lived the open wound of that double-edged sword of having survived. What remained in the ruins for her was nothing but her own stage four bone cancer. "With all this going on," she choked through her tears, "What's the point? I just want to go jump off the bridge." "Well" I said, "get your coat, and I'll walk down there with you." She laughed and consequentially decided to live, in spite of life's cruelty, unpredictability and insubstantiality.

Elsewhere (DuBose, 2015) I have discussed therapeutic care as "being-with" in being-for, being-alongside, and being-otherwise. This process is a collaborative one that is an engaged understanding for lived meaning. Being-for is a radical validation of who and how one is in one's existential situation, no matter what kind of being in the world is enacted. Being-alongside deconstructs and recontextualizes lived experience as unique ways of taking up ontological givens shared by us all. Being-otherwise brings in often overlooked or inattended experiences such as our possibilities or limitations in any given situation and may offer hermeneutical reframes of ways we are living out particular life situations. These ways of being-with occur simultaneously and equiprimordially; one way of being-with does not trump another, particularly regarding being-otherwise in relation to being-for, but this is exactly what often occurs when faced with meaninglessness.

The general prescription in the very sparse therapeutic literature on caring for meaninglessness is to help a person experiencing it to find meaning and assuage meaninglessness, with various concrete suggestions of how to do so, including those offered by many existential therapists. For instance, Yalom (1980) writes that "the effective therapist must help patients to look away from the question (of meaninglessness): to embrace the solution of engagement rather than plunge in and through the problem of meaninglessness" (p. 483). Furthermore, Yalom (1980) notes that " ... the therapist guides the patient toward engagement with others by first personally relating deeply and authentically with the patient" (p. 482).

Likewise, Frankl (1985) advises " ... turning suffering into a human achievement ... deriving from guilt the opportunity to change oneself for the better ... and deriving from life's transitoriness an incentive to take responsible action" (p. 162). Frankl (1985) goes on to suggest futural hope can provide the movement from meaninglessness to meaning: "It is a peculiarity of man that he can only live by looking to the future ... this is his salvation in the most difficult moments of his existence, although he sometimes has to force his mind to the task" (p. 94). Yalom (1980) quotes Frankl's response to a patient struggling with meaninglessness: "Don't focus on questions like this. Whatever the pathological process underlying your psychological affliction may be, we will cure you ... don't be concerned about the strange feelings haunting you. Ignore them until we make you get rid of them" (Yalom, p. 473).

Several techniques are offered by both Frankl and Yalom to cure meaninglessness, including dereflection, engaging with a cause, taking life as a gift, and with much discourse on the pathology of meaninglessness, such as Frankl's "existential vacuum." I agree with Yalom (1980) that meaningfulness can be "a by-product of engagement" (p. 482) and that engagement is central to the therapeutic process, but not as directional. Also, engagement is relative to each situation as is meaning, and the alienation often felt by others as a by-product of disengagement is also meaningful, albeit in a disturbing way. Prescriptive approaches to meaninglessness miss the important point that any one intervention may be helpful for one person and not for someone else. Engagement, for instance, may be frightening for someone traumatized by an intrusive world. Likewise, merely being with others does not erase meaninglessness.

Time and again, friends encourage other friends who are in meaninglessness to "get out and do something with friends." This can, in fact, make things worse. Not only is this approach mis-attuned to meeting the other where he or she is but also drives the pain of meaninglessness deeper by seeing it as an experience to be avoided or overcome like an allergen. This approach itself, though, spreads existential histamines of loneliness and shame and reinforces an already feared assumption that there is no place to talk about feeling that life is meaninglessness without being avoided or corrected.

Prescriptive approaches still reinforce that meaninglessness is pathological and actually simply do not listen to the dilemma faced by the one experiencing meaninglessness; accepting a prescription of try this or do this presumes an ability to value and find significance in this or that prescription. If one can follow such prescriptions, then one is living a different kind of meaning than meaninglessness.

The question of productive approaches to states of meaninglessness when thinking about therapeutic care must attend to the clandestine way "production" seeks to reestablish a commodification in the first place. Meaninglessness, though, is a confession that life has been de-commodified, that is, nothing's exchange value matters as it heretofore has in one's life, and nothing meaningful or of exchange value appears on the horizon. Meaninglessness reminds us of, if not liberates us toward, life's uselessness. In doing so, experience can be not only de-commodified but also de-instrumentalized (i.e., life's "isness" as only meaningful when producing or pragmatic). The very push to be productive, which often in therapeutic care means "get one over meaninglessness as a pathogen," paradoxically fuels an enframing that sets up further experiences of meaninglessness if what is proposed does not hold in current or future life circumstances. Even hermeneutical reframes of viewing the positive benefits of situations that seem hopelessly dour does not eliminate the pain of events, and, again, bifurcating these experiences against each other merely splits individuals into experiences that are "allowed and appropriate" and those that are not. Hence, therapeutically, this is why one allows meaninglessness to "be" without a "why" as Angelus Silesius, the seventeenth-century German mystic and poet, reminds us in his poetic expression that "the rose is without why," that is, without needing to justify its existence or point to causations to be corrected suggesting its illegitimacy.

The rush to cure meaninglessness isn't surprising in itself given the generally medically-modeled world of therapy-as-deficit correction but is somewhat surprising when existential therapists operate in like kind given that the history of the existential position critiques the very deficit-correction model they employ. This would include the privileging of meaning over meaninglessness, openness over closedness, authenticity over inauthenticity, freedom over confinement, good faith over bad faith, courage over cowardness, and so forth. At one time, we may focus on not being special in the sense that we are like every other human being and share ontological givens like anyone else but at another time grasp the dizzying vertigo of how free we are to attune in different ways to the same situation or to various situations. We then catch a glimpse of our radical incomparability in taking up our existential condition. In order to remain congruent with allowing the significance of any experience, to show itself as it is, in its own way, requires a receptive openness to lived meaning*less*ness-as-nothing-being-special, just like we would any other kind of lived meaning, and without the intent to replace it with purposeful, inspirational enhancement.

Being-otherwise may indeed bring into discussion heretofore inattended possibilities and reframes for an expanded sense of understanding one's situation, but not as a replacement of or as a promotion of specialness over the integrity of the confession that one is nothing special. Being-for radically validates the significance disclosed in this confession, which, when viewed ontologically, is courageous enough to receive one truth about the human condition. Being-alongside better understands the significance of what is validated in being-for and through descriptive clarification further unfolds the limitations and possibilities of what is radically validated, not replace it. Being-otherwise is not exchanging meaninglessness as nothing special for meaning as something special; it is bringing clarity to nothingness. What is successful in therapeutic outcome is predicated on attunement. This is easier when we are comfortable with that to which we are attuned, but attunement also calls for attunement to nothingness and to do so as nothingness. What is the place of nothingness?

> What is it like being in the world not feeling special? I feel like a ghost. In what ways? Like no one sees me. And if no one sees you? I will be lost, overlooked, unnoticed. And if so? I will miss out on something .... I guess sometimes I don't want to be noticed. Sometimes I just want to be normal. But I feel I have to be special to be loved. If I am special, then others will love me. Someone once told me that I should not want to be famous, as then I can't get away from others to be like everyone else. Rock stars, celebrities often yearn to just go to the supermarket or get gasoline at the service station, and can't because they are so special no one leaves them alone. They want to be anonymous. I suppose being special has different meanings for different people. This moment is like all other moments but is also unique in itself; we can't repeat exactly this moment.

We go into and through the meaninglessness. The only way "dwelling on it makes it worse" is when dwelling on it as something to be avoided or as listeners who fight against the gravity of this situation with impatient, fidgety, pitying comportment. Why not admiration of an ability to look into the abyss? This dwelling is a dwelling without a cure, without deliverance, and without transcendence, not on the way to hope, but as an end in itself. Hope often comes as a by-product but only if not a goal. It is without conclusions, footholds, safety lines, and deadlines. In order to be attuned to such a place, we can't aim at its transformation into something instrumental or valuable only according to how it functions for us or fits into our preestablished schemas of health and well-being.

Attuning to states of existence *as* meaningless, without any essentialist allegiances regarding how one should be and cease trying to transform it, paradoxically, brings additional meaning to these moments of contact, particularly if meaninglessness is understood as a meaningful experience. *Not trying to change it, correct it, fix it, cure it, and decontaminate it, which is what I mean by being with another in the space of being nothing special, is paradoxically what is transformative.* Spinelli (2015) notes that "Paradoxically, the willingness to tolerate, perhaps even embrace, a temporary engagement with meaninglessness serves to strengthen the lived value and validity of those meanings that emerge from a person's confrontations with the unknown, the unexpected and the uncertain" (p. 37). I would add: "and the experience of being nothing special."

I think this art of being-with in this way is disappearing. As instrumental and engineering-oriented technical therapeutic technique is becoming these days, our educational and training programs do not teach "presence" much anymore, particularly the ability to engage in a vigilant presence with another in the abyss. We teach having correct categorical diagnoses, consistent treatment plans, accurate reads of assessment materials, and memorization of neurotransmitters but no classes on doing nothing with someone in the abyss. Were there to be a class, the closest thing to it I know of is a clinical pastoral education unit in the emergency room or on the burn unit where what you bring into a person's world can't fix anything, thus developing the skill of how to be in situations of suffering we can't fix.

Mental health professionals, particularly psychologists, don't get much of this kind of education. It would require relating in a way that does *not* know and not in a false and feigned way but in a way that does not withdraw from the intensity of engaging fatalism by appealing to the certainties of metapsychological schemas and diagnostic classification. Rather, hope is communicated in the communion of being with another in hopelessness:

> He looked flatly at his therapist. No matter which way he turned, tried options just did not seem to hold juice. "I just don't want you to suicide," his therapist choked. "So, you want me to live so I can suffer?" was his retort. His eyes met his therapist's eyes, and his therapist said, "I just don't know what to tell you. I don't know what to do." He then smiled a smile of relief, recognition and communion. "I am not alone," he thought, and even entertained for a moment that an unfixable situation may indeed have its own significance after all.

The therapist often worries about having an answer for any and every situation. Indeed, the primacy of unknowing, uncertainty, and the unfixability of much of life is unfortunately avoided, in spite of continual clucking about existential finitude — we say it but don't often believe it. In doing so, paradoxically, the "knowing" therapist can amplify the aloneness of the one who experiences life's unanswerable quality. Moreover, offering answers to that which is inherently unanswerable can very well be patronizing and mis-attuned to the lived helplessness seeking respect from the one entrusted to care. The communion in this situation occurred when the therapist was *with* the other rather than *above* him; he cared by *not* knowing.

So what are the "takeaways" for therapeutic care?

- The way of caring suggested here is not an apathetic or passive stance, but one that intentionally brackets presumptive and simplified answers to nonnegotiable and irresolvable dilemmas, while remaining anticipatorily resolute for transitional horizons.
- *What is healing is not trying to heal meaninglessness.*
- The very act of engaged attunement with the experience of nothing being special communicates interpersonally that we will take up in a meaningful way this meaningless experience without flinching or privileging meaningfulness over meaninglessness.
- The act of *not* reaching to "fix," fixes, as imposed privileging is what has collapsed and is no longer tenable. Fixing, curing, correcting, ameliorating, repairing, rectifying, amending, and remedying all communicate that meaninglessness cannot stand on its own and, like any other way of being, does not have its own wisdom. Instead, explore, expand, and clarify the maelstrom of gale force-winded values in flux, of how worlds have morphed and died and, ironically, have created its own kind of freedom in a type of existential bardo state of no longer "there" while simultaneously "not yet."
- The meaningfulness of an engaged and respectful exploration of meaninglessness *is* the therapeutic care.

- The clinician who can provide the existential sanctuary for this exploration of meaninglessness becomes familiar with her or his own value of meaninglessness as much as those for whom she or he cares, including how meaninglessness exposes the grand charades proposing either that the mutable is eternal or the eternal is immutable. Meaninglessness draws open the curtain on both imposters.
- A respect that does not bifurcate nor privilege meaning-as-positive over meaninglessness-as-negative offers more unconditional hospitality and acceptance to those persons who seek our care, even when in states of existence that frighten or disturb us. Moreover, such respect guards against prescriptive impositions of how one should live, including prescriptive suggestions of how to engineer us away from meaninglessness.
- Our lived experience of permanence is through living decisively into impermanence, even if without purpose or completion—particularly so. That this moment, too, will pass away is both sad and hopeful, a limitation and a possibility: Both call for respect, which is the heart of what is suggested for therapeutic practice as we conclude these reflections.
- Meaninglessness itself can become a strange way of avoiding meaninglessness if it takes the stance that "nothing has held, so nothing will hold; life is permanent or is not life at all." This is meaninglessness' attempt to choke off itself, to conclude rather than stay in the flux and steward its value.

How shall we live in such flux? John Caputo (2013), in his book, *The Insistence of God: A Theology of Perhaps*, put it his way:

> The intensity of life is a function of its transiency, which is the issue of "perhaps." Impermanence intensifies existence. The very precariousness of things makes them precious …. The fact that things have come about by the most extraordinary strings of cosmic luck and singular sequences of cosmic cycling and are vulnerable to the slightest shift in cosmic circumstances does not lessen but only magnifies their preciousness. (p. 227)

It takes courage to sit with an openness to the meaning of meaninglessness, with the recognition that the gods have fallen. Touching the horizon of meaninglessness without looking for the occluded sun, where we find that we are not so special after all, may very well be the most special encounter possible.

References

American Psychological Association Presidential Task Force on Evidence-Based Practice. (2006). Evidence-based practice in psychology. *American Psychologist, 61*, 271–285.

Bergner, R. (1998). Therapeutic approaches to problems of meaninglessness. *American Journal of Psychotherapy, 22*(1), 72–87.

Caputo, J. (2013). *The insistence of God: A theology of perhaps*. Bloomington, IN: Indiana University Press.

Craig, E. (2012). Existential psychotherapy, discipline and demarche. In L. Barnett & G. Madison (Eds.), *Existential therapy: Legacy, vibrancy and dialogue*. London: Routledge.

Crumbaugh, J., & Maholick, L. T. (1964). An experimental study in existentialism: The psychometric approach to Frankl's concept of noogenic neurosis. *Journal of Clinical Psychology, 20*, 200–207.

DuBose, T. (2015). Engaged understanding for lived meaning. *Journal of Contemporary Psychotherapy, 45*(1), 25–35.

Flanagan, O. (2009). *The really hard problem: Meaning in a material world*. Cambridge, MA: MIT Press.

Fox, M. (2009). *The remarkable existentialists*. Amherst, NY: Humanity Books.

Frankl, V. (1985). *Man's search for meaning*. New York, NY: Washington Square Press.

Kierkegaard, S. (1941). *Concluding unscientific postscript* (Swenson, D., & Lowrie, W., Trans.). Princeton, NJ: Princeton University Press for American Scandinavian Foundation.

Kim, J., Seto, E., Davis, W., & Hicks, J. (2014). Positive and existential psychological approaches to the experience of meaning in life. In A. Batthyany & P. Russo-Netzer (Eds.), *Meaning in positive and existential psychology* (pp. 221–233). New York, NY: Springer.

Sartre, J. -P. (1956). *Being and nothingness: An essay on phenomenological ontology* (Barnes, H., Trans.). New York, NY: Philosophical Library.

Schurmann, R. (1987). *Heidegger on being and acting: From principles to anarchy*. Bloomington, IN: Indiana University Press.

Spinelli, E. (2015). *Practising existential therapy: The relational world* (2nd ed.). London: Sage.

Steger, M. F., Frazier, P., Oishi, S., & Kaler, M. (2006). The Meaning in Life Questionnaire: Assessing the presence of and search for meaning in life. *Journal of Counseling Psychology, 53*, 80–93.

Yalom, I. (1980). *Existential psychotherapy*. New York, NY: Basic Books.

Part III
Thriving: Integrative Meaning-Oriented Perspectives and Interventions for Human Thriving

Meaning, Medicine, and Healing

Thomas R. Egnew

> *Whether he wants to be or not, the doctor is a storyteller and he can turn our lives into good or bad stories, regardless of the diagnosis. Anatole Broyard (1992, p. 53)*

Introduction

The advances of medicine in the developed world have arguably wrought miracles. But the very forces that have helped medicine progress have at the same time created considerable liabilities for both physicians and patients and underscored the value of existential and positive psychology. The veneration of technology and the quest for efficiency that are hallmarks of contemporary society have permeated medicine to render medical care increasingly impersonal (Cassell, 1993; Gibes, 2014). While technology has contributed to medicine's power to prevent, detect, treat, and manage disease, it has also distanced patients from doctors by focusing on the physical aspects of disease to the exclusion of the personal experience of illness. "Since technology deprives me of the intimacy of my illness, makes it not mine but something that belongs to science," prostate cancer patient Anatole Broyard (1992) opined, "I wish my doctor could somehow repersonalize it for me" (p. 47). To depersonalize a patient's illness experience is to turn away from the patient's suffering, while the press for efficiency has undermined the trust embodied in the doctor-patient relationship that makes it "sacred" (Gibes, 2014, p. 310). Patients thus find themselves experiencing more invasive and prolonged treatment but feeling less support and caregiving from an overextended medical team.

In response to these changes, new models of care are increasingly involving therapists in medical treatment planning and implementation. Since medical training does little to prepare doctors to be interpersonally therapeutic, patients may find little guidance from their doctor for how to cope with their illnesses. Therapists can

---

T.R. Egnew, Ed.D., L.I.C.S.W. (✉)
Tacoma Family Medicine, Tacoma, WA, USA
e-mail: Thomas.Egnew@multicare.org

fill an important role in helping patients to not only cope but also to learn and grow from their illness experiences. Therapists working closely with physicians or within medical contexts may discover fulfilling career opportunities, from consulting to augment physicians' personal therapeutic skills to helping patients manage the ravages of serious illness. This requires an appreciation of the forces that shape and challenge physicians, a grasp of the existential impact of serious illness on patients, and an awareness of how physicians and therapists might collaborate to help patients holistically heal.

In this chapter, I shall emphasize three points: firstly, that holistic healing involves the transcendence of suffering, occurs other than biophysically, and is a viable option when cure is impossible. This requires that those providing care engage the patient's experience of illness and suffering. Secondly, that suffering arises from a loss of meaning accompanying the illness experience and is related as a personal narrative. Transcendence of suffering involves helping patients find meaning, which obliges those helping to be skilled in the nuances of narrative competence. And lastly, that the work of the healer inevitably involves the existential aspects of a patient's life, which necessitates connecting with patients on levels relatively uninformed by professional education. Typical of holistic healing, these concepts are not distinct entities but are interrelated and interdependent.

Medicine in the Postmodern World

That medicine is at the height of its technical prowess while simultaneously under siege is a paradox. Modern medicine rose through the twentieth century on the efficacy of its scientifically derived biomedical model (Starr, 1982). The biomedical narrative of disease came to dominate the narrative about acceptable healing practices in the developed world so as to become the folk medicine of the modern world (Kleinman, 1988). But science has proved a two-edged sword. The power to produce miracle cures also spawned iatrogenesis—pain, illness, impairment, and death—as collateral damage (Illich, 1982). Further, biomedical successes have created a growing population of chronically ill patients whose complex needs now constitute "the single greatest challenge" to medical practice (Wagner, 1998, p. 2). The medical service delivery system is tooled toward acute care, which saves lives but is poorly designed to meet the needs of chronically ill patients. Thus, modern medical science has ironically fostered a reality in which patients can be supported at the biological margins of life to suffer longer.

Additionally, a half-century of postmodern thought has influenced twenty-first century medicine, both conceptually and clinically. Evidence may be seen in medicine's customer service focus, its response to assertions that knowledge is historically relative and culturally impacted, and its growing appreciation of the importance of holistic healing (Morris, 2000). The aggressive promotion of its products and services, the efforts to develop new markets by medicalizing ever widening spheres of social life, and a focus on customer satisfaction as a measure of success denotes postmodern healthcare as a service industry. Practices borrowed from the entertainment industry are being used to increase patient satisfaction (Lee, 2004), despite evidence of questionable medical outcomes (Fenton, Jerant, Bertakis, & Franks, 2012; Zgierska, Miller, & Rabago, 2012). Medicine has become a lucrative industry that promotes medical services as commodities and devours mounting societal resources (Rastegar, 2004; Relman, 1980).

Medicine has responded to the questioning of its hegemony over healing practices by intensifying its scientific focus. It has emphasized evidence-based medicine (Sackett, Rosenberg, Gray, Haynes, & Richardson, 1996), the value of which is debatable (Henry, Zaner, & Dittus, 2007; Smith, 2008; Spielmans & Parry, 2010), and called for research into the alternative and complementary treatments competing with biomedicine for legitimacy (Committee on the Use of Complementary and Alternative Medicine by the American Public, 2005). Patient-centered medicine has gained popularity as an approach to clinical care that values patient perspectives (Stewart, Brown, Weston, McWhinney, & Freeman, 1995) and the patient-centered medical home—which includes mental health therapists in the treatment team—has become a popular model for managing chronic illness (Rosenthal, 2008). These are but a few of reactions of contemporary medicine to the influences of postmodernism.

Yet, the biomedical narrative remains challenged by "powerful alternative narratives that view human illness not as the malfunction of a biophysical mechanism but as the unique experience of a meaning-making and embodied cultural being" (Morris, 2000, p. 8). Some alternative narratives have arisen from within medicine itself, such as the calls to implement biopsychosocial (Engel, 1977), biopsychosocial-spiritual (McKee & Chappel, 1992), and social constructivist (Wilson, 2000) paradigms. But biomedicine with its biomedical model has largely rebuffed these efforts to remain the dominant narrative defining contemporary medicine while promoting a curative model of medical service delivery throughout the developed world (Fox, 1997).

The convulsions of postmodern medicine have greatly impacted both physicians and patients. In the development of marketplace medicine, physicians have become *providers* and patients *customers* (Krugman, 2011), with little appreciation of the fundamental changes to their relationship this entails (Brownlee, 2012). Coupled with the limitations of and challenges to biomedicine's claims to superior treatment, public trust in contemporary medicine has eroded (Lundberg, 2000; Mechanic, 1996), interest in complementary and alternative healing systems has risen (Eisenberg et al., 1998), and physician morale has plummeted (Crawshaw, 2000; Steiger, 2006). For patients who are chronically ill, biomedicine struggles to achieve its ancient goal to relieve suffering. Saving and prolonging life entail a moral obligation to accompany patients on their chronic illness journeys. Beyond the physical limitations of the biomedical paradigm, patients need support to deal with the existential implications of their experience of disease, illness, and suffering. Such support starts with understanding the experience of illness.

The Nature of Chronic Illness

Illness refers to the subjective human experience of disease (Moyers, 1993). While disease involves "disturbances in the structure or function of any part, organ, or system of the body," illness entails "feelings by which persons know themselves to be unwell" (Cassell, 1991, p. 49). Illness relates to the entirety of a person and to the meaning a patient ascribes to the experience which brought him or her to the attention of the doctor (Balint, 1964; Eisenberg, 1980).

Physicians and patients experience disparate realities when confronting illness. Physicians understand patients' complaints through a lens of biomedical diagnosis and treatment, while patients understand illness as a lived experience. This gap in perspectives must be bridged if doctors are to understand the chronically ill patient. To facilitate this, Kay Toombs (1987), who suffers multiple sclerosis, encouraged an "eidetic approach" (p. 228) involving perceptions of loss—lost wholeness and bodily integrity, certainty, control, freedom to act, and connection with the world as previously known—held in common by those who suffer serious illness. A vivid appreciation of these losses helps caregivers understand what illness means to a particular patient.

Illness threatens that which healthy individuals routinely take for granted (Baron, 1985; Murphy, 1990). It changes those actions, relationships, and perceptions of time through which identity is formed and maintained. The body undergoes a "metamorphosis" to become an "omnipresent and concrete threat to the self" (Toombs, 1993, p. 224). With time, illness becomes a "presence" experienced as "disability," the inability to engage the world in habitual ways, which leads to "the despoilment of identity that is the common fallout of the damaged self" whose future is no longer given and whose present is often distorted (Murphy, 1990, p. 110). Eventually, illness becomes central to identity. "I was my face," wrote Lucy Grealy (1995), disfigured in childhood by cancer of the jaw, "I was ugliness" (p. 7). The eidetic aspects of illness "transcend the peculiarities and particularities of different disease states and constitute the meaning of illness-as-lived" (Toombs, 1987, p. 229). Identity and illness meld in a shattered existence that is foreign to those who are well.

A patient experiences and understands illness-as-lived according to the "collectivity of his meanings," which is a function of the patient's life history (Cassell, 1979, p. 203). To understand the illness experience is to appreciate the meanings the patient attaches to that experience which, in turn, relate to the patient's experience of those existential concerns common to humanity: death, freedom, isolation, and meaninglessness (Yalom, 1980). These concerns are innate to experiencing chronic illness and are reflected as dynamic tensions in a patient's life.

Many chronic illnesses are progressively debilitating, which underscores "the tension between the awareness of the inevitability of death and the wish to continue to be" (Yalom, 1980, p. 8). The losses accompanying chronic illness often shatter the external structures through which persons make meaning and feel grounded and thus engender the tension between "our confrontation with groundlessness and our wish for ground and structure" (Yalom, 1989, p. 9). Chronic disease is experienced as isolation (Murphy, 1990; Remen, 1993), spawning tension between "our awareness of our absolute isolation and our wish for contact, for protection, our wish to be a part of a larger whole" (Yalom, 1989, p. 9). Lastly, chronic illness changes an individual's meaning structures, inevitably raising the question, "Why me?" (Murphy, 1990), and exacerbating the "dilemma of a meaning-seeking creature who is thrown into a universe that has no meaning" (Yalom, 1989, p. 9). To be chronically ill is to confront life's major existential quandaries.

Healing involves "addressing and resolving the *existential predicament* [italics added] of the person who is ill" (Toombs, 1993, p. 229), a task distinctly different than diagnosing and treating disease with the goal of cure. What is meant by existential can relate to existence, the meaning of existence, or striving to find concrete personal meaning in existence (Frankl, 2006). As chronic disease inevitably thrusts the ill person into questions concerning the meaning of life, holistic healing must attend to the dynamics of existential disease just as biomedicine addresses the mechanics of physical disease (Coulehan, 2009).

The Nature of Holistic Healing

Holistic healing may be defined as "the personal experience of the transcendence of suffering" (Egnew, 2005, p. 258). Other definitions include "a dynamic process of recovering from a trauma or illness by working toward realistic goals, restoring function, and regaining a personal sense of balance and peace" (Hsu, Phillips, Sherman, Hawkes, & Cherkin, 2008, p. 310); "being cured when possible, reducing suffering when cure was not possible, and finding meaning beyond the illness experience" (Scott et al., 2008, p. 3220); and "the process of restoring and preserving a sense of personal harmony that does not depend upon the integrity of the physical body" (Toombs, 1995, p. 98). Together, these definitions imply that holistic healing involves cure or recovery from disease, restoration of function, a sense of personal harmony, balance and peace, and reducing or transcending suffering. Yet, not all these qualities are applicable to the chronically ill.

With chronic disease, recovery may not be a credible option and restoring function may be impossible. Indeed, progressive debilitation leading to death may be the natural course of the disease. But achieving personal harmony, balance, and peace in the face of the debilitating illness remains possible. Transcending suffering arguably results in harmony, balance, and peace. It is a viable option for chronically and terminally ill patients, since healing so defined can occur other than biophysically and is independent of cure, impairment, pain, suffering, or death (Egnew, 2005). "Paradoxically," declared the founder of the modern hospice movement, Dame Cicely Saunders (2006), "death has been shown to be a place of healing, of growth through loss" (p. 162).

Holistic healing thus remains a potential despite illness, debilitation, and death, and provides an instrumental role for those caring for chronically and terminally ill patients. But what does it mean to transcend suffering? And how might caregivers aid in this process, function as healers? The answers to these questions lie in understanding suffering and its dynamics, appreciating transcendence, and grasping how to assist the process.

The Nature of Suffering

Cassell (1982) defined suffering as "the state of severe distress associated with events that threaten the intactness of the person" (p. 640). Other definitions include "an aversive emotional experience characterized by the perception of personal distress that is generated by adverse factors undermining the quality of life" (Cherny, Coyle, & Foley, 1994, p. 57); "an individual's experience of threat to self, a meaning given to events such as pain or loss" (Kahn & Steeves, 1996, p. 5); "perceived damage to the integrity of the self" (Chapman & Garvin, 1999, p. 2233); and "a syndrome of some duration, unique to the individual, involving a perceived relentless threat to one or more essential human values creating certain initially ominous beliefs and a range of related feelings" (Reed, 2003, p. 11). From these definitions, we can deduce that suffering is personal, individual, relates to threats to the integrity of self, and is experienced by the whole person, not just the body (Cassell, 1982; Mount, Boston, & Cohen, 2007).

Suffering ranges in intensity from distress (Cassell, 1982; Cherny et al., 1994; Coulehan, 2009) to misery, anguish, and agony (Reed, 2003). While not necessarily associated with pain (Cassell, 1982), though unremitting pain may certainly foster suffering, suffering is an existential angst of a different order than pain that relates to a sense of a loss of wholeness as a person (Chapman & Garvin, 1999). Dynamically, suffering arises with the disruption of previously held meaning structures and thus fills the chasm of meaninglessness patients experience (Kahn & Steeves, 1996). Postmodern thought has questioned many of the traditional forms by which people previously found meaning (Morris, 2000), creating what Frankl (2010) called an "existential vacuum ... the experience of a total lack, or loss, of an ultimate meaning to one's existence that would make life worthwhile" (p. 49). The relationship between suffering and meaninglessness is a central dynamic in transcending suffering.

Suffering is inevitable. This is the first of the Four Noble Truths of Buddhism and must be acknowledged to begin spiritual awakening. Suffering arises because of the human tendency to seek permanency in an ever-changing world. "The more we grasp," noted Kornfield (2008), "the more we experience suffering" (p. 247). Simply put, suffering arises when we are "not getting what we want or having to deal with what we don't want" (Dass & Gorman, 1985, p. 54). For Frankl (1962), suffering, along with guilt and transitoriness, are a "Tragic Triad" constituting the "primordial facts of man's existence" (p. 26). He believed that suffering and trouble "belong to life as much as fate and death" (Frankl, 1965, p. 89). Thus, to live is to suffer.

The themes associated with suffering involve isolation, hopelessness, helplessness, and loss and are associated with a sense of the disintegration of self, values and belief systems, and daily connections to the world (Kearsley, 2010). Sufferers may be rendered mute by their suffering, may struggle to find the words by which to express their experience, or may generate a new understanding of self to ameliorate suffering by reinstating or preserving their personal integrity (Cassell, 1982; Reich, 1989). Meaning in life differs not only from person to person but also within the same individual from moment to moment (Frankl, 2006). "Whether (and in what way) illness causes suffering," Toombs (1993) asserts, "depends upon the whole texture of meanings and values intrinsic to a particular patient's unique life narrative" (p. 228). Thus, suffering is carried as a singularly personal narrative (Moerman, 1983). To understand the sufferer, one must understand the narrative, for it is through story that one accesses the patient's state of suffering (Kearney, 1996).

Narrative and Suffering

"My initial experience of illness was as a series of disconnected shocks," Anatole Broyard (1992) wrote, "and my first instinct was to try to bring it under control by turning it into a narrative. Always in emergencies we invent narrative" (p. 19). Telling the story of suffering serves three purposes for the sufferer: to reconstruct the painful past and potentially gain distance from the suffering; to receive affirmation of the search for a new story in which a new self emerges from the suffering; and to help the sufferer find a language of interpretation that fosters the transcendence of suffering (Younger, 1995). Thus, telling the story of suffering helps the sufferer gain perspective, reconnect with the world, and forge a new identity. These purposes are in line with the relational outcomes of hope, trust, and being known that are characteristic of healing relationships (Scott et al., 2008). By simply hearing and affirming their stories of suffering, patients can be helped to holistically heal.

Physicians (and therapists) are responsible for helping patients construct their illness narratives (Brody, 1994). Through helping patients to edit their illness narratives, physicians and therapists assist them to author a healing story (Egnew, 2009). Suffering arises from changes in the relationship of the sufferer to self and those suffering feel alienated from a despised, disguised, or detached self (Younger, 1995). The despised self springs from negative evaluations of feeling compromised; the disguised self emerges as a false consciousness out of touch with feelings; and the detached self represents a disjunction between affect and activity. Narration plays a crucial role in transforming the sufferer's relationship to self by first acknowledging the change in relationship and then developing a story that reconciles the sufferer to self.

Yet, declaring the importance of narrative competence to managing suffering risks imposing a moral imperative on doctors and therapists without explicit guidance about how to accomplish the good end. This is akin to proclaiming that patients should not be allowed to die from appendicitis without teaching the surgical skills to remove the appendix. To avoid such a quandary, physicians and therapists must be trained to be competent in the skills of narrative medicine.

Understanding Narratives

According to Charon (2007), narrative competence involves "the capacity to recognize, absorb, metabolize, interpret, and be moved by stories of illness" and narrative medicine is practiced by "someone who knows what to do with stories" (p. 1265). The goal of narrative medicine is affiliation, a joining of those involved in the caring effort, for to inquire into the meanings of illness is to embark on a journey into relationships (Kleinman, 1988).

Illness stories take many forms: restitution, tragedy, quest, and chaos (Frank, 1998). The story preferred in Western culture is the recovery narrative in which the ill person recovers health and full functioning (Frank, 1995). Related to this are narratives that feature triumph over adversity (Conway, 2007). In these stories, the process of transformation in the face of illness mirrors the timeless structure of mythic hero stories: separation from the world as known, isolation and change, and return to the world transfigured to teach the lesson of life renewed (Campbell, 1968). Thus, the basic structure of an illness story involves the onset of illness, adjustment to illness, and the incorporation of illness into identity (Kerr, 2010). "The experience of illness is always the experience of both 'having' and 'being had'," observed Toombs (1995). "I not only 'have' the illness, it also 'has' me" (p. 99).

The dominance of the recovery narrative suppresses other stories of suffering, like those of anger and protest. To tell their tale, sufferers need relief from the burden of conforming to the expectations of a happy ending (Garden, 2010). Stories of tragedy portend no restitution or restoration; stories of chaos involve a shattered experience of illness with no emerging reorganization; and stories of quest feature a transformation unfolding with the end yet in sight. These are tales difficult to state and hear. They render both teller and listener vulnerable to the embarrassment, shame, and guilt (Lazare, 1987; Murphy, 1990) that accompany the radical loss of self-esteem produced by disability (Murphy, 1990; Price, 1994). Stories of illness may also be suppressed because of an inability to verbalize the experience (Garden, 2010). "Language supplies us with ways to express ever subtler levels of meaning," noted Grealy (1995, p. 44), "but does that imply language gives meaning, or robs us of it when we are at a loss to name things?"

Central to the sickness story is a threat to "the most cherished assumption we hold," personal indestructibility (Toombs, 1995, p. 99). The sickness story is thus a story of wreckage, as the present does not represent what the past was supposed to portend and the future is fearful to behold (Frank, 1995). "My history is no longer smooth and linear," Robert Murphy (1990) observed about his paralysis from a spinal tumor, "but bisected and polarized. And my long-range future does not really exist" (p. 26). So the story of sickness is a story of devastation, reflection, and, in the best of cases, restoration (Launer, 2002). Yet, even when restoration is not possible, holistic healing remains so, for the healing narrative is a story of fragmentation of identity, contemplation of ensuing suffering, and transcendence through acceptance and meaning.

Transcending Suffering

Transcendence means "transcending or lying beyond the limits of ordinary experience" (Webster's, 1979, p. 1230). Craigie (2010) described it as "the journey of letting go or making peace with the unchangeable elements of life" (p. 265). This involves a dynamic engagement of pain and suffering—confronting, considering, and moving beyond them to a new perspective. Suffering has traditionally been transcended through acceptance (Hayes & Smith, 2005; Mikulas, 1978) or by investiture with meaning (Frankl, 2006).

Identity is formed through attachments to life that are meaningful, the severing of which precipitates suffering by disrupting perceptions of personal integrity (Cassell, 1982; Kegan, 1982; Moerman, 1983). Acceptance of the change without pursuing or rejecting the severed attachments results in the transcendence of suffering (Hayes & Smith, 2005; Mikulas, 1978). Sufferers found relief, observed palliative care specialist Ira Byock (1994), when they "surrendered who they were to a new reality of who they are" (p. 13). "Achieving harmony in the face of illness," wrote Toombs (1995), "means learning to live with bodily disorder as a permanent way of being" (p. 102). In essence, suffering arises in the struggle between the patient's desire to maintain a personal identity that in reality has been compromised. By accepting the new reality, relinquishing the desire to have things different and accepting a new identity, suffering is transcended.

As suffering arises in the crisis of meaning that occurs when previous meaning structures are no longer applicable to the sufferer's experience of life (Barrett, 1999; Kahn & Steeves, 1996), suffering changes when it takes on meaning. Indeed, suffering ceases to be suffering "the moment it finds a meaning" (Frankl, 2006, p. 113). This is no placebo effect, since placebos are inert whereas meaning is "richly alive and powerful" (Moerman & Jonas, 2002, p. 474). The challenge for doctors and therapists alike is to help patients discover meaning in their experience.

If suffering is produced and alleviated primarily by the meaning attached to experience (Brody, 1987), how is meaning generated? Meaning is discovered through work or dedication to a cause, through love or relationship, or through the attitude one takes toward suffering that cannot be avoided (Frankl, 2006). As existential psychiatrist Irvin Yalom (1989) observed, "the last gift a parent can give to children is to teach them, through example, how to face death with equanimity" (p. 92). Even death can be a gift infused with meanings that salve its sting. This generation of meaning involves "self-transcendence," the capacity to transcend oneself "either toward another human being or toward meaning" (Frankl, 1988, p. 18). So it is through connection to someone or something outside oneself that meaning is created or discovered. Frankl (2010) believed humans have a will to meaning, "the basic striving of man to find and fulfill purpose" (p. 35). Frankl's observations explain how meaning eases the tensions surrounding the existential issues of death, freedom, isolation, and meaninglessness to help patients transcend suffering.

Meaning is created through relationships that ameliorate the sense of isolation suffering patients feel. Through their will to meaning and self-transcendence, patients become connected with something beyond themselves and are no longer alone. The freedom to choose how they respond to circumstances, even those beyond their control, means patients are not helpless despite the most dire situations. By restructuring values and finding meaning, patients uncover ground and structure to generate hope and overcome loss. Frankl believed it is through meaning that humans can come to terms with and survive the worst of conditions. He was fond of quoting Neitzsche: "He who has a *why* to live for can bear almost any *how*" (Frankl, 2006, p. 104). Acceptance is thus the progeny of meaning which in turn fosters transcendence of suffering. A healer helps patients find a "why" to transcend their suffering.

Physicians and Therapists as Healers

McWhinney (1997) observed that healers recognize and acknowledge suffering, understand the meaning of the illness for the patient, are present in times of need, and provide hope—be it for survival, future spiritual realization, or the present moment. "To be a healer," McWhinney (1997) noted, "is to help patients find their own way through the ordeal of their illness to a new wholeness" (p. 95). Ultimately, it is the patient who must find that meaning which transcends his or her suffering, but the process may be facilitated through a therapeutic relationship. To be a healer, then, is to be "someone who helps other people heal themselves" (Davis-Floyd & St. John, 1998, p. 70). This requires both a skilled physician or therapist and a particular type of therapeutic relationship.

Healing requires compassion, touch, and dialogue (Sulmasy, 1997), so a healer must empathically understand suffering, be consoling, and possess narrative competence. Compassion literally means *to suffer with* another and empathy fosters compassion. Empathy is the medium by which compassion is expressed and has beneficial physiological effects on both healer and patient (Adler, 2002). Basic empathic skills involve recognizing when emotions may be present but not directly expressed, inviting exploration of these unexpressed feelings, and effectively acknowledging feelings so that patients feel understood (Suchman, Markakis, Beckman, & Frankel, 1997). Empathy is the foundation of the healing relationship.

The skin is the largest organ and cutaneous contact is our first medium of communication (Montagu, 1978). Physicians, unlike therapists, are socially sanctioned and expected to touch patients. They can therefore use touch as a way to build trust, establish connection, demonstrate compassion, and provide comfort and healing (Osmun, Brown, Stewart, & Graham, 2000). Doctors can actively use emotional and physical intimacy to demonstrate empathy, while therapists are generally constrained to touching patients empathically to create emotional intimacy. For either physician or therapist, empathy must be explicitly expressed as "empathy withers in silence" (Spiro, 2009, p. 1178).

Empathy is facilitated by a type of projective identification with the patient through the recognition of oneself in the patient (Stein, 1985). To be with another empathically requires one to "lay aside your own views and values in order to enter another's world without prejudice" (Rogers, 1980, p. 143). This facilitates dialogue, the aim of which goes beyond the understanding of any one person to gain insights that cannot be individually achieved (Senge, 1990). The conditions necessary for dialogue to occur include the suspension of assumptions, collegiality, and a facilitator skilled in "seeing the flow of meaning and seeing the one thing that needs to be said now" to help participants observe their own thinking (Bohm, 1965; Senge, 1990, p. 247). Psychiatrist Carl Hammerschlag noted that healers "listen to the stories of their patients and feed it back in language and metaphor that the patient understands" to encourage patients to reflect upon their stories (Egnew, 1994, p. 146).

Such a relationship draws the healer and the patient into what philosopher Martin Buber called an *I-Thou* relationship. *I-Thou* relationships involve those profound experiences of another that "give meaning to our lives and make us fully human" (Buber, 1958, p. 34). As such, *I-Thou* relationships are difficult to describe. They reside in the relational space generated by an encounter, are not reducible to causal or temporal frameworks, and are two-way relationships based in dialogue which cannot be forced but are instead generated from openness to their presence by both parties. *I-Thou* relationships foster a "connexional" experience, a transpersonal dimension that bonds healer and patient and changes the patient's story "from being abstract and distant to being immediate and felt, as if we were inside it" (Matthews, Suchman, & Branch, 1993, p. 974). Using such a connexion, physician-healers help patients connect with sources of meaning that allow them to transcend their suffering.

In contrast, Buber described *I-It* relationships that are determined by objective temporality as one-way relationships characterized by experiencing and using objects. Healing cannot occur through *I-It* relationships, for in this realm those dispensing care and patients "may meet, but not encounter, speak but not reveal, and hear but not listen. Two concurrent monologues masquerade as dialogue" (Cohn, 2001, p. 172). In such an interpersonal vacuum, suffering may be exacerbated (Cassell, 1982).

Scott et al. (2008) developed a Healing Relationship Model, the processes of which involve valuing, appreciating power, and abiding. Valuing is akin to what Rogers (1961) described as unconditional positive regard and is the source of the nonjudgmental stance necessary for dialogue to occur. Appreciating power reflects the recognition of the inherent asymmetry in physician-patient relationships and the fiduciary obligation of the healer to use this asymmetry to serve patients. Abiding reflects a continuity of caring actions in an enduring relationship. These processes of healing are comparable to the processes involved in Buber's conceptions of teacher-student and therapist-client *I-Thou* relationships (Scott, Scott, Miller, Stange, & Crabtree, 2009). So, healing occurs in the space occasioned by the healer-patient encounter and is brokered through authentic dialogues that help patients find meaning to transcend suffering.

To support healing relationships, healers must be present (Craigie, 2010; Kane, 2003), for while they can pretend to know or care, they "cannot pretend to be there"

(Phillips & Haynes, 2001, p. 274). This requires not only physical presence but also psychological mindfulness (Epstein, 1999), an awareness of the impact of the encounter on both parties and a nonjudgmental observation of experience that supports presence and fosters dialogue. Healers appreciate that listening for stories is something more acute than listening to them (Welty, 1998), and they must be willing to bear the vulnerability of being open to the patient's brokenness (Cassell, 1991). This is facilitated by an awareness of the healer's own brokenness. Indeed, in many traditions the call to be a healer is reflected through suffering dramatic physical or psychological wounds (Achterberg, 1987–1988).

The concept of the wounded healer, the idea that healing springs from brokenness not strength, is a particularly robust theme in the literature regarding healing. Recognizing woundedness serves a healing purpose by encouraging connection in the healing relationship. The knowledge of our personal weakness softens defensiveness and "strengthens our helping hand" (Dass & Gorman, 1985, p. 66), as the healer connects with the patient from an awareness that pain and suffering arise from "the depth of the human condition which all men share" (Nouwen, 1979, p. 88). Accepting the shadow of their brokenness, healers need not be fearful of nor retreat from the brokenness of others.

The awareness of woundedness fosters trust and promotes a mutual exchange of healing. "It's our woundedness that allows us to trust each other. I can trust another person," explained physician Rachel Remen, "only if I can sense that they, too, have woundedness, have pain, have fear" (Moyers, 1993, p. 344). Woundedness thus brings a quality of authenticity to the healing connection which affirms and heals both parties. As Tumulty (1978) observed, "for a physician, healing of yourself takes place through the healing of others" (p. 142). The same may be said of therapists.

There is utility in doctors and therapists bringing their "soiled humanity" (Hammerschlag, 1993, p. 151) to their relationships with patients since the "more conscious we are in dealing with our own suffering, the more sensitive we will be in treating the pain of others" (Dass & Gorman, 1985, p. 86). Being comfortable with one's own wounds allows one to accept and understand the wounds of another and thus to be present to provide the "touch, trust, understanding, comfort and healing" that patients seek (Phillips & Haynes, 2001, p. 274). An awareness of shared woundedness grounds the therapeutic relationship in authenticity.

Medicine for the Twenty-First Century

As we move into the twenty-first century, holistic healing poses theoretical and practical challenges to contemporary medicine. Theoretically, the personal, individual nature of suffering does not lend itself to exploration through the scientific research paradigms valued by biomedicine (Frank, 2001) and incorporated into academic psychology. Science makes no room for beliefs not provable by positivistic research methodology (Groopman, 2004); if a phenomena cannot be measured, it is considered suspect in science's world of "objectivity." Suffering, like illness, is comprehensible only through the subjective experience of the sufferer. It occurs as a threat to the integrity of personhood and does not fit neatly into the narrative of objectivity by which medicine and psychology are conceived and practiced. Thus, to ask physicians and therapists to entertain suffering is to ask them to depart from their scientific models and embrace the world of human experience.

Three languages describe human experience: "I-language," "We-language," and "It-language" (Wilber, 1996, p. 121). I-language reflects the truth of personal subjective experience while We-language involves the intersubjective or cultural dimensions of truth. It-language is objective, neutral, value free—the language of truth as determined through science. All three languages are necessary to describe reality, but the Enlightenment paradigm "reduced all I's and all we's to mere its" (Wilber, 1996, p. 123). As the personal, subjective experience of illness and suffering is revealed in I- and We-language, the language of science is rendered mute. In the narrative of suffering, the subjective becomes the objective, for suffering is its own illness and can only be healed when so acknowledged (Vallurupalli & Vesel, 2012).

It is thus not surprising that increasing numbers of patients are seeking treatment outside the purview of biomedicine. The appeal of complementary and alternative medicine may in part be related to a greater willingness of its practitioners to engage the existential level of patient concerns, to not "shy away from some of the big questions surrounding illness: Why has this sickness happened to me? Why do people get sick despite living well? Why do some people die 'before their time'?" (Wright, Watson, & Bell, 1996, p. 169). The use of integrative medical approaches may be as much an indication of the hunger of suffering patients to explore the existential aspects of their illness experience as it is a reflection of the efficacy of the treatments offered. Thus, contemporary medicine faces the dilemma of engaging patients' existential concerns or losing them. One response has been to increasingly recognize the value of therapists as a vital part of the treatment team.

The doctor-patient relationship remains the enduring keystone of medical care (Engel, 1973) and therapists are an extension of that therapeutic liaison. Within the intimacy of this person-to-person encounter lies the potential to engage patients biomedically and existentially. Wilber's observations regarding the language of human experience closely reflect Buber's appreciation of *I-Thou* and *I-It* relationships. Biomedicine uses the *I-It* language of Cartesian reductionism to diagnose and treat disease. Physicians move between *I-It* and *I-Thou* relationships (Scott et al., 2009), at the least in gathering a history that inevitably reflects a patient's subjective experience (Haidet & Paterniti, 2003), to both treat disease and care for the sick person. Therapists perform a similar dance when translating personal history and symptoms into diagnostic algorithms that suggest treatment strategies. Herein lies the potential for doctors and therapists to become healers. Engaging the patient's story allows them "to cross into the life of the other" (Yalom, 1989, p. 18) to create a healing connection.

The healing *I-Thou* relationship involves a spontaneous, subjective, reciprocal, recognition and acceptance of a unique other (Cohn, 2001). The narrative of the ensuing encounter embodies I- and We-language as the patient reveals the experience of meaninglessness in the present moment. To so embrace the patient's being through an *I-Thou* relationship inherently affirms the patient as a suffering person. These in-the-moment encounters embody that presence necessary to the healing relationship (Craigie, 2010; Kane, 2003; Kearsley, 2012), since patients seldom verbalize their emotions spontaneously or directly but, instead, tend to offer clues. If invited to elaborate, they may then express their emotional concerns directly. Patient clues are an invitation to explore the patient's perspective of the illness (Mauksch, Dugdale, Dodson, & Epstein, 2008), as "the deliberate and open acknowledgement of suffering frequently opens the door for other fears or worries not previously expressed" (Wright et al., 1996, p. 168). As the patient's story of suffering unfolds in the subsequent dialogue, physicians and therapists can suggest edits that nourish meaning and cultivate healing.

Physician or therapist anxiety about such an exploration can limit the healing potential of the therapeutic relationship. Trained to fix problems and be in control (Stein, 1990), physicians may hesitate to address existential issues for which they perceive no scientifically-derived, evidence-based answers. Doctors and therapists may limit patient storytelling to maintain diagnostic clarity, avoid uncomfortable emotions, and maintain efficiency (Hunter, 1991; Levinson, Gorawara-Bhat, & Lamb, 2000; Marvel, Epstein, Flowers, & Beckman, 1999; Waitzkin, 1991). Yet, patients invited to discuss personal issues rarely speak for an inordinate amount of time; healers can develop skills to end such episodes and revisit them in continuity contacts (Branch & Malik, 1993); and some work can be done via short telephone calls that demonstrate empathy and understanding (Egnew, 2011). Still, the patient may need to address existential and spiritual issues that physicians and therapists feel poorly prepared to entertain.

Illness invites a wake-up call about life, which encourages spiritual dialogue as the meaning of life is queried or reviewed (Wright et al., 1996). The issue of spirituality has been contentious within medical circles (Koenig et al., 1999; Sloan, Bagiella, & Powell, 1999). But the spiritual dimension of human existence contributes to a sense of health and well-being and a growing body of research validates the value of encouraging patients' abilities to find meaning in their experience (Baker & Stern, 1993; Johnson et al., 2011). Herein lies the potential for patients to experience the meaning and purpose in life, connection to others, transcendence, and spiritual energy that supports holistic healing (Waldfogel, 1997). Thus, Broyard (1992) desired a physician who could "treat body and soul" (p. 40), for healing is "a work of spirit" (Remen, 1988, p. 5).

For Frankl (2000), issues of meaning are related to self-transcendence and spirituality, which he termed "ultimate meaning." Meaning cannot be given an individual, but life never ceases to offer meaning "up to its last moment, up to our last breath" (Frankl, 2000, p. 141). He believed that humans should "understand that life expects something" from them (Frankl, 1965, p. xiii), that we are called by life to meaning and "the more comprehensive the meaning, the less comprehensible it is ... necessarily beyond comprehension" (Frankl, 2000, p. 143). Part of personhood is reflected in a transcendent self (Cassell, 1982) that can neither be objectively studied nor fully comprehended—lest it not be transcendent (Campbell, Moyers, &

Flowers, 1991) — but can be engaged in a healing journey. "Over the years," wrote disfigured Lucy Grealy (1995), "my perspective on 'what it was all about' has shifted, but the most important point then was that there *was* a reason that this was happening to me ... I undertook to see my face as an opportunity to find something that had not yet been revealed" (p. 180). Even disfigurement can become a portal toward meaning.

In ethical, existential, and ontological senses, suffering related to health care is a matter of neglect and uncaring where patients' existential suffering is unseen and they are not viewed as a whole human beings (Arman, Rehnsfeldt, Lindhom, Hamrin, & Eriksson, 2004). A conundrum for twenty-first century medicine is therefore not so much a challenge of the paradigms through which medicine is practiced as a call for physicians and therapists to explore patients' existential suffering and personally help them to find meaning in their experience of illness so to transcend suffering and heal. "The most powerful therapeutic tool you'll ever have," observed evidence-based medicine guru David Sackett, "is your personality" (Smith, 2003, p. 1431). Nowhere is this more evident than in instances of chronic illness and palliative care where biomedical curative paradigms no longer apply and clinicians are called to a "medical ministry" (Frankl, 1988, p. 5). Postmodern physicians and therapists must therefore entertain the meaning patients ascribe to their experience of disease and illness and nurture dialogue so as to help patients find meaning in their illness experience (Frankl, 2010). Inevitably, this draws them into the realm of spirituality, at the very least in the provision of hope.

From Pathology to Positivity and Meaning

Hope lies at the heart of healing, but to help others find hope requires knowing them in depth (Groopman, 2004). Whether doctors can be healers who help patients find hope in an era of industrialized medicine with clinic volumes curtailing meaningful dialogue is arguable. A medical service delivery system focused on holistic healing would be comprised of skilled physicians supported by care teams involving therapists for an efficient dispersal of service. It would, at the least, provide universal access to continuity medical care; equitably reimburse spending time with patients as opposed to doing things to them; and allocate parity in mental health funding. "Compassionate" hospitals would have a staff that "has a deep awareness of, and respond to, the suffering that arises from illness" (Kearsely & Youngson, 2012, p. 457). Such is the task of medical service delivery systems in the twenty-first century. Affecting this change requires data that indicates the efficacy of creating such a supportive system. Fortunately, a growing body of knowledge has demonstrated the value of positive and existential psychology to patient care. The limitations of this chapter allow but a cursory summary of a robust inquiry.

As regards the value of meaning, research has shown that the discovery of meaning is important to developing a positive psychological state in patients experiencing severe stress (Folkman, 1997); is linked to better disease trajectory and decreased mortality in HIV-positive patients (Bower, Kemeny, Taylor, & Fahey, 1998); reduces suffering in terminally ill patients (Chochinov et al., 2005); and is evident in those able to find a sense of well-being and wholeness though facing serious illness (Mount et al., 2007). We know that social support extends breast cancer survival rates (Spiegel, Boom, Kraemer, & Gottheil, 1989) and there is evidence that discerning life purpose may lead to the spontaneous remission of cancer (Ventegodt, Morad, Hyam, & Merrick, 2004). Research is also documenting the importance of existential issues and their relationship to suffering in a variety of serious illnesses (Albinsson & Strang, 2003; Bolmsjö, 2001; Goldner-Vukov, Moore, & Cupina, 2007; Lee, 2008). Data such as these suggest that addressing existential concerns has meaningful benefits for patients.

Likewise, the influence of positive psychology on health has been increasingly explored with encouraging results. We have learned that shifting attention from dysfunction and pathology to optimal functioning and positive emotions improves mental health and well-being (Kobau et al., 2011). We know that developing resilience and a positive psychological perspective reduces susceptibility to the common cold (Cohen, Doyle, Turner, Alper, & Skoner, 2003) and supports diabetes management and glycemic control (Yi-Frazier, Hilliard, Cochrane, & Hood, 2012). Further, it appears that positive emotions in early life are associated with longevity (Danner, Snowdon, & Friesen, 2001), that positive emotions appear to support spiraling emotional well-being (Fredrickson & Joiner, 2002), and that a positive reinterpretation to trauma and adversity lessens distress and supports growth (Linley & Joseph, 2004). Studies such as these have demonstrated the remarkable health benefits associated with positive psychology.

Existential and positive psychology offer medicine an avenue for moving away from its pathology-oriented focus to a perspective that better supports holistic healing, particularly in cases of chronic illness and palliative care. But to achieve such system change requires doctors and therapists well-trained in the detection, assessment, and management of suffering. They must be exposed to role models who actively assess suffering at the bedside and in the consultation (Cassell, 1999), reflect issues of suffering in their case histories (Donnelly, 1996), and transparently articulate their experience of the patient and their efforts to engage the patient's suffering in their care plans (Egnew & Wilson, 2011). They must learn the communication techniques that draw out stories of suffering (Launer, 2002) and help patients reattach to the human community from which illness has separated them (Brody, 1994). Lastly, they must have protected time to thoughtfully cultivate moral perspectives which allow their humanism to thrive (Branch, 2000). Curricula supporting these learning needs would likely require a refocusing of many prevailing professional education paradigms. Such is the charge to prepare professionals for healthcare service in the twenty-first century.

Ultimately, to balance humanism with scientific progress, contemporary medicine will need to emphasize relieving suffering as much as it focuses on diagnosis and treatment. This will inevitably involve expanding the focus of care to address the patient's total pain (Saunders, 1966) — physical, mental, social, and spiritual — which will inherently involve the use of therapists. Diagnosing and treating disease has become confused with caring for sick persons, making medicine "a prisoner of its own success" (Will, 1994, p. 74). Population management may help prevent disease and maintain function, but medicine will never succeed in undoing the genetic code that makes us mortal. The need for a guide in both living and dying (Farber, Egnew, & Herman-Bertsch, 2002; Nuland, 1994) is the ground in which both doctors and therapists stake their claim as healers.

Frank (1995) argued that life's temporality gives meaning to existence and biomedicine has assumed responsibility for extending the temporality of lives. So meaning must be at the center of medicine's caring efforts and doctors and therapists must strive to develop the moral imagination (Engel, Zarconi, Pathtel, & Missimi, 2008) essential to helping patients transcend suffering by investing their lives with meaning and dignity (Chochinov, 2007). Thus is the task of postmodern medicine: to encourage the exploration of meaning in those lives saved and extended, for "even a helpless victim of a hopeless situation, facing a fate he cannot change, may rise above himself, may grow beyond himself, and by so doing change himself. He may turn a personal tragedy into a triumph" (Frankl, 2006, p. 146). How medicine evolves to address this challenge will define its soul in the twenty-first century.

Key Takeaways

- Contemporary medicine has produced an ever-growing population of patients who live to suffer longer with chronic illnesses which inevitably involve the existential aspects of a patient's life. Yet, medicine and physicians are poorly positioned, both from training and service delivery system aspects, to address the existential predicaments inherent in a patient's suffering.
- While not curable, many chronically and terminally ill patients can be healed, since healing can occur despite illness, impairment, or death. Therapists can augment healthcare efforts by supporting the process of healing, the transcendence of suffering.
- To assist patients to transcend suffering, therapists must understand the existential meaning of a patient's illness experience and how suffering may be transcended. This requires relational skills to both listen for and elicit the story of suffering and to explore avenues of meaning and acceptance through which patients may transcend their suffering.
- Patients must find healing for themselves, but therapists who can skillfully facilitate dialogue concerning the existential issues associated with serious illness; who can mindfully manage their own impulses to either avoid pathos or to reflexively attempt to remedy the patient's suffering; and who can reflect positive areas for growth through the illness experience can help patients along their path to healing.
- While exploring a patient's experience of serious illness can be challenging, therapists who help chronically and terminally ill patients to heal may discover this to be some of the most satisfying and fulfilling work of their careers.

References

Achterberg, J. (1987–1988). The Wounded Healer: Transformational journey in modern medicine. *Shaman's Drum, 11(Winter)*, 19–24.

Adler, H. M. (2002). The sociophysiology of caring in the doctor-patient relationship. *Journal of General Internal Medicine, 17*, 883–890.

Albinsson, L., & Strang, P. (2003). Existential concerns of families of late-stage dementia patients: Questions of freedom, choices, isolation, death, and meaning. *Journal of Palliative Medicine, 6*, 225–235.

Arman, M., Rehnsfeldt, A., Lindhom, L., Hamrin, E., & Eriksson, K. (2004). Suffering related to health care: A study of breast cancer patients' experiences. *International Journal of Nursing Practice, 10*, 248–256.

Baker, C., & Stern, P. N. (1993). Finding meaning in chronic illness as the key to self-care. *Canadian Journal of Nursing Research, 25*, 23–26.

Balint, M. (1964). *The doctor, his patient, and the illness* (Rev. ed.). New York, NY: International Universities Press.

Baron, R. J. (1985). An introduction to medical phenomenology: I can't hear you while I'm listening. *Annals of Internal Medicine, 103*, 606–611.

Barrett, D. A. (1999). Suffering and the process of transformation. *Journal of Pastoral Care, 53*, 461–472.

Bohm, D. (1965). *The special theory of relativity*. New York, NY: W.A. Benjamin.

Bolmsjö, I. (2001). Existential issues in palliative care: Interviews of patients with amyotrophic lateral sclerosis. *Journal of Palliative Medicine, 4*, 499–505.

Bower, J. E., Kemeny, M. E., Taylor, S. E., & Fahey, J. L. (1998). Cognitive processing, discovery of meaning, CD4 decline, and AIDS-related mortality among bereaved HIV-seropositive men. *Journal of Consulting and Clinical Psychology, 66*, 979–986.

Branch, W. T. (2000). Supporting the moral development of medical students. *Journal of General Internal Medicine, 15*, 503–508.

Branch, W. T., & Malik, T. K. (1993). Using 'windows of opportunities' in brief interviews to understand patients' concerns. *Journal of the American Medical Association, 269*, 1667–1668.

Brody, H. (1987). *Stories of sickness*. New Haven, CT: Yale University Press.

Brody, H. (1994). "My story is broken, can you help me fix it?" Medical ethics and the joint construction of narrative. *Literature and Medicine, 13*, 79–92.

Brownlee, S. (2012, April 23 & April 30). The doctor will see you—If you're quick. *Newsweek, CLIX*, 46–50.

Broyard, A. (1992). *Intoxicated by my illness*. New York, NY: Fawcett Columbine.

Buber, M. (1958). *I and Thou* (2nd ed.). New York, NY: Scribner.

Byock, I. (1994). When suffering persists. *Journal of Palliative Care, 10*, 8–13.

Campbell, J. (1968). *The hero with a thousand faces* (2nd ed.). Princeton, NJ: Princeton University Press.

Campbell, J., Moyers, B. D., & Flowers, B. S. (1991). *The power of myth*. New York, NY: Anchor Books.

Cassell, E. J. (1979). The subjective in clinical judgment. In H. T. Engelhardt Jr., S. F. Spicker, & B. Towers (Eds.), *Clinical judgment: A critical appraisal* (pp. 199–215). Dordrecht: D. Reidel Publishing.

Cassell, E. J. (1982). The nature of suffering and the goals of medicine. *New England Journal of Medicine, 306*, 639–645.

Cassell, E. J. (1991). *The nature of suffering and goals of medicine*. New York, NY: Oxford University Press.

Cassell, E. J. (1993). The sorcerer's broom: Medicine's rampant technology. *Hastings Center Report, 6*, 32–39.

Cassell, E. J. (1999). Diagnosing suffering: A perspective. *Annals of Internal Medicine, 131*, 531–534.
Chapman, C. R., & Garvin, J. (1999). Suffering: The contributions of persistent pain. *Lancet, 353*, 2233–2237.
Charon, R. (2007). What to do with stories. *Canadian Family Physician, 53*, 1265–1267.
Cherny, N. I., Coyle, N., & Foley, K. M. (1994). Suffering in the advanced cancer patient: A definition and taxonomy. *Journal of Palliative Care, 10*, 57–70.
Chochinov, H. M. (2007). Dignity and the essence of medicine: The A, B, C, and D of dignity conserving care. *British Medical Journal, 335*, 184–187.
Chochinov, H. M., Hack, T., Hassard, T., Kristjanson, L. J., McClement, S., & Harlos, M. (2005). Dignity therapy: A novel psychotherapeutic intervention for patients near the end of life. *Journal of Clinical Oncology, 23*, 5520–5525.
Cohen, S., Doyle, W. J., Turner, R. B., Alper, C. M., & Skoner, D. P. (2003). Emotional style and susceptibility to the common cold. *Psychosomatic Medicine, 65*, 657.
Cohn, F. (2001). Existential medicine: Martin Buber and physician-patient relationships. *The Journal of Continuing Education in the Health Professions, 21*, 170–181.
Committee on the Use of Complementary and Alternative Medicine by the American Public. (2005). *Complementary and alternative medicine in the United States*. Institute of Medicine of the National Academies. Washington, DC: National Academies Press.
Conway, K. (2007). *Illness and the limits of expression*. Ann Arbor, MI: University of Michigan Press.
Coulehan, J. (2009). Compassionate solidarity: Suffering, poetry, and medicine. *Perspectives in Biology and Medicine, 52*, 585–603.
Craigie, F. C., Jr. (2010). *Positive spirituality in health care*. Minneapolis, MN: Mill City Press.
Crawshaw, R. (2000). Diminished medical morale syndrome. A profession's impairment. *Journal of the South Carolina Medical Association, 96*, 304–309.
Danner, D. D., Snowdon, D. A., & Friesen, W. V. (2001). Positive emotions in early life and longevity: Findings from the nun study. *Journal of Personality and Social Psychology, 80*, 804–813.
Dass, R., & Gorman, P. (1985). *How can I help?* New York, NY: Knopf.
Davis-Floyd, R., & St. John, G. (1998). *From doctor to healer: The transformative journey*. New Brunswick, NJ: Rutgers University Press.
Donnelly, W. J. (1996). Taking suffering seriously: A new role for the medical case history. *Academic Medicine, 71*, 730–737.
Egnew, T. R. (1994). *On becoming a healer*. (Unpublished doctoral dissertation). Seattle University, Seattle, WA.
Egnew, T. R. (2005). Defining healing: Transcending suffering. *Annals of Family Medicine, 3*, 255–262.
Egnew, T. R. (2009). Suffering, meaning, and healing: Challenges of contemporary medicine. *Annals of Family Medicine, 7*, 170–175.
Egnew, T. R. (2011). "I know this must have been a difficult day for you:" Personal care in a patient-centered medical home. *Family Medicine, 43*, 435–436.
Egnew, T. R., & Wilson, H. J. (2011). Role modeling in the clinical curriculum. *Family Medicine, 43*, 99–105.
Eisenberg, L. (1980). What makes persons "patients" and patients "well"? *The American Journal of Medicine, 69*, 277–286.
Eisenberg, D. L., Davis, R. B., Ettner, S. L., Appel, S., Wilkey, S., Van Rompay, M., & Kessler, R. C. (1998). Trends in alternative medicine use in the United States, 1990–1997: Results of a follow-up national survey. *Journal of the American Medical Association, 280*, 1569–1575.
Engel, G. L. (1973). Enduring attributes of medicine relevant to the education of a physician. *Annals of Internal Medicine, 78*, 587–593.
Engel, G. L. (1977). The need for a new medical model: A challenge for biomedicine. *Science, 196*, 129–136.

Engel, J. D., Zarconi, J., Pathtel, L. L., & Missimi, S. A. (2008). *Narrative in health care*. Oxon: Radcliffe Publishing Ltd.
Epstein, R. M. (1999). Mindful practice. *Journal of the American Medical Association, 282*, 833–839.
Farber, S. J., Egnew, T. R., & Herman-Bertsch, J. L. (2002). Defining effective clinician roles in end-of-life care. *The Journal of Family Practice, 51*, 153–158.
Fenton, J. J., Jerant, A. F., Bertakis, K. D., & Franks, P. (2012). The cost of satisfaction: A national study of patient satisfaction, health care utilization, expenditures, and mortality. *Archives of Internal Medicine, 172*, 405–411.
Folkman, S. (1997). Positive psychological states and coping with severe stress. *Social Science and Medicine, 45*, 1207–1221.
Fox, E. (1997). Predominance of the curative model of medical care. A Residual Problem. *Journal of the American Medical Association, 278*, 761–763.
Frank, A. W. (1995). *The wounded storyteller: Body, illness, and ethics*. Chicago, IL: University of Chicago Press.
Frank, A. W. (1998). Just listening: Narrative and deep illness. *Families, Systems & Health, 16*, 197–216.
Frank, A. W. (2001). Can we research suffering? *Qualitative Health Research, 11*, 353–362.
Frankl, V. E. (1962). Logotherapy and the challenge of suffering. *Pastoral Psychology, 13*(5), 25–28.
Frankl, V. E. (1965). *The doctor and the soul*. New York, NY: Knopf.
Frankl, V. E. (1988). *The will to meaning*. New York, NY: Meridian.
Frankl, V. E. (2000). *Man's search for ultimate meaning*. New York, NY: Basic Books.
Frankl, V. E. (2006). *Man's search for meaning: An introduction to logotherapy*. Boston, MA: Beacon.
Frankl, V. E. (2010). *The feeling of meaninglessness*. Milwaukee, WI: Marquette University Press.
Fredrickson, B. L., & Joiner, T. (2002). Positive emotions trigger upward spirals toward emotional well-being. *Psychological Science, 13*, 172–175.
Garden, R. (2010). Telling stories about illness and disability: The limits and lessons of narrative. *Perspectives in Biology and Medicine, 53*, 121–135.
Gibes, J. P. (2014). Technique in medicine and its implications for the biopsychosocial model. *International Journal Psychiatry in Medicine, 47*, 309–316.
Goldner-Vukov, M., Moore, L., & Cupina, D. (2007). Bipolar disorder from psychoeducation to existential group therapy. *Australian Psychiatry, 15*, 30–34.
Grealy, L. (1995). *Autobiography of a face*. New York, NY: Harper Perennial.
Groopman, J. E. (2004). *The anatomy of hope: How people prevail in the face of illness*. New York, NY: Random House.
Haidet, P., & Paterniti, D. A. (2003). "Building" a history rather than "taking" one. *Archives of Internal Medicine, 163*, 1134–1140.
Hammerschlag, C. A. (1993). *The theft of the spirit: A journey to spiritual healing with native Americans*. New York, NY: Simon & Schuster.
Hayes, S. C., & Smith, S. (2005). *Get out of your mind and into your life: The new acceptance and commitment therapy*. Oakland, CA: New Harbinger Publications.
Henry, S. G., Zaner, R. M., & Dittus, R. S. (2007). Moving beyond evidence-based medicine. *Academic Medicine, 82*, 292–297.
Hsu, C., Phillips, W. R., Sherman, K. J., Hawkes, R., & Cherkin, D. C. (2008). Healing in primary care: A vision shared by patients, physicians, nurses and clinical staff. *Annals of Family Medicine, 6*, 307–314.
Hunter, K. M. (1991). *Doctor's stories: The narrative structure of medical knowledge*. Princeton, NJ: Princeton University Press.
Illich, I. (1982). *Medical nemesis: The expropriation of health*. New York, NY: Pantheon.
Johnson, K. S., Tulsky, J. A., Hays, J. C., Arnold, R. M., Olsen, M. K., Lindquist, J. H., & Steinhauser, K. E. (2011). Which domains of spirituality are associated with anxiety and

depression in patients with advanced illness? *Journal of General Internal Medicine, 26,* 751–758.

Kahn, D. L., & Steeves, R. H. (1996). An understanding of suffering grounded in clinical practice and research. In B. R. Ferrell (Ed.), *Suffering* (pp. 3–27). Sudbury, MA: Jones and Bartlett Publishers.

Kane, J. (2003). *How to heal: A guide for caregivers.* New York, NY: Helios Press.

Kearney, M. (1996). *Mortally wounded: Stories of soul pain, death and healing.* Dublin: Marino Books.

Kearsely, J. H., & Youngson, R. (2012). "Tu Souffres, Cela Suffit": The compassionate hospital. *Journal of Palliative Medicine, 15,* 457–462.

Kearsley, J. H. (2010). Therapeutic use of self and the relief of suffering. *Cancer Forum, 34(2),* Retrieved from http://wwww.cancerforum.org.au/Issues/2010/July.html.

Kearsley, J. H. (2012). Wal's story: Reflections on presence. *Journal of Clinical Oncology, 30,* 2283.

Kegan, R. (1982). *The evolving self.* Cambridge, MA: Harvard University Press.

Kerr, L. (2010). Always the same story: Familiar narrative structures in Oliver Sacks and Nancy Mairs. *Family Medicine, 42,* 97–99.

Kleinman, A. (1988). *The illness narratives.* New York, NY: Basic Books.

Kobau, R., Seligman, M. E. P., Peterson, C., Diener, E., Zack, M. M., Chapman, D., & Thompson, W. (2011). Mental health promotion in public health: Perspectives and strategies from positive psychology. *American Journal of Public Health, 101,* e1–e9.

Koenig, H. G., Idler, E., Kasl, S., Hays, J. C., George, L. K., Musick, M., Larson, D.B., Collins, T.R., Benson, H. (1999). Religion, spirituality, and medicine: A rebuttal to skeptics. *International Journal of Psychiatry in Medicine, 29,* 123–131.

Kornfield, J. (2008). *The wise heart.* New York, NY: Bantam Books.

Krugman, P. (2011, April 21). Patients are not consumers. *The New York Times.* Retrieved from www.nytimes.com/2011/04/22/opinion/22krugman.html?_r=1.

Launer, J. (2002). *Narrative-based primary care: A practical guide.* Oxon: Radcliffe Medical Press.

Lazare, A. (1987). Shame and humiliation in the medical encounter. *Archives of Internal Medicine, 147,* 1653–1658.

Lee, F. (2004). *If Disney ran your hospital: 9½ Things you would do differently.* Bozeman, MT: Second River Healthcare Press.

Lee, V. (2008). The existential plight of cancer: Meaning making as a concrete approach to the intangible search for meaning. *Support Care Cancer, 16,* 779–785.

Levinson, W., Gorawara-Bhat, R., & Lamb, J. (2000). A study of patient clues and physician responses in primary care and surgical settings. *Journal of the American Medical Association, 284,* 1021–1027.

Linley, P. A., & Joseph, S. (2004). Positive change following trauma and adversity: A review. *Journal of Traumatic Stress, 17,* 11–21.

Lundberg, G. D. (2000). *Severed trust: Why American medicine hasn't been fixed.* New York, NY: Basic Books.

Marvel, M. K., Epstein, R. M., Flowers, K., & Beckman, H. B. (1999). Soliciting the patient's agenda: Have we improved? *Journal of the American Medical Association, 281,* 283–287.

Matthews, D. A., Suchman, A. L., & Branch, W. T., Jr. (1993). Making "Connexions": Enhancing the therapeutic potential of patient-clinician relationships. *Annals of Internal Medicine, 118,* 973–977.

Mauksch, L. B., Dugdale, D. C., Dodson, S., & Epstein, R. (2008). Relationship, communication, and efficiency in the medical encounter. *Archives of Internal Medicine, 168,* 1387–1395.

McKee, D. D., & Chappel, J. N. (1992). Spirituality and medical practice. *Journal of Family Practice, 35,* 205–208.

McWhinney, I. R. (1997). *A textbook of family medicine* (2nd ed.). New York, NY: Oxford University Press.

Mechanic, D. (1996). Changing medical organization and the erosion of trust. *Milbank Quarterly, 74*, 171–189.
Mikulas, W. L. (1978). Four noble truths of Buddhism related to behavior therapy. *Psychological Record, 28*, 59–67.
Moerman, D. E. (1983). Physiology and symbols: The anthropological implications of the placebo effect. In L. Romanucci-Ross, D. Moerman, & L. Tancredi (Eds.), *The anthropology of medicine: From culture to method* (pp. 156–167). South Hadley, MA: J. F. Bergin Publishers.
Moerman, D. E., & Jonas, W. B. (2002). Deconstructing the placebo effect and finding the meaning response. *Annals of Internal Medicine, 136*, 471–476.
Montagu, A. (1978). *Touching: The human significance of the skin* (2nd ed.). New York, NY: Harper & Row.
Morris, D. B. (2000). How to speak postmodern: Medicine, illness, and cultural change. *Hastings Center Report, 30*, 7–16.
Mount, B. M., Boston, P. H., & Cohen, S. R. (2007). Healing connections: On moving from suffering to a sense of well-being. *Journal of Pain and Symptom Management, 33*, 372–388.
Moyers, B. (1993). *Healing and the mind*. New York, NY: Doubleday.
Murphy, R. F. (1990). *The body silent*. New York, NY: Norton.
Nouwen, H. J. M. (1979). *The wounded healer*. New York, NY: Image Books.
Nuland, S. B. (1994). *How we die*. New York, NY: Knopf.
Osmun, W. E., Brown, J. B., Stewart, M., & Graham, S. (2000). Patients' attitudes to comforting touch in family practice. *Canadian Family Physician, 46*, 2411–2416.
Phillips, W. R., & Haynes, D. G. (2001). The domain of family practice: Scope, role and function. *Family Medicine, 33*, 273–277.
Price, R. (1994). *A whole new life*. New York, NY: Scribner.
Rastegar, D. A. (2004). Health care becomes an industry. *Annals of Family Medicine, 2*, 79–83.
Reed, F. C. (2003). *Suffering and illness: Insights for caregivers*. Philadelphia, PA: F. A Davis Company.
Reich, W. T. (1989). Speaking of suffering: A moral account of compassion. *Soundings, 72*, 83–108.
Relman, A. S. (1980). The new medical-industrial complex. *The New England Journal of Medicine, 303*, 963–970.
Remen, R. N. (1988). Spirit: Resource for healing. *Noetic Sciences Review, (Autumn)*, 5–9.
Remen, R. N. (1993). Wholeness. In B. Moyers (Ed.), *Healing and the mind* (pp. 343–363). New York, NY: Doubleday.
Rogers, C. R. (1961). *On becoming a person*. Boston, MA: Houghton Mifflin.
Rogers, C. R. (1980). *A way of being*. Boston, MA: Houghton Mifflin Company.
Rosenthal, T. C. (2008). The medical home: Growing evidence to support a new approach to primary care. *Journal of the American Board of Family Medicine, 21*, 427–440.
Sackett, D. L., Rosenberg, W. M., Gray, J. A., Haynes, R. B., & Richardson, W. S. (1996). Evidence based medicine: What it is and what it isn't. *British Medical Journal, 312*(7023), 71–72.
Saunders, C. (1966). The last frontier. *Frontier, 1966(Autumn)*, 183–186.
Saunders, C. (2006). Templeton prize speech. In *Cicely Saunders: Selected writings 1958–2004* (pp. 157–162). Oxford: Oxford University Press.
Scott, J. G., Cohen, D., DiCicco-Bloom, D., Miller, W. L., Stange, K. C., & Crabtree, B. F. (2008). Understanding healing relationships in primary care. *Annals of Family Medicine, 6*, 315–322.
Scott, J. G., Scott, R. G., Miller, W. L., Stange, K. C., & Crabtree, B. F. (2009). Healing relationships and the existential philosophy of Martin Buber. *Philosophy, Ethics, and Humanities in Medicine, 4*, 11. doi:10.1186/1747-5341-4-11
Senge, P. M. (1990). *The fifth discipline: The art and practice of the learning organization*. New York, NY: Doubleday/Currency.
Sloan, R. P., Bagiella, E., & Powell, T. (1999). Religion, spirituality, and medicine. *The Lancet, 353*, 664–667.
Smith, R. (2003). Thoughts for new medical students at a new medical school. *British Medical Journal, 327*, 1430–1433.

Smith, G. S. (2008). Envisioning the successful integration of EBM and humanism in the clinical encounter: Fantasy or fallacy? *Academic Medicine, 83*, 268–273.
Spiegel, D., Boom, J. R., Kraemer, H. C., & Gottheil, E. (1989). Effect of psychosocial treatment on survival of patients with metastatic breast cancer. *Lancet, 2*(8668), 888–891.
Spielmans, G. I., & Parry, P. I. (2010). From evidence-based medicine to marketing-based medicine: Evidence from internal industry documents. *Bioethical Inquiry, 7*, 13–29.
Spiro, H. (2009). The practice of empathy. *Academic Medicine, 84*, 1177–1179.
Starr, P. (1982). *The social transformation of American medicine*. New York, NY: Basic Books.
Steiger, B. (2006). Survey results: Doctors say morale is hurting. *Physician Executive, 32*, 6–15.
Stein, H. F. (1985). What is therapeutic in clinical relationships. *Family Medicine, 17*, 188–194.
Stein, H. F. (1990). *American medicine as culture*. Boulder, CO: Westview Press.
Stewart, M., Brown, J. B., Weston, W. W., McWhinney, I. R., & Freeman, T. R. (1995). *Patient-centered medicine. Transforming the clinical method*. Thousand Oaks, CA: Sage Publications.
Suchman, A. L., Markakis, K., Beckman, H. B., & Frankel, R. (1997). A model of empathic communication in the medical interview. *Journal of the American Medical Association, 277*, 678–682.
Sulmasy, D. P. (1997). *The Healer's calling: Spirituality for physicians and other health care professionals*. New York, NY: Paulist Press.
Toombs, S. K. (1987). The meaning of illness: A phenomenological approach to the patient-physician relationship. *The Journal of Medicine and Philosophy, 12*, 219–240.
Toombs, S. K. (1993). The metamorphosis: The nature of chronic illness and its challenge to medicine. *Journal of Medical Humanities, 14*, 223–230.
Toombs, S. K. (1995). Healing and incurable illness. *Humane Medicine, 11*, 98–103.
Tumulty, P. A. (1978). The art of healing. *The Johns Hopkins Medical Journal, 143*, 140–143.
Vallurupalli, M., & Vesel, T. (2012). Hidden suffering. *Journal of Palliative Medicine, 15*, 362–363.
Ventegodt, S., Morad, M., Hyam, E., & Merrick, J. (2004). Clinical holistic medicine: Induction of spontaneous remission of cancer by recovery of the human character and the purpose of life (the life mission). *TheScientificWorldJOURNAL, 4*, 362–377.
Wagner, E. H. (1998). Chronic disease management: What will it take to improve care for chronic illnesses? *Effective Clinical Practice, 1*, 2–4.
Waitzkin, H. (1991). *The Politics of medical encounters: How patients and doctors deal with social problems*. New Haven, CT: Yale University Press.
Waldfogel, S. (1997). Spirituality in medicine. *Complementary and Alternative Therapies in Primary Care, 24*, 963–975.
Webster's New Collegiate Dictionary. (1979). Springfield, MA: G. & C. Merriam Company.
Welty, E. (1998). *One writer's beginnings*. Cambridge, MA: Harvard University Press.
Wilber, K. (1996). *A brief history of everything*. Boston, MA: Shambhala.
Will, G. F. (1994, March 7). Facing the skull beneath the skin of life. *Newsweek*, p. 74.
Wilson, H. J. (2000). The myth of objectivity: Is medicine moving towards a social constructivist medical paradigm? *Family Practice, 17*, 203–209.
Wright, L. M., Watson, W. L., & Bell, J. M. (1996). *Beliefs: The heart of healing in families and illness*. New York, NY: Basic Books.
Yalom, I. D. (1980). *Existential psychotherapy*. New York, NY: Basic Books.
Yalom, I. D. (1989). *Love's executioner*. New York, NY: Perennial Classics.
Yi-Frazier, J. P., Hilliard, M., Cochrane, K., & Hood, K. K. (2012). The impact of positive psychology on diabetes outcomes: A review. *Psychology, 3*, 1116–1124.
Younger, J. B. (1995). The alienation of the sufferer. *Advances in Nursing Science, 17*, 53–72.
Zgierska, A., Miller, M., & Rabago, D. (2012). Patient satisfaction, prescription drug abuse, and potential unintended consequences. *Journal of the American Medical Association, 307*, 1377–1378.

Integrative Meaning Therapy: From Logotherapy to Existential Positive Interventions

Paul T.P. Wong

Introduction

This chapter focuses on meaning-enhancing positive interventions from both positive psychology (PP) and existential psychology perspectives. It is a continuation of the same endeavor found in the current author's chapter on Frankl's meaning-seeking model (Wong, 2014). This earlier chapter focused on the intersection and integration of Frankl's concepts and PP research on meaning. The present chapter goes one step further by focusing on the underlying paradigm that facilitates such integration for both research and interventions.

More specifically, the current chapter makes the case that integration between PP and existential psychology results in existential positive psychology (EPP) (Wong, 2010), which is largely inspired by Frankl's theme of positive meaning potentials in sufferings. This logical progression can be referred to as "second wave positive psychology" (PP2.0) because it represents a synthesis of thesis (negative existential focus) and antithesis (PP1.0). Thus, the emerging PP2.0 is an inevitable scientific progression and provides the proper paradigm for meaning-oriented research and interventions.

Given the mounting evidence regarding the vital role of meaning in well-being and healing (Batthyany & Russo-Netzer, 2014; Steger, Sheline, Merriman, & Kashdan, 2013; Wong, 2012a), it is expected that meaning-enhancing interventions will be important in applied PP. Unfortunately, meaning-oriented interventions remain underdeveloped, as compared to happiness-inducing interventions and strengths-enhancing interventions. In contrast, both logotherapy (Frankl) and meaning therapy (Wong) focus almost exclusively on meaning-enhancing interventions.

P.T.P. Wong, Ph.D., C.Psych (✉)
Meaning-Centered Counselling Institute, Inc.,
13 Ballyconnor Court, Toronto, ON, Canada, M2M 4C5
e-mail: drpaulwong@gmail.com

Part of the reason for the lack of development in meaning-enhancing interventions in PP may be due to the assumption that when people are happy and successful, meaning is superfluous—there seems to be no need for meaning. Therefore, PP has devoted most of its energy to happiness research and happiness-inducing interventions.

From both personal experiences and research, it is known that people are more likely to engage in a quest for meaning when things go wrong (Wong & Weiner, 1981). Furthermore, meaning makes suffering more bearable and enables people to be more resilient (Frankl, 1985; Wong & Wong, 2012). In fact, most of the profound insights into meaning in life have been discovered by those who have gone through extreme suffering (Frankl, 1985; Guttman, 2008).

This chapter proposes PP2.0 (Ivtzan, Lomas, Hefferon, & Worth, 2015; Wong, 2011) as the necessary paradigm for meaning-oriented interventions. The main differences between the beginning stages of PP and PP2.0 will be discussed in detail later in this chapter. Suffice to say that PP2.0 has become necessary for two main reasons:

1. The simple-minded focus on only the positive is no longer defensible because positives and negatives are often connected—there is a bright side to the negatives and dark side to the positives. Therefore, the dialectic rather than binary principle is more applicable to the reality of human experiences.
2. Life is hard and full of suffering for most people. One cannot focus on the pursuit of happiness and assume that the problem of suffering will simply go away. PP2.0 emphasizes that one needs to confront and embrace the dark side of human existence in order to achieve authentic happiness and resilience.

Since PP2.0 is informed by existential psychology and based on the insights of Frankl, it is also known as existential positive psychology (EPP) (Wong, 2009, 2010). Thus, the unique contribution of PP2.0 or EPP is that it maintains the importance of confronting the dark side of human existence in order to achieve meaning, authentic happiness, and resilience.

From the perspective of PP2.0, this chapter will first introduce logotherapy and classical logotherapy interventions. Then, it will introduce integrative meaning therapy, which extends logotherapy by incorporating existential positive interventions. In other words, integrative meaning therapy is broader than logotherapy and includes other positive interventions (e.g., the gratitude exercise) that are informed by PP2.0 and have meaning as their underlying integral construct.

Research has consistently demonstrated that our behavior is a function of person-situation interactions (Mischel, 1968). However, PP2.0 or EPP proposes that, at a deeper level, our behavior is also a function of the interaction between personal beliefs and the universal condition of human existence. For example, according to a well-known saying from William James, "Believe that life is worth living, and your very belief will help create the fact" (James, 2000, p. 240). Thus, if a person believes that there is inherent meaning in the human condition regardless of circumstances, such affirmation will have an overall adaptive influence on his/her behavior in various situations. The adaptive benefits of functioning beliefs are a fruitful area of PP research.

Meaning Enhancing Positive Interventions from PP1.0

The most commonly recommended positive interventions include enhancing positive emotions, expressing gratitude, and identifying character strengths followed by finding new opportunities to use them (Seligman, Steen, Park, & Peterson, 2005). There are actually very few meaning-enhancing interventions in the PP literature. Most of the publications in this area are written by Parks and Rashid, the two coauthors of Seligman's initial article on positive psychotherapy (Seligman, Rashid, & Parks, 2006).

In a recent review article, Parks and Biswas-Diener (2013) ask the rhetorical question whether positive interventions are just "selling old wine in a new bottle" (p. 140). In fact, most of the positive interventions reported predate Seligman's launching of the PP movement in 1998. What makes the current research on positive interventions unique is its experimental rigor.

Sin and Lyubomirsky (2009) define positive interventions as those aimed at cultivating positive feelings, positive behaviors, or positive cognitions. Parks and Biswas-Diener (2013) define positive interventions in terms of their focus on positive topics; positive mechanisms or positive outcome variables; and promoting wellness rather than fixing weaknesses. Most PP interventions are designed to help the nondistressed improve themselves rather than to provide therapy for the clinical population (Parks & Biswas-Diener, 2013).

More recently, Foody, Barnes-Holmes, and Barnes-Holmes (2013) provide a more complete statement regarding positive psychology interventions:

> The primary goal of positive psychology is to identify the positive aspects of an individual's personality and to harness these in the service of achieving optimum human functioning. In other words, strategies for promoting well-being lie at the heart of this psychological movement. (pp. 178–179)

Thus, the domain of PP and positive interventions is clearly oriented toward happiness. In recent years, meaning has emerged as a hot research area for PP (Batthyany & Russo-Netzer, 2014; Hicks & Routledge, 2013; Wong, 2012b). However, both the PP literature and the current author's personal conversations with leading positive psychologists indicate that there has been less research on meaning-enhancing interventions as compared to happiness-inducing or strengths-based interventions.

Empirical Support for Positive Meaning Interventions

Parks and Biswas-Diener (2013) provide a balanced review of positive interventions, pointing out both their successes and limitations. Surprisingly, the only meaning intervention they covered was expressive writing. They are correct in pointing out that most meaning interventions involve personal narratives to make sense of traumatic or stressful events (e.g., Pennebaker & Seagal, 1999). In contrast, the benefits of expressive writing on positive experiences are less clear-cut. Lyubomirsky,

Sousa, and Dickerhoof (2006) found that participants who wrote about a past positive event reported lower life satisfaction as compared to a control group. Writing about one's positive future was beneficial (Sheldon & Lyubomirsky, 2006), but Parks and Biswas-Diener point out that even this approach did not work with some individuals.

Parks and Biswas-Diener's (2013) coverage of interventions related to social connections is relevant to meaning intervention, since meaning is generally defined as service to others (Frankl, 1985; Seligman, 2004). This area of research is primarily related to altruistic behaviors toward others. Dunn, Aknin, and Norton (2008) report that spending money on others results in enhanced happiness, and this finding has been replicated in many other countries (Aknin et al., 2013).

Parks and Biswas-Diener (2013) conclude that manipulations that increase social connections can enhance personal happiness. From a meaning perspective, such manipulations result in happiness precisely because it is a natural by-product of serving others or self-transcendence, as Frankl (1985) has maintained. Consistent with the enduring spiritual teaching that it is more blessed to give than to receive, Frankl nails down the biggest spiritual secret of living a meaningful and fulfilling life—we do not ask what we can get from life, but ask what life demands of us. Such self-transcendence is the key to meaning and happiness, because it is at the heart of our spiritual nature. Unfortunately, often due to too strong a focus on personal happiness, most first wave positive mental health professionals may not as profoundly recognize the meaning and significance of Dunn et al.'s (2008) finding.

The simple-minded focus on happiness leads to some experiments that are of questionable value from a meaning perspective. For example, Lyubomirsky, Sheldon, and Schkade (2005) investigated whether engaging in an act of kindness per day for a week or five acts of kindness in a single day leads to increases in well-being. This is an interesting study with respect to personal happiness, but from the standpoint of meaning, it has dubious value. To translate this finding to practice, does it mean that one should refrain from doing a kind deed, even when the situation demands it, so that one can "cash in" more happiness by doing all kind deeds in one day? In other words, does this study encourage callous calculation devoid of compassion? Wouldn't we rather encourage people to perform random acts of kindness every day, because this is good for both those who practice it and their society?

The same can be said about gratitude exercises. Parks and Biswas-Diener (2013) point out that sometimes such exercises may actually result in negative feelings rather than increased happiness. For example, Parks recognizes that the Gratitude Visit exercise does not work or even backfires for some individuals from Asian-American backgrounds (Parks & Biswas-Diener, 2013). Does this mean that gratitude is desirable only in certain situations, simply because it does not increase one's happiness? Shouldn't one rather maintain an attitude of gratitude for the overall benefit of improving one's relationships and spiritual maturity at a deeper level?

In Buddhist psychology, as well as in traditional cultures, there is a consistent teaching that people should be grateful. Take, for instance, the popular Chinese saying, "Whenever you drink, remember its source." This means that when you eat, be grateful to the farmers who grew the crops and the cook who prepared the dish for you. When you are aware of your existence, be grateful to your parents who gave birth to you and raised you. Such teachings on attitude change can avoid the problem of doing contrived gratitude exercises inappropriately, whether it is sending a gratitude letter or paying a gratitude visit.

A positive attitude of gratitude has more to do with virtue rather than personal feelings of happiness. One may express such gratitude in the appropriate manner that is called for by each situation. Frankl (1985) consistently emphasizes the importance of situational demands and the need to be sensitive to their meaning potential. This contextual approach is clearly more realistic and flexible than the prescription of any specific gratitude exercise.

Recently, Foody et al. (2013) emphasized that "gratitude exercises should avoid a focus on what is felt over what is valued in order to encourage self as process" (p. 188). Similarly, in meaning therapy, gratitude interventions focus on the virtue and process of becoming a better and more grateful person, because such an appreciative and grateful attitude may have more pervasive benefits on well-being and meaning.

Positive Psychotherapy

Another area of applied PP is positive psychotherapy (PPT) (Seligman et al., 2006). Recently, Rashid et al. (2014) have provided a detailed description of PPT:

> PPT, unlike traditional therapeutic paradigms, purports that problems do not necessarily reside entirely inside participants. Hence, it is not in favor of the New Age mantra: *To Change Life, Change Your Attitude*. Instead, PPT acknowledges that well-being and depression are engendered and maintained by complex interactions between individuals and their environments. PPT doesn't purport to oversimplify this complexity. It weighs symptoms and strengths, vulnerabilities and opportunities, skills and deficits realistically—without minimizing or ignoring either. In this regard, Positive Psychotherapy is a misnomer; we would prefer to call it a balanced therapy—but it is far less appetizing than PPT. In striking the balance, PPT equally considers positive emotions and strengths and negative symptoms and disorders. (p. 162)

Clearly, the description emphasizes the need to strike a balance between "symptoms and strengths, vulnerabilities and opportunities, skills and deficits realistically" (Rashid et al., 2014, p. 162). However, in a careful examination of the actual session-by-session description, the present author has found little evidence of a balanced approach that pays equal attention to symptoms, weaknesses, and negative emotions. Most of the sessions cover the typical PP variables, such as positive emotions, character strengths, and gratitude.

Their only reference to the dark side is about "bad memories." Consistent with their positive bias, bad memories are interpreted as being bad for you: "the role of bad memories is discussed in terms of how they undermine one's resilience" (Rashid et al., 2014, p. 164). In contrast, from a meaning perspective, bad memories can be good if one learns to confront, transcend, and make a coherent narrative out of them.

Moreover, there is no evidence that meaning is included in the program, even though they claim that PPT is designed to build "positive emotions, strengths, and *meaning*, in addition to undoing symptoms" (Rashid et al., 2014, p. 161; emphasis added).

Another limitation of PPT is that it attempts to dismiss the importance of attitude change in transforming one's life. Attitude change is not simply a "New Age mantra." There is substantial literature on the psychology of attitude change. An attitude is "a relatively enduring organization of beliefs, feelings, and behavioral tendencies toward socially significant objects, groups, events or symbols" (Hogg & Vaughan, 2005, p. 150). As such, interventions designed to change one's attitude may have more pervasive and enduring effects than interventions focused on behavioral or cognitive change. Attitude modification is an essential part of logotherapy and meaning therapy. Future research is needed to determine the relative efficacy of meaning-oriented attitude modification as compared to happiness-oriented positive interventions.

Mainstream mental health professionals have also recognized the importance of meaning in life in psychotherapy (Hill, Kline, et al., 2015; Ryff et al., 2014):

> The cure is thus not defined by the alleviation of emotional discomfort, or the attainment of some ideal feeling state, but by being able to take constructive action in one's life—i.e., being able to live a full and meaningful existence, rather than be ruled by passing emotions. (Ryff et al., 2014, p. 12)

Recent attempts to integrate PP and action and commitment therapy (ACT) (Kashdan & Ciarrochi, 2013) have significantly expanded meaning-oriented interventions and moved closer to logotherapy and meaning therapy in terms of placing more emphasis on values and actions rather than the feeling good and hedonic outcome measures. In doing so, they provide a "framework for sustaining fulfillment even in the face of pain and setbacks" (Steger et al., 2013, p. 243).

Steger et al.'s (2013) chapter is exceptionally helpful in introducing meaning-oriented interventions from this new framework. This approach offers "'larger and larger patterns.' Meaning in life research directly addresses how behaviors and values, as a holistic unit, bring one's life into harmony by serving a greater purpose" (Steger et al., 2013, p. 262). They recognize the following main themes that are closely related to logotherapy and meaning therapy.

1. *Mobilizing values.* The aim of this intervention is to identify and explore the values that clients can act on. For example, one can ask clients to talk about "what they stand for, what they believe in, what makes them proud about their own conduct, and so on" (Steger et al., 2013, p. 255). This line of questioning serves to push clients to discuss their values that benefit both them and the world.
2. *What the World Needs Now.* This intervention strategy approaches the value issue from what the world demands of the client. "Continued dialogue can help clients find the most magnetic need in the world. When paired with the 'mobilizing values' intervention, people can be helped to find a purpose they care about and articulate some rough ideas about how they would like to pursue it" (Steger et al., 2013, p. 256).

Importantly, Steger et al. (2013) recognize that meaning is inherently related to self-transcendental value:

> Although most meaning in life theorists are agnostic about what kinds of meaning are 'best,' several have argued that as people mature, their meaning in life becomes increasingly

directed at a greater good that transcends their momentary, individualistic desires. This notion of self-transcendence is often a descriptor used of people experiencing a mindful mindset (Brown, Ryan, & Creswell, 2007). (p. 261)

However, while they acknowledge the importance of values and self-transcendence, their epistemological assumptions are still similar to those of the earlier stages of PP.

It should also be noted that in the larger literature on trauma and its treatment (Janoff-Bulman, 2006, 2010) as well as posttraumatic growth (Calhoun & Tedeschi, 2006; Tedeschi & Calhoun, 2012), the concept of meaning indeed plays an important role, but such interventions are not generally considered PP interventions, which are generally seen as those based on variables and mechanisms in PP research (Parks & Biswas-Diener, 2013).

The Need for PP2.0

As stated in the Introduction, PP2.0 takes a larger view of recognizing both the infinite human potentials for good and for evil. In other words, it adds an additional existential dimension to provide greater depth for the human phenomena of meaning, happiness, and virtue (Wong, 2015).

Focusing on a person's strengths does not mean ignoring the dark side of human existence, which includes personal problems and illnesses (Saleebey, 2011). Similarly, Simmons and Lehmann (2013) believe that the most promising positive approach is to simultaneously increase one's strengths and remediate one's deficiency. They strongly argue for a balanced approach:

> The argument for balance in addressing the human experience in assessment and evaluation is quite the opposite of what has been referred to as the "happiology" construct in which all that matters is a focus on human happiness and well-being (Peterson, 2006, p. 7). As Snyder, Lopez, and Pedrotti (2011) note, "it is very tempting to focus on just the good (or the bad) in the world, *but it is not good science* and we must not make this mistake in advancing positive psychology" (p. 8). (Simmons & Lehmann, 2013, p. 21)

They also recognize the importance of contributions prior to Seligman's PP movement. These include transcendent experiences (James, 1902/1958), Frankl's (1985) concept of self-transcendence, Maslow's (1943, 1968) self-actualization, Rogers' (1961) ideas about the fully functioning person, and Antonovsky's (1979) concept of *salutogenesis*.

Consistent with logotherapy and meaning therapy, Simmons and Lehmann (2013) emphasize that effective intervention depends on the following foundational assumptions regarding humanistic and existential values:

1. Individual value and dignity.
2. Optimism in recovery and growth.
3. Dialectic perspective of positive and negative.
4. Intrinsic meaning in life.
5. Personal responsibility and collaborate effects.

With respect to the promotion of meaningful instrumental activities, Proctor and Linley (2014) also advocate a balanced approach to developing both character strengths and relative character weaknesses. As well, they favor a more holistic approach:

> Finally, spirituality, positive religious coping, and daily spiritual experiences have also been [shown] to be positively related to positive affect and life satisfaction among young people (Van Dyke et al., 2009). These results suggest that holistic approaches to increasing well-being should consider the use of positive religious coping strategies among youths who are religious and the role of spirituality in early adolescents' psychological well-being. (Proctor & Linley, 2014, p. 209)

In earlier publications, such as Batthyany and Russo-Netzer (2014) and Wong (2011, 2012b), the differences and similarities between PP and existential-humanistic psychology have been discussed. Table 1 represents a summary of the differences between PP1.0 and PP2.0, which incorporates much of the prior discussions.

Perhaps the most significant difference is PP2.0's conceptualization of a dialectic and interactive approach as shown in Fig. 1.

According to this model, there are constant interactions between positive and negative sides and internal and external factors. Positive mental health does not only depend on positive internal and external factors; it can also benefit from overcoming character defects and external obstacles. For example, overcoming external obsta-

Table 1 Contrast between PP1.0 and PP2.0

PP1.0	PP2.0
Dichotomous and binary.	Dialectical and interactive.
Focuses on the positive only.	Focuses on both the positive and the negative.
Emphasizes positive emotions.	Emphasizes responsible action.
Avoids the topics of suffering and death.	Embraces of the topics of suffering and death as precondition for authentic happiness.
Flourishing achieved through focusing on the positive and avoiding the negative.	Flourishing achieved only through confronting the dark side of human existence.
Happiness oriented, self-fulfillment focused.	Meaning oriented, self-transcendence focused.
Direct pursuit of happiness may backfire.	Direct pursuit of meaning leads to authentic happiness.
Truncated understanding of well-being.	Complete understanding of well-being in the midst of suffering.
Focuses on elements of well-being, such as behavior, cognition, affect, and so on.	Focuses on the whole person, taking a holistic and person-centered approach.
Distinct from humanistic-existential psychology.	Informed by humanistic-existential psychology.
Based on the positivist paradigm.	Based on the humble science perspective.
Based on empirical findings from psychological laboratories.	Based on empirical findings from both psychological and real-life "laboratories."
Based on individualist culture.	Based on both individualist and collectivist cultures.

```
                    INTERNAL FACTORS
                           ▲
     Character defects         Character strengths
     Handicaps                 Talents

NEGATIVE      ◄──────────────────►    POSITIVE
(Deficits)                            (Resources)

     Obstacles                 Opportunities
     Social Isolation          Social Support
                           ▼
                    EXTERNAL FACTORS

     A dynamic, dialectic two-dimensional model of mental health
```

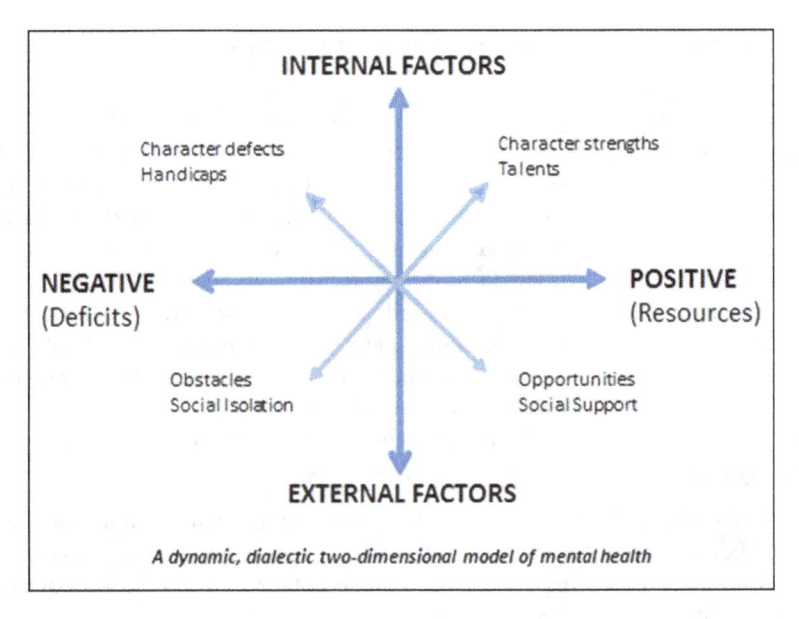

Fig. 1 A dialectic and interactive model of mental health

cles can increase the character strength of persistence, and social support can help a person overcome their handicaps. This interactive model increases both the scope and flexibility of positive interventions.

It is encouraging that leaders in ACT have explicitly recognized the need to move toward PP2.0. Hayes (2013) provides abundant evidence to demonstrate the contextual limits of positive traits as well as the binary dichotomous approach toward human experiences and traits.

> In this area, the acceptance and mindfulness traditions can add something useful to positive psychology as it transitions into "Positive Psychology 2.0" (Wong, 2011). Contextual behavioral scientists and practitioners are well suited to this task because their focus on context affords a more dynamic and less judgmental approach to human experience (Hayes, 2013, p. 307).

Meaning-Enhancing Interventions in Logotherapy

Lukas (2015) points out logotherapy's unique contribution of providing positive meaning and healing in times of suffering:

> No science can explain the meaning of illness, guilt, and pain in this world. Neither can psychology. But the assertion of the logotherapist is that human beings are fundamentally equipped to find meaning even in illness, guilt, and pain by lifting themselves spiritually beyond them and perhaps even finding their own destiny in the process. (p. 58)

The Objective Criteria of Meanings and Values

The key concept of logotherapy is the will to meaning (Frankl, 1988). Frankl has a unique view of equating the will to meaning with the spiritual nature of self-transcendence. Frankl (1985) recognizes that the perception of meaning is subjective, as it varies from person to person and situation to situation. However, he also points out the main objective criteria of self-transcendence—the touchstone of meaning—getting beyond oneself in the service of God, other people, or a greater cause. Furthermore, bigger is not necessarily better, because a greater purpose needs to be ethically responsible to self, others, and a Higher Authority. Such objective requirements are needed to prevent another Hitler or holocaust. This emphasis on ethical responsibility is missing in positive interventions.

In addition, Frankl (1985) has also identified the following three objectives or enduring values as the pathways of meaning:

1. *Creative value.* Devote your life to doing something creative and unique for the well-being of others. Everybody can make a unique contribution; everyone is at least good for something. Remember that it is not the nature of the work or career but the attitude you bring that matters the most.
2. *Experiential value.* Be mindful of what is happening around you rather than always thinking about yourself. Paying attention to what is around you will leave you less time to feel miserable. If you have an appreciative attitude, you will find beauty and meaning even in the most mundane experiences. The idea is getting the focus away from yourself toward what is happening around you here and now.
3. *Attitudinal value.* You can always take the stand of maintaining a defiant attitude. This is the last freedom that no one can take it away from you. This type of spirit says, "You can destroy me, but you cannot defeat me." It helps maintain human dignity. Being able to exaggerate and laugh at your problems (as in the case of paradoxical intention) reflects this value.

In contrast to the behavioral focus in positive intervention, logotherapy emphasizes the following five attitudes as essential for living a meaningful life (Frankl, 1985):

1. An affirmative attitude toward life and human potentials (believing in the intrinsic meaning in life and the human capacity for freedom and self-transcendence).
2. A responsible attitude toward life as a whole and the demands of concrete situations.
3. A creative attitude toward any kind of work we do (the creative value).
4. An appreciative attitude toward life as a whole and daily experiences (the experiential value).
5. A defiant attitude toward sufferings that are beyond our control (the attitudinal value).

Furthermore, there are at least five ways to modify one's attitude according to logotherapy:

1. Identify one's spiritual need for meaning and self-transcendence through Socratic dialogue.
2. Distance oneself from the situation and habitual ways of responding.
3. Decide to take a positive and defiant stance toward fate and adversity.
4. Consult one's innate conscience and core values.
5. Implement an attitude that is consistent with one's most cherished meaning and beliefs.

The Value of Self-Transcendence

With respect to cultivating an attitude of self-transcendence, Lukas (2015) proposes the following elements in logotherapy:

1. Switching from blaming others for problems to assuming responsibility to find solutions.
2. Switching from selfish pursuits (ego) to serving others or a worthy cause (logos) as in the case of dereflection.
3. Becoming motivated by the fulfillment of spiritual longings rather than immediate need gratification.
4. Being willing to suffer and sacrifice for the greater good or a higher purpose.
5. Being willing to let go of what cannot be changed and transcend unavoidable suffering and losses.
6. Being open to the meaning potentials of every situation and life as a whole.
7. Activating one's spiritual dimension to discover what really matters.

It is particularly worth noting that logotherapy emphasizes the spirit of self-sacrifice, which is missing in other meaning-enhancing interventions. This is the spirit of willingly and intentionally enduring suffering in order to achieve a meaningful goal. Consistent with the thinking of PP2.0, suffering is not only a reality to be accepted, but also a necessity to be embraced in order to survive and thrive. The present author hypothesizes that those who are willing to accept a small self-sacrifice for a worthy cause are more likely to live a meaningful life and achieve some measure of greatness in public or humanitarian services.

According to Lukas (2015),

> Frankl wrote about "giving meaning" (*Sinn geben*) as a form of "sacrificing something" (*preisgeben*), which must be done for the sake of the meaning to be actualized. Nevertheless, it is extremely difficult for a person spoiled by the affluence of the present Western culture to make a sacrifice, even when it would be meaningful and the value gained would be great. (p. 210)

One of the many profound insights from Frankl is this: Sacrifice is a beneficial spiritual exercise in pursuing self-transcendence and meaning.

The present author has recently developed a Self-Transcendence Measure as part of his research related to the Templeton Grant on Virtue, Meaning and Happiness (Wong, 2015). This scale was designed to provide a reliable and valid measure of Frankl's conceptualization of self-transcendence (Wong, in press).

1. I assume full responsibility for my life and my behavior.
2. I consider it a privilege and joy to suffer for my family and friends.
3. I take good care of myself so that I can take good care for those who depend on me.
4. I contribute money and effort to uplift society and humanity.
5. I care about other people's well-being, even when they are unrelated to me.
6. My purpose in life is to serve others, even when it entails personal sacrifice.
7. I practice civic responsibility in order to create a better society.
8. I experience deep satisfaction from serving God or a great worthy cause.
9. I feel spiritually connected with God or the cosmos.
10. My faith or hope extends beyond my external situations and physical existence.
11. I am responsible to develop my full potential in order to give my best to society.
12. I am willing to take risks and accept challenging responsibilities.

Individuals are asked to rate how each statement is characteristic of them on a five-point rating scale, ranging from "Not At All" to "A Great Extent." This scale can be used for meaning therapy to monitor people's progress in the pursuit of self-transcendence.

The unique key to healing in logotherapy and meaning therapy is to activate clients' spiritual will to meaning in a creative way that suits clients' unique predicaments, personal history, and personality. Such spiritual activation may be summed up as three meaning-enhancing interventions:

1. *Exploration*. This first step usually involves exploration in past instances or current situations in which clients show some inkling or trace of self-transcendence. That is, times in which they express selfless interest in another person or a worthy cause and some urge or personal responsibility to do what is right or what really matters.
2. *Insight*. The second step involves helping clients gain some insight of the noble, spiritual side of themselves that is so different from their culturally conditioned egotistic, materialistic thinking. It is like a ray of light breaking through the darkness and ignorance of their mind regarding the spiritual virtue of self-transcendence.
3. *Implementation*. The third step involves awakening the clients' willingness to implement their insights, knowing that people are not only good and life is not like living in Disneyland. Only through a bold and realistic view that people are capable of both good and evil and the world is full of potential for meaning and goodness in the midst of suffering, violence, and death can we develop a PP robust enough to be relevant to the suffering masses.

Wong's Existential Positive Interventions

The present author's integrative meaning therapy (MT) is an intervention that evolves from Frankl's logotherapy (Wong, 2012a). Different from Frankl's classic logotherapy, MT is pluralistic and emphasizes the application of contemporary meaning research findings, such as in the sources of meaning (Wong, 1998), the meaning-mindset (Wong, 2012c), and components of meaning (Wong, 2011). A good example of such integration can be found in the current author's chapter on Frankl's meaning-seeking model (Wong, 2014).

The Practice of Integrative Meaning Therapy

MT is actually a pluralistic approach (Cooper & McLeod, 2010), open to incorporating cognitive behavior therapy (CBT), narrative therapy, and so on. For example, there are at least five ways to overcome irrational anxiety according to MT. The following shows a combination of CBT, MT, and logotherapy:

1. Recognize that the anxiety is irrational (Rational thinking).
2. Exaggerate it to the point of laughing at it (Paradoxical intention).
3. Stop rumination and switch attention to a worthy task (Dereflection).
4. Recognize it is of no consequence in the larger scheme of things (Double vision).
5. Believe that everything will work out at the end (Affirming faith).

The main difference between Cooper and McLeod's (2010) approach and Wong's is that the latter's pluralistic outlook is integrative with meaning as the central organizing construct. Thus, the commonality between different approaches of psychotherapy has to do with the basic human capacity for meaning-seeking and meaning-making.

Existential Positive Interventions of Pursing Meaning

On the basis of all available research, Wong (2012a) has concluded that meaning consists of four fundamental components: Purpose, Understanding, Responsibility, and Enjoyment/Evaluation (PURE). The empirical support on the adaptive benefits of purpose, understanding (coherence), enjoyment (positive affect) is enormous (Batthyany & Russo-Netzer, 2014; Wong, 1998, 2012b).

Consistent with Frankl (1985), responsibility is recognized as a fundamental ingredient of meaning, which is often missing in meaning research and meaning-oriented PP interventions. However, there is a large literature in social-personality research bearing on the importance of responsibility in mental health and well-being. For example, responsibility is related to research on locus of control

(Lefcourt, 2014), attribution of responsibility (Weiner, 1993), and self-determination theory (Ryan & Deci, 2000). In psychotherapy, there is also the emphasis on helping clients shift from blaming others and situations to assuming personal responsibility for one's well-being and future based on the aforementioned literature on responsibility.

PURE, as a comprehensive definition of meaning, also provides a flexible framework of existential positive interventions and encourages the pursuit of meaning along any of these pathways according to the unique need of each client. Here is a typical example of how one can use the PURE framework in meaning therapy:

1. Explore clients' stated *purpose* and motivations for change and their preferred future without their problems,
2. Help clients gain new *understanding* and insight of their own difficulties and stuck-ness,
3. Lead clients to embrace their freedom and *responsibility* to implement actions based on their self-efficacy beliefs, personal strengths, and available resources, and
4. Guide clients to *experiment* with whether their actions would bring about positive change; if not, then, they need to either modify their goals or actions.

The exploration, insight, and implementation elements of MT are similar to what Hill, Kanazawa, et al. (2015) identify as basic skills in working with meaning in life issues as reported by experienced psychotherapists. The last point regarding behavioral experimentation is similar to what is commonly used in CBT.

From a slightly difference perspective, PURE is similar to ACT's intervention of enhancing committed action (McCracken, 2013). Existential positive interventions cover the following steps after spiritual activation as described earlier:

1. Work with the client to develop a realistic and measurable action plan.
2. Empower and contract the client to carry out their commitment, one step at a time.
3. Use the double-system strategy to identify and resolve difficulties (through ABCDE; see section below, "Existential Positive Interventions of Resilience") and return to their original goal (through PURE).
4. Use the double-vision strategy to link their therapy goal to larger life goals or some higher purposes.

Existential Positive Interventions of Resilience

On the basis of empirical research regarding meaning and resilience (Wong & Wong, 2012), the present author has identified five elements as essential in coping with adversity: Acceptance, Belief, Commitment, Discovery, and Evaluation/Enjoyment (ABCDE). Wong (2012a) explains how these functions work together to achieve resilience. Basically, this involves a journey of self-discovery, self-reflection, and self-acceptance, along with the journey of overcoming and transcending adversities and suffering.

In the ABCDE process, acceptance is an essential existential component. Acceptance of a painful emotion is never an end in its own right, but rather an overall life attitude of accepting life as it is. Unless people confront and accept the dark side of human existence, they will have difficulty experiencing healing and flourishing. Six main reasons why acceptance is an important intervention are that it:

1. Increases our tendency to accept life in its totality,
2. Increases self-compassion in spite of our limitations,
3. Increases our acceptance of other imperfect human beings,
4. Reduces harsh self-judgment,
5. Reduces complaints about our own misfortunes, and
6. Reduces fear of uncertainties and misfortunes.

An existential gratitude exercise is perhaps the best example of existential positive intervention, in contrast with gratitude exercises as usual. The emphasis is placed on cultivating gratitude by internalizing it as an essential virtue rather than practicing the gratitude exercise as a way of increasing personal hedonic feelings. For example, instead of writing about three good things, three daily blessings can be emphasized:

1. Be thankful for being alive with all its opportunities for creative contributions.
2. Be thankful for family members, friends, and all those who have contributed to your life.
3. Be thankful for our home, the beautiful planet earth.

Such an existential gratitude exercise is not only deeper and broader than the Three Good Things Exercise or Gratitude Visit of mainstream positive interventions, but is also more relevant to people in all life circumstances and ethnic-cultural contexts. If one meditates on the above three areas daily, it will make one a better and happier person. The current author invites positive mental health professionals to compare this existential gratitude exercise of Three Blessings with any other gratitude exercise.

Further Research

A research agenda inspired by PURE and ABCDE includes the following:

1. The adaptive benefits of self-transcendence based on the above Self-Transcendence Scale as well as experimental manipulations of preferring some self-sacrifice for others.
2. The adaptive benefits of beliefs in the intrinsic values and meaning of life as compared to those who do not share such beliefs.
3. The adaptive benefits of training grit or commitment in pursuing a worthy goal.

Over the past 20 years, the current author has given workshops on integrative meaning therapy to all kinds of mental health workers—from psychologists, mental health therapists, and counsellors, to GP psychotherapists and clinical nurses. According to their feedback, they find that the general frameworks of PURE and ABCDE, as well as the evidence-based components of these frameworks, provide considerable flexibility and confidence in their clinical practices. In other words, they find these frameworks cover additional areas of classic logotherapy due to the recent progress in PP research on meaning and positive interventions.

Perspective is Everything

As Thomas Aquinas' treatment of the will has been succinctly summarized, "The things that we love tell us what we are" (Kreeft, 2012, p. 183). In other words, the things we love and pursue reveal our true nature. According to Aquinas and Frankl, we are physical, psychological, and spiritual beings, and our truest selves, free from earthly concerns and egotistic interests, are spiritual selves, interested in the ideals of meaning, authenticity, and compassion.

Beyond one's physical needs for pleasure and comfort (Freud) and beyond psychological needs for power and fame (Adler), what one loves and cares deeply about reveals the hidden aspects of the spiritual need for meaning (Frankl). The task of logotherapy and meaning therapy is to activate the spiritual virtue of self-transcendence as the pathway to meaning.

A simple perspective change can transform one's life for the better. Perspective change is a powerful tool for psychotherapists and coaches. What is unique in logotherapy or MT is that perspective change is fundamental to reorienting clients from egotistic concerns of pleasure and success to the meaning-mindset of being responsible for the well-being of others and its resulting deep satisfaction.

Like ACT, meaning therapists also ask clients questions like, "What do you care about (values, personal strivings)?" "What do you really want in life?" and "What really matters?" However, existential positive interventions go beyond values clarification and the identification of personal goals; they are also designed to awaken clients' personal responsibility for self-transcendence as described in spiritual activation (see the section above, "The Value of Self-Transcendence").

MT also emphasizes the role of values, but it goes beyond personal strivings, because it also attempts to awaken the hidden spiritual value of longing for the "self-transcendent good." The purpose is to help one discover life's calling and became what one was meant to be. A slight change to the self-transcendent perspective can change how one sees life and how one lives.

Furthermore, the emphasis in MT is not on flexibility per se, but on the adaption of the responsibility to be flexible in order to change from ego to logos. The advantage of this shift away from an egotistic orientation represents a basic switch from egotistic pursuits to self-transcendence.

Existential positive interventions, based on a broad and positive explanatory system regarding human nature or the human condition, can offer people infinite possibilities of meaning and hope in the midst of unavoidable suffering. They seem more realistic and relevant to most people who are struggling with the hardship and seeming absurdity of human life. It is hoped that the second wave of positive psychology (PP2.0) will devote more research on existential positive interventions as the most promising direction to develop meaning-enhancing interventions.

Key Takeaways

- Positive interventions can become more realistic and relevant to the suffering masses if they include an existential dimension, which acknowledges that suffering and anxiety are inevitable aspects of being alive.
- Existential positive interventions are based on the assumption that one is to embrace and transform the dark side of human existence in order to find authentic happiness and resilience.
- The dialectical principle works best in existential positive interventions because it aims to bring out the bright side in negative situations and prevent the dark side in positive situations. Thus, this principle is more likely to optimize positive functioning than the binary approach of only focusing on the positives.
- The PURE and ABCDE frameworks not only provide a flexible meaning-oriented intervention, but also give therapists the confidence that all the individual components in these frameworks have considerable empirical support from both positive psychology and existential psychology.

References

Aknin, L. B., Barrington-Leigh, C. P., Dunn, E. W., Helliwell, J. F., Burns, J., Biswas-Diener, R., … Norton, M. I. (2013). Prosocial spending and well-being: Cross-cultural evidence for a psychological universal. *Journal of Personality and Social Psychology, 104*(4), 635–652. doi:10.1037/a0031578
Antonovsky, A. (1979). *Health, stress and coping*. San Francisco, CA: Jossey-Bass.
Batthyany, A., & Russo-Netzer, P. (Eds.). (2014). *Meaning in existential and positive psychology*. New York, NY: Springer.
Calhoun, L. G., & Tedeschi, R. G. (Eds.). (2006). *Handbook of posttraumatic growth: Research and practice*. Mahwah, NJ: Erlbaum.
Cooper, M., & McLeod, J. (2010). *Pluralistic counselling and psychotherapy*. Thousand Oaks, CA: Sage.
Dunn, E. W., Aknin, L. B., & Norton, M. I. (2008). Spending money on others promotes happiness. *Science, 319*(5870), 1687–1688. doi:10.1126/science.1150952
Foody, M., Barnes-Holmes, Y., & Barnes-Holmes, D. (2013). On making people more positive and rational: The potential downsides of positive psychology interventions. In T. Kashdan & J. Ciarrochi (Eds.), *Mindfulness, acceptance, and positive psychology: The seven foundations of well-being* (pp. 166–193). Oakland, CA: New Harbinger.

Frankl, V. E. (1985). *Man's search for meaning* (Revised & updated ed.). New York, NY: Washington Square Press.
Frankl, V. E. (1988). *The will to meaning: Foundations and applications of logotherapy* (Expanded ed.). New York, NY: Meridian.
Guttman, D. (2008). *Finding meaning in life, at midlife and beyond: Wisdom and spirit from logotherapy*. Santa Barbara, CA: Praeger.
Hayes, S. C. (2013). The genuine conversation. In T. Kashdan & J. Ciarrochi (Eds.), *Mindfulness, acceptance, and positive psychology: The seven foundations of well-being* (pp. 303–319). Oakland, CA: New Harbinger.
Hicks, J. A., & Routledge, C. (Eds.) (2013). *The experience of meaning in life: Classical perspectives, emerging themes, and controversies*. New York, NY: Springer.
Hill, C. E., Kanazawa, Y., Knox, S., Schauerman, I., Loureiro, D., James, D., … Moore, J. (2015). Meaning in life in psychotherapy: The perspective of experienced psychotherapists. *Psychotherapy Research, 17*, 1–16. doi:10.1080/10503307.2015.1110636
Hill, C. E., Kline, K., Bauvan, V., Brent, T., Breslin, C., Calderon, M., … Knox, S. (2015). What's it all about? A qualitative study of meaning in life for counseling psychology doctoral students. *Counselling Psychology Quarterly, 28(1)*, 1–26. doi:10.1080/09515070.2014.965660
Hogg, M., & Vaughan, G. (2005). *Social psychology* (4th ed.). London, UK: Prentice-Hall.
Ivtzan, I., Lomas, T., Hefferon, K., & Worth, P. (2015). *Second wave positive psychology: Embracing the dark side of life*. London, UK: Routledge.
James, W. (1902/1958). *The verities of religious experience*. New York, NY: New American Library.
James, W. (2000). *Pragmatism and other writings*. New York, NY: Penguin.
Janoff-Bulman, R. (1992/2010). *Shattered assumptions: Towards a new psychology of trauma*. New York, NY: Simon & Schuster.
Janoff-Bulman, R. (2006). Schema-change perspectives on posttraumatic growth. In L. G. Calhoun & R. G. Tedeschi (Eds.), *Handbook of posttraumatic growth: Research and practice* (pp. 47–67). Mahwah, NJ: Erlbaum.
Kashdan, T., & Ciarrochi, J. (Eds.). (2013). *Mindfulness, acceptance, and positive psychology: The seven foundations of well-being*. Oakland, CA: New Harbinger.
Kreeft, P. (2012). *Socrates meets Kant: The father of philosophy meets his most influential modern child*. South Bend, IN: St Augustine's Press.
Lefcourt, H. M. (2014). *Locus of control: Current trends in theory & research*. New York, NY: Psychology Press.
Lukas, E. (2015). *The therapist and the soul: From fate to freedom*. Charlottesville, VA: Purpose Research.
Lyubomirsky, S., Sheldon, K. M., & Schkade, D. (2005). Pursuing happiness: The architecture of sustainable change. *Review of General Psychology, 9(2)*, 111–131. doi:10.1037/1089-2680.9.2.111
Lyubomirsky, S., Sousa, L., & Dickerhoof, R. (2006). The costs and benefits of writing, talking, and thinking about life's triumphs and defeats. *Journal of Personality and Social Psychology, 90(4)*, 692–708. doi:10.1037/0022-3514.90.4.692
Maslow, A. H. (1943). A theory of human motivation. *Psychology Review, 50*, 370–396. doi:10.1037/h0054346
Maslow, A. H. (1968). *Toward a psychology of being*. New York, NY: Wiley.
McCracken, L. (2013). Committed action. In T. Kashdan & J. Ciarrochi (Eds.), *Mindfulness, acceptance, and positive psychology: The seven foundations of well-being* (pp. 128–139). Oakland, CA: New Harbinger.
Mischel, W. (1968/1996). *Personality and assessment*. Mahwah, NJ: Erlbaum.
Parks, A. C., & Biswas-Diener, R. (2013). Positive interventions: Past, present, and future. In T. Kashdan & J. Ciarrochi (Eds.), *Mindfulness, acceptance, and positive psychology: The seven foundations of well-being* (pp. 140–165). Oakland, CA: New Harbinger.
Pennebaker, J. W., & Seagal, J. D. (1999). Forming a story: The health benefits of narrative. *Journal of Clinical Psychology, 55(10)*, 1243–1254. Retrieved from http://poetryforpersonalpower.com/wp-content/uploads/2011/10/health-benefits-of-forming-a-story.pdf

Proctor, C., & Linley, P. A. (2014). Life satisfaction in youth. In G. A. Fava & C. Ruini (Eds.), *Increasing psychological well-being in clinical and educational settings* (Vol. 8, pp. 199–215). Dordrecht, NL: Springer.

Rashid, T., Anjum, A., Chu, R., Stevanovski, S., Zanjani, A., & Lennox, C. (2014). Strength based resilience: Integrating risk and resources towards holistic well-being. In G. A. Fava & C. Ruini (Eds.), *Increasing psychological well-being in clinical and educational settings* (Vol. 8, pp. 153–176). Dordrecht, NL: Springer.

Rogers, C. D. (1961). *On becoming a person: A therapist's view of psychotherapy*. Boston, MA: Houghton Mifflin.

Ryan, R. M., & Deci, E. L. (2000). Self-determination theory and the facilitation of intrinsic motivation, social development, and well-being. *American Psychologist, 55*(1), 68–78. doi:10.1037/0003-066X.55.1.68

Ryff, C. D., Love, G. D., Miyamoto, Y., Markus, H. R., Curhan, K. B., Kitayama, S., ... Karasawa, M. (2014). Culture and the promotion of well-being in East and West: Understanding varieties of attunement to the surrounding context. In G. A. Fava, & C. Ruini (Eds.). *Increasing psychological well-being in clinical and educational settings* (Vol. 8, pp. 1–19). Dordrecht, NL: Springer.

Saleebey, D. (Ed.). (2011). *The strengths perspective in social work practice* (6th ed.). New York, NY: Allyn & Bacon.

Seligman, M. E. P. (2004). *Authentic happiness: Using the new positive psychology to realize your potential for lasting fulfillment*. New York, NY: Free Press.

Seligman, M. E. P., Rashid, T., & Parks, A. C. (2006). Positive psychotherapy. *American Psychologist, 61*(8), 774–788. doi:10.1037/0003-066X.61.8.774

Seligman, M. E. P., Steen, T. A., Park, N., & Peterson, C. (2005). Positive psychology progress: Empirical validation of interventions. *American Psychologist, 60*(5), 410–421. doi:10.1037/0003-066X.60.5.410

Sheldon, K. M., & Lyubomirsky, S. (2006). How to increase and sustain positive emotion: The effects of expressing gratitude and visualizing best possible selves. *The Journal of Positive Psychology, 1*(2), 73–82. doi:10.1080/17439760500510676

Simmons, C. A., & Lehmann, P. (2013). *Tools for strengths-based assessment and evaluation*. New York, NY: Springer.

Sin, N. L., & Lyubomirsky, S. (2009). Enhancing well-being and alleviating depressive symptoms with positive psychology interventions: A practice-friendly meta-analysis. *Journal of Clinical Psychology: In Session, 65*, 467–487. doi:10.1002/jclp.20593

Steger, M. F., Sheline, K., Merriman, L., & Kashdan, T. B. (2013). Using the science of meaning to invigorate values-congruent, purpose-driven action. In T. Kashdan & J. Ciarrochi (Eds.), *Mindfulness, acceptance, and positive psychology: The seven foundations of well-being* (pp. 240–266). Oakland, CA: New Harbinger.

Tedeschi, R. G., & Calhoun, L. G. (2012). Pathways to personal transformation: Theoretical and empirical developments. In P. T. P. Wong (Ed.), *The human quest for meaning: Theories, research, and applications* (2nd ed., pp. 559–572). New York, NY: Routledge.

Weiner, B. (1993). On sin versus sickness: A theory of perceived responsibility and social motivation. *American Psychologist, 48*(9), 957–965. doi:10.1037/0003-066X.48.9.957

Wong, P. T. P. (1998). Implicit theories of meaningful life and the development of the Personal Meaning Profile (PMP). In P. T. P. Wong & P. Fry (Eds.), *The human quest for meaning: A handbook of psychological research and clinical applications* (pp. 111–140). Mahwah, NJ: Erlbaum.

Wong, P. T. P. (2009). Existential positive psychology. In S. Lopez (Ed.), *Encyclopedia of positive psychology* (Vol. 1, pp. 361–368). Oxford, UK: Wiley Blackwell.

Wong, P. T. P. (2010). What is existential positive psychology? *International Journal of Existential Psychology and Psychotherapy, 3*, 1–10.

Wong, P. T. P. (2011). Positive psychology 2.0: Towards a balanced interactive model of the good life. *Canadian Psychology, 52*(2), 69–81. doi:10.1037/a0022511

Wong, P. T. P. (2012a). From logotherapy to meaning-centered counseling and therapy. In P. T. P. Wong (Ed.), *The human quest for meaning: Theories, research, and applications* (2nd ed., pp. 619–647). New York, NY: Routledge.

Wong, P. T. P. (Ed.). (2012b). *The human quest for meaning: Theories, research, and applications* (2nd ed.). New York, NY: Routledge.

Wong, P. T. P. (2012c). What is the meaning mindset? *International Journal of Existential Psychology and Psychotherapy, 4*(1), 1–3.

Wong, P. T. P. (2014). Viktor Frankl's meaning seeking model and positive psychology. In A. Batthyany & P. Russo-Netzer (Eds.), *Meaning in existential and positive psychology* (pp. 149–184). New York, NY: Springer.

Wong, P. T. P. (2015). The meaning hypothesis of living a good life: Virtue, happiness, and meaning. Retrieved from http://www.drpaulwong.com/the-meaning-hypothesis-of-living-a-good-life-virtue-happiness-and-meaning/

Wong, P. T. P. (in press). The development of a new Self-Transcendence Measure based on Frankl's concept. *International Journal of Existential Psychology and Psychotherapy.*

Wong, P. T. P., & Weiner, B. (1981). When people ask "Why" questions and the heuristic of attributional search. *Journal of Personality and Social Psychology, 40,* 650–663.

Wong, P. T. P., & Wong, L. C. J. (2012). A meaning-centered approach to building youth resilience. In P. T. P. Wong (Ed.), *The human quest for meaning: Theories, research, and applications* (2nd ed., pp. 585–617). New York, NY: Routledge.

Nostalgia as an Existential Intervention: Using the Past to Secure Meaning in the Present and the Future

Clay Routledge, Christina Roylance, and Andrew A. Abeyta

Meaning in life is a fundamental human motive (Frankl, 1997; Maslow, 1968), and has critical implications for mental and physical health and well-being (Hicks & Routledge, 2013). Meaning can be thought of as the belief that one is living a life of purpose and significance (Baumeister, 1991; Heintzelman & King, 2014). Additionally, meaning has been defined as the feeling that the world is a predictable and reliable place, and that we can come to understand it with some sense of certainty (Antonovsky, 1993; Baumeister & Vohs, 2002).

Psychologists have long been interested in the value of perceiving life as meaningful. For example, according to Abraham Maslow (1968), having a meaningful framework for one's life is a fundamental human need, and exists in a hierarchy of needs alongside basic physical needs such as food, water, and shelter. Drawing on his experience surviving a Nazi concentration camp, Viktor Frankl (1997) conceptualized meaning as derived through one's work and contributions to society, social relationships, as well as the ability to persevere through suffering. His conceptualization of meaning contributed to his development of Logotherapy, an existential psychotherapy predicated on the notion that attaining a sense of meaning is critical to human survival. Carl Rogers' person-centered therapy (1951, 1961), a product of humanistic psychology, focuses on allowing clients to discover meaning as a way to achieve self-actualization and ultimately positive self-regard. Thus, according to Rogers, the therapeutic process should allow clients to learn to have a positive self-concept, which will in turn facilitate meaning-making.

The common thread among these and other theoretical accounts is that humans need meaning to live and live well—as mentioned, many of these theories have been used to develop therapies aimed at improving people's quality of life. Indeed, empirical

---

C. Routledge, Ph.D. (✉) • C. Roylance, M.S • A.A. Abeyta, M.A
Department of Psychology, North Dakota State University,
Minard Hall, Fargo, ND 58102, USA
e-mail: clay.routlege@ndsu.edu

research shows that feeling that one's life is meaningful contributes to people's health and well-being. For example, people with meaning report feeling healthier than those who lack meaning (Steger, Mann, Michels, & Cooper, 2009). Also, perceiving life as meaningful is associated with greater ability to cope with stress (a protective health factor; Park, 2011), and greater happiness and satisfaction with life (Park, Park, & Peterson, 2010). Not only do those with meaning live healthier lives, they live *longer* lives (Boyle, Buchman, Barnes, & Bennett, 2010; Krause, 2007). Particularly as people age, meaning in life appears to be a protective factor against mortality and age-related cognitive deficits (Boyle, Barnes, Buchman, & Bennett, 2009).

Conversely, feeling that one's life is meaningless is associated with many negative psychological health consequences, such as depression (Mascaro & Rosen, 2005), suicidality (Ungar, Ungar, & Kim, 2011), and substance abuse (Kinnier, Metha, Keim, & Okey, 1994). Among military veterans with posttraumatic stress disorder (PTSD), deficits in meaning in life are associated with severity of symptoms (Owens, Steger, Whitesell, & Herrera, 2009).

In addition, meaning is an important component of a wide range of psychological interventions. Therapies that encourage meaning-making have been found to be effective for treating depression (Santos et al., 2013) and alcohol abuse (Singer, Singer, & Berry, 2013). Additionally, a great deal of work has focused on how meaning-making through expressive writing can have health benefits (Pennebaker, 1993, 2004). Research has established that expressive writing helps people make meaning, especially after facing trauma (Park & Blumberg, 2002). The resulting health benefits have ranged from improved immune functioning (Pennebaker, Kiecolt-Glaser, & Glaser, 1988), better psychological adjustment to living with cancer (Park, Edmondson, Fenster, & Blank, 2008), and better physical health amongst cancer survivors (Creswell et al., 2007). Thus, especially when people are facing hardships, the ability to find meaning offers protection from harm, both physically and psychologically.

In sum, those who have meaning enjoy the benefits of longer, better lives. And those who lack meaning are at greater risk of experiencing negative health and well-being outcomes. Perceiving life as meaningful is such a core need, that meaning-making may not only have a place in clinical settings, it may be crucial. We now turn our attention to nostalgia and how it contributes to meaning in life.

Nostalgia

The term "nostalgia" was coined in 1688 by the Swiss medical student Johaness Hofer (1688/1934). The word comes from two sounds: *nostos* (return to the native land) and *algos* (pain). Therefore, nostalgia as originally conceived means the pain caused by the desire to return to one's native land. Hofer viewed nostalgia as a medical disease afflicting Swiss soldiers and mercenaries who travelled from their

Alpine homes to the plains of Europe to wage war. Symptoms of this disease included constant thinking about home, sadness, anxiety, irregular heartbeat, insomnia, loss of thirst, disordered eating, physical weakness, and fever (see Routledge, Wildschut, Sedikides, & Juhl, 2013). Hofer proposed that nostalgia was a "cerebral disease" (Hofer, 1688/1934, p. 387) resulting from "the quite continuous vibrations of animal spirits through those fibers of the middle brain in which impressed traces of ideas of the Fatherland still cling" (Hofer, 1688/1934, p. 384).

In the twentieth century, nostalgia became viewed as less of a medical disease and more of a psychological condition. For psychologists from the psychoanalytic tradition, nostalgia represented an "acute yearning for a union with the preoedipal mother, a saddening farewell to childhood, a defense against mourning, or a longing for a past forever lost" (Kaplan, 1987, p. 466). Nostalgia was considered to be an unpleasant state associated with difficulties of individuation or separation (Neumann, 1949/1971; Peters, 1985) or even a subconscious yearning to return to one's fetal state (Fodor, 1950).

By the mid twentieth century, the view of nostalgia as a psychological disorder started to wane. Scholars began to distinguish the feeling of homesickness (the longing for home) from the broader longing for the past that characterizes nostalgia (McCann, 1941). Psychologists became particularly interested in homesickness and the distress associated with young people's transitions away from the home environment (Hendrickson, Rosen, & Aune, 2010; Kerns, Brumariu, & Abraham, 2008; Thurber & Walton, 2007) and largely neglected the concept of nostalgia. Importantly, by the late twentieth century, most scholars no longer equated nostalgia with homesickness. In fact, researchers in marketing and consumer psychology viewed nostalgia as a positive state, predictive of preferences for products associated with one's past (e.g., Holbrook & Schindler, 1994, 1996).

More recently, social psychologists have sought to enhance understanding of nostalgia by elucidating the content of nostalgic memories and identifying the psychological states that trigger nostalgia as well as the psychological consequences of engaging in nostalgia (see Routledge et al., 2013). This work has rehabilitated the construct of nostalgia. Nostalgic memories tend to be happy memories. These memories can contain negative emotions, but they typically follow a redemptive affective sequence in which feelings of longing and loss give way to feelings of happiness and gratitude (Abeyta, Routledge, Roylance, Wildschut, & Sedikides, 2015; Wildschut, Sedikides, Arndt, & Routledge, 2006). Nostalgic memories are also largely social in nature (Abeyta et al., 2015; Wildschut et al., 2006), and often involve time spent with friends, family, and romantic partners. However, nostalgic memories also predominantly feature the self (Wildschut et al., 2006). Thus, though these memories almost always involve others, the self is the protagonist. Finally, nostalgic memories are meaningful memories. They involve personally cherished life experiences (e.g., graduations, weddings, family vacations, holidays, religious rites of passage; Wildschut et al., 2006). In sum, when people engage in nostalgic reflection they are revisiting personally treasured and generally positive life experiences shared with close others.

Nostalgia serves a number of psychological functions. Notably, engaging in nostalgia increases positive affect (but not negative affect), self-esteem, and feelings of social connectedness (Wildschut et al., 2006). In addition, nostalgia is triggered by negative psychological states (e.g., loneliness) and serves to restore psychological adjustment (e.g., feelings of social support; Wildschut et al., 2006; Zhou, Sedikides, Wildschut, & Gao, 2008). In short, in contrast to historic views, recent empirical research reveals that nostalgia is a psychological resource that people can employ to protect or promote psychological health and well-being in the face of distress (see Routledge et al., 2013).

In the present chapter, we describe research identifying nostalgia as a meaning-making resource. Specifically, we review studies demonstrating that (1) nostalgia contributes to perceptions of meaning, (2) threatened meaning increases nostalgia, (3) nostalgia mitigates the effects of various meaning-relevant threats (mortality salience, expectancy violations, boredom), and (4) nostalgia improves psychological well-being and reduces distress for people with meaning deficits. We conclude by discussing the potential for the future development of nostalgia-based clinical interventions.

Nostalgia Predicts Meaning

The first question is whether nostalgia positively contributes to perceptions of meaning in life. In two studies we (Routledge et al., 2011) tested the potential for nostalgia to be related to meaning. In the first study, we measured nostalgia proneness (Routledge, Arndt, Sedikides, & Wildschut, 2008). Specifically, participants responded to items such as "How often do you experience nostalgia?" on a scale ranging from *very rarely* to *very frequently*. Subsequently, participants completed two measures of the perceived presence of meaning in life. These were the Purpose in Life scale (e.g., "My personal existence is purposeful and meaningful"; Crumbaugh & Maholick, 1964) and the Presence subscale of the Meaning in Life Questionnaire ("I have a good sense of what makes my life meaningful"; Steger, Frazier, Oishi, & Kaler, 2006). Providing evidence that nostalgia is a source of meaning, nostalgia proneness was positively and significantly correlated with both meaning measures.

In our next study (Routledge et al., 2011), participants listened to popular songs and rated how nostalgic each song made them feel and the extent to which each song made them feel that life is worth living. Results provided further support for a link between nostalgia and meaning in that the more people reported that a piece of music made them feel nostalgic, the more they reported that the music made them feel like life is worth living. This indicates that when people feel nostalgic while listening to music, they also feel that life is very meaningful.

Reid, Green, Wildschut, and Sedikides (2015) found a similar pattern of results with scent-evoked nostalgia. In this research, participants were presented with tubes containing various scented oils (e.g., pumpkin pie spice, eggnog, cotton candy), instructed to smell each oil and indicate how nostalgic each scent made them feel. The researchers also asked participants to indicate the extent to which each scent made them feel "life is meaningful" and "life has a purpose." The more a scent generated nostalgia, the more participants reported that it made them feel like life has meaning and purpose. In all, these studies link the experience of nostalgia to perceptions of meaning in life.

Experimentally Induced Nostalgia Increases Meaning

A number of experimental studies offer evidence that nostalgia is not merely associated with meaning, it actually generates meaning. We (Routledge et al., 2011) utilized multiple nostalgia inductions to test nostalgia's potential to enhance meaning. In one study, we used music lyrics to induce nostalgia. Specifically, in an initial session, participants provided a list of songs that make them nostalgic. Weeks later, participants returned to the lab and received lyrics from the songs that either they (nostalgia condition) or another participant (control condition) had indicated as being nostalgic. Subsequently, participants completed the Presence subscale of the Meaning in Life Questionnaire (Steger et al., 2006). Participants who received their own nostalgic song lyrics reported higher meaning in life than participants who received non-nostalgic lyrics.

We (Routledge, Wildschut, Sedikides, Juhl, & Arndt, 2012) demonstrated the same effect with a nostalgia writing induction. Specifically, we provided university student participants in the nostalgia condition with a dictionary definition of nostalgia and asked them to bring to mind and write down four keywords concerning an experience of nostalgia (Wildschut et al., 2006). We instructed participants in a control condition to bring to mind and write down four key words related to a desired future event. All participants then completed the Presence subscale of the Meaning in Life Questionnaire (Steger et al., 2006). Again, inducing nostalgia increased meaning when compared to a control condition (a desired future event). University students have a number of meaningful major life events ahead of them (e.g., graduation, finding a career, marriage, starting a family), and thinking about these future desired events could presumably increase meaning. Thus, finding that nostalgia heightens meaning relative to a desired future event condition provides strong evidence that the past is an important existential resource, and may even be more powerful than thinking about an appealing future. In a subsequent series of studies, we (Routledge et al., 2012) replicated this effect of nostalgia increasing meaning with a different control condition (i.e., memory of a recent positive event) and measure of meaning (i.e., search for meaning in life).

In all, a number of studies using distinct experimental manipulations indicate that nostalgia increases meaning in life. When people revisit their personally treasured past experiences that make them feel nostalgic, they report greater perceptions of meaning in life.

Threats to Meaning Trigger Nostalgia

Nostalgia increases meaning, but do people naturally turn to nostalgia when meaning is under threat? To answer this question, we (Routledge et al., 2011) conducted an experiment in which we induced meaninglessness and measured nostalgia. Specifically, participants were randomly assigned to read one of two philosophical essays. To induce meaninglessness, one essay concerned the cosmic insignificance of the human species. It served to remind participants that human life is extremely short and that, relative to the timeline of the universe or even our own planet, human existence is relatively recent and brief. It also explicitly asserted that humans are no more objectively meaningful than any other form of biological life. The other essay (the control condition) concerned the limitations of computers. In a pilot study, we found that both essays were judged to be equal in the extent to which readers found them to be engaging, interesting, and original. However, the meaning threatening essay decreased perceptions of meaning relative to the control essay. After participants read one of the two essays, they responded to a measure of state nostalgia (e.g., "I feel nostalgic at the moment"; Wildschut et al., 2006). Results supported the notion that people employ nostalgia in response to threats to meaning. Participants who read an essay about the insignificance and meaninglessness of human life reported higher levels of nostalgia than participants who read an essay about the limitations of computers.

In a series of studies, van Tilburg, Igou, and Sedikides (2013) further explored meaninglessness as a nostalgia trigger. They specifically focused on the experience of boredom as a threat to meaning that leads to nostalgia. Boredom increases feelings of purposelessness and motivates people to seek out meaning (van Tilburg & Igou, 2011, 2012). Thus, boredom might inspire nostalgia, a meaning-making resource.

First, van Tilburg and colleagues (2013) investigated whether or not boredom would lead people to engage spontaneously in nostalgic reverie. Participants were randomly assigned to a high or low boredom condition. In the high boredom condition, participants were asked to copy 10 references about concrete mixtures from a Wikipedia entry. Participants in a low boredom condition were only asked to copy two references. Participants then responded to a single item on how boring they found the reference copying task. Next, participants were asked to bring to mind a past memory. Half of the participants were specifically instructed to bring to mind a nostalgic memory (nostalgic memory condition) and half were instructed to bring to mind a past memory (the word nostalgia was not used; unspecified memory condition). Finally, all participants completed a nostalgia questionnaire (Wildschut et al., 2006).

Results supported the proposal that boredom increases nostalgia. First, participants found the high boredom task significantly more boring than the low boredom task. Not surprisingly, participants who were specifically instructed to bring to mind a nostalgic memory reported higher nostalgia than participants in the unspecified memory reflection task. Critically though, the boredom induction moderated this effect. In the low boredom condition, participants in the nostalgia memory condition felt significantly more nostalgic than participants in the unspecified memory condition. However, in the high boredom condition, participants in the unspecified memory condition felt just as nostalgic as participants in the nostalgia memory condition. Further, within the unspecified memory condition, high boredom participants were significantly more nostalgic than low boredom participants. In short, participants in the high boredom condition turned to nostalgia even without being prompted. In two additional experiments using a different boredom task, the researchers replicated this effect.

After establishing that boredom triggers nostalgia, the researchers sought to determine if the need for meaning in life was responsible for the effect of boredom on nostalgia. Participants were randomly assigned to a high or low boredom task (i.e., copying 10 or two references about concrete mixtures), responded to items assessing the extent to which they would currently like to do something meaningful or purposeful (search for meaning), and then completed a nostalgia measure. The high boredom condition increased the search for meaning and nostalgia. In addition, search for meaning fully mediated the relationship between boredom and nostalgia. The researchers then replicated this pattern of results with dispositional measures. That is, participants responded to items indicative of trait boredom (e.g., "How often do you experience boredom?"), completed a search for meaning scale (e.g., "I am looking for something that makes my life feel meaningful"; Steger et al., 2006), and finally, completed a measure of nostalgia proneness (Routledge et al., 2008). Replicating the experimental findings, trait boredom predicted search for meaning and nostalgia proneness and the relationship between boredom and nostalgia was mediated by search for meaning. Taken together, van Tilburg and colleagues' (2013) research demonstrates that people naturally become more nostalgic when their perceptions of meaning are threatened by boredom.

In all, a number of studies evidence that nostalgia is triggered by experiences that undermine meaning. Whether people are facing heavy questions about their cosmic insignificance or merely experiencing a lack of meaningful engagement because they are performing a boring task, they become nostalgic.

Nostalgia Counters Threats to Meaning

Nostalgia contributes to meaning and threatened meaning increases nostalgia. However, does nostalgia protect people from threats to meaning? To begin, we (Routledge & Arndt, 2005) proposed that nostalgia might prove to be an important resource for coping with existential threats related to meaning. This proposal was based upon a framework derived from terror management theory (TMT; Greenberg, Pyszczynski, & Solomon, 1986). According to TMT, humans strive for self-preservation but are highly self-aware and able to project the self forward in time, and thus uniquely able to realize that death is inevitable. This awareness of death has the potential to generate a great deal of personal distress and can undermine perceptions of meaning in life. The theory proposes that people are able to, for the most part, avoid the terror associated with the awareness of death by investing in structures (e.g., family, religion, social identities) that make life seem meaningful. Through living meaningful lives, people feel like they have made lasting and important contributions to society that symbolically allow them to transcend mortality.

In support of TMT, a large body of research demonstrates that experimentally heightened awareness of mortality (mortality salience) leads to heightened investment in socially and culturally derived meaning-providing structures and that such investment reduces the cognitive accessibility of death-related thoughts (Greenberg, Solomon, & Arndt, 2008) as well as psychological distress (e.g., anxiety; Routledge & Juhl, 2010; Routledge et al., 2010). We (Routledge & Arndt, 2005) proposed that nostalgia is a psychological resource that people can employ to reassure themselves that their lives are meaningful when facing existential threats that could undercut meaning.

In a series of studies, we (Routledge et al., 2008) tested the proposal that nostalgia serves to counter meaning-relevant existential threat. We specifically hypothesized that if nostalgia is a meaning-providing resource then, like other meaning-providing resources, it will mitigate the effects of death-related cognition. In the first study, we measured individual differences in nostalgia proneness (e.g., "How often do you engage in nostalgia?") and manipulated death-related cognition with a well-established mortality salience induction (Rosenblatt, Greenberg, Solomon, Pyszczynski, & Lyon, 1989). Specifically, in the experimental condition, participants were instructed to spend a few minutes reflecting on their mortality. In the control condition, participants reflected on an anxiety-provoking experience not related to death: dental pain. Next, participants completed a meaninglessness scale (e.g., "All strivings in life are futile and absurd"; Kunzendorf & Maguire, 1995). We hypothesized that thinking about one's mortality would increase perceptions that life is meaningless, but only among individuals low in nostalgia proneness. Results supported this hypothesis. People who regularly engage in nostalgia were shielded from the meaning-sapping effect of thinking about death.

These results indicate that nostalgia helps protect meaning when people think about death. But does nostalgia actually help reduce death-related cognition? Previous research demonstrates that when mortality is made salient, investment in meaning-proving structures (e.g., religion) reduces the accessibility of death thoughts (Greenberg et al., 2008). Since nostalgia promotes meaning, we hypothesized that nostalgia would reduce the accessibility of death thoughts after such thoughts are activated via a mortality salience induction. In one study, we measured nostalgia proneness and then induced mortality salience using the same induction previously described. In another study, we manipulated nostalgia by having participants write about an experience of nostalgia or an ordinary past experience (Wildschut et al., 2006). In both experiments, the dependent variable was death-thought accessibility (DTA). Specifically, participants received a list of incomplete word stems, some of which could be completed with death or non-death-related words (e.g., COFF_ _ could be COFFIN or COFFEE; Greenberg, Pyszczynski,

Solomon, Simon, & Breus, 1994). Participants were instructed to complete each word stem. More death-relevant stem completions correspond to greater accessibility of death cognitions, and a higher DTA score.

Both studies provided support for the hypothesis. Mortality salience increased the accessibility of death-related thoughts, but only at low levels of nostalgia (when nostalgia proneness was measured) and in the ordinary condition (when nostalgia was manipulated). When people are reminded of death, both trait and experimentally induced nostalgia counter the resulting death-thoughts, and reduce their cognitive accessibility.

We (Juhl, Routledge, Arndt, Sedikides, & Wildschut, 2010) also tested whether nostalgia would mitigate mortality salience-induced death anxiety. If nostalgia reduces the accessibility of death thoughts, we reasoned it would also reduce death anxiety. To test this, we assessed nostalgia proneness, manipulated mortality salience, and assessed death anxiety with the 8-item Death of Self subscale from the Revised Collett-Lester Fear of Death Scale (Lester, 1990). For this scale, participants indicate how anxious they feel about different aspects of death (e.g., "the shortness of life", "the total isolation of death"). Mortality salience increased death anxiety, but only among individuals low in nostalgia proneness. People who regularly engage in nostalgia were shielded from the death anxiety that contemplating death causes.

We (Juhl et al., 2010) further considered the potential for nostalgia to influence other well-established meaning-related consequences of death awareness. One way in which people respond to mortality salience is by clinging to group memberships and social identities. Group identities are a powerful source of meaning—individuals die, but the groups they belong to typically continue to exist indefinitely. In other words, groups offer enduring meaning—the feeling that one is part of something that transcends physical death. Since groups offer transcendent meaning, people respond to mortality salience by favoring their own group and disliking other groups (Greenberg et al., 2008). If nostalgia provides meaning, it should reduce the need to defend one's meaning-providing group following mortality salience.

We (Juhl et al., 2010) hypothesized that people who regularly engage in nostalgia (high proneness individuals) would not respond to mortality salience with the typically observed ingroup bias. To test this prediction, we measured nostalgia proneness (Routledge et al., 2008), manipulated mortality salience as described before, and then asked participants to evaluate an essay critical of their university (a salient group identity for college students). Students were told they were reading an essay authored by a fellow student, which then asserted that their university is not as good as everyone thinks it is and that attending it was a big mistake. After reading the essay, participants responded to items evaluating the essay (e.g., "How much do you agree with this person's opinion?") and the author (e.g., "How much do you think you would like this person?"). As hypothesized and consistent with past research, mortality salience increased negative evaluations of the essay and essay author. When people are reminded of mortality, they are not tolerant of those who derogate a group they belong to. However, this effect only occurred among individuals low on nostalgia proneness. People who frequently utilize nostalgia did not feel compelled to defend their university identity, or derogate someone who undermined that identity.

We (Routledge, Juhl, Abeyta, & Roylance, 2014) also considered the potential for nostalgia to mitigate some of the more socially problematic consequences of death awareness. As previously noted, research identifies mortality concerns as a contributing factor to ingroup bias, as well as intergroup conflict (Greenberg et al., 2008). Building on this work, further studies sought to determine if the existential threat of death awareness contributes to aggressive and even self-harming behaviors, inasmuch as such actions may be associated with the defense of a meaning-providing identity. Our physical bodies tie us to our mortal nature. Therefore, when faced with the option, we may at times be willing to sacrifice our transient physical self in the service of attaining a more meaningful and symbolically immortal self that is derived from social and cultural identities. In support of this possibility, Pyszczynski and colleagues (2006) found that in response to mortality salience, Iranian college students indicated increased positivity toward martyrdom attacks against the United States as well as increased willingness to consider joining the cause. Similarly, we (Routledge & Arndt, 2008) found in a sample of British students that mortality salience increased endorsement of items such as "I would die for England" and "My personal safety is not as important as the continuation of the British way of life."

We (Routledge et al., 2014) proposed that nostalgia, because it provides meaning, may mitigate mortality salience provoked willingness to self-sacrifice. We tested this possibility in two studies. In the first study, American university students completed a measure of nostalgia proneness (Routledge et al., 2008), were randomly assigned to think about their mortality or the experience of extreme pain, and then completed a measure of nationalistic self-sacrifice (e.g., "I would die for my nation"; Routledge & Arndt, 2008). As in past research, mortality salience increased nationalistic self-sacrifice. However, this effect was only observed among those scoring low in nostalgia proneness. People who regularly engage in nostalgia did not respond to the heightened awareness of death with an increased willingness to self-sacrifice for their nation.

In our second study, we (Routledge et al., 2014) expanded this analysis in a number of ways. Specifically, we focused on religious self-sacrifice and thus recruited a sample of adults who indicated being religious. Instead of manipulating mortality salience, we administered the same measure of death thought accessibility mentioned previously (a word stem completion task; Greenberg et al., 1994). Previous research indicates that naturally occurring high death-thought accessibility predicts outcomes similar to when such thoughts are made accessible via a mortality salience experimental induction (Routledge et al., 2010). Next, participants were randomly assigned to bring to mind and spend a few minutes writing about either an experience of nostalgia or a recent ordinary autobiographical experience (Wildschut et al., 2006). Finally, participants completed a measure of self-sacrifice similar to the one previously discussed. However, this time, instead of assessing nationalist self-sacrifice, we assessed religious self-sacrifice with items such as "I would die for my religion."

Further indicating that nostalgia counters meaning-related threat, results indicated that death thought accessibility was a significant predictor of religious self-sacrifice, but only in the non-nostalgic control condition. Inducing nostalgia thus disrupted the relationship between accessible death thoughts and willingness to engage in religious self-sacrifice. In this case, nostalgia appears to provide an alternative means of managing existential concerns about mortality.

Overall these findings demonstrate that nostalgia counters the threat of death awareness, but does nostalgia help people cope with other meaning-relevant threats? Indeed, studies demonstrate that nostalgia mitigates a wide range of threats to meaning besides mortality salience. For example, we (Routledge et al., 2011) demonstrated that nostalgia reduces defensive responses to arguments that life is objectively meaningless. In this study, participants were first randomly assigned to bring to mind and briefly write about a nostalgic or ordinary autobiographical experience (Wildschut et al., 2006). Next, participants were randomly assigned to read either the meaninglessness essay or limitations of computers essay previously described. Finally, participants were asked to evaluate the essay and the author with items such as "The author is a reliable source" and "The essay is convincing in conveying its point." We proposed that participants should respond more negatively to the meaning threat essay than the limitations of computers control essay. That is, people should want to defend meaning by negatively evaluating the meaning threat essay and author. However, if nostalgia serves as a meaning resource, then participants who were first given the opportunity to engage in nostalgia should be less in need of defending meaning, and thus less inclined to negatively evaluate the meaning threat essay and author.

Results were consistent with this proposal. In the non-nostalgic control condition, participants who read the meaning threat essay evaluated it and the author more negatively than participants who read the essay on the limitations of computers. In the nostalgia condition, no such effect emerged. In fact, for participants who read the meaning threat essay, nostalgia increased positivity toward the essay and author. Nostalgia apparently reduced the need to defend against meaning threat.

Theory and research suggest that perceiving the world as structured and predictable contributes to perceptions of meaning (Juhl & Routledge, 2012; Landau et al., 2004; Proulx, Heine, & Vohs, 2010; Vess, Routledge, Landau, & Arndt, 2009). An orderly, predictable, and stable world (i.e., a meaningful world) provides the foundation for establishing the sense that one's life has meaning. Consistent with this idea, Proulx and colleagues (2010) found that viewing stimuli that violates expectations about the world (e.g., absurd art) increased the desire to see the world in a clear, unambiguous, and orderly way (need for structure; Thompson, Naccarato, Parker, & Moskowitz, 2001), which the authors interpreted as evidence for threatened meaning (i.e., structure seeking as meaning-making).

We (Routledge et al., 2012) employed the paradigm utilized by Proulx and colleagues (2010) to determine if nostalgia mitigates an expectancy violation meaning threat. Specifically, participants were presented with a piece of art on a computer screen and were then told to spend a few minutes studying the piece of art because they would later be asked to explain the meaning of it. Participants viewed either the absurd or representational art used by Proulx and colleagues (2010). Specifically, in the absurd art condition, participants viewed Rene Magritte's *The Son of Man*. This painting challenges expectations about the visual world, as it consists of an unexpected juxtaposition of objects—an apple hovering in front of a man's face. In the representational art condition, participants viewed John Constable's *Landscape With a Double Rainbow*. This painting displays a rainbow on the beach. Next, participants were asked to bring to mind and briefly write about a nostalgic or recent positive past experience. Participants then completed the previously described Presence subscale of the Meaning in Life Questionnaire (Steger et al., 2006).

In support of the proposal that nostalgia counters meaning threat, participants who were told that they were going to have to make sense of the absurd art reported significantly lower levels of perceived meaning in life (as opposed to participants told that they were going to have to make sense of the representational art), but only in the non-nostalgic recent positive experience condition. For those who received the nostalgic prime, nostalgia eliminated the effect of needing to make sense of absurd art on meaning. In fact, for participants who were instructed to try and make sense of absurd art, those who brought to mind a nostalgic experience reported significantly higher levels of meaning than those who brought to mind a positive recent past experience. Thus, nostalgia protects meaning when people are exposed to stimuli that violate their expectations about the visual world.

Further nostalgia is not only triggered by boredom, as we previously discussed, but serves as an antidote by restoring meaning following experiences of boredom. Specifically, van Tilburg and colleagues (2013) induced boredom with the reference copying task previously described. They then instructed participants to bring to mind a memory from the past and then assessed state nostalgia. Subsequently, participants reported how much that memory gave them a sense of meaning and completed the Presence subscale of the Meaning in Life Questionnaire (Steger et al., 2006). The researchers used structural equation modeling to test the relation between variables. Results supported the proposal that nostalgia regulates meaning threat, in that boredom increased nostalgia and nostalgia in turn predicted increased meaning in life.

In all, studies identify nostalgia as a resource that helps counter a wide range of meaning threats. Nostalgia mitigates the effects of heightened death awareness on perceptions of meaning, the accessibility of death-related cognition, death anxiety, ingroup bias, and the willingness to self-sacrifice in the service of a meaningful group identity. Nostalgia reduces defensive responses to philosophical arguments about the cosmic insignificance of human life and also preserves meaning when people's expectations are violated, or when they are engaged in a boring task.

Nostalgia as an Intervention for People Lacking Meaning in Life

The studies described thus far provide evidence that nostalgia has potential as an existential resource or intervention. A critical remaining question though is whether nostalgia actually helps those who are suffering from meaning deficits. Nostalgia increases meaning and counters threats to meaning, but does it lead to positive psychological outcomes for people who currently perceive their lives as meaningless? In two studies, we (Routledge et al., 2011) tested this possibility. In the first study, we measured dispositional levels of meaning with the Purpose in Life scale (e.g., "My personal existence is purposeful and meaningful"; Crumbaugh & Maholick, 1964). We then randomly assigned participants to bring to mind and briefly write about either a nostalgic or ordinary event from their lives (Wildschut et al., 2006). After this manipulation, participants completed the State Vitality Scale (Ryan & Frederick, 1997), which includes items such as "At this moment, I feel alive and vital" and "I am looking forward to each new day." We assessed vitality because it is an indicator of eudaimonic well-being (i.e., well-being derived from meaning) and a critical component of adaptive psychological functioning.

People who lack meaning in life should report low vitality. Our findings supported this prediction: low purpose in life was significantly associated with low vitality. However, nostalgia successfully mitigated this effect. That is, the relationship between meaning and vitality became non-significant in the nostalgia condition. For people who scored low on dispositional meaning, nostalgia increased vitality. This result indicates that nostalgia promotes psychological well-being for those who perceive their lives as lacking meaning.

People who perceive their lives as meaningless may be at high risk for experiencing stress in challenging situations (Park & Folkman, 1997). We (Routledge et al., 2011) tested the potential for nostalgia to buffer the heightened stress experienced by people with meaning deficits by utilizing a well-established experimental stress paradigm: the Trier Social Stress Test (TSST; Kirschbaum, Pirke, & Hellhammer, 1993; Kudielka, Hellhammer, & Kirschbaum, 2007). First, participants reported their current perceptions of meaning ("My life has meaning"). Then, we administered a baseline measure of subjective stress. In this measure, participants indicated the extent to which they currently feel "jittery," "fearful," and "ashamed." Participants were then randomly assigned to bring to mind and briefly write about a nostalgic or ordinary autobiographical experience (Wildschut et al., 2006).

The next part of the study was the TSST, which consists of a public speaking and arithmetic task that has been shown to reliably increase psychological stress responses (Schlotz et al., 2008). For the task, two research assistants dressed in laboratory coats entered the room and were seated at a desk facing the participant. The experimenter then told the participants that they would be playing the role of a job candidate for the vacant position of a tour guide and that they needed to prepare a 5-min introduction with the goal of trying to convince the panel of research assistants that they are suitable for this position. The participants were provided with paper and pencil and given 3 min to prepare their presentations. After the preparation time expired, one of the panel members instructed the participants to make their presentations. If the participants finished before 5 min, a panel member instructed them to continue. After this task, a panel member instructed the participants to subtract serially the number 17 from 2023 as fast and accurately as possible. Participants were instructed to start over each time they made a mistake. This task lasted for 5 min. Immediately following this task, the participants again responded to the stress items previously administered at baseline. They were then given a 30 min rest period and then responded to the stress items one final time.

Results supported the assertion that nostalgia helps people with meaning deficits cope with stressful experiences. First, subjective stress increased immediately after the stressful job interview task, and returned to baseline levels when assessed again 30 min later. However, trait levels of meaning and induced nostalgia determined the level of stress people felt right after the stressful task. Specifically, in the control condition, subjective stress was higher for those low in trait meaning than those high in trait meaning immediately after the stressor task. This indicates that without intervention, low meaning in life increases vulnerability to stress. However, nostalgia mitigated this effect, and decreased subjective stress. In fact, nostalgia decreased subjective stress for the low meaning participants, dropping it to levels similar to high meaning participants. In short, nostalgia eliminated the stress-vulnerability associated with deficits in meaning in life.

The Future of Nostalgia: Potential Clinical Interventions

To date, no research has operationalized nostalgia as a clinical or therapeutic intervention, and tested such an intervention on clinical populations. However, research has supported the efficacy of clinical interventions that make use of autobiographical reflection as a means of promoting meaning. These interventions capitalize on the natural tendency for people to engage in reminiscence and life review across the lifespan, but that becomes increasingly prevalent in old age. Reminiscence and life review broadly refer to the recall of experiences from the past (for a comprehensive review, see Webster, Bohlmeijer, & Westerhof, 2010). Reminiscence theory proposes that autobiographical reflection can lead to positive or negative psychological outcomes (Hallford & Mellor, 2013; Webster et al., 2010). On the one hand, reminiscence to revive feelings of bitterness is negatively related to mental health and well-being. On the other hand, reminiscence for identity and problem-solving purposes tends to be linked with positive psychological health and well-being (Cappeliez & O'Rourke, 2006; Webster, 1997).

Recognizing the mental health implications of reminiscence, researchers have focused on the efficacy of clinical interventions that make use of autobiographical reflection. These methods look to capitalize on types of reminiscence that promote positive functioning and reduce the impact of negative types of reminiscence. In general, reminiscence interventions can be characterized as falling into one of three categories: simple or unstructured reminiscence, structured reminiscence or life review, or life-review therapy (Webster et al., 2010; Westerhof, Bohlmeijer, & Webster, 2010).

Simple or unstructured reminiscence is the most informal and least guided of the interventions. Simple reminiscence occurs naturally in groups, like when a group of friends gets together to share stories about past experiences. Likewise, simple reminiscence interventions tend to be facilitated in group settings (e.g., in nursing home communities) and consist of group members responding to positive memory prompts by sharing their personal experiences. These interventions tend to be focused on goals like increasing a sense of community and promoting positive feelings. We propose that when people are engaging in this type of reminiscence, they are likely bringing to mind nostalgic experiences and feelings, and the extent to which this form of reminiscence is psychologically beneficial may be related to the extent to which it implicates nostalgia. However, this proposal needs to be tested empirically.

Structured reminiscence or life-review interventions offer a more guided experience relative to simple reminiscence interventions. Structured interventions typically occur one-to-one instead of in groups. The focus of structured reminiscence is to review the lifespan while focusing on integrating positive and negative experiences. These interventions promote self-acceptance and a sense of self-continuity. Further, structured reminiscence interventions make use of reminiscence to solve problems and reframe negative past events. Again, nostalgia may be a critical component to the success of this kind of intervention. Recent research indicates that nostalgic reflection promotes self-continuity, that people naturally turn to nostalgia when they experience feelings of self-discontinuity, and that nostalgia-inspired self-continuity promotes psychological health (Sedikides, Wildschut, Routledge, & Arndt, 2015). Thus, nostalgia may prove to be an important facet of structured reminiscence or life-review interventions, due to its implications for self-continuity. Again, research is needed to evaluate nostalgia's role in this kind of intervention.

Life-review therapy is highly structured and typically applied only in psychotherapeutic settings. A number of clinical approaches to life-review therapy focus specifically on using autobiographical reflection as a means of encouraging self-continuity and perceptions of meaning in life (Watt & Cappeliez, 2000; Westerhof, Bohlmeijer, van Beljouw, & Pot, 2010). Unlike unstructured reminiscence and structured life-review interventions, life-review therapy is typically aimed at individuals with severe depression or anxiety who tend to experience distress related to negative memory biases. The ultimate goal of these therapies is to alleviate depression and anxiety by integrating positive and negative memories into a cohesive and meaningful life story, as well as moving people away from reminiscence about negative events and reminiscence to alleviate boredom. Since nostalgia has been shown to decrease stress and anxiety and promote well-being, even for those with meaning deficits or who are experiencing threats to meaning (see Routledge et al., 2013), nostalgia might serve as an important component of life-review therapy. Nostalgia involves remembering cherished or personally meaningful life events. Similarly, a number of approaches to life-review therapy encourage people to adopt a more adaptive view of their past by emphasizing positive memories in terms of how they contribute to life's meaning (Bohlmeijer, Valenkamp, Westerhof, Smit, & Cuijpers, 2005; Watt & Cappeliez, 2000). Thus, bringing to mind nostalgic memories may help people reframe their life narratives by making salient experiences high in meaning.

Overall, research has supported the efficacy of reminiscence interventions. A recent meta-analysis by Pinquart and Forstmeier (2012) provides the most comprehensive review of the effectiveness of reminiscence interventions across a number of well-being and clinical outcomes. Using data from 128 studies, they found that relative to control groups, participants randomly assigned to receive some form of reminiscence intervention experienced significant improvement (pre-intervention to post-intervention) on nine outcomes. Specifically, reminiscence interventions led to significant increases in purpose in life, cognitive performance, feelings of personal mastery, social integration, ego integrity, and general well-being. Further, reminiscence interventions led to significant decreases in death anxiety, depressive symptoms, and mental health symptoms more generally. Reminiscence interventions were most effective in alleviating depressive symptoms and promoting ego-integrity. Even though the three types of reminiscence interventions produced significant improvements on all nine outcomes, the authors found that life-review therapy had a significantly larger effect on reducing depression than did simple reminiscence or structured reminiscence. Further research has established that forms of life-review therapy (i.e., creative reminiscence therapy) are efficacious in part by increasing perceptions of meaning in life (Westerhof, Bohlmeijer, van Beljouw, et al., 2010; Westerhof, Bohlmeijer, & Webster, 2010). Thus, life-review therapy is recognized as the gold standard of reminiscence interventions for treating depression and anxiety (Hallford & Mellor, 2013).

In all, research clearly identifies nostalgia as an existential resource that promotes meaning in life and helps people cope with experiences that threaten meaning. Though psychologists have yet to create a nostalgia-specific therapy, the broad effectiveness of other types of autobiographical therapeutic interventions suggests nostalgia may have therapeutic value. First, nostalgia may already be an important feature of reminiscence and life-review therapies because they involve reflecting on life experiences from the past. Second, since nostalgia involves revisiting life experiences that people find meaningful, then explicitly integrating nostalgia exercises into existing reminiscence or life-review therapies may improve their effectiveness. Future research should consider these possibilities.

Key Takeaways

- Nostalgic memories are typically memories that people consider to be personally significant or cherished. That is, they are memories of momentous life experiences.
- Engaging in nostalgic reflection boosts psychological health by increasing positive mood, self-esteem, feelings of belongingness, optimism about the future, and perceptions of meaning in life.
- Nostalgia not only increases a sense of meaning, it also reduces the distress that people who lack meaning often experience. In this way, nostalgia is an excellent coping resource for people struggling with meaning deficits.
- Both writing about a nostalgic memory and listening to music that makes one feel nostalgia have been shown to successfully increase feelings of meaning in life.

References

Abeyta, A. A., Routledge, C., Roylance, C., Wildschut, T., & Sedikides, C. (2015). Attachment-related avoidance and the social and agentic content of nostalgic memories. *Journal of Social and Personal Relationships, 32*, 406–413.
Antonovsky, A. (1993). The structure and properties of the Sense of Coherence scale. *Social Science & Medicine, 36*, 725–733.
Baumeister, R. F. (1991). *Meanings of life*. New York, NY: Guilford Press.
Baumeister, R. F., & Vohs, K. D. (2002). The pursuit of meaningfulness in life. In C. R. Snyder & S. J. Lopez (Eds.), *Handbook of positive psychology* (pp. 608–618). New York, NY: Oxford University Press.
Bohlmeijer, E., Valenkamp, M., Westerhof, G., Smit, F., & Cuijpers, P. (2005). Creative reminiscence as an early intervention for depression: Results of a pilot project. *Aging & Mental Health, 9*, 302–304.
Boyle, P. A., Barnes, L. L., Buchman, A. S., & Bennett, D. A. (2009). Purpose in life is associated with mortality among community-dwelling older persons. *Psychosomatic Medicine, 71*, 574–579.
Boyle, P. A., Buchman, A. S., Barnes, L. L., & Bennett, D. A. (2010). Effect of a purpose in life on risk of incident Alzheimer disease and mild cognitive impairment in community-dwelling older persons. *Archives of General Psychiatry, 67*, 304–310.
Cappeliez, P., & O'Rourke, N. (2006). Empirical validation of a model of reminiscence and health in later life. *The Journals of Gerontology. Series B, Psychological Sciences and Social Sciences, 61B*, 237–244.
Creswell, J. D., Lam, S., Stanton, A. L., Taylor, S. E., Bower, J. E., & Sherman, D. K. (2007). Does self-affirmation, cognitive processing, or discovery of meaning explain cancer-related health benefits of expressive writing? *Personality and Social Psychology Bulletin, 33*, 238–250.
Crumbaugh, J. C., & Maholick, L. T. (1964). An experimental study in existentialism: The psychometric approach to Frankl's concept of noogenic neurosis. *Journal of Clinical Psychology, 20*, 200–207.
Fodor, N. (1950). Varieties of nostalgia. *Psychoanalytic Review, 37*, 25–38.
Frankl, V. E. (1997). *Man's search for ultimate meaning*. New York, NY: Insight Books/Plenum Press.
Greenberg, J., Pyszczynski, T., Solomon, S., Simon, L., & Breus, M. (1994). Role of consciousness and accessibility of death-related thoughts in mortality salience effects. *Journal of Personality and Social Psychology, 67*, 627–637.
Greenberg, J., Pyszczynski, T., & Solomon, S. (1986). The causes and consequences of a need for self-esteem: A terror management theory. In R. F. Baumeister (Ed.), *Public self and private self* (pp. 189–212). New York, NY: Springer.
Greenberg, J., Solomon, S., & Arndt, J. (2008). A basic but uniquely human motivation: Terror management. In J. Y. Shah & W. L. Gardner (Eds.), *Handbook of motivation science* (pp. 114–134). New York, NY: Guilford Press.
Hallford, D., & Mellor, D. (2013). Reminiscence-based therapies for depression: Should they be used only with older adults? *Clinical Psychology: Science and Practice, 20*, 452–468.
Heintzelman, S. J., & King, L. A. (2014). Life is pretty meaningful. *American Psychologist, 69*, 561–574.
Hendrickson, B., Rosen, D., & Aune, R. K. (2010). An analysis of friendship networks, social connectedness, homesickness and satisfaction levels of international students. *International Journal of Intercultural Relations, 35*, 281–295.
Hicks, J., & Routledge, C. (Eds.). (2013). *The experience of meaning in life: Classical perspectives, emerging themes, and controversies*. New York, NY: Springer.
Hofer, J. (1934). Medical dissertation on nostalgia (C. K. Anspach, Trans.). *Bulletin of the History of Medicine, 2*, 376–391. (Original work published 1688).
Holbrook, M. B., & Schindler, R. M. (1994). Age, sex, and attitude toward the past as predictors of consumers' aesthetic tastes for cultural products. *Journal of Marketing Research, 31*, 412–422.

Holbrook, M. B., & Schindler, R. (1996). Market segmentation based on age and attitude toward the past: Concepts, methods, and findings concerning nostalgic influences on customer tastes. *Journal of Business Research, 37*, 27–39.

Juhl, J., & Routledge, C. (2012). The effects of individual differences in trait self-esteem and mortality salience on search for meaning. *Journal of Personality and Social Psychology, 99*, 897–916.

Juhl, J., Routledge, C., Arndt, J., Sedikides, C., & Wildschut, T. (2010). Fighting the future with the past: Nostalgia buffers existential threat. *Journal of Research in Personality, 44*, 309–314.

Kaplan, H. A. (1987). The psychopathology of nostalgia. *Psychoanalytic Review, 74*, 465–486.

Kerns, K. A., Brumariu, L. E., & Abraham, M. M. (2008). Homesickness at summer camp: Associations with the mother-child relationship, social self-concept, and peer relationships in middle childhood. *Journal of Developmental Psychology, 54*, 473–498.

Kinnier, R. T., Metha, A. T., Keim, J. S., & Okey, J. L. (1994). Depression, meaninglessness, and substance abuse in 'normal' and hospitalized adolescents. *Journal of Alcohol and Drug Education, 39*, 101–111.

Kirschbaum, C., Pirke, K. M., & Hellhammer, D. H. (1993). The 'Trier Social Stress Test'–A tool for investigating psychobiological stress responses in a laboratory setting. *Neuropsychobiology, 28*, 76–81.

Krause, N. (2007). Longitudinal study of social support and meaning in life. *Psychology and Aging, 22*, 456–469.

Kudielka, B. M., Hellhammer, D. H., & Kirschbaum, C. (2007). Ten years of research with the Trier Social Stress Test--Revisited. In E. Harmon-Jones & P. Winkielman (Eds.), *Social neuroscience: Integrating biological and psychological explanations of social behavior* (pp. 56–83). New York, NY: Guilford Press.

Kunzendorf, R. G., & Maguire, D. (1995). *Depression: The reality of "no meaning" versus the delusion of negative meaning. Unpublished manuscript.* Lowell, MA: University of Massachusetts.

Landau, M. J., Johns, M., Greenberg, J., Pyszczynski, T., Martens, A., Goldenberg, J. L., & Solomon, S. (2004). A function of form: Terror management and structuring the social world. *Journal of Personality and Social Psychology, 87*, 190–210.

Lester, D. (1990). The Collett–Lester fear of death scale. *Death Studies, 14*, 457–468.

Mascaro, N., & Rosen, D. H. (2005). Existential meaning's role in the enhancement of hope and prevention of depressive symptoms. *Journal of Personality, 73*, 985–1014.

Maslow, A. H. (1968). *Toward a psychology of being* (2nd ed.). New York, NY: Wiley.

McCann, W. H. (1941). Nostalgia: A review of the literature. *Psychological Bulletin, 38*, 165–182.

Neumann, E. (1971). *The origins and history of consciousness* (R. F. C. Hull, Trans.). Princeton, NJ: Princeton University Press. (Original work published 1949).

Owens, G. P., Steger, M. F., Whitesell, A. A., & Herrera, C. J. (2009). Posttraumatic stress disorder, guilt, depression, and meaning in life among military veterans. *Journal of Traumatic Stress, 22*, 654–657.

Park, C. L. (2011). Meaning, coping, and health and well-being. In S. Folkman (Ed.), *The Oxford handbook of stress, health, and coping* (pp. 227–241). New York, NY: Oxford University Press.

Park, C. L., & Blumberg, C. J. (2002). Disclosing trauma through writing: Testing the meaning-making hypothesis. *Cognitive Therapy and Research, 26*, 597–616.

Park, C. L., Edmondson, D., Fenster, J. R., & Blank, T. O. (2008). Meaning making and psychological adjustment following cancer: The mediating roles of growth, life meaning, and restored just-world beliefs. *Journal of Consulting and Clinical Psychology, 76*, 863–875.

Park, C. L., & Folkman, S. (1997). Meaning in the context of stress and coping. *Review of General Psychology, 1*, 115–144.

Park, N., Park, M., & Peterson, C. (2010). When is the search for meaning related to life satisfaction? *Applied Psychology: Health and Well-Being, 2*, 1–13.

Pennebaker, J. W. (1993). Putting stress into words: Health, linguistic, and therapeutic implications. *Behaviour Research and Therapy, 31*, 539–548.

Pennebaker, J. W. (2004). *Writing to heal: A guided journal for recovering from trauma and emotional upheaval.* Oakland, CA: New Harbinger Publications.

Pennebaker, J. W., Kiecolt-Glaser, J. K., & Glaser, R. (1988). Disclosure of traumas and immune function: Health implications for psychotherapy. *Journal of Consulting and Clinical Psychology, 56,* 239–245.

Peters, R. (1985). Reflections on the origin and aim of nostalgia. *Journal of Analytical Psychology, 30,* 135–148.

Pinquart, M., & Forstmeier, S. (2012). Effects of reminiscence interventions on psychological outcomes: A meta-analysis. *Aging and Mental Health, 16,* 541–558.

Proulx, T., Heine, S. J., & Vohs, K. D. (2010). When is the unfamiliar the uncanny? Meaning affirmation after exposure to absurdist literature, humor, and art. *Personality and Social Psychology Bulletin, 36,* 817–829.

Pyszczynski, T., Abdollahi, A., Solomon, S., Greenberg, J., Cohen, F., & Weise, D. (2006). Mortality salience, martyrdom, and military might: The great Satan versus the axis of evil. *Personality and Social Psychology Bulletin, 32,* 525–537.

Reid, C. A., Green, J. D., Wildschut, T., & Sedikides, C. (2015). Scent-evoked nostalgia. *Memory, 23,* 157–166.

Rogers, C. R. (1951). *Client-centered therapy; its current practice, implications, and theory.* Oxford: Houghton Mifflin.

Rogers, C. R. (1961). *On becoming a person: A therapist's view of psychotherapy.* Boston, MA: Houghton Mifflin.

Rosenblatt, A., Greenberg, J., Solomon, S., Pyszczynski, T., & Lyon, D. (1989). Evidence for terror management theory I: The effects of mortality salience on reactions to those who violate or uphold cultural values. *Journal of Personality and Social Psychology, 57,* 681–690.

Routledge, C., & Arndt, J. (2005). Time and terror: Managing temporal consciousness and the awareness of mortality. In A. Strathman & J. Joireman (Eds.), *Understanding behavior in the context of time: Theory, research, and applications* (pp. 59–84). Mahwah, NJ: Erlbaum.

Routledge, C., & Arndt, J. (2008). Self-sacrifice as self-defence: Mortality salience increases efforts to affirm a symbolic immortal self at the expense of the physical self. *European Journal of Social Psychology, 38,* 531–541.

Routledge, C., Arndt, J., Sedikides, C., & Wildschut, T. (2008). A blast from the past: The terror management function of nostalgia. *Journal of Experimental Social Psychology, 44,* 132–140.

Routledge, C., Arndt, J., Wildschut, T., Sedikides, C., Hart, C., Juhl, J., … Scholtz, W. (2011). The past makes the present meaningful: Nostalgia as an existential resource. *Journal of Personality and Social Psychology, 101,* 638–652.

Routledge, C., & Juhl, J. (2010). When death thoughts lead to death fears: Mortality salience increases death anxiety for individuals who lack meaning in life. *Cognition and Emotion, 24,* 848–854.

Routledge, C., Juhl, J., Abeyta, A., & Roylance, C. (2014). Using the past to promote a peaceful future: Nostalgia proneness mitigates existential threat induced nationalistic and religious self-sacrifice. *Social Psychology, 45,* 339–346.

Routledge, C., Ostafin, B., Juhl, J., Sedikides, C., Cathey, C., & Liao, J. (2010). Adjusting to death: The effects of mortality salience and self-esteem on psychological well-being, growth motivation, and maladaptive behavior. *Journal of Personality and Social Psychology, 99,* 897–916.

Routledge, C., Wildschut, T., Sedikides, C., Juhl, J., & Arndt, J. (2012). The power of the past: Nostalgia as a meaning-making resource. *Memory, 20,* 452–460.

Routledge, C., Wildschut, T., Sedikides, C., & Juhl, J. (2013). Nostalgia as a resource for psychological health and well-being. *Social and Personality Psychology Compass, 7,* 808–818.

Ryan, R. M., & Frederick, C. (1997). On energy, personality, and health: Subjective vitality as a dynamic reflection of well-being. *Journal of Personality, 65,* 529–565.

Santos, V., Paes, F., Pereira, V., Arias-Carrión, O., Silva, A. C., Carta, M. G., … Machado, S. (2013). The role of positive emotion and contributions of positive psychology in depression treatment: Systematic review. *Clinical Practice and Epidemiology in Mental Health, 9,* 221–237.

Schlotz, W., Kumsta, R., Layes, I., Entringer, S., Jones, A., & Wüst, S. (2008). Covariance between psychological and endocrine responses to pharmacological challenge and psychosocial stress: A question of timing. *Psychosomatic Medicine, 70*, 787–796.

Sedikides, C., Wildschut, T., Routledge, C., & Arndt, J. (2015). Nostalgia counteracts self-discontinuity and restores self-continuity. *European Journal of Social Psychology, 45*, 52–61.

Singer, J. A., Singer, B. F., & Berry, M. (2013). A meaning-based intervention for addiction: Using narrative therapy and mindfulness to treat alcohol abuse. In J. A. Hicks & C. Routledge (Eds.), *The experience of meaning in life: Classical perspectives, emerging themes, and controversies* (pp. 379–391). New York, NY: Springer Science+Business Media.

Steger, M. F., Frazier, P., Oishi, S., & Kaler, M. (2006). The Meaning in Life Questionnaire: Assessing the presence of and search for meaning in life. *Journal of Counseling Psychology, 53*, 80–93.

Steger, M. F., Mann, J. R., Michels, P., & Cooper, T. C. (2009). Meaning in life, anxiety, depression, and general health among smoking cessation patients. *Journal of Psychosomatic Research, 67*, 353–358.

Thompson, M. M., Naccarato, M. E., Parker, K. H., & Moskowitz, G. B. (2001). The personal need for structure and personal fear of invalidity measures: Historical perspectives, current applications, and future directions. In G. B. Moskowitz (Ed.), *Cognitive social psychology: The Princeton Symposium on the Legacy and Future of Social Cognition* (pp. 19–39). Mahwah, NJ: Lawrence Erlbaum Associates Publishers.

Thurber, C. A., & Walton, E. A. (2007). Preventing and treating homesickness. *Pediatrics, 119*, 843–858.

Ungar, T., Ungar, A., & Kim, M. (2011). Comments on meaninglessness and suicidal risk. *The International Forum for Logotherapy, 34*, 72–75.

van Tilburg, W. A. P., & Igou, E. R. (2011). On boredom and social identity: A pragmatic meaning-regulation approach. *Personality and Social Psychology Bulletin, 37*, 1679–1691.

van Tilburg, W. A. P., & Igou, E. R. (2012). On the meaningfulness of behavior: An expectancy x value approach. *Motivation and Emotion, 37*, 373–388.

van Tilburg, W. A. P., Igou, E. R., & Sedikides, C. (2013). In search of meaningfulness: Nostalgia as an antidote to boredom. *Emotion, 13*, 450–461.

Vess, M., Routledge, C., Landau, M. J., & Arndt, J. (2009). The dynamics of death and meaning: The effects of death-relevant cognitions and personal need for structure on perceptions of meaning in life. *Journal of Personality and Social Psychology, 97*, 728–744.

Watt, L. M., & Cappeliez, P. (2000). Integrative and instrumental reminiscence therapies for depression in older adults: Intervention strategies and treatment effectiveness. *Aging and Mental Health, 4*, 166–177.

Webster, J. D. (1997). The reminiscence functions scale: A replication. *International Journal of Aging and Human Development, 44*, 137–148.

Webster, J. D., Bohlmeijer, E. T., & Westerhof, G. J. (2010). Mapping the future of reminiscence: A conceptual guide for research and practice. *Research on Aging, 32*, 527–564.

Westerhof, G. J., Bohlmeijer, E. T., van Beljouw, I. M. J., & Pot, A. M. (2010). Improvement in personal meaning mediates the effects of a life review intervention on depressive symptoms in a randomized controlled trial. *The Gerontologist, 50*, 541–549.

Westerhof, G. J., Bohlmeijer, E., & Webster, J. D. (2010). Reminiscence and mental health: A review of recent progress in theory, research and interventions. *Ageing and Society, 30*, 697–721.

Wildschut, T., Sedikides, C., Arndt, J., & Routledge, C. (2006). Nostalgia: Content, triggers, functions. *Journal of Personality and Social Psychology, 91*, 975–993.

Zhou, X., Sedikides, C., Wildschut, C., & Gao, D. G. (2008). Counteracting loneliness: On the restorative function of nostalgia. *Psychological Science, 19*, 1023–1029.

Caring and Meaning in Psychotherapy

Ofra Mayseless

Introduction

The purpose of this chapter is to highlight the crucial and fundamental place of caring in meaning and purpose in life and in psychotherapy. Psychotherapy is a helping profession and as such its core essence relates to caring; the caring of the therapist for the client. This caring is often embedded within certain conceptual framework and relies on professional skills and on the therapist's personality, warmth, and character and is an essential and defining component of the therapist-client relations. This chapter goes beyond this obvious fact and underscores the key role of caring in human life, its centrality in human search for meaning and purpose in life, and the ramifications of such realizations to psychotherapy.

The *caring motivation* is an intrinsic and fundamental human motivation that involves a universal *need to give care*. Furthermore, the caring motivation is encompassing and includes a variety of manifestation with close others and strangers and even with nonhuman entities all resting on similar biological and neural basis and demonstrating similar psychological dynamics (Mayseless, 2016). Such motivation reflects an innermost core of human nature, is a major source of meaning and purpose, and is strongly connected to individuals' self-actualization. It is therefore imperative to attend to the ramifications of this fact when trying to help others find meaning in their life, flourish and actualize their deep and high potential.

Accordingly any psychotherapeutic intervention should acknowledge the centrality of this caring motivation as a source for meaning for the therapist who chose to engage in caring in his/her profession *and* as an important and central arena for life meaning for all clients. This is especially true for meaning-oriented interventions that adopt a humanistic perspective such as logotherapy which embraces a

---

O. Mayseless, Ph.D. (✉)
Faculty of Education, University of Haifa, Abba Khoushy Ave 199, Haifa 3498838, Israel
e-mail: ofram@edu.haifa.ac.il

"caring and compassionate approach to health care" (Marshall & Marshall, 2012; introduction to Chapter 3) and positive psychotherapy which is based on the tenets of positive psychology and views meaning and positive relationships as key components of well-being (Seligman, 2011).

The Centrality and Significance of the Caring Motivation in Psychotherapy and in Human Life

Caring is central and pivotal to psychotherapy at various levels and spheres. The first and most obvious connection relates to the core of psychotherapy which is a helping profession. As a helping profession, it is geared to help others heal and repair psychological wounds, faulty relationships, and problems in functioning, gain emotional and cognitive well-being, find meaning in life, and move toward self-actualization, thriving and flourishing. In this sense psychotherapy is a profession whose core practice involves providing care, and this caring constitutes its fundamental character. But psychotherapy is not only about caring acts; the motivation underlying such acts is crucial too. Psychotherapeutic caring acts are often unsuccessful unless accompanied by the caring motivation—an other-oriented motivation to care, tend, nurture, and help other entities grow, thrive, heal, and develop (Mayseless, 2016).

In fact mutual, warm and trusting rapport between psychotherapists and clients has been identified as core aspect in very diverse forms of interventions and often showed the strongest association with psychotherapy's success (Horvath & Symonds, 1991; Martin, Garske, & Davis, 2000). Specifically, psychotherapy is most successful when psychotherapists really care about their patients or clients: when they feel empathy, kindness, compassion, and respect toward them and want to alleviate their suffering and help them find meaning, heal, and thrive because they care about them. This does not obliterate the importance of professional expertise, clinical knowledge, and skills but underscores a fundamental truism that psychotherapy is first and foremost a meeting between people and only when such meeting is authentic and involves acceptance, respect, trust, and care—clients can heal and thrive building upon it. This depiction is true for any kind of psychotherapeutic intervention but even more so for those situated within the humanistic tradition or the transpersonal tradition—a perspective that underscores human potential to transcend the self and expand it beyond "regular" self-actualization (Maslow, 1971).

Such depiction underscores the importance of *receiving and experiencing* good and optimal care in "real life" and in psychotherapy to be able to heal wounds, thrive, and flourish. A large number of traditions have underscored such relational need and advocated for a view of people as interconnected and people-oriented rather than being mostly individuated and autonomous (e.g., Keltner, 2009; Noddings, 1984/2003; Taylor, 2002). These include, for example, attachment theory which has provided a convincing evolutionary explanation for the innate and primary need to connect and to attach to others and a strong empirical foundation that demonstrated that such innate basic need is indeed universal and characterizes us "from cradle to the grave" (Bowlby, 1969/1982; Cassidy & Shaver, 2008; Mikulincer & Shaver, 2007).

Similarly, eminent feminist scholars provided convincing arguments that the human species is a relational species—growing within and through relationships (e.g., Gilligan, 1982; Josselson, 1996). Within psychotherapeutic circles, object relations theories, and in particular the relational turn within dynamic-oriented psychotherapies, stress the importance of real interpersonal relations and the primacy of the need to have actual close relations with others (Wiseman, 2016). However, most of these paradigms focus on the need *to receive* love, closeness, appreciation, and company and less about the need to care, namely, the motivation *to give* love and appreciation and to help an entity heal, develop, and thrive. Such motivation to care is distinct (though connected) to the motivation to receive care and be loved (see discussion of these issues in Mayseless, 2016).

Giving care as a practice and a motivation is central in human nature. It has developed as part of the human species evolutionary past and is vital and crucial for its existence. Without being cared for as infants and children, individuals would not have survived, and without being able to rely on care in the form of emotional support, instrumental help, provision of information, appreciation, and acknowledgement, survival post childhood and adulthood years would have also been compromised. Following this logic, most of the research and theorizing of care focused on the importance and significance of care to the *care-receiver*.

However, this depiction is only one facet of the innate human nature. Besides the innate need to connect and to receive care, we all have an innate complementary motivation to give care and help other entities heal, grow, and thrive (Mayseless, 2016). From an evolutionary point of view, it is clear why the caring motivation is fundamental and necessary. A species like the human species where newborns cannot survive without care would become extinct if the human species did not have an innate motivation to respond with care to the needy and fragile and to emotionally attach to their infants in a caring capacity, namely, to form *caring bonds*. In such bonds, people take responsibility and commit themselves to see to it that the other person's well-being is maintained and enhanced. In such caring bonds, individuals not only respond with care and become active when the other person is in need but remain vigilant and observe the other person and his or her whereabouts to be able to identify a situation needing intervention even if the other person is not aware of the problem.

The innate and encompassing caring motivation has been discussed and studied as part of a variety of conceptual paradigms such as evolutionary, developmental, biological, psychological, cultural, and spiritual. Some of these large literatures are briefly discussed here. The recognition of the critical necessity of care for survival as babies, children, and adults led to the development of a large number of evolutionary models to explain mothering and fathering, support for kin, cooperation in small groups, and even generosity with strangers. Consequently, today within evolutionary accounts of human behavior there is a strong agreement that caring and the motivation to care to kin and non-kin is hardwired in human ancestral nature and helps the survival of the human species (see summary in de Waal, 2009).

Such intrinsic motivation to care is seen already at very early stages of development. Developmental research has documented that 1-year-old babies demonstrate intrinsic motivation to help adults in household tasks, to bring or point to out-of-reach objects that adults need and to comfort others in distress (Davidov, Zahn-Waxler, Roth-Hanania, & Knafo, 2013). Fourteen-month-old babies do so intrinsically, even without prompts from adults and even when they have to surmount obstacles on the way (a pile of toys) or when they are in the middle of play with an attractive toy (Warneken & Tomasello, 2006, 2007, 2013). In toddlerhood, they help close others and strangers, and, in fact, a major part of socialization relates to streamlining such innate motivation by teaching children when, to whom, and how to help others rather than to arouse it (Hay, 1994).

Furthermore, an intricate neural and biological circuitry that is implicated in care in its diverse forms such as mothering, fathering, helping strangers, assisting friends, volunteering, and generosity has been discovered (Decety, 2010). Some of the most indicative findings that caring is encompassing and involves a large variety of caring relations and care situations relate to the neurohormone oxytocin which has been implicated in diverse kinds of care. For example, levels of oxytocin were associated with mothers' sensitive and concordant interactions with their baby. Such connection has also been observed with nonbiological mothers' and with fathers' interactions with their baby (Feldman, 2012). Oxytocin has also been associated with higher levels of trust as part of an economic game and with generosity and money donations among adults (Kosfeld, Heinrichs, Zak, Fischbacher, & Fehr, 2005). Moreover, the same brain areas that were implicated in showing empathic response with a baby have also been implicated in empathy for romantic partner, for friends, and for strangers (Decety, 2010).

Furthermore, historical and anthropological accounts (e.g., Murdock, 1981) as well as international surveys conducted for the past 10 years identified the universal prevalence of caring acts (Charities Aid Foundation, 2013). These include both reactive care to an encountered need or distress in others and proactive care that spontaneously emanates from the person as an intrinsic wish to care. Care that is proactive involves actively looking for situations, people, and circumstances where help, care, and contribution to the welfare of others can be provided. Interestingly, such proactive care is very broad and is not limited to connections within intimate relations. Individuals look to care for familiar acquaintances and for strangers such as when assisting neighbors, contributing to charity, mentoring at-risk children, and volunteering in sports (Mayseless, 2016). Such universal enactment of the innate caring motivation is not restricted to other people, and individuals also care for animals, plants, the earth, and even to abstract causes such as the environment or future generations.

Erikson (1963) related to such universal motivation in his famous life-span developmental model and suggested that the developmental task of middle adulthood is generativity—the investment in the welfare of future generations broadly defined to include parenting, mentoring, taking care of the environment, being involved in the community, and more (McAdams & De St Aubin, 1992). However, the caring motivation as depicted here is broader than generativity in that it starts emerging from very early on, at the same time that the self begins to form and when the first intimate intersubjective space develops and characterizes human life throughout the life-span as a continuous vital stream of caring reflected in affect, cognition, relationships, and deeds. Furthermore, caring is enacted in a variety of contexts, some clearly relevant to the next generations (e.g., caring for own children) and others not so (e.g., caring for ailing neighbor, cooperating with friends). It is thus central and fundamental in a much larger sense than Erikson's notion of generativity.

Altogether, the extant research shows that such universal and fundamental caring motivation is embedded in human evolutionary past, human neural and biological makeup, and individuals' interpersonal relations and cultures (Keltner, 2009; Mayseless, 2016; Taylor, 2002).

Caring as a Central and Pivotal Way to Meaning and Self-Fulfillment

Caring as a motivation is so central in human nature not only because it sustains human life and culture but also because it is a primary source of life meaning. Different accounts using a variety of samples, cultures, and age groups, as well as a variety of research methods, have converged on a few major domains in individuals' lives that accord them a sense of purpose and meaningfulness (Bar-Tur, Savaya, & Prager, 2001; Emmons, 2005; Little, 1998; Steger, Kashdan, Sullivan, & Lorentz, 2008; Wong & Fry, 1998). Two of the most frequent ones involve caring: one is caring for and about known others as part of close relationships, and the other is caring for the community or for future generations, often termed "service" or "self-transcendence." Both have been most central in all accounts and across cultures and were thus suggested as principal anchors in individuals' meaning and purpose in life.

Why is caring such a central path to life meaning and purpose? The answer to this enigma may be given on several levels of explanations. One of the explanations relates to the often arduous and difficult nature of care. For example, unlike other basic motivations, such as hunger or sleep, and despite being a central source of joy, parenting, frequently described as the most characteristic manifestation of the caring motivation, is often associated with negative emotions, such as exhaustion, fatigue, anger, and frustration (Hansen, 2012). Thus, hedonic please may not always be a viable proximal reason for engaging in caring. The sense of life meaning and purpose that is associated with caring is often cited as the deep psychological reason why such "investment" is worth it and how it is maintained (White & Dolan, 2009).

At a different level of explanation, caring may be so strongly associated with life's meaning because it is associated with our *daimon*, "spirit," or "true self" as a species. This is closely related to the distinction between eudemonic and hedonic types of happiness or well-being discussed and studied mostly within the realms of positive psychology (Ryan & Deci, 2001; Ryff & Singer, 2006). This term (*daimon*), and *eudaemonia* (happiness in the sense of flourishing) in particular, was discussed in Hellenic philosophy and particularly in Aristotle's *Nicomachean Ethics* but was also later elaborated by other philosophers (see a discussion by Waterman, 1990). The *daimon* refers to the potentials which represent the greatest fulfillment in living that individuals are capable of. Realizing these potentials or advancing in efforts to realizing them prompts a sense of *eudaemonia*. Caring is one central way of fulfillment of such a 'true self' and spirit (Frankl, 1946/1963) and hence its enactment provides individuals with a sense of meaning and purpose and an intense experience of happiness of the *eudaemonic* nature.

What is the unique characteristic of the "true self" that caring expresses? It is suggested that caring reflects a core quality of the "authentic" self (the *daimon*) which involves the capacity and potential to extend and transcend the self. A central defining feature of human "true" nature is that the human species is a caring species that strives to give and to facilitate thriving in the world. Hence, actualizing and fulfilling this caring nature is a core manifestation of *self*-actualization, be it by parenting, by volunteering, by mentoring, by adopting a pet, by tending a garden, by lending a hand to a neighbor, by defending the reputation of a friend, or by benefitting future generations through fighting injustice. In all of these endeavors, individuals extend themselves beyond their personal self to something that is greater than their self—extending themselves to the intimate intersubjective space, to the community, to nature, or to the universe at large. Thus, self-actualization does not have to mean self-indulgence or self-focus, but a realization of the authentic nature of the self which involves, among other things, extending beyond the self and caring. People actualize their true *self* when they help *others* thrive and help make the world a better place, and through such engagement *they* also thrive and find a deep meaning and purpose to their lives. *Caring is thus, not just one thing that humans do. It is intimately tied to human nature, self-actualization, and life meaning. Paradoxically, therefore, it is through a benevolent involvement in something other and greater than one's self that people appear to express the self in one of the most authentic and profound ways.*

Caring and the Spiritual Realm

The personal conviction of many including Frankl the father of logotherapy (e.g., Frankl, 1946/1963, 1986, 1969/1988; Hart, 2014; Maslow, 1971) ties this central caring motivation in human nature to a spiritual core. By "spiritual," it is meant "the aspect in us which is divine, which gives us life as we know it, and through which we know ourselves as humans; it is that sphere which we share with all other things in the universe and with the Cosmos itself" (Mayseless, 2016, p. 346). For some of the readers, the spiritual may be viewed as nonexistent and in particular as something that is beyond research and hence not relevant to the thesis of this chapter. Indeed although the prevalence and centrality of care in people's life as well as its centrality as a significant way to express and discover life meaning have been empirically studied and demonstrated, the connection between caring and the spiritual is not part of empirical science. So for those who may feel uneasy with this section of the chapter, please, just skip this part and go directly to the next one.

Several central spiritual traditions view the divine as epitomizing love, giving, protection, forgiveness, compassion, and caring. Many of these traditions and in particular their esoteric and mystical schools of thought, such as the Islamic Sufis, the Christian Gnostics, the Advaitan Hindus, and the Zen Buddhists, as well as a large number of perspectives developed within new religions and contemporary spiritualities (Heelas, 1996), further hold that all humans are in essence divine. This divine essence, which involves benevolence and caring, was expected to be brought to the fore through spiritual practices, and this process was conceived as the ultimate purpose of life on earth. These faiths consider the caring motivation an expression of the sacred nature of humans. Spiritual development was thus perceived as involving a process of becoming more empathic, caring, compassionate, and giving. Such expectation though articulated differently in the various traditions can be found in Christianity, Buddhism, Judaism (in particular in Jewish Kabbalah), and a large number of contemporary spiritualities.

For example, one of the most important spiritual traditions in which human spiritual nature is conceived as giving, providing, and "bestowing" is Kabbalah ("receiving" in Hebrew) which is a school of thought concerned with the mystical aspects of Judaism. According to one of the most central interpretations of the Kabbalah (Ashlag, 2005), humans are a vessel (*Keli* in Hebrew) with a will and desire to receive without limits. But they also have a spiritual light—a soul—and hence an inner spiritual desire to bestow which mirrors the divine qualities. This desire needs to be developed in order to transform selfishness and egoistical desire—the desire to receive—into altruistic desire, the desire to give and devote oneself to loving and cherishing others. Such giving is deemed the expression of life's ultimate purpose and reflects the essence of the divine—the spiritual light—inside each person. Altogether, spiritual traditions worldwide view the divine as reflecting or embodying the ultimate care and expect humans to live their lives by bringing this aspect of spiritual nature shared with the divine to the fore and radiating it to others.

Similar views were voiced by Frankl, the founder of logotherapy who maintained that the inner realm of existence is spiritual and relates to the noetic dimension in life (Frankl, 1946/1963). Frankl suggested that through connection to such core the person becomes more open to the transcendental dimension and can experience ultimate reality and discover and realize his or her ultimate life meaning and purpose. He further suggested that caring (love using his terms) (Frankl, 1946/1963, p. 59) "is the ultimate and highest goal to which man can aspire."

These frameworks as well as a large number of other perspectives in psychology (Hart, 2014; Maslow, 1971; Pargament, 2007) suggest that caring is one of the manifestations of human spiritual and divine core. It is certainly not the sole one but a central one. Caring and compassion are also conceived as expressing the "divine" in us, because through care individuals connect to all that exists and transcend their finite existence and through care individuals *create*—they give and sustain life and help it heal, grow, and thrive. By caring, people contribute to the ongoing force of life with its beauty, abundance, and multitude of emanations. The enactment of care is therefore a fulfillment and an actualization of a central aspect of human spirit, and its successful enactment provides people with the deep and profound sense of satisfaction and meaning that reflects the mysterious and unique realization of the divine within them.

The Place of Caring as a Source for Meaning in Logotherapy and Positive Psychotherapy

The discussions so far have significant ramifications to psychotherapy as they relate to the defining elements of human life and in particular underscore that the capacity to enact the innate caring motivation is intimately connected to the capacity to live the good and worthy life—life with meaning, purpose, and eudaemonia.

Both positive psychotherapy—psychotherapy based on positive psychology notions (Rashid, 2009; Seligman, Rashid, & Parks, 2006) and logotherapy—one of the most central existential psychotherapies (Fabry, 1994; Frankl, 1946/1963, 1969/1988; Graber, 2004; Lukas, 1984; Marshall & Marshall, 2012; Wong, 2010, 2012) stress the centrality and importance of meaning and both discuss how meaning can be attained or created. The basic tenet of logotherapy is that we have a universal and fundamental will to meaning—a deep seated need and capacity to search for meaning and to find meaning and a responsibility to discover and fulfill it. Creating or discovering meaning is viewed as the central task of psychotherapy involving a process of extending and transcending the self through connection with the noetic (often thought of as the spiritual) dimension in life. Meaning is achieved through answers that individuals give to life as it presents itself to them, and the answers are deemed unique for each individual.

Positive psychology and the psychotherapy that relies on its notions relate to meaning as *one* of several (few) domains of life that are implicated in happiness and well-being. Seligman, one of the founders of positive psychology (Seligman & Csikszentmihalyi, 2000), postulated three such domains in an earlier theory relating to authentic happiness: *the pleasant life, the engaged life, and the meaningful life* (Seligman, 2004). In a latter conceptualization, he talked about flourishing and well-being and discussed meaning as one of five aspects of the full spectrum of well-being. In this latter version he included the three former dimensions plus *relationships* and *achievement* and all were conceived as contributing to human flourishing (Seligman, 2011). He too viewed meaning as involving extending beyond the self. Specifically, the meaningful life can be achieved by using one's personal strengths in belonging and especially in serving something bigger than the self, such as religion, politics, family, community, and nation.

Both paradigms also discuss and relate to caring as an important and central aspect in life, often using other terms than caring. For example, in logotherapy Frankl (1946/1963, 1986, 1969/1988) maintained that caring is one central way by which the noetic (spiritual) dimension in life can be expressed. Frankl referred to three central categorical values in life which to his view provide pathways to exercise the will to meaning. These include *creative value* (giving something to the world through creative works), *attitudinal value* (choosing one's attitude—specifically choosing how to understand, interpret, and react to the world and life, in particular in the face of suffering and pain), and *experiential value* (receiving something from the world through experiencing, appreciating, and gratitude). He accorded central place to caring as an expression of the human will to meaning and tied the capacity to transcend through caring to *experiential value*. In doing so, he used the term love which is a broader term than caring and encompasses other aspects besides giving, such as the needy side—the need to be loved.

Specifically he suggested that "The most important example of experiential values is the love we feel towards another. Through our love, we can enable our beloved to develop meaning, and by doing so, we develop meaning ourselves!" He then even restated it more strongly as a profound insight:

> The truth - that Love is the ultimate and highest goal to which man can aspire. Then I grasped the meaning of the greatest secret that human poetry and human thought and belief have to impart: The salvation of man is through love and in love. (Frankl, 1946/1963, pp. 58–59)

This inspiring realization indeed refers to one of the central manifestation of caring, that of deep love to another person as part of intimate relationships. Yet caring as conceptualized here is much broader and includes many other experiences and actions, such as compassion for animals, care for future generations, volunteering to help inmates, and mentoring at work. It does not necessitate a formation of an intense caring bond, though of course such bond epitomizes caring in one of the most profound way.

Furthermore, caring is relevant not only to the experiential value but also to the creative one as caring often involves creating a work or doing a deed. In fact, Frankl refers to such venue when he discussed self-actualization as ensuing from self-transcendence:

> The more one forgets himself--by giving himself to a cause to serve or another person to love--the more human he is and the more he actualizes himself. What is called self-actualization is not an attainable aim at all, for the simple reason that the more one would strive for it, the more he would miss it. In other words, self-actualization is possible only as a side-effect of self-transcendence. (Frankl, 1946/1963; p. 133).

Thus, service of a cause, one of the expressions of the innate and encompassing caring motivation, has also been described as fulfillment of the will to meaning as part of the creative categorical value.

Frankl mentioned intimate love as one expression and service as another and provided many examples of his own kind, generous, and empathic choices and acts in the concentration camp (Frankl, 1963/1946). Yet other endeavors of care (e.g., generosity, helping acquaintances, organizational citizenship behaviors) were much less discussed by him, and especially he did not conceptually combine the variety of expressions of care under one overarching term and did not discuss them all as manifestations of the same caring core. Consequently, the fundamental place of caring as a pathway to self-transcendence and ultimate meaning is often underrepresented and has not been accorded the central place it deserved at least within conceptualizations of psychotherapeutic interventions in logotherapy.

For positive psychology and positive psychotherapy which is based upon it, caring is viewed as one of 24 central human strengths. It is categorized as part of the humanity category which includes three values: love (e.g., loving and being loved), social intelligence, and kindness (Peterson & Seligman, 2004). Kindness includes generosity, nurturance, care and compassion, altruism, and "niceness," and these are sometimes discussed as part of the strengths of the heart which also include love and gratitude (Park & Peterson, 2008). Interestingly the strengths of the heart were found to be more strongly associated with well-being than more cognitively oriented strengths (e.g., creativity, appreciation of beauty and love of learning; Park, Peterson, & Seligman, 2004; Park & Peterson, 2008).

Accordingly, within positive psychology, positive relations are highly valued as sources of well-being, happiness, and flourishing (Kauffman & Silberman, 2009; Rashid, 2009; Ryff & Singer, 2006). Often, in these depictions caring, the giving side, is not distinguished from the receiving side and from other qualities of the heart such as gratitude that may be expressed by counting one's blessing. Yet, positive psychology and psychotherapy do appear to underscore the distinct importance of the giving side when they discuss and study other positive endeavors that express the caring motivation such as generosity (Dunn, Aknin, & Norton, 2014; e.g., spending money on others as compared to on oneself) and the active expression of gratitude to someone else as in the "gratitude visit" exercise (Seligman, Steen, Park, & Peterson, 2005). These two exercises that involve expressions of the caring motivation as well as other exercises such as engaging in acts of kindness (e.g., Lyubomirsky, Dickerhoof, Boehm, & Sheldon, 2011) have been amply used and studied in positive psychology interventions with a variety of people (e.g., college students, people suffering from depression, clients in couple therapy, psychiatric patients, youth) demonstrating the powerful positive effect of engaging in caring on the caregiver's well-being (Lyubomirsky, Sheldon, & Schkade, 2005; Sin & Lyubomirsky, 2009).

However, the essential connection between caring and meaning has been less salient in writings and research within positive psychology and psychotherapy. One of the reasons might be that caring is not directly tied to transcendence (another category of strength) and meaning (one of the domains contributing to flourishing) but is rather categorized as part of kindness and interpersonal strengths (Seligman et al., 2006). Thus, when Seligman et al. (2006) present the basis of positive psychotherapy and discuss the meaningful life, caring does not come up as one of the ways to construe meaning and self-transcend but is mostly viewed as part of the engaged life especially with regard to close others. Even in the new model of well-being that provides a revised basis for positive psychotherapy, the PERMA (positive emotions, engagement, relationships, meaning, and achievement) Seligman (2011) discusses caring as part of being engaged in relationships and not as part of the meaning aspect. Thus caring within relationships is viewed as important for well-being but is less salient as source of meaning and transcendence. Still because meaning within positive psychology is conceived as seeking to embed one's life in something greater than oneself, caring for future generations or engagement in service to community that are also part of caring do count as sources for meaning.

It appears that logotherapy and positive psychotherapy view and depict the place of caring a bit differently. Within logotherapy, caring either as love for a closed one or as giving oneself "to a cause to serve" is conceived as a potential pathway to express and create meaning and as an expression of the human spirit through self-transcendence. Within positive psychotherapy, caring is considered one of the central character strengths and as part of one's well-being in the relationship arena. It is less viewed as connected to the meaningful life, though some of its manifestations (e.g., service to the community) are discussed as pathways to meaning.

What is important to the thesis of this chapter is that in both of these paradigms there appears to be a differentiation among caring within close relations (love and compassion), caring as service, and daily kind and generous acts that are not part of a loving bond or service. This segregation hinders the capacity to view the bigger picture and understand that all these different manifestations are expressions of the same comprehensive and deep underlying caring motivation. Such a motivation is manifested in different ways and in a large variety of circumstances, but these all are manifestations of the general caring motivation despite their differences. Together they create a web of caring which seems to flow naturally from an inner source, sustaining us as a species, defining the human nature, and occupying a fundamental place in life meaning and purpose. Consequently, though scholars in both traditions discuss the association between meaning and caring, the salience of this connection is not as clear as it should be and it sometimes get lost in the host of ways and names that are used to describe it.

A Plea to Accord the Caring Motivation and Its Fundamental Connection to Life's Meaning the Place It Deserves in Psychotherapy

Being one of the cornerstones of one's *daimon* and a central arena for life meaning and purpose, the caring motivation need to be nurtured in any kind of psychotherapy but even more so in therapeutic interventions that are geared to help others thrive and reach self-fulfillment such as existential and positive psychotherapy. In these psychotherapies, in particular, we need to acknowledge the centrality of the caring motivation and consequently help clients and therapists realize their capacity to find meaning and transcend themselves through care with others as well as in the relationship between the therapist and the client.

The insights regarding the significance of the caring motivation, its innate and fundamental nature, and its primary connection with self-actualization, life meaning, and one's spiritual core have several ramifications with regard to the practice of psychotherapy. First, therapists who have chosen caring as a profession need to acknowledge and understand the centrality of this pathway to meaning in their life, observe and listen to the place of caring in their life, and examine the extent to which they are truly authentic in this choice and in their caring relations with their clients. Most often today, training programs for psychotherapists emphasize skills, professional capacity, and knowledge and place less focus on asking therapists to connect to their *daimon* and their caring motivation and understand the place of caring in their life meaning and purpose. The skills and knowledge are crucial, but we also need to cultivate self-awareness, clear mind, and authenticity of the therapist, qualities that are necessary to help them help clients ask themselves "what is the meaning of my life." These qualities need to be nurtured in psychotherapists throughout their career.

Second, within psychotherapy, caring of the therapist and the client should be appreciated, nurtured, and cultivated. Although caring is innate and fundamental, not everyone is in a position to express it in a way that is optimal, fulfilling, and provides meaning. Just as we see individual differences in the expression of other fundamental motivations (e.g., hunger), individuals greatly differ in their capacity to care and the extent to which they care in a judicious, balanced, and optimal way. Thus, the caring motivation—the motivation to help sustain (preserve) an entity and help it grow and thrive—though innate, still undergoes a highly sophisticated process of conscious and unconscious learning to allow individuals to engage in good and optimal caring and to choose caring that reflects each person's *daimon* and is meaningful to them. To be able to extend ourselves this way and to give care most people first need to be able to receive care and to care for and about themselves (Eisenberg, Fabes, & Spinrad, 2006). Therapeutic encounters need therefore ascertain: (1) that people receive care and learn to accept it and enjoy it; (2) that people learn to care about themselves, their needs, and their wishes and to recognize and accept their limitations; and (3) that their own intrinsic caring motivation is nurtured, respected, encouraged, and welcomed.

Receiving care and caring about and for oneself are often part of the general goals of almost any psychotherapy. Being able to "receive," accept, and make use of at least some of the care, empathy, and help offered by the therapist is almost a precondition for psychotherapy's success and especially for the capacity to explore meanings and purpose in life. Most psychotherapeutic traditions deal with these issues and discuss ways to help clients trust their psychotherapist and accept the care offered. Learning to care about and for oneself, love and cherish the person that one is, and investing in feeling good and worthy are often major goals for people inside and outside of psychotherapy. In contrast to the last part—the nurturance of the motivation and the capacity to give care might be often overlooked in psychotherapy.

To illuminate this issue a story that I heard from one of my colleagues is presented. The colleague recounted a situation that happened to her in a group that she was leading as a therapist on a weekly basis. On one of the occasions, she came rather distraught because her young child was seriously ill with high fever, and she felt totally out of control. She still came to the session but then received a phone call that the fever went up and she needs to hurry back home. She burst into tears and was at a loss. People in the group helped her by providing advice and comforting, suggesting to drive her back home which one of them eventually did and helped her gather her things. A few days later, her child felt better, and she came back the next week feeling very bad about her bursting and collapsing, apologizing and saying that she was the one who needed to care for them and how bad she feels that they actually had to reverse the roles and care for her. To her surprise, people in the group reacted differently than she was expecting. They said that they used the same tools that they learned from watching her, that it felt good to be able to help her, and that it showed them their strengths and capacities.

This, for her, was a major breakthrough—understanding that part of caring in the therapist's role is also the capacity to receive care from the clients, that they too needed to care, and that in the same way that she derives meaning in her life from helping others—they too felt that helping was very meaningful for them. This was a very different way of looking at her role as a psychotherapist.

This story underscores the importance of cultivating the clients' capacity to care in psychotherapy with its ensuing sense of meaning and the importance of allowing clients to exercise care in psychotherapy including in their relations with the therapist. This should be done judiciously while taking into consideration processes of transference and countertransference and the distinct role of the therapists that need to be on guard not to fulfill their needs for reassurance, security, power, and the like at the expense of the clients' needs. The claim advocated here refers to the inclusion of a measure of authentic encounter where both parties are first and foremost humans, and the realization that in this encounter, though one is the therapist and the other is the client, both parties give *and* receive.

How such delicate dance could be achieved? Several suggestions for therapists are provided here. First, as described in previous sections, therapists need to be aware of the place caring plays in their life and its association with their meaning and purpose in life. By reflecting on these issues and understanding and acknowledging them, a more authentic personal stance is created, and this can facilitate a similar process of authenticity in their relations with their clients and in the clients themselves.

Second, therapists can also focus on observing how caring is experienced in the client's life and how it is enacted and in particular discern to what extent such enactment resonates with the client's authentic and deep-sited self. Individuals greatly differ in how much they want to engage in caring, what kinds of provisions they like to give and to whom (Mayseless, 2016). Thus, although caring, as a general endeavor, is universally volitionally exercised, the specifics of such care are quite diverse and reflect gross individual differences. Such individual differences are highly relevant to the life meaning that individuals associate with caring. Extant research demonstrates that optimal care needs to be intrinsically and volitionally given in a balanced manner and needs to take into consideration both the caregiver's and the care-receiver's fundamental needs and concerns (See review in Mayseless, 2016, chapter 14). Hence, the nurturance of the caring motivation should be done judiciously. Caring as a motivation would be associated with self-fulfillment and meaning *only* when it is intrinsically and volitionally based and when it reflects the person's connection to his or her authentic core.

This is most clearly seen in volunteering. Some people prefer to volunteer with children, others with adults; some like to help in sports, others with inmates, and yet others by tending the ill. Indeed research found that volunteering becomes beneficial for the volunteers and positively affects their life meaning and psychological and physical health only when it is volitionally chosen and practiced with other-oriented rather than self-oriented motivation (e.g., Clary et al., 1998; Konrath, Fuhrel-Forbis, Lou, & Brown, 2012). Thus, just as people are expected to be the ones who find and create their own meaning in life (Frankl, 1946/1963), caring too needs to be individually chosen to become a major source of meaning, purpose, and self-transcendence.

Premature encouragement, even well-meant one, to be prosocial and to tend to others, may often come at the cost of the provision of an unbalanced care and may often reflect an egoistic-based care, namely, care that is geared to satisfy the caregiver's own needs for reassurance, self-worth, or overcoming guilt rather than the needs of the other. Similarly blocking or ignoring client's wishes to be caring toward the therapist or others may stifle the budding of the client's wish to transcend the self through caring. The biblical tale of Cain demonstrates how painful it is to have one's gift of care rejected by a caregiving authority figure—in Cain case, God—and how devastating the results of this rejection can be. Fairbairn, an eminent pioneer of object relations theories, expressed this very eloquently with regard to children's needs:

> The greatest need of a child is to obtain conclusive assurance (a) that he is genuinely loved as a person by his parents, (b) that his parents genuinely accept his love (Fairbairn, 1952; p. 39).

Though clients are not children and therapists are not parents, genuinely accepting the love and care that some clients want to bestow as part of psychotherapy may be an empowering encounter for both sides.

Concluding Remarks

The therapeutic arena invites an authentic encounter between therapists and clients. Such encounter has the potential to allow both sides to express and enjoy their innate, fundamental, and spiritually based capacity to care. In such expression of the caring motivation, both parties can find deep meaning and purpose, and clients can learn how to use this pathway of caring to discover and create their own life meaning also outside the encounter. Caring in that capacity is very broadly defined to include love, kindness, generosity, and service in close relations and with strangers as well as with nonhuman entities and in caring for abstract causes.

To do this, therapists need to understand and enjoy their own caring in psychotherapy and elsewhere and to deeply understand and acknowledge the meaning and self-transcendence that such care, especially in therapy, offers them. Therapists could also go even deeper and recognize the connection of the caring dimension to their deep, authentic self and the noetic/spiritual dimension of their existence. Such deep understanding could offer them the will and the freedom to authentically help clients find and create their own meaning through care. Furthermore, the centrality of care as a fundamental human motivation and part of one's *daimon* and as a central way of expressing one's self-transcendence needs to be salient within therapeutic encounters. As part of these encounters, caring would need to be experienced and discussed as well as appreciated and nurtured as a central facet of one's core existence. Such focus in psychotherapy, existential, and positive as well as other kinds of psychotherapy will render caring—the capacity to extend ourselves, connect, and help another entity heal and thrive—its pivotal role in human experience, life meaning, and flourishing.

Key Takeaways

- An intrinsic, innate, and fundamental need to give care—*the caring motivation* is central in human nature. Caring is broadly defined to include love, kindness, generosity, and service in close relations and with strangers as well as with nonhuman entities (a pet, a garden, the environment) and abstract causes. Extant research shows that such universal caring motivation is embedded in human evolutionary past and its diverse manifestations rest on similar biological and neural basis and show similar psychological dynamics.
- Furthermore, extant research demonstrates that caring is one of the most central sources of meaning and purpose and is strongly connected to individuals' self-actualization.
- Caring is thus not just one thing that humans do. It is intimately tied to human nature, self-actualization, and life meaning. Through a benevolent involvement in something greater than one's self, people appear to express the self in one of the most authentic and profound ways.
- It is therefore important to attend to the ramifications of this fact when trying to help others find meaning in their life, flourish and actualize their deep and high potential.
- Consequently, any psychotherapeutic intervention should acknowledge the centrality of this caring motivation as a source for meaning for the therapist who chose to engage in caring in his/her profession and as an important and central arena for life meaning for all clients.

- Based in humanistic perspective, both logotherapy and positive psychotherapy discuss the importance of meaning in life and the importance of caring. However, both do not fully acknowledge the breadth of the caring motivation, and both do not fully address the strong and inherent connection between caring and meaning in life.
- The therapeutic arena invites an authentic encounter between therapist and clients that has the potential to allow both sides to express and enjoy their innate, fundamental, and spiritually based capacity to care. In such expression, both parties can find deep meaning and purpose and clients can learn how to use this pathway of caring to discover and create their own life meaning also outside the encounter.
- One implication is the need of therapists to acknowledge and understand the centrality of caring and its connection to meaning in their *own* life and to examine the extent to which they are truly authentic in their caring relations with their clients.
- Another implication relate to the importance of cultivating the clients' capacity to care with its ensuing sense of meaning in psychotherapy. In therapeutic encounters, caring would need to be experienced and discussed as well as appreciated and nurtured as a central facet of one's core existence.
- This needs to be done in a judicious and authentic manner. Caring needs to be individually chosen to become a major source of meaning, purpose, and self-transcendence. Premature encouragement, even well-meant one may often come at the cost of the provision of an unbalanced or an egoistic-based care. Similarly blocking or ignoring client's wishes to be caring toward the therapist or others may stifle the budding of the client's wish to transcend the self through caring.

References

Ashlag, Y. (2005). *Introduction to the Book of Zohar*. Toronto, ON: Laitman Kabbalah Publishers.

Bar-Tur, L., Savaya, R., & Prager, E. (2001). Sources of meaning in life for young and old Israeli Jews and Arabs. *Journal of Aging Studies, 15*(3), 253–269.

Bowlby, J. (1982). *Attachment and loss: Vol. 1. Attachment*. New York, NY: Basic Books (Original work published 1969).

Cassidy, J., & Shaver, P. R. (Eds.). (2008). *Handbook of attachment: Theory, research, and clinical applications* (2nd ed.). New York, NY: Guilford Press.

Charities Aid Foundation. (2013). *World Giving Index 2013: A global view of giving trends*. Retrieved from https://www.cafonline.org/PDF/WorldGivingIndex2013_1374AWEB.pdf.

Clary, E. G., Snyder, M., Ridge, R. D., Copeland, J., Stukas, A. A., Haugen, J., & Miene, P. (1998). Understanding and assessing the motivations of volunteers: A functional approach. *Journal of Personality and Social Psychology, 74*, 1516–1530.

Davidov, M., Zahn-Waxler, C., Roth-Hanania, R., & Knafo, A. (2013). Concern for others in the first year of life: Theory, evidence, and avenues for research. *Child Development Perspectives, 7*(2), 126–131.

de Waal, F. B. M. (2009). *The age of empathy: Nature's lessons for a kinder society*. New York, NY: Three Rivers Press/Random House.

Decety, J. (2010). The neurodevelopment of empathy in humans. *Developmental Neuroscience, 32*(4), 257–267.
Dunn, E. W., Aknin, L. B., & Norton, M. I. (2014). Prosocial spending and happiness using money to benefit others pays off. *Current Directions in Psychological Science, 23*(1), 41–47.
Eisenberg, N., Fabes, R., & Spinrad, T. L. (2006). Prosocial development. In N. Eisenberg & W. Damon (Eds.), *Handbook of child psychology: Vol. 3. Social, emotional, and personality development* (6th ed., pp. 646–718). New York, NY: Wiley.
Emmons, R. A. (2005). Striving for the sacred: Personal goals, life meaning, and religion. *Journal of Social Issues, 61*, 731–745.
Erikson, E. H. (1963). *Childhood and society* (2nd ed.). New York, NY: Norton.
Fabry, J. (1994). *The pursuit of meaning* (Rev. ed.). Abilene, TX: Institute of Logotherapy Press.
Fairbairn, W. R. D. (1952). *Psychoanalytic studies of the personality*. London: Tavistock.
Feldman, R. (2012). Parent–infant synchrony: A biobehavioral model of mutual influences in the formation of affiliative bonds. *Monographs of the Society for Research in Child Development, 77*(2), 42–51.
Frankl, V. E. (1946/1963). *Man's search for meaning* (3rd ed.). New York, NY: Simon & Schuster.
Frankl, V. E. (1986). *The doctor and the soul: From psychotherapy to logotherapy* (3rd ed.). New York, NY: Vintage Books.
Frankl, V. E. (1969/1988). *The will to meaning: Foundations and applications of logotherapy*. New York, NY: The World Publishing Co.
Gilligan, C. (1982). *In a different voice: Psychological theory and women's development*. Cambridge, MA: Harvard University Press.
Graber, A. V. (2004). *Viktor Frankl's logotherapy: Method of choice in ecumenical pastoral psychology* (2nd ed.). Lima, OH: Wyndham Hall Press.
Hansen, T. (2012). Parenthood and happiness: A review of folk theories versus empirical evidence. *Social Indicators Research, 108*(1), 29–64.
Hart, T. (2014). *The four virtues: Presence, heart, wisdom, creation*. New York, NY: Atria.
Hay, D. F. (1994). Prosocial development. *Journal of Child Psychology and Psychiatry, 35*(1), 29–71.
Heelas, P. (1996). *The New Age movement: The celebration of the self and the sacralization of modernity*. Oxford: Blackwell.
Horvath, A. O., & Symonds, B. D. (1991). Relation between working alliance and outcome in psychotherapy: A meta-analysis. *Journal of Counseling Psychology, 38*(2), 139–149.
Josselson, R. (1996). *The space between us: Exploring the dimensions of human relationships*. Thousand Oaks, CA: Sage.
Kauffman, C., & Silberman, J. (2009). Finding and fostering the positive in relationships: Positive interventions in couples therapy. *Journal of Clinical Psychology, 65*(5), 520–531.
Keltner, D. (2009). *Born to be good: The science of a meaningful life*. New York, NY: Norton and Company.
Konrath, S., Fuhrel-Forbis, A., Lou, A., & Brown, S. (2012). Motives for volunteering are associated with mortality risk in older adults. *Health Psychology, 31*, 87–96.
Kosfeld, M., Heinrichs, M., Zak, P. J., Fischbacher, U., & Fehr, E. (2005). Oxytocin increases trust in humans. *Nature, 435*, 673–676.
Little, B. R. (1998). Personal project pursuit: Dimensions and dynamics of personal meaning. In P. T. P. Wong & P. S. Fry (Eds.), *The human quest for meaning: A handbook of research and clinical applications* (pp. 193–212). Mahwah, NJ: Erlbaum.
Lukas, E. (1984). *Meaningful living: Logotherapeutic guide to health*. Cambridge, MA: Schenkman.
Lyubomirsky, S., Dickerhoof, R., Boehm, J. K., & Sheldon, K. M. (2011). Becoming happier takes both a will and a proper way: An experimental longitudinal intervention to boost well-being. *Emotion, 11*(2), 391–402.
Lyubomirsky, S., Sheldon, K. M., & Schkade, D. (2005). Pursuing happiness: The architecture of sustainable change. *Review of General Psychology, 9*(2), 111–131.

Marshall, M., & Marshall, E. (2012). *Logotherapy revisited: Review of the tenets of Viktor Frank's logotherapy*. Ottawa, ON: Ottawa Institute of Logotherapy.

Martin, D. J., Garske, J. P., & Davis, M. K. (2000). Relation of the therapeutic alliance with outcome and other variables: A meta-analytic review. *Journal of Consulting and Clinical Psychology, 68*(3), 438–450.

Maslow, A. (1971). *The farther reaches of human nature*. New York, NY: Viking.

Mayseless, O. (2016). *The caring motivation: An integrated theory*. New York, NY: Oxford University Press.

McAdams, D. P., & de St Aubin, E. (1992). A theory of generativity and its assessment through self-report, behavioral acts, and narrative themes in autobiography. *Journal of Personality and Social Psychology, 62*(6), 1003–1015.

Mikulincer, M., & Shaver, P. R. (2007). *Attachment in adulthood: Structure, dynamics, and change*. New York, NY: Guilford Press.

Murdock, G. P. (1981). *Atlas of world cultures*. Pittsburgh, PA: University of Pittsburgh Press.

Noddings, N. (2003). *Caring: A feminine approach to ethics and moral education* (2nd ed.). Berkeley, CA: University of California Press (Original work published 1984).

Pargament, K. I. (2007). *Spiritually integrated psychotherapy: Understanding and addressing the sacred*. New York, NY: Guilford Press.

Park, N., & Peterson, C. (2008). The cultivation of character strengths. In M. Ferrari & G. Poworowski (Eds.), *Teaching for wisdom* (pp. 57–75). Mahwah, NJ: Erlbaum.

Park, N., Peterson, C., & Seligman, M. E. P. (2004). Strengths of character and well-being. *Journal of Social and Clinical Psychology, 23*, 603–619.

Peterson, C., & Seligman, M. E. P. (2004). *Character strengths and virtues: A handbook and classification*. New York, NY: Oxford University Press.

Rashid, T. (2009). Positive interventions in clinical practice. *Journal of Clinical Psychology, 65*, 461–466.

Ryan, R. M., & Deci, E. L. (2001). On happiness and human potentials: A review of research on hedonic and eudaimonic well-being. *Annual Review of Psychology, 52*, 141–166.

Ryff, C. D., & Singer, B. H. (2006). Best news yet on the six-factor model of well-being. *Social Science Research, 35*, 1103–1119.

Seligman, M. E. (2004). *Authentic happiness: Using the new positive psychology to realize your potential for lasting fulfillment*. New York, NY: Simon & Schuster.

Seligman, M. E. (2011). *Flourish: A visionary new understanding of happiness and well-being*. New York, NY: Simon & Schuster.

Seligman, M. E. P., & Csikszentmihalyi, M. (2000). Positive psychology: An introduction. *American Psychologist, 55*, 5–14.

Seligman, M. E., Rashid, T., & Parks, A. C. (2006). Positive psychotherapy. *American Psychologist, 61*(8), 774–788.

Seligman, M. E., Steen, T. A., Park, N., & Peterson, C. (2005). Positive psychology progress: Empirical validation of interventions. *American Psychologist, 60*(5), 410–421.

Sin, N. L., & Lyubomirsky, S. (2009). Enhancing well-being and alleviating depressive symptoms with positive psychology interventions: A practice-friendly meta-analysis. *Journal of Clinical Psychology, 65*(5), 467–487.

Steger, M. F., Kashdan, T. B., Sullivan, B. A., & Lorentz, D. (2008). Understanding the search for meaning in life: Personality, cognitive style, and the dynamic between seeking and experiencing meaning. *Journal of Personality, 76*, 199–228.

Taylor, S. (2002). *The tending instinct: Women, men, and the biology of relationships*. New York, NY: Henry Holt.

Warneken, F., & Tomasello, M. (2006). Altruistic helping in human infants and young chimpanzees. *Science, 311*(5765), 1301–1303.

Warneken, F., & Tomasello, M. (2007). Helping and cooperation at 14 months of age. *Infancy, 11*, 271–294.

Warneken, F., & Tomasello, M. (2013). Parental presence and encouragement do not influence helping in young children. *Infancy, 18*, 345–368.

Waterman, A. S. (1990). The relevance of Aristotle's conception of eudaimonia for the psychological study of happiness. *Journal of Theoretical and Philosophical Psychology, 10*(1), 39–44.

White, M. P., & Dolan, P. (2009). Accounting for the richness of daily activities. *Psychological Science, 20*(8), 1000–1008.

Wiseman, H. (2016). The quest for connection in interpersonal and therapeutic relationships. *Psychotherapy Research, 6*, 1–19.

Wong, P. T. P. (2010). Meaning Therapy: An integrative and positive existential psychotherapy. *Journal of Contemporary Psychotherapy, 40*(2), 85–99.

Wong, P. T. P. (2012). From logotherapy to meaning-centered counseling and therapy. In P. T. P. Wong (Ed.), *The human quest for meaning: Theories, research, and applications* (2nd ed., pp. 619–647). New York, NY: Routledge.

Wong, P. T. P., & Fry, P. S. (Eds.). (1998). *The human quest for meaning: A handbook of research and clinical applications*. Mahwah, NJ: Erlbaum.

Character Strengths and Mindfulness as Core Pathways to Meaning in Life

Hadassah Littman-Ovadia and Ryan M. Niemiec

The term *positive psychology* originated with Abraham Maslow, a humanistic psychologist, who first coined the term in his 1954 book *Motivation and Personality*. Maslow did not like how psychology concerned itself mostly with dysfunction and disorder, arguing that it did not have an accurate understanding of human potential. He emphasized how psychology successfully shows our negative side by revealing much about our illnesses and shortcomings, but not enough on our virtues or aspirations (Maslow, 1954). The scientific study of positive psychology emerged in the late 1990s as a call to social scientists to bring greater attention to what's best in people, relationships, and organizations. Martin Seligman (1999) acknowledged the tremendous gains that had occurred in traditional psychology in the assessment, diagnosis, and treatment of mental disorders, addictions, and other problems over the preceding century. However, in comparison, only a paucity of studies had addressed happiness, positive traits, positive subjective experiences, and positive institutions. Since that time, thousands of studies have been published in the domain of positive psychology, scholarly journals have emerged (e.g., *Journal of Positive Psychology*), and institutions have been created to dedicate a focus to one or more aspects of this work (e.g., VIA Institute on Character). In this chapter, we will discuss some of this research and target a few of the topics that fall under this umbrella (character strengths, mindfulness, and meaning) and offer points around the integration therein.

H. Littman-Ovadia, Ph.D. (✉)
Department of Behavioral Sciences and Psychology, Ariel University,
P.O. Box 3, 40700 Ariel, Israel
e-mail: hadassaho@ariel.ac.il

R.M. Niemiec, Psy.D.
VIA Institute on Character, 312 Walnut Street, Suite 3600, Cincinnati, OH 45202, USA

Xavier University, Cincinnati, OH, USA

Character Strengths

What Are Character Strengths?

Character strengths are positive human traits that influence human thoughts, feelings and behavior, providing a sense of fulfillment and meaning (Park, Peterson, & Seligman, 2004). Character strengths have different moral values than those of aptitudes, and unlike aptitudes, character strengths can be developed. According to the positive psychology literature, for a trait to be considered a character strength, most of the following criteria must be met: (1) a strength must contribute to fulfillment and to the good life; (2) a strength must be morally valued in its own right; (3) the expression of a strength does not diminish people; (4) almost every parent wants their child to have the strength; (5) there are rituals and institutions in a society that support the strength; (6) the strength is universal, valued across philosophy, religion, politics, and culture—past and present; (7) there are people who are profoundly deficient in one or more strengths; (8) the strength is measurable; (9) there are prodigies and paragons that reflect the strength in profound ways; and (10) the strength is distinct in and of itself, from other strengths and positive qualities (Peterson & Seligman, 2004; Seligman, 2015). Following the research of 55 scientists over a number of years, 24 character strengths were found to meet these and other criteria, and to be ubiquitous across cultures. The result is what is known as the VIA[1] Classification of character strengths and virtues and is assessed using the VIA Inventory of Strengths (VIA Survey). Table 1 outlines this framework. Following this groundbreaking classification system in 2004, scientists have published over 200 peer-reviewed articles using the VIA Survey measurement tool and VIA Classification (see www.viacharacter.org for a review of studies). For example, studies have empirically shown that the endorsement and application of strengths is correlated with positive individual outcomes, such as increased happiness, meaning in life, job satisfaction, and decreased depression (e.g., Littman-Ovadia & Steger, 2010; Seligman, Steen, Park, & Peterson, 2005), to name a few.

In their book, *Character Strengths and Virtues* (CSV), Peterson and Seligman provided a positive alternative to the well-known and widely used *Diagnostic and Statistical Manual of Mental Disorders* (*DSM-5*). The CSV provided what some refer to tongue-in-cheek as the anti-DSM, but more specifically the CSV represents a common language for researchers and practitioners in psychology, and in the field of positive psychology in particular. The CSV is considered to be a cornerstone of the field. In the VIA Classification, Peterson and Seligman (2004) identified 24 character strengths from an original pool of hundreds, and classified them

---

[1] VIA originally stood for "Values in Action" however the name was changed to emphasize the focus of this work which is the scientific exploration of character, not values per se. "VIA" is a word that stands on its own, in Latin meaning "the path," and refers to the nonprofit organization that initiated and champions this character strengths work (VIA Institute on Character), the systematic classification system (VIA Classification), and the psychological measurement tool assessing strengths of character (VIA Survey).

Table 1 The VIA classification of character strengths and virtues

- *Wisdom*: cognitive strengths that entail the acquisition and use of knowledge
  - *Creativity* [originality, ingenuity]: Thinking of novel and productive ways to conceptualize and do things; includes artistic achievement but is not limited to it
  - *Curiosity* [interest, novelty-seeking, openness to experience]: Taking an interest in ongoing experience for its own sake; finding subjects and topics fascinating; exploring and discovering
  - *Judgment* [open-mindedness, critical thinking]: Thinking things through and examining them from all sides; not jumping to conclusions; being able to change one's mind in light of evidence; weighing all evidence fairly
  - *Love of Learning*: Mastering new skills, topics, and bodies of knowledge, whether on one's own or formally; related to the strength of curiosity but goes beyond it to describe the tendency to add systematically to what one knows
  - *Perspective* [wisdom]: Being able to provide wise counsel to others; having ways of looking at the world that make sense to oneself/others
- *Courage*: emotional strengths that involve the exercise of will to accomplish goals in the face of opposition, external or internal
  - *Bravery* [valor]: Not shrinking from threat, challenge, difficulty, or pain; speaking up for what is right even if there is opposition; acting on convictions even if unpopular; includes physical bravery but is not limited to it
  - *Perseverance* [persistence, industriousness]: Finishing what one starts; persevering in a course of action in spite of obstacles; "getting it out the door"; taking pleasure in completing tasks
  - *Honesty* [authenticity, integrity]: Speaking the truth but more broadly presenting oneself in a genuine way and acting in a sincere way; being without pretense; taking responsibility for one's feelings and actions
  - *Zest* [vitality, enthusiasm, vigor, energy]: Approaching life with excitement and energy; not doing things halfway or halfheartedly; living life as an adventure; feeling alive and activated
- *Humanity*: interpersonal strengths that involve tending and befriending others
  - *Love* [capacity to love and be loved]: Valuing close relations with others, in particular those in which sharing and caring are reciprocated; being close to people
  - *Kindness* [generosity, nurturance, care, compassion, altruistic love, "niceness"]: Doing favors and good deeds for others; helping them; taking care of them
  - *Social Intelligence* [emotional intelligence, personal intelligence]: Being aware of the motives/feelings of others and oneself; knowing what to do to fit into different social situations; knowing what makes other people tick
- *Justice*: civic strengths that underlie healthy community life
  - *Teamwork* [citizenship, social responsibility, loyalty]: Working well as a member of a group or team; being loyal to the group; doing one's share
  - *Fairness*: Treating all people the same according to notions of fairness and justice; not letting feelings bias decisions about others; giving everyone a fair chance
  - *Leadership*: Encouraging a group of which one is a member to get things done and at the same time maintain good relations within the group; organizing group activities and seeing that they happen
- *Temperance*: strengths that protect against excess
  - *Forgiveness* [mercy]: Forgiving those who have done wrong; accepting others' shortcomings; giving people a second chance; not being vengeful
  - *Humility* [modesty]: Letting one's accomplishments speak for themselves; not regarding oneself as more special than one is

(continued)

Table 1 (continued)

– *Prudence*: Being careful about one's choices; not taking undue risks; not saying or doing things that might later be regretted
– *Self-Regulation* [self-control]: Regulating what one feels and does; being disciplined; controlling one's appetites and emotions
• *Transcendence*: strengths that forge connections to the universe and provide meaning
– *Appreciation of Beauty and Excellence* [awe, wonder, elevation]: Noticing and appreciating beauty, excellence, and/or skilled performance in various domains of life, from nature to art to mathematics to science to everyday experience
– *Gratitude*: Being aware of and thankful for the good things that happen; taking time to express thanks
– *Hope* [optimism, future-mindedness, future orientation]: Expecting the best in the future and working to achieve it; believing that a good future is something that can be brought about
– *Humor* [playfulness]: Liking to laugh and tease; bringing smiles to other people; seeing the light side; making (not necessarily telling) jokes
– *Spirituality* [religiousness, faith, purpose]: Having coherent beliefs about the higher purpose and meaning of the universe; knowing where one fits within the larger scheme; having beliefs about the meaning of life that shape conduct and provide comfort.

© Copyright 2004–2017, VIA Institute on Character. Reprinted with permission. All rights reserved. www.viacharacter.org

into six broader virtues: (1) wisdom and knowledge (includes the strengths of creativity, curiosity, judgment/critical thinking, love of learning, and perspective/wisdom); (2) courage (including bravery, honesty, perseverance, and zest); (3) humanity (including kindness, love, and social intelligence); (4) justice (including teamwork, fairness, and leadership); (5) temperance (including forgiveness, humility, prudence, and self-regulation); and (6) transcendence (including appreciation of beauty and excellence, gratitude, hope, humor, and spirituality/religiousness). These six virtues are the core features traditionally valued by philosophers and religious scholars; they are universal and are likely grounded in human biology (Peterson & Seligman, 2004). Peterson suggested that while the 24 strengths are the "good" in a person, their absence, opposite or excess is the "ill" in a person (Seligman, 2015). However, this theoretical proposal has not yet been tested empirically.

The Benefits of Character Strengths

One of the most interesting findings to emerge from the research is the importance of what is termed *signature strengths*. Signature strengths are those strengths that typically emerge highest in one's results profile on the VIA Survey and are viewed as those strengths most core or essential to the individual's identity. Research continues to investigate how many signature strengths individuals have. While early research suggested three to five and while the convention of many researchers is to limit individuals' quantity to five, research from the VIA Institute finds that many people believe they have far more than five core signature strengths (Mayerson, 2013). The use of individuals' most signature strengths of character seems to have particularly positive effects: Seligman and colleagues (2005) and Gander and colleagues (2013) have found that using one's signature strengths (defined as the five most dominant core strengths) in new and different ways for a number of days led to significant increases in happiness and decreases in depressive symptoms. These effects were sustained at a 6-month follow-up. Similar results with signature strengths interventions have been achieved with different populations, e.g., youth (Madden, Green, & Grant, 2011), older adults (Proyer, Gander, Wellenzohn, & Ruch, 2014), people with traumatic brain injuries (Andrewes, Walker, & O'Neill, 2014), and students (Linley, Nielsen, Gillett, & Biswas-Diener, 2010). Working students who made use of at least two of their signature strengths in a new way over a 2-week period reported higher levels of harmonious passion for their work, which was also associated with an increase in their well-being (Forest et al., 2012). In a similar way, applying signature strengths at work was linked with perceiving work as a calling (Harzer & Ruch, 2012) and with positive effects on performance (Engel, Westman, & Heller, 2012).

The endorsement of character strengths has been linked with a host of positive psychological outcomes, such as life satisfaction and positive affect (Littman-Ovadia & Lavy, 2012), self-acceptance, a sense of purpose in life, environmental mastery, physical and mental health (Leontopoulou & Triliva, 2012), coping with daily stress (Brooks, 2010), and resilience to stress and trauma (Park & Peterson, 2006, 2009). Recently, Littman-Ovadia and Lavy (2015) pointed to *perseverance* as the character strength most highly associated with work performance and most negatively associated with counter-productive work behaviors.

Although strengths endorsement is important and beneficial, an individual's ability to use his or her strengths is much more important in predicting job and life satisfaction (Littman-Ovadia & Steger, 2010). The use of character strengths seems to promote academic goal-achievement for college students, which in turn is associated with greater well-being (Linley et al., 2010). Recent evidence from a diary study has shown daily strengths deployment as a mood-repair mechanism (Lavy, Littman-Ovadia, & Bareli, 2014a).

These studies demonstrate the importance of strengths endorsement and deployment for various positive outcomes at work and in life in general. Indeed, Littman-Ovadia and Steger (2010) found that both recognition and active use of strengths in vocational activities were related to greater vocational satisfaction, greater well-being, and a more meaningful experience in work and in life.

Beyond contributing to the individual's own well-being, character strengths also enhance the welfare of others in the individual's social environment (Niemiec, 2013; Peterson & Seligman, 2004), specifically his or her partner. Evidence from a study of adolescent couples in a dating context provides support for this claim, indicating that certain character strengths of each partner (i.e., women's forgiveness and men's perseverance, social intelligence, and prudence) are associated with the other partner's life satisfaction (Weber & Ruch, 2012). Strengths endorsement and deployment in married couples were recently found to be important for both partners' life satisfaction (Lavy, Littman-Ovadia, & Bareli, 2014b).

Mindfulness

Core Concepts

The literature on mindfulness consists of two distinct (albeit related) concepts. One is derived from contemplative, cultural, and philosophical traditions such as Buddhism, and involves the cultivation of a moment-to-moment, non-judgmental awareness of one's present experience (Kabat-Zinn, 1994). This concept of mindfulness is practiced mainly through formal and informal meditation and mindful living practices (Nhat Hanh, 1979; Niemiec, 2012). The second concept of mindfulness is derived from Western scientific literature, and is defined as a mindset of openness to novelty in which the individual actively constructs categories and distinctions (Langer, 1989). More recently, scientists in the field of mindfulness gathered to conceptualize an operational definition of mindfulness in order to offer greater consistency for this construct in future studies. This group arrived at a two-part definition of mindfulness: (1) mindfulness involves the self-regulation of attention; and (2) an attitude of curiosity, openness, and acceptance (Bishop et al., 2004). This definition, which was to provide guidance for the field, is what will be most instructive for this chapter.

The practice of mindfulness derives from ancient Buddhist meditation practices from over 2500 years ago, and is described as the experience of consciously attempting to focus attention on the present moment, in a non-judgmental manner, where one attempts to not dwell on discursive, ruminating thought, putting aside past and future distractions (Shapiro, 1982). Niemiec (2014) summarized Stern's (2004) present moment phenomenology as a brief, not necessarily verbal experience that is just long enough to capture the shortest of holistic happenings (groupings of thoughts, feelings, actions, or sensations) currently in our awareness or consciousness. Mindfulness, then, is contrasted with the habitual mind, the automatic processing that our minds are busy with on a daily basis, the activities or mind wanderings we go by without much attention or effort (Niemiec, 2014; Segal, Williams, & Teasdale, 2013). As a "way of being," mindfulness can be applied to any moment-to-moment experience (Kabat-Zinn, 1994). As such, mindfulness can be considered not only as a technique or an exercise, but should rather be looked at as a path to building greater awareness of the present moments in our experiences (Niemiec, 2014).

A meta-analysis conducted by Sedlmeier and colleagues (2012) sought to understand the effects of mindfulness-based meditation, examining 163 studies and their reported effects on outcomes such as anxiety, concentration, and well-being. Overall, the results indicated that mindfulness has a global positive effect, generally having a positive impact across psychological variables, although effects are stronger on negative emotional variables rather than cognitive ones.

To date, a number of mindfulness-based interventions have been developed. The most notable program is Mindfulness-Based Stress Reduction (MBSR) (Kabat-

Zinn, 1982, 2003), an effective treatment for daily life stress and stress-related symptoms (Praissman, 2008). Other notable programs include: Acceptance and Commitment Therapy (ACT) (Hayes, Strosahl, & Wilson, 1999), Mindfulness-Based Cognitive Therapy (MBCT) (Segal et al., 2013) and Dialectical Behavior Therapy (DBT) (Linehan, 1993). Many more mindfulness-based interventions exist, with the aim of repairing physical or mental health conditions (see Cullen, 2011).

Correlates

All of these mindfulness-based interventions share the goal of alleviating problems and symptoms, and indeed, a recent meta-analysis supports that mindfulness is beneficial in reducing symptoms of anxiety and depression. Khoury and colleagues (2013) examined the effects of mindfulness-based interventions across 209 studies with more than 12,000 participants. It is important to note that this meta-analysis sought to better isolate the effects of mindfulness, looking at interventions such as MBCT and MBSR, and therefore excluded therapies that included mindfulness as part of another treatment, such as DBT and ACT. This meta-analysis pointed to mindfulness therapies' potential in decreasing clinical and non-clinical levels of anxiety and depression at post-treatment, with results maintained or improved at follow-up. Mindfulness-based interventions were also shown to increase mindfulness itself (as measured in the various studies), the levels of which in-itself strongly correlated with the above-mentioned clinical outcomes, pointing to the key role mindfulness may play in the effectiveness of these therapies.

Practicing mindfulness has been shown to have positive effects across a wide range of domains in one's everyday life. In examining mindfulness and relationships, Kowalski et al. (2014) showed that mindfulness was related to the feeling of happiness and decreased expression of pet peeves among partners. In examining mindfulness for organizational and personal well-being, Baccarani, Mascherpa, and Minozzo (2013) demonstrated that practicing mindfulness for 4 weeks increased well-being, self-control, general health and vitality, while anxiety and depression were decreased. Desrosiers, Klemanski, and Nolen-Hoeksema (2013) set out to examine the connection between the facets of mindfulness (observing, describing, acting with awareness, non-judging, and non-reacting to inner experiences [Baer et al., 2008]) and depression and anxiety, finding that all facets of mindfulness, with the exception of observing, were negatively and significantly related to depression and anxiety. Van Dam, Hobkirk, Sheppard, Aviles-Andrews, and Earleywine (2014) examined mindfulness with respect to the same five facets as above, demonstrating that mindfulness therapy lowered anxiety, depression, and perceived stress. In another example, Desrosiers, Vine, Klemanski, and Nolen-Hoeksema (2013) found that mindfulness was negatively related to depression and to anxiety, mediated by rumination and worry, respectively.

In addition, many positive associations have been found between mindfulness and flourishing-related outcomes, such as subjective well-being, positive affect, life satisfaction, psychological well-being, optimism, self-regulation, self-compassion, positive relationships, vitality, creativity, health, longevity, and a range of cognitive skills (Baer, Smith, & Allen, 2004; Brown & Kasser, 2005; Brown & Ryan, 2003; Brown, Ryan, & Creswell, 2007; Carson, Carson, Gil, & Baucom, 2004; Keng, Smoski, & Robins, 2011).

Integration of Character Strengths and Mindfulness

Theoretically, there has been little discussed about the overall integration and mutual impact of mindfulness and character strengths. In the original VIA classification work (Peterson & Seligman, 2004), links were drawn between character strengths and Buddhist mindfulness training, not unlike the traditions of Tibetan Buddhism which has drawn close links between meditation and the strengths of compassion and wisdom (Chodron, 1997). As mentioned earlier, Bishop and colleagues (2004) defined mindfulness as involving two character strengths: self-regulation of one's attention and curiosity to allow for an attitude of openness and acceptance. Baer and Lykins (2011) argued that mindfulness meditation can facilitate the cultivation of strengths and can increase well-being. The time one spends using character strengths correlates with the levels of mindfulness one has (Jarden et al., 2012).

For a review of research exploring the links between mindfulness and each of the particular 24 character strengths, see Niemiec (2014). By way of a couple of examples, creativity and judgment were found to correlate with mindfulness (Sugiura, 2004), and hope/optimism was increased as a result of mindfulness practice (Carson et al., 2004).

Some research has drawn from the work of Thich Nhat Hanh (1998, 2009), linking in detail how the Five Mindfulness Trainings are connected with character strength use (see Niemiec, 2012). Niemiec and colleagues (2012) voiced how these two human elements have the potential for growth and self-improvement, as well as highlighted more explicitly how a connection between mindfulness and character strengths exists. They argued that there is a potential for integrating the two practices together, to create a virtuous circle of positive impact, or, as they elude—an upward positive spiral (Fredrickson, 2001). In this way, they explained how mindfulness can help one to express character strengths in a way that is balanced and sensitive to context, and also that character strengths can bolster an individual's mindfulness practice by overcoming typical obstacles and barriers—thus supercharging mindfulness (Niemiec, 2014). Furthermore, due to the nature of character strengths interventions (e.g., selecting a character strength to apply to a real-life situation), there is a practical foundation that enables a ready-made pathway for mindfulness, and consequently, mindful living (Niemiec, 2012).

Meaning and Purpose

Core Concepts and Research

Meaning in life is the perception of a purpose, significance or mission in life, and its role in positive human functioning was noted by Frankl (1965) long before positive psychology existed as we know it today (Littman-Ovadia & Steger, 2010; Steger, 2009). Since the turn of the century, meaning has been receiving much attention, and there is a growing body of research showing that finding meaning in life is indicative of well-being, good mental health, and decreased psychopathology (Vella-Brodrick, Park, & Peterson, 2009). As such, meaning is one of the higher correlating constructs (besides engagement and pleasure) with life satisfaction, and is a key player among these three pathways to a happy life (Peterson, Park, & Seligman, 2005).

Meaning can be found in any context an individual is part of, be it a religious institution or work (Duckworth, Steen, & Seligman, 2005). In assessing the components of well-being, a meaningful life has been described as one that serves a higher purpose, and provides a lasting meaning to a life that matters (Peterson et al., 2005). Proyer, Annen, Eggimann, Schneider, and Ruch (2012) argued that such a purpose can be seen in those that choose a military career — a career that is meant to serve the greater good. Their study examined the role of the three orientations to happiness in career satisfaction, with only the meaningful life playing a significant role in its prediction.

Littman-Ovadia and Steger (2010) have further demonstrated the role of meaning in life, showing its significant relationship to satisfaction in work and life, in working and volunteering groups. Satisfaction in the latter group further supports the notion of life satisfaction and well-being being derived from an activity perceived to be serving a higher purpose.

Regardless of the context, considering the significant contributions that meaning has on satisfaction in the various domains, on well-being, and happiness as a whole, individuals strive to achieve a meaningful life (Duckworth et al., 2005). When considering the amount of time spent there, it is of no surprise that constructs like meaning should be examined at the workplace (Littman-Ovadia & Steger, 2010). As such, it is also natural that people should strive to find work that is meaningful, "work that is both significant and positive in valence" (Steger, Dik, & Duffy, 2012, p. 323).

In their study comparing volunteer and paid workers, Littman-Ovadia and Steger (2010), among other variables, examined the relationship between meaning and satisfaction from life, work, and well-being. Their volunteer and working samples demonstrated a strong connection between having meaning in their volunteer activity/work and life satisfaction.

As such, meaningful work, providing one with a sense of higher purpose, is integral to the sense of *calling* (Steger, Pickering, Shin, & Dik, 2010). Calling is the perception one's work has toward fulfilling one's destiny, the opportunity to enjoy one's work while being good at it. Seeing one's work as a calling allows one to experience all three orientations of happiness—engagement, meaning, and pleasure—through the work place (Harzer & Ruch, 2012). To further support this notion, research conducted on calling indicates that experiencing one's work as a calling is linked to increased work and life-related well-being (Duffy, Bott, Allan, Torrey, & Dik, 2012).

McKnight and Kashdan (2009) theorized that a purpose in life is the ultimate aim around which all aspects of one's life, one's behaviors and goals, are organized. In terms of the basic elements of purpose, it (1) stimulates behavioral consistency, (2) generates appetitively motivated behaviors, (3) stimulates cognitive flexibility, (4) aids in efficient resource allocation for greater productivity, and (5) stimulates higher level cognitive processing. They suggested a three-dimensional theory, such that the following three concepts can describe purpose: (1) scope—the breadth of the purpose's influence across the various domains in life; (2) strength—the actions, thoughts, and emotions that purpose influences within its scope; and (3) awareness—the attention paid to the purpose, influenced by the scope and strengths of the purpose (e.g., if one's purpose is broad in scope and is strong, one is very likely to be more aware of it). The aspects that allow one to organize one's life toward one's purpose are interrelated, and once a certain cognitive or behavioral cue is activated, the entire network is activated and is brought to one's awareness. Organizing all the necessary cues through the purpose-centered framework lightens one's cognitive load. When one is unaware of one's purpose, resources necessary for its achievement are much less organized. A purpose in one domain does not mean that one cannot have a purpose in another, and it may be beneficial to have the opportunity to work toward a second purpose when the first becomes too difficult. That being said, having too many purposes may make cognitive resources difficult to allocate. Among the benefits of purpose are the organization of emotions, buffering against stress and increased resilience. Ultimately, McKnight and Kashdan (2009) suggested that purpose is influential in health and well-being.

In support of the latter point, Hill and Turiano (2014) set out to examine the effect of purpose on longevity. Longevity was examined longitudinally (14-year follow up) across different age groups, showing that purpose was significantly associated with longevity regardless of age, such that its benefits are demonstrated across the lifetime.

Integration of Character Strengths and Meaning

Peterson, Ruch, Beermann, Park, and Seligman (2007) conducted an initial study examining the relationship of character strengths and the three modes of existence according to authentic happiness orientations (Seligman, 2002)—the pleasurable, engaging, and meaningful existence. While all 24 strengths significantly accounted for some of the variance in all three orientations to happiness, the effect was the largest in the meaningful orientation. In turn, meaning was the stronger predictor of life satisfaction. Meaning was most strongly associated with the character strength of religiousness/spirituality, with the character strengths of zest, hope, and gratitude also revealing high correlations with meaning.

When examining individual strengths, zest, curiosity, gratitude, and hope emerged with the strongest associations with all three modes of existence—the pleasurable, engaging, and meaningful existence (Brdar & Kashdan, 2010). These specific strengths also showed the highest associations with the three most important human needs according to self-determination theory (SDT; Ryan & Deci, 2001)—satisfaction of autonomy, relatedness, and competence needs—as well as with life satisfaction (Brdar & Kashdan, 2010). Looking at meaning specifically, Brdar and Kashdan (2010) found that a meaningful life was significantly correlated with all 24 strengths.

The role of character strengths and meaning has also been considered at the workplace. Specifically, Littman-Ovadia and Steger (2010) examined the deployment and endorsement of character strengths in two samples of volunteers and a sample of working adults. Deploying strengths at work provided key links to meaning among both young and middle-aged volunteers, and adult working women. Among adult volunteers and paid workers, endorsing strengths was related to meaning. Together, these findings provide a model for understanding how strengths may play a role in explaining how both volunteer and paid workers find meaning.

Finally, a study conducted by Allan (2015) found not only that all 24 strengths were positively correlated with a meaningful life, but that a balance in certain strengths was also related to a meaningful life. High agreement in the pairs of kindness and honesty, love and social intelligence, and hope and gratitude were related to the experience of a meaningful life. If this harmony is important, these results indicate that for a meaningful life, it is important to develop all, rather than a few, character strengths.

In Peterson and colleagues' study (2007), it was found that the path to life satisfaction and the strengths of religiousness/spirituality and perspective was mediated by meaning. Berthold and Ruch (2014) examined satisfaction in life in non-religious and religious people. Their results indicated that those that practice their religion score higher on the strengths of kindness, love, hope, forgiveness and spirituality, and report a more meaningful life.

Character strengths-based interventions were shown to increase happiness (meaning being a key concept in defining happiness) with lasting effects in Seligman and colleagues' (2005) Internet-based study. In a later study, Gander, Proyer, Ruch, and Wyss (2013) replicated Seligman and colleagues' (2005) study and demonstrated that the intervention of *using a character strength in a new way* had not only increased happiness, but also alleviated symptoms of depression, and its effects lasted for 6 months after the intervention. The study also showed the benefits of utilizing more specific strengths-based interventions, such as the *gratitude visit*, on well-being. Proyer, Ruch, and Buschor (2013) have also tested the effects of character strengths-based interventions on happiness, also operating under Seligman and colleagues' (2005) definition of happiness. Although, instead of looking at signature strengths, Proyer and colleagues (2013) compared the effects applying strengths that are highly correlated with life satisfaction (zest, humor, curiosity, gratitude, and hope) versus those strengths that do not often correlate with life satisfaction (appreciation of beauty and excellence, creativity, kindness, and love of learning) and a group that received no strengths intervention of any sort, finding that both character-strengths groups reported increased life satisfaction and happiness.

Kerr, O'Donovan, and Pepping (2015) examined the effects of gratitude or kindness interventions in a clinical setting, where individuals were asked to list things they were grateful for or list the kind acts they had committed, respectively. Although there was an increase in satisfaction with life, the study did not find that either intervention increased meaning in life, as measured by the Purpose in Life test (rather than the *Authentic Happiness Inventory*, which is commonly used to assess happiness on its components, including meaning in life). It is also important to note that the study used rather small groups of roughly 16 participants in each of its three groups (kindness, gratitude, and control).

Integration of Mindfulness and Meaning

With the potential that mindfulness has for experiencing the self and surroundings, it seems natural to examine the effects that such a process could have on one's meaning in life.

In attempting to validate a mindfulness assessment, the Five Facet Mindfulness Questionnaire (FFMQ; Baer et al., 2008), mindfulness was checked against measures of psychological symptoms, as well as measures of psychological well-being. Purpose, and within it meaning, was one of the core elements measuring psychological well-being. Mindfulness was found to be positively correlated to well-being across a sample consisting of meditators, students, and a community sample, which was generally highly educated. It is important to note that only among practicing meditators was there a relationship between well-being and the observing facet of mindfulness (noticing or attending to internal or external experiences, such as smells), suggesting that experienced meditators are practiced in unbiased, rather than selective, observing of stimuli.

Jacobs et al. (2011) were the first to set out and examine the effects of mindfulness directly on meaning in life, as part of the purpose in life scale of Ryff's (1989) well-being scale. Although this is the same well-being scale used in Baer's (2009) study, here only the purpose in life scale was attended to, such that meaning in life could be better isolated. The participants of the study were instructed by a Buddhist scholar and practitioner in "the cultivation of attentional skills and the generation of benevolent mental states" (Jacobs et al., 2011; p. 668). While no significant changes were reported by the waitlisted controls, meditation participants experienced a significant improvement in their levels of meaning, as well as mindfulness itself, and a decrease on measures such as neuroticism.

In a study conducted by Kögler et al. (2015) examining the effects of existential behavioral therapy (EBT) on informal caregivers to palliative patients, mindfulness was found to be significantly correlated to meaning in life. Although the study did not find that EBT had an impact on meaning, and nor was that relationship mediated by mindfulness, it was found that meaning in life increased significantly when mindfulness was practiced in a formal and informal manner, frequently and infrequently.

Most recently, Allan, Bott, and Suh (2015) attempted to link mindfulness to meaning in life, finding that it was positively correlated to the latter. However, they attempted to do so with the mediation of SDT, finding that awareness positively mediated the effect of mindfulness on meaning, indicating that awareness may be the key factor in explaining the role of mindfulness in meaning.

Practice Considerations

Based on this exciting research that is unfolding around character strengths, meaning, and mindfulness, as well as the integration of these areas, there are a number of considerations we suggest for practitioners. We discuss these ideas from two general perspectives: (1) single targeted interventions—brief strategies designed to elevate mindfulness of character strengths and life meaning; and (2) multifaceted integration programs—Here, we focus on mindfulness-based strengths practice (MBSP), a comprehensive, manualized program integrating character strengths and mindfulness that has been found in pilot studies to boost meaning and purpose for participants.

Targeted Interventions

Based on the emerging science, the use of signature strengths is aligned with individuals tapping into harmonious passion (Forest et al., 2012), a variable consistent with concepts relating to purpose and meaning. Moreover, interventions involving the use of signature strengths have been successful across several populations and cultures, and thus are a core element of the following interventions. We order these three interventions around time orientation—an intervention around past use, present use, and future use.

Source of Meaning

This exercise involves looking to the past.

1. Wong (1998) has suggested seven central sources of meaning: relationships, intimacy, self-transcendence, self-acceptance, fairness, spirituality/religion, and achievement. As you review this list of potential sources where people commonly find greater meaning, name the two that have been the strongest sources of meaning in your life up until now.

2. As you think about these two sources of meaning, consider how your character strengths (signature strengths and other strengths) have helped you capitalize on each in the past. Journal about the ways in which your character strengths have served as pathways to manifest these sources of meaning.

Strengths Alignment

This exercise looks at current work tasks and the potential of greater strengths use when engaging in these tasks. Researchers are drawing important links between signature strengths use and work that is a "calling" experience (Harzer & Ruch, 2012). This intervention on "aligning strengths" highlights this effect.

1. List the five tasks that you do most frequently at work (e.g., filing, leading team meetings, emailing clients, making sales calls, etc.).
2. Review your top seven strengths in your character strengths profile from the VIA Survey.
3. Write down one way you can use any one of your top strengths with each of the five work tasks (e.g., using kindness to lead a team meeting with sensitivity to others' needs, using creativity to offer different perspectives when making a sales call, etc.).
4. Explain *how* you will bring the character strength forth in the given task.

Point of clarification: This alignment exercise is asking individuals to both *match* one strength with each task (it is okay to repeat strengths more than once) and *describe* how they will do the task with their character strength in mind.

What Matters Most?

This "what matters most?" intervention, which builds upon the best possible self exercise (Meevissen, Peters, & Alberts, 2011), invites individuals to look to the future:

1. Imagine your not-so-distant future—perhaps 6 months or 1 year from now. Name one area of your life that matters most to you—something that is so important and meaningful to you that you'd like to improve it (e.g., increasing happiness in marriage, graduating from college, improving physical health).
2. List one way in which each of your five strongest signature strengths could be used as a "pathway of meaning" to help you improve this area and would therefore assist you in deepening your experience of what matters most.

This exercise immediately brings individuals to a key source of meaning and provides an immediate, easy-to-use, energizing, and individualized mechanism (signature strengths) as a pathway for getting there.

Multifaceted Integration Programs

Here we focus on the first program designed to integrate mindfulness and character strengths to foster a number of positive outcomes, including meaning—Mindfulness-Based Strengths Practice (MBSP).

In merging the conceptual, scientific, and practical links between mindfulness and character strengths, and in integrating cross-cultural pilot group feedback, Niemiec (2014) developed MBSP—a program designed to explicitly focus on what is best in people. The rationale behind this link lives in the definition of each concept, as practicing mindfulness assumes the deployment of such character strengths as self-regulation and curiosity, while the mindful deployment of character strengths is the strengthening of mindfulness itself. As such, "the practice of mindfulness *is* strengths, and the practice of strengths *is* mindfulness" (Niemiec, 2014, p. 104).

MBSP involves didactic input, strength meditations, exercises, and discussions to encourage participants to enhance their engagement with life and to increase levels of meaning, improve problem-management, and catalyze flourishing (Niemiec, 2014). The program has substantive roots from existing and empirically tested and validated mindfulness programs, such as MBSR and MBCT. More specifically, the program is built from Thich Nhat Hanh's mindfulness work based on mindful living (Nhat Hanh, 1993), and on the other hand, it is grounded from the character strengths research developed by Peterson and Seligman (2004). The unique aspect of MBSP is how mindfulness—usually a quiet and often calming approach—is combined with the energy and engagement that strengths provide, providing a unique synergy between these two forces of positive psychology (Niemiec, 2014).

The motivations for practicing meditation usually stem from the desire to deal with psychological emotional problems, and/or expand consciousness (Sedlmeier et al., 2012), and MBSP was created to support both, but is particularly aligned with the latter. Niemiec (2014) noted that MBSP can be likened to a third wave approach to psychological treatment, since it targets more meaningful living. This is also reflected in approaching MBSP as a practice, rather than "therapy," as the goal is to improve and grow, rather than fix and perfect. As a result, MBSP is perfectly placed as a practice for any therapist, coach, consultant or even the general consumer, whether or not they have previous experience with mindfulness or character strengths.

In essence, MBSP operates from four universal assumptions of human beings (Niemiec, 2014). Firstly, individuals have the power to build their character strengths and mindfulness. Secondly, people can use their mindfulness ability and their character strengths to deepen self-awareness, foster insight, build a life of meaning and purpose, build relationships, and to reach their goals. Thirdly, individuals practiced in MBSP can use their core qualities in a more balanced and proficient manner. Finally, applying character strengths to mindfulness practice and mindful living will encourage individuals to become more consistent, as well as enabling themselves to reap more benefits from their mindfulness practice.

As a result of participating in a course of MBSP sessions, clients report clear experiences of growth. Niemiec (2014) explained that this growth is sometimes incremental, in which individuals are just beginning to challenge their old ways, while others experience the growth as an awakening, some reporting that they wish they could have gone through the process years earlier. In more operational terms, the changes can be subtle, substantial, or both—an individual may experience subtle changes between each session, amounting to a substantial change at the last session, when compared to when they had just started. The program is composed of eight, 2-h group sessions spanning over 8 weeks, though adaptations frequently occur. See Table 2 for a listing of the core themes of each week.

Table 2 MBSP sessions and topic areas

Session	Core topic	Description
1	Mindfulness and autopilot	The autopilot mind is pervasive; insights and change opportunities start with mindful attention.
2	Your signature strengths	Identify what is best in you; this can unlock potential to engage more in work and relationships and reach higher personal potential.
3	Obstacles are opportunities	The practice of mindfulness and of strengths exploration leads immediately to two things—obstacles/barriers to the practice and a wider appreciation for the little things in life.
4	Strengthening mindfulness in everyday life	Mindfulness helps us attend to and nourish the best, innermost qualities in ourselves and others, while reducing negative judgments of self and others; conscious use of strengths can help us deepen and maintain a mindfulness practice.
5	Valuing your relationships	Mindful attending can nourish two types of relationships: relationships with others and our relationship with ourselves. Our relationships with ourselves contribute to self-growth and can have an immediate impact on our connection with others.
6	Mindfulness of the golden mean	Mindfulness helps to focus on problems directly and character strengths help to reframe and offer different perspectives not immediately apparent.
Optional retreat	MBSP ½-day retreat	Mindful living and character strengths apply not only to good meditation practice but also to daily conversation, eating, walking, sitting, reflecting, and the nuances therein (e.g., opening the refrigerator door, turning a doorknob, creating a smile). This day is therefore, a *practice* day.
7	Authenticity and goodness	It takes character (e.g., courage) to be a more authentic "you" and it takes character (e.g., hope) to create a strong future that benefits both oneself and others. Set mindfulness and character strengths goals with authenticity and goodness in the forefront of the mind.
8	Your engagement with life	Stick with those practices that have been working well and watch for the mind's tendency to revert back to automatic habits that are deficit-based, unproductive, or that prioritize what's wrong in you and others. Engage in an approach that fosters awareness and celebration of what is strongest in you and others.

Each session focuses on a different aspect of mindfulness and character strengths, leading to the integration of the two concepts and their application in everyday life, problems, relationships, and planning for the future. MBSP suggests the weekly completion of experiential practices and exercises between sessions, allowing for deeper integration and benefit.

To be sure, MBSP is based in strong research foundations, however, it cannot yet be viewed as an evidence-based approach. Pilot research is promising, with participant-reports consistently noting benefits to meaning, purpose, well-being, management of problems, and other valued outcomes. Pilot studies reveal positive results relative to control groups (Briscoe, 2014; Niemiec, 2014) and case studies with several organizations have been reported (Niemiec & Lissing, 2016). As of this writing, randomized-controlled trials are underway (including a comparison of MBSP and CBT) and practitioners are testing and adapting it to a number of client populations and settings, including organizations, schools, teachers, parents of children with and without disabilities, young mothers, young adult entrepreneurs, people with severe mental illness, and caregivers, to name a few. Practitioners bring positive feedback from the field, reporting on a variety of positive effects they witnessed in their clients and students. One example of a unique benefit of MBSP that is frequently observed and reported is the strengthening and building of positive relationships (Niemiec & Lissing, 2016) — a finding that if found in future empirical studies may potentially have a robust association with life meaning and purpose. These successful feasibility and pilot studies warrant further research on MBSP as an intervention program to boost meaning, purpose, positive relationships, well-being, and other valued outcomes.

Future Recommendations

The field of positive psychology has unique and compelling aims to enhance flourishing in the general population (Seligman, 2011). Therefore, the creation and the scientific validation of interventions, practices, and programs for improving and enhancing positive qualities, not only reducing and alleviating problems (Parks & Biswas-Diener, 2013), needs to be established in order to accomplish these aims.

There appear to be substantial positive associations for mindfulness practices and character strengths practices; however, less is known about their interactions, synergistic outcomes, and relations with meaning and purpose. The targeted interventions we suggest offer some potential pathways for making strides in the practice of these areas. In addition, research suggests multi-component mindfulness therapies are more effective than mindfulness alone (Vøllestad, Nielsen, & Nielsen, 2012), thus programs such as Mindfulness-Based Strengths Practice are well-positioned to be enhancers of meaning.

Key Takeaways

- The endorsement of character strengths have been linked with life satisfaction and positive affect, self-acceptance, a sense of purpose in life, environmental mastery, physical and mental health, coping with daily stress, and resilience to stress and trauma. Character strengths also enhance the welfare of others in the individual's social environment.
- The deployment of character strengths have been linked with job and life satisfaction, academic goal-achievement, and positive affect. The deployment of signature strengths, in new and different ways, increases happiness and decreases depressive symptoms.
- Mindfulness is beneficial in reducing clinical and non-clinical levels of anxiety and depression at post-treatment, with results maintained or improved at follow-up. Practicing mindfulness has positive effects across a wide range of domains in one's everyday life. Many positive associations have been found between mindfulness and flourishing-related outcomes, such as subjective well-being, positive affect, life satisfaction, psychological well-being, optimism, self-regulation, self-compassion, positive relationships, vitality, creativity, health, longevity, and a range of cognitive skills.
- Mindfulness can help one to express character strengths in a way that is balanced and sensitive to context, and character strengths can bolster an individual's mindfulness practice by overcoming typical obstacles and barriers—thus supercharging mindfulness.
- All 24 strengths have been linked with a meaningful life. Harmony and balance between strengths are also important for a meaningful life. Thus, any of the 24 character strengths can be targeted in an intervention or improved upon.
- Mindfulness practice has been linked with a meaningful life.
- Interventions that integrate these areas can be deployed across time orientation— the past can be used to target "sources of meaning" and the character strengths pathways, the present can be emphasized by examining the "alignment of signature strengths" with work tasks (linked with meaning/calling), and the future can be called upon with the "what matters most?" exercise that links strengths with a positive vision of oneself in the future.
- Mindfulness-based strengths practice (MBSP), a comprehensive, manualized program integrating character strengths and mindfulness, has been found in pilot studies to boost meaning and purpose for participants.

References

Allan, B. A. (2015). Balance among character strengths and meaning in life. *Journal of Happiness Studies, 16*, 1247–1261. doi:10.1007/s10902-014-9557-9

Allan, B. A., Bott, E. M., & Suh, H. (2015). Connecting mindfulness and meaning in life: Exploring the role of authenticity. *Mindfulness, 6*, 996. doi:10.1007/s12671-014-0341-z

Andrewes, H. E., Walker, V., & O'Neill, B. (2014). Exploring the use of positive psychology interventions in brain injury survivors with challenging behavior. *Brain Injury, 28*, 965–971.

Baccarani, C., Mascherpa, V., & Minozzo, M. (2013). Zen and well-being at the workplace. *TQM Journal, 25*(6), 606–624. doi:10.1108/TQM-07-2013-0077

Baer, R. A. (2009). Self-focused attention and mechanisms of change in mindfulness based treatment. *Cognitive Behaviour Therapy, 38*(1), 15–20.

Baer, R. A., & Lykins, E. L. M. (2011). Mindfulness and positive psychological functioning. In K. M. Sheldon, T. B. Kashdan, & M. F. Steger (Eds.), *Designing positive psychology: Taking stock and moving forward* (pp. 335–348). New York, NY: Oxford University Press.

Baer, R. A., Smith, G. T., Lykins, E., Button, D., Krietemeyer, J., Sauer, S., Williams, J. G. (2008). Construct validity of the Five Facet Mindfulness Questionnaire in meditating and nonmeditating samples. *Assessment, 15*(3), 329–342. doi:10.1177/1073191107313003

Baer, R. A., Smith, G. T., & Allen, K. B. (2004). Assessment of mindfulness by self-report: The Kentucky Inventory of Mindfulness Skills. *Assessment, 11*(3), 191–206.

Berthold, A., & Ruch, W. (2014). Satisfaction with life and character strengths of non-religious and religious people: It's practicing one's religion that makes the difference. *Frontiers in Psychology, 5*, 876. doi:10.3389/fpsyg.2014.00876

Bishop, S. R., Lau, M., Shapiro, S., Carlson, L., Anderson, N. D., Carmody, J., ... Devins, G. (2004). Mindfulness: A proposed operational definition. *Clinical Psychology: Science and Practice, 11*(3), 230–241.

Brdar, I., & Kashdan, T. B. (2010). Character strengths and well-being in Croatia: An empirical investigation of structure and correlates. *Journal of Research in Personality, 44*(1), 151–154. doi:10.1016/j.jrp.2009.12.001

Briscoe, C. (2014). *A study investigating the effectiveness of mindfulness-based strengths practice (MBSP)*. Thesis submitted to University of East London.

Brooks, J. E. (2010). *Midshipman character strengths and virtues in relation to leadership and daily stress and coping*. Unpublished doctoral dissertation, Howard University, Washington, DC.

Brown, K. W., & Kasser, T. (2005). Are psychological and ecological well-being compatible? The role of values, mindfulness, and lifestyle. *Social Indicators Research, 74*(2), 349–368. doi:10.1007/s11205-004-8207-8

Brown, K. W., & Ryan, R. M. (2003). The benefits of being present: Mindfulness and its role in psychological well-being. *Journal of Personality and Social Psychology, 84*(4), 822–848. doi:10.1037/0022-3514.84.4.822

Brown, K. W., Ryan, R. M., & Creswell, J. D. (2007). Mindfulness: Theoretical foundations and evidence for its salutary effects. *Psychological Inquiry, 18*(4), 211–237. doi:10.1080/10478400701598298

Carson, J. W., Carson, K. M., Gil, K. M., & Baucom, D. H. (2004). Mindfulness-based relationship enhancement. *Behavior Therapy, 35*(3), 471–494. doi:10.1016/S0005-7894(04)80028-5

Chodron, P. (1997). *When things fall apart: Heart advice for difficult times*. Boston, MA: Shambhala.

Cullen, M. (2011). Mindfulness-based interventions: An emerging phenomenon. *Mindfulness, 2*, 186–193.

Desrosiers, A., Klemanski, D. H., & Nolen-Hoeksema, S. (2013). Mapping mindfulness facets onto dimensions of anxiety and depression. *Behavior Therapy, 44*(3), 373–384. doi:10.1016/j.beth.2013.02.001

Desrosiers, A., Vine, V., Klemanski, D. H., & Nolen-Hoeksema, S. (2013). Mindfulness and emotion regulation in depression and anxiety: Common and distinct mechanisms of action. *Depression and Anxiety, 30*(7), 654–661. doi:10.1002/da.22124

Duckworth, A. L., Steen, T. A., & Seligman, M. E. P. (2005). Positive psychology in clinical practice. *Annual Review of Clinical Psychology, 1*(1), 629–651. doi:10.1146/annurev.clinpsy.1.102803.144154

Duffy, R. D., Bott, E. M., Allan, B. A., Torrey, C. L., & Dik, B. J. (2012). Perceiving a calling, living a calling, and job satisfaction: Testing a moderated, multiple mediator model. *Journal of Counseling Psychology, 59*(1), 50–59. doi:10.1037/a0026129

Engel, H. R., Westman, M., & Heller, D. (2012). *Character strengths, employees' subjective well being and performance: An experimental investigation.* (Unpublished doctoral dissertation). Tel-Aviv University, Tel-Aviv.

Forest, J., Mageau, G. A., Crevier-Braud, L., Bergeron, E., Dubreuil, P., & Lavigne, G. L. (2012). Harmonious passion as an explanation of the relation between signature strengths' use and well-being at work: Test of an intervention program. *Human Relations, 65*(9), 1233–1252. doi:10.1177/0018726711433134

Frankl, V. E. (1965). *The doctor and the soul: From psychotherapy to logotherapy.* New York, NY: Vintage Books.

Fredrickson, B. L. (2001). The role of positive emotions in positive psychology: The broaden-and-build theory of positive emotions. *American Psychologist, 56*(3), 218–226. doi:10.1037/0003-066X.56.3.218

Gander, F., Proyer, R. T., Ruch, W., & Wyss, T. (2013). Strength-based positive interventions: Further evidence for their potential in enhancing well-being and alleviating depression. *Journal of Happiness Studies, 14*(4), 1241–1259. doi:10.1007/s10902-012-9380-0

Harzer, C., & Ruch, W. (2012). When the job is a calling: The role of applying one's signature strengths at work. *The Journal of Positive Psychology, 7*(5), 362–371. doi:10.1080/17439760.2012.702784

Hayes, S. C., Strosahl, K. D., & Wilson, K. G. (1999). *Acceptance and commitment therapy: An experiential approach to behavior change.* New York, NY: Guilford Press.

Hill, P. L., & Turiano, N. A. (2014). Purpose in life as a predictor of mortality across adulthood. *Psychological Science, 25*(7), 1482–1486. doi:10.1177/0956797614531799

Jacobs, T. L., Epel, E. S., Lin, J., Blackburn, E. H., Wolkowitz, O. M., Bridwell, D. A., ... Saron, C. D. (2011). Intensive meditation training, immune cell telomerase activity, and psychological mediators. *Psychoneuroendocrinology, 36*(5), 664–681. doi:10.1016/j.psyneuen.2010.09.010

Jarden, A., Jose, P., Kashdan, T., Simpson, O., McLachlan, K., & Mackenzie, A. (2012). [International Wellbeing Study]. Unpublished raw data.

Kabat-Zinn, J. (1982). An outpatient program in behavioral medicine for chronic pain patients based on the practice of mindfulness meditation: Theoretical considerations and preliminary results. *General Hospital Psychiatry, 4*(1), 33–47.

Kabat-Zinn, J. (1994). *Wherever you go, there you are.* New York, NY: Hyperion.

Kabat-Zinn, J. (2003). Mindfulness-based interventions in context: Past, present, and future. *Clinical Psychology: Science and Practice, 10*(2), 144–156.

Keng, S., Smoski, M. J., & Robins, C. J. (2011). Effects of mindfulness on psychological health: A review of empirical studies. *Clinical Psychology Review, 31*(6), 1041–1056. doi:10.1016/j.cpr.2011.04.006

Kerr, S. L., O'Donovan, A., & Pepping, C. A. (2015). Can gratitude and kindness interventions enhance well-being in a clinical sample? *Journal of Happiness Studies, 16*(1), 17–36. doi:10.1007/s10902-013-9492-1

Khoury, B., Lecomte, T., Fortin, G., Masse, M., Therien, P., Bouchard, V., et al. (2013). Mindfulness-based therapy: A comprehensive meta-analysis. *Clinical Psychology Review, 33*(6), 763–771. doi: 10.1016/j.cpr.2013.05.005

Kögler, M., Brandstätter, M., Borasio, G. D., Fensterer, V., Küchenhoff, H., & Fegg, M. J. (2015). Mindfulness in informal caregivers of palliative patients. *Palliative & Supportive Care, 13*(1), 11–18. doi:10.1017/S1478951513000400

Kowalski, R. M., Allison, B., Giumetti, G. W., Turner, J., Whittaker, E., Frazee, L., et al. (2014). Pet peeves and happiness: How do happy people complain? *The Journal of Social Psychology, 154*(4), 278–282. doi:10.1080/00224545.2014.906380

Langer, E. J. (1989). *Mindfulness.* Reading, MA: Addison-Wesley/Addison Wesley Longman.

Lavy, S., Littman-Ovadia, H., & Bareli, Y. (2014a). Strengths deployment as a mood-repair mechanism: Evidence from a diary study with a relationship exercise group. *The Journal of Positive Psychology, 9*(6), 547–558. doi:10.1080/17439760.2014.936963

Lavy, S., Littman-Ovadia, H., & Bareli, Y. (2014b). My better half: Strengths endorsement and deployment in married couples. *Journal of Family Issues.* doi:10.1177/0192513X14550365

Leontopoulou, S., & Triliva, S. (2012). Explorations of subjective wellbeing and character strengths among a Greek University student sample. *International Journal of Wellbeing, 2*, 251–270.

Linehan, M. M. (1993). *Cognitive-behavioral treatment of borderline personality disorder.* New York, NY: Guilford Press.

Linley, P. A., Nielsen, K. M., Gillett, R., & Biswas-Diener, R. (2010). Using signature strengths in pursuit of goals: Effects on goal progress, need satisfaction, and well-being, and implications for coaching psychologists. *International Coaching Psychology Review, 5*, 6–15.

Littman-Ovadia, H., & Lavy, S. (2012). Character strengths in Israel: Hebrew adaptation of the VIA inventory of strengths. *European Journal of Psychological Assessment, 28*(1), 41–50. doi:10.1177/1069072715580322

Littman-Ovadia, H., & Lavy, S. (2015). Going the extra mile: Perseverance as key character strength at work. *Journal of Career Assessment,* 1–13. doi:10.1177/1069072715580322

Littman-Ovadia, H., & Steger, M. F. (2010). Character strengths and well-being among volunteers and employees: Towards an integrative model. *The Journal of Positive Psychology, 5*, 419–430.

Madden, W., Green, S., & Grant, A. M. (2011). A pilot study evaluating strengths-based coaching for primary school students: Enhancing engagement and hope. *International Coaching Psychology Review, 6*, 71–83.

Maslow, A. H. (1954). *Motivation and personality.* New York, NY: Harper.

Mayerson, N. M. (2013). Signature strengths: Validating the construct. Presentation to International Positive Psychology Association, Los Angeles, CA, 82–83. doi:10.1037/e574802013-112

McKnight, P. E., & Kashdan, T. B. (2009). Purpose in life as a system that creates and sustains health and well-being: An integrative, testable theory. *Review of General Psychology, 13*(3), 242–251. doi:10.1037/a0017152

Meevissen, Y. M. C., Peters, M. L., & Alberts, H. J. E. M. (2011). Become more optimistic by imagining a best possible self: Effects of a two week intervention. *Journal of Behavior Therapy and Experimental Psychiatry, 42*, 371–378.

Nhat Hanh, T. (1979). *The miracle of mindfulness: An introduction to the practice of meditation.* Boston, MA: Beacon.

Nhat Hanh, T. (1993). *For a future to be possible: Commentaries on the five mindfulness trainings.* Berkeley, CA: Parallax Press.

Nhat Hanh, T. (1998). *The heart of the Buddha's teaching.* New York, NY: Broadway.

Nhat Hanh, T. (2009). *Happiness.* Berkeley, CA: Parallax Press.

Niemiec, R. M. (2012). Mindful living: Character strengths interventions as pathways for the five mindfulness trainings. *International Journal of Wellbeing, 2*(1), 22–33.

Niemiec, R. M. (2013). VIA character strengths: Research and practice (The first 10 years). In H. H. Knoop & A. Delle Fave (Eds.), *Well-being and cultures: Perspectives on positive psychology* (pp. 11–30). New York, NY: Springer.

Niemiec, R. M. (2014). *Mindfulness and character strengths: A practical guide to flourishing.* Cambridge, MA: Hogrefe Publishing.

Niemiec, R. M., & Lissing, J. (2016). Mindfulness-based strengths practice (MBSP) for enhancing well-being, life purpose, and positive relationships. In I. Ivtzan & T. Lomas (Eds.), *Mindfulness in positive psychology: The science of meditation and wellbeing* (pp. 15-36). New York: Routledge.

Niemiec, R. M., Rashid, T., & Spinella, M. (2012). Strong mindfulness: Integrating mindfulness and character strengths. *Journal of Mental Health Counseling, 34*(3), 240–253.

Park, N., & Peterson, C. (2006). Methodological issues in positive psychology and the assessment of character strengths. In A. D. Ong & M. van Dulmen (Eds.), *Handbook of methods in positive psychology* (pp. 292–305). New York, NY: Oxford University Press.

Park, N., & Peterson, C. (2009). Character strengths: Research and practice. *Journal of College and Character, 10*, 1–10.

Park, N., Peterson, C., & Seligman, M. E. P. (2004). Strengths of character and well-being. *Journal of Social and Clinical Psychology, 23*, 603–619.

Parks, A. C., & Biswas-Diener, R. (2013). Positive interventions: Past, present, and future. In T. B. Kashdan & J. Ciarrochi (Eds.), *Mindfulness, acceptance, and positive psychology: The seven foundations of well-being* (pp. 140–165). Oakland, CA: Context Press/New Harbinger Publications.

Peterson, C., Park, N., & Seligman, M. E. P. (2005). Orientations to happiness and life satisfaction: The full life versus the empty life. *Journal of Happiness Studies, 6*(1), 25–41. doi:10.1007/s10902-004-1278-z

Peterson, C., Ruch, W., Beermann, U., Park, N., & Seligman, M. E. P. (2007). Strengths of character, orientations to happiness, and life satisfaction. *The Journal of Positive Psychology, 2*(3), 149–156. doi:10.1080/17439760701228938

Peterson, C., & Seligman, M. E. P. (2004). *Character strengths and virtues: A handbook and classification*. New York, NY: Oxford University Press.

Praissman, S. (2008). Mindfulness-based stress reduction: A literature review and clinician's guide. *Journal of the American Academy of Nurse Practitioners, 20*(4), 212–216. doi:10.1111/j.1745-7599.2008.00306.x

Proyer, R. T., Annen, H., Eggimann, N., Schneider, A., & Ruch, W. (2012). Assessing the "good life" in a military context: How does life and work-satisfaction relate to orientations to happiness and career-success among swiss professional officers? *Social Indicators Research, 106*(3), 577–590.

Proyer, R. T., Gander, F., Wellenzohn, S., & Ruch, W. (2014). Positive psychology interventions in people aged 50-79 years: Long-term effects of placebo-controlled online interventions on well-being and depression. *Aging & Mental Health, 18*(8), 997–1005. doi:10.1080/13607863.2014.899978

Proyer, R. T., Ruch, W., & Buschor, C. (2013). Testing strengths-based interventions: A preliminary study on the effectiveness of a program targeting curiosity, gratitude, hope, humor, and zest for enhancing life satisfaction. *Journal of Happiness Studies, 14*(1), 275–292. doi:10.1007/s10902-012-9331-9

Ryan, R. M., & Deci, E. L. (2001). On happiness and human potentials: A review of research on hedonic and eudaimonic well-being. *Annual Review of Psychology, 52*, 141–166. doi:10.1146/annurev.psych.52.1.141

Ryff, C. D. (1989). Happiness is everything, or is it? explorations on the meaning of psychological well-being. *Journal of Personality and Social Psychology, 57*(6), 1069–1081. doi:10.1037/0022-3514.57.6.1069

Sedlmeier, P., Eberth, J., Schwarz, M., Zimmermann, D., Haarig, F., Jaeger, S., & Kunze, S. (2012). The psychological effects of meditation: A meta-analysis. *Psychological Bulletin, 138*(6), 1139–1171. doi:10.1037/a0028168

Segal, Z. V., Williams, J. M. G., & Teasdale, J. D. (2013). *Mindfulness-based cognitive therapy for depression: A new approach to preventing relapse* (2nd ed.). New York, NY: Guilford.

Seligman, M. E. P. (1999). The president's address. *American Psychologist, 54*, 559–562.

Seligman, M. E. P. (2002). *Authentic happiness*. New York, NY: Free Press.

Seligman, M. E. P. (2011). *Flourish: A visionary new understanding of happiness and well-being*. New York, NY: Simon and Schuster.

Seligman, M. E. P. (2015). Chris Peterson's unfinished masterwork: The real mental illnesses. *The Journal of Positive Psychology, 10*(1), 3–6. doi:10.1080/17439760.2014.888582

Seligman, M. E. P., Steen, T., Park, N., & Peterson, C. (2005). Positive psychology progress: Empirical validation of interventions. *American Psychologist, 60*, 410–421.

Shapiro, D. H. (1982). Overview: Clinical and physiological comparisons of meditation with other self-control strategies. *American Journal of Psychiatry, 139*, 267–274.

Steger, M. F. (2009). Meaning in life. In S. J. Lopez & C. R. Snyder (Eds.), *Oxford library of psychology* (pp. 679–687). New York, NY: Oxford University Press.

Steger, M. F., Dik, B. J., & Duffy, R. D. (2012). Measuring meaningful work: The Work and Meaning Inventory (WAMI). *Journal of Career Assessment, 20*(3), 322–337. doi:10.1177/1069072711436160

Steger, M. F., Pickering, N. K., Shin, J. Y., & Dik, B. J. (2010). Calling in work: Secular or sacred? *Journal of Career Assessment, 18*(1), 82–96. doi:10.1177/1069072709350905

Stern, D. N. (2004). *The present moment: In psychotherapy and everyday life*. New York, NY: Norton.

Sugiura, Y. (2004). Detached mindfulness and worry: A meta-cognitive analysis. *Personality and Individual Differences, 37*(1), 169–179. doi:10.1016/j.paid.2003.08.009

Van Dam, N. T., Hobkirk, A. L., Sheppard, S. C., Aviles-Andrews, R., & Earleywine, M. (2014). How does mindfulness reduce anxiety, depression, and stress? An exploratory examination of change processes in wait-list controlled mindfulness meditation training. *Mindfulness, 5*(5), 574–588. doi:10.1007/s12671-013-0229-3

Vella-Brodrick, D., Park, N., & Peterson, C. (2009). Three ways to be happy: Pleasure, engagement, and meaning—Findings from Australian and US samples. *Social Indicators Research, 90*(2), 165–179. doi:10.1007/s11205-008-9251-6

Vøllestad, J., Nielsen, M. B., & Nielsen, G. H. (2012). Mindfulness- and acceptance-based interventions for anxiety disorders: A systematic review and meta-analysis. *British Journal of Clinical Psychology, 51*(3), 239–260. doi:10.1111/j.2044-8260.2011.02024.x

Weber, M., & Ruch, W. (2012). The role of character strengths in adolescent romantic relationships: An initial study on partner selection and mates' life satisfaction. *Journal of Adolescence, 35*(6), 1537–1546.

Wong, P. T. P. (1998). Spirituality, meaning, and successful aging. In P. T. P. Wong & P. S. Fry (Eds.), *The human quest for meaning: A handbook of psychological research and clinical applications* (pp. 359–394). Mahwah, NJ: Lawrence Erlbaum.

Strategies for Cultivating Purpose Among Adolescents in Clinical Settings

Kendall Cotton Bronk and Susan Mangan

Viktor Frankl (1959), a world-renowned psychiatrist and Nazi concentration camp survivor, believed the primary reason people sought psychological help was because they lacked purpose in their lives. He referred to the void of meaning as an existential vacuum, and he believed that experiencing such a state leads individuals to feel bored, anxious, depressed, and, under dire circumstances, suicidal. He argued that because of the potentially serious consequences of leading a life of purposelessness, mental health professionals should strive to help their clients identify a meaningful reason for living.

Over the past 20 years, in large part inspired by Frankl's theory on the importance of purpose, research on the construct has increased substantially (Bronk, 2013). The research literature has offered clearer definitions for both *purpose* and *meaning* and has identified ways that leading a life of purpose not only protects against negative states but also encourages positive ones. The present chapter briefly reviews leading conceptions of purpose and meaning and outlines points of intersection and distinction between them. It positions purpose in particular as a construct central to positive youth development. Additionally, it offers three empirically based approaches that mental health professionals can take to help all young people discover a meaningful and productive purpose in life. Finally, it concludes with a call for better communication between mental health professionals and researchers, in hopes that such discussions will generate additional strategies for effectively cultivating purpose among adolescents in clinical settings.

K.C. Bronk, Ph.D. (✉)
Quality of Life Research Center, Claremont Graduate University,
1227 N. Dartmouth Ave., Claremont, CA 91711, USA
e-mail: kcbronk@cgu.edu

S. Mangan, M.A.
Department of Psychology, Claremont Graduate University,
150 E. 10th Street, Claremont, CA 91711, USA

Purpose and Meaning

While Frankl (1959) used the terms *purpose* and *meaning* interchangeably, more recent work has distinguished them. According to the dominant model of purpose, the construct refers to *a stable and enduring intention to accomplish something that is at once personally meaningful and at the same time leads to productive engagement in some aspect of the world beyond the self* (Damon, Menon, & Bronk, 2003). This model describes a purpose in life as a personally meaningful goal. It refers not to a short term end, but instead to a far horizon aim that orients and directs more near term objectives. For example, individuals find purpose in creating new art forms, improving their communities, and pursuing socially beneficial careers. In this way, a purpose is distinguished from more immediate objectives, such as graduating from high school or finding a date, which are fairly readily accomplished and often serve as intermediary steps toward more enduring aims. Additionally, a purpose in life differs from a dream in that it represents a goal an individual is actively engaged in pursuing. Rather than merely contemplating a personally significant objective, purpose is evidenced by the investment of time, energy, and other resources in pursuit of its attainment. Beyond this, a purpose is not only meaningful to the individual pursuing it, but it is also significant in some way to the broader world. A purpose in life is motivated at least in part by a desire to make a difference in the world beyond the self.

While a dominant model of purpose has emerged, no such model of meaning yet exists (Steger, 2012). Scholars have proposed various models; however, most feature a prominent role for purpose. In most models purpose represents one piece of the bigger picture of meaning. In one such conception, purpose, value, self-worth, and efficacy are conceived of as the "four needs of meaning" (Baumeister, 1991). In another model, purpose represents one of the three descriptors of meaning in which meaning is defined as "the cognizance of order, coherence and purpose in one's existence, the pursuit and attainment of worthwhile goals, and an accompanying sense of fulfillment" (Reker & Wong, 1988, p. 221). In yet another model purpose and comprehension, which refer to how individuals make sense of the world and their role in it, comprise the two dimensions of meaning (Steger, Frazier, Oishi, & Kaler, 2006).

Regardless of which conception of meaning is applied, it is clear that purpose and meaning are closely related constructs. Despite this, scholars rarely discuss exactly how they compare and how they contrast. While definitions of meaning vary, most suggest it refers to something broader than purpose. We propose there are at least three important ways in which *purpose* refers to a narrower subset of personally significant sources of *meaning*. First, whereas meaning refers to anything that is personally significant, a purpose in life refers only to personally significant *goals* or *aims*. A walk in the woods may represent a meaningful experience, while working to preserve the environment may represent a purposeful one. In this way, a purpose in life inspires a productive source of motivation (Damon, 2008; McKnight & Kashdan, 2009).

Second, a purpose in life has an external quality not captured by meaning. Not only are purposeful aims personally meaningful, but they also are motivated in a significant way by a desire to make a difference in the broader world. Personally meaningful goals or aims that are driven by purely self-oriented motives do not represent purposes. We can imagine an adolescent who spends years amassing as many Facebook friends as possible. This activity may be meaningful, but since it is motivated by a desire to make a difference only in the individual's life and not in the world beyond the self, it would not qualify as a purpose.

Finally, purpose and meaning often reference different time horizons. A source of meaning may be lasting, such as when one finds meaning in a special relationship, or it may be fleeting, such as when one finds meaning in watching a shooting star. Purpose, on the other hand, always represents an enduring intention. It is a far horizon aim that serves an orienting function over a lengthy period of time. Though it may evolve, the essence of purpose lasts for a long time, usually for years and sometimes for a lifetime (Bronk, 2012).

Despite these subtle distinctions, purpose and meaning are clearly related. The better we understand what gives our lives meaning, the better we can visualize ways of progressing toward personally significant goals that stretch beyond the self (Damon et al., 2003). Based on these points of overlap and distinction, we can see that while not all sources of meaning qualify as purposes, all purposes include a central element of personal meaning.

As noted above, Frankl (1959) used the terms interchangeably, and he failed to offer a definition of either purpose or meaning in his seminal *Man's Search for Meaning*. However, in his book he refers to a sense of personal significance motivated by a desire to influence the world beyond the self. Similarly, in other publications, Frankl (1966) explains that a constitutive characteristic of purpose is that it is always directed toward something other than the self. Pursuing purpose requires being open to the world. As a concentration camp inmate, he noticed that of the prisoners who were given the opportunity to live, those who survived, like himself, felt they had some reason to keep going. In some cases they had a person they needed to stay alive for, in others they had unfinished business they needed to complete. In either case, there was some reason—beyond the self—that these individuals needed to stay alive, and this imbued their lives with a sense of significance. Frankl felt he needed to survive so he could share with the world profound insights regarding the important role of purpose to human survival. He promised himself that if he lived he would share widely the lessons he had gleaned about the centrality of purpose to mental health. Based on Frankl's emphasis on the beyond the self-dimension of personal significance and on his frequent writings about the importance of self-transcendence to the discovery of purpose, it seems clear that Frankl would have identified more closely with contemporary conceptions of purpose than meaning.

Benefits of Purpose

Leading a life devoid of purpose has been associated with a variety of psychological problems. As Frankl predicted, the lack of purpose has been found to correlate with boredom (Bargdill, 2000; Drob & Bernard, 1988), depression (Bigler, Neimeyer, & Brown, 2001), anxiety (Bigler et al., 2001), and even hopelessness and suicide ideation (Dixon, Heppner, & Anderson, 1991; Edwards & Holden, 2001; Harlow, Newcomb, & Bentler, 1986; Heisel & Flett, 2004; Kinnier et al., 1994). Purposelessness is also related to substance abuse (Coleman, Kaplan, & Downing, 1986; Padelford, 1974; Sayles, 1994; Schlesinger, Susman, & Koenigsberg, 1990). Frankl (1959) may well have been right when he predicted that a significant portion of clients who present for counseling probably do so at least in part due to a lack of purpose in life.

Likely as a result of his experience as a concentration camp inmate, Frankl (1959) conceived of purpose primarily as a buffer against suffering. While purpose is consistently inversely related to a range of negative experiences, it is more than just this. Purpose also contributes to human thriving (Bronk, 2013; Damon, 2008). Fueled in part by the positive psychology movement (Seligman & Csikszentmihalyi, 2000), researchers have become increasingly interested in the ways in which leading a life of purpose can help people achieve optimal states. Empirical studies find that individuals who cultivate a meaningful sense of direction for their lives tend to live longer, experience better physical and psychological health, and enjoy happier, more hopeful, and more satisfying lives (Boyle, Barnes, Buchman, & Bennett, 2009; Bronk, Hill, Lapsley, Talib, & Finch, 2009; French & Joseph, 1999; Gillham et al., 2011; Lewis, Lanigan, Joseph, & de Fockert, 1997; Melnechuk, 1988; Peterson, Parks, & Seligman, 2005).

Purpose During Adolescence

While individuals benefit from leading lives of purpose at all points in the lifespan, more recent studies suggest purpose may be particularly beneficial during adolescence. Adolescence is most commonly defined as the stage of life that begins with the onset of puberty and concludes with the full assumption of adult roles.

One reason purpose is particularly relevant to young people has to do with the relationship between purpose development and identity formation. Erikson (1968, 1980) was the first to propose that purpose and identity were related. He argued that similar to purpose, fidelity to a set of values and beliefs serves as an indicator of healthy identity growth. As individuals reflect on who they hope to become, they are also likely to consider the things they most hope to accomplish in their lives (Bronk, 2011). The process of reflecting on one naturally stimulates reflection on the other. In this way, the exploration of purpose corresponds to the exploration of identity, and adolescents who discover a meaningful purpose in life emerge with a stronger sense of who they are and how they fit into the broader world (Burrow, O'Dell, & Hill, 2010).

Another way purpose is particularly relevant during the adolescent stage of life has to do with the important sense of direction it provides. Adolescence is a time when possibilities can seem endless (Steinberg, 2014). The wide variety of curricular, professional, personal, and social options can be exciting. However, encountering seemingly infinite options can also be overwhelming. The array of possibilities can leave young people unsure of the best course of action, and as a result, late adolescents, especially those in their twenties, may experience a sense of drift. Finding a purpose in life can provide a roadmap, helping young people navigate this stage of life and moving them forward in a productive direction (Damon, 2008). Like a compass, a purpose in life can orient young people along a constructive and personally meaningful course. Knowing where they want to end up helps adolescents make productive decisions regarding school, work, and relationships.

Purpose has also been linked to positive academic outcomes for adolescents. For instance, compared to others, youth with purpose are more likely to possess characteristics associated with academic success, including grit (Hill, Burrow, & Bronk, 2016), resiliency (Benard, 1991), an internal locus of control (Pizzolato, Brown, & Kanny, 2011), and academic efficacy (Solberg, O'Brien, Villareal, Kennel, & Davis, 1993). Perhaps not surprising, emerging research also finds that compared to other young people, youth with purpose perform better in school (Benson, 2006; Pizzolato et al., 2011). It has been argued that adolescents, propelled by a personally meaningful and highly motivating purpose, know why they are in school and thus work hard without feeling stressed; consequently, they are more likely to stay in school and excel academically (Damon, 2008). Underscoring this theory is research that concludes that youth with purpose describe their schoolwork as more personally meaningful (Yeager & Bundick, 2009).

Because purpose facilitates identity development, provides an important sense of direction, and is associated with academic success, the construct has been identified as a critical component of leading conceptions of positive youth development (Benson, 2006; Bundick, Yeager, King, & Damon, 2010; Damon, 2004; Lerner et al., 2005). Given the widespread benefits associated with purpose, mental health professionals should not limit their efforts to fostering purpose to only those clients with more severe diagnoses. Instead, they should strive to help *all* adolescents discover and pursue the things that matter most to them.

Fostering Purpose Among Adolescents in Clinical Settings

Despite the central role of purpose in supporting positive youth development, the construct is rare. Empirical studies find that only about one in five adolescents reports having a clear purpose in life (Damon, 2008). Given the benefits and rarity of purpose, it stands to reason that more needs to be done to foster far horizon, personally meaningful aspirations among youth. The good news is that although a purpose ultimately comes from within, studies suggest there are steps mental health professionals can take to help young people discover and act on the things that matter most to them. In this section, we outline three empirically derived approaches to fostering purpose among all adolescents, including those who are in challenging and flourishing periods of life.

Not only is it possible to cultivate purpose in the lives of young people, but a small body of research suggests that doing so may be feasible in clinical settings.

Relatively few studies have sought to intentionally cultivate purpose, but those that have found that even relatively brief and straightforward interventions can be effective (Bronk, 2013; Koshy & Mariano, 2011). For instance, in a recent study researchers surveyed college students twice over a 9-month period. In between, a portion of the students also participated in 45-min interviews about the things that mattered most to them (Bundick, 2011). Months later, these individuals reported significantly higher purpose scores than the others, suggesting that while more enduring interventions may have more lasting impacts, even relatively brief discussions, appropriate for clinical settings, can increase rates of purpose.

Perhaps the oldest and most well-known therapeutic strategy designed to foster purpose is Viktor Frankl's (1959) logotherapy, which means "healing through meaning." Logotherapy is based on three principles, the first of which states that people have a *will to meaning*. In other words, people want to find significance in their lives. The search for purpose represents the search for our ultimate source of motivation, which drives more proximal objectives. The next principle holds that life has meaning under all circumstances, even the most miserable ones, and the last principle maintains, consistent with a positive youth development orientation, that *all* individuals are capable of discovering a purpose for their lives.

More contemporary approaches to fostering purpose tend to validate the basic premises of logotherapy. Research suggests there are at least three productive routes through which mental health professionals can effectively cultivate purpose among adolescents. Each considers purpose from a different starting point. The first approach starts with a grateful mindset. Helping young people focus on the many blessings in their lives triggers reflections not only on what others have done for them but also on how they might want to contribute to others and the world beyond themselves. The second approach considers purpose from a goal setting perspective. Individuals are encouraged to imagine their ideal future and consider the steps they need to take to realize their best prospects. Finally, since purpose emerges when individuals apply personal talents to address meaningful issues in the broader world, the third approach to nurturing purpose involves reflecting on personal values and identifying skills. Each of these approaches is outlined in greater detail below.

Gratitude. The first approach to cultivating purpose involves first encouraging a focus on blessings. A purpose in life is motivated by a desire to contribute to the broader world in a productive and meaningful way. To inspire this kind of beyond the self drive, it can be useful to encourage young people to engage in the practice of gratitude, which encompasses several steps. First, practicing gratitude requires a recognition of the way or ways in which adolescents have been blessed. Second, young people should acknowledge that someone has incurred a cost in order to help them, and finally, they should recognize that the blessing was intentionally given to benefit them (Froh & Bono, 2011). Encouraging adolescents to focus on each of these components is critical to fostering the beyond the self mindset that can predispose individuals to developing a purpose in life.

William Damon (2008), a leading scholar of purpose among adolescents, suggests that holidays, such as Thanksgiving, provide built-in opportunities to start discussions about gratitude. Mental health professionals can ask adolescents to reflect and elaborate on the things and people for which they are thankful. Socratic discussions, in which mental health professionals probe young people about the experience of gratitude, can help adolescents identify ways they have benefited and consider ways they might want to give back. This means that along with asking *what* questions (e.g., What are you grateful for?), mental health professionals should pose *why* questions (e.g., Why are you grateful for this? Why was this experience meaningful to you? Why do you think this person chose to help you in particular? Damon, 2008).

In addition to encouraging adolescents to talk about the experiences, opportunities, and relationships for which they are grateful, empirical studies find that activities can also be effective in cultivating gratitude. For instance, adolescents can be asked to record three to five blessings each week in a gratitude journal. A recent study found that this activity increased not only rates of gratitude but also rates of well-being among young people (Froh, Sefick, & Emmons, 2008). Another way to cultivate gratitude is to ask adolescents to write a letter to someone for whom they are grateful, recounting the ways this person has blessed them (Froh, Kashdan, Ozimkowski, & Miller, 2009). Hand delivering the letter can be a powerful experience, increasing the experience of gratitude. Finally, one of the simplest and most direct ways of fostering gratitude involves teaching adolescents about benefit appraisals (Froh & Bono, 2011). This entails encouraging adolescents to reflect on both the *benefits* recipients receive and the *costs* benefactors incur. This relatively straightforward exercise has been found to significantly increase adolescents' tendency to practice gratitude.

Not only does cultivating gratitude contribute to well-being among middle school (Froh et al., 2008; Froh, Yurkewicz, & Kashdan, 2009) and high school youth (Emmons & McCullough, 2003), but it can also predispose them to developing a purpose in life (Damon, 2008). Over the past 15 years, the first author has conducted hundreds of interviews with adolescents about their purposes in life. Young people often report being inspired to contribute to the world beyond themselves by some experience for which they feel grateful. For instance, in a recent study of rural youth (Bronk, Finch, Youngs, & Hunt, under review), a college student told us about her religious purpose:

> I want to do whatever the Lord wants me to do and follow wherever He wants me to go. I just feel really called to the missionary field, so after graduating I would love to go to other countries and just try to make a small difference there.

She repeatedly identified feeling blessed as a primary reason for wanting to care for those in need, and by the time we interviewed her, she had been actively involved in missionary work in Haiti following the earthquake, in New Orleans following Hurricane Katrina, and in Iowa following massive flooding. When asked why she found purpose in following her religious convictions and serving others, she explained,

> As I grew up, I'd say in junior high, starting to go on mission trips and different things, I just had a whole different view on (religion), and seeing that it's not just strict rules. It's about a relationship with Jesus and following him and just to see how many blessings I've received through that. And yeah, just realizing that my purpose in life is not about me.

As a result of the gratitude she experienced, she planned to dedicate her life to serving others. Her gratitude clearly inspired a deep commitment to a caring purpose in life.

Certainly not all young people discover such a profound purpose, but in this same study, another adolescent reported being inspired by his teacher. His math teacher was not only a proficient instructor, but he was also a supportive mentor who took the time to listen to and support him while his parents were going through a difficult divorce. As a result, this young man wanted to become a teacher so he too could help young people. Yet another young woman talked about wanting to become a healthcare professional after watching a particularly dedicated nurse care for her cousin during a lengthy hospitalization.

Focusing on the things youth are grateful for often leads not only to an enhanced appreciation for the good things in their lives, but also to a desire to share those blessings with others (Damon, 2008). Fostering gratitude seems to predispose young people to purpose in at least two ways (Bronk, Mangan, Baumsteiger, & Hunt, under review). First, gratitude encourages the action-oriented, beyond the self thinking that is core to purpose. The experience of contemplating blessings or reflecting on the people and experiences for which individuals are grateful leaves people feeling strongly inclined to reciprocate, and this can take the form of a more generalized desire to contribute to the world beyond the self in a personally meaningful manner. The second way gratitude can set the stage for the development of purpose is through social relationships. Gratitude has been referred to as a kind of social glue that binds people to one another (Emmons, 2007). Individuals who practice gratitude are more likely to have close friends and mentors, and these two resources have been found to contribute to the development of purpose (Bronk, 2012; Damon, 2008; Park, 2011). In these ways, cultivating gratitude can serve as a useful pathway to the development of purpose.

Goal setting. Another route to fostering purpose involves goal setting. To foster the development of a purposeful aim, adolescents should be encouraged to identify long-term, personally significant goals and to reflect on the steps required to reach those aims. In this section, we offer two ways mental health professionals can help adolescents identify and work toward personally meaningful goals.

The first approach applies a version of the best possible selves intervention (King, 2001). The modified best possible selves activity asks adolescents to imagine, in as much detail as possible, what their lives would look like in roughly 10 years if everything went according to plan. Adolescents are encouraged to talk about the activities they would engage in, the people who would be in their lives, and the things that would be most important to them. They are also asked to consider why this image of the future is particularly meaningful; why questions can help highlight the purpose behind their plans (e.g., "In the future I hope to be working as a doctor, helping my patients and supporting my family." Why would this be important to you? "I guess I really want to help others, through my role as a parent and a physician"). Once adolescents have a clear picture in mind of the positive aims they hope to accomplish, encourage them to reflect on the more short-term objectives they need to achieve to make their ideal future a reality. In short, goal setting discussions help youth identify the aims they most hope to accomplish and the steps required to reach those aims.

Whereas the modified best possible selves intervention focuses more on goal creation, this second approach focuses more on goal pursuit. In particular, it emphasizes cultivating the motivation and means to pursue meaningful goals. This approach utilizes hope therapy to foster purpose. According to researchers, hope is comprised of two components: agency, or motivation to work toward desired aims, and pathways, or knowledge of varied routes to achieving desired aims (Snyder, 2002; Snyder et al., 1991). Researchers often refer to this as the "will and ways" model of hope; people who are truly hopeful are motivated to reach their most meaningful goals and know how to go about doing so. Hopeful individuals display more positive emotional states, including friendliness, happiness, and a more positive attitude toward pursuing their future goals (Snyder et al., 1991; Snyder et al., 2002; Snyder, Michael, & Cheavens, 1999). They also tend to experience lower rates of anxiety and depression and—of particular interest here—higher rates of purpose (Feldman & Snyder, 2005; Snyder et al., 1991).

A couple of empirical studies find that hope and purpose are related and that inspiring hope can support the development of purpose. The first of these studies suggests that adolescents who have identified a purpose for their lives are content when they feel motivated to work toward personally meaningful aims (Bronk et al., 2009). The second of these studies determined that hopeful goal setting can contribute to increases in purpose. In this study, individuals participated in an 8-week hope therapy program where they identified goals and focused on cultivating the will and ways to reach those goals. Purpose was assessed before and after the intervention, and significant increases in the construct were evident following the intervention (Cheavens, Feldman, Gum, Michael, & Snyder, 2006). This suggests mental health professionals should help adolescents develop the motivation and discover the pathways to achieving the aims that matter most to them as a means of helping young people progress toward their purpose in life.

Of course, the modified best possible selves and hope therapy approaches are not incompatible ways of fostering purpose. Mental health professionals can utilize both approaches. Initiating discussions aimed at helping young people identify their most meaningful goals (goal planning), finding routes they can take to achieve those goals (pathways thinking), and supporting the motivation to work toward them (agency thinking) will help encourage the growth of purpose (Cheavens et al., 2006).

When the focus is on establishing long-term, meaningful aims, goal setting, through the best possible selves intervention or through hope therapy, can be an effective means of fostering purpose. Similar to cultivating gratitude, encouraging a sense of hope is beneficial for all young people, not just those with severe diagnoses. Through both of these goal-setting activities, mental health professionals should encourage adolescents to reflect on a particular kind of goal. Specifically, adolescents should be encouraged to contemplate far horizon aims motivated, at least in part, by a desire to contribute to the world beyond the self. Discussing how to set, attain, and motivate to achieve these kinds of larger than the self aspirations can facilitate healthy identity development and connect adolescents to personally significant purposes in life.

Identify values and skills. Finally, individuals discover purpose when they are able to apply distinctive talents to address personally meaningful issues in the broader world (Damon, 2008). Therefore, the third approach to fostering purpose involves helping young people identify both personally meaningful values and special skills they can use to contribute to the world beyond the self.

Personal values provide the foundation for purpose formation and identity development (Damon, 2008; Erikson, 1968, 1980). During adolescence, young people reflect on their religious, political, ethical, and moral beliefs. They contemplate the values they were raised to appreciate and their relevance to their lives and future plans. Developing a coherent value system is an important indicator of healthy identity development (Erikson, 1968, 1980).

While values clarification typically occurs spontaneously during this stage of life, it does not happen in a vacuum. It is a social process, whereby young people compare their developing value structure with established systems of belief. Young people born into a particular religious tradition, for instance, may compare their religious tenets with the principles that guide other faith traditions to arrive at a personally meaningful value system. Mental health professionals can serve a facilitative role, helping young people intentionally consider and organize their most significant beliefs and draw connections between personally meaningful values and future aims. Young people who value the environment might be encouraged to explore professional and volunteer opportunities that allow them to actively engage in protecting the natural world, for example.

In addition to aiding young people in the process of identifying their personal values and linking them to meaningful goals, mental health professionals can help adolescents reflect on their personal strengths. Career planning interventions designed to help young people identify personally meaningful career paths have effectively applied this approach to help young people find and pursue work that matters to them. Make Your Work Matter (Dik, Steger, Gibson, & Peisner, 2011) is a purpose-centered career planning intervention designed for adolescents. It consists of questionnaires and activities adolescents complete to identify their interests and skills. Counselors review the results with young participants to help adolescents explore and pursue career options that utilize their talents. Compared to other adolescents, young people who participate in these counseling sessions report a stronger sense of direction in their career choices, a clearer recognition of their interests, and a greater level of preparedness for the future.

Another purpose-focused career planning program designed to foster purpose engaged adolescents in a series of bimonthly discussions held over the course of 18 weeks in which a counselor encouraged students to reflect on and talk about the things that mattered most to them (Pizzolato et al., 2011). Compared to students in a control group, the young people in the treatment condition reported significantly higher purpose scores. This again suggests that encouraging youth to discuss the aims that matter most to them and helping them to identify ways they can work toward those goals is key to the development of purpose. While these approaches were designed for use in career planning settings, they should be effective in more general counseling contexts as well.

The values reflection and skills identification approach offers mental health professionals a way to capitalize on the normal course of identity development to foster purpose. By helping to make the process of interest, value, and skill identification more intentional and by linking young people's budding beliefs and talents to personally meaningful career and extracurricular pursuits, mental health professionals can help young people discover a productive purpose for their lives.

Conclusion

Only relatively recently have psychologists recognized purpose as an important component of positive youth development. Early studies sought to identify what a purpose in life was and to better understand the nature and prevalence of the construct (Bronk, 2013). As a result of this line of inquiry, we know that purpose is a relatively rare feature among typical youth. Given that relatively few young people currently benefit from leading lives of purpose, recent empirical studies have begun to explore effective ways of fostering an enduring sense of meaning and productive engagement more widely. However, this work is just getting underway. To date, few empirically based programs designed specifically to foster purpose among adolescents exist. Much more research is needed in this area.

Drawing on initial efforts to foster purpose in varied contexts, the present chapter proposes three tacks mental health professionals can take to cultivate a sense of purpose in life among adolescents in therapeutic settings. These methods approach purpose from different vantage points, including gratitude, goal setting, and values clarification. Despite their different entryways, however, these approaches are similar to one another in that each shares a focus on fostering purpose through two steps. First, each approach encourages adolescents to think seriously about the far-reaching aims that matter most to them. Rarely are adolescents given the space or time to consider what it is they want to accomplish in their lives. Asking probing questions in an open-minded spirit can facilitate this process. Second, adolescents are urged to consider how they can make progress toward these aims. This process may require both long-term and more immediate planning. It may also involve putting young people in touch with groups of like-minded peers and mentors who can help them learn how to pursue their purposes in life (Bronk, 2012).

The guidelines set forth in the present chapter are just that, guidelines. To learn how to most effectively apply these general approaches, an open and on-going dialogue between mental health professionals and researchers is needed. We hope that mental health professionals who read this chapter and try some of these strategies—and perhaps others—will share their experiences with us. We are eager to learn more about the strategies that work best.

Frankl discovered his own purpose in life during the Holocaust. He realized he had to live long enough to share with others his profound insight regarding the need for purpose and meaning in supporting the mental health of individuals in dire situations. Today we recognize that all people, not only those who are suffering, can benefit from leading lives of purpose. We also recognize that while the development of purpose can occur at any stage in the lifespan, it is particularly likely to take root during adolescence, when young people are exploring who they are and what they hope to accomplish in their lives. Clearly, we have learned a good deal about purpose since Frankl first introduced the construct as a relevant one for mental health professionals. However, much work remains to be done, especially around how to most effectively cultivate purpose among youth. We hope the empirically based strategies proposed here offer a useful starting point for this important endeavor.

Key Takeaways

- Emerging research suggests mental health professionals may represent viable candidates for the promotion of purpose among adolescents. To that end, the present chapter outlines three empirically based approaches mental health professionals can take to cultivate meaningful and productive purposes in life. Each approach considers purpose from a different perspective.
- The first approach involves nurturing a grateful mindset. Helping young people focus on the blessings in their lives triggers reflections not only on what others have done for them but also on how they might want to contribute to the world beyond themselves.
- The second approach involves setting long-term goals. Youth are encouraged to imagine their ideal future and consider the steps they need to take to realize their best prospects.
- Finally, since purpose emerges when individuals apply personal talents to address meaningful issues in the broader world, the third approach to cultivating purpose involves helping youth clarify their personal values and identify their strengths.

References

Bargdill, R. W. (2000). The study of boredom. *Journal of Phenomenological Psychology, 31*, 188–219.
Baumeister, R. F. (1991). *Meanings of life*. New York, NY: Guilford.
Benard, B. (1991). *Fostering resiliency in kids: Protective factors in the family, school, and community*. Portland, OR: Northwest Regional Educational Laboratory.
Benson, P. L. (2006). *All kids are our kids: What communities must do to raise caring and responsible children and adolescents* (2nd ed.). San Francisco, CA: Jossey-Bass.
Bigler, M., Neimeyer, G. J., & Brown, E. (2001). The divided self revisited: Effects of self-concept clarity and self-concept differentiation on psychological adjustment. *Journal of Social and Clinical Psychology, 20*, 396–415.

Boyle, P. A., Barnes, L. L., Buchman, A. S., & Bennett, D. A. (2009). Purpose in life is associated with mortality among community-dwelling older persons. *Psychosomatic Medicine, 71*(5), 574–579.

Bronk, K. C. (2011). Portraits of purpose: The role of purpose in identity formation. *New Directions for Youth Development, 132*, 31–44.

Bronk, K. C. (2012). A grounded theory of youth purpose. *Journal of Adolescent Research, 27*, 78–109. doi:10.1177/0743558411412958

Bronk, K. C. (2013). *Purpose in life: A critical component of optimal youth development.* New York, NY: Springer.

Bronk, K. C., Finch, H. W., Youngs, A., & Hunt, D. (under review). *Contextual and social supports for rural youth purpose.*

Bronk, K. C., Hill, P. L., Lapsley, D. K., Talib, T., & Finch, W. H. (2009). Purpose, hope, and life satisfaction in three age groups. *The Journal of Positive Psychology, 4*(6), 500–510.

Bronk, K. C., Mangan, S., Baumsteiger, R., & Hunt, D. (under review). *The relationship between purpose and gratitude.*

Bundick, M. J. (2011). The benefits of reflecting on and discussing purpose in life in emerging adulthood. *New Directions for Youth Development, 132*, 89–103.

Bundick, M. J., Yeager, D. S., King, P. E., & Damon, W. (2010). Thriving across the lifespan. In R. M. Lerner, M. E. Lamb, A. M. Freund, & W. F. Overton (Eds.), *Handbook of life-span development: Cognition, biology and methods* (Vol. 1, pp. 882–923). Hoboken, NJ: John Wiley & Sons.

Burrow, A. L., O'Dell, C., & Hill, P. L. (2010). Profiles of a developmental asset: Youth purpose as a context for hope and well-being. *Journal of Youth and Adolescence, 39*, 1265–1273.

Cheavens, J. S., Feldman, D. B., Gum, A., Michael, S. T., & Snyder, C. R. (2006). Hope therapy in a community sample: A pilot investigation. *Social Indicators Research, 77*(1), 61–78.

Coleman, S., Kaplan, J., & Downing, R. (1986). Life cycle and loss: The spiritual vacuum of heroin addiction. *Family Process, 25*, 5–23.

Damon, W. (2004). What is positive youth development? *The Annals of the American Academy of Political and Social Science, 591*, 13–24.

Damon, W. (2008). *The path to purpose: Helping our children find their calling in life.* New York, NY: Free Press.

Damon, W., Menon, J., & Bronk, K. C. (2003). The development of purpose during adolescence. *Applied Developmental Science, 7*(3), 119–128.

Dik, B. J., Steger, M. F., Gibson, A., & Peisner, W. (2011). Make Your Work Matter: Development and pilot evaluations of a purpose-centered career education intervention. *New Directions for Youth Development, 132*, 59–73.

Dixon, W., Heppner, P., & Anderson, W. (1991). Problem-solving appraisal, stress, hopelessness, and suicide ideation in a college population. *Journal of Counseling Psychology, 38*, 51–56.

Drob, S. L., & Bernard, H. S. (1988). The bored patient: A developmental existential perspective. *Psychotherapy Patient, 3*(3-4), 63–73.

Edwards, M. J., & Holden, R. R. (2001). Coping, meaning in life, and suicidal manifestations: Examining gender differences. *Journal of Clinical Psychology, 57*, 1517–1534.

Emmons, R. A. (2007). *Thanks! How the science of gratitude can make you happier.* New York, NY: Houghton Mifflin.

Emmons, R. A., & McCullough, M. E. (2003). Counting blessings versus burdens: An empirical investigation of gratitude and subjective well-being in daily life. *Journal of Personality and Social Psychology, 84*, 377–389.

Erikson, E. H. (1968). *Identity: Youth and crisis.* New York, NY: W. W. Norton.

Erikson, E. H. (1980). *Identity and the life cycle* (paperback). New York, NY: W.W. Norton & Company Inc.

Feldman, D. B., & Snyder, C. R. (2005). Hope and the meaningful life: Theoretical and empirical associations between goal–directed thinking and life meaning. *Journal of Social and Clinical Psychology, 24*(3), 401–421.

Frankl, V. (1959). *Man's search for meaning.* New York, NY: Washington Square Press.

Frankl, V. (1966). Self-transcendence as a human phenomenon. *Journal of Humanistic Psychology, 6*(2), 97–106.

French, S., & Joseph, S. (1999). Religiosity and its association with happiness, purpose in life, and self-actualization. *Mental Health, Religion, & Culture, 2*, 117–120.

Froh, J. J., & Bono, G. (2011). Gratitude in youth: A review of interventions and some ideas for application. *NASP Communique, 39*(5), 26–28.

Froh, J. J., Kashdan, T. B., Ozimkowski, K. M., & Miller, N. (2009). Who benefits the most from a gratitude intervention in children and adolescents? Examining positive affect as a moderator. *The Journal of Positive Psychology, 4*, 408–422.

Froh, J. J., Sefick, W. J., & Emmons, R. A. (2008). Counting blessings in early adolescents: An experimental study of gratitude and subjective well-being. *Journal of School Psychology, 46*, 213–233.

Froh, J. J., Yurkewicz, C., & Kashdan, T. B. (2009). Gratitude and subjective well-being in early adolescence: Examining gender differences. *Journal of Adolescence, 32*, 633–640.

Gillham, J., Adams-Deutsch, Z., Werner, J., Reivich, K., Coulter-Heindl, V., Linkins, M., ... Seligman, M. E. P. (2011). Character strengths predict subjective well-being during adolescence. *The Journal of Positive Psychology, 6*(1), 31–44. doi:10.1080/17439760.2010.536773

Harlow, L. L., Newcomb, M. D., & Bentler, P. M. (1986). Depression, self-derogation, substance use, and suicide ideation: Lack of purpose in life as a mediational factor. *Journal of Clinical Psychology, 42*(1), 5–21.

Heisel, M. J., & Flett, G. L. (2004). Purpose in life, satisfaction with life, and suicide ideation in a clinical sample. *Journal of Psychopathology and Behavioral Assessment, 26*(2), 127–135.

Hill, P., Burrow, A., & Bronk, K. C. (2016). Persevering with positivity and purpose: An examination of purpose commitment and positive affect as predictors of grit. *Journal of Happiness Studies, 17*, 257. doi:10.1007/s10902-014-9593-5

King, L. (2001). The health benefits of writing about life goals. *Journal of Personality and Social Psychology Bulletin, 27*(7), 798–807.

Kinnier, R., Metha, A. T., Keim, J. S., Okey, J. L., Adler-Tabia, R., Berry, M. A., & Mulvenon, S. W. (1994). Depression, meaninglessness, and substance abuse in "normal" and hospitalized adolescents. *Journal of Alcohol and Drug Education, 39*(2), 101–111.

Koshy, S. I., & Mariano, J. M. (2011). Promoting youth purpose: A review of the literature. *New Directions for Youth Development, 132*, 13–29.

Lerner, R. M., Lerner, J. V. L., Almerigi, J. B., Theokas, C., Phelps, E., Gestsdottir, S. ... von Eye, A. (2005). Positive youth development, participation in community youth development programs, and community contributions of fifth-grade adolescents: Findings from the first wave of the 4-H study of positive youth development. *Journal of Early Adolescence, 25*(1), 17–71.

Lewis, C. A., Lanigan, C., Joseph, S., & de Fockert, J. (1997). Religiosity and happiness: No evidence for an association among undergraduates. *Personality and Individual Differences, 22*, 119–121.

McKnight, P. E., & Kashdan, T. B. (2009). Purpose in life as a system that creates and sustains well-being: An integrative, testable theory. *Review of General Psychology, 13*(3), 242–251.

Melnechuk, T. (1988). Emotions, brain, immunity, and health: A review. In M. Clynes & J. Panksepp (Eds.), *Emotions and psychopathology* (pp. 181–247). New York, NY: Plenum.

Padelford, B. L. (1974). Relationship between drug involvement and purpose in life. *Journal of Clinical Psychology, 30*, 303–305.

Park, S. D. (2011). *Big questions, worthy dreams: Mentoring emerging adults in their search for meaning, purpose, and faith*. San Francisco, CA: Jossey-Bass.

Peterson, C., Parks, N. S., & Seligman, M. E. P. (2005). Orientations to happiness and life satisfaction: The full life versus the empty life. *Journal of Happiness Studies, 6*, 25–41.

Pizzolato, J. E., Brown, E. L., & Kanny, M. A. (2011). Purpose plus: Supporting youth purpose, control, and academic achievement. *New Directions for Youth Development, 132*, 75–88.

Reker, G. T., & Wong, P. T. P. (1988). Aging as an individual process: Toward a theory of personal meaning. In J. E. Birren & V. L. Bengston (Eds.), *Emergent theories of aging* (pp. 214–246). New York, NY: Springer.

Sayles, M. L. (1994). Adolescents' purpose in life and engagement in risky behaviors: Differences by gender and ethnicity. (Doctoral dissertation, University of North Carolina at Greensboro, 1994). *Dissertation Abstracts International, 55*, 09A2727.

Schlesinger, S., Susman, M., & Koenigsberg, J. (1990). Self-esteem and purpose in life: A comparative study of women alcoholics. *Journal of Alcohol and Drug Education, 36*, 127–141.

Seligman, M. E. P., & Csikszentmihalyi, M. (2000). Positive psychology: An introduction. *American Psychologist, 55*(1), 1–14.

Snyder, C. R. (2002). Hope theory: Rainbows in the mind. *Psychological Inquiry, 13*(4), 249–275.

Snyder, C. R., Harris, C., Anderson, J. R., Holleran, S. A., Irving, L. M., Sigmon, S. T., et al. (1991). The will and the ways: Development and validation of an individual-differences measure of hope. *Journal of Personality and Social Psychology, 60*, 570–585.

Snyder, C. R., Michael, S., & Cheavens, J. (1999). Hope as a psychotherapeutic foundation for nonspecific factors, placebos, and expectancies. In M. A. Huble, B. Duncan, & S. Miller (Eds.), *Heart and soul of change* (pp. 179–200). Washington, DC: American Psychological Association.

Solberg, V. S., O'Brien, K., Villareal, P., Kennel, R., & Davis, B. J. (1993). Self-efficacy and Hispanic college students: Validation of the college self-efficacy instrument. *Hispanic Journal of Behavioral Sciences, 15*, 80–95.

Steger, M. F. (2012). Making meaning in life. *Psychological Inquiry, 23*, 381–385.

Steger, M. F., Frazier, P., Oishi, S., & Kaler, M. (2006). The Meaning in Life Questionnaire: Assessing the presence of and search for meaning in life. *Journal of Counseling Psychology, 53*, 80–93.

Steinberg, L. (2014). *Age of opportunity: Lessons from the new science of adolescence*. New York, NY: Houghton Mifflin Harcourt.

Yeager, D. S., & Bundick, M. (2009). The role of purposeful life goals in promoting meaning in life and schoolwork during adolescence. *Journal of Adolescent Research, 24*(4), 423–452.

Meaning Centered Positive Group Intervention

Paul T.P. Wong

Introduction

Meaning-centered positive group work has much to recommend itself for three reasons: (1) It is an effective way to give positive psychology (PP) away (Wong, 2012a); (2) it is economic and can help many people at the same time; and (3) it is relevant to all people because of its focus on universal existential concerns (Lukas, 1986/2014; Yalom, 1995). According to Corey (2009), existential groups have the potential of helping participants be more honest with themselves, more open-minded in their perspectives, and more aware of what makes life meaningful. Such objectives can be beneficial to ordinary people.

Logotherapy or meaning therapy, as a distinct school of existential therapy, is most relevant to PP and psychotherapy because it is unique in its optimistic outlook and emphasis on personal growth and spirituality (Frankl, 1986; Wong, 2010a, 2014a).

Leontiev's Life Enhancement Group Work

Leontiev's (2015) group work represents a shift from the analysis of what is wrong to existential principles of how to grow psychologically; in other words, it is a move from therapy to coaching. It takes three full days to complete the group work. The focus is on understanding general existential principles and applying them to help participants think about their own long-term problems in a more adaptive way.

P.T.P. Wong, Ph.D., C.Psych (✉)
Meaning-Centered Counselling Institute, Inc.,
13 Ballyconnor Court, Toronto, ON, Canada M2M 4C5
e-mail: drpaulwong@gmail.com

The axiom of the group work is that everyone has needs and strives toward fulfilling them. The assumptions are that they will be able to cope with their long-term problems, both solvable and unsolvable ones, once they achieve a deeper understanding of the world and their role in it.

Lukas' Dereflection Groups

In contrast to Leontiev, who begins with participants sharing their long-term problems, Lukas (2014) discourages participants from talking about their problems. She calls her group work "dereflection groups," as her main focus is to redirect the members' orientation away from their problems to positive and meaningful activities. The assumption is that such a reorientation is needed in order to achieve self-transcendence. Thus, her group work is positively oriented and meaning-enhancing in terms of both objective and methodology.

Consistent with Frankl's (1986) logotherapy, Lukas (2014) argues that self-transcendence is the best possible positive intervention because it offers the following to her clients: (1) It broadens their values; (2) it opens the door for them to discover something worthy of self-transcendence; (3) it protects them from egocentricity; and (4) it enables them to find meaning directly and happiness indirectly, through their pursuit of self-transcendence. At the core of Lukas' meaning-centered group intervention is giving her clients "a picture of a human being that gives hope and courage" (p. 43).

Wong's Meaningful Living Group

Rather than leaving it to the group members to bring up positive materials for group discussion, as in Lukas' group, the present author gives a lecture prior to group discussion that provides the content and conceptual tools for group members to learn important principles of meaningful living. The main message is that it is never too late to become what one is meant to be—it simply begins with taking personal responsibility to make meaningful changes, one step at a time.

The Meaningful Living Group meetings were advertised on MeetUp and the present author's INPM website. Each cycle consisted of 12 sessions between an introduction and a concluding celebration. The introduction familiarized potential members with the objectives and methodology of the groups. The concluding session briefly wrapped up and was followed by a party where certificates were given to individuals who had completed at least 10 of 12 sessions.

In the present author's experience, these lessons were offered every other week free of charge. On average, there were 20 people in attendance over three cohorts. Two facilitators conducted the small group discussion after the lecture. The group discussion could last more than an hour, depending on the preferences of the group members, but never longer than one and a half hours.

During orientation, potential participants are informed that the group is to be considered a guided journey to discover how to live a happy and meaningful life based on the science of PP and meaning therapy. Furthermore, they are told that research shows there is more to life than being happy (Smith, 2013) and that meaning and purpose are necessary for living a good life (Wong, 2014b). Participants are then challenged with three basic questions about how to make life worth living:

1. Everyone has only one life—how do you get it right the first time?
2. Life is short and finite—how do you make the most of it?
3. Everyone wants a better life—how do you achieve it?

Finally, participants are informed that through the lectures, group discussions, and take-home exercises, they can make progress in finding answers to these important questions. The introduction is concluded with an invitation to join the important journey of self-discovery and self-improvement.

Lesson 1: Who Am I? Discover The True Self You Never Knew

Socrates' famous quote, "Know Thyself," is a philosophical and psychological imperative. It applies to every major area of psychology, from self-acceptance to self-esteem, from self-defence to personal growth. Almost every significant aspect of well-being and mental health is related to self-knowledge.

The Importance of Self-Knowledge

Self-knowledge is the foundation for building a meaningful and fulfilling life. The journey of healing depends on recognizing our own brokenness and weaknesses; the pathway of flourishing depends on acknowledging our intrinsic value and strengths. Unfortunately, many people are afraid to find out the truth about themselves, especially in regard to their "dark side" with its problems. However, we are each unique and worthy human beings despite the things that we fear to face. In accepting ourselves, we will find liberation and empowerment.

The negative consequences of not knowing your real self include:

- Choosing the wrong career or mate,
- Acting inappropriately and encountering unnecessary frustration,
- Wandering in the wilderness and feeling lost,
- Going through life without feeling like you are living,
- Feeling uncomfortable in your own skin, and/or
- Experiencing mental health problems and relational issues.

Self-Acceptance as a Precondition for Positive Change and Personal Growth

The antidote of self-deception is self-acceptance. Self-acceptance enables us to honestly and realistically conduct self-assessment in order to make necessary changes. Self-acceptance means embracing yourself as you are, both your potentials and your limitations. Inner pain often serves as a warning sign that something is wrong in your life and changes are urgently needed.

In fact, a healthy self-concept depends on self-acceptance. Accepting one's inherent value and worth as a human being provides an unshakable foundation for personal growth. This positive affirmation also includes acknowledging one's capability of making positive changes and pursuing what really matters. This sense of self-worth and self-confidence comes when you face and accept yourself as you really are rather than as what you think other people expect you to be. True self-esteem does not depend on superficial characteristics, but on accepting your uniqueness and intrinsic value.

Each of us can live a better life by becoming a better person, regardless of our current conditions and life circumstances, if we continue on the journey of self-discovery and meaning-seeking.

Who Are You? What Is Your True Self?

Your true self is bigger than your occupation, your performance, and even your problems. You have more potential than you realize, so do yourself a favor by finding out more about yourself. It is important to understand that the true self is a constantly evolving system, involving many different dimensions: physical, psychological, social, and spiritual. We can seek improvement in any of these dimensions. Therefore, there is always hope for constant improvement toward congruence between where you are now and where you want to be.

Central to this self-discovery is answering the important existential questions of "What am I living for?" or "What am I striving for?" Your answer to these questions will, to a large extent, determine the direction and destiny of your life.

Exercises

- Describe the "real you" in one sentence.
- Ask your best friend to describe the "real you" in one sentence.
- What kind of person do you want to be five years down the road?
- What might be your blind spots?
- What aspects of yourself do you have the most difficulty facing?

Lesson 2: What Really Matters in Life?

The next step of self-discovery is exploring your values and discovering what matters to you and what makes your life worthwhile.

What Really Matters to You

There are two pillars to a meaningful life: self-transcendence and authenticity. Self-transcendence means living for something bigger than ourselves. Authenticity means being true to yourself and taking care of your own well-being. These two pillars are interdependent: You must be true to your calling and develop your full potential in order to give your best in serving others.

Self-Determination and Goal-Setting

Our capacity for self-determination enables us to transcend any and all the determining forces in life. The biggest tragedy in life is people allowing their fears, society, or even parents dictate how they live their lives.

You can start setting new goals right where you are at this moment. Think of the kind of projects you have always wanted to do. Select one that reflects your interests and values the most, such as reconciliation with your loved ones or going back to school to complete your education. It is important that you start engaging in an activity that has intrinsic value—worth doing in its own right—such as volunteering or learning a new skill or subject. The more intrinsic your core values, the less dependent you will be on contingencies or external circumstances. The more self-transcending your life goals are, the more meaningfulness you will experience.

Exercises

- How much is your life worth? $1,000,000 or more?
- Is the value of your life dependent on your career or profession?
- When is the pursuit of meaning a more promising approach to achieving a worthy life than the pursuit of happiness or wealth?

Lesson 3: What Is the Meaning-Mindset and Its Benefits?

Dr. Viktor Frankl was the first and most influential psychotherapist who discovered the vital role of meaning in healing and well-being. According to Frankl (1985), the most effective way to attain healing and wholeness is through the

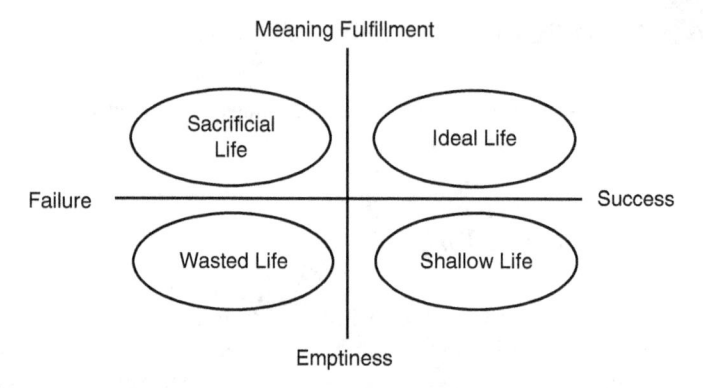

```
                    Meaning Fulfillment
                            |
          _____          |          _____
         /        \         |         /        \
        ( Sacrificial )     |       (  Ideal Life )
         \   Life   /       |         \        /
          ‾‾‾‾‾‾‾‾          |          ‾‾‾‾‾‾‾‾
Failure _____|_____ Success
          _____          |          _____
         /        \         |         /        \
        ( Wasted Life )     |       ( Shallow Life )
         \        /         |         \        /
          ‾‾‾‾‾‾‾‾          |          ‾‾‾‾‾‾‾‾
                            |
                        Emptiness
```

Fig. 1 The meaning-mindset versus the success mindset

spiritual path of discovering meaning. By introducing the vertical meaning dimension and its intersection with the success dimension (Fig. 1), Frankl revolutionized how we define a truly successful life. This graph summarizes what we have learned so far quite well.

The two axes represent two fundamentally different life orientations. One orientation is primarily concerned with how to live a meaningful life—one that is virtuous and focused on serving a higher purpose or the greater good. The other orientation is primarily concerned with how to get ahead in the world, particularly in terms of money and fame. People with this orientation are primarily concerned about personal gains. The above figure, modeled after Frankl (1985), places people into four categories.

If your life is empty, even success remains shallow because it is devoid of significant substance. A commentary on Henry David Thoreau's spirituality states, "Without a rich inner life, we must fill our existence with things from 'outside,' and that makes for a shallow life" (Anders, 2012, p. 144). If your life is not only empty but also unsuccessful according to society's standards, it will be a wasted one of suffering in vain. It is not difficult to identify people in this category, who feel bitter and angry toward life.

The good news is that when people see themselves and their lives with the meaning-mindset, they cannot fail. Even when their pursuit of a purposeful mission is met with suffering and death, such as in the cases of Gandhi and Martin Luther King, Jr., their lives are still objectively meaningful and admirable. As Lukas (2014) has emphasized, self-sacrifice is a necessary ingredient of self-transcendence; those who are not willing to make any sacrifices seldom accomplish anything significant.

The two orientations of the meaning-mindset and success-mindset exert pervasive influences on our lives and society, from career choices and character strengths to civic virtues and community development. It is difficult to develop a harmonious, compassionate, and virtuous society without a significant number of people subscribing to the meaning-mindset.

The Meaning-Mindset and the Spiritual Dimension

According to Frankl (1985), the meaning-mindset involves a shift of basic orientation from ego to logos. This shift of perspective enables us to see clearly the meaning advantages listed in the last lesson. We cannot see clearly the value of meaning and virtue if we are consumed by misguided ambitions for power, wealth, and fame; nor can we appreciate the joy of serving others if we are obsessed with pursuing physical pleasures and cheap thrills. Once we are spiritually awakened, we will begin to see things differently and perceive meaningful moments of beauty and goodness even in ordinary events, as Lukas (2014) has described.

Spiritual activation plays a big part in shifting our attention from everyday busyness to meaningful living. There are three stages in spiritual activation: (1) exploring one's core values and assumptions, as discussed in the last lesson; (2) awakening one's insight into the benefits of meaning-orientation, as discussed in this lesson, and (3) implementing one's insight, as will be discussed in the next lesson.

Exercises

- Complete the Life Orientation Scale (Wong, 2012b) (http://www.drpaulwong.com/dr-wongs-psychological-tests/)
- Write a brief paragraph entitled, "This I Believe." Describe what you believe to be most valuable and important in life.

Lesson 4: What Is the Foundation for a Meaningful Life? Understand the Three Basic Tenets of Logotherapy

In this lesson, we will focus on the three interconnected basic tenets of logotherapy (Frankl, 1985, 1986): (1) the freedom of will, (2) the will to meaning, and (3) the meaning of life. One cannot just accept only one or two of these three tenets; they have to be embraced as an integrated package for a good reason, as follows.

Freedom of Will

The freedom of will is not about being free to do or say whatever one wants. What Frankl has in mind is the radical spiritual freedom we have against all the deterministic forces of the environment, genes, and fate.

Frankl also differentiates between responsibility and responsibleness. The former comes from possessing the freedom of will. The later refers to exercising our freedom to make the right decisions in meeting the demands of each situation: "Existential analysis aims at nothing more and nothing less than leading [people] to consciousness of their responsibility" (Frankl, 1986, p. 275).

To be able to transcend our situations and assume responsibility to do the right thing is the most liberating and empowering message. To all those who say that they cannot change their lives because of depression, poverty, or other limiting factors, we can always choose to adopt a positive attitude or make some small change that is under our control.

Will to Meaning

Once we exercise our spiritual freedom of will, we will be able to make very different choices. We will be able to choose to pursue meaning and self-transcendence by doing what is right and responsible. The will to meaning is "the basic striving of [people] to find and fulfill meaning and purpose" (Frankl, 1988, p. 35). The will to meaning is possible because of the human capacity to transcend one's immediate circumstances.

The will to meaning represents a universal spiritual longing, a noble desire to be truly human. It provides an innate motive to serve a higher purpose and an innate sense of moral responsibility to do what is right.

The implementation of self-transcendence represents the last stage of spiritual activation—doing something for the good of others out of a sense of ethical responsibility. This could be a small gesture of offering a cup of water to a thirsty person, or going out of one's way to help a friend in need. Any practice of the will to meaning and self-transcendence will grant us a deep sense of satisfaction.

Meaning of Life

If oxygen is necessary for physical health, we have to assume that it is available everywhere on planet earth. Similarly, if meaning is necessary for our spiritual and mental health, we can assume that meaning is available everywhere in this world. Frankl (1985) makes a compelling case that meaning is even available in Nazi death camps.

However, while meaning potentials are available in every situation, it is up to us to discover it. "According to logotherapy, we can discover this meaning in life in three different ways: (1) by creating a work or doing a deed; (2) by experiencing something or encountering someone; and (3) by the attitude we take towards unavoidable suffering" (Frankl, 1985, p. 133).

By making use of the meaning triangle of attitude, creativity, and experience, we can overcome both the tragic triad and the neurotic triad. The tragic triad consists of pain, guilt, and death (Frankl, 1985). These negative experiences make us more aware of our needs for meaning and spiritual aspiration. Frankl (1985, 1986) has observed that people are willing to endure any suffering if they are convinced that this suffering has meaning. Thus, suffering without meaning leads to despair.

Exercises

- How would you encourage a friend who has lost his job and is in despair?
- If you believe that there is purpose in life and there is a reason for your existence, how would that make you more resilient?
- What kind of freedom can you have in a very oppressive situation?

Lesson 5: What Are the Sources and Ingredients of Meaning? The PURE Model

In the present author's ground-breaking research on sources of meaning (Wong, 1998a), hundreds of people from all walks of life were asked what contributes to an ideal meaningful life, if money were not an essential. It was found that there are eight sources of meaning and the good life: achievement, acceptance, transcendence, intimacy, relationship, religion, fairness, and positive affect (emotions).

It is understandable why relationships are rated as the most important. We are social beings; it is only normal that we will feel that life is empty and meaningless if we are isolated and without friends. Positive affect is also expected because scientific research has repeatedly demonstrated a close connection between meaning and happiness. What is most instructive in these findings is that society plays an important role. We feel that it is important that society provides fair treatment or equal opportunities.

Wong (1998a) answers the fundamental question of what we need to do to achieve meaningfulness. Now, we need to answer another fundamental question of what constitutes meaningfulness. Although perceived meaning is subjective, it is possible to identify the fundamental constituents of meaning.

Wong's PURE Model of Meaning

What are the basic components of meaning? Based on PP research on meaning (Batthyany & Russo-Netzer, 2014; Hicks & Routledge, 2013; Wong, 2012c), Wong has identified Purpose, Understanding, Responsibility, and Enjoyment/Evaluation or PURE as the constituents of meaning.

Purpose refers to both the direction and priorities of one's life. *Understanding* has to do with making sense, not only of ourselves, but also our role in the world. *Responsibility* reminds us that we are accountable to others and a higher authority. A clear sense of personal responsibility is a prerequisite for a civil society and ethical decisions. Finally, *enjoyment/evaluation* sums up the joy and self-regulation of a life well lived. Together, the PURE unit functions as the scaffold to build a better future for the self and society.

The meaning research literature has provided ample support regarding the importance of purpose, understanding, responsibility, and positive emotions (please see Wong's "From Logotherapy to Existential Positive Interventions" chapter in this volume for research support for these four components).

Exercises

- Complete at least one of the three measurements of meaning below and indicate which area of your life is the most meaningful and which area is the least meaningful:
  - Wong's (2013a) PURE test
  - Wong's (1998b) Personal Meaning Profile (PMP)
  - Steger, Frazier, Oishi, and Kaler's (2006) The Meaning in Life Questionnaire
- Describe the one thing you have done in your life that is most meaningful to you.
- Examine your beliefs and reflect on which beliefs are not functional or adaptive and need modification.
- Ask yourself whether the assumption or belief that life has intrinsic meaning and value is functional or dysfunctional.

Lesson 6: How Do I Find Happiness in Difficult Times?

Everybody wants happiness. It is easy to be happy when everything goes your way and when your every dream is fulfilled. Unfortunately, for most people, life is not a smooth path, nor is it a joyride. The challenge is how to find happiness in the midst of uncertainty and adversity.

Lyubomirsky (2007) argues that 40 % of our happiness is under our intentional control, regardless of circumstances and genes; however, this simplification has been questioned (Biswas-Diener, 2013). She introduced several happiness-enhancing techniques, such as practicing gratitude, forgiveness, goal setting, and mindfulness and has extended Seligman's (2004) *Authentic Happiness* based on additional research findings.

Other research in positive psychology has also shown that happy people are more likely to be open to see the good in their lives (Fredrickson, 2001), have meaning in their lives (Emmons, 2003; Steger et al., 2006), and enjoy loving relationships

(Peterson, 2013). Thus, our happiness depends not only on skills, but also on who we are—our mindset, meaningfulness, and relationships.

In addition to happiness, we also need meaning (Smith, 2013; Wong, 2014b). King, Hicks, Krull, and Del Gaiso (2006) have found that positive affect and meaning in life are related, and that the former may have more effect on the latter. However, it is hypothesize that longitudinal research will show that meaning as measured by active engagement with what really matters and relating well to significant people in our lives will predict positive affect more than the reverse. Pattakos and Dundon's (2015) *The OPA Way* lends further support to this meaning hypothesis.

Most of the positive psychology of happiness is based on the assumption that happiness is the final good, and that we can live a happy life by directly pursuing it. In contrast, Frankl (1985) and Wong (2011) propose that if we pursue meaning instead, happiness will become a by-product of meaning, as explained in the last few lessons. This chapter has shown that Wong's (1998a) eight sources of meaning are connected with happiness and made the case that the process of pursuing meaning and self-transcendence is sufficient to endow life with meaning and deep satisfaction (Wong, 2014a), even in difficult times.

Five Myths of Happiness

1. You can have instant happiness.
2. You can have lasting happiness.
3. Everyone has a fixed set point for happiness.
4. Money can buy happiness.
5. The happiness formula is a scientific equation.

Recently, Robert Biswas-Diener (2013) has debunked the above myths:

> If you think about it, it is nonsensical to speak about 40 % of your happiness being the result of personal choices. Further, within an individual it does not make sense to separate genetics from circumstances and personal choices. All three interact and mutually influence one another. In the end, it is the spirit of the pie chart that people warm to: the notion that you have some control over your own happiness. Rest assured, that sentiment is correct.

According to the meaning hypothesis, you can still have authentic happiness even when you go through trying times, because such happiness is not dependent on external circumstances but on living a meaningful life of self-transcendence.

Exercises

- Try to help someone who is less fortunate than you. Describe how you feel afterward.
- If you are bored with pleasurable activities, try something that challenges your intellect, courage, or skill.
- Discover the joy of letting go of something that has been bothering you.

Lesson 7: How Do I Maintain Hope in Desperate Situations? Tragic Optimism

Chance and fate intervene. Bad things happen. The best-planned project goes wrong. In this world, nothing is certain and nothing can be guaranteed—macro forces can defeat even our best and most careful efforts. The challenge is this: How can we maintain a sense of hope in a meaningful future in desperate or seemingly hopeless situations?

It took the horror of Nazi death camps for Frankl (1985) to discover the power of tragic optimism (TO). He defined TO as "an optimism in the face of tragedy" (p. 162). His chapter on the case for TO "addresses present day concerns and how it is possible to 'say yes to life' in spite of all the tragic aspects of human existence. … It is hoped that an 'optimism' for our future may flow from the lesson learned from our 'tragic' past" (Frankl, 1985, p. 17).

His own defiant spirit and courage in the most hopeless, helpless situation bears witness to the power of TO. In addition to the defiant attitudinal value, he also enjoyed the experiential value of watching a beautiful sunset and the creative value of working on his book with scraps of paper. Thus, he demonstrated that by meditating on the meaning triangle, we can experience meaning and optimism.

Unlike other kinds of hopes, TO cannot be crushed by adversities or catastrophes because, like true gold, it is purified in the crucible of suffering and rooted in an abiding inner value. Frankl (1985) aptly states, "The consciousness of one's inner value is anchored in higher, more spiritual things, and cannot be shaken by camp life" (p. 83).

Wong's Five Ingredients of Tragic Optimism

Wong (2005) has developed a psychological model of TO and proposed that it comprises the following components:

- *Acceptance of what cannot be changed*. By definition, TO depends on confronting and accepting the bleak reality as experienced.
- *Affirmation of the inherent meaning and value of life*. This is the turning point; the affirmation of life is the cornerstone of TO. Without firmly believing in the possibility of meaning in all aspects of human existence and the intrinsic value and dignity of human life, it would be difficult to experience optimism in the face of tragedy.
- *Self-transcendence*. This represents an action dimension of stepping out of oneself and becoming reoriented toward helping others or serving a greater purpose.
- *Faith in a higher being and/or others*. Faith in a higher being has been a source of strength and optimism to countless individuals in practically hopeless situations. Faith represents a flickering light at the end of the tunnel.

- *Courage to face and overcome adversity.* Courage may be considered the master virtue, because all the other components hinge on courage—the heroic and defiant human spirit. Acceptance requires courage; so does affirmation. Stepping out of our comfort zone to help others or to serve a higher purpose also requires the courage to be vulnerable. One cannot be optimistic without the courage to face an unknown and uncertain future.

Exercises

- How does meaning make tragic optimism stronger than other types of hope that are simply based on positive thinking and confidence in one's own competence?
- Think of a task that you have been avoiding because of its difficulty and high risk of failure. How would the concept of tragic optimism empower you to complete this task?

Lesson 8: What Are the Practical Steps to Build Resilience? The ABCDE Model

It takes resilience to bounce back after failure and setback. The defiant human spirit and the human capacity for meaning-making are very powerful tools at our disposal. Wong's ABCDE model (Wong, 2012d) incorporates both the meaning triangle and Wong's (2005) tragic optimism as a framework to overcome and transcend all kinds of adversities.

There are two possibilities after a tragic or traumatic event. Some become bitter and experience depression or posttraumatic stress disorder, while some become better and experience posttraumatic growth. The following are the components of the pathway of resilience, as represented by the acronym ABCDE.

1. *Acceptance*: *the reality principle.* Acceptance does not mean giving up or resignation; it simply means accepting what cannot be changed—the trauma, the loss, and the dark side of the human condition. It means accepting areas of "fate" which are beyond our control with courage and hope.
2. *Belief*: *the faith principle.* Belief primarily means affirming the three basic tenets of logotherapy. It means that there is always some area of freedom in which we can act responsibly and courageously.
3. *Commitment*: *the action principle.* Commitment simply means moving forward and carrying out one's responsibility with resolve, regardless of feelings or circumstances. This brings us back to the PURE strategy of striving to fulfill one's responsibility no matter what, because it is the right thing to do and it is part of one's life mission. Real change is possible only when one takes the first concrete step in a new direction.

4. *Discovery: the 'Aha!' principle.* Discovery involves learning something new about the self and life. It means that as we dig deeper into our resources and explore further, we discover hidden strengths and resources. This is consistent with Wong's (2012e) deep-and-wide hypothesis of the adaptive benefits of adversity and negative emotions.
5. *Evaluation: the self-regulation principle.* Evaluation means continuing to monitor and make the necessary adjustments to ensure some progress. If nothing seems to work and there is no reduction of symptoms and no improvement in the pursuit of positive life goals, then some adjustments will be necessary. This involves reflecting on one's life and assessing the opportunities and risks.

Exercises

- Currently, what is the most stressful thing in your life? Apply the ABCDE Strategy and find out whether it works for you.
- Discover an area of freedom in which you can exercise any of the three values of Frankl's meaning triangle, and discover whether it affects your life in a positive way.

Lesson 9: How Do I Live Life to the Fullest? The Yin-Yang Way

Life is a continuous series of problems and opportunities. The challenge confronting us is how to achieve our life goals by overcoming obstacles and making the best use of opportunities. This lesson focuses on how to manage our avoidance and approach tendencies in an adaptive way.

Wong (2011) emphasizes the Yin-Yang way as the basis for second wave positive psychology (PP2.0) or existential positive psychology (EPP; 2010a) because it avoids these two extremes and integrates positives with negatives. Just like the Yin-Yang symbol, life is a balancing act between positives and negatives. In fact, each positive experience contains the seed of self-destruction; each negative one contains the seed of personal growth. The Yin-Yang approach avoids the excesses of the pursuit of happiness and success, while allowing us to discover the potential benefits of negative experiences.

Basically, life involves a series of approach and avoidance conflicts. In every situation, there are always two options: "go" or "no go." If you choose to go ahead with your plan, you can rely on the PURE principle to ensure that you are pursuing something meaningful and worthwhile. However, in the process of goal striving, there will always be bumps in the road or real obstacles. These setbacks will make you consider the other option of "no go." This thought will trigger the ABCDE process to evaluate how to overcome the difficulty.

The continuous interactions between approach and avoidance represent a constant tension between Yin and Yang. Optimal functioning is possible when we do not invest all our energy in the futile pursuit of an unrealistic and unattainable goal. Similarly, we would not be living fully if we readily gave up and spent most of our days in avoidance mode. The positive system seeks to do what is desirable and what holds out the promises of a better future. The aversive system serves as a warning about what is wrong and threatening. There is a downside to the approach system and an upside to the avoidance system. We can optimize the positives in our lives by focusing on the meaning-elements in both systems.

Exercises

- Count your blessings in a negative situation you currently experience.
- Consider the hidden dangers of success when all your dreams are realized.
- In everyday situations, how do you balance the positives and the negatives so that you feel good at the end of each day?

Lesson 10: Why Do Other People Matter? The Practical Spirituality of Self-Transcendence

We are all interconnected in some way. That is both a blessing and a curse. We cannot live without other people. We are hardwired for each other—from babies' attachment to their parents to adults' bonding with their lovers, intimate relationships are the main source of our security, happiness, and well-being. In addition, a healthy family, community, and society are all built on good interpersonal relationships.

One of the challenges before us, as individuals and as a society, is how to strike a balance between self-interest and the welfare of others. Other people matter (Peterson, 2013), because relationships matter a great deal for the good life. To transform an inhumane society into a kinder and gentler community, we need to value people more than self-gain. We all gain at the end when we place other people's well-being above self-centered concerns.

Self-Transcendence

Self-transcendence simply means that only when we redirect our focus from self-interest to something bigger than ourselves can we experience meaning in life. Both Abraham Maslow (1993) and Viktor Frankl (1985) have come to the conclusion that self-transcendence represents the highest level of personal development. Frankl is more explicit in pointing out that self-transcendence represents our spiritual nature as well as our deepest yearning. It is our spiritual dimension that separates us from all other creatures and makes us truly human.

Frankl's three levels of self-transcendence (Wong, 2016):

1. *Seeking ultimate meaning.* To reach beyond our physical and intellectual limitations and gain a glimpse of the invisible wonders of the transcendental realm.
2. *Seeking situational meaning.* To be mindful of the meaning potential of the present moment with an attitude of openness, curiosity, and compassion.
3. *Seeking one's calling.* To reach beyond self-actualization and pursue a higher purpose for the greater good. This involves engagement and striving to achieve a concrete meaning in life, that is, a life goal of contributing something of value to others.

At all three levels, we are motivated by the intrinsic need for spiritual meaning. If we can cultivate these three levels of self-transcendence, we will develop a spiritual lifestyle that is good and healthy for individuals as well as society. The more we practice self-transcendence based on the meaning-mindset, the more it will be better for others and ourselves. It is a win-win strategy.

Exercises

- Think of a relational conflict in your life. What difference would it make if you thought in terms of "we" instead of "me" in this situation?
- Have you ever made amends in order to repair a broken relationship? If not, what holds you back?
- What is your communication style? Do you think that your communication style might be part of your relational problems? Fill out the Individual Communication Style Profile below.

Individual Communication Style Profile		
© Paul T. P. Wong, PhD		
Cold	I---1---2---3---4---5---I	Warm
Laid-back	I---1---2---3---4---5---I	Intense
Indirect	I---1---2---3---4---5---I	Direct
Guarded	I---1---2---3---4---5---I	Open
Judgmental	I---1---2---3---4---5---I	Appreciative

Lesson 11: What Should I Do When I Feel Stuck? The Double-Vision Strategy

Do you feel trapped in a bad relationship or stuck in a dead-end job? Do you feel discouraged by setbacks because all your struggles seem to be futile? We all have such moments and do not know how to resolve our personal predicaments.

This lesson introduces the double-vision strategy, which can be very helpful in problem solving.

The paradox is that, sometimes, the more we focus on finding a solution to these problems, the more confused and frustrated we become. However, when we step back, expand our vision, and look at the big picture, such as the universal human condition or a higher being, we begin to see our problems in a different light—this shift in perspective enables us to find new solutions.

What Is Personal Is Often Universal

What seems to be a personal problem may be related to a universal human condition. For example, one's anxiety about sending off a daughter or son to another city for post-secondary education may reflect one's existential anxiety about aging and dying.

The double-vision strategy is helpful in pursuing one's life goals if you take a larger view of life. When we keep in mind our higher purpose, we will be less likely defeated by small setbacks along the way. To use a chess game analogy, we do not mind sacrificing a pawn in order to checkmate our opponent's king. To use a sport analogy, we need to keep one eye on the ball and the other on the goal.

When we strive for an ideal as our life purpose, we are more willing to overcome similarly insurmountable problems and hardships. It is by keeping our eye on the big picture that we can deal with small, everyday problems more effectively.

The Double-Vision Strategy

The double-vision strategy simply means you keep one eye on your situational problem and another on your future meaning to be fulfilled. The bigger your vision of the future, the more effective your double-vision strategy. The biggest vision will involve not only the future generations of humanity, but also involve the transcendental realm or a higher being. If you are convinced that you have received a calling from above and are thus striving for the greater good of future generations, then you will not be defeated by opposition, setbacks, or personal problems.

The problem with most people is that they never look beyond their self-imposed prison. They never have the courage to venture out of their cave. Therefore, they will only live in a shadowy land without any idea of what life is like under the sun. A person with a double-vision is no longer preoccupied with everyday busyness and personal problems; such people are able to live on a higher plane and at a deeper level, because they know that their transient earthly life is only an instrument for accomplishing something far greater than they are.

As one of the most popular Chinese sayings goes, "If you step back from your immediate problem, the horizon will broaden and the sky will open up," the double-vision strategy represents a change in perspective as well as a change of value from ego to logos.

Exercises

- How can the double-vision strategy make your life happier and more productive?
- Learn to pause and reflect. This exercise of self-reflection is an effective way to ponder the big picture. For example, reflect on the questions, "Who am I?" "What is my place in the universe?" "What is my life mission?" or "What is God's purpose for my life?"
- Is it worthwhile devoting one's life to pursuing one's calling, even when it does not yield any monetary reward or recognition?

Lesson 12: Learn The Meaning-Centered Pathways to Well-Being

We have now come to the end of our journey of self-discovery. We are now able to pull all the lessons together and have an overview of how meaning plays a central role in living the good life. Meaning not only leads to well-being, but also protects us against distress.

Snyder and Lopez (2007) are correct in proposing the formula: Happiness + Meaning = Mental Health. Wong (1998a) has found that the sources of meaning predict both the presence of well-being and absence of mental illness. This has been replicated and extended to prospective studies (Mascaro, 2014; Mascaro & Rosen, 2008).

However, when people are going through very difficult times, meaning, rather than positive emotions, becomes more important in maintaining some level of well-being (Frankl, 1985; Wong, 2011). According to the meaning-centered approach to well-being, the ABCDE strategy serves the function of transforming negatives into positives, as well as making suffering more bearable. The ABCDE acronym stands for acceptance, belief, commitment, discovery, and enjoyment/evaluation. A detailed account on how these components contribute to resilience and well-being in adverse situations has been discussed in previous works (Wong, 2010b; Wong & Wong, 2012).

In addition, the important role of hope in maintaining one's well-being and health has been well documented (Snyder, 2000). Hope provides the motivation to strive and improve one's life. However, in extreme situations, such as the Holocaust or dying from incurable cancer, one needs a different kind of hope, which is found in Frankl's (1985) concept of tragic optimism.

Therefore, meaning provides at least three pathways toward a healthier and happier life that is both resilient and optimistic. When we cultivate the meaning-mindset and practice self-transcendence, we are on a very promising path toward healing and wholeness. More recently, Wong (2014c) has provided a more detailed integrative model indicating how meaning contributes to our well-being, as seen in Fig. 2.

MEANING-BASED MODEL OF WELL-BEING AND MENTAL HEALTH

```
                    Complete Mental
                  Health and Flourishing
                           ↑
  Reduced Negativity &                    Broaden-and-Build
       Increased                          Model of Positive
    Resourcefulness      Personal Growth,     Emotions
           ↑            Character Strengths, &      ↑
                          the PURE Model
                            (Factor II)
   Deep-and-Wide Theory                  Experience of Positive
    of Effective Coping                    Emotions (Factor I)
        (Factor III)
                         Sources of meaning
```

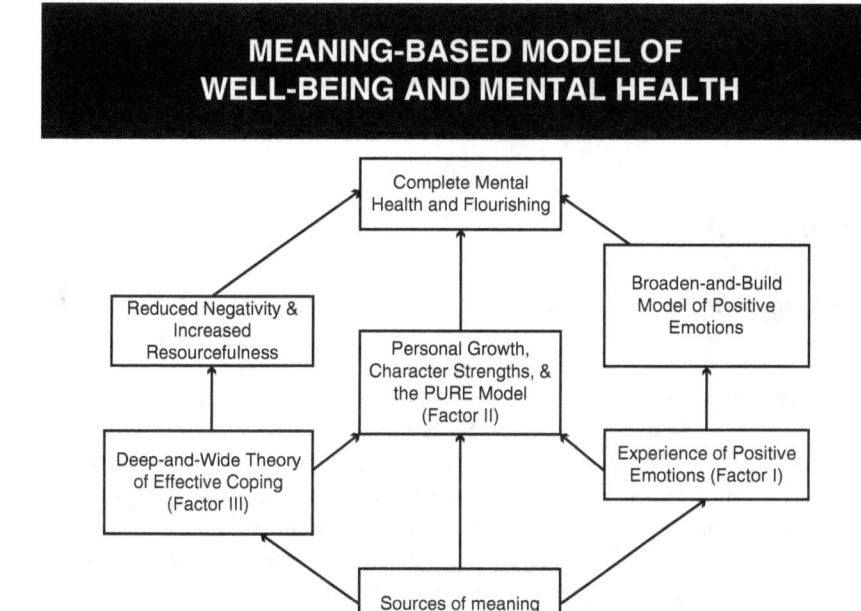

Fig. 2 A meaning-centered model of positive mental health

A meaning-centered holistic model of complete mental health recognizes both the presence of positive emotions and the reduction and transformation of negative emotions and symptoms. Both of these objectives can be achieved through the pursuit of meaning, as shown in Fig. 2 (refer to Wong, 2014c for details). The plain path toward complete positive mental health is through self-transcendence rather than the self-centered pursuit of personal happiness and success. Thus, it is dependent on having a meaning-mindset and an appreciative and defiant attitude, rather than positive feelings and favorable circumstances.

The good life is not just a matter of positive thinking and positive effect, but also a matter of living out a meaningful life in a technological culture and toxic world. It will be both selfish and delusional to think that we can live a happy life by ourselves, without caring about the world in which we live—a world that is polluted by injustice, violence, and evil. Meaningful living is about being a light to shine through the darkness.

Exercises

- Identify an unhappy situation in your life. Try to use meaning-seeking or meaning-making as a way to help you feel better.

- Describe an experience in which you felt good about yourself in going through a very difficult situation because of your decision to practice self-transcendence.
- How will you use the meaning approach to help a friend who is struggling with depression, anxiety, or despair?

Meaning Manifesto

The Meaningful Living Group MeetUp concludes with the below meaning manifesto, which summarizes the main points of the 12 lessons. We celebrate the conclusion of the MeetUp with a dinner and the awarding of certificates of completion.

"Life is much more than the everyday busyness of making a living or striving for personal success. Life is much more than a constant struggle of coping with harsh realities by fighting or escaping. Life can be lived at a deeper level and on a higher plane by adopting a *meaning-mindset* as your basic life orientation.

Your life has intrinsic meaning and value because you have a unique purpose to fulfill. You are endowed with the capacity for *freedom* and *responsibility* to choose a life of meaning and significance. Don't settle for anything less. No matter how confusing and bleak your situation, there is always beauty, truth, and meaning to be discovered, but you need to cultivate a *mindful* attitude and learn to transcend self-centeredness.

Don't always ask what you can get from life, but ask what life demands of you. May you be awakened to your sense of responsibility and the call to *self-transcendence*. You become fully human only when you devote your life to serving a higher purpose and the common good.

Let your inner goodness and *conscience* be your guide. Let compassion be your motive and may you see the world and yourself through the lens of *meaning and virtue*. You will experience transformation and authentic happiness when you practice meaningful living. Now, go forward with courage and integrity and pursue your ideals against all odds with the *defiant human spirit*."

Key Takeaways

- There is mounting evidence in the research literature concerning the vital role played by meaning in life in enhancing well-being and buffering against stress. Meaning-centered positive group work has much to contribute to the mental health movement because it educates participants regarding their essential need for meaning and the basic principles and skills of meaningful living.
- This group intervention is based on both the positive psychology research of meaning and the existential insights and principles of Frankl's logotherapy and Wong's integrative meaning-centered therapy. Therefore, it can be used for both community-based groups interested in personal development and various clinical groups that address meaning in life issues.

- For each session, the group activity consists of a mini lecture by a psychologist, followed by group discussions and take-home exercises. All activities are designed to focus on the optimistic outlook of positive changes regardless of circumstances.
- The 12 lessons cover important questions such as "Who am I?" "What really matters in life?" and "How can I find happiness in difficult situations?" These lessons draw upon scientific findings and clinical insights. The applications of the principles of meaningful living answer these universal concerns while taking into account each participant's personal context.
- Participants learn Frankl's concept of the meaning-mindset. When life is viewed from this perspective, life takes on more meaning; even adversities are transformed into challenges and opportunities. Participants also learn the Yin-Yang principle of existential positive psychology, which is capable of transforming all negative life experiences into ones that are positive.

References

Anders, M. (2012). *What you need to know about spiritual growth: 12 lessons that can change your life*. Nashville, TN: Thomas Nelson.

Batthyany, A., & Russo-Netzer, P. (Eds.). (2014). *Meaning in positive and existential psychology*. New York, NY: Springer.

Biswas-Diener, R. (2013, April 1). 5 myths of positive psychology. *Psychology Today*. Retrieved from https://www.psychologytoday.com/blog/significant-results/201304/5-myths-positive-psychology.

Corey, G. (2009). *Theory and practice of counseling and psychotherapy* (8th ed.). Belmont, CA: Brooks/Cole.

Emmons, R. A. (2003). Personal goals, life meaning, and virtue: Wellsprings of a positive life. In C. L. M. Keyes (Ed.), *Flourishing: The positive person and the good life* (pp. 105–128). Washington, DC: American Psychological Association.

Frankl, V. E. (1985). *Man's search for meaning* (Revised & updated ed.). New York, NY: Washington Square Press.

Frankl, V. E. (1986). *The doctor and the soul: From psychotherapy to logotherapy* (3rd ed.). New York, NY: Vintage Books.

Frankl, V. E. (1988). *The will to meaning: Foundations and applications of logotherapy* (Expanded ed.). New York, NY: Meridian.

Fredrickson, B. L. (2001). The role of positive emotions in positive psychology: The broaden-and-build theory of positive emotions. *American Psychologist, 56*(3), 218–226. doi:10.1037/0003-066X.56.3.218

Hicks, J. A., & Routledge, C. (Eds.). (2013). *The experience of meaning in life: Classical perspectives, emerging themes, and controversies*. Dordrecht, NL: Springer.

King, L. A., Hicks, J. A., Krull, J. L., & Del Gaiso, A. K. (2006). Positive affect and the experience of meaning in life. *Journal of Personality and Social Psychologist, 90*(1), 179–196. doi:10.1037/0022-3514.90.1.179

Leontiev, D. A. (2015). Experience processing as an aspect of existential psychotherapy: Life enhancement methodology. *Journal of Contemporary Psychotherapy, 45*(1), 49–58.

Lukas, E. (1986/2014). *Meaning in suffering: Comfort in crisis through logotherapy*. Birmingham, AL: Purpose Research.

Lyubomirsky, S. (2007). *The how of happiness: The scientific approach to getting the life you want*. New York, NY: Penguin Press.

Mascaro, N. (2014). Meaning sensitive psychotherapy: Binding clinical, existential, and positive psychological perspectives. In A. Batthyany & P. Russo-Netzer (Eds.), *Meaning in positive and existential psychology* (pp. 269–289). New York, NY: Springer.

Mascaro, N., & Rosen, D. H. (2008). Assessment of existential meaning and its longitudinal relations with depressive symptoms. *Journal of Social and Clinical Psychology, 27*(6), 576–599. doi:10.1521/jscp.2008.27.6.576

Maslow, A. H. (1993). *The farther reaches of human nature.* City of Westminster, UK: Penguin.

Pattakos, A., & Dundon, E. (2015). *The OPA! way: Finding joy and meaning in everyday life and work.* Dallas, TX: BenBella Books.

Peterson, C. (2013). *Pursuing the good life: 100 reflections on positive psychology.* Oxford, UK: Oxford University Press.

Seligman, M. E. P. (2004). *Authentic happiness: Using the new positive psychology to realize your potential for lasting fulfillment.* New York, NY: Simon & Schuster.

Smith, E. E. (2013, January 9). There's more to life than being happy. *The Atlantic.* Retrieved from http://www.theatlantic.com/health/archive/2013/01/theres-more-to-life-than-being-happy/266805/.

Snyder, C. R. (Ed.). (2000). *Handbook of hope: Theory, measures, and applications.* San Diego, CA: Academic.

Snyder, C. R., & Lopez, S. J. (2007). *Positive psychology: The scientific and practical explorations of human strengths.* Thousand Oaks, CA: Sage.

Steger, M. F., Frazier, P., Oishi, S., & Kaler, M. (2006). The Meaning in Life Questionnaire: Assessing the presence of and search for meaning in life. *Journal of Counseling Psychology, 53*, 80–93.

Wong, P. T. P. (1998a). Implicit theories of meaningful life and the development of the personal meaning profile. In P. T. P. Wong & P. S. Fry (Eds.), *The human quest for meaning: A handbook of psychological research and clinical applications* (pp. 111–140). Mahwah, NJ: Erlbaum.

Wong, P. T. P. (1998b). Personal meaning profile (PMP) [Questionnaire]. Retrieved from http://www.drpaulwong.com/documents/wong-scales/personal-meaning-profile.pdf.

Wong, P. T. P. (2005). Viktor Frankl: Prophet of hope for the 21st century. In A. Batthyany & J. Levinson (Eds.), *Anthology of Viktor Frankl's logotherapy.* Tusla, AZ: Zeig, Theisen, & Tucker.

Wong, P. T. P. (2010a). What is existential positive psychology? *International Journal of Existential Psychology and Psychotherapy, 3*, 1–10.

Wong, P. T. P. (2010b). Meaning therapy: An integrative and positive existential psychotherapy. *Journal of Contemporary Psychotherapy, 40*(2), 85–93. doi:10.1007/s10879-009-9132-6

Wong, P. T. P. (2011). Positive psychology 2.0: Towards a balanced interactive model of the good life. *Canadian Psychology, 52*(2), 69–81. doi:10.1037/a0022511

Wong, P. T. P. (2012a, June 22). Giving positive psychology away: Meaningful living meetups. *Positive Psychology News Daily.* Retrieved from http://positivepsychologynews.com/news/paul-wong/2012062222849.

Wong, P. T. P. (2012b). Life Orientation Scale (LOS) [Questionnaire]. Retrieved from http://www.drpaulwong.com/dr-wongs-psychological-tests/.

Wong, P. T. P. (Ed.). (2012c). *The human quest for meaning: Theories, research, and applications* (2nd ed.). New York, NY: Routledge.

Wong, P. T. P. (2012d). From logotherapy to meaning-centered counseling and therapy. In P. T. P. Wong (Ed.), *The human quest for meaning: Theories, research, and applications* (2nd ed., pp. 619–647). New York, NY: Routledge.

Wong, P. T. P. (2012e). Toward a dual-systems model of what makes life worth living. In P. T. P. Wong (Ed.), *The human quest for meaning: Theories, research, and applications* (2nd ed., pp. 3–22). New York, NY: Routledge.

Wong, P. T. P. (2013a). The PURE test [Questionnaire]. Retrieved from http://inpm.org/wp-content/uploads/2011/08/Meaningful-Living-Project-Exercise-6-PUREtest.pdf.

Wong, P. T. P. (2014a). Viktor Frankl's meaning-seeking model and positive psychology. In A. Batthyany & P. Russo-Netzer (Eds.), *Meaning in positive and existential psychology* (pp. 149–184). New York, NY: Springer.

Wong, P. T. P. (2014b). From attunement to a meaning-centred good life: Book review of Daniel Haybron's Happiness: A very short introduction. *International Journal of Wellbeing, 4*(2), 100–105. doi:10.5502/ijw.v4i2.5

Wong, P. T. P. (2014c). Meaning in life. In A. C. Michalos (Ed.), *Encyclopedia of quality of life and well-being research* (pp. 3894–3898). New York, NY: Springer.

Wong, P. T. P. (2016). Meaning-seeking, self-transcendence, and well-being. In A. Batthyany (Ed.), *Logotherapy and existential analysis: Proceedings of the Viktor Frankl Institute* (Vol. 1). Cham, NL: Springer.

Wong, P. T. P., & Wong, L. C. J. (2012). A meaning-centered approach to building youth resilience. In P. T. P. Wong (Ed.), *The human quest for meaning: Theories, research, and applications* (2nd ed., pp. 585–617). New York, NY: Routledge.

Yalom, I. (1995). *The theory and practice of group psychotherapy* (4th ed.). New York, NY: Basic Books.

Index

A

Acceptance and Commitment Therapy (ACT), 103, 275, 389
Acceptance, Belief, Commitment, Discovery and Evaluation/Enjoyment (ABCDE), 336, 337
Adolescents, 407, 410–418
Alcohol use disorder (AUD), 204
Alcoholics Anonymous (A.A.), 204
Aligning strengths, 396
Assessment skills, 191
Authentic Happiness Inventory, 394
Authentic self, 377

B

Bhutanese refugees, 99
Biological perspective, 182–183
Biopsycho-existential model, 183
Biopsychosocial resilience, 182

C

Cambodian refugees, 99
Cancer, 187
Cardiovascular disease (CVD), 172, 173, 186, 188, 193
Caring
   meaning and self-fulfillment, 367–368
   and spiritual realm, 368–370
Caring motivation, 363
   attachment theory, 364
   care -receiver, 365
   caring bonds, 365
   Erikson's notion, generativity, 367
   evolutionary models, 365

historical and anthropological accounts, 366
human species, 365
interpersonal relations, 365
intrinsic motivation, 366
life-span developmental model, 366
neural and biological circuitry, 366
neurohormone oxytocin, 366
patients/clients, 364
proactive care, 366
psychotherapy, 364
self-actualization, 364
socialization, 366
warm and trusting rapport, 364
Character strengths, 384–387
   benefits, 386–387
   and mindfulness, 390
Character Strengths and Virtues (CSV), 384
Chronic illness
   biomedical diagnosis and treatment, 302
   healing, 303
   metamorphosis, 302
Chronic pain, 172, 173, 186, 188–189, 193
Chronic/life-threatening disease, 177, 185
Clinical symptoms, 1
Clinicians' perspective
   functions and concepts, 8
   meaning-oriented psychologies, 7
   metaphysics, 7
   nonreductionism, 8
   therapeutic experience, 8
Cognitive-Behavior Therapy (CBT), 173, 274
   collaborative empiricism, 224
   emotions, 224
   GCM, 225
   guided discovery, 224
   vs. logotherapy, 234–235

Cognitive-Behavior Therapy (CBT) (*cont.*)
   meaning, 225
   vs. positive psychology, 233–234
   REBT, 223
Cognitive process, 267
Coping
   duality in life, 175
   existential, 179–180
   medical information, 190
   and transcending, 193
Coping effectiveness training, 274
Counselling, 64, 65
Cultural diversity, 115

D
Dadaab refugee, 100
Deficit-based psychology, 6
Depression
   CBT, 238
   integrative model, 238, 239
   logotherapy, 238
Dereflection technique, 231, 237, 239
Despair, 246–249, 258
Diagnostic and Statistical Manual of Mental Disorders, Fifth Edition (*DSM-5*), 232, 384
Diagnostic Statistical Manual, 95
Dialectical Behavior Therapy (DBT), 389
Disaster mental health, 150, 158, 161
Discongruence, 185
Displaced refugees, 102
Distress, 98
Diversity of Refugee Experiences, 92–95
Double-Vision Strategy, 438–440

E
Eidetic approach, 302
El Colectivo Aquí y Ahora Foundation (CAYA)
   comorbid mental health problems, 208
   group interventions, 211
   implementation, 209
   motivations, 207
   multi-component model, 207
   psychoeducation, 209
   relapse prevention, 208
   self-distancing, 210
End-of-life care, 245, 246, 249
English-speaking philosophy, 18
Ethnopolitical conflicts with six levels, 93
Ethnopolitical warfare, 89–90
   causes of displacement, 93
   diversity of refugee experiences, 92

outcomes of displacement, 93, 94
   primary and secondary control, 90–92
   refugees fleeing, 102
Eudaimonic approach, 2
Eudaimonism, 23, 24
Existential analysis, 61, 64, 75, 77, 79, 190
Existential Behavioral Therapy (EBT), 394, 395
Existential Positive Psychology (EPP), 335
   broad and positive explanatory system, 339
   MT (*see* Meaning Therapy (MT))
   PURE (*see* Purpose, Understanding, Responsibility and Enjoyment/Evaluation (PURE))
   resilience, 336, 337
Existential psychology. *See also See* Existential Positive Psychology (EPP)
   meaning of life, 111
   positive *vs.* humanistic psychology, 112–114
   spirituality, 112
Existential psychotherapy, 283
Existential skills, 191
Existential therapy, 246
Existential threat, 349, 350, 352
Existential vacuum, 201, 206, 207

F
Five Facet Mindfulness Questionnaire (FFMQ), 394
Forced population movements, 95
Formative *vs.* facilitative intervention, 135
Frankl, V.E., 61–63, 180, 182, 190, 191, 323, 324, 326, 327, 329, 332, 334, 335, 338
Frankl's theory, 230, 407
Franklian therapy, 191
Freedom of will, 429

G
GCM. *See* Generic Cognitive Model (GCM)
Generic Cognitive Model (GCM), 225
Genetic counselling, 171, 186, 190

H
Healing
   compassion, 308
   definition, 303
   empathy, 308
   I-Thou relationship, 309
   soiled humanity, 310
   woundedness, 310

Index

Healing medicine
  biomedical model, 300
  biomedicine, 301, 310
  evidence-based medicine, 301
  languages, 311
  self-transcendence and spirituality, 312
  therapeutic relationship, 312
  treatment planning and implementation, 299
Health professionals, 1
Heritable diseases, 189–190
Human coping, 11
Human maturity, 6

I
I-It relationships, 309, 311
Individual Meaning-Centered Psychotherapy (IMCP), 249
  attitudinal sources of meaning, 253–254
  cancer and meaning, 251–252
  creative sources of meaning, 254–255
  experiential sources of meaning, 255
  historical sources of meaning, 252–253
  pilot study of, 250
  purposes, 250
  sources of meaning, 250, 251
  transitions, 255–256
  treatment manual, 250
Integrated meaning-centred clinical–aetiological model, 184
Integration
  logotherapy, 234
  positive psychology, 235
Integration cognitive-behavior therapy, 233
Integrative psychotherapy, 223
I-Thou relationship, 309, 311

K
Karnofsky Performance Rating Scale (KPRS), 248
Knowledge, 2, 20, 39, 66, 100, 104, 124–126, 140, 150, 152, 178, 189, 216, 241, 261, 264, 275, 300, 310, 313, 364, 374, 385, 386, 415, 425

L
Leontiev's Life Enhancement Group Work, 423–424
Lesbian, Gay, Bisexual, Transgender and Queer (LGBTQ), 118, 121
Life review, 356–358

Logotherapy, 4, 103, 190, 207–211, 323, 412, 423, 429–431
  British NICE guidelines, 62
  CAYA logotherapeutic treatment model (*see* El Colectivo Aquí y Ahora Foundation (CAYA))
  and CBT, 234–235
  dereflection, 231
  existential vacuum, 206
  Frankl's anthropology centres, 62
  individuals experience meaning in life, 62
  lack of validation, 62
  MCT trials, 62
  meaning, 231–233
  meaning-based coping styles, 63
  meaning-centered therapeutic process, 231
  meaning-centered practitioners, 62
  meaning-enhancing positive interventions (*see* Meaning-enhancing interventions)
  noetic dimension, 230
  personal recovery, 63
  policymakers, 63
  and positive psychology, 63, 235–236
  resilience, 237
  standardisation, MCT, 62
  SUD, 206
  training institutions, 62
Lukas' Dereflection Groups, 424

M
Maladaptive behavior, 225, 237, 239
Man's Search for Meaning, 409
Manichean Gnostic deliverance, 285
MCGP for Breast Cancer Survivors (MCGP-BCS), 257
MCGP in Cancer Survivors (MCGP-CS), 258
McNemar test, 213
MCP for Caregivers (MCP-C), 256–257
Meaning, 408–409
  CBT, 225
  and character strengths, 392–394
  core concepts and research, 391–392
  and mindfulness, 394–395
  mortality and age-related cognitive deficits, 344
  nonsacred, 40
  positive psychology, 228–229, 313–315
  sanctification, 53
  self-actualization, 343
  spirituality, 37
Meaning connections, 133, 135, 138, 141, 142

Meaning in life
  Anglo-American philosophers, 27
  client's attitudes, 27
  client's life, 31
  client's values, 31
  deliberation and volition, 28
  egalitarian terms, 30
  hypothesis, 31
  intelligence, 28, 29
  intimacy, 30
  life period, 27
  meaning-making, 151
  measurement, 212–213
  participants, 212
  philosophical reflection, 28
  procedures, 213
  self-development, 29
  subjectivism, 27, 30
Meaning in Life Dimensional Scale (MLDS), 212–215
Meaning in Life Questionnaire (MLQ), 228, 229, 237, 285
Meaning insight devices
  broader meaning-making contexts, 140
  characteristic of Socratic dialogue, 141
  classification, 136, 139
  deep emotional reactions, 141
  formative self-directed, 141
  formative self-interventions, 140
  in-depth dynamic psychotherapy, 142
  Life Enhancement (LE) methodology, 142
  meaning-focused intervention, 142
  nontherapeutic, 141
  Pollyanna effect, 141
  reflexive discovery, 140
  reflexive self-analysis, 140
  self-facilitation, 141
  sense-making task, 140
  sexual drives, 140
Meaning intervention, mental health care, 59, 65–68, 70
  Acceptance and Commitment Therapy and dignity therapy, 80
  clinical–aetiological assumptions
    absolute hierarchy, 66
    clinical and aetiological assumptions, 70
    conceptualisation, 65
    correlational and functional evidence, 67
    definitions, 68
    empirical research, 65
    experience, 67
    Franklian value triad, 68
    hypothesis, 65
    inauthentic or externally, 66
    psychological well-being, 66
    sociological causes, 65
    treatment manuals, 68
    types of, 67
    validation, 65
    values, 68
  depression or anxiety, 80
  effectiveness, 78–79
  individuals perceive, 50, 52, 59, 270–271
  MCT (see Meaning-Centred Therapy (MCT))
  meta-analyses, 79
  psychopathology, 81
  risk, 82
  screening, 81
  session structure, 76–78
  systematic literature review of therapies, 72–73
  thematic analyses, 69–70
  therapeutic sensitivity, 82
  time and energy, 59
Meaning in life, 430–431
Meaning Therapy (MT)
  CBT, 335
  logotherapy, 328
  PURE framework, 336
Meaning-based intervention, 205, 216, 217
Meaning-Centered Group Psychotherapy (MCGP), 248, 249
Meaning-centered holistic model, 441
Meaning-centered intervention, 202, 215–217
Meaning-centered positive group work, 423
Meaning-Centered Psychotherapy (MCP)
  adolescents and young adults with cancer, 257–258
  advanced cancer, 245
  bereaved parents, 257
  consensus conference, 245
  core principles, 258
  end-of-life support, 246
  Frankl's basic concepts, 246
  IMCP, 250–256
  IOM reports, 245
  MCGP, 248–249
  MCGP-BCS, 257
  MCGP-CS, 258
  MCP-C, 256–257
  Memorial Sloan Kettering Cancer Center, 246
  model of, 247–248
  participants, 248
  Viktor Frankl's logotherapy, 258
Meaning-Centred Therapy (MCT), 62, 71–76, 188, 190–195

approaches, 80
assumptions, 61
behavioural–cognitive machines, 60
benefits, 81
conceptual dissimilarities, 80
counselling, 64
de-reflection techniques, 61
effectiveness, 80
fundamental clinical and aetiological assumptions, 60
literature review, 60
logotherapy (see Logotherapy)
meaning-related questions, 82
modulation of attitudes, 61
narrative approach, 64
nondeterministic therapeutic approach, 61
nontherapeutic approaches, 64
paradoxical intention(s), 61
photography, 64
psychologists and psychiatrists, 60
self-transcendence, 61
skills
  assessment, 71
  existential, 74–75
  meaning-specific, 71–74
  relational–humanistic, 75–76
  spiritual and mindfulness, 76
standardisation and systematic research, 59
systematic and directive techniques, 63
theoretical ABCDE model, 64
training, therapists, 59
Meaning-changing interventions
  broader superordinate context, 131
  classification, 134–136
  complexity, 131
  human sciences and public discourse, 131
  meaning and meaning-making, 132
  professional psychotherapy and counseling settings, 131
  self-intervention, 132–133
  volition, 133–134
Meaning-enhancing intervention
  logotherapy, 332
  self-transcendence, 333–335
  values, 332
Meaninglessness
  assumptions, 284
  being nothing special, 287, 288, 292
  being special, 287
  being-alongside, 289, 291
  being-for, 289
  being-otherwise, 289, 291
  by-product of engagement, 290
  clinical syndrome, 283

concrete suggestions, 290
confidentiality, 286
culprit/nemesis, 284
de-commodified and de-instrumentalized, 291
deficit correction, 284
deficit-correction model, 287, 291
descriptive clarification, 286
evaluative and devaluative assessments, 286
existential cocaine, 287
existential therapy and positive psychology, 284
false dichotomy, 284
feelings of being special, 289
Frankl's response, 290
hermeneutical reframes, 291
hierarchical bifurcations, 285
hopelessness, 293
human achievement, 290
illegitimacy, 291
instrumental and engineering-oriented technical therapeutic technique, 292
life's unanswerable quality, 293
manifestations, 284
meaning-centric living, 288
mental health professionals, 293
meta-analysis, 283
nothingness, 292
ontological beings, 288
ontological nature, 285
person seeking care, 288
person's situation, 289
phenomenology, 286
pre-established schemas, 292
prescriptive approaches, 290
rank-ordered scales, 288
self-made human being, 286
significance as inherently ontological, 285
therapeutic care, 289, 293, 294
thriving and altruism, 285
transcendence, 287
valuations, 286
Meaning-making devices
  capacity, 137
  commercial advertising, 138
  crystallization, 137
  existential choice, 139
  facilitative intervention, 138
  formative self-correcting intervention, 137
  implicitly, 137
  inner mental work, 139
  interpersonal manipulation, 136
  meaning-related arguments, 139
  meaning-related choice, 138

Meaning-making devices (*cont.*)
  mechanisms, volitional regulation, 136
  paradoxical reversal effect, 137
  self-esteem, 138
  self-evident, 138
  simple choice, 138
  type of intervention, 137
  unconscious defenses, 137
Meaning-making model, 264–266
  adaptive emotion-regulation skills, 159
  adjustment process, stressful life events, 263
  global meaning
    beliefs, 264
    goals, 264
    subjective feelings, 264
  indicators of adjustment, 266
  positive reappraisal, 154
  situational meaning
    appraised event, 264
    assimilation *vs.* accommodation processes, 265
    automatic *vs.* deliberate processes, 265
    discrepancy, 264, 265
    meanings made, 265–266
    search for comprehensibility *vs.* search for significance, 265
Meaning-mindset, 429, 442
Meaning-oriented interventions
  academic achievement, 2
  compartmentalization, 4
  happiness-enhancing interventions, 2
  human existence, 7
  logotherapy, 6
  metaphysics, 5
  methodological factors, 5
  personal narratives, 3
  phenomenological method, 7
  philosophical problems, 4
  psychological terms, 3
  psychologists and psychiatrists, 5
  research studies, 3
  researchers and practitioners, 2
  sublimation/compensation, 6
  therapeutic mechanisms, 3
Meaning-specific skills, 191
Mental health
  mind/activities, 29
Mental health professionals, 415
Mental illness, 8
Meta-analysis, 173, 182, 187, 193
Microaggressions, 124–125
Mindfulness
  and character strengths, 390
  core concepts, 388–390
  correlates, 389–390

Mindfulness-Based Cognitive Therapy (MBCT), 389, 397
Mindfulness-Based Strengths Practice (MBSP), 395, 397–400
Mindfulness-Based Stress Reduction (MBSR), 388, 389, 397
MLDS. *See* Meaning in Life Dimensional Scale (MLDS)
MLQ. *See* Meaning in Life Questionnaire (MLQ)
Motivation and personality, 383
Multicultural psychology
  character and identity, 120–122
  courage, 118
  cultural myths, 117
  ethnicity, 119
  eudaimonic perspectives, 124, 125
  existential psychology, 116–117
  freedom, 118
  heightened perceptual wisdom, 120
  individual and collective meaning, 123–124
  microaggressions, 124–125
  misapplications, 124
  nonverbal and implicit communications, 121
  positive psychology, 114–116
  prejudice and discrimination, 124
  sustaining and non-sustaining meaning, 122
Multiculturalism, 10
Multifaceted integration programs, 395, 397–399

N
Narrative medicine
  disability, 306
  suffering, 305
NCCN Clinical Practice Guidelines, 248
Nihilism, 283
Nostalgia
  absurd art condition, 354
  boredom condition, 349
  DTA, 350
  existential threat, 349, 350, 352
  experimental study, 347
  life review, 356
  meaning deficits, 354, 355
  meaning-making resource, 346, 348
  memory, 345
  non-nostalgic control condition, 353
  reminiscence, 356–358
  scent-evoked, 346
  self-sacrifice, 352
  structural equation modeling, 354
  symptoms, 345
  TSST, 355

Index

O
Oncology, 187
Oxytocin, 366

P
Paired-samples *t*-test, 215
Pathways to meaning in life, 383–400
Perceived control and psychological functioning, 90
PERMA (Positive emotions, Engagement, Relationships, Meaning and Achievement), 372–373
Personal values, 416
PIL—SF. *See* Purpose in Life test—Short Form (PIL—SF)
Positive interventions. *See* Existential Positive Psychology (EPP)
Positive psychology (PP), 37, 96–98, 100, 383, 384, 391, 397, 399, 423
  vs. CBT, 233–234
  happiness, 229–230
  vs. humanistic psychology, 112–114
  vs. logotherapy, 235–236
  meaning, 313–315
  meaningfulness, 229–230
  meaning-seeking model, 323
  MLQ, 228
  PERMA model, 226
  PP1.0, 325–327
  strengths-based assessment, 226
  usage, 227
  VIA-IS, 228
  well-being therapy, 227
Positive psychotherapy (PPT)
  ACT, 328
  attitude, change, 328
  logotherapy, 328
  MT, 328
  self-transcendental value, 328, 329
Positive reappraisal. *See* Reflective rumination
Post-traumatic growth (PTG), 266
  greater appreciation of life, 157
  positive reappraisal (reflective rumination), 154
  relationships, 156
  self-efficacy, 155, 156
  spiritual development, 157, 158
Post-traumatic Growth Inventory (PTGI), 271
Post-traumatic stress disorder (PTSD), 95, 344
Potentially traumatic event, 150, 151
PP1.0, 327
  feelings and cognitions, 325
  happiness, 325
  PP, 325–327
  PPT (*see* Positive psychotherapy (PPT))
  vs. PP2.0, 330
Primary appraisal, 179
Psychology of religion, 50
Psychotherapy, 62, 64, 75, 76, 191
  academic department, 26
  attitudinal value, 371
  authentic happiness, 370
  caring motivation, 363, 370, 373, 377
  caring motivation and fundamental connection to life's meaning, 373–376
  client's pleasure, 24
  client's self-realization, 26
  client's *welfare*, 18
  creative value, 371
  dominant approaches, 18
  eudaimonism, 23, 26
  experiential value, 371
  generosity, 372
  human flourishing, 370
  human motivation, 363
  kindness, 372
  kindness and interpersonal strengths, 372
  logotherapy, 370, 373, 378
  love, 372
  moral *constraints*, 17
  myriad points of therapy, 17
  objective conceptions, 23
  PERMA, 373
  positive relations, 372
  profound insight, 371
  psychological intervention, 24
  ramifications, 377
  relationships, 371
  sacrifice, 24, 25
  self-psychology, 23
  self-realization, 26
  self-transcendence, 371, 372, 377
  social intelligence, 372
  suicide, 26
  theoretical approach, 23
  theoretical level, 18
  therapist-client relations, 363
  unbalanced/egoistic-based care, 378
PTSD. *See* Post-traumatic stress disorder (PTSD)
PURE. *See* Purpose, Understanding, Responsibility and Enjoyment/ Evaluation (PURE)
PURE Model of Meaning, 431–432
Purpose, 408–409
  benefits, 409–410
  during adolescence, 410–411

Purpose in Life (PIL), 285
Purpose in Life test—Short Form (PIL—SF), 232, 233, 237
Purpose, Understanding, Responsibility and Enjoyment/Evaluation (PURE), 335, 336

R

Rational Emotive Behavior Therapy (REBT), 223
REBT. *See* Rational Emotive Behavior Therapy (REBT)
Recovery-oriented cognitive therapy, 225
Reflective rumination, 154
Refugees, 90–100, 102–105
  adaptive functioning, 90
  Bhutanese, 99
  Cambodian, 99
  Dadaab camp, 100
  displaced, 102
  perceiving control, 99, 100
  psychological experience, 95, 96
  redefining, 96–97
  security, meaning, and coping, 97–99
Relational–humanistic skills, 191
Religion
  sexual functioning, 48
  spiritual, 42
Reminiscence
  autobiographical reflection, 356
  depression and anxiety, 358
  efficacy, 357
  life-review interventions, 357
Resilience, 90, 94, 96, 97, 99, 101, 102, 104, 105
  cognitive-behavior strategy, 234
  existential aloneness, 152
  internal and environmental resources, 151
  logotherapy, 237
  meaning-centered approach, 153
  relapse prevention strategy, 237
Response to Stress Questionnaire (RSQ), 91
14-item Resilience Scale (RS-14), 233

S

Sacred. *See* Sanctification
Salutogenesis, 329
Sanctification
  body, 50
  desecration, 51–53
  environment, 50
  forgiveness, 40
  marriage, 46
  mindfulness/meditation, 53
  moments, 44
  nonrelational aspects, 43
  parent–child relationship, 47
  prevalence rate, 42
  religion, 42, 46
  sacred loss, 51–53
  sacred obligation, 41
  sexual behavior, 47–48
  social justice, 40, 51
  spirituality, 37
  strivings, 48, 49
  theistic and nontheistic, 39–40
  works, 49
Second Wave Positive Psychology (PP2.0)
  ACT, 331
  dialectic and interactive model, 330, 331
  humanistic and existential values, 329, 330
  personal problems and illnesses, 329
  vs. PP1.0, 330
  salutogenesis, 329
Secondary appraisal, 179
Secondary Control and Adversity, 101–102
Secondary control, benefits, 101
Self-acceptance, 426
Self-determination and goal-setting, 427
Self-Determination Theory (SDT), 393, 395
Self-directed *vs.* other-directed intervention, 134
Self-efficacy, 91, 92, 99, 104, 105, 155, 156
Self-esteem, 425, 426
Self-knowledge, 425
Self-transcendence, 367, 424, 427, 428, 430, 433, 437, 438, 440–442
  Frankl's conceptualization, 334
  logotherapy, 333
  meaning-enhancing interventions, 334
Single targeted interventions, 395
Spinal cord injury (SCI), 267–271
  ACT, 275
  autonomy and social integration, 262
  CBT, 274, 275
  conceptualization, 276
  coping effectiveness training, 276
  discrepancy, 277
  global meaning, 266–267, 277
  health professionals, 274
  hypothesized discrepancy, 272
  meaning-centered group psychotherapy approach, 276
  meaning-making model, 261, 266
  meaning-making process, 277
  meanings made, 272–273
  mental health, 277
  physical impairments, 262

Index

post-traumatic stress disorder, 262
reeducation and vocational trainings, 262
searching and finding meaning, 273–274, 277
self-efficacy, 275
situational meaning
   appraisals, 267
   assimilation *vs.* accommodation processes, 269
   automatic *vs.* deliberate processes, 268, 269
   comprehensibility *vs.* significance searching, 269
   discrepancy, 267–268
   person's values and priorities in life, 271
   PTG, 271
   reappraisals, 270
   rehabilitation discharge, 271
   retrospective approach, 271
   self and identity, 270
   self-perception, 270
   vocational reintegration, 270
social environment, 274
third wave behavior therapies, 275
traumatic/nontraumatic etiology, 261
Spiritual and mindfulness skills, 191
Spiritual dimension, 10
Spirituality, 10, 37, 54
Strengths-based approaches, 160, 226, 233, 238
Strengths-oriented cognitive-behavior therapy, 225
Subjective well-being
   acceptance of responsibility, 19
   clients of suffering, 19
   human nature, 22
   individual interpretations, 20
   mental illness, 20
   objective approach, 19
   point of therapy, 22
   rehabilitation, 22
   schizoid tendencies, 21
   self-satisfaction, 22
   stability, 21
   theoretical reflection, 21
Substance use disorders (SUD)
   alcohol usage, 202, 203
   AUD, 204
   CBT, 205
   depression and stress, 202
   gender differences, 203
   logotherapy, 206–207
   maladaptive coping strategy, 201
   McNemar test, 213
   meaning in life, 201–218
   meaning-based interventions, 216, 217
   mental illness, 216

paired-samples t-test, 215
12-step model, 215
Suffering
   definition, 304, 305
   narrative, 305
   transcendence, 307–308

T

Targeted interventions, 395–396
Terror Management Theory (TMT), 3
Tertiary appraisal, 179
The Insistence of God: A Theology of Perhaps, 294
The Remarkable Existentialists, 284
Therapeutic relationship, 308, 310, 312
Tragic optimism (TO), 434
Transcending perspective, 180
Transformative learning, 267
Traumatic injury, 261
Trier Social Stress Test (TSST), 355
12-step model, 213, 215

U

United Nations Office on Drugs and Crime (UNODC), 201

V

Values Awareness Technique (VAT), 231
Values In Action Inventory of Strengths (VIA-IS), 226, 228, 235, 237
VIA
   classification, 390
   classification of character strengths and virtues, 385–386
   Inventory of Strengths, 384
   Survey measurement tool, 384
VIA-IS. *See* Values In Action Inventory of Strengths (VIA-IS)
Volition, 133–134

W

Well-being therapy, 227, 233
Will to meaning, 1, 6, 61, 66, 67, 101, 112, 183, 184, 191, 207, 211, 230, 231, 232, 236, 246, 307, 332, 334, 370, 371, 412, 429, 430
World assumptions, 174–176
World Health Organization (WHO), 262

Y

Yin-Yang approach, 436

CPSIA information can be obtained
at www.ICGtesting.com
Printed in the USA
BVHW012119230122
626998BV00002B/24